This chronology of Florentine theatrical works
is dedicated with deep affection, appreciation and respect
to the memory of Dr. Federico Ghisi and to Signora Evelina Ghisi
in recognition of their warm support,
encouragement and unfailing hospitality.

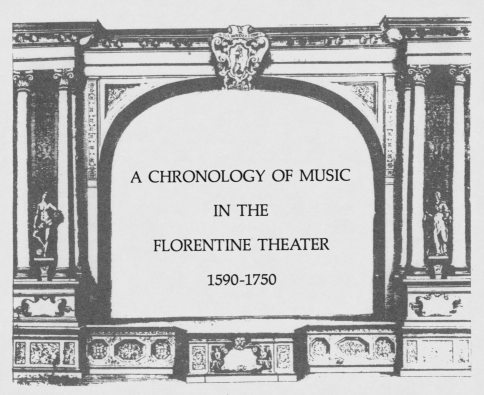

A CHRONOLOGY OF MUSIC

IN THE

FLORENTINE THEATER

1590-1750

OPERAS, PROLOGUES, FINALES, INTERMEZZOS

AND

PLAYS WITH INCIDENTAL MUSIC

by

Robert Lamar Weaver

and

Norma Wright Weaver

DETROIT STUDIES IN MUSIC BIBLIOGRAPHY ✱ NUMBER 38

INFORMATION COORDINATORS, INC. ✱ 1978 ✱ DETROIT

172314

PUBLISHED BY
INFORMATION COORDINATORS, INC.
1435-37 RANDOLPH STREET, DETROIT, MICHIGAN 48226

BOOK DESIGNED BY VINCENT KIBILDIS

CONTENTS

ILLUSTRATIONS

TABLES

PREFACE

OUR CHRONOLOGY has been a family undertaking. It has been "in progress," give or take a few years of dormancy, for more than twenty years, and consequently it has engaged more than one generation: mothers Rae Weaver and Tekla Wright, niece Meg Westley, and son Raymond Weaver have all taken their turns at solving problems of research, reading catalogues, copying material, and the like. We must first, then, express our gratitude to the family for their willing and quite capable assistance, even at times when the reasons for all this tedious labor were not very clear.

The appearance of the family at the entrance to European libraries must have caused consternation among their staffs: mother, father, grandmother, and children of unimpressive years all in a row. Fortunately in most cases the librarians most generously tolerated our family enterprise, the intrusion upon their routines and the transgression against the spirit, if not the letter, of their rules. Over a twenty-year period, we have had frequently to call upon librarians, especially in Italy, of course, for their help. We cannot recall a single instance in which that help was not generously given, and our list of librarians to whom we have reason to be grateful reads like a bibliographical reference work. However, it would be gross dereliction not to mention among them Sig. Sergio Paganelli of the Civico Museo in Bologna, Maestro Mario Fabbri of Florence, Dr. Claudio Sartori of Milan, and Dr. Giancarlo Savino of Pistoia.

To name all of the scholars who have assisted us in this project would, likewise, require a separate chapter. But the most generous and helpful among the many *seicentisti* has been Dr. John Hill of the University of Pennsylvania who has shared both information and his great skill and knowledge of archival research. To him we owe much appreciation and gratitude.

The exceptional ability and skill of designer Vincent Kibildis and compositor Joy Hick, both of Information Coordinators, were, of course, essential to the high physical quality of the volume, but we feel in addition that we owe them a great debt for their patient understanding of the necessity for the many corrections, alterations, and additions that occurred as the result of continued work even during the process of preparing the manuscript for publication.

Finally we must recognize the deeply appreciated financial assistance from the Fulbright Commission. The initial steps toward the realization of the chronology were taken with the support of a student scholarship to Italy in 1952-1953. One of the most productive later periods was spent in Vienna working in the National Library under a Fulbright research fellowship in 1966-1967. Several grants were also given by the Committee on Faculty Research of George Peabody College and in 1974 the college granted a sabbatical leave for the purpose of completing the research for the chronology. The University of Louisville generously granted assistance to their newly-arrived scholars for last minute corrections and research in 1975.

We hope that our effort to illuminate one of the last grandeurs of Florentine history in some measure is worthy of the assistance and support of all these friends and colleagues.

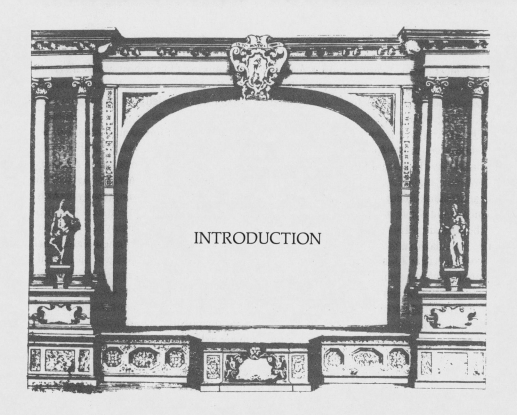

INTRODUCTION

UNTIL THE YEARS FOLLOWING the Second World War, Florentine opera remained a neglected subject, excepting always that extraordinary time in which the form itself was born. To be sure there were certain subjects that were probed more deeply than others, that is, the comedies at the Pergola between 1657 and 1662, and the brilliant era of the productions at Pratolino under the patronage and personal direction of Prince Ferdinando di Medici from 1679 to 1710. Indeed, the studies piled one upon another on the subjects of the Pergola and Pratolino with a degree of repetitiousness, beginning with Alessandro Ademollo's *I primi fasti del teatro della Pergola* (Milano, 1885) and following with Pavan's *Saggio di cronistoria teatrale fiorentina: serie cronologica delle opere rappresentate al teatro degli Immobili* (Milano, 1901), G. Piccini's *Storia aneddotica dei teatri fiorentini.* l. *Il teatro della Pergola* (Firenze, 1919) under the pseudonym of Jarro, and finally Ugo Morini's *La Reale Accademia degli Immobili e il suo teatro La Pergola* (Pisa, 1926). Concerning Ferdinando's operas, Leto Puliti published in his *Cenni storici della vita del Serenissimo Ferdinando dei Medici* (Firenze, 1874) a list of operas, maestri, performers, etc., gleaned from the correspondence of the prince, and Renzo Lustig expanded the available information to a small degree in his article, "Per la cronistoria dell'antico teatro musicale. Il teatro della Villa Medicea di Pratolino" in *Rivista musicale italiana* XXVI (1929).

The first attempt to broaden the view from the narrow perspectives of these studies was Robert Weaver's dissertation for the University of North Carolina (1958) *Florentine Comic Opera of the Seventeenth Century* (University Microfilms, L.C. no. MIC 58-5975), the principal theses of which were published in "Opera in Florence, 1646-1731" in *Studies in Musicology* (Chapel Hill, 1969). Included in the dissertation as Appendix II, p. 332, is a list of librettos, 1597-1741, which is the first stage in the development of the present chronology.

The most comprehensive study, however, to have appeared in the post-war years is Mario Fabbri's article on "Firenze" in the *Enciclopedia dello spettacolo* V (1958), wherein the real productivity and character of Florentine opera was revealed for the first time in an important general reference.

Quite recently three new publications have appeared of great importance. The first is the magnificent catalogue printed in conjunction with an exhibition of 1975 in Florence promoted by the Amministrazione Provinciale di Firenze by the title of *Il luogo teatrale a Firenze*, Catalogo a cura di Mario Fabbri, Elvira Garbero Zorzi, and Anna Maria Petrioli Tofani (Milan: Electa Editrice, 1975). Two articles publish new material: one by Lorenzo Bianconi and Thomas Walker, "Dalla 'Finta pazza' alla 'Veremonda': storie di Febiarmonici," in the *Rivista italiana di musicologia* X (1975), 379-454; and the second by John Walker Hill, "Le relazione di Antonio Cesti con la corte e i teatri di Firenze," in the same journal in volume XI (1976, no. 1, pp. 27-47). The latter makes public perhaps the richest archival resources unearthed in recent years. Hill's article publishes information drawn from the archives of the Sorgenti which he discovered in the Archivio di Stato di Firenze.

Our chronology obviously and appropriately presents the most copious supply of information thus far. But it may hardly be said that the possibilities are herein exhausted. (Rather it might be said that it is the authors who are exhausted.) In particular, the manuscript resources in libraries and archives are barely scratched, in spite of certain notable items extracted from such resources. Among these the most important are the archives of the Accademia Infuocati from 1699 existing in the Biblioteca ed Archivio Communale di Firenze in via S. Egidio. These records have never, to our knowledge, been cited or described though their existence surely has been known to a number of scholars in the field. We can add to these records Filza 631 of the *Reggenza* (i.e., the government of Francesco di Lorena, who as the consort of Maria Theresa resided in Vienna) in the Archivio di Stato di Firenze. The contents of this filza consist of requests to the Reggenza for permission to use the Cocomero Theater, sometimes signed by the impresarios of touring troupes, sometimes by academic impresarios and sometimes by the superintendent of the theater, the Marchese Scipione Capponi. Normally the requests are granted in the form of a marginal approval in an appropriately illegible bureaucratic scrawl. Occasionally complexities or conflicts require longer replies, in which cases copies of letters, chiefly from the Conte di Richecourt, appear in the filza. Hence the filza is in part the complementary correspondence to that which is the subject of an index in the Infuocati archives: *Indice della Filza I di Negozi escrittime dell'Accad.a degl'Infuocati dal 1712 al 1762 fatto l'anno 1776 dal Canc.e Aless.o Romoaldo Scurtij Provved.e della d.a Accademia*. The actual documents which Scurtij indexes have disappeared, but because the order of Reggenza 631 corresponds so closely to that of the index, it very nearly supplies the information which the lost documents would have contained.

Among a number of diaries we have examined, which are listed in the bibliography, two most useful sources are the diaries in the Marucelliana Library, one by G. B. Fagiuoli and the other by Nicolò Susier. Both have been known for some time and excerpts have been published by various scholars, but again the first systematic use appears in the present chronology. However, we cannot claim to have ferreted out all information in the diaries. Besides being humanly frail in our fulfillment of the tedious task of reading these diaries, the diaries themselves are in the most distressing states of decomposition. Some pages are impossible to separate. In the case of the Susier, the library has withdrawn it from use, and consequently we have been forced to rely upon a microfilm of the diary, which is even more difficult to read than the original, and upon two glosses of the musical information, one a nineteenth century manuscript deposited in the Biblioteca Nazionale, and the other made by Professor John Hill, who was perhaps the last scholar allowed to read the diary itself. The difficulty of reading it is demonstrated by the variations between our reading of the microfilm and the two glosses. The great Settimanni diaries in the Archivio di Stato di Firenze have not really been given their due attention, and anyone desiring to dig further into such sources might do well to begin there and continue with several more diaries at the Archivio di Stato which we have not had time to examine.

Letters are a special branch of archival research and the most difficult resource to use effectively without a vast expenditure of time. We have been able to make only a limited investigation of the Magliabecchi Collection in the Biblioteca Nazionale di Firenze and the correspondence of G.B. Fagiuoli in the Moreniana, and a more intensive (but still far from exhaustive) one of the Medici Archives. In the last named, the letters of Francesco de Castris and of the Cardinal Francesco Maria de' Medici stand out as remarkably vivid accounts of that kind of gossip and trivia capable of investing the duller and more accurately detailed information of librettos with new life. Unfortunately, the cardinal's handwriting is indecipherable though the letters are in a good state of preservation. We are positive that the letters contain more information than that little we have extracted.

We have done a reasonable job of scanning the letters of Mattias de' Medici but the letters of other members of the Medici family should be examined more carefully. Vittoria della Rovere, from the collection of prologues dedicated to her in the Archivio di Stato, appears to have been somewhat more interested than supposed in opera or at least drama with some music, and her letters might contain something of interest. The roles of Cardinals Leopoldo and Francesco Maria as patrons also emerge from the chronology with enhanced importance, suggesting that perhaps their correspondence, at least in the years of their activity as patrons of opera, would be productive material for research. As for Cosimo III's correspondence, we can say only that the scholar who approaches it must do so as a self-sacrifical rite.

The most important letters are those of Ferdinando de' Medici. But in view of the several scholars at work presently on the letters and because of Puliti's charts, the essential information, we felt, was available. Unfortunately, the more we sifted through Puliti's information the more we realized that it was essentially useless and that we had to examine the letters ourselves. Not that Puliti was inaccurate: we have found remarkably few errors, even of omission. But he was injudicious and undiscriminating. He listed singers, for example, who were mentioned in letters without regard for the contents of the letters. Hence some of those listed as "patronized" by Ferdinando were in fact rejected; some of them merely passing through Florence and sending their respects; some were asking only for passports and recommendations; and some of the composers and poets sending their works unbidden by the prince and could never have claimed his patronage. While for our own purposes we have generally been able to discipline Puliti's uncontrolled information, we cannot claim to have exhausted Ferdinando's correspondence, concerning which we will report in more detail below.

In the Biblioteca Nazionale Centrale di Firenze and the Archivio di Stato there are numerous volumes entitled *Poesie varie* or some such in which prologues, intermezzi, finales, and occasionally whole dramas with incidental music will be found. Often these works contain information about the performances, and the otherwise very sketchy outlines of the known academic activities are thereby filled in. But other collections of such material in the Riccardiana, Moreniana, Marucelliana, and the Laurenziana are yet to be investigated.

Other untapped sources are travelers' guides of which substantial lists are available in Gaetano Imbert's *La vita Fiorentina nel seicento* (Firenze, 1906). Eric Cochrane's *Florence in the Forgotten Centuries 1527-1800* (Chicago, 1973) contains a copious bibliography of both diaries and travelogues, but unfortunately the structure of the bibliography makes it necessary to read the entire bibliography to cull them out.

One of the disappointing aspects of our research has been the paucity of scores. Altogether we have been able to identify only three new scores: *Le nozze in sogno*, 1665[1]*, *L'amante di sua figlia* 1683[4], both of which are anonymous, and Alessandro Melani's *Il sospetto senza fondamento*, 1691[3]. Astonishingly enough, apart from the scores of the Camerata and of Marco da Gagliano at the beginning of the century, there are only eight identified scores out of some 53 Florentine first performances. To the three mentioned above can be added only Cavalli's *Ipermestra*, 1658[3]; Jacopo Melani's *Il potestà di Colognole*, 1657[1], and *Ercole in Tebe*, 1661[1]; Alessandro Melani's *Carceriere di se medesimo*, 1681[1], and Pollaroli's *Tito Manlio*, 1696[5] (arias only).

After 1700 the statistics are no better and furthermore grossly inaccurate under any counting because of the impossibility of any degree of security in attributing the scores.

The question of attributions is the most vexing problem of all. It is no exaggeration to say that the attributions of librettos and scores of operas in Italy and within the period covered by the present chronology are in a state of massive confusion and contradiction throughout the literature and reference works devoted to the subject. There is not a single reference work that is even reasonably reliable beyond the level of thoroughly authenticated librettos and scores. Even the monumental *Enciclopedia dello spettacolo*, by far the best reference available, will be discovered to have attributed the same score to more than one composer, particularly where performances outside of Rome, Venice, and Vienna are concerned. We cannot claim to have remedied the situation more than somewhat in a restricted area. We have questioned every attribution. The results are sometimes more confusing than helpful, we do not doubt, and at other times more frustrating than instructive, for we are forced into either airy speculation or a deadly series of *anonimi*. By nature we are inclined to the former, which places us in spiritual and intellectual harmony with many Italian scholars. But we implore the reader to recognize and accept speculation for exactly what it is: no more than indications of possible avenues of further investigation. Our own chronology provides an example of the ill effects that obtain when too-hasty encyclopedists fail to distinguish between speculation and fact: the long attribution of the score of *Il Girello* to Filippo Acciajuoli on the basis of a clever but fallacious speculation by Ademollo to the effect that the score to the first performance of *Il Girello* was by the librettist, Filippo Acciajuoli, has found its way into authoritative encyclopedias and the error has contributed in a small way to the failure by historians to recognize both the quality and the importance of the setting by Jacopo Melani.[1]

Much more irresponsible has been the misinformation created by the misuse of poor old Allacci. Allacci and his editors were not less human in their frailties than modern

---

* The arabic superscript following a year date refers to the entry in the main chronology. All other superscripts, in *italics*, are footnote references.

[1] The whole problem of *Il Girello* is discussed in Weaver, "*Il Girello*."

bibliographers, and they have their failures here and there. They, too, were too dependent upon previous sources, as Thomas Walker has demonstrated in his article, "Gli errori di 'Minerva al tavolino' " in *Venezia e il melodramma nel Seicento. Atti del Convegno internazionale* (Venezia, 1972). But they are not responsible for all of the nonsense that has been created by subsequent bibliographers and cataloguers. Sesini, Pavan, Morini and others have long made attributions by simply looking in Allacci for the nearest date to a given anonymous libretto, and presto! there is a librettist and a composer. Needless to say, such encyclopedias as Manferrari's and Casella's merely repeat the misinformation mindlessly.

To add insult to injury, too frequently things have been read in Allacci which are not actually there. We quote an entry as a case in point: "ASTIANATTE. Dramma rappresentato l'anno 1701–in Pratolino. 1701 in 8–Poesia del Dott. Antonio Salvi, Fiorentino, di Lucignano.–*Replicato nel Teatro di S. Gio. Grisostomo di Venezia l'anno* 1718 in 12– Musica di Marc-Antonio Bononcini, Bolognese." Readers of the entry assume that the attribution of the music to Bononcini applies to both publications of the libretto. Hence the music for Pratolino is attributed to Bononcini by Sesini, Manferrari, Loewenberg, and the article by Werner Bollert in the redoubtable *Musik in Geschichte und Gegenwart.* More thoughtful examination of Allacci will show that attributions of composers are intended to apply only to each publication of the libretto. They are neither cumulative nor retrospective. That is, if four libretti are listed of which the third has an attribution of the music, that attribution does not apply either to the first two nor to the fourth. *Replicato* refers to the libretto, not the music.

As a well-intentioned step in the right direction we have said so if a given libretto is in fact without an attribution of either poet or composer. Or if the libretto was published elsewhere with the name of the poet appended, we have stated so as the only secure method of determining the author. The majority of the librettos can be identified with a proper author, ignoring the degree to which the original has been altered by some unknown poet (or worse). The situation for the composers is more confused. Most of the musical settings of librettos must be declared anonymous. But wherever it seems useful we have noted performances in other cities where the composer is identified in librettos, strengthening the correlations by comparisons of the librettos and occasionally by noting common performers. However, the reliability of such comparisons of texts and performers should be understood to be quite limited, not only as means of determining the facts (i.e., identical texts do not mean absolutely that the same music was used, and even less is it certain that the same music was used simply because one or more singers sing the same roles in different cities), but also because of the limitations of time and funds available to the authors. We have been able to make a substantial number of complete comparisons but the majority of the comparisons have been restricted to portions of the librettos, that is, the first and last scenes of each act. A serviceable technique, one would suppose, but there remains the possibility that some diabolical poetaster retained those precise scenes while transforming the entire remainder of the libretto. Several cases occur where the second poet has retained the argument, the characters, and even the scenes, but has changed all of the text! The nature and scope of the comparisons we have attempted to make clear in each case so that the researcher will have some idea of the reliability of the information based upon the comparisons.[2] An unhappy percentage of the librettos has

---

2 For example, compare *Il trionfo della continenza considerato in Scipione Affricano* (Perugia, Ciani e Desiderij, 1677) with *Generosa Continenza di Scipione Affricano* (Bologna, Longhi, 1677) both in I Bc.

not been compared at all. Sometimes Sesini and Sonneck speak of their own comparisons in a way that allows the use of their work to fill in the gaps. But a vast amount of work will still have to be done in the way of comparisons before the librettos will yield up solidly dependable evidence of the repetition of the music in various cities. Comparisons should also be made between librettos and scores, especially in the instances of scores first performed outside of Florence.

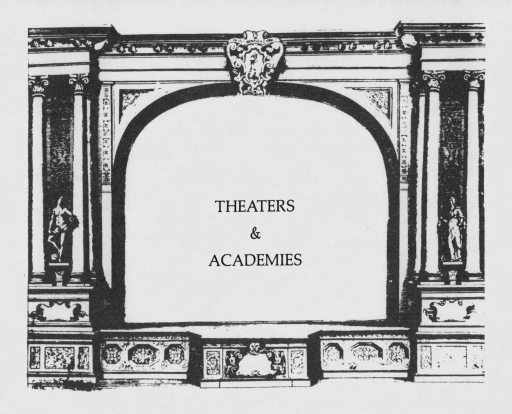

THEATERS
&
ACADEMIES

I. 1590-1644

During the first period, stages were built for each performance in locations that were not permanently or exclusively theaters but large rooms in the Palazzo Vecchio, Uffizi, or Medicean palaces, or in private palaces. Performances also took place in temporary arenas with *ad hoc* stages and machinery in outdoor gardens, courtyards, city squares, and even on floats on the Arno. The three largest rooms in the city were the Salone dei Cinquecento of the Palazzo Vecchio, the Sala di Don Antonio or more simply, the Salone di Palazzo

19

Pitti, and the Teatro Mediceo agli Uffizi. At least the first and last had permanent raised-platforms at one end, but the rooms were actually assembly halls or ballrooms used for other purposes than theatrical performances. Stadium-like bleachers lined the sides of the rooms while the central floor was left clear to accommodate ballets performed by the members of the court. The stages were connected by steps with the main arena, and characteristically the musical drama overflowed the limits of the stage by way of the steps to fill the arena. The platform was not enclosed so that whatever staging or machinery was necessary had to be housed in a temporary structure. The Salone dei Cinquecento still exists very much in the form given it in the sixteenth century, lacking only the bleachers along the walls which, in any case, were probably temporary wooden structures themselves. Well-known prints of the staging of the *Veglia della liberatione di Tirreno* (1617) show the similarity between the Teatro agli Uffizi and the Sala dei Cinquecento.

While performances in private palaces or the villas of the Medici continued at least sporadically during the entire seventeenth century, at no other time was the production of such theatricals so great or so attentively noted by diarists. The reason is not difficult to imagine: the wealthy noble families were following the example of the Medicean court by participating in pastorales and mascheratas in their own palaces. Obviously, staging was done upon individually constructed stages which, while not lacking in costly splendor, must have been relatively miniature. Performances are recorded at the following palazzi: Corsi, Riccardi, Camerata presso Fiesole (Ninfeo), Montalvi, Strozzi, Gherardesca, del Nero, Rinaldi, and at Medicean villas, Casino Mediceo di San Marco, Casa di Don Giovanni de' Medici, and the Poggio Imperiale.

A unique feature of the first period also is the performances of the juvenile academies. One must assume that institutions of learning for young nobles and wealthy merchants existed at all times and that they would have made public performances of some sort. But the notice of them in diaries and in published librettos is curiously restricted to the first part of the seventeenth century. The fact is again a sign of the remarkable conjunction between theatrical entertainment and ordinary social expression that seems to have been everywhere exceptionally strong at that time. Pedagogical drama, if you will excuse the jargon, was nourished by a resurgent neo-Platonism and vigorously reinforced by Jesuitic theories of education, whereby music was taught to youth as a means of tempering and ennobling character.[1] It was further made feasible because of current standards of miniature *ad hoc* staging. A generation of noblemen who were to be the founders of later dramaturgical academies grew up performing religious and secular musical dramas (if not actually operas).

There is some difficulty in being certain of the meaning of *compagnia* (i.e., whether it means a company of professional *comici*), but we suspect that the "Giovani della Compagnia d'Alberto" that performed *I morti e i vivi* at the Casino Mediceo in 1602[2] * is an early example of a pedagogical academy. In 1618[4] in the Palazzo Pitti there was a pastorale performed "by the sons of Leone de' Nerli and by other young Florentine nobles" which also probably belongs in this category. But more certainty can be attached to the productions of an academy maintained by Jacopo Cicognini called the "Compagnia di S. Giorgio,"

---

* The arabic superscript following a year date refers to the entry in the main chronology. All other superscripts, in *italics*, are footnote references.

[1] For a fascinating discussion of seventeenth century neo-Platonism and its expression through the participation of society in opera, see Robert Isherwood, in *Music in the Service of the King* (Ithaca: Cornell University Press, 1973), pp. 1-54.

in 1622[1] and 1622[3], the performers of which are named. Among them is the future librettist, Giacinto Cicognini, son of Jacopo. Cicognini's company evidently passed soon afterwards under the sponsorship of an ecclesiastical order, since his young men next performed under the name of "Venerabili Compagnia di Agniolo Raffaelo detta la Scala" and his librettos are dedicated to the honorable "Padri e Fratelli."

Although we assigned to the second period the ascendancy of the academies, some were active during the first period as well, but in contrast to the following period, they performed in private houses and, with the glaring and remarkable exception of the Camerata, restricted their performances to intermezzi, mascherate, cocchiate, and the like. The list of *conversazione* or *accademie* must, of course, begin with the Camerata of Count Bardi, whose activities are so well-known that they hardly need to be recounted. But, so far as we know, a statement to be found in a libretto of *Gli amorosi affanni*, a *tragedicomedia pastorale* by Vincenzio Panciatichi published in Venice in 1606 (see 1601), has not been recognized. Panciatichi says in his letter to the reader that his fable was performed "in the place called 'Camerata' near Fiesole, rebaptized 'Ninfeo,' where the Florentine poets and musicians met under the leadership of the Count Bardi."

For a brief period between 1623[1] and 1628[2] the Accademici Rugginosi performed. In 1623[3] the Incostanti mounted the famous intermedii by Filippo Vitali. The Infiammati are recorded in 1626[2] in the performance of *La finta mora* and again in 1630 in a prose play with a prologue and intermezzi for music. The Percossi, whose membership included the poet Salvador Rosa and comedy writer G.B. Ricciardi met beginning in 1646 under the patronage of Giovanni Carlo de' Medici to perform improvised comedies, according to Maylender, but no texts or librettos of musical or spoken dramas produced by the Percossi have been found. Therefore they are not registered in the chronology. The circumstances are similar in the case of the Elevati, successors of the Camerata, who, Maylender says, were founded by Marco da Gagliano about 1607 and continued at least to 1621. But since no published librettos or descriptions of specific performances in Florence have been found, they do not appear in our chronology except as a reference (1600[1-3]).

II. 1644-1678

During the second period permanent theaters were built modeled on the theaters of Venice. The manner in which the theaters were used was, however, determined by the presence of the academicians in all theatrical entertainments other than performances by traveling troupes of *comici*. The academies were the very body and soul of Florentine life in the mid-seventeenth century. The great academies of the Renaissance were restricted to comparatively small honorary associations of humanists, each of whom maintained a powerful sense of individuality. But in the seventeenth century it is as if the Renaissance *uomo universalis* became gregarious and highly social. Flourishing as never before or afterwards, the academies were the channel through which flowed with extraordinary energy the social and intellectual expression of the city and its principality. The historian Galluzzi described the spirit of the reign of Ferdinando II (d. 1670) with undisguised enthusiasm:

> Upon the traces of Bacon and of Galileo arose in Italy a spirit ardent for the perfecting of knowledge, the breaking of the ancient yoke (of ignorance), the rediscovering of truth and the conquering of error; the communication of sentiments and ideas was believed the most efficacious means of realizing these

intentions, and to that purpose assemblies were formed dedicated solely to the end of self-perfection. . . . The Nobility and qualified persons participated therein with pleasure, since with these assemblies easily were combined pastimes and diversions.[2]

As in all aspects of cultural life of the period of Ferdinando and his brothers, the theater was dominated by academies. Together with the uncertainties of Medici patronage, the dominance was responsible for the irregularity of performances, for the lack of seasons predictable and defined, for the brevity of any one season or the number of performances given any one opera, and the great variety of types from spoken prose comedies and tragedies to plays with incidental music and to opera. To a large degree the *bel canto* style exemplified by the scores of Cesti and Melani owes its simple, melodic, and dance-like character to the academic environment wherein performers were likely to be amateur academicians.

The theaters were operated by the academies as quasi-public and commercial ventures, and for those purposes the theaters were conceded to itinerant troupes of *comici*. But the primary purpose of the theaters was to provide opportunity for performances and activities by the academicians themselves, and the sale of tickets was no more than a means of financing their own academic pleasures. Of course, on special occasions, for visits of foreign dignitaries, and for wedding festivities, the theaters were used by the Medicean court which then generously contributed to the cost of the production. Individual members of the Medici family as patrons contributed regularly to the costs of the academic theatricals, but how much and how frequently seems to have depended, apart from special occasions, entirely upon the particular Medici prince. Some, like Gian Carlo, were munificent; others, like Cosimo III, were stingy.

The second period thus begins with the founding of the Accademia dei Concordi in 1644, for the purpose of promoting "the study of mathematics, the exercise of dance and fencing and of other cavalier activities; the reading of comedies and the performance of good music."[3] To attain these ends they imposed dues upon the members which were used in part to engage a fencing master, a music master, and a master of mathematics.

However, the period takes on substance only with the foundation of the Immobili in 1649 and the signing of a contract with Niccolò degli Ughi for the construction of a theater for the Immobili in via del Cocomero in 1650. Mattias de' Medici had already in 1645 become interested in the construction of a theater in Siena and had for that purpose corresponded with Francesco Maria Zati in Venice asking him for descriptions and plans of Venetian theaters.[4] Zati replied with praise for the Grimani Theater but added that it was "too long, with the result that those who face the stage could hardly hear the performers" and that the prince should reduce his plan to two rows of boxes instead of the four of the

---

[2] "Sulle traccie di Bacone e del Galileo sorgeva in Italia uno spirito ardente di perfezionare le cognizione, scuotere l'antico giogo, ritrovare la verità, e vincer gli errori; il communicare i sentimenti e le idee fu creduto il più efficace mezzo per conseguirne l'intento, e perciò si formarono delle assemblee indirizzate unicamente allo scopo di perfezionarse. . .la Nobilità e le persone qualificate vi si occupavano con piacere, poichè con esse facilmente si combinavano i passatempi e il divertimento." Galluzzi, Vol. IV, p. 126.

[3] ". . . lo studio delle matematiche, l'esercizio del ballo e della scherma e di altri cavallereschi esercizi; la lettura di commedia e fare della buona musica." Morini, p. 1.

[4] I Fas: Med. 5472, c. 9-13.

Grimani.[5] Zati's recommendations must have still been in the mind of Giovanni Carlo
de' Medici when he, as the protector of the Immobili, stipulated in the contract with Ughi
that a theater of 36 boxes in two rows be built.[6] Estimates made by John Hill[7] on the
basis of the sale of tickets by the Sorgenti for a performance of *Erismena* (1661[3]) are that
the Cocomero possessed only 15 boxes and seated only 506 (at least that is the maximum
number of tickets sold) on the ground floor. Apparently even so late as this year, the
original plans had not yet been realized. The theater after two major reconstructions in the
eighteenth century still stands, now in melancholy subjugation to the movie. Reconstruction
has added a third row of boxes and heightened the stage, but it is still remarkably small.
When we visited it we were not allowed to pace the stage, but by eye we would judge it to
be about 25 feet wide and quite shallow. A square screen of a size common about 1940
fills the entire space.

The contract of 1650 left the actual ownership of the houses and land in the hands of
Ughi and his heirs. No academy or patron in the period under consideration owned the
theater: whoever used it only rented it from the Ughi. This fact led to continual conflict
between the academies using the theater and the Ughi. Even in the eighteenth century
when the theater was rented on a secure and continuing basis by the Infuocati, litigation
over the use of precise houses and space and over the rights of the academy was continuous,
filling to overflowing the archives of the Infuocati described in the introduction to this
work. On one occasion the conflict escaped the boundaries of legality and propriety.
Fagiuoli recounts that on June 25, 1727[3], "Cav. Piero Ughi beat up Paperini [the publisher]
because for the comedy they are reciting now in via del Cocomero entitled *La Caccia in
Etolia* he had not said [on the libretto's title page] 'in the Teatro Ughi' but said 'in the
Teatro di via del Cocomero.' "

The combination of the two factors, the smallness of the theater as proposed, and the
lack of control by the Immobili (or, one might suppose, by the patron) must have quite
early, even before the theater had been completed, seemed too restricted to satisfy the
ambitions of Giovanni Carlo and the wealthier members of the academy. For on July 12,
1652, he laid the foundation stone of the theater in via della Pergola. The Pergola was
planned on a considerably more sumptuous scale on designs by the architect Ferdinando
Tacca. The stage is generous with a depth just short of being equal to the length of the
auditorium itself. A print of the seventeenth century which views the auditorium from the
stage shows a loggia or platea raised above the orchestra floor surmounted by three tiers of
boxes and arranged in an ingeniously angled design that afforded excellent views of the stage
from all boxes. The pattern is closer to a triangle than to the bulging horseshoe of the
present design.

In the second constitution of the Immobili of 1651 conserved in the Biblioteca
Marucelliana two separate bodies were recognized: the first were named *accademici proprietari*
and were expected to contribute money (they had in fact been those who had provided the
means of constructing the theater). These members, in addition to special contributions,
were regularly subject to a membership tax. The second class of members were the "aggregati"
or associates who were obligated to give their labor and talents to the academy for the

---

5 Bianconi and Walker, p. 435.
6 Fabbri, "Firenze," c. 382.
7 P. 35.

performance of comedies, ballets, combattimenti, etc., including the surveillance of the theater during performances. These were exempted from paying the tax. Electoral offices of *Principe*, *Provveditore*, and *Segretario* were established. The final power of decision concerning whatever activity was placed in the hands of the Protector, in which position Cardinal Giovanni Carlo de' Medici was reaffirmed. The activities were to be similar (but expanded) to those of the Concordi and likewise there were to be engaged masters of ballet, fencing, jousting, and horsemanship, while the objective was declared to be the achievement of the highest perfection in all the noble undertakings of the Academy. To spur on reluctant members a fine of 15 scudi was provided for uncooperative behavior of members who refused to do their assigned tasks in the comedies and festivals.[8]

By 1657 the Pergola was sufficiently finished to permit its inauguration in the carnival of that year with a performance of *Il potestà di Colognole*, libretto by Giovanni Andrea Moniglia and music by Jacopo Melani, a work that has largely established the historical importance of the theater. Over the next five years the Immobili produced comedies of the same type and in addition two feste teatrali, *Ipermestra* with music by Francesco Cavalli and *Ercole in Tebe* by Jacopo Melani, both settings of librettos by Moniglia. But the form of the deed conceding the land to Gian Carlo in perpetuity and the great financial contribution to the academy by him became, after his death in January of 1663, a source of grief to the academicians and their theater. It was closed because of litigation by the heirs of Gian Carlo and by claims against his estate from his death to 1718[3] except for the wedding festival for Ferdinando di Toscana and Violante di Baviera in 1689[5] and for occasional horse-ballets performed by the Accademia dei Nobili. The Pergola, however, has received a sufficiency of attention, and for more information we refer the reader to the bibliography outlined in our introduction. The Cocomero, on the other hand, has been sorely neglected in spite of the fact that operatic life in Florence in the second and third periods of our history depended upon the Cocomero after its beauteous competitor had quite fainted away.

We cannot say when the Cocomero was finished precisely but we would venture to say 1655. Several proposals have been put forward by various historians for the opening opera.[9] *La Deidamia*, performed in the carnival of 1650[1], is too early since the contract to build the theater was not signed until later the same year. A publication by Bonardi of *Giasone*, of which the dedication is signed on May 15, 1650, is again too early, and moreover the publisher remarks that he was forced to republish it because he ran out of copies and the demand still continued. Hence the publication was not for the occasion of a performance. In another publication of the same libretto dated January 11, 1651[1], the publisher, this time Onofri, repeats exactly the same statement and adds in his dedication

---

[8] Hill, n. 15, quotes the principal objectives from the *Capitoli*.

[9] Pandolfini says (quoted by Piccini, p. 1): "Quegli accademici [the Immobili] presero fitto dal Signor Niccolo Ughi 'uno stanzone' in via del Cocomero . . . e a loro spese vi eressero un Teatro ove si recitarono diverse Commedie, ma riuscendo il luogo troppo augusto pensarono a provvedersi d'un altro più dilato." However, Pandolfini writing in 1753 cannot be depended upon without some other confirmation to have set down the precise sequence of events. Pandolfini's history is in the Biblioteca Nazionale di Firenze (see bibliography). John Hill tells us that the archives of the Sorgenti contain expenses for various kinds of building material which, not being pertinent to his article, were not alluded to there. Certainly the entries would show that the theater was not altogether finished even in 1655.

to Filippo Franceschi that he took the opportunity of dedicating it to him because Franceschi "was near to his happy wedding. . . when more than at any other time it is deemed appropriate to read similar compositions." Obviously the publisher knows nothing of any performance. With the performance of *Alessandro Vincitor di se stesso* in the carnival of 1654[1] a more likely candidate is found. It was indeed performed largely through the efforts of Mattias de' Medici who began correspondence engaging the performers as early as 1652. But postponement followed postponement, yet without a mention of the reason in unequivocable terms. Bianconi and Walker, p. 443, n. 260, speculate that the last delay was caused by the performance of an opera in Bologna in late 1653 by Anna Francesca Costa who had been engaged to sing in *Alessandro*. On the other hand, constant delay of opening night is a well-known, endemic hazard for those who are in charge of inaugural opening nights of a theater a-building. What is dubious about this choice is that the libretto has no hint of being the signal of so auspicious an event and even less of being the product of an academy, Infuocati or otherwise. The dedication, vacuous and vain, is signed by a singer, which would be an impropriety if it were an academic opera. The only clue is the dedication to Gian Carlo, who was the patron of the first academy to occupy the Cocomero, the Sorgenti. Still the theater might have been near enough to completion for a performance to take place.

Finally, only in July of 1654[2] is the via del Cocomero faintly connected with some kind of theatrical: a "Festa rappresentata da gl'Accademici Sorgenti" for Cosimo III's birthday. But even then the description in the libretto plainly says that the academicians gathered in via del Cocomero for the beginning of a parade that, "after making the tour of via del Cocomero twice, thence proceeded to the Palazzo Pitti. . . ." The academy is not necessarily *in* the theater yet, though some identification with the location has been formed.

The role of the Sorgenti in the history in Florence has been very obscure: that which has been known has been also ignored; and much of what the academy actually accomplished has been unknown. In one of the most important discoveries in the history of Florentine opera in recent years, Professor John Hill has published the contents of an archive belonging to the first years of the Sorgenti, 1655-1663. These archives clearly prove that the Cocomero is in the hands of the Sorgenti during these years. Here, in order to establish the continuity of the occupation of the theater itself, we will need to examine the evidence concerning the tenancy and existence of the Infuocati.

Ugo Morini, pp. 1-3, is the authority for the statement now found throughout historical literature (that treats the subject at all) to the effect that the Infuocati were created when Giovanni Carlo took some thirty-two of the richest and noblest of the Immobili with him to the new location in via della Pergola in 1652 and that the remainder, assuming a new title, Accademia degl'Infuocati, stayed in via del Cocomero under the patronage of the Grand Duke Ferdinando II, where they occupied themselves with the production of spoken comedies. No one has undertaken a challenge of the accuracy of his statement. We do so now.

Concerning Morini's information, he is probably basing his statement ultimately upon Palmieri Pandolfini's brief history of the Immobili written in 1753 and cited above. While the substance is much as Morini says, Pandolfini does not actually name the academy remaining in via del Cocomero. There is also an anonymous nineteenth century history of the Immobili in the Archivio di Stato di Firenze (Arch Med. Miscellaneo di Acquista 308/8) that is a gloss of documents from the archives of the Immobili. Like Pandolfini, the

TABLE I

Performances at the Cocomero 1665-1674

Year	Work	Poet	Dedicatee	Performers
1665[2]	Intermezzi	Pietro Susini *Member of Sorgenti*		Sorgenti
1665[1]	Nozze in Sogno	Pietro Susini	Carlo de' Medici	Infuocati
1666	Artemisia	Niccolo Minato	March. G.V. Salviati *1686 Immobili member*	comici
1667[1]	Egisto	Giovanni Faustini	Leopoldo de' Medici	comici
1668[1]	Rivalità favorevole	Ximenes Aragona *later known to be a member* *of Infuocati* Music by Pietro Sanmartini *associated with Sorgenti*	Leopoldo de' Medici	Infuocati?
1669[1]	Scipione Affricano	Niccolo Minato	Leopoldo de' Medici	comici
1669[2]	Antioco	Anonymous	Leopoldo de' Medici	comici
1670[1]	Girello	Filippo Acciajuoli *1686 Immobili member*[10]	Domenico Caccini *1686 Immobili member* Niccolo Strozzi *aristocrat!*	comici
1670[2]	La Dori	Apolloni	Margherita d'Orleans	comici
1672[1]	Incostanza del Fato	Anonymous	March. M.M. Bartolomei *Protettori* *among 3* Carlo Taddei *Immobili member*	Adamisti
1674	Tacere et Amare	G.M. Moniglia[11] *wrote comedies for Immobili*	Cosimo III	Infuocati

[10] Morini gives the membership list contained in the constitution of 1686. See also in Biblioteca Marucelliana, Ms C. 136, *Capitoli dell'Accademia degl'Immobili*, p. 5; Hill, n. 8.

[11] The evidence of the existence of the Infuocati prior to 1665 most difficult to overcome in order to sustain our hypothesis is the statement contained in the preface to *Il potestà di Colognole* in G.A. Moniglia's *Poesie drammatiche* III (1689), p. 3: "[This drama] was repeated in Florence [in 1661[6]] for the visit of the Archduke Ferdinando Carlo d'Austria *nel teatro de' SS. Accademici Infuocati.*" It should be noted he is saying *in the theater*, not *by the academicians.* By contrast, on p. 380 he says of *Tacere et 'amare*, "This present drama was performed in the Teatro di Via del Cocomero *da' SS. Accademici Infuocati.*" Moniglia may be merely identifying the theater by the academicians in control of the theater at the time he wrote the preface. Throughout his prefaces he takes pains to emphasize the nobility of his patrons and audience; hence he would have no cause to record any connection with the Sorgenti. On the other hand, the libretto of 1661[6], which is silent about the academy and theater, does make a tenuous link with *Orontea* (1661[4]), a libretto that does name the Sorgenti.

anonymous author describes the events without naming the academy that remained in via del Cocomero. One begins to suspect that Morini simply supplied the missing name by using that of the academy which in the eighteenth century was in *de facto* possession of the Cocomero theater.

The first solid record of the Infuocati is a libretto of 1665[1], *Le nozze in sogno* by Pietro Susini and music, to judge by the quality of the score, by various amateur composers in the academy. Prior to that date we know of no other document or reference in diaries to the Infuocati, nor does Morini cite any. On the contrary, when the Infuocati are reorganized in 1699, their own review of the history of the Cocomero reaches back to the rental of the Cocomero by the Sorgenti in 1661 (the climactic year of operatic performances by the Sorgenti: see 1661[3-6] and 1662[2]) and omits any reference to the existence of the Infuocati in the seventeenth century. Ferdinando's patronage is likewise undocumented and, because of the lack of librettos dedicated to him, doubtful.

To simplify the exposition of the data Table I, *opposite*, shows performances that can be assigned with some security to the Cocomero for the lack of any other theater from 1665 until 1674.

Before attempting an exegesis of these data, a few more should be thrown in. Priorato Gualdo Galeazzo includes an entry on page 65 about the Infuocati:

> 4. Accademia de gl'Infuocati *moderna* [italics ours] in cui sono ascritti 34.
> nobili Fiorentini, ne d'altri sorte vi s'ammettono. Vi si sono rappresentate
> opere musicali bellissime. Il Protettore di questa era il Serenissimo Principe
> [Cardinale!] Carlo, & ogn'anno si muta il Console.

In the absence of any documentation for the protection of Ferdinando II, the quotation from Galeazzo plus the dedication of the first libretto (1665[1]) makes that of Carlo more substantial.[12] Carlo died in 1666. Hence the appearance thereafter of Leopoldo on the title pages indicates that he has succeeded to the position. Galeazzo's description of the Infuocati as *moderna* follows his description of the Immobili and seems to reinforce the notion that the Infuocati chronologically follow the former, whom he describes as the academy of Cardinal Giovanni Carlo of Glorious Memory.

Next it should be noted that the various theatricals and plays produced a very mixed group of people not very consonant with Morini's designation of the Infuocati as the less and the Immobili as the more aristocratic. Furthermore, Galeazzo says that the Infuocati were limited to thirty-four of the nobility exclusively: the parallel with the thirty-two membership of the Immobili is striking. Reinforcement of a close relationship between the Immobili and the Infuocati comes in the presence of two members of the Immobili among the dedicatees, together with another member of one of the most noble of Tuscan families, the Strozzi, and of Filippo Acciajuoli among the librettists.

The Infuocati, if they seem actually consistent with the character of the Immobili, contrast strongly with the Sorgenti, the tenants of the Cocomero until 1665. Hill lists

---

[12] From the dedication: "Whence. . . one hopes the more. . . that the incomparable benignity of Your Highness (Carlo) will be pleased to make [the academicians of the Infuocati] enjoy with some partiality the fruits of your sublime protection." The wording is important since one weakness in our argument is that, in most cases, a dedicatee is not a protector of the academy. See the varied dedications of the librettos of the Sorgenti prior to 1665. In fact, the appearance of Carlo and Leopoldo on the title pages speaks of a far more distant relationship between these men and the Infuocati than that between Giovanni Carlo and either of his two academies.

seventy-two members including people of diverse talents from performers to painters, none patrician. Obviously all that is required for membership is to have a dramatic talent and to be willing to contribute it to the academy. Yet, despite the contrast, the first libretto for the Infuocati is by Pietro Susini, member of the Sorgenti, and *Rivalità favorevole* of 1668 is a collaboration in one form or another between a member of the noble Infuocati, Ximenes, and another associate of the Sorgenti, Sanmartini. The existence of the printed libretto of *Nozze in sogno* which cites the Infuocati and of a manuscript of intermezzi which cites the Sorgenti in the same year and by the same author begins to take on significance: comic opera and intermezzi, both done as the first cooperative venture of the two academies forced to use the same theater. The disappearance of the Sorgenti implies that the Infuocati, being noble and wealthy, more or less overshadowed the former until 1679, at which time the Sorgenti have built their own theater.

All of this fits with a reconstruction in this manner:

1649   Founding of the Immobili, Giovanni Carlo protector.

1650   Contract for the Cocomero, for some unexplained reason on a quite modest scale (perhaps Mattias' influence).

1652   Construction of the Pergola begun while Cocomero was still unfinished, but this time on a larger scale appropriate to the status of the Immobili.

1655   Cocomero at least partially finished. Giovanni Carlo becomes patron of the Sorgenti, a large society of commoners interested in participating directly in all types of theatricals themselves.

1657   Opening of the Pergola.

1663   Death of Giovanni Carlo. Pergola closed.

1664   Cosimo III becomes protector of Immobili.

1665   An alternate academy is organized for the nobles, the Infuocati, who move into the Cocomero. The Sorgenti contribute to productions but yield precedence to the Infuocati. Card. Carlo becomes protector of the Infuocati (and probably the Sorgenti).

1667   Card. Leopoldo becomes protector after death of Carlo.

1679   Sorgenti reestablish their independence with the construction of a theater (in piazza del Grano?).

How unhappy and frustrating must have been those years following the death of Gian Carlo! The unfortunate Immobili were not only deprived of their theater but were saddled with Cosimo as their protector, just at the time that the rest of Italy and much of Europe were enjoying the fresh excitement of opera. On his own admission Cosimo did not like music and musicians, and furthermore, his French wife, Marguerite d'Orlèans, who did, was proving a bit more than he could handle, both as prince and as grand duke. His father in the 1660's kept sending him off on travels intended to give him more worldly polish and attractiveness in the eyes of Marguerite, a hopeless enterprise as it turned out. Things were bad enough as long as Ferdinando lived, but after his death she became a plague to the court until finally in 1675, having produced three children by Cosimo, she declared her studding days over and departed for France.

The situation could not have been other than most awkward and sensitive to the aristocrats of the Immobili, hamstrung yet not daring to affront Cosimo by simply resigning from the Immobili and founding a new academy in order to be rid of him. After all, had Cosimo really wished to reopen the Pergola, there is no doubt that he could have done so. A comparison with the way in which Prince Ferdinando handled a quite similar situation in Livorno later is instructive (see below, p. 35), and he did in fact reopen the Pergola for his wedding in 1689. The only recourse of the dispossessed nobles would have been to give their support (while remaining officially enrolled in the Immobili) to a new academy with as little noise about it all as possible.

What better construction may we place on the bit of elegant reticence contained in the libretto of *La regina Floridea* (1678[2]) wherein the gentlemen of a new *conversazione* rejoice in the patronage of Francesco de' Medici and recall the loss of Cardinal Leopoldo (who died in 1675) which so grieved them that they did not "desire for a long time to hear upon the stage either grave Melpomene or playful Talia, who for a space of thirty years under the authoritative patronage of such a Prince (Leopoldo), sometimes with the title of the Affinati and sometimes with *another name*, were made familiar to us . . . ." If the author is unconcerned to name the Affinati, why not the Infuocati? And why did the "Infuocati" of 1699, who were in fact of lower social status than the Caccinis, the Strozzis, and the Acciajuolis, and others of the Immobili-Infuocati, choose to ignore the existence of the academy in the seventeenth century totally, finding their history to have originated instead in the Sorgenti?[13] One must wonder if there were not some bitterness still present in 1699 at the reorganization of the Infuocati that led these haute bourgeoisie to forget their seventeenth century noble predecessors. Maylender reflects the blindness of the eighteenth century Infuocati when he begins his history of the Infuocati with the early eighteenth century (undoubtedly he had access to the archives), saying that "The protection of the Infuocati was assumed from the beginning by the prince Ferdinando dei Medici and after his death, Cosimo III delegated this obligation to Camillo Vitelli, to whom succeeded the marchese Scipione Maria Capponi." (Alas, Maylender is all wrong: Prince Ferdinando became protector only in 1704, five years after the reorganization; Vitelli and Capponi were appointed *provveditori*, not protectors; and Gian Gastone followed Ferdinando as protector. But the point remains valid.)

Having eliminated the Infuocati before 1665, we can return to the Sorgenti in order to consider their membership and thus to clarify somewhat the relations among the three academies, the Immobili, the Sorgenti and the Infuocati. Hill in n. 12 lists the membership. Like the Immobili, it is divided into people who are expected to contribute money (Accademici Solventi, et Obbligati alle Tasse) and those who contribute labor and talent

---

[13] The earliest *Capitolo dell'Accademia degl'Infuocati*, dated September 1, 1699, describes the group as a "new conversazione limited to twenty members" under the protection and patronage of Saint Andrea Corsini. The reference to the Sorgenti is in a legal brief beginning "Osservazione sopra l'esposto nel memoriale dell'Ill.mo Sig. Carlo Filippo Ughi." One "capitoli" speaks of reconstituting the "ancient academy," but we believe it to be a later composition, for it concludes with a continuing membership roll from 1701 to February 10, 1919. I Fac: Infuocati, Busta 1.

(Accademici Esenti dalle Tasse et altri pagamenti, essendo obbligati ad altri impieghi per l'appresso Cause). None of the former are nobility. It is interesting to encounter Antonio Guerretti who may be the father or grandfather of the Antonio Guerretti who is an impresario at the Cocomero in the eighteenth century (1710^6 to 1741^3). Also present are Mario Calamari, playwright, and Ferdinando Tacca, architect of the Immobili. In the second group are members who are expected to dance, to make costumes, to recite spoken roles, to sing, to play instruments, to work the machines, to copy manuscripts, to be prompters, to write, to paint, to compose music, and one gentleman to go out, that is, one supposes, to travel about buying necessary supplies, engaging singers, and running errands in general. The singers include Antonio Ruggiero, listed as a singer and a painter, Michele Mosi, Niccola Coresi, as a singer and an instrumentalist, and Antonio Rivani. All of these sang in 1658^1 at the Pergola. Rivani, in fact, sang in all of the productions at the Pergola from 1657^1 until 1663. Jacopo Melani is listed as a composer and he likewise was called upon regularly to supply scores for the Immobili. Obviously it was a common practice for the Immobili to call upon the Sorgenti for assistance in their operas at the Pergola. The relationship between the Sorgenti and the Infuocati naturally falls into the same pattern.

The Sorgenti must have felt very much the underdogs in the Cocomero once the Infuocati settled in, and such circumstances provided sufficient motivation for the Sorgenti's having built another theater for themselves of which the inaugural work is probably *Donna saggia può ciò che vuole*, a prose comedy with a prologue for music by Pietro Susini, appropriately enough. It was, as the title page indicates, performed in 1679^3 by the Sorgenti in their "new theater." Unfortunately, it does not locate the theater. However, Quadrio[14] says that the Sorgenti had a theater first "in piazza del Grano, then moved to via dell'Anguillara, and presently (1752) are to be found behind S. Remigio." By observing the alternate periods of activity and inactivity (a method made hazardous by the modest nature of the Sorgenti's theatrical productions, not often requiring the publication of librettos), one can guess that the Sorgenti were in piazza del Grano around 1679^3, in via dell'Anguillara from 1684^5 to 1701^3, and about 1742^{10} were located behind S. Remigio.

Besides the new theater of the Sorgenti, two other small academic theaters open during the second period: in 1669^4 the Imperfetti are first recorded in a theater in Borgo Tegolaio. Later, in 1673^2, another academy used the same theater, this time the Rinvigoriti. In 1676^1 the Imperfetti perform in a new theater, one having a history through the remainder of the period covered in this chronology, the theater in the Corso de'Tintori. In 1689^4, the Imperfetti are replaced by the Cadenti, and thereafter the theater is as often identified by the name of that academy as by the name of the street.

L'incostanza del Fato in 1672^1 seems to present another solution to the problem of the incapacity of the Immobili, that is, to organize *ad hoc* academies to sponsor individual operatic performances. The patron and dedicatee is Marchese Mattias Bartolommei, a playwright himself, and the "Protectors of the drama" are three noblemen, one of whom, Carlo Taddei, is a member of the Immobili in both the lists of 1648 (founders) and 1686. The academicians who sign the dedication are the Adamisti, unknown to Maylender and represented in the chronology by this one entry. This solution appears more frequently during the third period of our history.

---

14 Tomo VII (*Indice universale*), p. 10.

Before concluding this narrative of the second period in Florentine theatrical history, we must draw attention to the dedication of *La Dori* in 1670[2] to Margherita Luisa, Principessa di Toscana, Cosimo's unhappy wife, by the actress who played the role of Dori. It is a pathetic sign of the agitation in the Medici household. La Dori is the ancestor of *Die Entfuehrung aus dem Serail*, the story of the escape from a harem by a beautiful Christian princess. Margherita had to delay her escape until 1675, when Louis XIV finally gave her permission to enter a convent near Paris. In the year following its performance in Florence, *La Dori* was given in Rome at the special insistence of Maria Mancini Colonna, and *she* ran away from *her* philandering husband that very same opera season! Without even asking Louis's permission!

III. 1678-1711

The third period in the history of the theaters coincides with the patronage of opera maintained by Francesco Maria and Ferdinando de' Medici, the inaugural events being the performances of *La Regina Floridea* at Francesco's palace, the Casino di S. Marco, in 1678[2], and in the following year of *Con la forza d'amor* at Ferdinando's villa at Pratolino. The two men, though uncle and nephew respectively, were close to each other in temperament, taste, and age: in 1678 Francesco was 18 and in 1679 Ferdinando was 16, ages which in the seventeenth century were quite sufficiently advanced for young princes to establish their own courts.

Francesco must be given the credit for initiating the new era of Florentine opera, and undoubtedly it was his influence that encouraged his nephew to follow his example. Like Giovanni Carlo before him, Francesco established an academy, called in this case the *Conversazione del Casino di S. Marco*. *La Floridea* is their first effort. In the dedication to Francesco they exult that the drought which had afflicted the Florentine stage ever since the death of Leopoldo in 1675 (they are being generous: they should have said since the death of Giovanni Carlo!) has come to an end with the "acquisition of the most felicitous Protection which Your Highness has so condescendingly deigned to concede to us [and because of which,] seized by supreme joy, we undertake with secure confidence to recall upon the stage the more delightful and precious Muses, [Melpomene and Thalia]."

From 1678[2] until 1682[1] the new conversazione produced one opera each year. In the first two years the season was not specified, but in the next two they were performed in October and November respectively, which suggests a coordination with Ferdinando's operas, which, beginning in 1679[2], took place in September. Possibly the arrangement allowed the same singers to perform in succession. We have no explanation for the hiatus between 1682[1] and 1686[3], the year of the next production by the Conversazione del Casino, but thereafter Francesco became cardinal and, as his diary shows, he spent much of his time in Rome. The Casino still doubtless continued periodically to perform other theatricals on the order of the prose (?) comedy *Il Cid* in 1691 (see 1694[1]), but the only other opera occurs in 1695[2]. Otherwise Francesco apparently chose when in Florence to join Ferdinando at Pratolino rather than to sponsor his own operas.[15]

---

[15] See letters to Francesco de Castris listed under manuscripts in the bibliography.

COSIMO I
1519-1574
Duke 1537
Grand Duke 1569

FRANCESCO I
1541-1587
Grand Duke 1574

Don Antonio
natural son?

FERDINANDO I
1543-1609
Grand Duke 1587
= Cristina di Lorena
d. 1637

Carlo
Cardinal 1615
d. 1666

Francesco
d. 1614

COSIMO II
1590-1621
Grand Duke 1609
= Maria Maddalena
d'Austria
d. 1631

Francesco
d. 1634

Giovanni Carlo
1611-1663
Cardinal

FERDINANDO II
1610-1670
Grand Duke 1621
= Vittoria della
Rovere *d. 1694*

COSIMO III
1642-1723
Grand Duke 1670
= Margherita Luisa
d'Orleans *d. 1721*

Anna Maria Luisa
Ludovica
1667-1743
= Giovanni
Guglielmo
Elettore Palatino
del Reno

GIAN GASTONE
1671-1737
Grand Duke 1721
= Anna Maria von
Saxe-Lauenberg

Don Giovanni
natural son
d. 1621

Lorenzo
d. 1648

Caterina
= Ferdinando
Gonzaga
Mantua

Maddalena

Claudia Felicitas
= *1.* Federigo della
Rovere *Urbino*
2. Leopoldo
d'Austria *Tyrol*

Vittoria della
Rovere *d. 1694*

Mattias
1613-1667

Leopoldo
1617-1675
Cardinal 1667

Anna
= Ferdinando
Carlo d'Austria

Margherita
= Odoardo Farnese
Parma

Francesco Maria
1660-1711
Cardinal 1686-1709
= Eleonora Gonzaga

THE MEDICI
1519-1737

Ferdinando
1673-1713
= Violante Beatrice
di Baviera *d. 1730*

SEMPER

Ferdinando by far eclipsed his uncle in the strength, effectiveness, and continuity of his efforts to revive opera in Tuscany. Possessed by a passion for music, he assumed control over musical affairs in all corners of Tuscany and exhibited a desire for power that might also be a measure of the degree to which his father excluded him from any real political power. He was, as is well-known, a capable and talented musician in his own right, being an accomplished cembalist. In fact, since he occupied himself with every detail of his productions of opera at Pratolino, it can be assumed safely that he directed from the harpsichord. His intervention throughout Tuscany was doubtless a reinforcement and an encouragement of good music, but it also sometimes must have been a weighty musical despotism.

The direct outlet for his passion was primarily the theater he had constructed in his villa at Pratolino[16] and secondarily, especially towards the end of the century, the Florentine theaters. But since the need in these cases for correspondence was limited to engaging singers (of which more will be said later), the view of his manner of operating through and controlling his academies is obscure. However, Ferdinando was not content to restrict his passion for opera to his own personally directed productions at Pratolino or to the encouragement of performances in Florence, for he obviously felt a mission to bring opera to all of the major cities of Tuscany. His method was to encourage the foundation or in some cases, revival of dramaturgical academies, the Avvalorati in Livorno, the Intronati in Siena, others in Pisa, Lucca, and Pistoia. His vigorous dedication to opera found men to match it and many who hoped to benefit from his largesse. Even small towns appealed to him. The Accademici Ricomposti of Terra d'Anghiari wrote a humble petition in 1702 (I Fas [Med 5903, c. 789]) for his protection, and likewise in 1705 (I Fas [Med 5903, c. 790]), the Accademici Rinascenti of Poppi, a village of perhaps a thousand souls. Francesco Antonio Pistocchi was emboldened by his long correspondence with Ferdinando to propose that Ferdinando become the patron of the Filharmonici of Bologna which he naturally refused as being outside of his dominion (I Fas [Med 5905, cc. 100 and 348]). But in Livorno Ferdinando's efforts met with reluctance and bitter complaints; and out of these complaints, all addressed to Pier Antonio Gerini, his *maestro di camera*, comes an extraordinarily vivid picture of Ferdinando's *modus operandi.*[17]

Among Tuscan cities of that time, Livorno was comparatively industrial and commercial. In a modest degree it fattened on rivalries among commercial interests of Spain and England and so its dependence upon Florence was not quite so abject as that of cities of the Arno. Its bourgeoisie, made up of businessmen, traders, merchants and seamen, had little interest in spending good hard-earned cash on aristocratic and academic frivolities like opera, and they said so to Gerini in language more vivid and heated than eloquent.

The first opera which Ferdinando promoted in Livorno was Scarlatti's *Pompeo* in 1688. However, the carteggio of letters begins only in late 1696. In 1697 Ferdinando expanded his ambitions for Livorno and the sparks began to fly.

On July 19, 1697, the governor of Livorno, Marchese Alessandro del Borro, wrote to Gerini about his difficulties in rounding up the academicians necessary for performing and financing the opera for the next carnival.

---

[16] Fabbri, *A. Scarlatti*, reproduces between pages 36 and 37 a view of the Villa Medicea di Pratolino and the plan of the third floor where the theater was located.

[17] All of the following letters concerning Livorno are found in I Fas: Med. 5909.

As soon as I had understood the command of the most serene crown prince
given to me by your Lordship in his most gentle letter of the 16th of the
current month in which I was charged with putting together the necessary
number of academicians for the comedies which will be done in the coming
carnival, I undertook myself the task of reestablishing and restoring, as I
presume at this point, the number of 16 academicians, the same as last year.
However, I have not met with success so easily as one might suppose, because
these gentlemen complain that they sustained a loss of seven hundred pieces,
owing to the little attention on the part of those who spent money, and
particularly because of the *Piazza morte* [complimentary tickets] held at the
gate whereby dozens of people were admitted at the pleasure of Parenti [a
member of the Academy who probably was in charge of the gate] without
having regard for the people of the proper academicians, many of whom
declared themselves to be offended, especially the signori Huigens and
Sologni. Hence to keep these academicians loyal, who profess a particular
ambition to meet the will and desire of His Serene Highness and more
importantly to capture their good will in the future, it would appear
opportune to think about better regulating this conduct.

One should note not only the internecine struggle but the wording that leaves little doubt
about the origins of this academy: the Marquis is putting it together upon orders from
Ferdinando. It is hardly springing up as a spontaneous burst of cultural activity. The
governor's letters year after year continue to remark on the reluctance of the gentlemen to
accept their appointed duties.

The carteggio overflows with problems, many of which are clearly solved by princely,
law-bending pressures. In 1698 the Stanzio delle Commedie rented normally by the
Avvalorati was closed by the heir of the owner, Mattias Francesco Bonfigli. Of course, the
situation could not be tolerated. While only one-half of the correspondence, that is,
Bonfigli's, is preserved, his growing anxiety over his confrontation with Ferdinando, is
pathetically reflected in his own letters (c. 24, 25, 36, 44). At the last minute, in January
1699, Bonfigli capitulates, grants the theater and frantically apologizes, protesting his desire
to please the prince.

The largest problem is the lodging of the singers who were quartered on the citizens like
a conquering army. One much harassed merchant, Francesco Salamoni, had had quite enough
of these annual guests by 1698 when he complained (c. 82) that he had been putting up
musicians and their families since 1693 and that the previous year he had been forced to
entertain Elena Garofalini, a Bolognese singer in the service of the Duke of Mantua, who
arrived with a sister, a brother and a servant, all apparently in the last stages of acute
malnutrition. He went so far as to send Gerini a complete accounting for all of his income
and expenditures for the entire year in order to convince him that he really could not afford
to accept these ravenous singers and their entourages. It did him no good except that his
guests were changed to instrumentalists, presumably a much more humble breed compared
to the opera stars. From 1703 to 1706 he accepted a young theorbist, Niccolo Susier (the
same man who wrote the diary so useful to the chronology of Florentine opera), without
complaints. The large number of the members of the family and their servants accompanying
a singer was a frequent complaint. Marchese del Borro passed on another bill, obviously much
to his embarrassment, that one host insisted be paid to him (c.82): "for the performance
in 1698 for food for Signora Maria Landini, her husband, a chamberlain, a servant and a
lackey for seventy-one days, beginning December 11, 1697, and ending February 19, 1698,

and in addition food for her brother who arrived the 13th and departed the 31st of January, in all 150 mori."

The burghers crossed the Prince to their peril. What was the particular form the power of the Prince took is not clear. One can only observe the results. Alamanni Veneroso on December 7, 1696, wanted and expected La Florentina but instead La Romana, a woman,[18] whoever she was, of extravagant ways, arrived. Veneroso promptly threw her out in the streets, bag, baggage, and claque (c. 97). Ten days later he grovelled (c. 98). He had only been trying to accommodate the wishes of the Prince who had assigned him La Florentina and how was he to know these people were not trying to force him to disobey the Prince's commands? La Romana was indeed not very well liked, that is, if la Romana is the same singer who is the subject of another irate letter, this time from Francesco Ternesi. On November 14, 1702, after agreeing to take a violoncello player, he continues (c. 76), "But I do not want on any account that animal who usually comes here in other years because it is impossible to come out of it with honor because, accustomed to Rome, nothing is found, not any kind of amusement at Livorno, no matter how noble or honorable, that will content her and free me from insults and tortures."

In Florence the resistance to Ferdinando's ambition was assuredly less heated. But there were other complications beyond our ability to assess: the conflict between Ferdinando and Cosimo III that bears some similarity to the contention between George I and his son, the Prince of Wales, during Handel's time. In Florence the question was to go or not to go, depending upon whom one wished least to offend.

Doubtless, as in other matters, G. F. Young in *The Medici*[19] exaggerates Cosimo's boorish and oppressive character. Despite Piccini's[20] quotation to the effect that at his own wedding Cosimo wanted nothing to do either with musicians or music, he did mellow sufficiently to attend the opera at Pratolino in 1701[5] and 1702[4], though any other attendance is certainly unnoticed by the diarists. And it is difficult to believe that singers of the Grand Duke's *musici ordinari* such as Ippolito Fusai and Filippo Melani could have sung at Pratolino in 1679 without the at least grudging approval of Cosimo. Still there was friction and, as a memorial written in 1688 by Francesco Redi[21] shows, the two communicated with each other through ambassadors. Later Francesco de Castris, one of the favorite singers of both Ferdinando and Francesco de' Medici, became the intermediary, and when Cosimo, enraged, violently objected to dealing with such a person, de Castris was forced into exile in Rome.

Whatever the causes, whether court intrigue or academic objections to or reluctance to undertake the expenses of opera, the effects in Florence are visible. One sign is the stubborn problem of the Pergola. It is simply incredible that had the Grand Duke wished the theater to be opened, it would not have been opened, and his attitude during Ferdinando's negotiations to open it during the celebration of his wedding is reluctant and unwilling beneath the diplomatic gloss of Redi's memorial. Where Ferdinando could use the legal apparatus to force Bonfigli to keep the theater in Livorno open, rights of heirs notwithstanding, he is powerless in Florence itself. He tried. In 1688 he replaced Cosimo as the protector of the Immobili having probably instigated the reorganization of the academy in 1686.

---

[18] The most likely singer is Isabella de Angelis Romana who sang in Florence, 1700[3], and previously in 1699 in Livorno.

[19] Pp. 710-716

[20] P. 38.

[21] Reproduced in Fabbri, *A. Scarlatti*, opp. 44.

The immediate objective was to obtain the theater for the approaching wedding of Ferdinando and Violante Beatrice di Baviera in 1689 which was duly celebrated by a performance of *Il Greco in Troia*. But afterwards the academy relapsed into inactivity and the theater, splendidly restored for this one occasion, closed again until 1718 except for a few displays of horsemanship on the part of the Accademia dei Nobili.

The Infuocati and the theater in via del Cocomero fared somewhat better, but stability and continuity still eluded both the academicians and any would-be commercial impresarios. Between 1674, when the Infuocati were last heard from, and 1687, only two operas are performed, both of them with texts by Ludovico Adimari, who very likely paid at least for the publication of the libretto himself, if not for a substantial portion of the total costs. According to entries in diaries, the Infuocati performed in 1687 one or another of the *Lisimaco*'s current in that year; another unknown opera in 1688; *Adelaide* for the wedding festivities of 1689, and then two operas in the carnival of 1690, one dedicated to Ferdinando and the other to Violante di Baviera. But another unexplained lacuna intervenes between 1690 and 1698 that is filled by a strange series of academies whose librettos are all dedicated to either Ferdinando or to Violante and whose dedications are filled with obscurity. The names of the academies are testimony that something is amiss: Volante (1690), Improvisi (1690), Innominati (1692), Efimeri (1692), Saggiati (1693); and then silence for two years. As if exhausted from the efforts to think up pathetic names for themselves, from 1696 until 1704[5] the academicians do not identify themselves on the librettos. As if it were all hopeless anyway, no dedications are written, and the theater is not named. During this time the Infuocati, if they actually existed, are reorganized. Charters of 1699, 1700, and 1701-1706 are found in the Infuocati Archives. At first it is evident that there is no real continuity of membership and that the backers of the opera are organizing themselves on an annual basis, writing a rental contract with the Ughi each year.

The smaller theaters were erratically active during this third period, among them the most continuously so being the Sorgenti, whether in piazza del Grano or in via dell'Anguillara, followed by the rarer Cadenti in corso de' Tintori, and the still rarer Rinvigoriti in Borgo Tegolaio. For a brief five years a conversazione "al Canto de' Carnesecchi dal Centauro" devoted itself to performances of opera imported from Rome in 1684[1], 1685[1], 1686[2], and 1688[3]. Al Canto de' Carnesecchi is, it would seem, a location between Florence and Fiesole; however, we wonder whether that is only the location of its usual meetings and whether the performances actually took place in the Cocomero. If so, the missing year may be filled by *Lisimaco* (1687[1]) which would fit into their Roman operas if one chose the Pasquini setting. Also, since the Infuocati are not active during these years, the Centauro would appear to be another academy like the Adamisti and the several in the last decade who rent the Cocomero briefly. However brilliant their five-year existence, they disappeared utterly after 1688, and significantly Settimanni does not record any performance by them in the celebrations for the wedding of Ferdinando in 1689, one year after their last performance. The Teatro della Venerabile Compagnia di Giovanni Evangelista, normally occupied with oratorio, ventured into secular though moralizing drama on two occasions: 1683[1] and 1696[1]. One oddity is something called the *stanza* de' Rifritti (1682[2]).

Only one new theater, "nuovo e bel," went up during the third period. It was located by a diarist in Borgo Ognissanti in 1692. Another theater described as being "in Porta rossa" (1694[1]) may have been a temporary theater since it was never heard from again.

In summary, then, the third period is the expression above all of the determined ambition of Ferdinando de' Medici to make Florence an operatic capital to equal the great cities of Europe. Both his devotion and his tyranny can be recognized as contributory to the characteristics of the period: the great increase in number of performances and at the same time the remarkable instability of the academies, whose membership must have found the organizations at times to be a tool whereby the prince could extort directly or indirectly money for his operas. Adding to their problems as well as to the prince's would have been the disapproval of Cosimo for all such goings-on. It must have discouraged some of the wealthier and more powerful families from participating and given others by disposition already disinclined to do so good excuse for their refusal. All of these circumstances would have created a situation in which the devoted men at the top of Ferdinando's academies were few in number who, in order to exist at all, would have been forced to organize and to reorganize the academies as the base of the membership evaporated. New members would have had to be recruited (as the governor of Livorno had done) like conscripts for an army, since the wealthy or not-so-wealthy merchants would have been reluctant indeed to shoulder the cost of the productions. Economically the period is one of decline in Tuscany, and Florence was in no position to bid in the same market as Venice, Vienna, Rome and Paris. The financial crisis reported in 1690[2] was probably only too common. But such things would not have deterred Ferdinando. The whole bootstrap operation which had as its objective the raising of Florentine opera above the level of amateur theatricals depended upon one thing: Ferdinando's ability to provide singers. He did so, as we shall recount in the following essay.

IV.   1699-1737

Beginning with *Muzio Scevola* (1696[3]), a continuous series of librettos having standardized appearance is published in Florence without any indication of the theater, an academy, a dedication (except 1696[4] and 1703[4] both dedicated to Violante Beatrice di Baviera) or a protector. The lack of all of these things at once occurs very infrequently and at no other time with such consistency and continuity. The series ends only with *Il più fedele fra i vassali* (1704[5]). All, excepting *Il Girello* (1697[5]), a burlesque, and *Il sospetto non ha fondamento* (1699[6]), a pastorale, are dramas previously performed in Venice, Naples, Rome, etc. From 1696[3] to 1697[6] the seasons are not stated, but thereafter the season appears on the title pages and by 1698[2,3,6] it is apparent that the seasons have become standardized at two operas during carnival and one in the autumn, i.e. November. From 1698[6] the singers are listed in most librettos and a continuity based upon them is possible. The continuity is joined by increasingly frequent references in Fagiuoli's diary that confirm the use of the Cocomero or the "teatro degl'Infuocati." Then in 1699 the archives of the Infuocati confirm that the academy has been reorganized. In 1704 the libretto declares the opera to be under the protection of Ferdinando.

The earlier operas in the series from 1696[3] to 1698[3] could reasonably be assigned to the Cocomero on the basis of the consistency of the whole series, but we have, with perhaps unaccustomed restraint, refrained from doing so in view of the unusually vigorous activity at the Sorgenti and Cadenti theaters and of Fagiuoli's entry quoted in 1698[1]. Our beginning of this fourth period in 1699 is arbitrarily based upon the existence of documents which confirm a reorganization that probably was in effect as early as 1696[3] and which made possible regular performances at the Cocomero.

The earliest records are a rental agreement and the rules and regulations (the *capitoli*) both dated the first of September, 1699, and signed by the academicians of the Infuocati. In the first, Giovanni Batista Ruggierj agreed to pay scudi 105 for the year's occupancy of the "grand room and rooms (stanzone e stanze) of the theater in via del Cocomero in order to do comedies." The payment went to the Marchese Ferdinando Bartolommei (perhaps a governmental representative or representative of the Ughi family). It is signed by twenty academicians of the Infuocati "under the protection of S. Andrea Corsini," who, as a fourteenth century Florentine saint, would have as a protector been uncritical and undemanding but unfortunately miserly as well.

The constitution of *capitoli* of 1699 (see footnote *13*) is a very simple, businesslike, legal document having a much more bourgeois character than the 1651 Immobili constitution with its insistence on cavalieresque exercises and imperative goals of perfection. The men who sign both the rental agreement and the constitution of 1699 are of respectable families but there are no noblemen among them and, although the membership is limited to twenty, the quality of birth is not mentioned as a requirement. Filippo Niccolini who, as is revealed in 1699[6], was elected *provveditore*, was a lawyer. Gregorio Barsotti became an impresario in 1731[2]. Francesco Maria Ricci was a banker. Other families are Miccinesi, Riccioli, Montucci, Archi, Landi, and Berzini. The title and summary of the provisions follow:

> *Capitoli dell'Accademia degl'Infuocati posti sotto il patrocinio di S. Andrea Corsini*, 1699; a "new conversazione with a membership of twenty located in the grand room of via del Cocomero or the rooms annexed to the same settled upon them by Sig. Carlo Ughi under the agreement with Sig. Gio. Batista Ruggieri."

1. All members will share expenses equally.

2. Membership maintained on a yearly basis. Members must give six months' notice of withdrawal before the first of September each year.

3. Resigning members may appoint a successor, but, failing to do so, must continue to pay their portion of the expenses.

4. Payment of the rent of the theater is to be in advance and prorated among the members.

5. Members in arrears within fifteen days are automatically "licensed" but are still liable for the amounts owed.

6. Procedures for withdrawal are established.

7. Officers to be elected are: *provveditore* (who reports in April and September subject to fines for failure to do so) and a *servo* on salary to care for the theater.

8. Provision that, if expenses decline, by reason (for example) of a rise in profits from the gaming tables (*Trattenimenti del gioco*), the profit will be applied to the rental of the theater and the cost to each member appropriately recalculated.

9. *Provveditore* must keep books and minutes of meetings. He has the power to pay ordinary expenses but must consult the academy before paying extraordinary expenses.

10. The *provveditore* will call meetings.

11. Concerns the notification of actions taken at meetings to be sent to absent members.

12. Establishes voting rules and the limits of majority rule.

13. In the absence of action by the *provveditore* the *servo* may call a meeting.

14. The academicians may participate in any comedies done by Ruggiero but only under the rules stated in the rental agreement.

We could not find a rental agreement for 1700, though there must have been one. But there is a list of members in 1700 which shows an almost total change in membership. The general class is the same. Again the nobility is conspicuously absent. The number of men is twenty-seven, compared with twenty-one the preceding year, and twenty-four in 1701. These facts tend to reinforce the view expressed above, that, at least until 1701, the "academies" were *ad hoc* organizations rarely, if ever, outlasting a year. Possibly a rotation among a large group had been in operation during the 1690s.

In 1701 the Infuocati were definitively reorganized on a more permanent basis. Again there exists a rental agreement and a *capitoli*. The rental contract of October 31, 1701, is for five years, and this time the contract is with Senator Alamanno Ughi (but signed by his son, Carlo Lorenzo Ughi) to whom the payment is due of eighty-two scudi in advance every six months. The contract is much more explicit than that of 1699.

The academicians are granted the right to concede the theater to whomever they wish in order "to do recitations or comedies, whether in music or in prose," without Ughi's having the right to "make any opposition whatsoever" or to "pretend to any sort of emolument." Among various items, the most curious is a provision for the purchase of all of the theatrical costumes (*tutti gl'Abiti da commedia*) by the academicians for sixty-two scudi, whence it appears that the Ughi had retained ownership of the costumes, probably renting them along with the theater. The furnishings also are the property of the Ughi and the contract is very specific about what the academicians are allowed to do with them.

We are not entirely sure about the proper dating of the *capitoli* that purports to be contemporary with the rental agreements. We think it may be a copy of the original in which a few minor alterations have taken place. The title reads: *Capitoli dell'Accademia degli'Infuocati posti sotto il Patrocinio di S. Andrea Corsini e sotto la protezione del Ser. mo Principe Ferdinando di Toscana* (without date). It concludes with a list of all members continuing to February 10, 1919. Its contents are interesting, though without further examination it may not be assumed to be a primary source. It speaks of the resolution to reassume the ancient Academy degli Infuocati composed of twenty-four united *cittadini*. The officers in contrast to 1699 have been augmented to a *console*, two *consiglieri*, a *provveditore*, a *sotto provveditore*, and a *segretario*. The Academicians vow to sponsor at least ten masses to celebrate the festival of S. Andrea Corsini.

An agreement dated 1702 initiated a long series of attempts over the years to enlarge the theater. The same carton contains contracts for enlargements in 1754 (to raise the roof and add another order of balconies), in 1764, and others in the nineteenth century, including a proposal to build a new theater "nel posto della Pallacorda da S. Maria Nuova [*sic*]." The wording of the 1702 agreement, quite apart from any revelation it contains about the theater itself, illuminates the tangled relationship between the Ughi and the academies using the theater, which has all the earmarks of the eternal conflicts of landlord and tenant. Carlo Ughi is addressed as the *padrone di detti effetti* (the *stanzone e stanze*) *e mobili* (furnishings) and he is held responsible for seeing that all properties are in good condition and serviceable for the purposes of the academy. Under these conditions obviously improvements to the theater will be the subject of constant contention between owners and tenant. It is not surprising that an enormous portion of the Infuocati archives are filled with legal briefs.

Once established the academy does operate with sufficient efficiency to do operas every year with rare interruptions (see carnival 1709) except for official state mourning. The protection of Ferdinando is acknowledged (though not always) from 1704 until his death in 1713. His influence cannot be documented, but he must have contributed money, as Gian Gastone did later, and his recruitment of singers is occasionally to be spotted in his correspondence. Prior to 1704 none of his correspondence seems directly related to performances other than Livorno and Pratolino, though suspiciously, singers he engaged for Pratolino in the fall turn up in the casts of the Cocomero. For example, he requested from the Duke of Mantua the services of Cattarina [*sic*] Azzolini (**I** Fas Med. 5885: c. 22) for Pratolino and acknowledged his indebtedness to the same duke for sending Regina Polastri to Livorno in the late summer of 1700 (c. 23). Both singers performed at the Cocomero in the following carnival. His own singers make up a large portion of those performing at the Cocomero as will be seen by comparing the casts with the list of Ferdinando's singers on page 68. In one of the rare signs of some accommodation between Cosimo and Ferdinando, but as always through intermediaries, Cosimo granted Filippo Balatri, a ducal musician, permission to sing in 1703[4] at the expressed desire of Ferdinando before, it should be noted, he became the official protector.

After he became officially the protector, he wrote to ask for singers specifically for his academy. To the Duke of Modena he wrote on July 21, 1705: "This theater of Florence being under my protection, I regard the Impresarios with a special inclination; for which reason I cannot deny them my more ardent supplications toward Your Highness that you may concede to them Gio. Batta Roberti for the approaching recitation of autumn and of carnival . . . ."[22]

The policies of the academy concerning the operatic fare offered to the public were obviously to bring to Florence the dramatic poetry in fashion in Rome, Venice and Vienna: the works of Zeno, Noris, Silvani, and the like. Between 1696 and 1704, out of twenty-eight librettos only one, *Il Girello*, by Filippo Acciajuoli (1697[5]) is by a Tuscan and that was performed first in Rome, 1668. Ferdinando was only slightly more inclined to use Tuscan poets at Pratolino during the same years. Antonio Salvi's *Astianatte* (1701[5]) and *Arminio* (1703[3]) are the only first performances by a Florentine. At Pratolino he was more concerned about the novelty of the music, spending much effort upon the choice of composer and then supervising and approving the results (even returning scores for alteration where they did not satisfy him), but he rarely favored composers around him such as Pagliardi, Bitti, Cattani, and de Castris in preference to outsiders such as Alessandro Scarlatti and Giacomo Perti. At the Cocomero, the situation is very unclear owing to the great lack of positive identification of composers. In the same period only the two operas, both by

---

[22] **I** Fas: Med. 5903, c. 455. Reply, c. 172.

Tommaso Albinoni in 1703[2,4] appear to be first performances. As for type, both theaters, Pratolino and Cocomero, mount *drami per musica* on end and when a burlesque (*Girello*, 1697[5]) or a pastorale (*Sospetto*, 1699[6]) is done, it stands out as a remarkable event.

After 1704 several noteworthy changes occur which may or may not stem from the active patronage of Ferdinando. First, the number of first performances of texts and/or music increases (see 1707[1], 1707[4], 1707[6], 1708[4], 1710[6]). Second, comic contrascenes and intermezzi are introduced (1703[2], 1704[6], 1711[3], 1713[3], 1715[4], etc.). Third, the first resurrection of a seventeenth century burletta or comic opera, *La serva favorita* (1705[5]) takes place, the first indication of an identity gradually assumed by the Cocomero as a comic theater. Finally Giuseppe Orlandini, maestro di cappella to Prince Gian Gastone, begins his long and fruitful association with the theater possibly as early as 1707[1].

As soon as the official year of mourning for Ferdinando, who died October 30, 1713, ended, Gian Gastone became the protector of the Infuocati. A house adjacent to those rented by the academy and belonging to the Medici was refurbished for use, at least in part, for gambling and connected with the theater by a passage leading directly to new rooms constructed in the first balcony for Gian Gastone, all at his expense. A *ricordo* in the Infuocati archives describes the auspicious occasion on November 25, 1714, when Gian Gastone first played (*si è giocato per la prima volta*), then ceremoniously passed into the theater, being met by the academicians whom he reaffirmed in his protection, to attend the opera, *Sesostri re d'Egitto* (1714[1]).

Among the financial records of the Infuocati, which are very sparse and haphazardly ordered, a summary of opera expenses and receipts in 1722 is more complete and informative than most of the records; therefore we quote it in full. The date must be *ab incarnatione* if it is to be related to a libretto by Antonio Salvi, that is, *Ginevra* (1723[2]).

EXPENSES

Opera	Scudi
In Musica	1180
Orchestra	248:2:3.4
Alle Strumentari	17:1
Carta Rigata	3:5:12.4
Al Copista	12
della per Rammentare	2:6
per nolo d'Abiti	220
In Velj	17.4.5
Evanti [?]	13:−:13.4
Per Cimsierj [chemiserie] per le donne	14.7
Calze di seta	13.9
Calze d' Bambagia per le comparsi	6:−6.8
Scarpe, e Stivaletti	13:5:
Olio, e Candele d'	62:3:−.2
Cera per Torcieri, moccoli, e stoppioni	7:4:17.
Spese di comparse, et altri operante sera per sera	124:5:1.2
Al Sig.ᵉ D. Salvi, e Sig. Salvini per regalo	21:3.
Spese d' Quartiere, per i Virtuosi	54:2.6
Spese diverse	73:5.9.8

RECEIPTS

Da Cav.[i] Interessati	323:5
Da Bullettini	608:6:15.4
Appalti	692:2:8.8
Palichetti [*sic*]	375:6.8.4
Stampatore dell'Opera	20:4
Appala d'Argine e Porte	38:4.13.4
Appalto di Circo	17.1
Dal Ser Gran Principe	47.4.6.8

"Appalla d'Argine e Porte" we take to mean open spaces for standing behind barriers and doors (to the boxes) and the "Appalto di Circo" to mean the rental of space in the top balcony which, judging by the amount, was not expensive. No totals are given, but the scudi alone show a small profit.

Notice the relatively small outlay for costumes. Plainly new costumes are not required for every role and the attendants needed only shoes and stockings. Altogether costumes cost less than the candles and lamp oil. One is reminded of the item above in the first rental contract wherein the new conversazione purchased costumes from the Ughi. The gifts to Salvi and Salvini are also quite low, being somewhat more than the cost of copying, probably because the libretto was old and needed only rewriting and because of the status of the gentlemen; that is to say, they are not common salaried persons. The interesting feature is the amount of Gian Gastone's decently generous contribution. In 1730 below, the dues-paying membership is only twenty-three. Assuming a like number in 1722, each member is contributing fourteen scudi; the prince, more than three times the average gift. To be noted also is the fact that the publisher paid for the privilege of publishing the libretto in return for which he retained the profit from the sales. *Bullettini* represent the proceeds from the sale of individual tickets; *Appalti* the subscriptions for boxes; and *Palchetti*, the sale of seats in boxes not otherwise subscribed.

As the operation of the theater developed under the new organization, the academicians themselves withdrew from direct involvement (compare 1665) in the productions leaving increasingly all responsibility in the hands of the impresarios, who were normally, but in the case of the Cocomero not always, members of the academy. This evolution is apparent in the late years of the reign of Gian Gastone, who himself withdrew from participation in any kind of social activity, but it becomes especially characteristic in the final period of our history. The choices of composer and musical director, the opera to be done and the singers devolved upon the impresario, a fact that is made clear by Susier's remark in 1748[16] that the impresario Grifoni had Pescetti come from Venice to compose and direct *Arminio* at the Pergola. As a halfway point in the evolution, so to speak, we can cite the disorderly collection of papers which Antonio Guerretti as impresario in 1730-1731 used to figure his expenses (the only papers of this sort to survive in such quantity in the archives).[23] The earliest documents concerning the operas of autumn, 1730, and carnival, 1731, are three

---

[23] The papers belonging to the productions from 1730[2] in autumn through the carnival of 1731[4] are found in Filze 23 (three letters and a contract), *Filze di ricevuti* (no. 44), 1730-1741, and Busta 44, *Conti e ricevuti diverse*.

letters and a contract engaging Sig.ª Maddalena and Monsieur Salvai to sing and play respectively in the two seasons. The letters and contract, shown on p. *259*, are signed by Giuseppe Orlandini who must be Guerretti's maestro di cappella. Next in order are scraps of paper including bills for the ordinary expenses of maintenance of the theater and a list of twenty-three academicians who have paid their dues. Among them is a scrap that appears to be Guerretti's rumination about a possible cast for *Serva nobile* (the roles in brackets are added):

[Leandro]	Contadino	Pertici
[Isabella]	Babbi	Inamorati [*sic*]
[Bruscolo]	Bruscolo	Romana?
[Leonora]	Vedova	Landrucci [for Landuzzi]
[Desso]	Tartaglia	Romana [crossed out]
[Anselmo]	Vecchio	Ristorini
?	L'altra donna	L'Ungherella

Curious list. Some parts are inappropriately cast. The parts in brackets are those of *Serva nobile*. The notion of using a female for the stuttering dolt is absurd and Guerretti crossed la Romana off. But Bruscolo would not be a better choice, as Guerretti's question mark suggests. Pertici would be more appropriately cast as the *vecchio*, a role he usually sings in other burlettos. We suspect that Landuzzi, a contralto who sings serious male roles in 1730[6] and 1731[3], would be a surprise in the role of a *vedova*. In any case, this cast never was realized. Perhaps Guerretti received better advice from Orlandini!

The payments registered for the autumn (we believe) are found in Busta 44, *Conti e ricevuti diverse*. The list is for both operas, being much too large for one opera, and includes singers who normally sing intermezzi, Lottini and Faini. On the reverse side are shorter lists which, we believe, pertain to the operas of the carnival. None are dated. But the operas can with reasonable certainty be identified by comparison with the published casts of 1730[6] and 1731[3] and by deduction.

LIST 1

	Paoli
Caffariello	120
Fontini	47.4.6.8
Barbieri	30.
Babbi	152.2.13.4
Landuzzini	133.2.6.8
Pertici	224.5.6.8
Baldi	457.1
Cerminati	247.4.6.8
Monticelli	190.3.6.8
Penna	94.4
Salvai	422.4
Lottini	70
Faini	90

LIST 2 *reverse of above*

Fontana	9-6-8
Barbierj	31-6-6-8
Babbi	141 6 6-8
Landuzzi	104 5 6 8
Pertici	199 1 10 -
Monticelli	133-7-6-8
Penna	81-3
Lotinj	39
Faini	20.6

LIST 3 *each is crossed off with indication of payment*

Fontana	59 3 13 4
Barbieri	31 6 6 8
Babbi	141 6 6 8
Pertici	145 6 3 4
Monticelli	133 2 6 8
A Lottini	
F Faini	36.4

LIST 4 *separate page*

Landuzzi	104.5.6.9
Baldi	266.4.13.4
Cerminati	164.5.6.8
Salvaj	333.2.6.8
Penna	81.3
Monticelli	133.2.6.8
Babbi	141.3.3.4

On page 7 of these sheets the writer lists the receipts daily from the first performance on October 19 through November 28, with twenty-eight performances in all. All are denominated "recita" except numbers 13, 14, 18, 24-27 which are marked "burletta."

Sundry receipts and expenditures follow giving individual payments to singers, payments for their costumes and oddments, out of which we present here a few items of some interest.

The Gran Principessa paid sc.19.3.13.4 for having the burletta performed "a Palazzo."

The sale and purchase of scores is recorded in a manner that demonstrates why so few remain. The score of *Vinceslao* (O.T. of *Fratricidio innocente*, 1730[6]) was sold before December 6, even before it was performed, the parts having been copied. On the 15th of December, Natale Gonnelli was paid sc.2.4 for an honorarium for having gone to Livorno for the score of *Serva nobile*. Curiously, on the same day sc.7 were paid to Gregorio Barsotti, who is listed in 1699 as a member of the academy, for the score of the same opera. The burletta had been performed in 1720[3] (Antonio Lottini, who is in the 1731[2] cast, sang Bruscolo in that performance!) and it may have been that Barsotti was the impresario in 1720 and the owner of that score. On the 20th of December another score, *Maschera levata al Vizio*, was bought from D. Giov. Batt.a Tappi. Payments for new music for *Timocrate* are registered as well: to Gio. Chinzer, sc.8.4, for one act; and to Gaetano Bracci, sc.17.1, for two acts. By adding both together, a sum, 25.5, is obtained that is near the average of the lowest paid singers for the operas. An entry of a payment to Gaetano [Bracci] for *Artaserse* may be for some portion of the score for that opera, perhaps substitute arias.

The reopening of the Pergola directly affected the Cocomero, and it seems to have strengthened a tendency to present burlettas or comic operas as an alternative and competitive offering to the serious operas at the Pergola. Resurrections of comedies of Villifranchi and Moniglia more or less brought up-to-date (1705^5, 1717^3, 1717^4, 1719^4, 1720^3, 1720^4, 1721^3, 1727^2, 1730^3, 1731^2, 1732^{11}, 1741^9) frequently intervene between the fare of standard serious operas. Remarkably few new comic operas were written, but those of Francesco Vanneschi, including one of the most famous of the century, *Commedia in Commedia* (1731^8) should be noted. A central figure in the cultivation of comic opera at the Cocomero is Pietro Pertici who first performs in the theater in 1725 in a serious role, Marco Fabio, in *Lucio Papirio* (1725^2). But by 1730^3 he has become a member of a company specializing in comic operas. Thereafter he periodically returns to the Cocomero, at other times touring Europe, returning finally to the Cocomero to found a national theater in 1750 (see below).

When last heard from, the Immobili had reconstructed the Pergola theater (largely at the expense of the Medici) and enlarged it to fifty boxes in three rows on a design by Ferdinando Sengher for the wedding festivities of 1689. But afterwards it was, according to the anonymous historian of *I Fas* (Med. Misc. d'acquista 308) left in total abandonment and menaced by threats of foreclosure by the *Provveditore* of the Wool Guild (by whom the land had originally been conceded). But, he continues, the threats were ended by the assistance of Cosimo III, and by a payment of 600 scudi registered in contracts of March 14 and November 27, 1717, by Notary Anton Filippo Ridolfi, chancellor of the academy and its first impresario in 1718. Two years after the theater opened, the Immobili adopted a new constitution which was published with the title of *Le leggi della nuova accademia degli Immobili fatte l'anno 1720 sotto la protezione dell'Altezza reale del Serenissimo Gio: Gastone Gran Principe di Toscana*. Firenze, per Fabio Benedetto Maria Verdi, Stampatore dell'Accademia, MDCCXXIII.[24]

In the meantime the Immobili did have some kind of existence, though what they were doing is anybody's guess. Apart from duns from the Wool Guild, they were in other financial straits in 1697 since Ferdinando had to intervene in order to protect Giovanni Taddei, a member of the academy, from responsibility for a debt owed by the Immobili to the Opera di Santa Maria del Fiore (the Duomo).[25] And in 1701, Ferdinando approved in a letter to Domenico Caccini of a new appointment to the post of beadle. In 1712 on June 20, a meeting took place to renew the attempts to restore the theater and the academy. Five years later success was finally attained.

The penury did not prevent a new reconstruction which enlarged the auditorium, brought the number of balconies to four, and the boxes to seventy-eight. Along with this information, I Fas (Med. Misc. d'acquista 308) adds a few statistics about the first performance. Twenty-

---

[24] Ms copy in I Fas: Med. Misc. di Acquista 204, n. 6.
[25] I Fas: Med. 5910, c. 485.

nine tickets for the boxes brought in 560 lire; each *accademico proprietario* (30) and each *accademico aggregato* (10) paid 28 lire for a total of 1120, and a grand total of 1680 lire. Costs rose rapidly, for in 1720 the academicians had to pay 42 lire for each of two seasons.

As in the case of the Cocomero, other types of entertainment were used to help defray the costs of the theater. The anonymous historian records that in 1728 on the last day of carnival a ball took place. "The Platea was illuminated by torches of white wax in the Venetian style and the stage was reduced to chambers (a gabinetti) with five grand chandeliers with candles. In them were three great tables, two for playing *bassetta* and one for *trentuno* (card games). These festival balls were multiplied in the succeeding years until there were seven per carnival." In the summer of 1737 a new rage, faro (farone) invaded the theater, and adjacent rooms were rented by the academy for this purpose. Such enterprises everywhere and at all times, alas, are more financially rewarding than opera, so the academy apparently demanded its share of the profit from, as our historian says, "games of hazard." They imposed fees upon the impresari that amounted to 420 lire for the theater, 175 for quarters for the singers and 70 for the gaming rooms.

As we observed of the Infuocati, the choice of what opera to do, whether to use new or old scores, and all facets of a given operatic performance were left to the impresario within the character assumed by the noble academicians; that is, at the Pergola only *opera seria* or *semi-seria* was done—no burlettas. After several presentations of comic intermezzi ($1718^{5, 6}$, $1719^{7, 8}$, 1725^{3-6}, 1726^5, 1727^1), ballet was substituted for the entr'actes in 1727^4 and, with the exception of intermezzi in 1731^9, 1732^6, and 1750^{21}, and a few years with no designated entr'actes of any sort, ballet became standard in the Pergola. Ballet had greater status, one supposes, suitable to the character of the Immobili; but also by comparison with the Cocomero the Pergola had a stage large enough for ballet.

Again since so much depended upon the impresario, there is little consistency about what composers and poets were employed though as the dominance of Zeno and Metastasio became established, the repetition of the texts became a trifle boring. As for the music, a few are first performances. Antonio Vivaldi (1718^3, 1727^1, 1728^6, and 1736^1) and L.A. Predieri (1718^4, 1719^1, 1719^8, 1720^2) rank as the two most frequent composers chosen to write new scores, though with so many anonymous scores no secure analysis of policies is at all possible. Giovanni Porta (1730^1) is given one premiere, and he is joined by two local musicians, Giuseppe Bencini (1726^5) who is a *virtuosa di camera* to Gian Gastone, and Don G.N. Ranieri Redi (1729^2), composer of sacred music who probably unwisely wrote a setting of *Viriate* at the insistence of the Grand Duke. Behind many of the anonymous scores inevitably lurks Giuseppe Orlandini. His *Arsace* (1731^9) is the first identified score by him at the Pergola, but it is not a premiere. The second score, *Ifigenia in Aulide* (1732^5), is a first performance, however, and how many of the long list of anonymous scores between *Ifigenia* and *Temistocle* (1737^1), his next premiere, were written by him cannot be determined.

Activity in the smaller theaters subsided notably during the last decade of the seventeenth century and the first of the next. We have no witnesses to tell us why but we do suspect that it resulted from the establishment on a regular commercial basis of the Infuocati followed by the Immobili. That is to say, it is the effect of restraint placed upon the other theaters, namely the Sorgenti, and the theaters in Corso de' Tintori, Borgo Tegolaio and Ognissanti, by the Medicean government in order to restrict performances of opera. The regulation of the theaters would have, of course, been a simple matter since the protectors of the academies were the Medici, and therefore the means of regulation would have left little trace. The force of governmental regulation will become perfectly obvious, however, once the Medici are gone and their place is filled by a bureaucracy of an absentee government in the final period of our history. The decline in activity is not to be discounted as an absence of historical record, for Giovanni Battista Fagiuoli's diary in this period is becoming ever more detailed, and it is doubtful that a significant event might have escaped his attention and certainly he would not have ignored continuing productions. What little record we do have of prose comedies performed by the academicians themselves is to be found in his diary.

The theaters of both the Cadenti (1697[1], 1698[11], 1700[1, 4], and 1701[3]) and the Sorgenti (1698[1, 4], 1699[3], 1701[3]) are active at the turn of the century, the latter performing a comic opera with a published libretto in 1699[3]. But after 1701[3] the Sorgenti are not registered by a publication or by a diarist until 1742[10]. The Cadenti continue sporadically to perform and since they manage to make Fagiuoli's diary primarily when he performs or when they perform his comedies, we may assume actually a more continuous history. But no operas are performed in the theater, and none of the prose comedies are published concurrently. Activity is recorded in 1705[2], 1706[5] (Istrioni), 1732[2] (note long silence), and 1734[4]. The Casino di San Marco likewise disappears excepting in 1700[4], still during the life of Francesco Maria, and after his death - 1713[1], 1713[4], 1716[2], and possibly 1717[2] (if our reading of "Cascine" is in error). Three new academies are recorded: the *Acerbi*, *Rimoti* and *Abbozzati*. The first two are ephemeral, the first performing a prose comedy by Fagiuoli in 1710[1] and the second intermezzi in "their theater," (1723[4]); for neither is ever heard of again. The Abbozzati (*abbozzare* means to make a rough draft; by extension, the title would seem to mean roughly, of course, the "sketched ones") are more intriguing. The librettos of 1735[5, 6] describe the comedies as *scherzi drammatichi* to be performed in the *teatrino delle figurine*. One is tempted to equate *figurine* with puppets, but we have found no dictionary, including the *Vocabolario della Crusca*, which will allow such a meaning. The prudent course is to accept the academy's name at face value and to presume the action was represented either by painted cardboard figures or by silhouettes. But they, like the first two, manage only one brief period of productivity.

By contrast with the lesser academies, evidently performances in private houses flourish as they had not since the first quarter of the seventeenth century. Here, however, the evidence may indeed be weighted by the degree of detail provided by Fagiuoli, himself an actor and dramatist, to whom there is no seventeenth century counterpart after Tinghi. Be that as it may, notable are six performances in Casa Palmieri in Fiesole (from 1690[2] to 1710[4]) and other private performances in the Poggio Imperiale (1704[3]), Casa Ulivieri (1705[3]), Giannetti (1706[3]), Marian Mattei (1719[3]), del Fortini (1733[2]), and in Villa Gorini (1717[5]).

One new theater is opened: the Coletti, functioning in 1726 since Fagiuoli gives out complimentary tickets to a merchant in that year.[26] After the first notice of a performance in 1726[4] when it is being used by a commedia dell'arte company, there is no record of it until 1732[12] when an intermezzo, *La Potenza del vino*, is written and performed by Domenico Guagni, an unlettered dramatist, the eighteenth century descendant of Pietro Susini. Guagni in the next period will play a prominent role in the development of comic theater in Florence.

---

26 | Fr: Fagiuoli Carteggio 3011, letter dated January 1, 1726.

V. 1737-1750

On April 10, 1738, the Prince of Craon reassured Scipione Capponi, *provedditore* of the Infuocati, that Duke Francesco di Lorena, the successor to the last of the Medici, Gian Gastone, and the ruler imposed upon Florence by agreement of the European powers, would condescend to become the protector of the academy,[27] and thus theatrical continuity was assured but under rather different terms. François de Lorraine was the consort of Empress Maria Theresa of Austria (crowned in 1745) and consequently he lived in Vienna leaving the government of Tuscany to a regency headed by Marc de Beauvau, a commoner by birth, a Falstaff to Francesco's Henry, who was elevated to the title of Prince of Craon precisely in order to make him at least nominally suited to the post assigned him by Francesco.[28] Dedications to Craon announce his preferences with a spate of burlettas at the Coletti Theater from 1742[3] to 1743[6]. Together with his more cultured friend and financial adviser, Emmanuel de Richecourt, who seems to have been the official responsible for the regulation of the theaters, he conceived the idea of establishing in 1750 at the Cocomero a national theater headed by Pietro Pertici. Also characteristic of this period is the large number of translations of French comedies and tragedies, a general trend notable in other capitals of Europe, but in Florence the French orientation of the Lorraine government must have reinforced the fashion.

The new government was not one to spend overmuch time lamenting a dead Medici, so, although Gian Gastone died in July, the Cocomero opened the carnival with a comic opera on December 29, 1737[7], dedicated to the Principessa di Craon, and the Pergola resumed its customary *opere serie* by the next month. No particular change is detectable in the first years of the Lorraine government. The names upon the title pages change to Craon, Archduchess Maria Theresa, and, of course, Francesco III as Duke and Francesco I as Emperor. Orlandini hastened to pay his respects to the new Duke and render thanks for having had his stipend renewed. In 1738[6] he and other musicians of the granducal establishment performed a grand cantata at the Pergola. But the Duke had not arrived yet so, as Susier remarks, the best they could do was to send the score to Vienna. The following year Francesco, Maria Theresa and their son Carlo arrived in Florence and attended *Arianna e Teseo* at the Pergola (1739[1]). This, however, was the only visit by the ducal family in the long years of Francesco's reign.

But other than these few changes matters progressed much as before; *opere serie* with ballets and masked balls at the Pergola, and a mixture of comedies, burlettas, *opere serie*, intermezzi, and *commedia dell'arte* at the Cocomero, with gambling not an inconsiderable attraction in both houses.

Our view of theatrical history is at this point in danger of being greatly altered by the quantity and quality of the available resources to the degree that what is visible may be an illusion created by the nature of the documents: first, the diary of Niccolo Susier in the Riccardiana library and second, the four volumes of the records of the Regency dealing with the regulation of the theaters (I Fas [Reggenza 629-632]). Together they form a record far more detailed than any other available to document another period. Nevertheless, trends which are particularly strengthened in the last decade are evident even discounting the effect

---

[27] I Fac: Infuocati, *Indice*.
[28] Cochrane, p. 346f.

upon our perception of the greater details supplied by our sources. These trends are the increase in the number of theaters, in the variety of the types of dramatic entertainments they offer, and the sheer quantity of their productions. Susier does in fact reveal these trends, though it is always possible that he might have changed his habits in making notations in his diary.

The title of the diary announces that he was a theorbist in the service of Ferdinando de' Medici. Both the original spelling of his name and the frequent Gallicisms in his diary prove that he was French. Upon entering his service as a "giovine studioso del suono di Tiorba, e Arcileuto," Ferdinando sent him to Modena in 1708 to study with Gheardo Ingoni, who promptly sent him back because Susier played so well that Ingoni had nothing to teach him, suggesting instead that perhaps Ferdinando could give him a better instrument.[29]

Susier's own contribution to the diary begins in earnest about 1738 with volume 9. The first eight volumes are copies of earlier diaries beginning in the beginning of the seventeenth century. These volumes were copied probably as a means of becoming acquainted with the history of his adopted country and of studying the language. Volume 8 (1728-1737) does have a few entries that have the generally phlegmatic and distant yet awkward style of his own writing, but only in volume 9 (1738-1741) do some of his own characteristics appear, chiefly a preoccupation with money (it seems very important to record at which theater one has to pay for entrance and whether a performer is worth his pay or leaves a large sum on dying). Presuming his age to be about sixteen in 1708, he obviously is about forty-six when the diary begins, which is surely old enough to be set in his ways. Hence changes in what and how much are recorded ought to be fairly accurate and consistent.

The number of theaters mentioned in the ten-year period from 1740-1750 rises to fourteen. Besides the Cocomero and Pergola, the Tintori, Coletti or Giardino, Borgo de' Greci, and Orsanmichele are active more than ten times, while the other eight are entered at least once. These are: Vangielisti (in Susier's spelling), Porta S. Apostoli, Porta S. Niccolo, Mercato Nuovo, in via S. Zanobi, the Sorgenti, S. Fridiano, and Albergo del Vecchio.

The schedule of performances at the six principal theaters comes closer to being continuous, the maximum being sixteen performances at the Cocomero in 1750. In the cases of the Cocomero and Tintori, this constancy, which would make the theaters financially much more profitable (their original purpose of supplying gentlemanly *passatempi* for the academicians having faded away), was attained by an increase in the frequency with which the theaters were rented to troupes of *comici* who performed all types of theatricals from *opera seria* to spoken drama, burlettas to improvised comedies.

The theaters continue to define their own characters and the fare they present. The Pergola never condescends to anything less than *seria*, give or take a few ballets, and the number of operas remains at the level of three or four each year. Never is the theater rented to troupes whether for opera or not. The Cocomero does everything; not turning away, for example, a troupe of English acrobats in 1740[4]. But the preference slightly inclines towards burlettas: some twenty-two are mounted from 1737[7] to 1750[11], while seventeen serious operas are done. The Coletti does not permit serious opera on its stage,

---

[29] Relevant correspondence in I Fas: Med. 5904, cc. 54, 55, 60, 62, 71, 78, 107, 435.

only burlettas, and if not burlettas, spoken dramas. The Cocomero and the Coletti thus compete with each other for audiences, but, interestingly enough, a series of burlettas beginning in 1742[9] and continuing through 1743[5] have casts that maintain some constant singers, finally including Pertici, which cast then transfers from the Coletti (1743[6]) to the Cocomero (1743[8]).

At Borgo de' Greci only prose comedies are shown, but at Orsanmichele prose comedies, some of them translations of French plays, are mixed with puppet (burattini) shows and "figurine" (silhouette?) shows with music.

Under the circumstances supervision of the theaters became more difficult. Conflicts among competing impresarios and heads of companies could only be resolved by the Regency. In Medicean days, of course, the protector could resolve virtually any conflict he wished. But the Regency was responsible to an absentee ruler, and therefore obligated to make decisions as bureaucracy must: by committees, through echelons, with official approvals, and paperwork. Troubles can be seen a-brewing in 1741[2] when the Regency was obligated to extricate the Infuocati from their own confusion created when the theater was rented to too many impresarios at once. Where else could such an episode lead other than to bureaucratic regulation?

All of this theatrical activity aroused a fierce competition, and competition was most keenly felt by the Immobili who, because of their noble status, perforce had to produce what was at once the most expensive and the least popular form of theatrical entertainment, namely, serious opera. The comments of Fagiuoli and Susier about the lack of attendance (while poor quality is found elsewhere) are directed towards the Pergola, e.g., Susier's remark concerning 1738[1] that "Cuzzoni and Senesino earn their money, but few people go," or even more pointedly in 1749[2] his observation that a comedy performed by a company of *Istrioni* at the Cocomero was "very pleasing and they did [their play] three times with a great crowd of people, which is not the case at the theater in via della Pergola, where they sell few tickets." One would not expect the noble gentlemen of the Immobili to tolerate such a state of affairs gladly.

One way for the academy to escape undue liability for a financial failure was to force the impresario to assume all risks. The resulting pressure was already great in 1707[2] when Michele Giusti in his address to the reader expressed his anguish and frustration with surprising candor in an age not often candid: "So much the more I hope [that you will support this drama] when you know of the fatigues, the disasters, and expenses suffered in order to perform this opera and to overcome the invidiousness of those who have used every possible means to impede this so noble diversion . . . ." An item in the *Indice* of the Infuocati archives (I Fac), the original documents of which are missing, is undated but even so it says a great deal: "the obligation of the instrumentalists to recognize the impresario as the debtor and not the academy."[30]

At least one impresario decided there was advantage in playing the Infuocati against the Immobili in a bid for the best arrangement for himself. The first time that Gaetano del Ricco

---

[30] *Obbligazioni dei musici sonatori di riconoscere pp debit^e l'impresario e non l'accad.^{ia}*. Evidently the musicians for the carnival of 1748 complained to the Regency who, in I Fas Reggenza 629, rebuked the academy for not paying on time. The last item of the index would correspond by the page number to the period and may have been the reaction of the academy to the complaint from the Regency, that is, the musicians were obligated to seek redress from the impresario, not the academy.

172314

switched from the Cocomero to the Pergola in 1746[9] he seems to have escaped censure. He even boasted a little about it. But the second time he got himself in trouble. In a letter addressed to the Emperor,[31] del Ricco complained that the Infuocati made claims against him, doubtless, that he should pay the rent of the theater in full even though he had transferred his operas, and he asked the Regency to settle the matter "according as it believe appropriate to equity and justice with the greatest promptitude possible." Hardly had the Regency received this complaint than it received another from Ugolino Grifoni saying that the Immobili were tardy in responding to his bid in June, 1748, for the use of the Pergola although he had already signed contracts with the "professori" for the opera and ballet. Consequently he wanted to use the Cocomero[32] from August 15 to October 20. Evidently he changed his plan again since he performed *Siroe* (1748[12]) at the Pergola, and again an item in the Infuocati index says, in eloquent brevity: "Obblig.e del Cav. Grifoni di prende il teatro p.la recita dell'op.e."

Being in the Pergola was no secure advantage. When del Ricco had succeeded in transferring to the Pergola, he found that he was losing money on *Caio Mario* (1747[11]) because the comedy at the Coletti, *Almansor re della china* (1747[12]) and the *Istrioni* (either the Grimani company or Marchesini's in 1747[9]) were capturing his audience. He appealed to the Regency to close those theaters on the nights he was performing his opera.[33]

It was all a little more than the Regency could take. In the spring a plan was devised to bring the theaters, the academies and their impresarios under better regulation.[34] The regulations start with the premise that the Immobili are the highest academy and deserving of deference from the others. The bias, of course, is natural and a standard attitude in favor of nobility of the century. It hardly needs documentation, but two instances of the thinking of the Regency are particularly pertinent. In the fracas of 1741[2] over the conflicting rental agreements made by the Infuocati, the argument was advanced by (we think) Scipione Capponi that he "would deem it always preferable to have *opere in musica* to Istrioni . . . the impresario moreover being a cavalier."[35] A similar decision protecting the Cocomero from the opening of smaller theaters was explained by Richecourt in similar if more condescending terms: " . . . I believe that it is good to have one (the Cocomero) theater open but that it would be prejudicial to the public good to allow a large number especially

---

[31] In I Fac, Infuocati: *Filza di Motupropri Descritti e Negozj diretti al Soprindente del Regio teatro del Cocomero*, no. 12, "Giov. Gaetano del Ricco . . . espone, come alle premure e istanze della nobiltà di Firenze, ha dovuto condescendere a transferare nel Teatro di Via della Pergola con notabile accrescimento di spese le Opere in Musica, che aveva destinato fare nel Teatro di Via del Cocomero, per il che presentendo che dalli Accademici di Via del Cocomero siano per suscitarsi più e diverse pretenzioni in notabile suo pregiudizio, e de' suoi Interessati Le quali non restando speditamente composti potrebbero sempre più pregiudicarli: supplica la S[ua] C[esarea] M[aestà] V[osignore] a degnarsi di quelli delegare, ed commettere a chi più le passa, e piacera, con ordine al medesimo, che sommariamente, e pettoralmente componga tutte le differenze in sorte o da insorgere fra detti Accademici di Via del Cocomero, e l'Oratore, secondo che credera conveniente all'equità, e alla Giustizia con tutta la maggior prontezza possibile: Che della grazia etc." Del Ricco had been impresario in the summer, autumn and carnival at the Pergola 1747[10, 11], 1748[6].

[32] I Fac, ibid, no. 14.

[33] I Fas: Reggenza 630, c. 126.

[34] I Fas: Reggenza 631, c. 59, *Capitoli J. del Piano p[er] l'Imperial Consiglio di Reggenza d'un nuovo Regolamento nell'occasione dell'Opere del Teatro di via della Pergola in ordine al viglietto di detto Consiglio del dì 15 Marzo 1747/8*. carteggio 58, Convenzione fra l'Accademia degl'Immobili . . . e degl' Infuocati. I Fac: Infuocati archives, *Filza di Motupropri*, cc. 13: a summary of the regulations dated July 6, 1748.

[35] " . . . mi do l'honor di dirle che stimerci, che fosse sempre preferibile l'opera in musica agl'Istrioni . . . essendo l'Impresario dell'opera un Cav.e tanto più . . . "

of little offshoots as is being proposed, which are good only for increasing the idleness of low people." [36] But obviously it was easier to win a favorable decision from the Regency than from those who bought tickets to the theaters.

Be that as it may, the regulation embodied in an "agreement" (the *convenzione* of May 22, 1748) between the Immobili and the Infuocati, that must not have been made without a certain exercise of power over the Infuocati, states simply that "the preference is given to [the theater] di via della Pergola, [the Regency] not wishing that the two be open at the same time for *opera in musica*." Further, concerning carnival the Immobili have until the end of the previous July to decide whether they wish to perform an opera and, failing a decision by that date, the Infuocati are free to perform what they wish in the following carnival. Similarly for the season of S. Giovanni (June 24 through July), the Immobili must decide before the last day of the preceding March whether they will have an opera, and before the last day of May for the autumn (November) season, in each case, the Infuocati then having their choice if the Immobili do not decide to do an opera. But nevertheless, the Immobili are obliged to allow the Infuocati one season of the three to perform an opera or burletta in music.

Once it had entered upon this kind of regulation, the Regency proceeded to compose rules for the internal behavior of the academy itself, and to govern both great and quite minor matters. The previous January it had already taken the step of abolishing gambling, [37] which certainly cut into the profits of the impresarios and the academicians though it may have improved the attention which audiences gave to the opera. The financial woes of del Ricco and Grifoni in the next years are probably directly related to this order. Separate orders were issued for the Infuocati and the Immobili, [38] similar in effect, but we will choose those of the Immobili.

First, the Regency denied the Immobili's petition that they transfer financial responsibility from themselves to the impresarios and insisted that the academy see to it that the impresario paid on time. To cover themselves, the academy was to demand from the impresarios a deposit of a thousand scudi and to pay to the academy the price of the saleable boxes (i.e., those not permanently reserved by the academicians, the Regency, etc.) and of the *piccionaja* (the pigeon roost, i.e., top balcony). These amounted to Scudi 1010 in carnival and 730 in autumn, prices being higher during carnival. The estimated total cost ordinarily is reckoned to be Scudi 6000, leaving some 2000 as the assumed risk of the academy. Now, the Regency cleverly insinuated, that is a sum large enough to induce the academy to take the further precaution of requiring that all expenditures be approved by a "Persona di confidenza" of the academy who will understand the academy's risk in not staying on top of those "deceits which an impresario can easily employ when he has the unlimited power to make agreements with third parties and to feign contracts and obligations (independently of what the Council

---

[36] ı Fas: Reggenza 631, c. 105. "[je] crois qu'il est bon d'avoir un theatre ouvert mais qu'il seroit prejudiciable au bien public d'en souffrir grand nombre surtout de petits tets qu'on les proposse, qui ne sont propres qu'a augmenter l'oisiveté du bas peuple ce 26 mars 1750. Richecourt."

[37] ı Fas: Reggenza 629, insert 11, no. 2 dated January 28, 1748. In 1747 the Regency considered curtailing a custom which allowed maskers to go up onto the stage during ballets. Del Ricco objected on the grounds that it would diminish his ticket sales, already too low. The abolition of the custom was, however, contained in Rule 18 of the Regulations of the Pergola discussed below. See n. 37. Del Ricco's objection in ı Fas: Reggenza 631, c. 83r,v.

[38] Infuocati in ı Fac: Infuocati archives; *Filza di Motupropri*, c. 15; for the Immobil, ı Fas: Reggenza 631, cc. 59r-60r and 114r-123v.

would like) to pay all the nonsense which by mischance or maliciousness the Impresario might have made. Such may always happen if the Impresa undertake a subject that has no standing in these Tuscan states, which is most often the case. . . ."[39]

If the academicians had any doubt about it, they surely recognized the dawn of a new era when this document was delivered at their door: *Regolamento da tenersi nelle Opere del Teatro di via della Pergola, tanto riguardo al decoro, e convenienza di quello, che agl' Interessi fra l'Accademia, e li Impresarj annuali, e all'Interesse di questi co'i Terzi ricavato dagli Ordini, e Approvazioni del Consiglio di Reggenza del Pmo Giugno 1748 sul Piano presentatogli' dall'Accademia.*[40]

There follow twenty-five articles of the most extraordinarily detailed rules beginning with a general declaration that all who have dealings with the academy must maintain the high decorum appropriate to an "assembly which lives under the auspices of His August Monarch," to instructions where patrons were to leave their portable chairs and traffic directions for people who arrive in carriages. After the moral imperatives, the relations between the two primary theaters are restated, then the requirement of deposit and security from the impresario is likewise repeated with a few loopholes closed up. The poor impresario is given one assistance. Much abuse must have resulted from uncomfortable pressures for the wholesale dispensation of free admissions. Rule 5 takes care of that. It lists those to whom the impresario cannot deny free entrance, most of whom seem to be practical choices: policemen (whose function is later described), a doctor, servants to attend the Palco dei Principi, and the like. Any other free passes can be issued only with the approval of the Imperial Council!

Number 7 specifies that rental of the theater with its appurtenances, the *scena di ballo* (?), gaming rooms, dressing rooms (*quartieri dei Professori*) can include no more than forty days prior to the first performance to one week following. Number 8 obliges the impresario to use only the publisher, artist, engineer, master bricklayer and carpenter of the academy. Next comes the appointment of a supervisor from the academy, a sort of officer-of-the-day. The regulations concerning the rental of boxes, individually and by subscription are the subject of paragraph 10, wherein the tariff for the entire house is set down with the stipulation that the prices cannot be changed without the consent of the Imperial Council. They range from 40 Scudi for the large box on the first order on ground level facing the theater to 2 or 3 Scudi up in the pigeon's roost. Rules 9 through 15 outline conditions

---

[39] I Fas: Reggenza 631, cc. 59r,v: ". . . non rimanendo assicurata, che di Soli Scudi 2000 in circa con le divisate sicurezze, e possa, come e di ragione, obbligar l'Impresario a Lasciare La Cassa di tutta la sua Economia in mano di Persona di confidenza di detta Accademia, e non gli sia permesso disporre cosa di rilievo nella sua Amministrazione senza il consenso di quell'Economo, che gli deputera. La medesima, e che quest'Economo deva esser pagato dall'Erario dell'Impresa, conoscendo benissimo con tutto questo l'Accademia il suo rischio di non rimanere a bastanza al coperto di quegl'inganni, che un Impresario fraudolento può ordire agevolmente, quando ha tutta la facoltà di contrattare con i terzi, e fingere Scritte, e obbligazioni independentemente da quella, che si vuole tenuta dal Consiglio a pagar tutto quel voto, che per disavventura, o malizia facesse l'Impresario, Lo che potra accadere tutte le volte, che prestera il nome all'Impresa un soggetto, che non possieda nulla in questi Stati, come succede per lo più, nel qual caso Supplica l'Accademia l'Imperial Consiglio di non condannarla, se ricusa concedere il Suo Teatro, allorche non trovi dipotersi cautelare da tanti rischj irreparabili." The reference to feigned contracts probably refers to a claim that Grifoni made against Clorinda Landi (1748[16]), that she had contracted to give him eight shares (caratti) in her performance at the Pergola as prima donna and that he had received only five. We would guess that the "shares" represent a kickback, hence the Regency's hostile reaction. See cc. 11-18v of the same filza.

[40] I Fas: Reggenza 631, c. 114-123r.

governing rentals and ticket sales, that is to whom, rights of academicians, penalties for not paying for subscriptions, and the arrest of counterfeiters. Numbers 17 and 18 deal with a uniquely eighteenth century phenomenon, the masques, the limitations of masks to evenings permitted by the Regency, the obligation to remove the mask for recognition at the entrance, but elaborate provisions whereby some maskers can be allowed to enter without identification.

The remainder of the numbers govern the behaviour of the audience. The deputy of the academy must intervene if there is "extraordinary applause that might be found indecent to the dignity of a theater qualified by the Protection of this Sovereignty."[41] Further, if the audience divides itself into claques in favor of this or that actor or ballet dancer, he must use his authority to the point of calling out the soldiers to remove the obstreperous members of the audience and, if he thinks it wise, to arrest and remove also the actor or dancer who occasions such behaviour (rule no. 20). "Equally," says rule no. 21, "it will be the duty of the Deputy to uphold the rights of the Impresario, when necessary, to make all of the employees obey and respect him, even to the point of constraining by force some one of them who at some time might fabricate excuses for not giving him the service to which he is obligated."[42]

Rule 22 forbids the impresario to raise the curtain any later than an hour and a quarter after the posted hour of the performance, unless the Deputy informs him that the Sovereign or his representative intends to come. The remaining three rules then take up such matters as where the servants shall stay while waiting for their masters, how many and whose servants can stand at the doors to the boxes, where the portable chairs are to be parked, the movement of carriages (via della Pergola was before and after the opera one-way and no one save the members of the Imperial Council could have his carriage turned around to go the opposite direction), and a provision for the arrest and automatic dismissal, whether the master would or no, of any coachman who parked his carriage and left it on the street.

How much closer 1748 seems to the twentieth century than even 1737, the last year of the Medicean era!

The Regency took in 1750 a remarkably forward-looking step by founding a national theater by which is meant, more than anything else, popular. One thinks by comparison of Josef II's theater in Vienna founded in 1778. The *Opera comique* is comparable only to a degree, and only after Rousseau's *Devin du Village* does its repertory begin to assume the generic definition and quality of the Tuscan National Theater at its inception. The idea came apparently from the Regency and its author was Richecourt, though Marc de Craon must have had much to do with it in view of his predilection for comedy (cf the dedications of the burlettas at the Coletti and Infuocati) and his association with the two men who were engaged to found the theater, Pertici and Guagni. It may also have been part of a move to reduce the role of the academicians, for it had the effect of expropriating the Cocomero.

Several notices of the events leading to the Tuscan National Theater exist, but the most detailed is a *memoria* in 1 Fas Reggenza 631, cc. 71r and v., which is an undated petition (but by the contents it must have been written about 1769) on behalf of Pertici who is in

---

[41] "Applausi straordinarj, che si trovassero indecenti alla dignità di un Teatro qualificato della Protezione del Suo Sovrano."

[42] "Parimente sara peso del Deputato di sostenere le ragioni dell'Impresario, quando occorresse di farlo ubbidire, e rispettare da tutti li operanti fino a costringere colla forza tal'uno di Essi, che qualche volta mendicasse pretesti, per non rendergli quel servizio, al quale si fosse obbligato."

danger at that time of being left without sustenance in his old age. Therefore it reviews the history of the foundation. We here present a gloss.

In 1749 Pertici and his wife returned from London (where they had been performing *Commedia in Commedia* and other burlettas) to Parma where he served for a salary of 350 Zecchini and quarters per year for two years. In 1750 Richecourt informed him of his intention to found a Tuscan theater with Pertici as the director with a lifetime pension of 100 Scudi per annum from Richecourt and in addition a lifetime appointment as director and impresario of the Cocomero theater with all the income attached to those positions. He obtained leave from Parma in order to be in Florence in the spring ($1750^{7,8,11}$). At the urging of Sen. Rucellai, Sig. Ab. Uguccioni, Mons. Votie, and Sig. Ab. Niccoli, secretary of Richecourt, he accepted the proposal. He pleased Richecourt, the government, the public and the academicians for four years. At the end of that time the academicians petitioned Richecourt for the return of the theater for five years with the understanding that Pertici would remain as director with a salary of 25 Scudi per·month. After the death of Richecourt in the meantime, the theater passed to another impresario for another five-year period but still retaining Pertici as the director with the same salary by order of the government. At the end, then, of nineteen years, he petitioned the government for the protection of his pension in his old age, citing his service to the city in establishing his company whose presence had added so much luster and given so much pleasure.

The Regency immediately had reason to protect its new Teatro Toscano from too much competition, repeating in effect the previously described scramble in 1747-1748. Three requests for permission to perform theatricals during the spring of 1750 at the same time as Pertici's proposed burlettas at the Cocomero were sent to the Regency. The discussion of the effect of these competitive proposals is rich in information. The proposers were:

> Matteo Arcangioli wished to perform in the "Teatro de' Cadenti posto nel Corso de Tintori."
>
> Luigi Vannini wished to open a theater in via Santo Egidio with burlettas "a pago... mezzo paoli."
>
> Antonio Bani and Company wished to perform prose comedies in the new Teatro dalla Croce Rossa.

A letter from Scipione Capponi to Roberto Pandolfini (c. 100) presented the arguments for not permitting the three performances (converting in the process Bani to Danti) and in doing so expands the view of what the Teatro Toscano was doing. There were two impresarios: Pertici and Domenico Guagni. The relationship between the two is not clear. In fact, there was some question in Guagni's mind, since later in the year he addressed a letter dated November 12, 1750, to Capponi raising the same question. He reminded Capponi that his "new" company for the past five years had been given an exclusive privilege of performing four days per week excluding days in which all public performances were forbidden and in which opera was being given at the Pergola (unless the day were Sunday in which case his company could perform regardless of an opera at the Pergola). Guagni wished to know if his privilege was to be continued. Without mentioning Pertici's Teatro Toscano of which the following year was to be the first official one, he must certainly have been wondering, in view of the appointment of Pertici by the government, if the academy still had the authority to grant him the use of the theater. Capponi replied affirmatively and added that if there were operas performed during carnival at the Cocomero (there being none at the Immobili), Guagni would be free to take his company to the Cadenti Theater in corso de' Tintori, which shows how little the academicians themselves had anything to say about what was done in their theaters. [43]

Returning to Capponi's letter to Pandolfini, Capponi says that he has asked Pertici his opinion of the effect the competing performances would have if permission to open were granted by the Regency. Pertici replied the damage would be great for he had already engaged his cast and he expected to spend no less than Scudi 1700, including the cost of the ballets. Further, he had come to Florence with the assurance that all other theaters would be closed during the performance of his burlettas. Then Pertici turned to the damage the proposed theatricals would cause to the prose plays and here the wording becomes ambiguous. (We translate as literally as possible in order to preserve Capponi's meaning.)

> . . . One was already preparing these prose comedies with Guagni, by
> searching for all the means for reuniting together [tautology original]
> that small number of young actors who were separated from the said
> Guagni, and who alone were judged capable of this training, which will
> become in fact impossible whenever these [actors] will have the hope
> of finding employment in other theaters, and without this union the
> assurance of the conceived project of forming a company of Tuscan
> actors capable of performances continuing a good part of the year will
> be entirely hindered. [44]

We interpret the opposition of "reuniting" and "separating" to mean that Guagni's troupe, having come to the end of its five-year contract, had broken up at the end of 1749, before Pertici had received news of Richecourt's plans. Therefore, the group, judged by Guagni and by Pertici to be the only one capable of achieving the goals of the Teatro Toscano, had had to be reassembled. Though there is only scattered evidence for this reconstruction of events we feel, in the main, it is convincing.

First about Guagni. It should be noted that his letter quoted above does not say in which theater his company had been performing in the preceding five years although he is writing about the next unspecified number of years at the Cocomero. A rapid survey of the schedule of performances at the Cocomero from 1745 to 1749 will show that in fact he could not have been performing in the Cocomero for there are only operas with known impresarios and singers, all of whom come and go, and are plainly not on five-year contracts, or there are performances by *comici* from other cities that very nearly fill up all remaining time between operas.

Guagni and his company were, however, at the Coletti instead, we think. He is first recorded performing in intermezzi, for which he has composed both text and music, in

---

[43] Letters in I Fac: Infuocati, *Filza di Motupropri*, c. 23.

[44] ". . . stimano che questa permissione sara per Loro di sommo pregiudizio, e il Pertici ha soggiunto, che tanto si e impegnato a venire a Firenze, e fare presentem[ent]e le Burlette in Musica, p[er] le quali non spendera meno, compresi i Balli di Scudi Mille Settecento, quanto che fu assicurato che in questo tempo non vi sarebbe stato altro Teatro aperto, e che doveva considerarsi ancora la perdita, che averebbe fatta nelle commedie recitate in prosa, p[er] le quali si andava già preparando con il Guagni, con cercare tutti li mezzi p[er] riunire assieme quel'piccolo numero di Giovani recitanti, che si sono separati dal detto Guagni, e che soli giudicati Capaci di questo esercizio, la qual'cosa diventera affatto impossibile tutto che volte che questi averanno la speranza di trovare impiego in altri Teatri, e senza questa unione andano del tutto impedito l'assicurazione del progetto ideato di formare una Compagnia di recitanti Toscani da potare continuare le Recite una buona parte del'anno."

1732[12] at the Coletti. The second role is sung by Gaetano Ciarli. Both perform the
intermezzi again at the Tintori in 1740[7]. The entry for 1742[13] seems to present the
possibility that Guagni was among impresarios of a spoken comedy at the Cocomero
performed with intermezzi sung by Pertici and his wife, Caterina Brogi. Next Guagni
turns up in a cast consisting of himself, Ciarli, Civili, Dori, and Giamberini in 1744[6] at
the Coletti, the troupe being significantly identified as a Florentine company.

Note carefully: in the preceding years beginning in 1742[3] and continuing in 1742[5],
1742[10], 1742[11], and 1743[6], a series of burlettas are performed at the Coletti which are
known elsewhere to be in the repertory of Pertici and his wife and a variable company but
they do not appear in the casts. In 1743[8] the same company moves from the Coletti to the
Cocomero performing another burletta. In 1743[9] Pertici and his wife join the cast of still
another burletta. Meanwhile the burlettas disappear from the schedule of the Coletti and
are replaced by spoken comedies from 1743[10] until 1749[7], about five years, when abruptly
the Coletti ceases its productions. From 1742 onwards there are, except in 1745, three or
four plays each year at the Coletti, but in 1750 there are none at all. Instead the Cocomero
which has alternated between opera and *istrioni* produces in 1750 twelve spoken comedies,
many translations of French drama. The conclusion that Pertici and Guagni are working
together, the first concentrating on burlettas and Guagni on spoken drama (including the
interesting performance of an opera libretto without the music in 1750[13]) is inescapable.
Moreover, Guagni has indeed already put together a Florentine company, so naturally
Pertici would have turned to him for assistance in order to build the Teatro Toscano.

The membership of the Teatro Toscano, we believe, is found on another one of those
scraps of paper in I Fac: Infuocati, Conti e Ricevuti. On the upper-left hand corner there
is a date: 1723, but it is a late addition and can be explained by a too-eager archivist who
wrote the date on the page simply because it followed a letter originally bearing a date of
1723. But 1723 is most improbable. We can say only that our date is, by contrast, probable.
The list is as follows:

NOTA DI PROVVISIONI ANNUALI

Al Sig. Poffi, e Consorte	300
Michele del Zanca	200
Frilli	42
Totti	51.3
Dori	51.3
Tosi	51.3
Marbizzi	51.3
Sorbi	34.2
Ciarli	34.2
Guagni	100
Alla Sig.ra Pecchioli sette scudi il mese, e il piccolo vestiario oppure scudi otto il mese, ed ella debe pensare a tutti	96
Alla Sig.ra Dei o cinque scudi il mese, come sopra, a sei	72
Alla servetta	36
	1120.2

Alla Sig.ra Puccini per recitare in musica Autunno, et carnivale 90

Circumstantial evidence that the list is in fact one of the first if not the first membership of the Teatro Toscano is as follows: (1) the presence of three of the cast of 1744[10], Guagni, Ciarli and Dori; (2) the title of "annual provisions," since at no previous time has there been any indication of a yearly salary paid to singers (the standard is an engagement of two seasons); (3) the coincidence of il Sig. Poffi's and his wife's salary of 300 scudi, which is the amount granted Pertici at the end of the first five-year period, that is, 25 per month logically arrived at by the new impresario simply as a continuation of the original agreement with Richecourt cited above (hence Poffi must be a nickname for Pertici); (4) the relationship between Pertici's and Guagni's salaries. (Who Michele is we have no idea, nor do we understand why Ciarli is paid so poorly.)

With Pertici and Guagni well in control of the Cocomero for the time being and with the backing of Richecourt, it is not to be wondered at that the Imperial Council unanimously voted to ban all other theaters besides, of course, the Pergola. No one, it seems, likes competition.

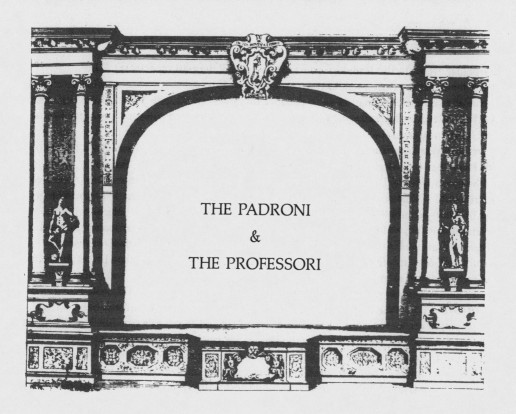

THE PADRONI
&
THE PROFESSORI

THAT OPERA WAS BORN in the midst of a *conversazione* of gentlemen is a well-known fact whose significance, in our opinion, has not been properly emphasized. It means simply that music moved from the private chamber to the ballroom of the same palace. Plainly the change from one room to another hardly lessened the dominance of the patrons or diminished the intimacy existing notably in the sixteenth century between the patrons and their artists. As the society of the sixteenth century thought of sacred and secular part music as a proper subject of their own activity, so they continued in the next century, sustained by a strong current of neo-Platonism and a new social consciousness, to regard opera and other theatrical forms which, of course, they invented, as designed for their pleasurable occupation, entertainment, education, and spiritual and social benefit. Consequently court and opera at times during the seventeenth century seem indistinguishable, as if opera were a transportation of the court at appropriate seasons to a higher plane of elegant artifice. As our own chronology has documented, nobility and haute bourgeoisie participated in operatic productions in all capacities: as poets, composers, singers, dancers, stage and costume designers, architects and more menial workers, all more or less willingly and joyfully occupied in creating flattering dramatizations of their own lives, positions, origins and undoubtable virtues in the sight of God and mankind.

They took the dramatic representation of themselves quite seriously, if we may include occasional cynicism as a serious mood. To represent Louis XIV and Cosimo III by Hercules on the stage was not ridiculous but a pleasing and instructive allegory, an invention to support magnificence appropriate (more so in the first case, to be sure) to the station and actual power of the rulers. Examples of the point are supplied by two opera-ballets by G.A. Moniglia and Jacopo Melani for performance in Pisa which translated by allegory

particular events in the Medicean court into a musical dramatic spectacle. Duke
Ferdinando II sent Cosimo on two voyages through Europe, as we have previously remarked,
in order to improve his manners and enhance his appeal to his wife Marguerite d'Orlèans.
Lest the allegory be missed, the prologues trace the itinerary of Cosimo's voyages. When
in 1669 he returned the first time he was represented as Aeneas arriving in Italy. The next
year he traveled again and appropriately after two long voyages he returned as Ulysses to
his Penelope. One might ask who was the actor and who the prince.

Such practices and attitudes could not fail to bring about the greatest intimacy between
patrons and artists, with both advantages and disadvantages to the artists. The advantages
are brilliantly exemplified by the Melani, the family of composers and singers, who rose
from the position of litterbearers for the Bishop of Pistoia to the Tuscan nobility in just
three generations by their skillful use of connections with various nobility of Tuscany,
Louis XIV, Mazarin, Queen Anne of France, Emperor Leopoldo, Clement IX, and the King
of Poland, not to mention the Medici.

This intimacy is typical from the beginning of opera to the death of Prince Ferdinando
in 1713, but it vanished rapidly in the beginning of the eighteenth century as the active
participation of the patrons and academicians waned and the dominance of the professional
musicians increased. The reasons for the change are many and complex: the economic
decline of the nobility, the end of the Medici and the beginning of absentee bureaucratic
government, and the commercialization of theaters. To demonstrate the point we must
examine the relationship between Ferdinando and his singers.

Ferdinando de' Medici

Just as Ferdinando exercised control over the academies, he assumed the right to make
appointments to all types of musical positions in Tuscany. When, for example, in 1703
Bartolomeo Melani, organist of the cathedral of Pistoia, died, the governor of Pistoia wrote
to Pier Antonio Gerini, Ferdinando's *maestro di camera*, immediately, recalling that Prince
Ferdinando had in 1693 ordered the governor to advise the Prince prior to conferring the
position of organist of the Cathedral if the need for an appointment should arise.[1] The
same filza in the Archivio di Stato in Florence contains many requests for singers, violinists,
and replacements thereof in churches large and small in Tuscany. In one instance (c. 488)
a position in the choir of the Duomo, St.a Maria del Fiore, was bestowed by the express
order of Ferdinando upon Romolo Birij. Such a policy placed all positions in the
principality in his hands and made all musicians, regardless of the actual source of the
income, his dependents. His relationship with his musicians was close, probably at times
too close for comfort, considering the enormous power seventeenth century rulers possessed
over the persons and property of their servants. Some few met unhappy fates as a result of
their dependence or of their inability to develop the proper courtier's diplomatic skill.
Galuzzi[2] says that Francesco de Castris, a singer in the service of Ferdinando, was so close to
the prince that Cosimo III, the Grand Duke, appealed to the singer when he wished to sway
the prince. De Castris was finally exiled from Tuscany because of his hold over the prince.

---

[1] I Fas: Med. 5910, c. 169.
[2] Lib. 7⁰, Tomo 4⁰, p. 289f.

Vittoria Tesi, a soprano also in the prince's service, was an innocent bystander who fell with De Castris. According to Fagiuoli's entry for April 4, 1753, Tesi was the daughter of De Castris' lackey. Acton[3] tells also of Ferdinando's affection for Giuseppe Petrilli, a male soprano who is recorded as having sung at Pratolino in 1679[2]* and 1684[3]. Petrilli got into trouble by presuming too much upon the prince's apparent intimacy.

Generally, however, the character that one sees behind the heavy veil of the protocol-ridden prose in Ferdinando's letters is warmhearted and compassionate and full of genuine concern for the problems, petty and grand, of his own musicians and of the musicians in Florence, even those not officially on his own staff. A touching, if still condescending and formal, sign of his attachment to musicians and artists was his habit of signing letters to such persons with "suo amorevole" in the place of the more frigid epistolary formulas.

With noblemen pretending to artistic ability he could be abrupt, but with artists and musicians never, although he might suffocate some poor creature with beautiful, meaningless prose. Stefano Romani, a singer of minor repute, wrote Ferdinando on October 2, 1706, a frightfully pitiful letter to remind the prince of *il povero Stefano* "who was nourishing himself on the many graces he had received from the Prince without merit."[4] The letter is filled with trembling. *Povero* Stefano knows that he has stepped far beyond his position by opening a correspondence with Ferdinando. Ferdinando's reply is a model of sweet, polite, and uncritical restraint and leaves the way open for continued correspondence. The exchange continues at least for a year. Romani's letters gain self-confidence and become newsy. Ferdinando's remain condescending and sympathetic but promise nothing. So far as the record is known Romani never even received an invitation to sing at Pratolino, a prize he was obviously angling for. These patient letters contrast strongly with a reply to a certain Count Niccolo Montemellini of Perugia who in 1703 and in 1707 sent Ferdinando some cantatas and, receiving a polite reply, presumed then to ask to be enrolled among the Prince's musicians. The proposal evidently offended Ferdinando, for his letter,[5] after the necessary elegance, coldly refuses with the half-stated rebuke "because I do not grant familiarity." [perche io non concedo Familiarità.] End of correspondence. The rebuke is to be understood in light of Montemellini's station as a nobleman who could not then be a familiar, i.e., servant of the household.

The essential charity of the man is shown in his brief relation with Isidoro Ceruti, *maestro di cappella* to the Count of Novellara. Ferdinando invited Ceruti on June 18, 1697, to stay with him[6] during the *villeggiatura* at Pratolino, for what purpose is unknown. Ceruti, an elderly composer of no great reputation, became sick and on December 6, 1697, Ferdinando wrote the count that Ceruti had not returned home because of the bad weather and his age,[7] but spring brought no improvement and still Ferdinando did not send him home. By November, 1698, Ceruti was ill from a "fiery scab" and approaching death, whereupon the count conceded him to Ferdinando's care for the remainder of his life.[8]

---

* The arabic superscript following a year date refers to the entry in the main chronology. All other superscripts, in *italics*, are footnote references.

[3] P. 160.

[4] I Fas: Med. 5903, cc. 233, 248, 263, 264, 332, 529, 538, 554, 625.

[5] I Fas: Med. 5888, c. 518; 5896, c. 286.

[6] I Fas: Med. 5882, c. 160.

[7] I Fas: Med. 5882, c. 273.

[8] I Fas: Med. 5882, cc. 343, 345, 386.

On the other hand, the prince could turn a deaf ear to the entreaties of Giuseppe Vecchi whose sad letter[9] (while recalling his past services in teaching Ferdinando's singers, specifically Raffaelo Baldi) declared he was on the point of starvation, or to the pleas of Alessandro Scarlatti, abandoned by Ferdinando for younger, more popular composers of the early eighteenth century.[10]

His own singers obtained their worth from him, one suspects. At times Ferdinando's letters seem to reveal a prince reduced to the role of booking agent, a good one to be sure, with status aplenty for the advantage of the singers, but nonetheless saddled with the problems of setting up their schedules, warding off unwanted invitations, interceding for them in difficulties with the police, intervening in legal procedures for their advantages, obtaining appointments in various military and bureaucratic positions for the members of the singers' families, and becoming involved even in private family matters.

A few examples of the problems he faced will have to suffice, so many and varied are the problems themselves. When Francesco de Castris came into the service of Ferdinando in 1687, he left the Bentivoglio family without his severance pay. Ferdinando took up his cause vigorously and, of course, successfully.[11] Invitations for his singers flowed in from all the major public and court theaters and from some not so major ones. Ferdinando easily pushed aside those invitations not likely to add glory to his own reputation and that of his singers. Luca Giustiniani and Carlo Grimani of Venice, the Dukes of Parma, Mantua, the Barberini, such would always find ready reception, but let a Signora Donna Benedetto Cornara Religiosa ask for singers to perform in a little drama her convent wants to do and vague plans for summer or spring operas which actually never get performed suddenly open up.[12]

Gerini found himself in the middle of a grand fracas[13] in 1697 because Antonio Ferrini, virtuoso of Ferdinando, had agreed to sing in a new theater which was being opened in Torino by Giacomo Maggi, otherwise known as the librettist of *Carlo re d'Alemagna* (1700^2) and other operas. His fee was settled at 90 *doppie*, quite a handsome honorarium. But when he saw the theater, he refused to sing because it was *poco decoroso* and, even more important, because the court was not going to attend! The circumstances were quite beneath the dignity of the virtuoso. Ferrini carried his outrage to Ferdinando who then obligingly withdrew his permission to sing. The impresari vented their fury in turn on poor Gerini, with what result we do not know.

If one could penetrate the prose, a series of letters exchanged between Ferdinando and Luca Giustiniano and Francesco Raggi (Genoa) about Maria Maddalena Musi, actually a virtuosa of the Duke of Mantua, but nonetheless a favorite of Ferdinando, would doubtless be amusing. Unfortunately all we can make of it is that Musi was not amused by something Giustiniani said about her to Raggi and the two gentlemen were greatly upset when she, disregarding all proprieties of station, complained directly about it to the Prince.[14] Musi later married a Bolognese nobleman, degli Antonij, but continued a personal (by seventeenth

---

[9] | Fas: Med. 5884, c. 445.
[10] See 1706^4.
[11] | Fas: Med. 5874: Judgment in Francesco's favor c. 117.
[12] | Fas: Med. 5880, c. 430f.
[13] | Fas: Med. 5908, cc. 109-122.
[14] | Fas: Med. 5878, cc. 237, 278, 279.

century standards) correspondence with Ferdinando, sending him holiday greetings and announcements of her growing family.

Ferdinando intervened in the familial relationships of Antonio Ristorini and his half-sister, Rosaura Mazzanti[15] with some heat and ferocity. Ristorini had brought legal action in 1710 to force his stepfather to give up custody of Rosaura. Infuriated, Ferdinando wrote to Senator Cav. Ranuzzi Cospi, his agent in Bologna, "I have heard with much disapprobation that this Antonio Ristorini uterine brother of the cantatrice Rosaura, daughter of Valentino Mazzanti, with improper method and objectives has proceeded to obstruct the fortunes of the sister by cutting off all opportunities which are offered to the same woman to go to recite outside the city and to profit from the talent that she enjoys in the profession of music. Whence I pray your Highness to call in this Ristorini and to talk to him in such a manner that he will desist from his self-interested persecution against his sister in stopping her from accepting the recitations offered her and that he will further cease speaking with little respect both for her and her father, from whose care, I understand, he would like to take her by his petition that is no example of sincere brotherly zeal."[16] Naturally, the Prince was heeded and Rosaura began singing at the Cocomero in Florence in 1712. Ristorini, who had been singing frequently in Florence before 1710, does not sing in Florence again until several years after the death of Ferdinand.

Ferdinando had a central purpose, of course, quite aside from his natural inclinations for his involvement, that purpose being to build up in Florence a school of singers capable of providing a corps of singers for the academic theaters of Florence as well as his own. As we have observed Florence was not in a position to compete with the Venetian theaters, the objective of international pilgrimages at carnival time, and a sign of this inability to compete is the infrequency with which famous Venetian singers performed in Florence or Pratolino during Ferdinando's lifetime. Yet obviously the singers had to be got somewhere. Two resources were open to him: the development of Florentine native singers and the creation of a circuit of pensioned singers in the service of neighboring princes.

The second method was readily adopted, if the matter was actually even consciously thought about, by a group of three princes, the Duke of Modena (Francesco followed by Rinaldo d'Este), the Duke of Mantua (Ferdinando Carlo Gonzaga) and Ferdinando de' Medici. From time to time others entered the circle: Rannuccio and Francesco Maria Farnese (Dukes of Parma), the Duchess of Zagarola, Cardinal Benedetto Pamphili, their excellencies of Venice, Grimani, Giustiniani and Tron, and others. But the constant exchange remained among the first three named.

Each prince maintained his own salaried singers who vaunted themselves as the virtuosi of this or that prince or duke. The singers were then available in a round robin of performances in the noble theaters, making a much greater variety of singers available to each and, one

---

[15] | Fas: Med. 5901, cc. 534, 535.

[16] "Al Senr Cav. Ranuzzi Cospi. Bol, 6 Agosto 1710 di Fir. Ho sentito con molto disapprovazione che cod^O Antonio Ristorini fratello uterino della cantatrice Rosaura figliuola di Valentino Mazzanti con modo, e fini non convenevoli processe di impedire ogni fortuna alla sorella col troncarla tutte le occasioni, che alla med^ma si offeriscono d'andare a recitar fuora e profitare sul talento che gode nella professione della musica; onde prego V.A. d'avere a Le' d^O Ristorini, e di parlar gli in modo che desista dallo suo interessate persecuzioni contro la sorella dall'impedirla le recitare che la venissero e dal parlare con poco rispetto, e di essa, e del Padre, dalla cura del quale ben li conosco che vorebbe levarla col Suo mendicato suo non sincero Zelo fraterno."

suspects, at a somewhat reduced price in view of the stability and the prestige afforded by the "protection" of the princes.

We cannot say without much more extensive research when this circuit of singers developed nor who was its chief organizer but it seems to take shape towards the latter years of the 1680s. Two samples of librettos of the Po Valley cities from the 1670s and 1680s show no signs yet of the ducal circuit. These are the casts of *Achille in Sciro* performed in Bologna at the Teatro Formagliari in 1673 (dedicated to Rinaldo d'Este). This cast consists of Ippolito Fusai, Giacomo Riccardini, Margherita Pia, Domenico Cecchi, Antonio Rivani, Andrea Genari, Ippolito Franci, and Antonio Ferrari, none of whom, according to Sartori's *Catalogo*, claim princely patrons, though Fusai is on the payroll of Grand Duke Cosimo and Rivani might have boasted of a connection with Giovanni Carlo de' Medici. Later, by 1694, Cecchi became a dependent of the Duke of Mantua. (The reader should note in passing that at least two singers of the era of Giovanni Carlo have survived into that of Ferdinando.) The second libretto is *Alcibiade* performed in the Teatro Ducale in Modena in 1685. In a list of nine singers, only one, Marco Antonio Origoni, whom Ferdinando engaged for Livorno in the carnival of 1691, claimed a patron, the others being simply identified by their native cities, Bologna, Turin, Ferrara, Reggio, and Naples. Again somewhat later some of them will announce their patrons.

The early casts, scanty as they are, at Pratolino depended almost entirely upon the *musici ordinari*, as Luca degl'Albizzi called them, that is, the musicians already in the employment of the ducal court, as is the case for 1679[2]. Only *musici ordinari* sing in 1684[3], and in 1685[3] only one singer, Niccola Paris from Naples, was brought in. In 1686[4] Giulio Cavaletti is a Roman but he is also in the service of Francesco Maria de' Medici which qualifies him among the *ordinari*. In 1687[3], Luca degl'Albizzi's letter implies a singer was brought from Rome, but that might be Cavaletti again.

The change to the ducal circuit begins to be suggested by 1688[5] and by Ferdinando's wedding opera of 1689[5]. The former opera had two singers, Francesco Grossi and Origoni, while the latter boasted three under the patronage of other princes: Domenico Ballerini, of the Duke of Mantua; Francesco Grossi, of the Duke of Modena; and Clara Sassi, of the Duke of Mantua. But the transition is even more pronounced elsewhere about the same time. In 1686, in *Alba soggiogata da' Romani,* performed in Reggio in the theater of Francesco II d'Este, seven of eight singers announced their patrons. Francesco de Castris and Carlo Antonio Zanardi are Ferdinando's virtuosi, Angiola Orlandi is his wife's (Violante di Baviera). Three claim the service of the Duke of Mantua: Francesco Ballarini, Ferdinando Chiaravalli, and Giovanni Buzzoleni, the first of whom later represented Ferdinando in Vienna. A seventh is a "musico del Co. Pinamonte Bonacossi," and the eighth stands alone. None are in the service of the Duke of Modena, patron of the theater.

Of nine members for *Aiace* performed in the Teatro Reggio of Milan in 1694 all proudly declare their patrons: Domenico Cecchi, Duke of Mantua; Giuseppe Scaccia, of Parma; Francesco Grossi, of Modena; Barbara Riccioni, of Mantua; Lucrezia Pontissi, of Mantua; Maddalena Musi, of Mantua; Marco Antonio Orrigoni, of Modena; Pietro Paolo Benigni, of Parma; and Antonio Predieri, of Parma. All of these singers except Riccioni and Benigni were at one time or another engaged by Ferdinando (Pontissi is listed by Puliti, p. 73, in 1689).

During the 1690s and early 1700s the fashion spread and the singers of the ducal circuit established a dominance over northern Italy and strong beachheads in Naples, Rome and Venice, of which we present a few examples.

Alba soggiogata da'Romani at the Teatro Malvezzi, Bologna, 1695

Pietro Mozzi	Ser. di Mantova
Garofalini	Ser. di Mantova
Mauro del Maures	Granduca di Toscana
Gioachino Berettini	Card. de' Medici
Lucretia Borgonzoni bolognese	
Girolamo Mellari	
Cristina Morelli	Ser. di Parma
Gio. Ant.o Archi	Virt. del can. Ercole Bonadrata di Rimini

Note: Neither del Maures nor Berettini are recorded in Florentine performances. Given the paucity of casts that fact may not be very significant.

Flavio Cuniberto at the Teatro Capranica, Rome, 1696

Sergio della Donna
Orazio, musico dell'Eccell. Sig. Duchessa Rospigliosi
Giuseppe Scaccia del Ser. di Parma
Carl'Andrea Clerici
Carl'Antonio Zanardi, del Ser. Gran. Pren. di Toscana
Raffaello [Baldi] del Ser. Gran. Pren. di Toscana
Gioseppe Argenti da Udine
G.B. Roberti, del Ser. di Modena
Ant.o Predieri, bolognese
Pietro Paolo Benigni, del Ser. di Parma

Gl'Amanti generosi at the Teatro di S. Bartolomeo, Naples, 1705

Caterina Gallerati, del principe di Toscana
Elena Garofalini, del Ser. di Mantova
Angiola Magliani, del Eminentissimo de' Medici
Maria Angelica Bracci
Niccola Grimaldi, R. capp. di Napoli
Maria Maddalena Fratini, del Card. de' Medici
Livia Mannini
Giuseppe Ferrari, del Ser. di Mantova

Achille placato at the Teatro Tron di S. Cassano, Venezia, 1707

Giuseppe Maria Boschi
Giambattista Roberti, del Ser. di Modana
Santa Stella, del Ser. di Modana
Francesca Vanini Boschi, del Ser. di Modena
Maria Domenica Pini, del Prin. di Toscana
Francesco de Grandis, del Ser. di Modena
Aurelia Marcello, di Venezia
Domenico Tollini, Virt. della S.M. Cesarea
Nicola Pasini
Santa Marchesini e Gio. Battista Cavana Interm.

Note: Marcello soon moved to Florence where she came under the protection of Violante di Baviera.

For the realization of his ambitions Ferdinando also encouraged the native singers of Tuscany. There was already a singer, Ippolito Fusai, a bass, who is first recorded in the role of Caronte in *Ercole in Tebe* (1661[1]) in the company of Antonio Rivani, also a Florentine, both of whom are in the cast of *Achille in Sciro* in Bologna in 1673 (cited above). Fusai was among the singers employed by Ferdinando at Pratolino in 1679[2] and 1686[4] and also in *Greco in Troia* in 1689[5]. His fame as a teacher grew one way or another (the cautionary note is sounded in view of the obvious connections through Violante di Baviera) so that in 1696 Giovanni Guglielmo–Johann Wilhelm–di Baviera sent his chamber singer, Andrea Fischer to Ferdinando so that he might study in the "Scuola del rinomato Fusai." Also Ferdinando sent singers from Florence or Tuscany to other teachers elsewhere for training. In 1692 he sent Raffaello Baldi to study in Rome with Giuseppe Vecchi;[17] in 1705; Marina Orsati, to study with Giuseppe Antonio Aldrovandini in Ferrara;[18] and in 1704, Andrea Guerri, to study with Francesco Pistocchi in Bologna.[19]

Among the Medici remotely interested in opera during Ferdinando's lifetime (Violante di Baviera outlived Ferdinando and, were the later years added, the list of her singers would be slightly longer), there were ample resources for the establishment of a large number of salaried singers. The following is a list by patron. The Grand Duke Cosimo's singers are merely on the ducal payroll and rarely claim his patronage in a published libretto. Those marked with an asterisk are known to be Florentines.

FERDINANDO DE' MEDICI

Giuliano Albertini*
Lucrezia Andrè
Raffaello Baldi*
Ortenzio Beverini*
Anna Maria Bianchi
Maria Maddalena Buonavia
Giuseppe Canavese
Francesco de Castris
Anna Maria Coltellini
Angiolina della Comare
Antonio Romolo Ferrini
Domenico Fontani*
Caterina Gallerati
Giovanni Domenico Graziani
Andrea Guerri
Anna Maria Lisi
Maria Domenica Marini
Maria Domenica Pini*
Vittoria Tarquini
Maria Maddalena Vettori
Carl'Antonio Zanardi

VIOLANTE DI BAVIERA

Gaetano Berenstadt
Francesca Cuzzoni
Maria Caterina Goslerin*
Giovanni Maria Morosi
Lorenzo Porciatti

CARD. FRANCESCO DE' MEDICI

Giulio Cavaletti
Maria Maddalena Fratini
Anna Maria Marchesini
Giovanni Batista Tamburini

ELEONORA DI TOSCANA

Filippo Rossi*

GRAND DUKE COSIMO

Mauro del Maures
Ippolito Fusai*
Filippo Melani
Vincenzio Ulivicciani

---

[17] I Fas: Med. 5878, c. 236; 5880, c. 489; 5882, cc. 400, 550; 5903, c. 372.
[18] I Fas: Med. 5903, c. 434, 447. Puliti says, p. 71, that he sent *Maria* Orsati to study with Aldrovandini in Bologna in 1696. We did not find this correspondence.
[19] I Fas: Med. 5903, c. 229.

With such encouragement a school of singers developed rapidly in less than twenty years. Several singers were able to establish themselves in the ducal circuit and thence make their way into the opera houses of Venice and Rome. The most important singers, exclusive of those listed above under their patrons were: Alessandro del Ricco, Giovanni Batista Franceschini, Rosaura Mazzanti, Giovanni Maria Morosi, Giovanni Battista Rapaccioli, Antonio Ristorini, Domenico Tempesti, and Vittoria Tesi.

The extraordinary increase in the number of Florentine singers is not due entirely to the efforts of Ferdinando. Such an increase could doubtless be duplicated in many of the ducal states, but certainly Ferdinando used his power and money to accelerate what was a peninsular phenomenon.

It is strange, however, that he took no pains to encourage the composers in Florence, although he frequently used Tuscan poets. There are no resident composers except G.M. Pagliardi to compare with the reputations of G.A. Moniglia, Cosimo Villifranchi and Antonio Salvi who, with Giuseppe Giacomini, provide a large percentage of the librettos. There is no indication that he engaged a *maestro di cappella* of his own, as did Gian Gastone later by his appointment of Giuseppe Maria Orlandini, nor does it appear that he formed a close relationship with a Tuscan composer as Giovanni Carlo did with Jacopo Melani. To be sure the problem is made difficult by the absence of any attribution of the music in the librettos (which, in fact, give no information about any person having anything to do with the productions at Pratolino) and many of the unidentified scores may be by local composers including G.M. Pagliardi, Benvenuti Cerri, Martino Bitti, Lorenzo Cattani, or Francesco de Castris.[20] Among these only Pagliardi established a reputation as a composer (Bitti was in much demand as a violinist and de Castris as a singer) outside of Florence. Pagliardi was *maestro di cappella* at S. Lorenzo and later at the Duomo and so he was obviously available. At the same time he was not, like Bitti and de Castris, one of Ferdinando's musicians. The same could be said of Cattani, the *maestro* at Pisa.

A list of the operas at Pratolino (see p. 70) shows that Ferdinando preferred to seek composers from Venice, Bologna and Rome rather than cultivate composers in Florence. The fact is somehow related to Ferdinando's musical taste and native talents. For texts he is willing to repeat old ones, altering them to suit his demands, as was the general custom, but for the music he apparently, at least, preferred[21] to choose music written by composers from various Italian centers.

The reorganization of the Infuocati in 1699 and the eventual reopening of the Pergola in 1718 profoundly affected the lives of the professional musicians. Without a shred of evidence, we would hazard a guess that the secure return of opera to Florence (not just at Pratolino and in provincial towns) was one of Ferdinando's greatest achievements. It could have been possible only with the amelioration of Cosimo's attitude, of which a sign was his intervention to reopen the Pergola. Whatever the cause, there set in a gradual crescendo of theatrical performances

---

[20] Besides the portions of the opera listed below, de Castris also wrote some arias since Ferdinando wrote Giuseppe Vecchi in 1692 (I Fas: Med. 5878, c. 305) thanking him for teaching Raffaello Baldi some of de Castris' arias.

[21] Fabbri, *A. Scarlatti*, p. 27, asserts that only new music by only *grandi musicisti* was performed at Pratolino. This is a slight exaggeration not supported by a sufficiency of facts. Cerri, Benini, Bitti, and de Castris are hardly great musicians, and Scarlatti's music for *Anacreonte*, 1698[5], most probably was not new. Furthermore, degl'Albizzi's observations in 1687[3] indicate that the prince at times had to modify his ambitions for financial reasons. Curtailment would probably have precluded the expense of a new score as well as other things.

TABLE II

List of Operas at Pratolino

Date	Opera	Librettist	Composer
1679[2]	*Con la forza d'amor*	Giov. Fil. Apolloni	Buonaventura Cerri
1680[2]	*Corindo*	Gius. Giacomini	——
1681[2]	*Rosalba*	Gius. Giacomini	——
1682	No opera known		
1683[3]	*Speziale di villa*	G.C. Villifranchi	——
1684[3]	*Speziale di villa*	G.C. Villifranchi	——
1685[3]	*Ifianassa e Melampo*	G.A. Moniglia	Giov. Legrenzi
1686[4]	*Finto chimico*	G.C. Villifranchi	——
1687[3]	*Pazzo per forza*	G.A. Moniglia	G.M. Pagliardi
1688[5]	*Tiranno di Colco*	G.A. Moniglia	G.M. Pagliardi
1689[10]	*Serva favorita*	G.C. Villifranchi	A. Scarlatti?
1690[6]	No opera known		
1691[4]	*Marco Aurelio*	A. Zeno?	——
1692[5]	*Trespolo oste*	G.C. Villifranchi	——
1693[4]	*Attilio Regolo*	M. Noris	G.M. Pagliardi
1694	No opera performed		
1695[4]	*Ipocondriaco*	G.C. Villifranchi	G.B. Benini
1696[5]	*Tito Manlio*	M. Noris	C.F. Pollaroli
1697[4]	Unknown opera was performed		
1698[5]	*Anacreonte*	D. Franc. Bussani	F. de Castris Martino Bitti Ales. Scarlatti
1699[8]	*Faramondo*	A. Zeno	C. Pollaroli?
1700[7]	*Lucio Vero*	A. Zeno	G.A. Perti? or C. Pollaroli?
1701[5]	*Astianatte*	A. Salvi	G.A. Perti
1702[4]	*Flavio Cuniberto*	M. Noris	A. Scarlatti
1703[3]	*Arminio*	A. Salvi	A. Scarlatti
1704[2]	*Turno Aricino*	S. Stampiglia	A. Scarlatti
1705[4]	*Lucio Manlio*	S. Stampiglia	A. Scarlatti
1706[4]	*Il Gran Tamerlano*	A. Salvi	A. Scarlatti
1707[3]	*Dionisio Re di Portogallo*	A. Salvi	G.A. Perti
1708[2]	*Ginevra Principessa di Scozia*	A. Salvi	G.A. Perti
1709[1]	*Berenice Regina di Egitto*	A. Salvi	G.A. Perti
1710[5]	*Rodelinda Regina de' Longobardi*	A. Salvi	G.A. Perti

that reached a climax in the 1740s by which time in a city of 120,000 four theaters were performing opera and several smaller theaters were occasionally entering the competition. Performances of all types of theatricals continued virtually year round. Carnival lasted from the end of December to Lent and until 1748 both the Cocomero and the Pergola performed one or two operas each. The season of 1730-1731 was something of a phenomenon; at the Cocomero four operas were produced, two *serie* and two *burlette* in alternation. The spring season began after Easter (even in the Octave) and lasted into May. The summer season began in June and lasted until August. The fall season normally divided into two segments, September and October, then November until Advent, though on one occasion permission was granted by the Reggenza to continue performances in Advent, normally, of course, a penitential season. Opera was not always performed in all seasons in all theaters, for it ranked only as the most elaborate form in a quite catholic passion for theater in all its forms. Commedia dell'arte, ballets, spoken dramas with and without music, comic intermezzi, tightrope acts, *saltimbancs*, and the like, whirled deliriously through the seasons in astounding variety. Within this craze for the theater, opera still made an impressive growth. Florence in the entire seventeenth century witnessed 118 registered performances of opera. In the fifty-one years following the reopening of the Cocomero in 1699, she heard more than 270 operas, not including intermezzi and other musical entertainments.

These events heralded a period of rapid expansion of the theaters to include a more general, if still largely bourgeois, audience, and under the impact of the expansion, the system of patronage built by Ferdinando quickly collapsed. The virtuosi supported by the last of the Medici and by Francesco di Lorena were very few indeed. Yet Ferdinando had achieved his goal and Florence continued to be a center capable of competing with other centers in the production of operatic singers, including Maria Maddalena Parigi, Giovanni Battista Pinacci, Pietro Pertici and his wife, Caterina Brogi, Antonio Lottini, Maria Maddalena Salvai, Prudenza Sani, Antonio Ristorini and Rosa Ungherelli, all of international fame during the century.

Altogether the growth of opera and the number of singers was phenomenal and the opportunities for making money correspondingly multiplied. But stability was the real cost of the new state of things for the singers (less so for other musicians). During the seventeenth century, such singers as Fusai, Ulivicciani, Vincenzio Melani, and Antonio Rivani could pass their entire professional lives in Florence. But in the eighteenth century such stability was rare.

In the first half of the eighteenth century identified singers performing in Florence numbered approximately 475. That figure could easily be raised by a third were all the singers known. Of these 475, over 350 performed in one to three operas. If one excludes the singers called to Florence by Ferdinando (d. 1713), there remain only twelve singers in the almost forty years that endure for twelve or more years, and it is plain that even those, like the Ristorini who considered Florence their home, are far more mobile than their seventeenth century predecessors. One is astonished at the unceasing parade of singers across the Florentine stage, a parade of course duplicated in major and minor principalities of Italy and in the capitals of Europe. The logistics seem awesome and it is a wonder how the impresarios managed to line up their casts in the free-for-all over such great distances that involved so many petty courts, theaters, and academies, and all without the aid of rapid communications, transportation, or computers! At the end of the seasons, the roads of Italy must have become clogged with the carriages of opera stars dashing from theater to theater. One suspects also that more than one cast was filled at the last minute by the impresario's snatching off the highway the first singer rushing by.

In view of the turmoil, the notion burgeons up that possibly logistics had as much to do with eighteenth century operatic reform as the Arcadian aesthetics, or at least we might say that for once aesthetics and practical necessity found a happy and harmonious union. The theaters would have been under great pressure for practical reasons to reduce the number of singers for a single opera to a fixed number (five or six) and the voicing to standards, i.e., two sopranos, two contraltos, tenor and bass, in order to make the casts as interchangeable as possible. Thus, as usually happened, the same group of singers could be hired to do two operas in one season or in adjacent seasons.

These pressures could be used to explain other Baroque phenomena: the standardized librettos of Zeno, Pariati and Metastasio, and the *pasticcio*, both being two slices out of the same pie. The first makes the second possible. The second in turn makes any one performance conveniently adjustable to the cast at hand. Table III, *opposite*, contains a series of casts for one opera, *Alessandro nell'Indie*, which show how singers repeat, exchange roles, learn new scores, etc. It is easy to see why the singers would want to retain arias from one opera in another, especially since these same singers would have been engaged in a similar juggling act with other operas in the same period.

The intermezzi, without attempting to dethrone the decisive role of the aesthetic debates of the Arcadi or the Aristotelian ideals that underlay the creation of *opera seria*, from another point of view are a practical and convenient method for turning, in a sense, all operas into *pasticcios*. Formerly, operas having eight to ten parts of which two at least were comic would have required particular casting for the comic roles just as for the serious ones. Under new arrangements, the performers for the intermezzi were a separate matter, and therefore the problem of the casting could be handled more easily by simply contracting with specialists who toured separately from the principal cast.

A cursory examination of the casts reveals a few ideas that are in general not accepted or thoroughly understood. First, in Baroque opera it was the common practice to use women in the male soprano and contralto roles, not merely as a stopgap for the lack of a suitable castrato, but for the purpose of obtaining the proper voicing, which, in the Baroque context, meant that heroic roles must have high tessiture. Women of great reputation sang male roles, some even specializing in singing *da huomo*. Examples are too abundant to attempt a list. An instance involving a famous soprano would be Vittoria Tesi's performance of Lotario in *Innocenza difesa* in 1721. An interesting scrap of paper in the Infuocati archives is a payment to a Sig. Galli as a commission to go "a Bologna per avere una donne di bel aspetto per far da uomo alla Sig.r Margherita Zani." Zani had sung several times in Florence between 1714 and 1725, but not in male roles. It was not always agreeable to the singer to perform such roles, for Clorinda Landi gave as her excuse for not singing a second opera at the Pergola in the carnival of 1748[16] that the impresario Grifoni had promised she would be the prima donna and not have to sing *da huomo*.[22] In modern performances it follows that the more appropriate arrangement is to use women in castrato roles rather than to transpose the roles.

Second, the common notion that a sharp distinction lay between the singers in *opera seria* and those of *opera buffa* is inaccurate. While the tendency to specialize in certain

---

[22] | Fas: Regg. 631, cc. 11-18r.

TABLE III

Casts for Alessandro Nell'Indie (Metastasio)

	Alessandro	Poro	Cleofile	Erissena	Gandarte	Timagene	Composer
Rome Carnival 1730	——	Carestini	——	——	Tolve	——	Vinci
Venice Carnival 1731	Berenstadt	——	Posterli	Stabili	Antinori	——	——
Milan Carnival 1731	——	Carestini	Tesi	Peruzzi	——	——	Predieri
Florence Carnival 1732	——	——	Posterli	——	——	——	——
Naples Carnival 1732	——	——	——	——	Tolve	——	Mancini
Reggio Carnival 1732	——	——	Turcotti	——	Antinori	——	Vinci
Venice Carnival 1732	Finazzi	——	Turcotti	——	Peruzzi	——	Pescetti
Brescia Carnival 1733	Finazzi	——	——	——	Poli	——	——
Bologna Carnival 1734	——	Finazzi	Peruzzi	——	Ferrari	——	Schiassi
Pisa Spring 1735	——	Saletti	——	——	——	——	——
Naples November 1736	Amorevoli	Carestini	Tesi	Giacomassi	——	——	Hasse
Parma Carnival 1736	Fontana	Ferrari	——	——	——	——	——
Venice Carnival 1736	Amorevoli	Castorini	Tesi	Giacomassi	Saletti	——	Hasse
Madrid 1738	——	Saletti	——	——	Uttini	Monticelli	Correlli
Prato Carnival 1736	Monticelli	Uttini	——	——	——	——	——
Mantua Carnival 1738	——	Castorini	——	Poli	——	——	Galuppi
Venice Carnival 1738	Tolve	Fontana	——	——	——	——	Hasse

characters is evident, numerous examples exist in which singers go from one type of role to another. The most famous of all buffa singers, Antonio Ristorini, sang serious roles in melodramas for more than seventeen years. Ristorini first appears in Florence in the role of Cleonte in *Lisimaco* (Sinibaldo and Pasquini) in 1690. He sings similar roles between 1703 and 1710. After an interval of absence he returns to sing a secondary role in *Scanderbegh* (Salvi and Vivaldi), the opera performed for the reopening of the Pergola. In the same season he performs the intermezzi at the Pergola with his wife Rosa Ungherelli. They both sang in *Il Trionfo della Costanza* (Zeno and an unknown composer) at the Cocomero in 1709[3]. After 1718 the pair rapidly acquires international fame as intermezzo singers. Francesca Cuzzoni, while she had sung earlier in *opera serie* elsewhere, made her Tuscan debut in the role of Leonora in a revised version of Moniglia's comic opera, *Tacere et amare*, in Florence and Siena in 1717. The various companies organized by Pietro Pertici to perform comic operas at the Cocomero use a number of singers who at other times sing serious roles at both the Cocomero and the Pergola.

The selection of composers and of librettists undergoes some change as a result of the commercialization of the academies and their subjugation to bureaucratic control but the change is not quite so dramatic. Throughout the seventeenth century poets stood apart from the other creators of opera and drama. They were men of letters, graduates of the Studio di Pisa, for the most part, some of them noblemen, and an astonishing number of them were doctors. The composers initially seemed to be the social and intellectual peers of the poets. Jacopo Corsi and Jacopo Peri as composers were quite on the same level as Rinuccini, Chiabrera or Salvadori. But by the mid-seventeenth century a difference in education and social level is noticeable. Jacopo Melani is not of the same class as Giovanni Andrea Moniglia, a physician, the occupant of a chair at Pisa, member of the Accademia della Crusca, nor is he the peer of Filippo Acciajuoli, member of one of the oldest noble families in Florence and brother of a Cardinal; Cesti is not the equal of Cicognini. The Villifranchis, father and son, both are physicians, like Moniglia, and graduates of the Studio, as is Antonio Salvi, the serious-minded, after them. By comparison Cattani, Pagliardi, and Bitti are hardly above the status of common servants. The poet-dramatists include Marchese Mattias Maria Bartolommei and the star of all Tuscan dramatists, Giulio Rospigliosi, Cardinal and Pope.

There were seventeenth century writers of lesser rank as well. In fact one can draw a lower class lineage almost as continuous as the physicians'. Pietro Susini, of whom Negri in the *Scrittori fiorentini*[23] says that he exemplified that poets are born, not made, since he had very little education, was especially gifted as a comic poet and with his comedies won the admiration of Grand Duke Ferdinando II and Cardinal Leopoldo. Susini's contemporary and fellow member of the Sorgenti, Mario Calamari, belongs in this category, but his chief function here is to establish connections with Giovanni Battista Fagiuoli, the most prolific and gifted comic librettist and playwright of the late seventeenth and early eighteenth centuries; for Fagiuoli records in 1680[1] his performing as the ridiculous servant, his speciality, at Calamari's house, and again in 1683[1] where he identifies Calamari as the guardian of the Compagnia del Vangelista. The last of the lineage is Ab. Francesco Vanneschi, perhaps also the last of the Tuscan comic librettists. (We have traced him at least as far back

---

[23] P. 470. Negri also says he died in 1668, which we doubt since he apparently wrote topical poetry after that date. See Index of Librettists.

as 1673 when he is listed among the pages of Vittoria della Rovere and found him in the 1733 census of 1730 with an impressive list of ancestors: Francesco Maria di Cammillo Vettorie di Agniolo Franceschini.[24]) Vanneschi's contribution has long been obscured by incorrect attributions, but an examination of the items listed in the index of librettists will place him securely in the ranks of Tuscany's most individual and unique writers— comic librettists.

All of these men from Rinuccini to Salvi, from Susini to Vanneschi wrote not as professional dramatists but as gentlemen of one rank or another while claiming some other profession. Therefore the commercialization led to their near extinction. Perhaps more than any other way, they were affected by the standardization of the libretto. Even comic librettos were subjected to some stereotyping. The adoption of standard Zeno and Metastasio texts for serious opera was matched by an almost regulated revival of the comic librettos of Moniglia and Villifranchi until Vanneschi's librettos managed to hold the stage for a time from the 1730s onward.

The standardization was more stultifying in the case of *opera seria*. After Salvi there was no one who could displace the standard librettos, and the form seemed moribund already before the end of our era for the lack of a native poet. Richecourt was never recorded as having attended an *opera seria* at the Pergola or the Cocomero, a fact that amply expresses his feelings about the form. Hence he was moved to found the Teatro Toscano, and we cannot overrule his judgment that Tuscan comic opera was far more alive than *opera seria*, continually a more stereotyped and exotic entertainment. At last he went to the opera to see *I cicisbei delusi* in 1750[8] when, Susier tells us, he entertained at gambling.

The lot of the Tuscan composer, either native or adoptive, actually seems to have improved under the new commercial era. Exotic composers still had great attraction, and the works, including premieres, of Albinoni, Predieri, Vivaldi, Lampugnani, Fini, Latilla, Rinaldo, Pescetti and Leo certainly jostle the resident composers. But Lirone, Redi, Arrigoni and Chinzer, minor composers though they be, had their day, while we strongly suspect that Giuseppe Maria Orlandini dominated all other composers both at the Pergola and the Cocomero. So many of the first performances of Orlandini's operas elsewhere announce that the opera has been altered to adopt it to local tastes and the performing artists, a fact that always implies (but does not prove) that the performance is in fact not the first. If not, where else but Florence, Livorno or Pisa? Again security on the point escapes our grasp because of the enormous number of operas without indication of the composer. Of course Florentines knew who wrote it and in that case higher status (provided everyone knew) went to anonymity than to publication. Prince Ferdinando had set a perfect example of elegance and grandeur without revealing his own or anyone else's identity. Therefore, any attempt to make an accurate accounting of Orlandini's works must start with the suspicion, at least, that any anonymous Florentine libretto might have been set by Orlandini if other evidence fails to give a clue. The first instance in which Orlandini's music can be documented in a Florentine performance is *Amor generoso*, 1708[4]. A Bolognese libretto of 1713 for *Carlo Re d'Alemagna* entitles him *maestro di cappella* to Gian Gastone, then principe di Toscana. It is to be suspected that a large percentage of all the anonymous operas performed in Florence, where he became a resident impresario, are by

---

[24] *Decima Granducale* Libro 1º Arroti del Quartiere S. Spirito F. 2145; and *Provvisione diverse della Ser^{ma} Gran Duchessa Vittoria*, f. 200.

Orlandini between at least 1715 and his death in 1760. It is tempting to compare Florence with Vienna where the imperial maestros had an absolute monopoly on the composition of operatic scores (aside from the addition of any imperial compositions) but Orlandini was not supported by so powerful a prince. Gian Gastone was no dictator politically or artistically and Orlandini's position was not strong enough, therefore, to impose himself autocratically upon the two academies. So we cannot raise our thoughts above the level of a hunch.

Two composers need to be mentioned in closing simply because they so seldom appear. Francesco Maria Mannucci is positively credited with two compositions in 1710[6] and 1713[2], though he ought to have been more productive since he was sent as a youth by Ferdinando to study with Perti in Bologna.[25] With such a background how could he fail to have written operas? He is the *maestro di cappella* to the Grand Duke in 1713, in which position he continues after Cosimo's death in 1723 since in 1732[8] he is succeeded by Orlandini (i.e., Orlandini as maestro to Gian Gastone did not follow his patron when he became Grand Duke). Mannucci technically outranked Orlandini. Are some of the anonymous scores by Mannucci rather than Orlandini? And what are we to make of 1738[10], a death notice of a "good cembalist and composer" who yet has not left his name on any composition? These names can only remind us that to assign a composer to any anonymous setting is hazardous and futile besides.

---

[25] I Fas: Med. 5903, c. 158. Thereafter many of Perti's letters mention Mannucci.

A CHRONOLOGY OF MUSIC

IN THE

FLORENTINE THEATER

1590-1750

THE FORM OF THE ENTRIES

THE DATES IN THE OUTSIDE MARGIN of each entry (with the day in Arabic and the month in Roman numerals) are often quite arbitrary. They are not always precisely the date of performance.

The preferred date by which an entry is identified is, of course, the date or dates of performance. But such is not always the case. If only the date of the signature of a dedication or an imprimatur is available, then such a date is used, though the dedication date will normally precede the performance by days or even weeks and months, since it is related to the date of the publication of the libretto rather than its performance. Nevertheless, the dedication is an indicator of the season at least and as such often solves the problem of chronological order within the year. Despite these difficulties which prevent an indisputable chronological order, we have used a simple superscript number for each entry to identify its assigned chronological position within a given year; that is, 1657^2 identifies the second entry in that year.

A special problem is created by the Lady Day Calendar in use in Florence during this period. This calendar begins the year on March 25 instead of January 1. Hence, one can never be certain whether a date between January 1 and March 25 is the year actually stated or the year following. Nor can the researcher depend upon any absolute consistency in the system of dating by any letter-writer, editor, diarist, *etc.*, of the seventeenth and eighteenth centuries. In general we have observed that diarists will regularly use the Lady Day Calendar. The dates of dedications usually do also, but the date on the title page will be taken from the Gregorian Calendar, usually that is, but not always. Letters frequently carry both years, in which case there is no problem. Sometimes the use of a year preceding on the title page is not a Lady Day Calendar but rather is the result of the libretto's having been printed in

November or December preceding the carnival season following, even in cases where the libretto was intended for the second opera of the season which would begin performances in late January or February. Publishers and the academies would have found an early printing a useful means of advertising.

We have placed those operas of the carnival season that began their performances after Christmas in the last positions of the year preceding the carnival. Many of these first operas of the season are identified by the diarists and therefore naturally would appear under the dates the diarists supply. Unless forewarned this practice might lead to confusion. It should be noted, however, that the practice of beginning in December is eighteenth century. The earliest datable instance is 1698[10]. Despite Morini's assumptions, especially in respect to the comedies performed by the Immobili in the Pergola from 1657 until 1662, a beginning in December simply cannot be established.

Operas for which the date of performance can not be determined more precisely than the year are grouped alphabetically at the end of the year.

Beneath the date will be found the theater, the academy, or other location of the performance. If the location is in parentheses, it is an adduced location. Some problems arise because the academies do not always perform in one theater, nor is one theater necessarily limited to performances by one academy. The Pergola, excepting some horse-ballets mounted by the Accademia dei Nobili, remained exclusively in the hands of the Immobili for operatic performances. But the Cocomero was used until 1699 by other academies than the Infuocati. Likewise the smaller theaters do change academic hands.

In titles and quotations, brackets are used to indicate insertions of explanatory material not part of the original title or quotation. Parentheses are used to enclose dates or theaters that are not established with certainty. In a few cases, a major bibliographic source may cite a Florentine performance that is plainly an error. Given the habits of bibliographers these errors will be repeated endlessly. In the probably vain hope of cutting the chain of repetitions, we have retained these entries and marked them by enclosing the entire date and theater in parentheses.

The titles of existing librettos are given in capital letters. If the performance is known by an entry in a diary, letter, or other archival material or by a later publication, the title is in italics. Following the libretto title are the libraries in which it is located. The abbreviations are listed on pages 81-83.

The attribution of the text follows with any information supplied by the libretto itself in prefaces, arguments, and dedications. The second paragraph concerns the music, including the locations of scores. While we have made every effort to locate scores of operas performed first in Florence, we have made only a superficial search for imported scores and include the information for the convenience of the reader. Our principal recourse has been to Eitner, MGG, and the catalogues of the major libraries (including the catalogues published by the Associazione di musicologia italiana). But no attempt has been made to check the accuracy of these sources.

If the cast is given in the libretto it is printed in the chronology following the discussion of the musical attribution. In cases of Florentine first performances the *personaggi* are printed even where there are no actors in the hope that this listing will aid in identifying scores.

We make no claims to having discovered all librettos or all copies of librettos we have uncovered ourselves. Eventually the union catalogue of librettos may be completed by

Dr. Claudio Sartori who has accomplished impressive things of that nature already and is currently in the process of issuing xerox or microfilm copies of his comprehensive index. However, even he has not succeeded in obtaining complete cooperation of all Italian libraries and the work is to a degree still limited by the lack of separate catalogues of librettos in the Italian libraries. Librarians years hence will still be discovering librettos which in their collections are catalogued merely under the title or author without distinction from the general holdings of the library.

These limitations apply as well to our work, and if we have succeeded in ferreting out librettos where the librarians themselves would not have recognized them, it is because of luck and the limitations of the subject itself. Where libraries are specialized music libraries, normally there are no problems in obtaining a reasonably complete examination of their entire holdings. Similarly some national and university libraries have separate collections of librettos (as the Marucelliana) or have separate catalogues (as in the Braidense and Estense). But in other major libraries, namely the Vittorio Emanuele in Rome, the Florence National, the Vatican, the British Museum, and the Paris National libraries, the librettos are catalogued with the whole collection. Hence it is impossible to find librettos which are not already known by author or title or both, and we cannot be sure how much our fishing methods have caught of the holdings of librettos in these libraries. Authors are the smaller of the two problems. The number of librettists is not unreasonable and early in our research a comprehensive list could be used in working with any catalogue. But most of the librettos are anonymous and are consequently catalogued by title, and therefore one could expect to find a new libretto in any drawer of a catalogue! The subjects of operas tend to be limited and conventional, so a list of key words was developed such as *Amore*, *Nozze*, *Vecchio*, and including standard heroes. Ineluctably the procedure developed into repeated visits to the same libraries as new titles were discovered in one of them. It is obvious that there is no end to the procedure except as is demanded by time and money. The numerous references in diaries to unnamed operas in the chronology attest to the fact that not all have been discovered, but we are moved to publish the chronology anyway because first, twenty-odd years are enough to spend on a project of this nature, second, what we have accumulated does sufficiently illuminate the musical and dramatic productivity of Florence to allow historians to reassess the city's role in the history of opera in general, and finally, what remains to be uncovered, we believe, will not essentially alter the record here assembled.

A final observation is necessary about the dramatic works included in the chronology. Although the principal subject is opera, the chronology includes any work which appears to have used music in any portion: a prologue, finale, intermezzo, or incidental music. But we have in addition included some works which are entirely in prose merely for the convenience of the user. It was our experience that in the search for librettos and the like, it became necessary to maintain the titles of prose works in the chronology in order to avoid duplication of effort. The titles do crop up in bibliographies and catalogues without any indication of the nature of the texts, whether prose or poetry, with or without music. By retaining them in the publication of the chronology with descriptions of their texts we hope we may save music historians unnecessary effort and possibly be of some help to historians of literature and drama. But we must warn these latter that as a chronology of spoken drama the list is less carefully and inclusively compiled. We have not, for example, entered every prose comedy cited by Allacci. If copies were located, we made the entry in order to preserve that bibliographical datum, or if the title in Allacci contained information not otherwise available, then we included it.

We have used short titles of the recurrent bibliographical sources which we hope are sufficient to identify the complete work by referring to the bibliography.

LIBRARY SIGLA

A	**Austria**
Wgm	Vienna, Gesellschaft der Musikfreunde
Wn	Vienna, Österreichische Nationalbibliothek
Wu	Vienna, Universitätsbibliothek

B	**Belgium**
Bc	Brussels, Bibliothèque du Conservatoire royal de musique
Br	Brussels, Bibliothèque royale de Belgique

C	**Canada**
Tu	Toronto, University of Toronto Library

D	**Germany**
Bds	Berlin, Deutsche Staatsbibliothek
Dsl	Dresden, Sächsische Landesbibliothek
LEm	Leipzig, Musikbibliothek
Mm	Munich, Städtische Musikbibliothek
MÜps	Münster, Bibliothek des Priesterseminars
ROu	Rostock, Universitätsbibliothek
SW	Schwerin, Landesbibliothek
Tmi	Tübingen, Musikwissenschaftliches Institut der Universität
W	Wolfenbüttel, Herzog-August-Bibliothek
WD	Wiesentheid, Gräflich von Schönbornsche Musikbibliothek

DK	**Denmark**
Kk	Copenhagen, Det kongelige Bibliotek

E	**Spain**
Mn	Madrid, Biblioteca nacional

F	**France**
Pc	Paris, Bibliothèque du Conservatoire
Pn	Paris, Bibliothèque nationale

GB	**Great Britain**
Cfm	Cambridge, Fitzwilliam Museum

Lbm	London, British Museum
Lk	London, King's Music Library
Oc	Oxford, Coke Collection
I	**Italy**
Baf	Bologna, Accademia filarmonica
Bam	Bologna, Biblioteca della Cassa di Risparmio (Biblioteca Ambrosini)
Bc	Bologna, Civico Museo Bibliografico-Musicale *formerly* Liceo Musicale "G.B. Martini"
Bca	Bologna, Biblioteca comunale dell'Archiginnasio
Bu	Bologna, Biblioteca universitaria
Fac	Florence, Biblioteca comunale ed Archivio di Firenze
Fas	Florence, Archivio di Stato
Fc	Florence, Biblioteca del Conservatorio di Musica "L. Cherubini"
Fl	Florence, Biblioteca Mediceo-Laurenziana
Fm	Florence, Biblioteca Marucelliana
Fn	Florence, Biblioteca nazionale centrale
Fr	Florence, Biblioteca Riccardiana
Lg	Lucca, Biblioteca governativa (Biblioteca statale di Lucca)
Ma	Milan, Biblioteca Ambrosiana
MAC	Macerata, Biblioteca comunale "Mozzi-Borgetti"
Mb	Milan, Biblioteca nazionale Braidense
Mc	Milan, Biblioteca del Conservatorio "Giuseppe Verdi"
MC	Montecassino, Biblioteca dell'Abbazia
MOas	Modena, Archivio di Stato
MOe	Modena, Biblioteca Estense
Nc	Naples, Biblioteca del Conservatorio di Musica S. Pietro a Maiella
Nn	Naples, Biblioteca nazionale "Vittorio Emanuele III" *with* Bibl. Lucchesi-Palli
PAc	Parma, Sezione musicale della Biblioteca Palatina presso il Conservatorio "Arrigo Boito"
PEc	Perugia, Biblioteca comunale Augusta
PIu	Pisa, Biblioteca universitaria
PLcom	Palermo, Biblioteca comunale
PS	Pistoia, Archivio capitolare della Cattedrale
PSc	Pistoia, Biblioteca comunale Forteguerriana
PScr	Pistoia, Casa Rospigliosi
Rca	Rome, Biblioteca Casanatense

Rn	Rome, Biblioteca nazionale centrale "Vittorio Emanuele II"
Rsc	Rome, Biblioteca musicale Santa Cecilia (Conservatorio)
Rvat	Rome, Biblioteca Apostolica Vaticana
Sc	Siena, Biblioteca comunale degli Intronati (Museo etrusco)
Tn	Turin, Biblioteca nazionale universitaria
Vcg	Venice, Casa di Goldoni, Biblioteca
Vgc	Venice, Biblioteca e Istituto di Lettere, Musica e Teatro della Fondazione "Giorgio Cini"
Vnm	Venice, Biblioteca nazionale Marciana
VTc	Viterbo, Biblioteca comunale degli Ardenti
VTs	Viterbo, Biblioteca del Seminario Diocesano *with* Biblioteca Provinciale A. Anselmi
VO	Volterra, Biblioteca Guarnacciana

P	**Portugal**
Pla	Lisbon, Biblioteca do Palácio nacional da Ajuda

PL	**Poland**
WRu	Wroclaw, Biblioteka Uniwersytecka

S	**Sweden**
Sk	Stockholm, Kungl. Biblioteket
Uu	Uppsala, Universitetsbiblioteket

US	**United States**
A	Austin, University of Texas
Bp	Boston, Massachusetts, Public Library
BE	Berkeley, California, University of California
BL	Bloomington, Indiana, Indiana University Library
CA	Cambridge, Massachusetts, Harvard University Library *and* Houghton Library and Theater Collection
Chb	Chicago, Illinois, Private collection of Howard Mayer Brown
NYp	New York, New York, Public Library
U	Urbana-Champaign, Illinois, University Library
Wc	Washington, D.C., Library of Congress
Ws	Washington, D.C., Folger Shakespeare Library

ABBREVIATIONS OF TITLES

Most abbreviations in Italian texts have been completed, added letters being in brackets. However, common titles have usually been unaltered. Abbreviations of standard titles follow:

A.R.	Altezza Reale
A.V.R.	Altezza Vostra Reale *or* Reverendissima
Ab.	Abbate
Accad.	Accademico
Arcid.sa	Archiduchessa
Card.	Cardinale
Cav.e	Cavaliere
Clemen.mo	Clementissimo
D.	Don, Donna *or* Dottore
Duch.sa	Duchessa
Ecc.	Eccellenza
Em.mo	Eminentissimo
Fr.	Frate
G.D.	Gran Duca *or* Duchessa
G.P.	Gran Principe *or* Principessa
Ill.mo	Illustrissimo
Imp.le	Imperiale
M., Mons.	Monsieur
Pr.	Prete
Pren., Prpe., Princ.	Principe
Rev.mo	Reverendissimo
S.	Serenissima, Sua, *or* Santa
S.A.	Sua Altezza
S.A.R.	Sua Altezza Reale *or* Reverendissima *in the case of cardinals*
S.M.	Sua Maestà
Ser., Ser.ma	Serenissima
Sig., Sig.r, Sig.ra	Signor *or* Signora
SS	Santi
Sigg. or SS	Signori
V.A.R.	Vostra Altezza Reale
V.A.S.	Vostra Altezza Serenissima
Virt.	Virtuoso *or* Virtuosa

ABBREVIATIONS

ab inc.   (*ab incarnatione*) - Lady Day calendar. Dates followed by *ab inc.* must be read as the following year in the Gregorian calendar.

c.   carta *or* letter

cc.   carta *or* letter (plural)

cap.   capitolo *or* chapter

carn   carnival

cod.   codex

col.   column

d.a   detta

d.o   detto

ecc.   eccetera *or* et cetera

f.   folio

F.   filza

fig.   figure

Magl.   Magliabecchi, **I** Fn

Med.   Archivio Mediceo, **I** Fas

Ms   Manuscript

n.   note

no.   number

opp.   opposite

o.t.   other title

p.   page

pt.   part

s.d.   without date

s.l.   without place

s.t.   without publisher

sc.   scudi (Italian currency)

suppl.   supplement

vol.   volume

CHRONOLOGY

1590¹ carn *Il satiro*, favola pastorale.

Text (lost): Laura Guidiccioni ne' Luchesini.

Music (lost): Emilio dei Cavalieri.
Information concerning this pastorale, as well as *La disperazione di Fileno*
and *Il giuoco della cieca* following is found in the dedication, *A'lettori*,
and *Avvertimenti* published in *Rappresentatione di anima et di corpo
nuovamente posta in musica del Signor Emilio del Cavaliere* (Roma:
Guidotti, 1600). The entire libretto is reprinted in Solerti, *Origini*,
pp. 1-39. The dedication remarks that the three pastorales were "recitate
alla presenza delle Serenissime Altezze di Toscana in diversi tempi: nel
1590 *il Satiro*, qual fu recitato anche un'altra volta; e lo stesso anno la
Disperazione di Fileno ritiratamente, e nel 1595 *il Giuoco della cieca*
alla presenza degli Illustrissimi Cardinali Monte e Mont'Alto e del Sereniss.
Arciduca Ferdinando. . ." The *A'lettori* reveals that Vittoria Archilei
sang in the *Disperazione*, and at the conclusion Laura Guidiccioni is cited
as the poet of all three pastorales, with Guarini's *Pastor fido* as the source
of the *Giuoco*. See further Solerti, "Emilio de' Cavalieri," p. 797.

1590² carn *La disperazione di Fileno*, favola pastorale.

Text (lost): Laura Guidiccioni.

Music (lost): Cavalieri. See above.

1595 29 x *Il giuoco della cieca*, pastorale.
Pal. Pitti
Text: Laura Guidiccioni after Guarini, *Pastor fido.*

Music: Cavalieri. Text and music are lost. Sonneck, "Dafne," p. 105, n. 1.

1598 carn, LA DAFNE d'Ottavio Rinuccini rappresentata alla Serenissima Gran Duchessa
1599 carn, di Toscana dal Signor Jacopo Corsi. Firenze, Giorgio Marescotti, MDC.
1600¹ on or B Bc; I Bc, Fn, Mb(2), MOe, PAc, Rca, Rsc.
before 18 i
Pal. Corsi Text: Rinuccini. Reprinted in Solerti, *Origini*, II, pp. 66-99.
1600² 21 i
Pal. Pitti Music: Jacopo Peri with some arias by Jacopo Corsi. Lost except for six
1600³ viii arias. It is not certain which, if any, of these surviving arias are by Peri.
Pal. Corsi Two arias in **B** Bc are ascribed in the original source to Corsi and have been
published by Panum, pp. 346f., by Panum and Behrend, pp. 218f.; Solerti,
Albori, I, suppl.; and Schneider, p. 109. A facsimile of a third, anonymous
aria in the same Ms is published by Wotquenne, pp. 46f. A fourth
anonymous aria from the same Ms has been identified and published by
Porter, pp. 108f. Ghisi, *Alle fonte*, pp. 10ff., reports two arias in **I** Fn,
which he ascribes to Peri, although, as Porter points out, p. 173, they are
actually anonymous. All six are published by Porter with a discussion of
their locations in the libretto.
Corsi, at some time before Peri set the text, wrote arias for *Dafne*
according to Peri's own statement in the *A'lettori* to his publication of
the score of *Euridice* (1600⁵). While, as Sonneck observes, it may not be
concluded that Corsi's arias were performed as a part of a setting primarily

by Peri, the qualification of the music by the diarist cited below as *dal Signor Jacopo Corsi* certainly strengthens the possibility.

Comment: Sonneck's hypothetical but soundly reasoned schedule of performances ("Dafne," pp. 102-10) is adopted here but adjusted under the assumption that the years (i.e., 1597-1599) are *stile fiorentina* or *ab incarnatione*, an adjustment suggested by Loewenberg and made explicit in *Luogo teatrale* (paragraph 6.8.1). The latter, however, retains the year of 1597 as the first performance and erroneously locates the performance on January 21, 1600[2], in Palazzo (or Casa) Corsi in place of the Palazzo Pitti.

The sources for each performance are as follows:

1598: In the *Ai lettori* to the publication of the score, *La Dafne* di Marco da Gagliano nell'Accademia degl'Elevati l'Affannato rappresentata in Mantova (in Firenze: Cristofano Marescotti, MDCVIII), Gagliano says that "in 1597 (one presumes *ab inc.*) [Peri's music for *la Dafne*] was performed in the presence of the most excellent Sig. Don Giovanni Medici and some of the principal gentlemen of our city." (Reprinted in Solerti, *Origini*, pp. 76-89.)

1599: Sonneck's deduction.

1600, January 18 (or before): Accounts of household expenses by Corsi's wife. Reported by Sonneck. The nature of the accounts precludes the certainty that the entry date is also the date of performance.

1600, January 21: The location is given precisely in *Storia d'etichetta* in I Fas published by Del Badia which says that on January 5 in the *Salone delle statue la pastorella in musica dal S. Emilio de' Cavalieri* was performed. On the next day in the same room there was a *commedia di Zani*, and on January 21, *la Pastorella in musica dal Signor Jacopo Corsi*. See also Solerti, *Musica*, pp. 19-22, and *Luogo teatrale, loc. cit.*, for other citations in diaries.

1600 viii: The household expenses maintained by Corsi's wife and reported by Sonneck.

These sources cannot be reconciled to one's total satisfaction with the famous history of *Dafne* which Ottavio Rinuccini included in his preface to *Euridice* (1600[5]), reprinted in Solerti, *Origini*, p. 40, and translated in Strunk, pp. 367-9. The original text is: "Ma pensiero sì fatto mi tolse interamente dall'animo M. Jacopo Peri: quando, udito l'intenzione del signor Jacopo Corsi e mia, mise con tanta grazia sotto le note la favola di *Dafne* (composta da me, solo per fare una semplice prova di quello che potesse il canto dell'età nostra) che incredibilmente piacque a quei pochi che l'udirono.

Onde, preso animo, e dato miglior forma alla stessa favola, e di nuovo rappresentandola in casa il sig. Jacopo, fu ella, non solo dalla nobiltà di tutta questa patria favorita, ma dalla serenissima Gran Duchessa e gli illustrissimi Cardinali Dal Monte e Montaldo udita e commendata." Strunk's translation arbitrarily makes "onde" modify "casa" rendering the passage thusly: ". . . Signor Jacopo . . . again represented it at his house, where it was heard and commended, etc." Actually "onde" is merely a connective between the two paragraphs and refers to the fact that the first experiment "incredibly pleased those few who heard it. *Wherefore*, Sig. Jacopo having taken heart and given better form to the same favola, and again performing it in his house, [*Dafne*] was heard and commended, etc." In this translation the passage is not quite so specific about the location of subsequent performances and would allow the possibility that the improved version was *first* performed in Casa Corsi (in 1599 and 1600) and *then* performed at the Palazzo Pitti before the grand duchess and the cardinals, which from the point of view of seventeenth century protocol is more likely than that the grand duchess went to the Casa Corsi. For which of the performances in 1600 the libretto was published is conjectural. Probably the one printing was used for all three.

1600⁴ 5 x
Pal. Vecchio

IL DIALOGO CANTATO NEL CONVITO REALE DA GIUNONE E MINERVA. . . . versi composti dal Signor Cavalier Battista Guarino, e messi in musica ottimamente dal Signor Emilio Cavalieri, Published in: *Descrizione delle felicissime nozze della Cristianissima Maestà di Madama Maria Medici Regina di Francia e di Navarra di Michelagnolo Buonarroti* (Firenze: Giorgio Marescotti, 1600).
I Fn, Vgc; US Wc.

Text: Dedication by Buonarroti signed 20 xi, that is, subsequent to the performance. Rolandi, p. 33; Solerti, *Musica*, p. 24 (text reprinted pp. 235-38); Nagler, p. 94. *Luogo teatrale*, pp. 102f., quotations from *Descrizione*.

Music (lost): Cavalieri.

1600⁵ 6 x
Pal. Pitti

L'EURIDICE d'Ottavio Rinuccini rappresentato nello sponsalitio della Christianissima Regina di Francia e di Navarra. Fiorenza, nella Stamperia di Cosimo Giunti, 1600.
I Bc, Fc, Fr, Mb, Rca, Rsc.

Text: Preface (Dedication) reprinted in Solerti, *Origini*, p. 40. Translation in Strunk, pp. 367-69. Rolandi, pp. 33ff.; Loewenberg, cols. 3, 4; *Luogo teatrale*, p. 144.

Music: LE MUSICHE DI Iacopo Peri, Nobil Fiorentino, SOPRA L'EURIDICE del Sig. Ottavio Rinuccini . . . Fiorenza, Giorgio Marescotti, 1600 [*ab inc.*].
    Preface and dedication reprinted in Solerti, *Origini*, pp. 43ff. The preface is translated in Strunk, pp. 373ff. See also Nagler, pp. 94f., but note errors. Peri says that Giulio Caccini composed the arias of Euridice and some of those of the shepherds and nymphs for the performance (though this music is not included in the score above). Dedication signed 6 ii 1600 [*ab inc.*]. Scores: B Bc; I Bc, Fc, Fl, Fn.

Cast: Mentioned in Peri's foreword (Solerti, *Albori*, pp. 2, 110): Aminta - Francesco Rasi; Pluto - Melchior Palantrotti; Dafne - Jacopo Giusti; Arcetro - Antonio Brandi; Euridice [by implication] - Vittoria Archilei; Orfeo - Jacopo Giusti. Instrumentalists: Gravicembalo - Jacopo Peri; Chitarrone - Don Garzia Montalva; Lira grande - Giovanbattista [Jacomelli] del Violino; Liuto grosso - Giovanni Lapi.

1600⁶ 8 x
Pal. Riccardi

RIME CANTATE NEL GIARDINO DEL SIGNOR RICCARDO RICCARDI con l'occasione d'una festa fatta quivi per la Reina. Firenze, D. Manzani, 1600.
I Vgc.

Text: Probably by Riccardi. Rolandi, p. 37 and plate 26; Solerti, *Musica*, pp. 25ff.; text pp. 239-60. Text also printed with erroneous attribution in Chiabrera, *Opere* (Napoli, Giordani, 1831).

Music (lost): Composer(s) unknown.

1600[7] 9 x
Uffizi

IL RAPIMENTO DI CEFALO. Rappresentato nelle nozze della Cristianissima Regina di Francia e di Navarra Maria Medici, di Gabriello Chiabrera. Firenze, Giorgio Marescotti, 1600.
I Bc, Fc, Fn(2), Rn, Rsc, Rvat, Sc.

Text: *Descrizione* by M.A. Buonarroti ascribes the intermedi to Giovanni de'Medici. Rolandi, pp. 38ff.; Solerti, *Musica*, p. 26; Molinari, pp. 43-49; *Luogo teatrale,* pp. 116-18 (date incorrectly given as 9 *maggio*).

Music: G. Caccini with some music by Stefano Venturi del Nibbio, Luca Bati and Pietro Strozzi. Music is lost, excepting two choruses and three airs which Caccini published in *Le nuove musiche* (1601). Loewenberg, cols. 3, 4; description in Nagler, pp. 96-100.

Cast (mentioned in Buonarroti's *Descrizione*, **1600[4]):** Francesco Rasi, Melchior Palantrotti and Jacopo Peri.

1600[8] 20 xii

L'EURIDICE composta in musica in stile rappresentativo da Giulio Caccini detto Romano. Firenze, Giorgio Marescotti, MDC. (Score) **A** Wn; **D** Bds, LEm; **I** Bc, Fn (2), Nc, Rsc, Rvat, Vnm (2); **US** Bp, Wc.

Text: Rinuccini.

Music: Giulio Caccini, whose dedication, published by Solerti, *Origini*, p. 50, and translated in Strunk, pp. 370-72, clearly states that this publication of the score was not for an actual performance (date shown is the date of the dedication) but rather for the purposes of establishing the composer's priority in the invention of the *stile rappresentativo*. That being the case there is, of course, no publication of the libretto separately from the score. The performance first took place in 1602[3].

1600[9]
Villa di
Camerata

L'AMICIZIA COSTANTE. Tragicomedia pastorale del Sign. Cavaliere Vincenzio Pánciatichi. Dedicata alla Sereniss. Maria Medici Christianissima Regina di Francia. Nelle reali nozze di S.M. col Christianissimo Enrico Quarto. In Fiorenza, per Filippo Giunti, 1600.
DK Kk; **I** Mb; **US** U.

Text: The text requires incidental music, including final choruses and ballets to each act, which are identified as intermezzi in a subsequent republication listed below.

Music (lost): Composer unknown.

Comment: Though no precise date can be established, it presumably would have been in October.

1601 4 xi

L'AMICIZIA COSTANTE. Tragicomedia pastorale del Cav. Vincenzio Panciatichi nella Accademia delli Spensierati il Sicuro. Rappresentata in Fiorenza alla Serenissima Maria Medici Christianissima Regina di Francia nelle regali nozze di Sua Maestà dal Signor Francesca Vinta. Fiorenze, Filippo Giunti, 1601.
C Tu.

Text: Dedicated on date shown by Francesca Vinta. Intermezzi by Jacopo Pagnini. The dedication indicates that the publication is commemorative of the performance represented by 1600[9] and not for a new performance.

Music (lost): Composer unknown.

Comment: The libretto was published subsequently in Venice: *Gli amorosi affanni* del Cavalier Vincenzo Panciatichi l'Agitato [*sic*!] Accademico Spensierato. [Venezia], Gio. Battista Ciotti senese, 1606, with six engravings of scenes. The dedication is signed by the author on February 25 in Florence and contains the following statement about the original performance in Florence: ". . .la favola fu rappresentata nel luogo detto Camerata presso Fiesole, rebattezzato Ninfeo, ove si riunivano i poeti e i musicisti fiorentini che facevano capo al conte Bardi." In **I** Mb; **US** U, Ws.

1602[1] 3 iv

The Cappuzi Diary: "Sua Altezza, trovandosi colla famiglia a Pisa, assiste a' divini uffici sul corridore della chiesa di S. Niccolò, attaccata al palazzo reale. Sua Altezza aveva fatto venire da Firenze i suoi musici, i quali eseguirono in detta chiesa tre cori stupendi in musica, diretti da Giulio romano, che oltre la moglie, aveva condotto seco anche le due figliuole, che cantarono assai bene." (We include the passage for its minor historical record of the Caccini family.)

1602[2] 16 v
Casino di D. Ant⁰ de'Medici

I morti e i vivi.

Text: J. Pagnini according to Solerti, *Musica*, p. 28. Allacci, col. 541, lists two comedies in prose by the title of *I morti vivi*, the first by Sforza degli Oddi, published in Perugia, 1576, and in Florence, in 1597, 1608, and 1617. The second is Jacopo Pagnini's prose comedy published in Florence in 1600. But some doubt must be raised that the present work is the same as either of Allacci's comedies. Both Solerti's diary and the Cappuzi Diary quoted below use the title shown which, of course, does not mean the same thing as the published title. Further, according to the Cappuzi Diary the comedy was *in musica*, i.e., not in prose.

Music (lost): Composer unknown.

Comment: The entry in the Cappuzi Diary reads: "Dopo desinare il granduca con tutta la famiglia stette a sentire la bella commedia intitolata *I morti e i vivi* recitata dai giovani della Compagnia dell'Alberto. La commedia era in musica coi suoi intermezzi e durò quattr'ore. V'intervenne molto gente, molte gentildonne e cavalieri fiorentini, e fu benissimo recitata sotto la direzione di Giovani Lapi." The location is provided by Solerti.

1602[3] 5 xii
Pal. Pitti

Euridice, favola pastorale.

Text: Ottavio Rinuccini (see 1600[5]).

Music: Giulio Caccini. The score was published in 1600[8], but it was not performed until the above date.

Comment: Solerti, *Musica*, p. 30; Loewenberg, col. 4; *Luogo teatrale*, p. 144. The Cappuzi Diary entry reads: "5 dicembre- A ore 24, avendo Sua Altezza fatto ordinare una pastorale per dare un poco di gusto e piacere alla Corte, e avendo fatto invitare un bel numero di gentildonne, salirono tutti nella sala detta del Sig.r Antonio [de' Medici] ove fu fatta una commedia nominata *Euridice* del Sig.r Ottavio Rinuccini, musicata e cantata e guidata da Giulio Caccini romano, musico di Sua Altezza. Durò due ore con grandissimo gusto degli invitati."

1602[4] 9 xii

The Cappuzi Diary: "Sua Altezza invitò tutte le gentildonne al festino di ballo. Si ballò dalle 24 alle 5 ore di notte. Sua Altezza fece una bellissima colazione ai Principi e agli invitati, servita dal Sigr. Del Bufulo. Dopo la colazione furono cantati tre cori dai musici vestiti da Ninfe e da pastori: ed eseguito un balletto di capriole, si continuò il ballo ancora fino all'ora detta."

1603 22 ix

LO ERRORE di Gio. Batista Gelli, Fiorentino. Firenze, nella Stamperia de'Giunti, 1603.
I Mb.

Comment: Prose comedy by Gelli as shown with five madrigals, one at the end of each act, in verse and probably intended for music. Dedication to Vincenzo della Fonte signed by the publisher Modesto Giunti on date shown above. The character of the publication suggests literary intentions rather than an actual performance.

**1604 26 x
Pal. Pitti**

LA DAFNE D'OTTAVIO RINUCCINI. Favola rappresentata al Serenissimo Duca di Parma dalla Serenissima Gran Duchessa di Toscana. Firenze, Cristofano Marescotti, 1604.
I Fn, Nc; **US BE.**

Text: Rinuccini (a reissue of 1600 with new title page).

Music (lost): J. Peri. Solerti, *Musica*, p. 34; *Luogo teatrale*, p. 144.

**1605 22 x
Casino di
D. Antonio
de'Medici**

IL NATAL D'ERCOLE di Michelagnolo Buonarroti. Favola rappresentata al Serenissimo Signor Don Alfonso da Este Principe di Modana, e all'Eccellentissimo Signor Don Luigi suo fratello, nella venuta loro a Firenze da Madama Serenissima di Toscana nel palazzo dell'Eccellentiss. Sig. Don Antonio Medici. Firenze, Giunti, 1605.
I Fn, Fr, Mb; **US Wc.** Autograph MS in I Fl (Buonarroti 58).

Music (lost): Pavan, Schatz MSS 11, cites Peri as the composer but Sonneck, p. 785, doubts that the work was for music, excepting the ballets. Solerti, *Musica*, p. 36 (Tinghi fails to mention music); *Luogo teatrale*, p. 87.

1608[1] ix?

La pietà di Cosmo ovvero Amore sbandito; Il pianto d'Orfeo.

Texts: Gabriello Chiabrera. Written for the wedding of Cosimo II de'Medici and Maria Maddalena d'Austria. No libretti found. Solerti, *Musica*, p. 44. Garboli, "Chiabrera," col. 625, suggests neither of these was performed for the lack of time. However, Allacci, cols. 69, 626, and 627, lists three separate librettos all published by Pavoni in Genoa in 1622 and each containing a statement that it was performed before the "Altezze Reale di Toscana sotto nome di Vegghia." The titles are *Amore sbandito, Il pianto d'Orfeo* and *La pietà di Cosmo.* Since Pavoni's publications are literary and commemorative, the date of publication is of no significance and the titles must refer to earlier performances.

Music (lost): Composer unknown.

For the following four works there is a description: Rinuccini, Camillo. *Descrizione delle feste fatte nelle reali nozze de' Serenissimi Principi di Toscana di Cosimo de 'Medici e Maria Maddalena Archiduchessa d'Austria* (Firenze: Giorgio Marescotti, 1608). Copy in I Fn bound with *Notte d'amore, Ballo e giostra de 'venti*, and *Argonautica*. (Also I Bc, Nc, Rca, Vgc.)

1608² 22 x
Pal. Pitti

NOTTE D'AMORE rappresentata tra danze nelle nozze del Sereniss. D. Cosimo de'Medici, Principe di Toscana, e della Serenissima Arciduchessa Maria Maddalena d'Austria. Firenze, Cristoforo Marescotti, 1608. I Fn, Rn, Sc.

Text: Francesco Cini. Solerti, *Musica*, pp. 45f., gives the title as: *La veglia della notte d'amore*; text pp. 261-74.

Music: One of the ballets by Lorenzo Allegri (or Lorenzo del Liuto) was published in *Primo libro delle musiche* as the first dance-suite. Ghisi, "Ballet," p. 429. Scores: I Fn, MOe, PSn.

Comment: *Luogo teatrale*, pp. 144-45, besides descriptions of the festivities, includes a Ms in I Fl (Buonarroti, cod. 81) which seems to be a report of the preparations for the celebrations of the wedding.

1608³ 25 x,
19 xi
Uffizi

IL GIUDIZIO DI PARIDE. Favola del S. Michelangelo Buonarroti: Rappresentata nelle felicissime nozze del Sereniss. Cosimo Medici Principe di Toscana e della Seren. Principessa Maria Maddalena Arciduchessa di Austria. Firenze, Sermartelli, 1607 and 1608. I Fn, Fr, Sc; Mss: I Fl.

Text: Buonarroti. Accompanied by six intermedii: I. *Il palazzo di Fama* by Lorenzo Franceschi, II. *Astrea* by Alessandro Adimari, III. *Il giardino di Calipso* by Giov. dei Bardi, V. *Vulcano* by Giov. Batt. Strozzi, and IV. *La nave di Amerigo Vespucci* and VI. *Il tempio della pace* by Buonarroti. Description of each in *Luogo teatrale*, pp. 120f.

Music: Anonymous fragments of the music for *Il giudizio* located by Ghisi, "Ballet," pp. 423ff., who deduces that the composers were probably the musicians of the Card. Montalto. In I Fc.

Comment: *Descrizione* by Camillo Rinuccini (Giunti, 1608) in I Fr. Engravings by Remigio Cantagallina of Giulio Parigi's scenery in Nagler, figs. 68-74, Molinari, figs. 11-17, and *Luogo teatrale*, figs. 8.30-32, which also lists various other descriptions contained in manuscripts.

1608⁴ 27 x
Pal. Pitti

BALLO E GIOSTRA DE'VENTI nella nozze del Serenissimo Principe e della Serenissima Principessa di Toscana, Arciduchessa d'Austria. Firenze, Giunti, 1608. I Fn, Sc.

Text: Lorenzo Franceschi. Invention by A.R. Sanseverino.

Music (lost): Composer(s) unknown.

Comment: A scenario rather than a libretto, this publication states the subjects of the scenes, lists the participants, and gives other details including the instruments used. Solerti, *Musica,* pp. 47ff (facs. of title page and a woodcut of the *giostra*).

1608⁵ 2 xi
In Arno

L'ARGONAUTICA rappresentata in Arno per le nozze di Cosimo II de'Medici con Maria Maddalena d'Austria. Firenze, Giorgio Marescotti, 1608. I Fn.

Text: Francesco Cini, according to C. Rinuccini's *Descrizione*, which also supplies date.

Music (lost): Composer (s) unknown.

Comment: See Nagler, pp. 111-15, for paraphrase of C. Rinuccini's *Descrizione*; also figs. 75-88 for engravings by Remigio Cantagallina of Giulio Parigi's barges.

1608⁶

CANZONE di Don Severo Bonini . . . per le felicissime nozze de' Serenissimi di Toscana, Don Cosimo Medici e Maddalena d'Austria. Firenze, Cristofano Marescotti, 1608. F Pn; US Ws.

1609¹ 25 i
Pal. Pitti

Notte d'amore, veglia.

Repetition of above (1608²). Solerti, *Musica*, pp. 45 and 55.

1609² 17 ii
Casa Montalvi

RIME DELLA BARRIERA FRA I TRACI, E L'AMAZONE. Rappresentata da nobile gioventù Fiorentina. In casa i Signori Montalvi a di 17. di Febbraio. 1608. Firenze, Volcmar Timan Tedesco, 1608. I Fn.

Text: Anonymous.

Music (lost): Composer (s) unknown. *Luogo teatrale*, p. 89. Especially since the date is included in the title, this year should be reckoned as *ab inc*. Not mentioned in Tinghi's diary.

1611¹ 9 ii
Casa di
D. Giovanni
de'Medici

LA DAFNE d'Ottavio Rinuccini. Rappresentata alla Sereniss. Gran Duchessa di Toscana dal Signor Jacopo Corsi. Firenze, Giorgio Marescotti, 1610. I Vgc.

Music: Jacopo Peri and Jacopo Corsi. See 1598.

Comment: The source for the date and location is Solerti, *Musica*, pp. 60f.

1611² 14 ii
16 ii
Pal. Pitti

Mascherata di ninfe.

Text: Ottavio Rinuccini. Solerti, *Musica*, pp. 62 and 63ff, *Albori*, pp. 283ff (*Descrizione* by Jacopo Cicognini). Original libretto not located. Nagler, pp. 116-18. See 1613³ below.

Music: Arias by Settimia and Francesca Caccini, Vittoria Archilei and Marco da Gagliano, recitatives by Jacopo Peri, and ballets by Lorenzo Allegri. Ghisi, "Ballet," p. 430. Fragments of Gagliano's music were published in his *Sesto libro de'madrigali a cinque voci* (I Bc). A portion of a recitative by Peri was published in facsimile in Ghisi, "An early 17th c. Ms," p. 51 (I Fc). One of Allegri's ballets was published in his *Primo libro delle musiche* as the second dance suite. (I Fn, MOe, PSn)

Cast: Vittoria Archilei, Settimia Caccini, Francesca Caccini, Antonio Brandi, Domenico Poggi.

Comment: The Cappuzi Diary contains a detailed description of the same mascherata performed on 16 ii which differs in some details from Cicognini's, particularly in an added rustic scene and a ballet, a *calata doppia*, a traditional Tuscan peasants' dance.

"Volendo Sua Altezza far piacere alla Granduchessa e alle Signore fiorentine e a tutta la Corte, fece preparare nella sala delle commedie una bella prospettiva raffigurante il mare di Livorno, con le tre torri, la Meloria, il Fanale, e nove galere.

Nel giorno indicato, nella presenza di un bell'auditorio, comparve sul mare un ricco carro col Granduca, la Granduchessa e 14 Dame di Palazzo e varî cavalieri vestiti a usanza di pesci marini, e le Dame da ninfe. Scesi dalla barca o carro, le dame e i cavalieri eseguirono un grazioso balletto in figura, in modo da formare tante lettere maiuscale, che riunite insieme dicevano *COSIMO E MARGHERITA*. A metà del ballo comparve in mare Nettuno col tridente, cantando graziose canzonette accompagnate dalle chitarre e da altri strumenti musicale. Dopo il ballo, il Granduca, seguito da'suoi cavalieri, si ritirò dalla sala per cambiarsi l'abito; la Granduchessa e le dame invece rimasero nel medesimo bizzarro abbigliamento. Rientrato Sua Altezza, continuò lo spettacolo nel modo seguente.

Giunse sulla scena, raffigurante le onde del Mare, in movimento, amene in una barca e due altre barche piene di pescatori dialogando tra loro in musica, circondati da scherzanti tritoni e da molte ninfe, che recavano moltissimo diletto agli spettatori.

Intanto di lì a poco si vide giungere in mare la *Dea Venere* [Cupid], tutt'affannata, in cerca di Venere e di Nettuno che avea smarriti e domanda di loro ai pescatori, i quali consolano la Dea aiutandola a ritrovarli, come poi avvenne con grande contento ed allegrezza di Lei e dei fuggitivi Dei.

Finito il ballo, uscirano di un bosco otto contadinelle belle, eleganti vestite, quattro di taffetta scarnatine con finali (?) color di mare e con pennocini in testa, molto vaghe e bizzarre; le altre quattro avevano i vestiti di taffetta colore di mare. Erano precedute da due araldi, anch'essi benissimi vestiti, e questi furono Agnolo Ricci maestro de'balli di Sua Altezza e messer Casimiro dell'Armajolo maestro di scherma. Ballarano, accompagnati dal suono delle chitarre, la *calata doppia*, con molto disinvoltura ed eleganza, incontrando il gusto dei sovrani e della nobile convitiva degli intervenuti. Dopo questo ballo si udirono nel bosco grida rumorosissime e subito dopo comparvero sul prato, accompagnati dal suono di quattro naccheroni e da due maestri di campo, otto uomini mascherati da leoni che tenevano in mano, con minacciosa, otto grossi e nodosi bastoni. Questi erano lottatori, i quali erano venuti per combattere contro chi gli avesse sfidati. Ecco di lì a poco uscir dal bosco un gran numero di uomini vestiti da satiri, tenendo anche'essi lunghi bastoni in mano, e saltellando sul prato, sfidarono i leoni alla lotta. Dopo grandi sforzi da tutt'e due le parti, i leoni rimasero vincitori, i quali afferrato i satiri a mezza vita, gli gettarono a bere nel vicino vivajo della fonte e sparirono dilegnadosi tra il fitto del bosco. Ricominciò il ballo, poi il canto e il suono degli strumenti, e dopo mezz'ora si presentarono improvisamente sulla scena tre uomini che leticavano tra loro, poi cominciarono a questionare col pubblico, dicendo che erano stati danneggiati grandemente dai signori villeggianti.

In questo tempo, al suono di pifferi ed altri strumenti rusticali comparvero sessanta persone vestite da Bertucce e da Bertuccioni e

cominciarano a dar noia, a molestare i recitanti provocando così le risa
degli spettatori, e dopo esser per un pezzo gesticalato e fatto mille
fuggonate, montarono come scoiattoli in cima agli abeti e di lassù
giocavano sui canapi messi a posta da un albero all'altro. Fu un
divertimento piacevole che incontro il gusto di tutto. Terminò la festa
alle 23 ore, dopo il quale fu imbandita una lautissima cena di confetture
e frutta per le gentil donne e le dame che rimasero grandemente contente
e sottisfatte. Finita la cena ognuno ringrazio i Sovrani e montati in lettiga
se ne ritornarono all loro case."

1611³ 25 v
Casino Mediceo

LA TANCIA. Commedia rusticale di Michelagnolo Buonarroti
nell'Accademia della Crusca detto L'Impastato. Firenze, Giunti, 1612.
I Fn, Rn. Autograph Ms in I Fl (Buonarroti 61).

Comment: Large sections for music, including whole scenes, though it is
primarily a spoken comedy. Intermedii: *De' frugnolatori, Delli
uccellatori, De' pescatori*, and *De' segnatori del grano*. Act V has no
intermedio but instead ends with a *Canzone a ballo* with solos for six
major roles and many ensembles. Frequently reprinted. Composer(s)
unknown.

The preface to the edition of 1612 states that "*La Tancia*, che l'anno
passato compari addobbata di quelli ornamenti, de'quali si degnarono
questi Sereniss. Principi onorarla, ritorna di nuovo a Città, e vuole
lasciarvisi ne'suoi semplici e rustici panni pur rivedere." The second clause
seems to indicate possibly that the 1612 edition was for literary purposes
only. Date and location in Solerti, *Musica*, p. 62 and *Luogo teatrale*,
p. 87.

1613¹ 16 ii
Pal. Pitti

MASCHERATA DI VILLANELLE DI CASTELLO. Ballo danzato nel regal
palazzo de' Pitti . . . dopo il battesimo del Principe Carlo, secondogenito
del Gran Duca Cosimo II. Firenze, Christoforo Marescotti, 1613.
I Fm, Fn, Rvat.

Text: Agnolo Ricci. Solerti, *Musica*, p. 69; *Albori* I, pp. 26-32. *Luogo
teatrale*, p. 145.

Music: Lorenzo Allegri's sixth dance suite in his *Primo libro delle musiche*
is probably for this ballet. Ghisi, "Ballet," p. 429. Scores: I Fn (2), MOe, PSn.

1613² 17, 19 ii
Uffizi

DESCRIZIONE DELLA BARRIERA, E DELLA MASCHERATA fatta in Firenze
a'XVII et a'XIX di Febbraio MDCXII [*ab inc.*] al Serenissimo Signor
Principe d'Urbino. Firenze, Bart. Sermartelli, 1613.
I Fn, Tn, Vgc.

Text: By Giovanni Villifranchi with additional ballets by J. Cicognini [not
G.A. Cicognini as stated in *Luogo teatrale*], A. Adimari, O. Rinuccini, and
A. Salvadori. Dedication signed Firenze, 20 Marzo, 1612 [*ab inc.*] by
Villifranchi. Solerti, *Musica*, p. 70; Nagler, pp. 119-25; and *Luogo teatrale*,
pp. 122f., which contains the most lengthy description, including an
interesting account of the introduction of the argument in the midst of
a ball at the Pitti Palace on February 3: a herald announced to the assembled
company that Love had driven Venus from his kingdom because of the
complaints of lovers and that she was about to take up her abode in Tuscany

where she would be defended by her champions, Cavalier Fidamante and Cavalier dell'Immortale Ardore.

Music: The seventh suite of dances from Lorenzo Allegri's *Primo libro delle musiche* was composed for these ballets. Ghisi, "Ballet," pp. 430ff. Scores: I Fn, MOe, PSn. On pp. 29-47 of the *Descrizione della Barriera* appears the COMPARSA DE'CAVALIERI DELLE STELLE MEDICEE nella BARRIERA combattuta l'anno 1613. Invenzione e versi da G.A. [*sic* for J.] Cicognini. See *Luogo teatrale*, p. 123.

1613³ 4 v
Pal. Pitti

MASCHERATA DI NINFE DI SENNA. Ballo danzato nel real palazzo del Gran Duca di Toscana per le felicissime nozze de gl'Illus. et Eccellentiss. il Signor Conte Mario Sforza Duca d'Unano e la Sig. Arnea di Loreno. Firenze, gl'Heredi del Marescotti, 1613.
I Fm, Fn, Rn, Rvat.

Text: Ottavio Rinuccini. Repetition with variations of 1611² 14 ii. Additions to text by Agnolo Ricci. Solerti, *Musica*, pp. 73f.; Ghisi, "Ballet," p. 430; Nagler, p. 118, implies incorrect year. *Luogo teatrale*, pp. 145f.

Music: See 1611².

Cast: Jacopo Peri - Nettuno; Vittoria Archilei - Tetide; Settimia e Francesca Caccini - Ninfe. Scenery by Giulio Parigi.

1613⁴
Casino Mediceo

La Cofanaria [del Francesco d'Ambra] recitato di nuovo dai fratelli della Compagnia nel Casino di S. Marco con intermezzi, prospettive, mutazioni di scene ad ogni atto, e con musica nuova.

Comment: Cited by Baccini, *Notizie*, p. 6, n. 1, quoting Arch. B. VIII No. 4 (Patrimonio Eccles.) in I Fas.

1614¹ 5 ii
Pal. Strozzi

MASCHERATA DI SELVAGGI. Ballo danzato nel palazzo del Sig. Lorenzo Strozzi presenti li Serenissimi Principi di Toscana. Firenze, Marescotti, 1613 [1614].
I Rvat.

Text: Rinuccini. See Solerti, *Musica*, p. 76. Reproduced in Solerti, *Albori*, II, p. 313. *Luogo teatrale*, p. 89, with print of a costume for a savage.

Music (lost): Composer (s) unknown.

1614² 6 ii
Pal. Pitti

SCHERZI E BALLI DI GIOVANETTE MONTANINE. Firenze, Valcmar Timan, s.d. but 1614.
I Fn, Fr.

Text: Giovambattista Ginori. Solerti, *Musica*, p. 80; reprint pp. 341-45 (Solerti's copy, evidently I Fr, lacked a title page). *Luogo teatrale*, p. 146.

Music (lost): Marco da Gagliano.

Cast: Sung and danced by eight noblemen directed by Santino Comesari, *maestro di ballo della famiglia granducale*.

1614³ 9 ii
Pal. Pitti

L'imperiale, balletto composta da Messer Agnolo Ricci, et l'aria da Pompeo, organista del Duomo.

Text and music (lost): Solerti, *Musica*, p. 80. Ghisi, "Ballet," p. 428, adds that Allegri composed the ballet music. Apparently this music is not included in Allegri's *Primo libro.*

Comment: Entries 1614[3-5] are ballets performed in succession on the same night to celebrate the birth of Mattias de' Medici.

1614[4] 9 ii
Pal. Pitti

BALLETTO fatto nel battesimo del terzogenito delle Serenissime Altezze di Toscana. Da Signori Paggi di S.A.S. Firenze, Pignoni, 1613.
I Fr.

Text: Ferdinando Saracinelli. See Solerti, *Musica*, pp. 80f.; reprint pp. 347-53. *Luogo teatrale*, p. 146.

Music: Recitatives (lost) by Peri. Ballet, "Elysian Fields," by Allegri. Published in the *Primo libro delle musiche* as the fourth dance suite. Ghisi, "Ballet," p. 431. Scores: I Fn, MOe, PSn.

Comment: Lorenzino tedesco, *sonatore di liuto*, i.e. Allegri, accompanied the arias. Ricci directed the ballets.

1614[5] 9 ii
Pal. Pitti

Alta [Altera?] Maria. Balletto.

Text (lost): Agnolo Ricci. Danced before the court by the princesses Maria [Maddalena d'Austria?] and Claudia [de Medici], Signora Leonora Orsini and Janira dal Bo. Solerti, *Musica*, p. 81.

Music: At least in part by Lorenzo Allegri and published as the third dance in his *Primo libro delle musiche*. Scores: I Fn, MOe, PSn.

1614[6] 11 ii
Pal. Pitti

IL BALLETTO DELLA CORTESIA. Fatto in Firenze dalle Serenissime Altezze di Toscana il dì 11 di Febbraio 1613 che fu introdotto da un'altro trattenimento rappresentato in'iscena. Firenze, Marescotti, 1613 [*ab inc.*].
I Fn, Fr.

Text: M.A. Buonarroti. The introductory dramatic dialog, a dispute between Passatempo and Gioco, was also written by Buonarroti, and was published by Solerti, *Musica*, pp. 281-339 (from Mss in I Fl) with Tinghi's description on pp. 81ff. See also *Luogo teatrale*, p. 146.

Music (lost): According to Tinghi by Jacopo Peri "et da [blank] maestro di cappella della chiesa de' Cavalieri di Pisa." Ghisi, "Ballet," p. 431, deduces the second composer to be Antonio Brunelli.

Comment: Danced by the Grand Duke [Cosimo II] and Grand Duchess [Maria Maddalena] and the court. Giulio Parigi designed the costumes. Agnolo Ricci "aveva curato lo spettacolo."

1615[1] 16 ii
Pal. Pitti

VEGGHIA DELLE GRATIE. Fatta ne' Pitti il carnovale dell'anno 1615. Firenze, G.A. Caneo, s. d.
I Fn (2), Rn (Vegghia only), Rvat.

Text: G. Chiabrera, reprinted in various editions of his works. Solerti, *Albori*, pp. 189ff. Performed in conjunction with the *Ballo delle Grazie*, invention by A. Ricci, and followed by two intermezzi, *La Gelosia scacciata da gli Amori* and *La Speranza guidata da Mercurio*, text, according to Garboli, "Chiabrera," cols. 624-25, by Chiabrera. Solerti, *Musica*, pp. 87f. *Luogo teatrale*, p. 147. See Allacci, col. 136, for edition of Genoa, 1622.

Music: Recitatives (lost) by Peri. The *Ballo* by Allegri. Published as the eighth dance suite entitled "Iris" in his *Primo libro delle musiche*. Ghisi, "Ballet," p. 432. Scores: **I** Fn, MOe, PSn.

1615² 24 ii
Pal. Pitti

BALLO DELLE ZINGARE. Rappresentato in Firenze nel Teatro dell'Altezza Serenissima di Toscana nel carnevale del l'anno 1614 [1615]. Firenze, Pignoni, 1614.
I Fn, Fr.

Text: F. Saracinelli. Invention by A. Ricci. Performed for the baptism of Mattias de' Medici. Solerti, *Musica*, p. 89; text pp. 355-65. *Luogo teatrale*, p. 147.

Music (lost): Francesca Caccini, who also sang.

1615³ 26 ii
Pal. Pitti

BALLO DI DONNE TURCHE INSIEME CON I LORO CONSORTI DI SCHIAVI FATTI LIBERI. Danzato nel real palazzo de' Pitti davanti alle Serenissime Altezze di Toscana. Firenze, Giunti, 1614 [1615].
I Fn (2), Rn.

Text and invention: By Alessandro Ginori. Solerti, *Musica*, pp. 93f.; reprint pp. 367-73.

Music: Marco da Gagliano. Eight numbers including a sinfonia published in *Musiche a una, due e tre voci* (Venetia, Amadino, MDCXV). Ghisi, "Ballet," p. 433, and E. Vogel, I, p. 263. Scores: **B** Bc; **I** Fl, Fn. Modern publication: University of California, Santa Barbara, *Series of Early Music*, Vol. 2.

Comment: Costumes by Jacopo Ligozzi; choreography by Santino Comesari.

1615⁴ 25 vii
In Arno

DESCRIZIONE DELL'ARRIVO D'AMORE IN TOSCANA IN GRAZIE DELLE BELLISSIME DAME FIORENTINE.
I Nn.

Text, invention, and music (music lost): F. Saracinelli. Solerti, *Musica*, p. 97. The Argument says in part:

> "Satio Amore di dar tormenti, e di veder penare l'anime a lui soggette . . . inviò il Gioco suo Ambasciatore il quale arrivato in Fiorenza cantando al cospetto de Serenissimi Padroni spiego alle bellissime Dame la sua Ambasciata colle seguenti ottave, mentre il superbo Teatro d'Arno era pieno di popolo per veder correre il palio delle fregate, trattenimento solito farsi ogn'anno per la festività di San Iacopo."

1616¹ 11 ii

GUERRA D'AMORE. Festa del Serenissimo Gran Duca di Toscana Cosimo Secondo fatta in Firenze il carnevale del 1615 [1616]. Firenze, Zanobi Pignoni, 1615.
I Fm, Fn (2), MOe; **US** NYp.

Text: A. Salvadori, Solerti, *Musica*, p. 102; Nagler, pp. 126 - 129, figs. 89-92.

Music (lost): Peri, Paolo Grazi, G.B. Signorini, and Giacomo del Turco. Ballets designed by Agnolo Ricci; floats, costumes by Giulio Parigi.

1616² 16 ii
Pal. Pitti

Balletto rusticale di contado fiorentini.

Text (lost): Saracinelli.

Music (lost): Peri and Allegri. Solerti, *Musica*, pp. 105f. Ghisi, "Ballet," p. 434, says the music is not contained in Allegri's *Primo libro.*

1616³ carn
Pal. Gherardesca

Orfeo dolente.

Text: Chiabrera. Published prior to the performance: *Favolette di Gabriello Chiabrera da rappresentarsi cantando* (Firenze: Pignoni, 1615). Solerti, *Origini*, p. 239, and *Musica*, p. 44; reprint, pp. 375-91. In the latter Solerti speculates upon the possibility of an earlier performance of the two favolette, *Il pianto d'Orfeo* (O.T. of above) and *La pietà di Cosmo* (see above 1608¹). Garboli, "Chiabrera," discards the possibility.

Music: ORFEO DOLENTE, musica di Domenico Belli. Diviso in cinque intermedi con li quali il Signor Ugo Rinaldi ha rappresentato l'Aminta favola boschereccia del Sig. Torquato Tasso. Novamente composta et data in luce. Venetia, R. Amadino, MDCXVI. For analysis of score see H. Riemann, *Handbuch* II, pt. 2, p. 288. Score: **PL** Wru.

1616⁴ 25 vii

PARTITA D'AMORE DAL BEL REGNO DI TOSCANA, per crudeltà delle Dame Fiorentine. Firenze, Pignoni, 1616.
I Fn.

Text: Saracinelli. Companion-piece for 1615⁴ 25 vii. The beginning of the text printed by Solerti, *Musica*, p. 109.

Music (lost): Composer (s) unknown.

1616⁵ 16 x
Piazza S. Croce

GUERRA DI BELLEZZA. Festa a cavallo fatta in Firenze per la venuta del Serenissimo Principe d'Urbino, l'Ottobre 1616. Firenze, Pignoni, 1616.
I Fm, Fn.

Text: Salvadori. Solerti, *Musica*, pp. 115ff. Libretto contains a brief description: Molinari, p. 68 and fig. 18. Nagler, pp. 129f., figs. 94-98.

Music (lost): Peri and Paulo Francesini. Ballets designed by Agnolo Ricci; costumes, chariots, etc., by Giulio Parigi.

1616⁶

Le ninfe d'Ardenna. Commedia pastorale in versi di Jacopo Lacchi, Fiorentino. In Firenze, Lodovico Timan, 1616.

Comment: Listed by Quadrio III.III.IV. p. 413, and also Allacci, col. 560. No copy located. No copy known to Sartori.

1617 6 ii
Uffizi

La liberazione di Tirreno e d'Arnea, autori del Sangue Toscano. Veglia reale.
I Fn (Palatino 251, ff. 134r-144v), and (Magl. II.IV, 252).

Text: Salvadori. Published for the first time in his *Poesie* I, pp. 300-315. Performed in three intermedii: *Primo intermedio della veglia della liberatione di Tirreno*; *Secondo intermedio dove si vide armarsi l'inferno*;

and *Terzo intermedio dove si vide venire Amore con tutta la sua corte a divider la battaglia.*

Music (lost): Marco da Gagliano with some music by Jacopo Peri.

Comment: Performed for the wedding of Ferdinando Gonzaga and Catherine de' Medici. See Beccherini, col. 1438; Molinari, p. 72 and figs. 19, 20; Nagler, pp. 131-33 and figs. 99, 100; Solerti, *Musica*, p. 121; and *Luogo teatrale*, pp. 123-25 and figs. 8.42-3.

1618¹ 3 ii
Casino Mediceo

LA GRECA SCHIAVA. Commedia di Giovanni Villifranchi da Volterra. Firenze, 1618, Giunti.
I Mb, Vnm.

Text: Prose comedy by G. Villifranchi. Dedication, dated 1 vi 1618, signed by Giandonato Giunti Giandonati and dedicated to Donato dell'Antella, speaks of a performance earlier in the year in Florence "con lode dell'autore, e de recitanti."

Comment: Date and location supplied by Solerti, *Musica*, p. 120. *Luogo teatrale*, pp. 87f.

1618² carn
Pal. del Nero

MASCHERATA DI COVIELLI. Ballo danzato nel palazzo del Sig. Alessandro del Nero. Firenze, Pignoni, 1618.
I Fn, Rvat.

Comment: Neither poet nor composer known. Not mentioned by Tinghi. Libretto cited by Solerti, *Musica*, p. 127. *Luogo teatrale*, p. 91.

1618³ 6 iii
Pal. Rinaldi
Accad. Storditi

L'Andromeda, favola marittima di Jacopo Cicognini scorso di penna in un corso di sole. Poesia drammatica del Sig. Giacomo Cicognini con la quale si descrive la favola d'Andromeda rappresentata musicalmente con real grandezza alla presenza del Serenissimo Leopoldo Arciduca d'Austria nel palazzo dell'Illustrissimo Sig. Rinaldi l'anno 1617 [1618].
I Fr (Ms).

Text: Cicognini.

Music (lost): Domenico Belli.

Comment: Information concerning this performance is found in a letter from Giulio Caccini to Andrea Cioli, secretary to the Grand Duke, which is in I Fas (Arch. Med. F. verde 1370, f. 57) and is quoted in full in *Luogo teatrale*, p. 90. See also Solerti, *Musica*, pp. 126-28.

1618⁴ 17 v
Pal. Pitti

The Cappuzi Diary: "Sua Altezza con l'Arciduchessa andò nella salla delle commedie dov'era all'ordine una commedina pastorale recitata dai figliuoli del Sgr. Leone de' Nerli e da altri nobili giovinetti fiorentini. Il soggetto era che Amore non volendo più stare in Corte si ritira in Arcadia. Il passo gli vien contrastato dalle ninfe e dai pastori, ma finalmente vince ed ottiene ospitalità. La commedia durò un'ora: dopo fecero un balletto di calata che piacque assai."

1618⁵ 25 vii
In Arno

DESCRIZIONE DELLA BATTAGLIA DEL PONTE FRA ABIDO, E SESTO NELL'HELLESPONTO. Festa rappresentata in Arno. Il dì 25 di luglio, 1618. Firenze, Zanobi Pignoni, 1618.

I Fn.

Comment: We have not been able to examine this *descrizione*.

1619[1] 11, 12 ii
Uffizi

La fiera.

I Fl (Mss. Arch. Buonarroti, cod. 64 [Autograph]).

Text: M.A. Buonarroti. Published for the first time together with *La Tancia* in Firenze, by Tartini, e Franchi, in 1726. The title of the 1726 edition continues: "Commedia recitata in Firenze nel carnevale dell'anno 1618 nel Teatro della gran sala degli Uffizj." The entire work consists of five separate comedies (each of five acts) which were intended to be performed in five successive evenings. Allacci, col. 343. Silvio d'Amico, col. 1331, states that only two were performed and that the performers were the *accademici del dottor Cicognini. Luogo teatrale*, p. 125, and fig. 8.46 (a sketch of a scene by Giulio Parigi).

Music (lost): Francesca Caccini and perhaps Gagliano. Solerti, *Musica*, p. 143, and Ghisi, "Ballet," p. 434. The Cappuzi Diary is similar in text to Tinghi's quoted by Solerti but it adds, "Sua Altezza andò in galleria e desinò nella Camera del Terrazzo della Galleria stessa per far provare con gli abiti una commedia detta *la Fiera* . . ." 200 performed, 3,000 attended. His date is February 18!

1619[2] 25 vii
In Arno

BATTAGLIA TRA TESSITORI E TINTORI. Festa rappresentata in Firenze nel fiume Arno il 25 di luglio 1619. Firenze, Cecconcelli, 1619.
I Fn.

Text: Salvadori. Solerti, *Musica*, p. 147ff.

Music: Composer (s) unknown.

1619 viii-1620 ix

Protracted illness of Cosimo II discourages dramatic performances. But Tinghi and Cappuzi Diaries contain several attempts to entertain the ailing duke.

1619[3] 15 viii

The Cappuzi Diary: "Alle 23 ore venire sotto le finestre di Sua Altezza Marco di Gagliano, maestro di Cappella, con tutti i musici e una gran quantità di gentiluomini fiorentini con strumenti, e cantarono due volte una loro composizione, la quale piacque assai a Sua Altezza e alle signore. L'argomento della canzone era intitolata *Gli amanti disperati*, e principiava così: Vaga stella d'Amor, diva bellissima . . ."

1619[4] 23, 25 ix
Pal. Pitti

Lo sposalizio di Medoro ed Angelica, commedia cantata in musica.

Text: Andrea Salvadori. Original libretto not found but a subsequent commemorative was published: IL MEDORO d'Andrea Salvadori rappresentato in musica nel palazzo del Serenissimo G. Duca di Toscana in Fiorenza per la elezione all'Impero della Sacra Cesarea Maestà dell'Imperatore Ferdinando Secondo, [etc.]. Fiorenza, Cecconcelli, 1623 (copies in GB Lbm; B Bc; I Fm, Fn, MOe, Rsc).

Music (lost): Marco da Gagliano and Jacopo Peri.

Comment: Cappuzi Diary is essentially the same as Tinghi's reported by Solerti, *Musica*, p. 149. Loewenberg, col. 10. *Luogo teatrale*, p. 148. See also 1626[1].

1620[1] 6 i   *Canzonette in lode della Befana.*

Text (lost): Andrea Salvadori.

Music: Francesca Caccini?

Comment: Tinghi and Cappuzi diaries are again quite similar. The performers were "la moglie e figliuoule di Giulio Caccini," to whom the Duke gave a ring inscribed: "Quest'anello vi do con un serpente: / Sta per insegna della gente a Corte / Ve l'ha fatto venir in man la sorte / Perche siete fra gli altri il più prudente." (Cappuzi)

1620[2] 26 ii   *La serpe* del [Giammaria?] Cecchi, commedia in prosa.

Comment: From the Cappuzi Diary: "Sua Altezza fece recitare la commedia detta *la Serpe* del Cecchi, recitata da tutte le fanciulle e dalla figliuola del Sigr. Curzio biccheria. La quale commedia fu recitata nella camera della Cappella e Sua Altezza stette levato e vestito puntualmente, al quale piacque assai la commedia per essere stata ben recitata. Non c'era altri ad ascoltarla che le dame di Palazzo e quelli della Camera di Sua Altezza."

1620[3] 3 iii
Pal. Pitti   *Mascherata.*

Comment: Tinghi as reported by Solerti, *Musica*, p. 153: ". . . venute le 24 ore S.A. entro nel lettino et stette alla porta della sua camera, dove era la Ser.ma et i sig.ri fillioli et sorelle et Madama Ser.ma dove comparse sei maschere vestite alla mantovana, et cantando fecero un ballo della galliarda, invitando le donne delle altre nazione a ballare. Et indì a poco comparse sei altre maschere vestite alla francese, dove con esse ballorno; et poi comparse sei altre maschere vestite alla spagniola, le quale anch'esse con l'altre maschere ballorno; et doppo comparse sei altre maschere vestite alla todesca, il quali fecero anch'esse il loro ballo; et poi tutte insieme et durorno un pezzetto . . . Vi era la Cecchina [Francesca Caccini] con le sue filliole, et altri musici in diversi abiti che cantorno in musica di belli versi . . . Fu composto da Gangelo Ricci."

1620[4] 26 x   *La regina Sant'Orsola.*

Text: Andrea Salvadori.

Music (lost): Marco da Gagliano.

Comment: Tinghi, as reported by Solerti, *Musica*, p. 156, describes a rehearsal of this *festa che s'ha da fare nelle future nozze* . . . The performance, projected for the wedding of the Prince of Urbino with Claudia de' Medici was prevented by the death of Cosimo II in February, 1621. It was revived in 1624[3] and 1625[1].

1620[5]   LA SFORZA DEL CORTIGIANO. Tragicomedia [in prose]. Firenze, Pietro Cecconcelli, 1620.
I MOe.

Text: Bernardino Azzi.

1621[1] 2 i   *S. Maria Maddalena.*

Text: J. Cicognini. Baccini, *Notizie*, p. 8. No mention of music.

Music (lost): Composer (s) unknown.

1621² 20 ii   *S. Giorgio liberatore di Silena.*

Text: J. Cicognini.

Music: Incidental music by Pietro Botti. Baccini, *Notizie*, pp. 8f.

1621 20 ii   Death of Cosimo II.

1622¹ 23, 27, 31 i;   *Il martirio di S. Agata della città di Catania.* Festa.
4, 7, 10, 13 ii
Compagnia di   **Text:** Jacopo Cicognini.
S. Giorgio
     Music: Prologue and six choruses by Marco da Gagliano; other incidental music by Francesca Caccini. (All music lost.)

Comment: Tinghi, quoted by Solerti, *Musica*, p. 162, records that "tutti i principi andarono alla compagnia di S. Giorgio in su la Costa a vedere recitare la festa . . . recitata da giovani di detta compagnia et da parte delli Accademici Incostanti . . . con intermedi et nugole ben intese et ben recitate." Baccini, *Notizie*, pp. 9-16, gives a full account of performers and costs. The performers are omitted here since they are exclusively the young gentlemen of the Academy. Notable among them is Giacinto Cicognini, the son of Jacopo, and future librettist. Repeated in 1622³.

1622² 7 ii   *Olimpia abbandonata da Bireno.* Intermedio.

Text: Salvadori. Solerti, *Musica*, p. 161. Text published in Salvadori's *Opere*, pp. 272-99.

Music (lost): Composer (s) unknown.

1622³ 22 vi   *Il martirio di S. Agata*, repetition of above (1622¹).
Casino Mediceo
     Text: J. Cicognini. Solerti, *Musica*, p. 162. Tinghi adds " . . . fata per l'occasione del ambasciatore di Spagnia, recitata da'giovanni della compagnia di S. Giorgio . . ." No libretto for either performance has been located. It was published two years later (copy in **I** Rvat): IL MARTIRIO DI S.ᵃ AGATA Rappresentazione del Dot. Jacopo Cicognini Accademico Incostante. Dedicata all'Ill.ᵐᵒ Sig.ʳ Cav.ʳᵉ Andrea Cioli Segretario di Stato del Serenissimo Gran Duca di Toscana et Gran Cancelliero dell'Ill. et Sacra Religione di S. Stefano. Firenze, Giunti, M.DC.XXIV.

Comment: The dedication, signed by Cicognini on 1 iv 1624, speaks of the performance listed above, adding that the first was "con la protezione e magnanimità del Signor Agnolo Sostegni . . ." and that the second under the protection of the Cardinal de'Medici was performed in the presence of the Cardinal Capponi and Conte di Monterei, ambassador of Spain. The *A ' lettori* ascribes the music of the chorus to Gagliano and the principal arias to Francesca Caccini, who is not mentioned by Tinghi. It concludes, "Il medesimo Martirio di S. Agata da me composto in Bologna l'anno 1614 in versi per potersi musicalmente rappresentare, fu poi da me ridotto in questa forma come più proporzionata per dilettare all'universale : . . ." Solerti, *Musica*, pp. 162f.; Allacci, col. 511. *Luogo teatrale* p. 88.

1622⁴ 27 xii
Compagnia di
Agniolo Raffaello
detta la Scala

Il gran natale di Christo Salvator nostro.

Text: J. Cicognini. Tinghi remarks, " . . . fu bella, e ben recitata, con buona musica . . . " Solerti, *Musica*, p. 164. The libretto was published during the visit of Prince Ladislao of Poland, though probably not for a performance:
IL GRAN NATALE DI CHRISTO NOSTRO dedicato al Ser.ᵐᵒ Ladislao Principe maggiore di Pollonia e Svezia. Del Dottor Jacopo Cicognini, Academico Incostante. Firenze, Giunti, 1625. Allacci, col. 511.

Music (lost): Composer unknown.

1622⁵

L'Orizia. Dramma per musica rappresentato in Firenze innanzi alle Altezze di Toscana sotto nome di Vegghie. Genova, il Pavoni, 1622.

Text: Gabriello Chiabrera. Published with other works of the author (Allacci, col. 581); therefore, the date is probably not the date of performance. Republished in Rome, 1711. Original publication unknown.

Music (lost): Composer unknown.

1623¹ 3 ii
Pal. Gherardesca
Rugginosi

LE FONTI D'ARDENNA. Festa d'arme e di ballo fatta in Firenze da dodici Signori Accademici Rugginosi il carnevale dell'anno 1623. Nel principato del Sig. Alessandro del Nero. Invenzione del Sig. Andrea Salvadori. Descritta dal Rugginoso Percosso. Dedicato al Serenissimo Guidobaldo Principe d'Urbino. Firenze, Cecconcelli, 1623.
I Bu, Fn, Fr, Rn; **US** Wc.

Text: (Invention by Salvadori) by Simone Carlo Rondinelli, a member of the Academy. Solerti, *Musica*, pp. 164ff.; Ghisi, "Ballet," p. 435. *Luogo teatrale*, pp. 90f.

Music (lost): Gagliano.

1623² 4 ii

Il voto d'Jefette osia Il voto d'Oronte.

Text: Jacopo Cicognini.

Music (lost): Composer unknown. Baccini, *Notizie*, pp. 16f.

1623³ carn
Casino Mediceo

INTERMEDII di Filippo Vitali fatti per la commedia degli Accademici Incostanti. Recitata nel palazzo del Casino dell'Ill.mo e Rev.mo Cardinale de Med.ci MDCXXII. Firenze, Cecconcelli, 1623. (Score)
B Bc.

Text: J. Cicognini. Performed with his prose comedy, *La finta mora* (see 1626²). Solerti, *Musica*, p. 168; text pp. 393-407; Ghisi, "Ballet," p. 433 (facsimile of frontispiece of above) and p. 435.

1623⁴ 20 xii

LA REGINA SANT'ORSOLA, s.l., s.d.
B Bc.

Text: Salvadori. Dedication signed by Salvadori 20 xii 1623. This printing may not have been for a performance since Solerti's diarist, Tinghi, is silent. Wotquenne, p. 114.

1624[1] 4,5 i
Compagnia del
A. Raffaello
alla P.za di S.ta
Maria Novella

Rappresentazione del Angiolo Raffaello, e di Tobia. Firenze, alle Scale della Badia. s.d.

Text: Jacopo Cicognini. Allacci, col. 844, lists above lost libretto of which he does not know the author. It was published subsequently: *La celeste guida, o vero l'Arcangelo Raffaello* rappresentazione sacra recitata nella Venerabile Compania dell'Arcangelo Raffaello detta la Scala in Firenze l'anno 1623 [1624]. Del Dottor Jacopo Cicognini, agli honorandi Padri e Fratelli della medesima compagnia. Venezia, Bernardo Giunti, 1625. Solerti, *Musica*, p. 171 and 185; Allacci, col. 176.

Music (lost): Marco da Gagliano.

1624[2] 28 ix
Poggio Imperiale

CANZONE DELLE LODI D'AUSTRIA. Cantata al SS. Arciduca Carlo dopo il banchetto alla Villa Imperiale della Granduchessa di Toscana. Firenze, Pietro Cecconcelli, 1624.
I Fn.

Text: Andrea Salvadori, according to the statement at the end of the libretto.

Music (lost): Jacopo Peri, as stated at the end of the libretto.

Comment: Sung by Francesco Campagniolo. Date supplied by Tinghi (see Solerti, *Musica*, p. 173). *Luogo teatrale*, p. 91.

1624[3] 6 x
Uffizi

ARGOMENTO DELLA REGINA SANT'ORSOLA rappresentazione d'Andrea Salvadori. Firenze, Cecconcelli, 1624.
I Fn.

Text: Salvadori. Published separately for the performance celebrating the visit of the Archduke Carlo of Austria. Libretto published the following year for the performance in honor of the visit of Ladislao Sigismondo listed below. Solerti, *Musica*, pp. 174ff.; *ibid.*, *Origini*, p. 242; Molinari, figs. 22-25; Nagler, pp. 134-37, figs. 102-7; *Luogo teatrale*, pp. 125-28, figs. 8.47, 48, 52, with detailed descriptions.

Music (lost): Marco da Gagliano. Scenery by Giulio Parigi with published engravings by Alfonso Parigi.

1625[1] 28 i
Uffizi

LA REGINA SANT'ORSOLA del S.r Andrea Salvadori Recitata in musica nel Teatro del Sereniss. Gran Duca di Toscana dedicato al Serenissimo Principe Ladislao Sigismondo, Principe di Polonia e di Suetia. Fiorenze, Cecconcelli, 1625.
I Bc, Fm, Fn, Fr, Mb, Rca, Rn, Rsc, Vgc.

Text: The libretto exists in three printings, all by Cecconcelli in the same year. The text is also the same but they differ in the following respects: 1. Title page as above; 2. With addition of the author's verses indicated on the title page by the insertion after the dedication of: *aggiuntivi Fiori del Calvario dello stesso autore*; and six engravings of the scenes, of which the first, *COUNCIL OF THE DEMONS AGAINST SAINT ORSOLA*, is shown on the *right*. 3. Without verses but with a more ample title page: LA REGINA SANTA ORSOLA, Virgine et Martire. L' Azzione Eroica di questa real Vergine recitata . . . (as above to *Toscana*) in Poesia Drammatica sotte le note di musica recitative, due volte con pompa degna dell'antica grandezza Romana e stata rappresentata a due de'maggiori Principi d'Europa; la prima

CONCILIO DI DEMONI CONTRO. S. ORSOLA
ATTO PRIMO

I Fn Palatino 12.8.I.20. *La Regina di Sant'Orsola*, 1625[1], *Concilio di demoni contro S. Agata.*
Scenery by Giulio Parigi, etching by Alfonso Parigi.

volta al Ser. Arciduca Carlo d'Austria & ultimamente al Serenissimo Ladislao Sigismondo, Principe, Principe di Polonia e di Svezia.

Dedication signed by Salvadori, 29 i 1625. Date of performance supplied by Tinghi. Solerti, *Musica*, pp. 174f. Preface comments that the work can be performed without music and that the published version is longer than the one performed.

Music (lost): Marco da Gagliano.

1625[2] 2 ii
Poggio Imperiale

LA LIBERAZIONE DI RUGGIERO DALL'ISOLA D'ALCINA. Balletto rapp.to in musica al Ser.mo Ladislao Sigismondo Principe di Polonia e di Suezia nella Villa Imp.le della Sereniss.ma Arcid.sa d'Austria, Gran Duch.sa di Toscana. Poesia di Ferdinando Saracinelli Balì di Volterra. Firenze, Cecconcelli, 1625.
I Fc, Fn, Rca.

Text: Saracinelli. Solerti, *Musica*, pp. 179f.; Molinari, p. 76 and figs. 26-29; Loewenberg, col. 11. Nagler, pp. 137f., figs. 108-12 (designs by Alfonso Parigi). *Luogo teatrale*, pp. 91ff., with two figs.

Music: LA LIBERAZIONE DI RUGGIERO DALL'ISOLA D'ALCINA. Balletto composta in musica dalla Francesca Caccini ne' Signorini Malaspina, [etc., as above]. Firenze, Cecconcelli, 1625. Score for above libretto. Reprint in Smith College Archives; excerpts in Goldschmidt. Also A. De la Fage. Scores: **F** Pc; **GB** Lbm; **I** Rca, Rsc, Vnm.

1625[3] 10 ii
Pal. del Card.
Carlo de'Medici
(Casino Mediceo)

LA PRECEDENZA DELLE DAME. Barriera nell'arena di Sparta, fatta dal Principe Gian Carlo di Toscana e da altri cavalieri giovanetti rappresentanti spartani, e spartane. Nella venuta a Fiorenze del Ser. Ladislao Sigismondo Principe di Polonia e Svezia. Invenzione del Sig. Andrea Salvadori. Firenze, Cecconcelli, 1625.
I Fn, Fr.

Text (as well as invention): Salvadori. Solerti, *Musica*, pp. 180ff., and Ghisi, "Ballet," p. 435. *Luogo teatrale*, p. 88.

Music (lost): Peri.

1625[4] (26?)

MASCHERATA DI DONZELLE DI GHINEA che cavalcando sopra le chiocciole mostrano una lodevole usanza de'lor paese. Fu messa in opere da Gio. del Sig. Giulio Parigi l'a. 1625 e piacque . . . COCCHIATA E MUSICA ch'ando dietro alla detta mascherata di donzelle more su le chiocciole.

Text: In Ms in I Fn attributed to A. Adimari. Not mentioned by Tinghi. Exact year made uncertain by the problem of the Lady Day calendar. Solerti, *Musica*, p. 185.

Music (lost): Composer unknown.

1626[1] 20 i
Uffizi

Intermedi rappresentati in Fiorenza al Serenissimo Leopoldo Arciduca d'Austria. *Atlante, overo l'Imperio di casa d'Austria* Intermed. P.mo / *Contrasto de' Venti nell'isola Eolia* Intermed. Secondo / *L'armi d'Achille dell'isola degl'eroi* Intermed. Terzo / *Balletto delle Muse e degl'Argonauti* Intermed. Quarto. Invenzione d'Andrea Salvadori.

I Fn (Magl. II.IV.22); Fr (Mor. 326), both Mss.

Text and invention: Salvadori. First published in the *Poesie*, vol. I, pp. 250ff.

Music (lost): Composer unknown.

Comment: According to Tinghi (Solerti, *Musica*, p. 186) these intermedi were previously performed with *Il Medoro* by "comici di Zanni con li intermedi apparenti." Solerti without justification assumes that the intermedi would have been without music. *Luogo teatrale*, pp. 128f., quotes Tinghi's reference to a "commedia pastorale recitata da nobili fiorentini . . ." See also p. 148. The two accounts are not compatible.

1626[2] 15 ii
Acad. degl'
Infiammati

LA FINTA MORA. Commedia del dott. Jacopo Cicognini Accademico Intronato dedicata all'Illustrissimo Sig. Roberto Capponi marchese di Monte Carlo in Regno. Firenze, Giunti, 1625.
I Fn.

Comment: Baccini, *Notizie*, p. 17, says intermedi by Filippo Vitali were performed at this time as well as in 1623[3]. The dedication speaks of the earlier performance. Solerti, *Musica*, p. 168, n. 2; *Luogo teatrale*, p. 88. All sources assume the publisher's date is *ab inc.*

1626[3] 22 ix
Pal. Pitti

La Giuditta. Azione sacra.

Text: Salvadori. The original libretto of the performance in honor of the visit of Cardinal Barberini in September, 1626, not found. First published in the *Poesie* of Salvadori, vol. I. Solerti, *Musica*, pp. 186f.; *ibid.*, *Origini*, p. 243.

Music (lost): Gagliano.

1626[4]

CLORI. Tragicommedia pastorale [in verso]. Firenze, Zanobi Pignoni, 1626.
I Sc.

Text: Camillo Lenzini. Allacci, col. 201.

1627[1] ii

Il martirio di S. Caterina.

Text (lost): Jacopo Cicognini. Baccini, *Notizie*, p. 18, mentions no music.

1627[2] 24 vi
Casa del Nero

MASCHERATA DI VECCHI INNAMORATI. Ballo danzato e cantato da gl'Accademici Rugginosi in casa dei Signori del Nero. Firenze, Cecconcelli, 1627.
I Fn.
Poet and composer unknown. Solerti, *Musica*, p. 187; Maylender vol. V, p. 73, *Luogo teatrale*, p. 91.

1628[1] 12 iii

IL SERAGLIO DEGL'AMORI fatto a gl'Ill.mi e Eccell.mi Signori Sposi. Il Sig. Duca Jacopo Salviati e la Signora Duchessa, Dorina Veronica Cibo. Epitalamio ballato e cantato. Firenze, Cecconcelli, MDCXXVIII.
I Rn.

Text: Dedication, signed by Cecconcelli, dated 12 iii, 1628, announces the poet as Andrea Salvadori. Solerti, *Musica*, p. 188.

Music (lost): Composer (s) unknown.

AMORE CHIEDE LA GELOSIA A PLVTONE

Alfonsus Paigius delj: et fecit 1628

I Fn Palatino (11) C.2.3.29. *La Flora*, 1628[3], Act III, scene 6: *Regno infernale*, Amore (Cupid) asks Pluto to release Jealousy. Charon plies the Styx in the background.

1628² 20 viii COCCHIATA DELLI ACCADEMICI RUGGINOSI. Fatta il dì 20 di Agosto 1628, e messa in musica da Filippo Vitali. Firenze, Cecconcelli, MDCXXVIII. I Fn, Rca.

Text: Poet unknown. Text consists of madrigals in six parts, and arias of one or more voices. Solerti, *Musica*, p. 188.

Music (lost): Filippo Vitali.

1628³ 14 x
Uffizi LA FLORA o vero IL NATAL DE' FIORI. Favola d'Andrea Salvadori, rappresentata in musica recitativa nel Teatro del Serenissimo Gran Duca, per le reali nozze del Serenissimo Odoardo Farnese, e della Serenissima Margherita di Toscana Duchi di Parma, e Piacenza, ecc. Dedicata a'Serenissimi Sposi. Firenze, Cecconcelli, 1628.
B Bc; I Fn, Fr, PAc, Rca, Rsc, Sc; US Wc.

Text: Salvadori. Contains five engravings by Alfonso Parigi, one of which is shown on the *left*. For reproductions see Solerti, *Musica*, pp. 189ff.; Molinari, p. 176 and figs. 30-33; Wotquenne, p. 72 opp.; Nagler, pp. 139-42, figs. 113-18; *Luogo teatrale*, pp. 129-31, figs. 8.59, 60, with descriptions of the other scenes designed by Alfonso Parigi. A reprint soon followed: LA FLORA overo IL NATALE DE' FIORI. Favola del Sig. Andrea Salvadori. [Title continues as above through the titles of the royal pair.] Aggiuntovi la Disfida d'Ismeno festa a cavallo del medesimo autore. Firenze, Pignoni, 1628.
I Bc, Fn.

Music: Gagliano. The score was subsequently published: LA FLORA del Sig. Andrea Salvadori. Posta in musica da Marco da Gagliano, Maestro di Cappella del Serenissimo Gran Duca di Toscana. Rappresentata nel Teatro del Serenissimo Gran Duca. Nelle reali nozze del Sereniss. Odoardo Farnese . . . e della Serenissima Principessa Margherita di Toscana. Firenze, Pignoni, 1628.

Comment: From the *A' lettori:* "Le musiche furono tutte del Sig. Marco da Gagliano, eccetto la parte di Clori, la quale fu opera del Sig. Jacopo Peri." Excerpts reprinted in Goldschmidt. Scores: I Bc, Nc, MOe.

1628⁴ 17 x
Pal. Pitti LA DISFIDA D'ISMENO. Abbattimento a cavallo con pistola, e stocco. Festa fatta in Firenze nelle reali nozze del Serenissimo Odoardo Farnese, e della Serenissima Margherita di Toscana, Duchi di Parma, e di Piacenza, ecc. Invenzione d'Andrea Salvadori. Firenze, Pignoni, 1628.
C Tu; D W; I Bc.

Text: Salvadori. The text is printed on pages 192ff. of the second libretto of *La Flora* listed above. From Tinghi's description, the performance took place in the *salone de' forestieri* in the Pitti. One squadron was led by the Duke, the second by Giancarlo de' Medici, a third by Mattias and a fourth by Don Lorenzo de' Medici. See Solerti, *Musica*, p. 192.

Music (lost): Composer (s) unknown.

1628⁵ (29?) MASCHERATA CAPRICCIOSA DI CALAI E ZETI che riconducono in mostra l'Arpie, e insieme tutti coloro che da esse furono offesi. Fatta dal figlio del Sig. Giulio Parigi, ingegnere di S.A.S. l'anno 1628. Firenze, Timan, s.d.

I Fn (lost).

Text: A. Adimari. In a Ms entitled *Poesie varie di Alessandro Adimari* in I Fn (Magl. II.I.92, cc. 101r-102v). No mention of composer. Not mentioned in Tinghi. Solerti, *Musica*, p. 188.

1628[6] (29?)
In Arno

MASCHERATA FATTA IN ARNO PER L'OCCASIONE D'UNA PIETANZA l'anno 1628 nel tempo che in Firenze si facevano fra la plege le Potenze.
I Fn (Magl. II.I.92, cc. 126r-127v).

Text: A. Adimari.

Music: Unknown.

1628[7] (29?)
Compagnia
dell'A. Raffaello

Il Trionfo di David.

Text: J. Cicognini, published subsequently: TRIONFO DI DAVID. Rappresentazione sacra del Dot. Jacopo Cicognini, Accademico Instancabile. Recitatata [sic] nella Venerabile Compagnia dell'Arcangelo Raffaello, detto la Scala alla presenza dell'Altezze Serenissime di Toscana l'anno 1628. In Fiorenza Dedicata a gli onorandi Padre e Fratelli di essa compagnia. Firenze, Pignoni, 1633. Solerti, *Musica*, p. 188; Baccini, *Notizie*, p. 7.

Music: Unknown.

1629[1] (?)
Pal. Pitti

Festa di S. Maria Maddalena da rappresentarsi nella Cappella della Serenissima l'anno 1629. Di Francesco Bracciolini.

Comment: Tinghi does not record performance. Solerti, *Musica*, p. 195.

1629[2] 6 viii
Pal. Pitti

I Caramogi. Palio e mascherata faceta fatta in Firenze il dì 6 agosto 1629.

Text: First printed in vol. I of Salvadori's *Poesie*, pp. 487-92. Tinghi records the palio which ended with a *cocchiata* in the courtyard of the Pitti. Solerti, *Musica*, p. 195, records a RISPOSTA DE' BEGL'IMBUSTI A' CARAMOGI. Palio, e mascherata fatta in Firenze il dì 28 d'agosto 1629. Firenze, Cecconcelli, 1629, which he tentatively attributes to A. Adimari.

1630 20 i
Infiammati

L'Ammalata.

Text: Giammaria Cecchi. Published in *Commedie inedite*. Firenze, Barbera, 1855, and again Le Monnier, 1856.

Music: Unknown. The prose play was performed with a prologue and *intermedi per musica*. And at the end there was a ballet for five youths "istruiti da un certo Giobata cappellaio." Baccini, *Notizie*, p. 19; performed by the Accademici Infiammati.

1634[1] 29 ii

La Siringa. Favoletta d'Alfesibeo Pastore Antellese cioè di me Mich.o Buon[arro]ti nella sua prima forma essendo poi variata come nel libro appare. Ma rifarsi da capo in altra guisa.
I Fr (Ms Buonarroti no. 75).

Text: Michelangelo Buonarroti. Performed in honor of the visit of Prince Alessandro di Polonia, brother of the king, Ladislao Sigismondo di Polonia, and accompanied by a *combattimento* in which all the gentlemen of Florence participated, as they had done in the comedy. Silvio d'Amico

provides date shown. Text printed in Solerti, *Musica*, pp. 519-88; also
pp. 196f. *Luogo teatrale*, p. 105.

Music (if any): Unknown.

1634[2]

Il valore. Melodramma allegorico per le nozze del Serenissimo
Ferdinando II Gran Duca di Toscana II con Donna Vittoria Principessa
d'Urbino.
I Rn.

Text: Pietro Bonarelli. Original libretto not found. Above in the author's
Poesie drammatiche, no. 3.

Music: Unknown. No evidence that it was actually performed.

Roles: Valore, Consiglio, Amore, Venere, Fama, Corilla, Clori, Megera,
Tenfane, Aletto, Apollo, Toscana.

1637[1] 8 vii
Cortile
Pal. Pitti

LE NOZZE DEGLI DEI. Favola dell'Abate Gio: Carlo Coppola rappresentata
in musica in Firenze nelle reali nozze de' Serenissimi Gran Duchi di Toscana
Ferdinando II e Vittoria Principessa d'Urbino. Firenze, Massi e Landi, 1637.
I Fm, Fn, Fr, MOe, Mb, Rca, Rn, Rsc.

Text: Coppola. Libretto contains seven engravings by Stefano della Bella of
the scenery of Alfonso Parigi. Scene 1 representing Florence is shown *overleaf.*

Music (lost): Rondinelli's *Relazione* (see below) says that the music was
written by five of the best composers of the city. Music "a cura di Ferdinando
Saracinelli."

Cast: Prince Gian Carlo de' Medici played a leading role, Eustachio. Ballets
by Agnolo Ricci. Two singers are mentioned: Paola and Settimia [Caccini]
who sang in the opera. See below (Bardi, p. 34).

Comment: Descriptions of the wedding festivities: (1) *Descrizione delle
feste fatte in Firenze per le reali nozze de' Serenissimi sposi Ferdinando II
Granduca di Toscana e Vittoria Principessa d'Urbino.* Firenze, Pignoni,
1637. In B Bc; I Mb, Rn; US Ws. This description is ascribed by Melzi,
I, p. 286, to Ferdinando de' Bardi. (2) *Relazione delle Nozze degli Dei,
favola dell'Abate Gio. Carlo Coppola alla Serenissima Vittoria Principessa
d'Urbino Granduchessa di Toscana.* Firenze, Massi, e Landi, 1637. By
Francesco Raffaello Rondinelli. (3) *Argomento delle Nozze degli Dei del
favola dell'Abate Gio: Carlo Coppola.* Fiorenze, Massi e Landi, 1637.
Both nos. 2 and 3 are in I Fn bound together. (4) Ms description by an
anonymous contemporary published in *Notizie istoriche italiane*, vol. II,
pp. 234-39. (5) Ms apparently containing plans for *Le nozze* entitled
Pensieri di machine, et altro p[er] *una festa nel Cortile de Pittj* in I Fn
(Magl. XXVII, 83). See Solerti, *Musica*, pp. 197-211; Molinari, pp. 176ff.,
figs. 62-68; Nagler, pp. 162-73, figs. 119-26; *Luogo teatrale*, pp. 140-43
figs. 9.37, 38, 43-44.

1637[2] vii
Pal. Pitti
(Boboli)

Armida e l'Amor Pudico. Festa a cavallo.

Text: Ferdinando Saracinelli. Bardi's *Descrizione* cited above in 1637[1]
publishes the text for two characters shown in the supposed title above.
The "invenzione de i Carri e d'altre macchine . . . fu commessa a Felice
Gamberai. "The scenes, each introduced with music, were coordinated

Parigi, Inu Stefa.⁰ Della
Deli: e. F.

PRIMA SCENA RAPRESENTANTE FIORENZA

I Fn 20.9.C.4. *Le nozze degli dei*, 1637[1], scene 1 (Prologo). Scene designed by Alfonso Parigi, etching by Stefano della Bella. Imeneo, goddess of marriage, with Honesty (left) and Fecundity (right), is descending to bless the wedding of Ferdinando de' Medici and Vittoria della Rovere. Three nymphs (downstage left) have risen out of the Arno to predict happy progeny for the couple. Note that Imeneo and her attendants are shown descending *and* descended on downstage right. Mercury descends upper left bringing the news of the joy of Jupiter. Florence is seen in the distance across the Arno.

by Agnolo Ricci. The squadrons were guided by Prince Gian Carlo and Don Pietro Medici.

Music (lost): Composers unknown. See *Luogo teatrale*, pp. 152-54.

1638^1 18 xi

LA GRISELSA. Favola pastorale del Dottore Andrea Baroncini. All'Ill. Sig. . . . Marchese Antonio Salviati. Fiorenza, Nesti, 1638.
I Rn.

Text: Dedication, signed as shown by author, states that the pastorale was "concepita ne'più verdi anni" but rewritten for performance in honor of the marriage of the Marchese.

Music: Unknown. Each of five acts ends with a *Coro*, which may indicate incidental music.

1638^2

LA SENARBIA. Comedia di Gio. Battista Benedetti Senese, nell'Accademia degli Ardenti il Rinovato. All'Illustriss. ecc. Bartolomeo Curini. Firenze, Francesco Onofri, 1638.
I Rn.

Text: Benedetti. In poetry but primarily without music. There are occasional indications of incidental music and the last act (fifth) has a *finale a due* for "Stalloccio e Pensiero cantano." However, from the dedication, this edition is for literary purposes. The performance took place in Siena in 1627 for the wedding of Flaminio Benedetti and Felice Pussi.

1639

L'Iride. Tragicommedia [in verse] di Giulio Pitti. In Firenze, Zanobio Pignoni, 1639. Cited by Quadrio III, II, III, p. 350. No copy known to Sartori.

1640

Flora feconda. Dramma per musica. Firenze, Amador Massi, e Lorenzo Landi, 1640.

Text: Margherita Costa, romana. Known only through Allacci, col. 363.

Music lost: Composer unknown.

1641 carn

S. Agata. Opera del Sig. Jacopo Cicognini con tutti i suoi intermedij in musica. Baccini, pp. 10ff.

1642 10 i

LI BUFFONI. Comedia ridicola di Margherita Costa romana. A Berardino Ricci cavaliero del Piacere detto il Tedeschino. Fiorenza, Amador Massi e Lorenzo Landi, 1641.
I Baf, Mb.

Text: Margherita Costa who signs the dedication 10 genn., 1641; dedication speaks of a performance during carnival. Dedicatory dates are usually *ab inc.*, hence the publication date is probably also.

Music (lost): Composer (s) unknown. The text is primarily in prose with a prologue, intermezzi, and occasional *canzonette* for music and dancing.

1644

Foundation of the Accademia dei Concordi for, among other purposes, the recitation of *commedie* in the Casino Mediceo of Don Lorenzo de'Medici in Via Parione. The Academy continued until the death of the patron 16 xi, 1648.

The only record of a performance by the Concordi is in **I Fas** (Misc. Medicea 49, c. 305) in a letter dated 16 i 1644 *ab inc.* from the Cardinale Imperiale to Giov. Poggi Cellesi expressing the cardinal's regrets that he cannot attend the "commedia del Casino del Principe Don Lorenzo."

1645[1] 14 ii
Stanzone di
Fiorenza Franco

La finta pazza.

Text: Giulio Strozzi.

Music (lost): Probably by Francesco Sacrati.

Comment: Bianconi and Walker, p. 402, report an undated notice in **I Fas** (Arch. Med. Fil. 5439, c. 325) which says that Giov. Paolo [*sic* for Battista] Balbi, Capo dell'Accademia de Feb'Armonici, had obtained permission to perform Giulio Strozzi's *Finta pazza* "con tutti l'Intermedii e mutatione di Scene, come l'hanno fatta a Venezia . . . " Filza 5431, cc. 145, 146, and 192, also concern this performance. Carta 192 gives the date of the first performance, the price of *mezza piastra per testa*, and the fact that the rental of *stanzini* had already brought in 500 scudi. Carta 146 states that singers from Rome were engaged because the Florentine singers did not wish to sing. It also contains enthusiastic praise of the performance as a whole and especially the costumes, scene changes, machines [voli], and ballets of bears, marmosets [gatti mammoni], and other inventions. There were two performances after Ash Wednesday.

1645[2] aut

Festa in musica.
No other details known. In a letter to the Principe di Palestrina [**I Rvat** (Barb. lat. 7242, ff. 39-42)], Mattias de' Medici requested the services of Niccola Paris, soprano, to perform in this *festa.*

1646[1] 10 v
Casa Corsini ?

CELIO. Drama musicale del dottor Hiacinto Andrea Cicognini rappresentato in Fiorenza l'anno M.DC.XLVI. All'Illustriss. Sig. Marchese Bartolomeo Corsini. Fiorenza, Franceschini e Logi, s.d.
B Bc; **I** Fc, Fn, MOe, Rn, Rsc.

Text: Dedication signed by Cicognini as shown. The *Al discreto lettore* states that the performed libretto was shorter than the published libretto.

Music: Baccio Baglioni and Niccolo Sapiti. Ricci, "Un melodramma ignoto," pp. 51-79; Ghisi, "Contributo," p. 64. Score: **I** Fn.

1646[2] 27 v
Cortile,
Pal. Pitti

EGISTO. Favola drammatica musicale di Gio: Faustini. Firenze, Franceschini e Logi, 1646.
I Fc, Rvat; **US** Wc.

Text: Faustini. Dedication to Cornelio Bentivoglio signed on date shown by Curtio Mannari (elsewhere Manara), machinist, who complains of the lack of time for the completion of his machines. The location given by Fabbri, "Firenze," col. 381.

Music: Cavalli. First performance Venice (S. Cassiano), 1643. Scores: **A** Wn; **I** Vnm.

1647
Infuocati [*sic*]

Xerse.
Text by N. Minati; music by Cavalli. Cited by Manferrari, I, p. 217, on the basis of a conjecture in Ademollo, *I primi fasti della Pergola*, p. 10. Entry suspect since neither the Academy nor the theater existed in 1647.

1649

Prologo per Musica fatto p[er] comando del Sig. Card. G. Carlo agl'Accad[emi]ci di Larione l'anno 1649.
I Fn (Magl. cl. VII, 359, pp. 663-71).

Text: [Antonio] Malatesti, as stated at the end of the prologue.

Music (lost): Composer(s) unknown.

Roles: Poro dio della Ricchezza, Fortuna, e Bellezza.

1649

Accademia degli Immobili organized under the patronage of Card. Giovanni Carlo de' Medici.

1650

Construction of the Teatro del Cocomero. See Morini, pp. 2ff.

1650[1] 11 i

LA DEIDAMIA. Dramma musicale di Scipione Herrico al Serenissimo Gran Duca di Toscana. In Venetia e di nuova in Firenze, nella stamperia di Amador Massi, 1650.
I Bc, Fm.

Text: Herrico. Dedication signed 11 Gennaio 1649 *ab inc.* by Gio. Batista Balbi, *e compagni*, the Feb-Armonici, i.e., by the impresario and his company of *comici* who performed the opera. First performance in Venice (Cavallerizzo), 1644.

Music (lost): Composer(s) unknown. Walker, "Gli errori," as quoted by Bianconi, col. 688, doubts the long accepted attribution (beginning with Ivanovich) of the music to Cavalli.

1650[2] 15 v

GIASONE. Drama musicale di D. Iacinto Andrea Cicognini, Accademico Instancabile. Al Serenissimo Principe Mattias di Toscana. In Fiorenze, Bonardi, 1650.
I Bc, Fn.
Dedication signed on above date by the Accademici Ineguali, a title that suggests precursors of the Sorgenti (see p. 27). The publisher explains in the *Ai lettore*: "L'Essermi mancate le copie del Giasone & essendomi cresciute le richieste di esso, mi ha necessitato a ristamparlo." This sentence is also to be found in the edition of Giuliani, Venice, 1650. Seemingly, then, the edition was literary rather than for a performance.

Music: Cavalli. First performance in Venice (S. Cassiano), 1649. Scores: B Bc; I Fn, Nc, Vnm. Excerpts in Eitner, *Publikationen* 12.

1650[3] 8 viii

ALIDORO IL COSTANTE. Canto fatto per comand.o del Ser.mo Cardinal Gian Carlo il dì 8 Agosto 1650. Composizione di Antonio Malatesti.
I Fn (Ms. Magl. VII, 359, pp. 584-91).

Text: Malatesti. One act.

Music (lost): Domenico Anglesi, according to Ms.

Roles: Alidoro, Rosalba, Morfeo ed le Larve, and Coro di fantasme.

1651¹ 11 ii IL GIASONE. Drama per musica del Sig. Giacinto Andrea Cicognini Accademico Instancabile all'illustrissimo Sig. Filippo Franceschi. Firenze, per l'Onofri, 1651.
I Lg.
It is clear from the dedication of this libretto set by Cavalli (see 1650¹) that this publication did not accompany a performance although Fabbri, "Firenze," col. 381, locates it in the Cortile of the Pitti Palace. On p. 4 the same statement is printed that appears in 1650¹; moreover the dedication says, "Le continue richieste . . . mi hanno indotto a ristamparlo, . . . ho stimato opportuno il presentarglielo, per essere V.S. Illustrissima in procinto di giocondissimi Imeneo . . . dove più che in altro tempo si riputa convenevole la letteratura di simili composizioni." The dedication is signed as shown by Francesco Onofri.

1651² LE QUERELE AMOROSE dialogo. Amore: 1. Amante non amato, 2. Amante geloso, 3. Amante tacito, 4. Amante dal doppio amore. In Firenze, Stamperia di S.A.S., 1651.
I Rn.
The text is dramatic and intended for music. However, there is no information about the poet, the composer, or the performance.

1652¹ 15 i
P.za di S.ta
Maria Novella
GIOSTRA RAPPRESENTATA IN FIRENZE AL SER.MO FRANCESCO DUCA DI MODANA.
I Fas (Med. 6424).

Text: Poet unknown. One scene. Pastoso, p. 39, no. 224, reports: "Per festeggiare, et onorare il Ser.mo Duca di Modana, se fece una superbissima giostra su la piazza di S. Maria Novella a lume di torce, la qual piazza era circondata attorno di palchi in forma d'amfiteatro, suigli palchi chi vi volse salire si pago 4, e 5 lire p[er] luogo, et insino ad una piastra; la festa riusci magnificentissima d'invenzione, carri, e musiche, e sopratutto p[er] il leggiadro comparire, e franco operare de i Cavalieri e fu stimato da i forestieri, che in grand.mo numero vi concorsero una festa veramente Regia." Settimanni on the same date 1651 *ab inc.* says that more than 1,500 costumed people participated and that it lasted until 5 *della notte*.

Roles: Melissa, Ruggiero, Bradamane, Coro di Cavalieri e Donzelle.

Music (lost): Composer(s) unknown.

1652² 25 iv
Pal. Pitti
COMBATTIMENTO E BALLETTO A CAVALLO. Rappresentato di notte in Fiorenza a' Serenissimi Arciduchi & Arciduchessa d'Austria Ferdinando Carlo, Anna di Toscana, e Sigismondo Francesco nel teatro contiguo al palazzo del Serenissimo Gran Duca. Firenze, St. di S.A.S. alla Condotta, 1652.
I Fas (bound in Settimanni Diaries), Fn, Rn.

Text: Benedetto Rigogli, as stated.

Music (lost): Composer(s) unknown.
Description and list of nobility, etc. Notice in Pastoso, p.37, no. 233, gives date of 28 iv. Settimanni's date shown above.

1652 12 vii Foundation stone of the Pergola Theater is laid by Card. Giovanni de'Medici.

The Accademia degli Immobili is divided. Those who move with the Cardinal retain the name and charter of the Immobili. Those who remain at the theater in via Cocomero take a new name: *degli Infuocati* with the Grand Duke Ferdinando de' Medici as their patron. This universally accepted information is provided by Morini, pp. 1-3. However, that the academy remaining in via del Cocomero is the Infuocati is unconfirmed by any other source. Activity by the Infuocati is not recorded in any document of the seventeenth century before 1665[1]. Instead the Sorgenti, registered first in 1654[2], produce a number of plays and operas at the Cocomero from 1657-1665 under the patronage of Gian Carlo de' Medici. All evidence, Morini aside, suggests that the division of the Immobili created the Sorgenti and that a general academic reorganization about 1665 was the origin of the Infuocati. See p. 27 above.

(1652)[3] *Veremonda, l'Amazzone d'Aragona.*
Allacci, col. 810, lists an opera by M. Bisaccioni and Cavalli performed in Venice in 1652. Manferrari under Cavalli states that an opera by the same title was performed in Florence. Both are mistaken. See Bianconi and Walker, p. 446.

1654[1] 15 i ALESSANDRO VINCITOR DI SE STESSO. Drama musicale del Sig. Francesco Sbarra gentiluomo Lucchese, al Serenissimo e Reverendissimo Principe Cardinale Gio. Carlo di Toscana. Firenze, Francesco Onofri, 1654. **GB** Lbm; **I** Bc, Mb.

Text: Sbarra. Dedication signed 15 i 1653 *ab inc.* by Sig.ra Anna Maria Sardelli (see Cast).

Music: Antonio Cesti. For argument that Allacci's attribution to Cavalli is incorrect, see Osthoft, pp. 13-43. Score: **I** Rvat.

Cast: Bianconi and Walker, p. 443, n. 260, report several attempts from 1652 until 1654 to mount *Alessandro* and to engage singers (**I** Fas [F. 5451, cc. 130, 214, 227, 454; F. 5419, cc. 918-19; F. 5371, cc. 71, 511-13]). Negotiations with some were unsuccessful: with "un Musico Castelli, Jacopo Melani (who was engaged in Venice), and Atto Melani (who refused the part of Apelle but asked for Alessandro, with what result is unknown). Two singers can be reasonably well assigned: Anna Francesca Costa, protected by Leopoldo de'Medici, and Anna Maria Sardelli who signed the dedication and sang the role of Campaspe. More information concerning Sardelli will be found in Bianconi and Walker, pp. 441-44. She sang the same part in Venice, 1651, with such success that she became known as *La Campaspe* and was celebrated or castigated in at least three poems: *Rollo delle Puttane*, a diatribe by Busenello (**I** Vnm: It. IX 458 [7032]), published by A. Livingston, p. 244; a sonnet by Torcigliani, published in the above-cited article by Osthoff, p. 16; and a third here reported for the first time, a satire attributed to Pietro Susini with the lengthy title of "Per la partenza di un castrato amato della Sig.ra Anna Maria [del] N[ero] Cortigiana, e cantatrice Romana detta Campaspe per haver recitata quella parte con gran applauso in una commedia in musica nella città di Firenze" in **I** Fn (Magl. VII, 362, pp. 289-95). Her dominance of the opera was such that a Ms prologue to the opera bears the title of her role:

PROLOGO DELLA CAMPASPE.

Text: Anonymous. Ms. in I Fn (Magl. VII, 359, pp. 775-87).

Music (lost): Composer unknown.

Roles: Notte, Terra, Fama, Giova, Saturno, Sole, Marte, Coro degli Iddei, Venere, Coro d'Amoretti.

1654[2] 14, 25 viii
Sorgenti

FESTA rappresentata da gl'Accademici Sorgenti nel giorno del felic.mo natale del Serenissimo Cosimo III Gran Principe di Toscana. Firenze, Lando Landi, 1654.
I Fr.

Text: Carlo Puccetti, according to handwritten insertion in I Fr. See Hill, pp. 31f.

Comment: Earliest libretto in which the Sorgenti are mentioned. It coincides with the earliest records of the academy (I Fas *S. Agnese* 218) reported by John Walter Hill, p. 31. Note 23 quotes the description in the libretto: "Nel giorno 14. d'Agosto 1654. giorno illustrato dal natale felicissimo del Sereniss. Cosimo Terzo Gran Principe di Toscana; gl'Accademici Sorgenti non poterono non mostrare publico segno d'allegrezza celebrando un tanto giorno con la descritta festa. Formorno un Carro d'eminenza altissimo, . . . Passeggiata con quest'ordine due volte la via del Cocomero illustrata con la presenza di tutti i Serenissimi Padroni, e dalla più scelta nobiltà di Dame, e Cavalieri si corse il Palio. Di poi con l'istesso ordine si porto il Carro al Palazzo de Pitti. . . ."

A second performance is recorded by Settimanni who errs in naming the academicians *Sorpresi*. On 25 viii the diary recounts: "Mercredi sera fu fatta ad un'ora e mezza di notte una festa dagli Accademici Sorpresi sulla Piazza di Santa Croce, consistente in un Carro Trionfale pieno di musici che cantarono in lode del Gran Principe Cosimo; qual Carro apparendosi alcuni giovani vi formavano sopra un balletto: e dietro di esso venivano molte persone mascherate a cavallo che soggermentavano li primi poeti greci e latini. Questa festa era già stata fatta nel cortile del Palazzo de' Pitti."

1654[3] 27 ix
2, 12 x

Ipermestra.

Text: G.A. Moniglia.

Music: Francesco Cavalli.

Comment: L. Bianconi, p. 692, quotes two letters by Atto Melani concerning private performances of Francesco Cavalli's score for G.A. Moniglia's *Hipermestra* (see 1658[3]). Portions of these letters had been published previously by Ademollo, *I primi fasti della musica*, p. 70, n. 1, but he did not catch the reference to *Ipermestra*. Bianconi has corrected Ademollo's oversight. The first letter of September 27, 1654 (I Fas: Arch. Med. F. 5452, cc. 747r-748r) speaks of an unnamed score, the first act of which had arrived in Florence. Atto and Leonora [Ballerini] sang it at the request of Card. Gio: Carlo de' Medici. The letter of October 2 (I Fas: Arch. Med. F. 5453, cc. 595r-596r) refers to the part of Ipermestra and to two performances, one in the chambers of the cardinal in Florence and the other

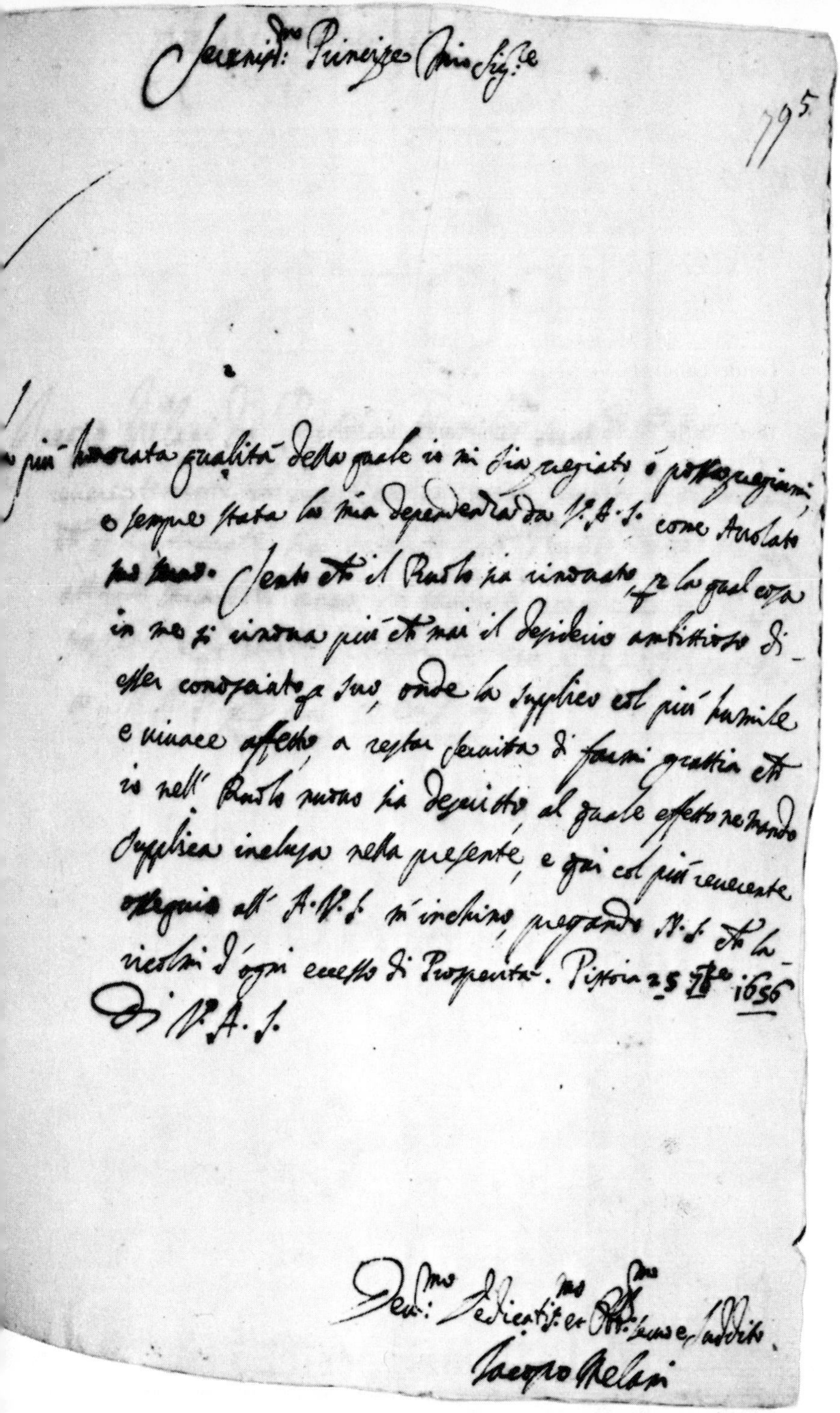

Sereniss.mo Principe Mio Sig.re

795

... più honorata qualità della quale io mi sia pregiato ò possa pregiarmi, è sempre stata la mia dependenza da V. A. S. come [illegible]. Sento ch'il Ruolo sia rinovato, per la qual cosa in me si rinnova più che mai il desiderio ambitioso di esser conosciuto per suo, onde la supplico col più humile e vivace affetto a restar servita di farmi grattia ch'io nell' Ruolo nuovo sia descritto, al quale effetto ne mando supplica inclusa nella presente, e qui col più reverente ossequio all' A. V. S. m'inchino, pregando N. S. che la ricolmi d'ogni eccesso di prosperità. Pistoia 25 7bre 1656

Di V. A. S.

Devotiss.mo Dedicatiss.mo et Obblig.mo Servo e Suddito
Jacopo Melani

I Fas, Arch. Med., Carteggio del Principe Mattias, Filza 5414/795.
Letter from Jacopo Melani, Pistoia, 25 ix 1656, asking for his reappointment to a position which apparently had been unfilled for an indefinite number of years.

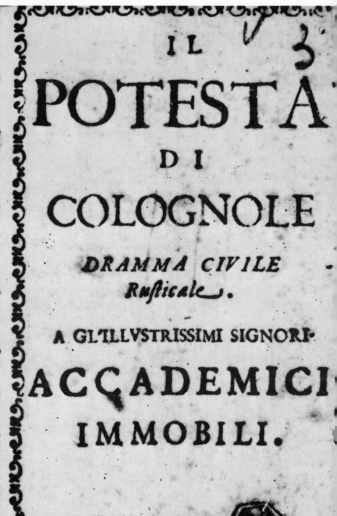

IL
POTESTÀ
DI
COLOGNOLE
DRAMMA CIVILE
Rusticale.

A GL'ILLVSTRISSIMI SIGNORI·
ACCADEMICI
IMMOBILI.

In Firenze, per il Bonardi 1657.
Con licenza de Superiori.

in the chambers of the Granduchess Vittoria della Rovere in Pratolino. The first of the performances was attended by Principe Leopoldo de' Medici and was performed with the assistance of various academic singers among whom were Count Bardi and the Marchese Niccolini.

For speculations about a performance in honor of the birthday of Vittoria della Rovere, see 1658[3].

1655[1] ca. 17 i
Cocomero
(Sorgenti)

Due commedie all'improvviso.   See Hill, p. 32.

1655[2] 20 ii
Cocomero
Sorgenti

La vendetta della sposa rapita. Commedia.

Comment: Four performances, ending on February 20. See Hill, p. 32.

1655[3]-56
inverno
Cocomero
Sorgenti

La donna più costante. Commedia con gl'intermedi in musica.

Text: Anonymous.

Music (lost): Jacopo Melani.

Comment: Performed twice. See Hill, p. 32.

1655[4]-56
inverno
Cocomero
Sorgenti

La Paolina, o vero Pudicizia schernita. Commedia.

Comment: One performance? See Hill, p. 32.

(1656)[1]
(Livorno)

IL GIASONE. Drama musicale del Dottore Giacinto Andrea Cicognini, accademico Instancabile. Fiorenze, Onofri, 1656.
I Fn, PAc, Rn.

Text: Cicognini. Dedication signed (without date) by Sig. G.B. Fiorillo Accademico Acceso: "Perche non isfuggano di sentire i successi del suo vivere i Fedeli su le Scene questo carnevale in Livorno, ragionevolmente ricorre sotto l'ombra della sua candide Crol . . . " Hence the opera was performed in Livorno. The entry is retained since the libretto is listed in bibliographies.

Music: Cavalli (see 1650[1]).

1656[2]
Pal. Pitti

INTERMEDIO DEL SIG.R MONTEMAGNI.
I Fn (Magl. VII 359, pp. 683-98).

Text: Montemagni.

Music (lost): Composer(s) unknown. At end: "Recitata in musica nella Comm[edi]a dei Paggi di S.A.S. l'anno 1656."

Roles: Antichità, Moda, e Tempo.

1657[1] 5 ii
Pergola
Immobili

IL POTESTÀ DI COLOGNOLE. Dramma civile rusticale. A gli Illustrissimi Signori Accademici Immobili. Firenze, Bonardi, 1657.
I Fn, Mb.

Text: G.A. Moniglia. Dedication signed on above date by il D[ott]. M[oniglia]. Title page is shown on the *left*.

Music: Jacopo Melani. The composer and performers are listed on the final page of the libretto. A. Bonaventura, p. 148, lists the performers of the prologue (without source) which are missing in the libretto. Scores: **D** Bds; **I** Fc, Rvat. Excerpts in Goldschmidt.

Cast: Anselmo - Michele Grasseschi; Isabella - Leonora Ballerini; Crezia - (dummy); Gora - Bartolomeo Mazzanti; Tancia - Antonio Rivani; Leonora - Elisabetta Nacci; Odoardo - Antonio Sirt; Desso Tartaglia - Carlo Righenzi; Leandro - Domenico Bellucci; Bruscolo - Simone Martelli; Flavio - Vincenzo Piccini; Ciapo - Carlo Guardini; Moro Monello - Moro di S.A. Rever. For prolog: L'Accademia - Vincenzo Piccini, Momo - Batistoni, Talia - Simone Martelli.

Comment: Preface to the comic opera in Moniglia's *Poesie dramatiche* III, p. 1, gives details of original performance. For argument that the opera season in Florence at this time did not begin, as frequently presumed, after Christmas but a few days before Carnival, see Weaver, *Florentine Comic Opera*, pp. 40ff.

1657² 28 ii
Cocomero
Sorgenti

La caduta del savio innamorato. Commedia.

Text: Mario Calamari. See 1691⁸.

Comment: Date given is final performance. See Hill, p. 32.

1657³ 28 ii
Cocomero
Sorgenti

Una commedia all'improvviso con gl'intermedi in musica.

Text: Anonymous.

Music (lost): Probably by Jacopo Melani, the academy's regular composer.

Comment: One performance. See Hill, p. 32.

1657⁴ 20 ix

Laurinda. Opera del Sig.ʳ Dottore Moniglia.
I Fn (Magl. Cl. VII c. 799, ff. 92-159v).

Text: Giovanni Andrea Moniglia. A prose comedy with prolog and three intermedi for music. The *Adornamenti* are listed: Un ballo d'Amori nel prologo in sei, un ballo di Cacciatori di Diana nel pr[im]o Intermedio, un ballo di Ninfe del fiume Liero nel secondo Intermedio, un ballo di Satiri nel ultimo Intermedio, La trasmutatione di Siringa in cane.

Music (lost): Composer unknown.

Roles: Pane Dio delle Selve, Due Satire suoi seguaci, Siringa Ninfa di Diana, Delfa nutrice di Siringa, Amore, Nisa Ninfa del Fiume Liero in Tessaglia.

Comment: There is no evidence that there was a performance. The date is that of the scribe who signs the manuscript of *Laurinda* twice, once at the end of the lst intermedio on September 14, 1657, and again at the end of the third on September 20. The collection of dramatic works, all copied by the same scribe, includes *Le fortunate gelosie del Re di Valenza* o vero *la Belmira*. Opera del Sig. Dottore Jacinto Andrea Cicognini composto in Venezia l'anno 1647 (ff. 1-91v); *Il Marito Ruffiano*. Opera del Susini (ff. 163-238, a prose comedy without prologue or intermedii); and *Opera tragica L'usurpator d'un Regnio* [sic] *Persago della Morte del Regniante* (ff. 243-320v, in prose likewise without prologue or intermedii).

1657⁵ 25 xi
Cocomero
Sorgenti

SCIPIONE IN CARTAGINE. Dramma musicale fatto rappresentare da gli Accademici Sorgenti nel loro teatro sotto la protezzione del Sig. Card. Gio: Carlo di Toscana. Firenze, Bonardi, 1657. Title page is shown *overleaf*. I Bc, MOe, Rn(2); US Chb.

Text: Dedication to Sig.ra Marchesa Giovanna dal Monte signed on above date by Giovanni Battista Rontini. The text on the authority of Allacci, col. 703, by G.A. Moniglia, which is probably the source for the same attribution by I. Carini, *L'Arcadia*, vol. I, p. 559. This libretto was not, however, published in the *Poesie dramatiche* of Moniglia. Fabbri's assertion in "Firenze," col. 381, that this is an early version of *Scipione Affricano* by N. Minato (see 1669¹) with music by Cavalli is erroneous. The libretto is entirely different. Anonymous Ms copy in I Fn (Magl. VIII, 356).

Music (lost): No mention of the composer is found in the libretto. However, if the libretto is indeed by Moniglia, the music was probably by Jacopo Melani, member of the Sorgenti and their regular composer, whose collaboration with Moniglia is well-established.

Roles: Filoro, Alarco, Scipione, Corali, Lucindo, Florisbe, Erifile, Rosmira.

Comment: The first opera performed by the Sorgenti, who previously have performed only prose comedies with or without prologues and intermedi for music. The payment records of the Sorgenti speak only of a *commedia in musica*. See Hill, p. 32.

(1657)⁶

Il Giasone.
Text by Cicognini, music by Cavalli. No libretto found. Cited by Fabbri, "Firenze," col. 381, probably in error for the Livorno, 1656, libretto.

1657⁷

MASCHERATA DI GALEONE, 1657.
I Fn (Magl. VII, 356, f. 198).

Text: Attributed at end of the mascherata to [Antonio?] Malatesti.

Music (lost): Composer unknown.

1658¹ 20 ii
Pergola

IL PAZZO PER FORZA. Dramma civile rusticale fatto rappresentarsi in musica da gl'illustriss. Sig. Accademici Immobili nel loro Teatro sotto la protezione del Sereniss. e Reverendiss. Principe Cardinale Gio: Carlo di Toscana essendo nel presente Semestre Principe dell'Accademia l'Illustrissimo Signore Lionardo Martellini. A' quattro Sig. Accademici Deputati per soprintendere alle musiche, Il Sig. March. Filippo Niccolini. Il Sig. March. Gio: Batt: Dal Monte. Il Sig. Piero del Sig. Piero Strozzi. Il Sig. Filippo Franceschi. Firenze, Bonardi, [s.d.].
I Fn, PAc, Rca.

Text: G.A. Moniglia who signs the dedication 20 February 1658. A shortened version of the libretto, which was set by Pagliardi (lost score) for performance at Pratolino in 1687³, appears in the two editions of the *Poesie dramatiche* of Moniglia. See Weaver, *Florentine Comic Opera*, pp. 49-56.

Music (lost): Jacopo Melani. He and the performers are listed on the final page of the libretto.

SCIPIONE

IN

CARTAGINE,

DRAMMA MVSICALE,

Fatto rappresentare

DA GLI ACCADEMICI
SORGENTI
Nel loro Teatro,

SOTTO *LA* PROTEZZIONE

Del Sereniss. e Reuerendiss. Princ. Card.

CIO: CARLO

D. TOSCANA ESTENSE

IN FIRENZE, Per Gio: Anton Bonardi.
Con licenza de' Super. · 6 7.

Left:
I MOe LXXXIII G.21.
Scipione in Cartagine, 1657[5],
first published libretto
naming the Sorgenti.

Above:
I Fn 60.5.284.
L'Hipermestra, 1658[3],
Act III, scene 17,
Palazzo di Venere,
Balletto finale.

Cast: Anselmo - Michele Grasseschi; Flavio - Carlo Righenzi; Leonora - Lisabetta Falbetti Nacci; Filandro - Vincenzo Piccini; Sgaruglia - Gio. Michele de Bar; Bellichino - Niccola Coresi; Beltramina - Simone Martelli; Isabella - Leonora Falbetti Ballerini; Trottolo - Simone Martelli; Leandro - Domenico Bellucci; Ligurino - Antonio Rivani; Moretta, Zingara - Il Moro di S.A. Reverendiss.; Coro di Zingari - Michele Mosi, Francesco Lionardi, Antonio Ruggieri, Niccola Coresi, Gio. Michele de Bar, Millone - Michele Grasseschi; Astrologo - Gio. Michele de Bar; Mattematico - Paolo Rivani; Soldato - Niccola Coresi; Ebreo - Michele Mosi; Donna vedova - Antonio Ruggieri; Donna Maritata - Francesco Lionardi.

1658² carn
Acc. Affinati

DI MALE IN PEGGIO. Commedia rappresentata in Firenze da Signori Accademici Affinati il Carnevale 1658.
I Bca (Ms. A 1080).

Text: Anonymous. In prose without prologue, intermezzi, finale or other musical texts. The performers (11) are listed but were not available at publication time.

1658³ 18 vi
Pergola

L'HIPERMESTRA. Festa teatrale rappresentata dal Sereniss. Principe Cardinale Gio: Carlo di Toscana per celebrare il giorno natalizio del real Principe di Spagna. Firenze, St. di S.A.S., 1658. Also a second printing: Firenze e Bologna, C. Ant. Peri, 1658.
A Wn; **B** Bc; **I** Bc, Fm, Fn(2), Mb, PAc, Rca, Sc; **US** Wc.

Text: G.A. Moniglia. Dedication signed by Moniglia June 12, 1658, but the *Descrizione della presa d'Argo, e degli amori di Linceo con Ipermestra, festa teatrale* (Firenze, 1658) states that the first performance took place *verso le 24 ore* on June 18. Dispatches to Modena (see Comments below) indicate that the first performance took place actually four days later. The *Descrizione*, by O.R. Rucellai, is frequently bound with the libretto, though sometimes it is a separate volume (e.g., **I** MOe). It was reprinted in Moniglia's *Poesie dramatiche*. The original libretto contains thirteen double-page plates, ten of which were reprinted in the *Poesie* with marginal trimming. Modern reproductions are fairly common: Wotquenne, pp. 87f.; Molinari, figs. 102-12 (commentary, pp. 178ff.); Haas, pp. 157f. The final scene, *PALACE OF VENUS*, is shown on the preceding page. Bianconi reprints portions of the *Descrizione* pertaining to the music of Cavalli, pp. 691f. See 1654³ above.

Music: Francesco Cavalli. Scores: **B** Bc; **I** Vnm.

Comment: The libretto does not contain a prologue. **I** Fas (Arch. Med. 6424, n. 9) is an anonymous prologue in manuscript clearly connected with the opera above. It is in two parts having the *interlocutori*, Sole, Coro di Hori, Venere, Theti, and Coro de Nereidi. The text is poetic with obvious signs of being intended for music. Connections with *Ipermestra* are established by references to three principal roles: Danao, Linceo and Hipermestra. Initially Sole sings of a special occasion: "al nascer di Vittoria," a salute to the birthday of the duchess common to a number of other dramatic works in this *filza*. Venere then announces her imminent departure for Tuscany: "Col mio vezzoso figlio oggi m'appresto / Sovra festose scene / Dagl'Immobili miei rese rotanti / Della Gran Donna a tranquillare il Ciglio." These lines could hardly be performed at the above performance of 1658 since that one celebrated the birth of the infanta of Spain. Besides, Vittoria's birthday was February 7, according to Fabbri, *Scarlatti*, p. 34, n. 44 (Litta says Vittoria's birthday was February 14). The Settimanni Diaries (I Fas) record on February 25, 1658 the repetition of the *calcio* in S. Croce. Then a different hand adds: "In questo tempo di Carnovale di detto anno 1658 nel loro Teatro di via della Pergola dagli accademici Immobili fù fatto recitare il Dramma intitolata *Il Pazzo per Forza* e *l'Ipermestra* - Poesie di Medico Dott.r Gio: Andrea Moniglia." Marginalia in still a third hand fill in information about the performance in the summer. To this evidence must be added the information found in the *Dispacci da Firenze* I MOas (Bianconi and Walker, p. 430, n. 246) that indicates preparations for the performance of *Hipermestra* as early as November 11, 1657, and a long period of continual postponement primarily because of the machines. A reasonable explanation for the prologue would be that the opera, the score being available in 1654[3], was in a sufficient state of preparation for the academicians to perform it for Vittoria's birthday without the machines and only for the court.

Bianconi, however, is of the opinion that the opera was commissioned as the inaugural opera for the Pergola theater in 1655 intended to take place in the carnival of that year and coinciding with the birthday of Vittoria della Rovere on February 7. Various matters caused the delay of the performance until after the actual opening of the theater with *Il potestà di Colognole* in the carnival of 1657[1], the principal reason for the delay being difficulties with the machinery. Supporting Bianconi's contention is the existence of a manuscript of the libretto which includes the prologue dedicated to Vittoria and mentioning the Immobili in I Rc 1294 (entitled "Egitto" and incorrectly ascribed to Giulio Rospigliosi). Such an interpretation of the evidence would require that the marginal comment in Settimanni's diary be written (and remain uncorrected) prior to an intended but unrealized performance in the carnival of 1658.

(1658)[4]	*Il Giasone.* Text by G.A. Cicognini, music by Francesco Cavalli. Cited by Loewenberg (ed. 1955). No libretto or reference found. See 1650[1].
1658[5] 28 xii **Cocomero** **Sorgenti**	*La forza del destino.* Commedia con gl'intermedi in musica. **Text (lost):** G.A. Moniglia. The most readily available text to equate with this comedy is *Laurinda* (1657[4]), which does contain intermedi. However, no other evidence exists linking the two. **Music (lost):** Probably by Jacopo Melani, the academy's regular composer. **Comment:** Three performances ending on December 28. See Hill, p. 32.
1659[1] carn **Pergola**	IL VECCHIO BALORDO. Dramma civile del Sig.r Dottore Gio: Andrea Moniglia. **Text:** There exist two Mss. I Fn (Magl. Cl. VII, c. 252) and Fl (Antinori 244) but no published libretto. It was not printed in the *Poesie* of Moniglia. The Mss. both carry the title given above. However, Ademollo, *I primi fasti del teatro*, p. 15, on the basis of the Archives of the Immobili, uses the title *Il vecchio burlato*, by which title it is generally recognized

in bibliographies. A reference in *La serva nobile* (1660[1]) also uses *burlato*. See Weaver, *Florentine Comic Opera*, pp. 58ff.

Music (lost): Jacopo Melani (attribution by Ademollo).

Roles: Commedia, Amore (prol.), Ascanio, Anselmo, Odoardo, Fernando, Lucrezia, Leonora, Petronella, Bestina, Piero Tartaglia, Betta, Gismondo, Frasia, Lisaura, Corali Moro.

1659[2] 5 iii
Cocomero
Sorgenti

La forza d'amore e di fortuna. Commedia con prologo in musica.

Text (lost): Mario Calamari.

Music (lost): Hill, p. 32, speculates that Pietro Sanmartini is the composer since he received a payment for tuning the harpsichord; hence, he may have played the harpsichord and composed the music. Sanmartini was a member of the *maestrato* of the Duomo, and as such certainly an available composer. See Castello, col. 1484. See 1668[1]. Four performances ending on March 5.

1660[1] 31 i
Pergola

LA SERVA NOBILE. Drama civile fatto rappresentare in musica dagl' Illustrissimi Signori Accademici Immobili nel loro teatro sotto la protezione del Ser. e Rev. Principe Cardinale Gio: Carlo di Toscana. A gl'Illustrissimi Signori Il Sig. March. Bartolomeo Corsini. Il Sig. Marc. Gio: Vincenzio Salviati. Il Sig. Cavalier Baldassar Suarez. Il Sig. Pier Giovanni Federighi. Firenze, nella Stamperia nuova all'Inseg. della Stella, 1660. GB Lbm; I Fn, Rca; S Uu.

Text: G.A. Moniglia, reprinted in the *Parte terza* of the *Poesie*. The dedication of the 1660 libretto signed January 31, 1659 [*ab inc.*], by Giuseppe Cocchini, the publisher. From the *A chi legge*: "Se questo Scherzo Drammatico perverrà in mano di Forestieri poco, o niente sarà per esser gustato, consistendo la maggior parte d'esso in proverbi, & idiotismi della Patria dell'autore, ai cittadini della quale è benissimo noto esser questa la quarta composizione nell'istesso stile, che gl'è uscita dalla penna."

Music (lost): Domenico Anglesi, who is listed with the performers on the final page of the libretto.

Cast: Anselmo - Michele Grasseschi; Leonora - Lisabetta Falbetti Nacci; Isabella - Leonora Falbetti Ballerini; Leandro - Antonio Rivani; Bruscolo - Simone Martelli; Desso - Carlo Righenzi; Fernando - Gio. Michele de Bar; Vaggia - Bartolomeo Mazzanti; Sandra - Giuseppe Toci; Cecia - Verginia Azzurrini; Lelio and Cincio - performers not named.

1660[2] 20 ii
Cocomero
Sorgenti

L'innocenza trionfo degl'inganni. Commedia.

Text (lost): Christofano Berardi, or Bernardi as spelled by Hill, p. 32.

Music: Probably a prose comedy.

Comment: Three performances ending on February 20.

1661[1] 8, 12,
22 vii; 7 viii
Pergola

ERCOLE IN TEBE. Festa teatrale rappresentata in Firenze per le reali nozze de' Serenissimi sposi Cosimo Terzo Principe di Toscana, e Margherita Luisa Principessa d'Orleans. Fiorenza, Nuova Stamperia all'Insegna della Stella, 1661.

B Bc; F Pn; GB Lbm; I Bc, Fn (4), Mb, PAc, Rn, Sc; US NYp, Wc.

Text: G.A. Moniglia. Dedication (2nd impression) signed by Moniglia June 25, 1661. Issued in two impressions, the first with the text only, the second with a *Descrizione* by Alessandro Segni and thirteen engravings of the scenes designed by Ferdinando Tacca. Two are shown *overleaf*. Eleven of the engravings are reproduced in Molinari, figs. 113-23 (see pp. 172 ff. for commentary). Wotquenne, opp. p. 59, reproduces three.

Music: Jacopo Melani, who is mentioned on p. 150 of the *Descrizione*. See Weaver, *Florentine Comic Opera*, pp. 238ff. for analysis of score. Scores: B Bc (modern copy); F Pn; I Pscr, Rvat; US Wc (modern copy).

Cast: The performers are not listed in the libretto. However, Ademollo, *I primi fasti del teatro*, p. 26, publishes the list taken from the archives of the Immobili. Ercole - Sig. Abate Cesti; Megera - Eleonora Ballerini; Ilo - Antonio Rivani; Teseo - Bartolomeo Melani; Iole - Lucia Rivani; Alceste - Domenico Bellucci; Lico - Vincenzio Piccini; Aristeo - Simone Martelli; Sifone - Carlo Righensi; Iolar - Moro di S.A.S.; Chitarro - Michele Grasseschi. Deities: Berecintia - Antonio Clementi; Giove - Ippolito Fusai; Giunone - Cosimo Orlandi; Venere - ——— ; Nettuno - Grossi [Siface] ; Plutone - Jacopo Acciari; Proserpina - Sebastiano Cioni; Mercurio - Sorentino; Gloria - Vincenzio Melani; Virtù - Sebastiano Cioni; Zeffiro - Pietro Galli; Elie - Sebastiano Cioni; Iride - Vincenzio Melani; Caronte - Ippolito Fusai; Aletto - Galletti; Radamante - Marco Giannetti; Minos - Gio. Michele de Bar.

Comment: Diarists Capponi, p. 93v; Pastoso, pp. 70f.: "Basti dire che cominciava all'un'ora di notte e finiva al far del giorno senza minimo tedio degli ascoltanti." Pastoso continues until p. 75 describing the festivities for the wedding including *Il mondo festeggiante* below. Bonazzini, p. 214, also writes a detailed description. An anonymous diarist (I Fas [Misc. Med. f. 39/5]) adds a few interesting and intimate details: "Vi furono tutti li Principi [de' Medici] , dove vi cenarono. Il Gran Duca fece però colazione. L'Arciduca [Ferdinando Carlo of Austria] stette sempre presso li sonatori attentissimo. La commedia riuscì nobilissima. Solo ebbe il difetto di troppo lunghezza che durò fino alle ore otto."

1661^2 1, 16 vii
Pal. Pitti

IL MONDO FESTEGGIANTE. Balletto a cavallo fatto nel teatro congiunto al palazzo del Sereniss. Granduca per le reali nozze dei Sereniss. Principe Cosimo terzo di Toscana e Margherita Luisa d'Orleans. Firenze, nella St. di S.A.S., 1661.
B Bc; I Bu, Fm, Fn, MOe.

Text: G.A. Moniglia. Contains one engraving, reproduced by Wotquenne, opp. p. 96, and *Descrizione*. Text and *Descrizione* reprinted in Moniglia's *Poesie*, I, 257, and 261 respectively.

Music (lost): Domenico Anglesi, who is mentioned on p. 61 of the libretto.

Comment: The record of the expenses (excluding music and musicians) is preserved in I Fas (Guardaroba F. 714). For diarists see *Ercole* above (1661^1).

I Fn Palat (11) C.2.4.11. *Ercole in Tebe.* 1661[1]. Scenes designed by Ferdinando Tacca. *Above*: Act V, scene 3, *Prigione: Lica prega Iole* (Prison: Lica beseeches Iole). *Below*: Act IV, scene 19, *Battaglia davanti alle mure di Tebe* (Battle before the walls of Thebes). Venus (left) and Juno (right) confront each other in the heavens.

1661³ 22 ii -
15 iii
Cocomero
Sorgenti

L'ERISMENA. Drama per musica di Aurelio Aureli, favola seconda dedicata all'Ill. Sig. Marchese Pietro Corsini. Firenze, Stamperia di S.A.S., 1661.
I Fc, Fm, Fn, Rn; US Chb.

Text: Aureli. Dedication, signed without date by the Accademici Sorgenti, speaks of an earlier performance in a theater *ne' più fastosi dell'Adriatico Lido* referring to the first performance in 1655 in Venice.

Music: Probably Francesco Cavalli. The reference to Venice probably applies both to the libretto and the music, but may, of course, apply only to the text. Score: I Vnm.

Cast: Maddalena Ottonaina (?), Anna, Vettoria, Carlo Righezzi [Righensi], Bartolomeo Melani, Bartolomeo Mazzanti, Sig. [Ippolito] Fusai, Sig. Franceschi, Sig. Galletti, Sig . . . del Sig. Nicolini. See Hill, p. 33.

Comment: The significance of *favola seconda* in the title probably is that the work is the second opera dedicated by the Sorgenti to Corsini. (It cannot mean to say that this is the second drama by Aureli who had written several librettos by this time.) Eight performances as follows - 22, 25, 28 February; 3, 6, 12, 14, and 15 of March.

1661⁴ 5 - 24 x
Cocomero
Sorgenti

L'ORONTEA. Dramma musicale del Dot. Giacinto Andrea Cicognini, rappresentato in Firenze nell'Accademia de' Sorgenti. Al Ser. Ferdinando Carlo Arciduca d'Austria. Firenze, Stamp. di S.A.S., 1661.
I Fn (This apparently unique libretto was destroyed in the flood of 1966.)

Text: G.A. Cicognini.

Music: Antonio Cesti. Dedication, signed by the academicians on date shown, speaks of previous performances in Venice (1649) and Innsbruck (1656), which confirms Cesti (who is not mentioned). Dedication published by F. Schlitzer, "Fortuna dell'Orontea," p. 81. See also Schlitzer, "L'*Orontea* di Antonio Cesti"; and N. Pirotta, "Tre capitoli su Cesti."

Scores: I Nc (excerpts), PAc, Rsc, Rvat. Recently edited by William Holmes for the Wellesley (Mass.) Edition, No. 11 (1973).

Cast: Sig. Abate [Antonio] Cesti, D. Tommaso, Sig. [Bartolomeo] Mazzanti, Sig. [Bartolomeo?] Melani, Vincenzino di Pistoia [Vincenzo Melani?], Giovanni Michele [de Bar], Vettoria e Giulia. See Hill, p. 33.

1661⁵ 25 x
Cocomero
Sorgenti

LA DORI overo LA SCHIAVA FEDELE. Dramma musicale dedicato al Ser. Ferdinando II Granduca di Toscana. Fiorenza, Insegna della Stella, 1661.
I Fm, Fn, Fr (Ms), Rsc.

Text: Giovanni [Apollonio] Apolloni, according to Allacci, col. 263, and Nino Pirotta "Apolloni." However, Schmidt, p. 455, n. 2, and Hill, p. 33, attribute this text to Giovanni Filippo Apolloni. The two librettists remain inextricably confused in dictionaries and bibliographies.

Music: Antonio Cesti.

Scores: A Wgm (excerpts), Wn; D MÜps; GB Lbm; I MOe, Nc (ariette), Vnm. Excerpts in Eitner, *Publikationen* 12.

Comment: The circumstances surrounding this performance are revealed by several sources: (1) Two letters exchanged between Cesti and

Salvator Rosa. Both letters are published by Schlitzer, "Una lettera inedita di A. Cesti," p. 93; and "Intorno alla Dori," p. 9; Cesti's letter appears in translation in Schlitzer, "A letter from Cesti to Salvator Rosa," pp. 150-52. Also it is quoted in Italian in Hill, p. 38, and again in a different translation in Schmidt, "Antonio Cesti's 'La Dori,' " p. 460. (2) A passage from Filippo Baldinucci, *Notizie*, pp. 588-89, the significance of which Schmidt points out on p. 461f. The passage is quoted in note 21. (3) The dedication of the above libretto which is signed by the Accademici Sorgenti without date. The entire dedication is printed in Schmidt, "Antonio Cesti's 'La Dori,' " p. 459, n. 15.

Despite misinterpretations, especially by Schlitzer, the conclusions to be drawn are as follows. Archduke Ferdinando of Austria, who was in Florence for the wedding festivities of Cosimo and Marguerite d'Orléans, ordered the performance by his musicians, including presumably Antonio Cesti, which was prepared in only four days. The performance took place on October 25 at the earliest (since *Orontea* was performed last on October 24) in the Cocomero theater, at that time rented by the Sorgenti as their theater.

Schmidt, p. 460, cites a scenario for an earlier performance in Innsbruck in 1657.

The *ossia* of *La Dori* is varied and confusing. Cesti in the above letter uses *La schiava fortunata* which is also another title for G.A. Moniglia's libretto, *Semiramide* (*La Schiava fortunata ossia Le risembianze di Semiramide e Nino*, Venice, 1674, with music by Cesti with alterations by Corradi and Ziani). (Allacci, col. 699) The Venetian libretto of 1663 uses *La schiava regia* or as Allacci would perversely have it, *Lo Schiavo Regio* (col. 263).

1661⁶ 6 x
Cocomero

IL POTESTÀ DI COLOGNOLE. Dramma civile rusticale. Al Serenissimo Ferd.do Carlo Arciduca d'Austria. Fiorenza, Insegna della Stella, ad istanza di Gio. Batista Rontini, s.d.
GB Lbm.

Text: Gio. Andrea Moniglia, not mentioned but see 1657¹. The dedication, signed by Rontini on date shown, says, "Faccendo io comparire alle stampe questi due scherzi drammatichi, alla protezione di V.A. devotamente gli dedico . . . " The first of the two *scherzi* must be *Orontea* (1661⁴).

Music: Jacopo Melani. See 1657¹.

Comment: The theater is identified by Moniglia in the preface to the edition in Vol. III of the *Poesie drammatiche*. One would assume that those singers in the Immobili's production would have repeated their roles, especially since *Orontea* and *Il Potestà* appear to be an exchange between the Archduke and the Medici of operas previously performed in their respective countries. The total absence in the libretto of any identification of an academic sponsor (Sorgenti, Infuocati, or Immobili) suggests that the Medici (probably Gian Carlo), and not an academy, are the sponsors.

1661⁷

LA FEDELTÀ D'ALCESTE. Dramma musicale di Girolamo Bartolommei, già Smeducci. In Firenze, Nella Stamperia di Francesco Onofri, 1661.
I Fn, Plu.

Dedication to Cosimo de' Medici signed without date by author. No mention of composer or actors. It is not possible to be certain that there ever was a performance from the dedication which says noncommitally: "...non diffido per questo, che sortendole di comparire su le Scene non potesse in qualche modo sodisfare a nobili, e virtuose Dame, godendo di rimirare dall'Inferno riscatata un tale Donna, che singolarissima nell'amore del suo Real Sposo, si rendesse perciò Gloria, e Corona del Loro nobiliss. Sesso." One hopes the good academicians of Florence recognized that the plot might be taken as offensive moralizing by the young bride of Cosimo and declined to mount it.

1662[1] 26 ii
Cocomero
Sorgenti

Commedia senza titolo del Sig. Mario Calamari cavata da D. Lopes della Viega.

Text: M. Calamari.

Comment: Five performances, ending with February 26. See Hill, p. 34.

1662[2] 29 xi -
13 xii
Cocomero
Sorgenti

LE FORTUNE DI RODOPE E DAMIRA. Dramma per musica di Aurelio Aureli dedicato alla Sereniss. Sig. la Principessa di Toscana nostra Signora. Firenze, nella Stamperia di S.A., 1662.
I Fc, Fn (destroyed).

Text: Aureli. Dedication signed on date shown by the Accademici Sorgenti.

Music: Score probably the same as Venice, 1657, that is, by P.A. Ziani, who is cited by Allacci, col. 369. Loewenberg, who does not list the Florentine libretto, does cite one for Livorno, May, 1661, with music by Ziani. Score: I Vnm.

Cast: Francesco Guerra, Girolama, Sig. [Bartolomeo?] Melani, Antonio [Rivani?], Giovanni Michele [de Bar], Maddalena [Ottonaini?] e Sig. [Bartolomeo] Mazzanti.

Comment: Five performances as follows - 29 November, 1, 7, 10, 13 December. See Hill, p. 34.

1662[3]

AMOR VUOL GIOVENTÙ. Scherzo drammatico musicale. Fiorenza, all'Insegna della Stella, 1662.
I Rn(2).

Text: Ludovico Cortesi, not mentioned, but cited in the titles of the librettos of Viterbo, 1659 (I Rca and Rvat) and Florence, 1664 below.

Music: Gio. Battista Mariani, according to the title page of the libretto of Viterbo. Scores: D MÜps; I MOe, Vnm.

(1662)[4]

Il Giasone.
Text by G.A. Cicognini, music by Francesco Cavalli. Cited by Loewenberg. Libretto not found.

1662[5]-63
Cocomero
Sorgenti

L'Erismena.

Cast: Girolama, Gabbriela di Lucca, Giovanni Michele [de Bar], Sig. [Bartolomeo] Melani, e Sig. [Bartolomeo] Mazzanti.

Comment: Repetition of 1661[3], according to Hill, p. 34. Three performances prior to the death of Gian Carlo on January 22.

1663
(Pergola)

Amor vuol inganno.

Text: G.A. Moniglia.

Music: Jacopo Melani.

Comment: According to the preface to the publication of the libretto in Moniglia's *Poesie dramatiche, parte terza*, pp. [299]-403, this opera was to be performed by the Accademici Immobili at the Pergola Theater. "Era stato messo in musica dal famoso Sig. Jacopo Melani, e n'erano di già stati distribuite le parti a li Recitanti, ma sopravenendo la sempre lagrimevol Morte di si gran Principe ne resto sospesa la Recita..." It was performed, however, in 1680[4].

Because of the confusion created by the Lady Day calendar, various dates will be found for the projected performance. Ademollo, *I primi fasti del teatro*, p. 32, and those basing their information on him (including the author's dissertation) give the date as 1662. The correct date (Fabbri, "Firenze," col. 384) is January 22, 1663, as is confirmed by Pastoso's entry, p. 85, no. 450, and by *Notizie* attributed to Pandolfini in I Fn, which are extracted from the archives of the Immobili. The comment in the *Notizie* reads: "Questa commedia benche si trovi che furono distribuite le parti, e preparato il Vestiario non credo fosse messa in Palco, perchè vedo che nel principio di Gennario 1662/63 si pensava al Vestiario, e a 22 del medesimo mese morì il Ser.mo Cardinale Gio. Carlo Protettore per il che credo che l'Opera non si proseguisse non trovando che più se ne parti."

Cast (as listed by Pandolfini without roles): Lucia Rivani, Leonora Falbetti Ballerini, Lucia Massai, Antonio Rivani, Domenico Bellucci, Paolo Rivani, Gio. Michele de Bar, Vincenzio Bonaccorsi, Carlo Righensi, Giovanni Grossi, Lorenzo Pettore, La Pollarolina, il ragazzo Cerroni.

1663 22 i

Pergola theater closed. Litigation over the property of the Cardinal and the lack of a patron among the Medici closed the theater until the wedding festivities of 1689[5] when *Il Greco in Troia* was performed. The Immobili Academy itself remained dormant until 1712.

1664

AMOR VUOL GIOVENTÙ. Scherzo drammatico musicale di Lodovico Cortesi. Fiorenze [e] Bologna, Gio: Battista Ferroni, 1664.
F Pc; I MOe.

Text: Cortesi.

Music: Giambattista Mariani. Scores: D MÜps; I MOe, Vnm. The score in I MOe is identical with the libretto.

1664 3 ix

Cosimo, Gran Principe di Toscana, became the protector of the Accademia degli Immobili. According to Morini, p. 11, the academy celebrated the event with *un trattimento musicale* in the theater in the presence of the Augusto Principe. However, Cosimo's patronage seems to have availed them little.

1665[1]
Cocomero

LE NOZZE IN SOGNO. Dramma civile rappresentato in musica nell'Accademia de' Signori Infocati dedicato al Sereniss.e Reverendiss. Principe Card.le Carlo de' Medici. Firenze, All'Insegna della Stella, 1665.

I Bc, Fn(2), MOe, Rca, Rn, Rsc, Rvat.

Text: Pietro Susini, who signs the dedication without date. This is the first recorded performance of the Infuocati. See 1652, and pp. 27-32: "La generosità de' Signori Infocati ha con si vaghi ornamenti arrichito questo mio Scherzo Drammatico, ch'egli insuperbito di quest'alta onoranza vuol comparire d'avanti a V.A.R. non tanto per una reverente espressione del suo giubilo, che per un devoto riconoscimento delle sue obligazioni. Questi Cavalieri, che l'anno con si graziosa magnificenza accolto nel lor Teatro, e quelli, che con le proprie voci l'anno reso nobilmente armonioso, si vantano d'essere i più ossequiosi ed obbligati servidori di V.A. . . . ; Onde . . . che si lusinga di più . . . che sia per compiacersi l'impareggiabil benignità dell'A.V. de fargli godere con qualche parzialità i frutti della sublime sua Protezione, . . ." Title page is shown *overleaf.*

Music: Anonymous. Score in F Pc. A page of the score is shown *overleaf.*

Comment: An entry in Weaver, "Opera," p. 69, no. 5, cites a libretto of this opera dated 1661, an error originating in a cataloguer's error at I Fn.

1665[2]
(Cocomero ?)
Sorgenti

INTERMEDIO DELLA CUCCAGNA del Sig. Pietro Susini rappresentati in musica nell'Accademia de' Sorgenti l'anno 1665. Primo intermedio che serve per prologo. Secondo Intermedio, Zerlino solo. Terzo intermedio, Bagni deliziosi. Quarto, ed ultimo, scena horrida.
I Fn (Ms. Magl. Cl. VII, B 868, f. 649-663v).

Text: Susini.

Music (lost): Composer(s) unknown.

1666 3 ii

ARTEMISIA. Drama per musica all'Illustriss. Sign. e Padron Colendiss. Il Sig. Marchese Gio: Vincenzio Salviati. Firenze, Francesco Onofri, 1666.
I Fn.

Text: Niccolo Minato, who is not mentioned. Dedication signed by Anna Caterina Venturi, probably a performer of the opera. First performance: Venice, 1656.

Music: Francesco Cavalli in the absence of any indication to the contrary. Scores: A Wn (fragments); I Vnm.

1667[1] 1 vii
Cocomero

L'EGISTO. Favola drammatica musicale di Gio. Faustini. Firenze, Stamperia di S.A.S., 1667.
F Pn; I Bc, Bu, Fn (destroyed), Rca, Rn.

Text: Faustini. Dedication to Leopoldo di Toscana signed without date by *I comici dell'Egisto*: "Comparisce di nuovo alla luce quell'opera dell'*Egisto*, che con applauso tanto segnalato illustro già le scene di questa fioritissima Patria, e sì per la perfezione di sua maravigliosa armonia, e per le riguardevoli circostanze, che l'accompagnarono riuscì sopra ogn'altro Drama famosa, . . ." The reference is to the previous performance in 1646[2].

Music: Cavalli, as seems fairly certain from the above quotation. See 1646[2].

Comment: A letter in the Vatican Archives from the papal nuncio, Lorenzo Lotti, states that the performance took place in *questo pubblico teatro.*

LE
NOZZE
IN SOGNO
DRAMMA CIVILE

Rappresentato in Musica

NELL'ACCADEMIA
DE' SIGNORI
INFOCATI
DEDICATO

AL SERENISS. E REVERENDISS.

PRINCIPE CARD.LE
CARLO
DE' MEDICI.

IN FIRENZE

All'Insegna della Stella. MDC
Con licenza de' Superiori.

Left:
I MOe LXXXIII.G.3[7].
Le nozze in sogno, 1665[1],
first libretto mentioning
the Infuocati.

Below:
F Pc Vm[4] 923.
Le nozze in sogno,
anonymous score for text
by Pietro Susini,
performed at the Cocomero, 1665[1].

This is the earliest indication that such a thing existed in Florence, that is, a theater open to the paying public. Undoubtedly the theater in question is the Cocomero since the Pergola was still closed.

1667² GLI AMANTI LADRI NOTTURNI COCCHIATA. Firenze, All'Insegna della Stella, 1667.
I Fm, Rn.
Brief (ten pages) libretto for music lacking any information about the poet, musicians, place of performance, etc. No dedication.

1668¹ 25 i LA RIVALITÀ FAVOREVOLE. Drama per musica al Sereniss. e Reverendiss. Principe Leopoldo Card. de' Medici. Firenze, nella Stamperia di S.A.S., 1668.
I Bc, Fm, Rca, Rn.

Text: Ximenes Aragona. Dedication signed on above date by Pietro Sanmartini, who Sesini says is probably the author of the text as well as the composer of the music. However, the Repertory of Granducale comedies in Fn (Magl. Cl. VIII, 40) ascribes the libretto to *Sig Cimenes* with *alcune cose del S. Siminetto.* The first name is probably an alternate spelling for Ottavio Ximenes Aragona or de Aragona, who is mentioned as the author first selected by the Accademici degli Infuocati to write the libretto for *Il Carceriere di se medesimo*, but who after his untimely death was replaced by Ludovico Adimari. Mazzuchelli, I, 928, records a *Vita del Venerabile Padre F. Benedetto da Poggibonsi* by Ximenes dedicated to Card. Carlo de' Medici published posthumously in 1689. The ascription of the music to Sanmartini does not seem justified either: he could as well be an impresario or an actor. Sesini was perhaps attempting to interpret the dedication which says, "Comparisce d'avanti al merito di V. Alt. Reverendiss. a farsi nota per mezzo delle note la Principessa Rosmira, or dir vogliamo la RIVALITÀ FAVOREVOLE, quale colla proporzione della sua esaltazione alle Porpora sacre, in breve spazio di tempo esposta su la riga d'aspirare della sua protezione . . ." See 1659².

Music (lost): Composer(s) unknown.

Roles: Idalba, Celindo, Pirro, Erasia, Evirallo.

1668²
Cocomero AMORE OPERA A CASO. Commedia [in prosa] di M[attias] M[aria] B[artolommei]. Agl'Illustriss. Signori Accademici Infocati. In Firenze, All'Insegna della Stella, 1668.
I Rn.
No prologue, finale or intermezzi for music. The undated Longhi edition of Bologna mentions the performance by the Infuocati *con non piccolo applauso.* Both editions contain a list of the works of Gia. Andrea Cicognini for the purpose of identifying false publications attributed to Cicognini.

1669¹
Cocomero SCIPIONE AFFRICANO. Dramma teatrale del Sig. Niccolo Minati, posto in musica del Sig. Fr. Cavalli l'anno 1664. e rappresentato nel Teatro di Firenze l'anno 1669. Dedicato al Ser. e Rev. Sig. Principe Card. Leopoldo di Toscana. Firenze, Stamperia di S.A.S., s.d.
I Baf, Bc, Rsc.

Text: Minati. Dedication signed without date by *I comici dello Scipione*.

Music: Cavalli. First performance in Venice, 1664. Score: I Vnm.

1669² 6 xii
(Cocomero)

L'ANTIOCO. Drama teatrale posto in musica dal Signor Francesco Cavalli e rappresentato in Firenze l'anno 1670. Dedicato al Sereniss. e Reverendiss. Sig. Principe Cardinale Leopoldo di Toscana. Firenze, Stamperia di S.A.S., s.d.
I Bc, Rn.

Text: Anonymous. Allacci, col. 95, lists three librettos by this title. The first, by Pietro Pariati, is later and not confused with this one. The second is the Florentine libretto above which he indicates is anonymous. The third is Niccolo Minato's libretto of Venice, 1658, with music by Cavalli, and repeated in Bologna, 1673, with the music of Gio. Luca Carpiani. This third is added in the second edition of Allacci. The Venetian libretto, according to Sonneck, p. 125, does not in fact bear the name of Cavalli as composer, nor does the Bologna one mention the composer (Carpiani signs the dedication but does not say anything that would indicate that he actually composed the music). The Florentine libretto, the only one to say specifically that the music was composed by Cavalli, is not the same libretto as Minato's for Bologna, 1673. The characters and the argument are identical, the scenes are similar, but the text is different. The dedication of the Florentine libretto, signed by the Comici del'Antioco on date shown, says: "Per rendere il nostro *Antioco* sempre mai glorioso vi concorse la vivacità d'un pellegrino Ingegno di questa Patria, che ne inventò l'Argomento, lo spirito d'un gentilissimo Cigno dell'Adria, che l'Opera vagamente distese, ed il valore impareggiabile del Sig. Francesco Cavalli, che con quella prodigiosa maestria, per cui s'e egli sopra ogn'altro più eccellente Professore inalzato l'ha merce di sua stupenda armonia costituito per ogni parte famoso."

Music: Francesco Cavalli, as stated.

1669³

LA SOFFERENZA VINCE LA FORTUNA. Commedia [in prosa]. Firenze e Bologna, per G. Longhi, 1669.
I Mb.

Text: Mattias Maria Bartolommei, according to Allacci, col. 727. No prologue, intermezzi, finale, or indication of incidental music. Listed by G. Martini (Ms in I Fn) under Bartolommei and by Quadrio III.II.III, p. 353.

1669⁴
Borgo Tegolaia
(Imperfetti)

GLI SPAZJ IMMAGINARJ. Prologo rappresentato in musica dagli Accademici Imperfetti a una commedia intitolata *Le stravaganze del caso*. In: *Raccolta di Opuscoli* by Giovanni Cosimo Villifranchi, p. 41. Two manuscript copies in I Fn: Magl. Cl. VII, 868, ff. 668-72 and Cl. VII, 187, f. 20. The latter is a collection of prologues by Villifranchi. Concerning the above it says: "Prologo recitato in Firenze l'anno 1669 in Borgo Tegolaia dove si fingono gli spazzi immaginari in Scena tutta bianca et in mezzo il globo del mondo a proporzione che vi possa stare un Personaggio nascosti rappresentante la Commedia. Composizione del S.D. Gio. Cosimo Villifranchi." The prose comedy is also by Villifranchi published in Bologna by Longhi without date with the title, ARMANDA, ovvero LE STRAVAGANZE DEL CASO. Allacci, col. 111.

1670[1] 20 i   IL GIRELLO. Drama musicale burlesco del Signor N.N. da rappresentarsi in Firenze l'anno 1670. Con la musica del Sig. Jacopo Melani raro ingegno del nostro secolo. Dedicato a gl'illustrissimi Signori Domenico Caccini e Niccolo Strozzi. Firenze, Stamperia di S.A.S., s.d.
I Bc.

Text: By Filippo Acciajuoli, who uses the pseudonym in the first libretto of Rome, 1668. Dedication, signed on above date by *I comici del Girello*, comments: "Non mancava al pregio del presente Drama burlesco del Girello, dopo aver riportati gli applausi maggiori ne' più famosi Teatri d'Italia, che d'incontrare l'approvazione dalla squisitezza degl'Ingegni Toscani. E con ragione la spera, mentre non solo alla bizarra vivacità della spiritosa Poesia ben si conosce per parto d'uno de' più graziosi Cigni dell'Arno; ma riceve pure dall'aggiustatezza di Toscano Maestro l'ornamento più soave dell' Armonia . . ." See Weaver, "Il Girello."

Music: Melani. Scores: **GB** Lbm; **I** MOe, Nc. Rvat; **P** La (Act I only); **US** Wc. Prologue by Alessandro Stradella.

I Fn II.I.290. Autograph score of *Enea in Italia* by Jacopo Melani (text by Giovanni Andrea Moniglia) performed in Pisa, 1670. The score is the only known autograph of the composer.

1670² 30 iv   LA DORI ovvero LA SCHIAVA FEDELE. Drama musicale dedicato alla Serenissima Margherita Luisa Principessa di Toscana. Firenze, nella Stamperia di S.A.S., 1670.
I MOe (2).

Text: G.A. or G.F. Apolloni, who is not mentioned. See 1661⁵. Dedication signed on above date by Elena Passarelli, who is probably the singer who performed the role of Dori since she pleads for the protection of Margherita Luisa on the grounds that the Queen was accompanied only by "la povertà de' miei talenti."

Music: Antonio Cesti. See 1661⁵.

(1670)³
Cocomero   *Nicomede.*
Fabbri, "Firenze," col. 382: ". . . nel 1670 al cospetto del card. de' Medici fu recitata dagli stessi accad. [degli Infuocati] la comm. *Nicomede*." No libretto found nor reference in diaries. See 1700⁵.

(1670)⁴   *Semiramide.* Firenze e Venezia, 1670.
Text by Moniglia. Music by Antonio Cesti. Cited by Quadrio III.IV.IV, 472. Doubtful since neither the Venetian libretto for 1670 nor the reprint in Moniglia's *Poesie dramatiche* of *Semiramide* speaks of the Florentine edition or performance.

1670 23 v   Death of Ferdinando II, Grand Duke of Tuscany. The preceding entries, if genuine, would of necessity have preceded Ferdinando's death since all theaters were closed afterwards for a year of mourning.

1671 3, 8 ix
Poggio Imperiale
and Pal. Pitti   Commedie in musica.
Pastoso, p. 131, no. 715: "Domenico a dì 30 Agosto 1671, entrò in Firenze il Duca Ferdinando di Mantova, e la Duchessa sua Madre . . . " [No. 716] "Martedi Pr.mo di Sett.re 1671 si fece la med.ma giostra detto sopra al cap. 712 nella Piazza, e Teatro di S. Maria Novella per trattenere e festeggiare i sudetti Principi . . . Il terzo giorno . . . la sera fù condotto al Poggio Imperiale a vedere una commedia in musica . . . Martedi 8 detto . . . la sera fu recitata una commedia in musica in Palazzo [Pitti] ." Capponi 273, p. 121, duplicates Pastoso.

1672¹ 25 i
Cocomero
Adamisti   L'INCOSTANZA DEL FATO. Drama musicale rappresentato nel Teatro di Firenze l'anno 1672. Consacrato all'Illustriss. Sig., e Pad. Colend. Il Sig. Marchese Mattias Maria Bartolommei. Firenze, Vangelisti, e Matini. s. d.
I Fc, Fn, Lg, Rn; US CA.

Text: Anonymous. Baron Francesco Maria del Nero, Conte Orlando del Benino, and Carlo Taddei are designated "Protettori del drama."
Dedication signed by *gli Accademici Adamisti* on above date. "Il Drama dell' *Incostanza del Fato* che tra'canori Cigni dell'Arno nel famoso Teatro di Flora è prossimamente per campeggiare . . . " Fabbri, "Firenze," col. 381, locates the performance at the Accademia degli Rinvigoriti for unknown reasons.

Music (lost): Composer unknown.

Roles: Pirro, Andromaca, Oreste, Ermiona, Pilade, Atreo, Batillo, Climante, Cleonilda, Erindo, Clitone, Orcane.

1672²
Imperfetti

Prologo. Rappresentato in musica in Firenze l'anno MDCLXXII dagli Accademici Imperfetti.
Published in the *Raccolta di Opuscoli* of G.C. Villifranchi, p. 3, *Descrizione* and text. Prologue performed with *Le cautele politiche*, of which no Florentine publication has been found. However, the prose comedy intended is probably G.B. Ricciardi's *Chi non sa fingere non sa vivere overo le cautele politiche* published by Longhi in Bologna without date. No composer mentioned.

1673¹
Casino

Lo Spedale. Prologo (e finale) alla Commedia intitolata *Ove forza non vale giova l'ingegno*.
From Villifranchi's *Raccolta di Opuscoli*, p. 67. On page 69 further information is added: "Rappresentato in Musica in Firenze l'an. MDCLXXIII. dagli Accademici del Casino." The prefatory *Vita* adds, p. xvi: "Ma sopra tutti questi [prologhi] famoso è la Spedale per la Commedia del March. Bartolommei da appellarsi veracemente la Vlasta, ma detta comunemente l'Ulasta, ovvero Ove forza non val, giova l'ingegno . . ." The popularity of the prologue is reflected in the existence of six manuscripts of it, all in I Fn (Magl. Cl. VII, nos. 187[3], 868, and 934, and Landau-Finaly 261).

1673²
Borgo Tegolaia
Rinvigoriti

Commedia rapp[resenta]ta dalli Accademici Rinvigoriti in Borgo Tegolaia. Diario in I Fn (Magl. Cl. VII, 757). In 1669⁴ the Imperfetti performed in this theater.

1674 7 i
Cocomero

TACERE ET AMARE. Dramma civile musicale rappresentato nell'Accademia degli Infuocati. Al Ser. Gran Duca di Toscana. In Firenze, Vangelisti e Matini, 1674.
B Bc; I Bc, Fn (destroyed), Mb.

Text: G.A. Moniglia, not mentioned, but he reprints the libretto in the *Parte Terza* of his *Poesie*, p. 380. Dedication signed January 7, 1673 [*ab inc.*] by the Accademici Infuocati. The *Prefazione* in the *Poesie*, p. 379, states: "Fù il presente Drama rappresentato nel Teatro di Via del Cocomero da' SS. Accademici Infuocati, e l'adornarono così gentilmente di Scene, d'Abiti, di Musica, di cui fù il compositore il Sig. Jacopo Melani, e di Balli, e d'Abbatimento, che riportolo universale applauso nelle molte, e molte replicate Recite, che se ne fecero, e tanto ne' Balli, che nell' Abbattimento tutti quegli, che operarono, furono Cavalieri Accademici."

Music (lost): Melani.

1676¹ 6 ii
Tintori
Imperfetti

La cortesia fra rivali. Commedia in prosa.
Text: Pietro Susini. Published in 1691⁶.
Comment: Fagiuoli: "A dì 6 [Febbraio, 1675 (*ab inc.*)]. Nell'Accad.a degli Imperfetti nuovamente eretta nel corso de' Tintori si fece un Op.a di Pier Susini intitolata *La cortesia fra rivali* ed io per la prima volta vi recitai facendo la parte di un paggio detto Rusteno, la quale parte era di poche parole, e non concludeva niente: onde ne riportai grand applauso."

The entry is the earliest account of the theater in the corso de' Tintori subsequently used by Accademici Cadenti.

1676² 7 ii?   *La Giocasta, regina d'Armenia.* Firenze, 1676.

Text: G.A. Moniglia, cited by Quadrio III.IV.IV.472. Published in the *Poesie, seconda Parte*, pp. 81-148, wherein the *Argomento* states: "Questo componimento fu chiesto dal Sig. cavaliere Antonio Cesti al serenissimo principe Mattias di Toscana, e l'A.S. mostrò all'autore desiderio di gratificare il Sig. cavaliere Cesti, laonde ne venne servita; ma partendosi poi il Sig. cavaliere dal servizio di S.M.C. e trattenendosi in Firenze alla corte di Toscana, si smarrì l'occasione di farlo comparire sù le scene, la quale (mancando la vita del Sig. Cesti) non s'è mai ritrovata, riserbataseglì non di meno tra le sue disavventure la gran fortuna di comparire presentemente alle stampe . . . "

The statement should be understood as referring directly only to Moniglia's original libretto, and under the term *misadventures* may lurk more than one unapproved revision. Certainly he is referring to the version "riformato al'uso di Venetia" which was published in Venice in 1677 and performed with music of Carlo Grossi (Sonneck, 559). He may also be referring to Quadrio's lost libretto. Circumstantial evidence that there was a Florentine performance is contained in a manuscript in I Fas (Med. F. 6424/6) of a *Prologo* (personaggi: Aria, Eolo e Garbinello) and *Licenza* by Pier Susini, both for music and containing references to *Giocasta* and to the celebration of the birthday of Vittoria della Rovere, Granduchessa di Toscana, whose birthday falls on February 7. The topical nature of the prologue and the absence of any reference to Mattias de' Medici indicate a performance subsequent to the original libretto described by Moniglia. However, an unresolved question is why a topical prologue was performed (i.e. 1676) so long after it had to have been written; for Susini, on the authority of Quadrio, III.IV.IV. p. 461, died in 1668. Quadrio's date is possibly an error (read 1686?). See 1678[1] and 1679[3] for activity after 1668.

1677 9 ii   AMORE E POLITICA. Tragicomedia dell Em.mo Sig.r Dottore Gio: Cosimo
Tintori   Villifranchi Volteranno.
Imperfetti   I Sc (Ms. G x1.70).

Text: Villifranchi. Manuscript with the appearance of an autographic draft, partly in prose, partly in poetry with ariette and duets. Although the ends of the acts are always poetic, the remainder shows no pattern of regular alternation.

Music (lost): Composer(s) unknown.

Comment: Fagiuoli records the performance on February 9, 1676 [*ab inc.*]: "Nell'accademia degl'Imperfetti si fece una Tragicomedia del Dr. Gio. Cosimo Villifranchi Med.co di Volterra, intitolata *Amore e Politica*, la quale ebbe gran'applauso per aver una bizzarra e nuova Opera, e benissimo recitata." See also Fagiuoli's comments concerning a second performance in 1700[4].

1678[1] 10 ii   PROLOGO. Si finge un poeta, che componga e sopraggiungi Pasquino.
Tintori   I Fn (Ms. Magl. Cl. VII, B 868, f. 643).
Imperfetti

Text: Pietro Susini. References to the play cite *L'onore impegnato per la conservazione del regno*, of which no publication has been located.

Comment: Fagiuoli records on February 10, 1677 [*ab inc.*]: "Nell' Accademia degl'Imperfetti si fece un opera del Susini intitolata *L'Onore impegnato per la conservazione del Regno* alla quale io recitai la parte di Silverio, che era di pochi parole, ed essendo [recitate] fieramente, ne anche quelle furon sentite; era la solita parte di Paggino."

1678[2]

Casino

LA REGINA FLORIDEA. Drama musicale che si rappresentata dalla Conversazione del Casino di S. Marco. Dedicato al Serenissima Principe Francesco Maria di Toscana Protettore. Firenze, il Vangelisti, e Matini, MDCLXXVIII.
I Fc.

Text: Quadrio, III.IV.IV.478, says: "L'Autore . . . come parisce dalla Lettera a Leggitori, fù Pietro Manni. Ristampata e recitato in Milano circa il 1684, e poi in Venezia nel 1687 con qualche Reforma fattagli da Giulio Pancieri." The *Lettera* to which he refers is not in the Florentine libretto. Nor does it appear in a libretto entitled simply FLORIDEA (Nicolini, Venice, 1688, but dedication signed November 22, 1687), listed by Sonneck, p. 520, which may or may not be the same libretto cited by Allacci for Venice, Niccolini, 1687. Pancieri himself is Milanese (Allacci, col. 364), so one must assume that Quadrio's information derives from the Milanese libretto which has not been located. If so, Quadrio's statement about the music given below must be considered doubtful until better evidence is found.

Music: According to Quadrio III.IV.IV.511, the music was composed by Francesco Rossi, Lodovico Busca, and Pier Simeone Agostini. Since Rossi was, as Quadrio says, the organist at S. Celso in Milan, it seems likely that the three composers' music was used in the Milan performance only, and it may not be presumed that the same music was used in Florence, as does Fabbri, "Firenze," col. 381.

Comment: The dedication of the Florentine libretto indicates that this is the first effort by a newly reorganized *conversazione* under the patronage of Card. Francesco Maria de' Medici: "Siccome nella perdita della Gloriosa Memoria del Serenissimo Card. Leopoldo di Toscana [d. 20 November, 1675], da estremo occupati, non ardimmo per molto tempo di far sentir sù le scene nè la grave Melpomene, ni la scherzosa Talia; le quali per lo spazio di trent'anni sotto l'autorevol Patrocinio di tanto principe, quando col titolo di Affinati, e quando con altro nome si erano a noi rese familiari, ed amiche; così ora all'incontro nell'acquisto della felicissima Protezione, che V.A.S. si è denignamente degnata concederci, da somma letizia assaliti, prendiamo sicurezza di richiamar le Muse più gioconde, e più care. Queste avendo veduto Floridea Dama straniera così generosamente onorata da V.A.S. co' suoi liberalissimi doni abbiamo speranza, che vogliano col tempo condurre in Abito pellegrino altre Dame, le quali riconoscendo l'origine da Fiorenza, possano esser più gradite all'A.V., alla di cui Real Presenza se ne viene in tanto l'istessa Floridea, più lieta, e fastosa in vedersi da Lei protetta, che d'esser fatta Spose. . . ." signed by the Conversazione del Casino.

The *Affinati* left little trace (see 1658[2]). The passage implies that the Conversazione del Casino was the successor to the Accademia degli Affinati. The Casino is recorded in 1673[1].

The reference to "altre dame" implies that the opera for the next year, *Adalinda*, had already been chosen.

1679[1]
Casino

ADALINDA. Favola dramatica a gl'Illustrissimi SS. dalla Conversazione del Casino da San Marco. Firenze, Vangelisti e Matini, 1679.
I Fc, Fn, Mb, MOe, PAc.

Text: Anonymous. The dedication, signed by Vangelisti and Matini, chides the academicians for being slow about ordering the libretto. The libretto is identical with one published in Milano, 1679. Title page is shown on the *right*.

Music: Probably by P.S. Agostino. Scores in I MOe and Rvat. The libretto of Milano, 1679, does not vary in its text from the score in I MOe, whence it is fairly safe to assume that the Florentine score is also by Agostino.

1679[2] ix?
Pratolino

CON LA FORZA D'AMOR SI VINCE AMORE. Componimento drammatico rusticale rappresentato in musica nella Villa di Pratolino. Firenze, Vincenzio Vangelisti, 1679.
I Fm, Fn, MOe, Rn.

Text: Giovanni [Filippo] Appolloni, as announced in the *A chi legge*, which also mentions the addition of a fourth part to the original three and some verses because of the brevity of the original. Title page is shown on the *right*.

Music: Buonaventura Cerri. On pp. 35f. of a Ms. in I Fn (Magl. Cl. VIII, 74), a two-page miscellany of *Notizie* about the life of Ferdinando, the author, A.F. Marmi, says of this opera, "L'autore del Dramma non si sa, ma la musica fù del Buonaventura Cerri."

Cast: The copy in I Fn lists the performers in handwriting: Nise Ninfa - Sr. Giuseppe Petrilli; Filli Ninfa - S. Bellieri; Silvio Pastore - D. Filippo Melani; Coridone Bifolco - Fusai.

Comment: This is the first of the series of operas performed at Pratolino by Principe Ferdinando de'Medici.

1679[3]
Sorgenti

DONNA SAGGIA PUÒ CIÒ CHE VUOLE. Commedia rappresentata da gli Accademici Sorgenti nel loro nuovo Teatro. Firenze, Vangelisti Stampatore Arcivescovale, 1679.
I Fn, Rca, Rn.

Text: Martini identifies the author as Pietro Susini, a fact unknown to Allacci (who cites an edition of Bologna, 1694), and to bibliographers in general. The text is prose; however, the prologue (*personaggi*: Ostinazione and Cavaliero peregrino) which is also presumably by Susini, is poetic and clearly intended for music. See 1694[2].

Music (lost): Composer(s) unknown.

Comment: The *A chi legge* reveals that, at least with regard to prose comedies, it is not the habit of the academies to publish the text; "Essendosi persuasi gli Accademici Sorgenti, che questo Componimento possa anche sotto l'occhio esser gradito, non meno di quello ch'è stato sopra la Scena, hanno voluto ch'io l'esponga con la stampa al guardo universale . . . "

Quadro VII (*Indice Universale*), p. 10, states that the Sorgenti had a

LE GARE
DELL' AMORE,
E DELL' AMICIZIA
COMMEDIA
DI LODOVICO ADIMARI

Recitata da' Caualieri della Conuerſazione di Borgo Tegolaia, e dall' Autore conſagrata.

ALL' ALTEZZA SER.
DEL PRINCIPE
D.FRANC.MARIA
DI TOSCANA.

IN FIRENZE

Alla Condotta. MDCLXXIX.
Con licenza de' Superiori.

I Fn 21.N.7.118.
Le gare dell'Amore, e dell'Amicizia, 1679[4],
comedy in prose
with prologue and finale in music.
First mention of
the theater di Borgo Tegolaio.

theater in the Piazza del Grano and afterwards in via dell'Anguillara, and finally behind S. Remigio until 1752. The location of this "new theater" is probably the Piazza del Grano. See p. 87.

1679⁴
Borgo
Tegolaia
(Imperfetti?)

LE GARE DELL'AMORE, E DELL'AMICIZIA. Commedia di Lodovico Adimari. Recitata da Cavalieri della Conversazione di Borgo Tegolaia e dall'Autore consagrato all'Alt. Ser. del Principe Franc. Maria di Toscana. Firenze, Condotta, 1679.
I Bca, Fn(2), Rn, Vgc.

Text: This first work by Adimari is in prose but with a prologue and finale in music. Dedication signed without date by Lodovico Adimari. *"Alle Dame della Conversazione*: Il più degno, e singolar motivo, che già prendessero i Cavalieri della nostra solita conversazione, di ragunarsi ne' giorni di Carnevale, e di quando, in quando, recitar privatamente qualche Commedia all'improviso, fù il solo desidero di render cosa grata a voi tutte, generosissime Dame, alle quale per debito, per volontà; e per congiunzione di sangue, si pregiano, e si pregieranno mai sempre, dover servire. Per l'istesso effetto presi io non meno a trasportare in volgar Toscano la presente Commedia, già scritta da famoso Compositore assai gentilmente nella Castigliana favella. Et in me potè tanto la giusta estimazione del vostro merito, che bramoso di portanerevene ad ogni mio rischio alcuna indubitabil prova, mi resolvei prontamente all' impresa; . . ." *A'Cavalieri* speaks of especial debt owed to Jacopo del Borgo, an academician who played the part of the ridiculous servant. A ballo closes the opera. Title page is shown on the *left*.

Music (lost): Composer(s) unknown.

1680¹ 26 ii
Casa Calamari

Con la moglie e con l'amico ci vuol flemma.
Fagiuoli 26 Febbr. 1679 [*ab inc.*] : "In casa del S.r Mario Calamari si recitò una commedia intitolata *Con la moglie* [*etc.*] , và fuori stampata sotto nome del Cicognini, ma è veram.te del S.r Av.to Cristofan Berardi: ed io vi recitai, e feci la parte del servo ridicolo, e fù la prima volta ch'io m'esponessi a q.ta parte; feci anche la parte di Florante altro servo, e in ultimo ballai ad un ballo di Pulcinelli, che ci fece Mesino Ballarino." Listed by Martini among prose comedies. Not in Allacci.

1680² aut
Pratolino

IL CORINDO. Favola boschereccia rappresentata in musica nella villa di Pratolino. Firenze, V. Vangelisti, 1680.
I Bc, Bu, Fc, Fn, Mb, MOe, Rn; US BE, Wc.

Text: Giuseppe Giacomini, according to Salvioli, p. 888.

Music (lost): Composer(s) unknown.

1680³ 1 x
Casino

SIDONIO overo IL RARO ESEMPIO DI COSTANZA E FEDE. Drama per musica dedicato dagli Accademici del Casino al Serenissimo Principe Franc. Maria di Toscana Protettore. Firenze, V. Vangelisti, s.d.
I Bc, Fm(2), Fn, MOe, Rca, Rn.

Text: Ab. Giuseppe Giacomini who is not mentioned, but according to catalogues of I Bc, I Rn, and Fabbri, "Firenze." The dedication sets down the ambition of the academicians to present new works, an idea which is seemingly accredited to the Principe: "Non tanto per manifestar quel pensiero, che nel punto istesso, che dalla Generosità di V.A.S. restammo assicurati del di Lei Benignissimo Patrocinio, concepimmo dentro noi medesimi rappresentare in questo Real Teatro, con apparato di nuove Scene, alcun'opera, che sotto Auspicj sì fortunati sortisse i suoi natali in Firenze; quanto per non mancare a quell'obbligo, che poi contraemmo con la Medesima A.V. nel dedicarle la Regina Floridea, di voler porre a esecuzione così giusto proponimento; abbiam preso ardire di comparire umilmente davanti V.A.S. con questo Drama . . ." It continues with a denial that there is any similarity to *Sidonio* of Francesco Melosio [Venice, 1642] except the title and the plot. Date supplied by dedication.

Music (lost): Composer(s) unknown.

1680⁴
Casa Corsini

La vedova, ovvero *Amor vuol inganno.*

Text: G.A. Moniglia. No libretto found for the performance of 1680. The information concerning it is found in the preface to the libretto published in Moniglia's *Poesie, parte terza*, p. 277: "Fù questo Drama composto dall'Autore per comandamento del Sereniss. e Reverendiss. Principe Cardinale Gio: Carlo di Toscana, per doversi rappresentare nel solito Teatro de' SS. Accademici Immobili sotto la Protezione della medesima Altezza Rever. e già era stato messo in Musica dal famoso Sig. Jacopo Melani e n'erano di già distribuite le parti a i Recitanti; ma sopravenendo la sempre lagrimevol Morte di sì gran Principe ne restò sospese la Recita; la quale dopo molti anni da una fiorita Conversazione di nobilissimi Cavalieri fù richiamata sù le scene l'anno 1680. nel Giardino del Sig. March. Bartolomeo Corsini vicino alla Porta al Prato con quella solennità maggiore, che può esser propria di tal componimento, e del Genio grande così ragguardevoli Cavalieri, con una scelta di Musici rappresentanti così rara, e perfetta, che non invidiò alcuna altra, che mai si fusse udita sopra i più rinomati Teatri; onde non recò ad alcuno maraviglia, se con applauso Universale venne sommamente gradito questo piacevole, e giocoso Componimento."

Music (lost): Jacopo Melani.

Roles: Marchionne, Frasia, Leonora, Isabella, Leandro, Flavio, Ligurino, Desso Geva, Moro, Tedesco, Franzese, Spagnuolo, tre contadinelle, Oste.

1680⁵

LA DANAE. Melodramma di Francesco Alfonso Donnoli Gentiluomo Montalcinese. All'Altezza Serenissima di Francesco Maria de' Medici Principe di Toscana. S.l., s.t., s.d.
I Bc, Fn, Mb, Rca.

Text: Donnoli. Extract (pp. 267-334) from a larger publication which has not been identified. Allacci lists this as a separate libretto. Dedication is dated Conegliano, December 1, 1680: "Più volte pensai, se deverò condurli in Teatro! Ma finalmente non hò ravvisati più bel teatro per loro, che lo sguardo Serenissimo dell'Altezza Vostra, giudicandomi a maggior gloria l'applauso d'un Gabinetto d'un Prencipe . . . che le voci d'un intiero popolo . . ." Hence the libretto is not published for a performance. It is not known whether it was ever set to music.

1680[6]   IL GIUGURTA. Melodramma di Francesco Alfonso Donnoli Gentiluomo Montalcinese. All'Altezza Serenissima di Francesco Maria de' Medici Prencipe Toscana. s.l., s.t., s.d. Extract following *La Danae* in unidentified publication.

    Lacks dedication, but preceding comments apply equally.

(1680)[7]   *Il Giasone.*
Text by Cicognini, music by Cavalli. Cited by Loewenberg (ed. 1955). No libretto found. Unknown to Bianconi. Probably an error.

1681[1] 24 i   IL CARCERIERE DI SE MEDESIMO. Drama per musica di L.A. rappresentato
Cocomero   nell'Accademia degl'Infuocati. Al Sereniss. Prencipe Francesco Maria di Toscana. Firenze, Vangelisti, 1681.
B Bc; I Bc, Fn(2), MOe, Mb, Rca, Rn; US Wc.

    Text: Ludovico Adimari, who signs the Dedication on above date, and comments therein: "Le medesime cagioni, che mi obbligarono a consacrare all'A.V.S. la mia prima Commedia [*Le gare dell'amore e dell'amicizia*, see 1679[4]] mi rendono di presente ardito ad offerirle questa seconda; la quale oltre a modo avventurosa riputar si deve, se dopo i molti applausi ricevuti ne i Teatri della Francia, dove già nacque, potrà vantarsi di comparir sù le nostre Scene in gran parte rabbellita da gli ornamenti del parlar Toscano ..." On page 5 he addresses the Accademici Infocati: "[L'ho composto] nello spazio brevissimo di ventitre giorni da principio a fine interamente condotto. So che molti de i Signori Accademici avrebbono con maggiore aspettazione ricevuta quest'opra dalla penna del Sig. Ottavio Ximenes Aragona, a cui l'avevano destinato; ma se egli sovrapreso da immatura morte, non pote terminarla. ed io nell'istesso carico, sono a lui succeduto, creder che dalla prudenza, e cortesia loro sarà la mia inabilità sostenuta, almeno, per non detrarre all'interezza del lor giudicio, che forse nella mia elezzione aver potrebbe troppo animosamente deliberato ... come per la squisitezza della musica, in ogni parte uguale al grido del Sig. [Alessandro] Melani, che l'ha composta."

    Music: Alessandro Melani. Scores: B Bc; F Pn; I Bc. Some of the score shown on *pages 152* and *153.*

1681[2] aut   ROSALBA. Drama rappresentato in musica nella villa di Pratolino. Firenze,
Pratolino   Vincenzio Vangelisti, MDCLXXXI.
I Bc, Fc, Fm, Fn (lost), MOe, Mb, Rn, Vgc.

    Text: Giuseppe Giacomini, who is not mentioned. The origin of the attribution has not been traced. It occurs in catalogues of I Fn and Rn.

    Music (lost): Composer(s) unknown.

    Roles: Rosalba, D. Felice, D. Alfonso, Irene, Alcaste.

1681[3] 12 xi   QUINTO LUCREZIO PROSCRITTO. Dramma musicale fatto rappresentare
Casino   de' Signori Accademici del Casino per festeggiare il giorno natalizio del Sereniss. Prencipe Francesco Maria di Toscana. Firenze, Vincenzio Vangelisti, 1681.
I Bc, Fc, Fm, Fn(2), Rca, Rn; US Wc.

Text: G.A. Moniglia, who is not mentioned. Dedication signed by the academicians on above date, the birthday of the prince. Reprinted in Moniglia's *Poesie, Parte prima*, p. 503.

Music (lost): Lorenzo Cattani who is mentioned in the *A chi legge*.

1682[1] 12 xi
Casino

IL CONTE DI CUTRO. Dramma civile fatto rappresentare da'Signori Accademici del Casino per festeggiare il giorno natalizio del Sereniss. Principe Francesco Maria di Toscana. Firenze, Vincenzio Vangelisti, 1682.
B Bc; I Bc, Fn, Rca, Rsc, Vgc.

Text: G.A. Moniglia. Dedication signed by the Accademici del Casino as shown. The libretto is also reprinted in the *Poesie, Parte terza*, p. 503.

Music (lost): Lorenzo Cattani. The copy in B Bc has a publisher's insert naming the composer, who is also named in Moniglia's *Poesie*.

1682[2]
Stanza
de'Rifritti

Prologo per musica per *La pazzia d'Orlando*.
Text by Giov. Battista Fagiuoli, published in the author's *Rime* V, pp. 252-58, where the year and location are given. The principal drama is probably by Prospero Bonarelli whose text will be found in his *Melodrammi*. Bonarelli's drama is also cited in a publication of Venice, 1635, by Allacci, col. 611. Since the work is specifically a melodrama, it was probably performed with music. However, since the only reference

Right and far right:
I MOe F. 730.
Il carceriere di se medesimo, 1681[1],
text by Ludovico Adimari,
music by Alessandro Melani,
performed by the
Accademia degl'Infuocati.

to the performance itself is in the title of the publication of Fagiuoli's prologue, the entry has been restricted to the prologue rather than the melodrama.

1683[1] 10 ii
Vangelista

La Mariene del [Giacinto Andrea] Cicognini (in prose). Fagiuoli, 10 Febbr. 1682 [*ab inc.*] : "Nella Compagnia del Vangelista a dì 10 Mercoledi si recitò una commedia del Cicognini intitolata la *Mariene*, ove io recita la parte di Friuvello servo ridicolo: ci assiste il S.r Mario Calamari Guard[iano] di detta Compagnia. È uomo peritissimo nella comica, e famoso compositore di comedie."

Allacci, col. 504, cites *Marienne, ovvero, Il Maggior Mostro del Mondo* (Perugia, Zecchini, 1656), Opera tragica (in prosa) by Giacinto Andrea Cicognini. It is, however, omitted among the works listed by Bruno Brunelli, "Giacinto Andrea Cicognini," though listed by Bartolommei (see 1668[2]).

1683[2] 24 ii

Il trionfo de'Brutti. Mascherata.
Brief description is found in Pastoso, f. 235, no. 947, on above date: "Fù fatta una bellissima mascherata del Ser.mo Pr.pe Fran.co Maria de Medici oggi cardinale. L'Invenzione fù *il Trionfo de' Brutti*, et era disposta in questo modo. Vedevasi sopra un superbiss.o carro nel più sublime luogo una bruttissima vecchia, la quale teneva a suoi piedi incatenata una bellissima Giovane; rappresentava la Vecchia, la Bruttezza,

e la Giovane, la Bellezza; tutto il resto del carro era pieno di musici, con
abiti bizzarri, ma con bruttissime maschere. Precedeva il Carro una copiosa
cavalcata di maschere, le quali similmente erano adottate di bizzarri e
curiosi abiti, adattati à diversi stati, gradi, e professioni, sì d'huomini, come
di donne, le quali tutte havevano bruttissime masche, le quale essendo fatte
à posta dal Foggini e Marcellini bravi scultori, al naturale rappresentavano i
più brutti mostacci della Città, che molto bene si riconoscevano. Era il
carro tirato da 12 bellissimi Destrieri, e per le strade della Città più conspicue,
al suono di diversi strumenti da fiato, si condusse su la Piazza di S. Croce
dove fermatosi nel mezzo di essa, dinanzi al Palco de'A.A. SS. fecero diverse
Sinfonie, dispensando gran quantità di Cartelli fatti da migliori Poeti della
Città in Lode della bruttezza e poi usciti girono più volti attorno li steccanati
col medesimo ordine la qual Mascherata piacque universalmente à tutto la
Città." Bonazzini, p. 329, and Susier are quite similar.

1683³ aut
Pratolino

LO SPEZIALE DI VILLA. Drama rappresentato in musica nella Villa di
Pratolino. Firenze, Vincenzio Vangelisti, 1683.
B Bc; I Fc, Fm, Fn, PAc.

Text: Giovanni Cosimo Villifranchi, who is not named. See Maffei,
pp. 27-47, for most authoritative source for attribution. See also 1704⁴.

Music (lost): Composer(s) unknown.

1683⁴
Cocomero

L'AMANTE DI SUA FIGLIA ovvero LA GENEROSITÀ ROMANE [sic] IN AMORE
SOTTO QUINTO FABIO MASSIMO. Drama di Ludovico Adimari, rappresentato
nell'Accademia degl'Infuocati. All'Altezza Serenissima di Cosimo III Gran
Duca di Toscana. Firenze, Vangelisti, s. d.
B Bc; I Bc, Fn, MOe, Rn, Vgc.

Text: Dedication signed by Adimari without date. The date of the libretto
is taken from the *Dizionario letterario Bompiani* (Firenze, 1956), I, 13.
The *Al lettore* states: "Lettore gentile ti prego istantemente voler gradire
questo mio secondo Drama qualunque egli sia, senza reprendere in esso la
disposizione de i due fili totalmente disgiunti; poiche ben io saprei
addurtene molti esempi per mia discolpa, nè tu potresti recarmi avanti
alcun precetto d'autorevol Maestro, che il vieti parlando strettamente in
tal genere di componimento. Quel poco d'amarognolo, che dovresti sentire
per così fatta disgiunzione, ho cercato, giusta il poter mio, smaltirlo con
la dolcezza del disteso, e con la facilità degli accidenti; Pure se ci te pare
altrimenti, quietati per questa volta; e per testimone di tua nobil cortesia
compatisci gli errori della stampa, cominciata, e terminata nello spazio di
tre giorni soli." The first drama: 1679⁴.

Music: Composer unknown. Score: F Pc.

1684¹ carn
Centauro

LA DONNA ANCORA È FEDELE. Drama musicale che si rappresentò dalla
Conversazione dal Centauro. Dedicato all'illustriss. e clariss. Sig., Sig. e
Padron Colendiss. Il Sig. Senatore Francesco Dati. Firenze, Vincenzio
Vangelisti, 1684.
I Bc, Fm, Fn (lost).

Text: Domenico Filippo Contini, who is not mentioned. Dedication
signed without date by the Conversazione del Centauro, but the opera is

declared to be the "onesto divertimento" of the present carnival.

Music: Possibly by Bernardo Pasquini, who composed the music for the first performance in Rome, 1676. G.F. Crain, I, p. 99, speculates that the music of Pasquini was used in part or entirely for Florence. It is most unlikely that an early version of Alessandro Scarlatti's score written for Naples, 1698, was used in Florence. Pasquini's score is in I MOe; Scarlatti's in I Nc.

1684² 23 i
Sorgenti

Apollo, l'Inganno, e'l Giovane, prologo per *L'Inganno vince l'inganno*. Commedia del S.r In.te [Mattias Maria] Bartolommei.

Text of prologue: Gio. Battista Fagiuoli, published in his *Rime piacevole*, pp. 259-70. No publication of a prose drama by Bartolommei by the above title found, but it may be supposed that Allacci's entry, col. 70, for *Amore non vuol Inganni*. Trattenimento scenico (in prosa) - Bologna Longhi, 1697, del March. Mattias Bartolommei, is another of Longhi's republication of plays performed by the Sorgenti (see 1694² and 1695⁶) and, therefore, is the drama entered here.

Comment: Fagiuoli records the performance, 23 Gennaio 1683 [*ab inc.*] : "Nell'Accad[emi]a de'Sorgenti si fece una commedia del S.r In[tenden]te Bartolomei intitolata *L'Inganno vince l'Inganno* alla quale io compori il Prologo [per musica] , ed recitai alla commedia la parte del Servo ridicolo." For possible location see p. 32.

1684³ 10 ix
Pratolino

LO SPEZIALE DI VILLA. Dramma per musica rappresentato in Pratolino. Firenze, Vincenzio Vangelisti, 1684.
I Fn (lost), MOe, Vgc.

Text: G.C. Villifranchi, who is not mentioned. See 1683³. This opera was the only opera to be repeated at Pratolino.

Music (lost): Composer unknown.

Cast: The performers are written in the libretto in I MOe as follows: Domenico Graziano, Giuseppe Petrilli, Carlo Ant.o Zanardi, Giuseppe Canavesi, Ant.o Panichi.

Comment: Fagiuoli, I, 37v. "A dì 10 [Sept. 1684] Andai a Pratolino à veder l'opera in musica che si recitò nella villa del S.r Pr.pe intitolata (blank)."

1684⁴ 16 x

URANIA FATIDICA. Commedia nuova da recitarsi nel gran teatro del mondo in quest'anno MDCLXXXV. capriccio astromantipoetico di Francesco Moneti da Cortona. Dedicato all'Illustrissimo Signore, Conte, e Cavaliere Bustico Davanzati Gentilhuomo Fiorentino. Firenze, Andrea Orlandini, alla Condotta.
I Mb, MOe, Rn.

Text: Moneti. *Al curioso Lettore*: "Già che ti vedo (o Lettore mio carissimo) cotanto amico di cose nuove, mi son risoluto di darti in quest'anno un Pronostico degli accidenti del Mondo in forma diversa da quella degl anni passati col farti rappresentare da i Pianeti una Commedia . . . In questa Commedia dunque, che ti propongo in quattro Atti divisa, che sono appunto le quattro Stagioni dell'anno sentirai in ogni quarta di Luna rappresentare da tutti i setti Pianeti una Scena, nella quale con poetici concetti spiegheranno i loro significati dedotti dalla celeste figura per quel tempo eretta, havendoci io per maggior diletto inscritto molte ariette sentenziose da mettere in Musica . . ." Signed by Andrea Orlandini on date shown.

Music (lost): Composer unknown.

Comment: It is not possible to decide whether this work was actually performed or even intended to be performed. The subject, while possibly spectacular, is not dramatic, and consists primarily of verses distributed through a weather almanac.

The difference between the date of title and of the dedication is unexplained.

1684⁵
Sorgenti

Prologo in musica per *La vita è un sogno.*

Text of prologue: Gio. Battista Fagiuoli, published in the author's *Rime piacevole*, V, pp. 270-76. The principal drama is probably the prose comedy by Giacinto Andrea Cicognini listed by Allacci, col. 822, in a Venetian publication of 1664. The *Rime* give the date and theater.

Music (lost): Composer unknown.

1685¹ carn
Centauro

L'IDALMA overo CHI LA DURA LA VINCE. Drama musicale che si rapresenta [*sic*] dalla Conversazione dal Centauro. Dedicato all'Illustriss. e Clariss. Sig., Sig. e Padron Colendiss. Il Sig. Senatore Francesco Dati. Firenze, Pietro Matini, s. d.
I Fn, Mb, Rn.

Text: G.D. de Totis, first performed with music by Bernardo Pasquini in Rome, 1680 (see Crain, I, pp. 122ff. and II, pp. 84ff.).

Music: Probably Pasquini. Score: F Pn.

Comment: The year is deduced from a comment in the dedication, signed by the Conversazione del Centauro: "Il vantaggio, che ha provato la nostra Conversazione nel dedicare a V.S. Illustriss. e Clariss. il Drama fatto recitare dalla medesima nell'anno trascorso, può scusare il nostro ardimento nel ricorrere di nuovo alla sua assistenze . . ." See 1684¹.

1685² 14 viii
Pal. Pitti

Il pellegrino.

Text: G.A. Moniglia. Original libretto not found (if published) but it was published in the *Poesie drammatiche, parte seconda*, p. [259]-323, with the title: *Il pellegrino.* Drama musicale rappresentato nelle camere della Serenissima Granduchessa Vittoria per solennizzare il giorno natalizio del Serenissimo Cosimo Terzo Granduca di Toscana. The prefatory note describes the work as a "piccolo componimento dramatico ristretto in due soli personaggi" performed by "due fanciulle di camera della serenissima granduchessa."

Music: Lorenzo Cattani, as stated in the *Poesie.*

Comment: The *Poesie* provides the year, and Cosimo's birthday is added.

1685³ aut
Pratolino

IFIANASSA E MELAMPO. Drama musicale rappresentato nella Villa di Pratolino. Firenze, Vincenzio Vangelisti, 1685.
B Bc; I Bc, Fm, Fn, Rn.

Text: G.A. Moniglia, not mentioned here, but the libretto is reprinted in the *Poesie, parte prima*, pp. 379-433. Argument traces story to Pausanius.

Music (lost): Giovanni Legrenzi as stated in the preface in the *Poesie*. First performance of music and libretto.

Cast: Francesco de Castris and Niccola Paris were engaged by Ferdinando. Gio. Domenico Graziani and Bastianino del Fusai, a student or child of Ippolito Fusai, are mentioned in other letters and possibly sang at Pratolino.

1685⁴

CALIGULA DELIRANTE. Melodrama per musica. Firenze, Vincenzio Vangelisti, 1685.
I Bc, Fc(2), MOe.

Text: Anonymous in all previous libretti as well as this one.

Music (arias): Gio: Maria Pagliardi, as stated in the above libretto on page 4. Pagliardi's score was used in Venice in 1672 and again in 1680 and probably in Rome and elsewhere (see Wotquenne, p. 35). A collection of arias in I Nc; full score in I Vnm.

1685⁵

LA GENEVIEFA. Dramma per musica. Firenze, St. di S.A.S., 1685.
I Fn (lost).

Text: Girolamo Gigli, according to the old catalogue of I Fn. No other copy of this unique libretto has been found. It is, however, probably for the performance in Siena mentioned in the dedication of the third edition (Siena, St. del Publico, 1689) listed by Wotquenne, p. 77. There Gigli says that his dedication to the Ill. Signori Convittori del Nobilissimo Collegio Tolomei di Siena is prompted by the fact that they first performed it in 1685. However, it should be noted that if there were two editions in 1685, the above might still indicate a Florentine performance following in the same year as the original in Siena.

Music (lost): Composer unknown.

1686¹ 9 ii
Sorgenti

Amor'e Sig[no] ria non voglion Comp[ars] a.
Fagiuoli, "A di 9 d.o. Se fece la p[rim] a commedia a Sorg[en] te *Amor'e Sig.ria non voglion Comp.a* ov'io recitai." The fact that Fagiuoli acted means the work is in prose. The interpretation of the final word is debatable. No record of a comedy of this title has been found.

1686² carn?
Centauro

TUTTO IL MAL NON VIEN PER NUOCERE. Drama musicale che si rappresenta dalla Conversazione del Centauro. Firenze, Pietro Matini, 1686.
I Bc, Fc, Fn.

Text: G.D. de Totis. First performed in Rome, 1681, with music by A. Scarlatti. Performed again in 1683 in Siena for the visit of Vittoria della Rovere (see Fabbri, *A. Scarlatti*, pp. 33f.), and again in Ravenna by the Accademici Riuniti in 1686 (in I Bu), which libretto is virtually identical to the Florentine one and which, while remaining mute about the poet and composer, does refer to an original performance in Rome.

Music: Probably by A. Scarlatti. Score in I MC and collections of arias in I Bc, Vnm, Rvat, and Nc (Zanetti, p. 83).

Comment: The season is suggested by the consistency in appearance and sources of the three librettos of the Conversazione del Centauro following their first opera in 1684[1].

1686[3] 25 v, 3 vi
Casino

GNEO MARZIO CORIOLANO. Drama musicale fatto rappresentare da' Signori Accademici del Casino sotto la protezione del Sereniss. Principe Francesco Maria di Toscana. Firenze, Vincenzio Vangelisti, s.d.
GB Lbm; **I** Bc, Bu, Fc, Fn, Mb, Rn, Vgc.

Text: G.A. Moniglia, reprinted in the *Poesie dramatiche, parte prima*, pp. [299]-378. Dedication signed May 25, 1686, by the Accademici del Casino. Prefatory note in the *Poesie* states that the libretto was written for Vittoria della Rovere who presented it after a year to Francesco Maria de' Medici.

Music (lost): Lorenzo Cattani, according to the prefatory note in the *Poesie*.

Comment: Fagiuoli: "A dì 3. Giugno 1686. Nel Casino si recitò il *Coriolano* dramma del S.r D.re Moneglia, dove recitarono Siface [G.F. Grossi] e Vincentino [?] primi professori del Mondo ed io vi fui ed ammirai non meno la composiz[ion]e del'Autore, che la disposiz[ion]e de i comici tutti valorosi, e fù fatto con ogni magnificenza sì di scene che di abiti prop[ri]a del Ser.mo Pr.pe Fran[ces]co sopraciò è Prot[et]tore della Accad[emi]a."

1686[4] 10,17 ix
Pratolino

IL FINTO CHIMICO. Drama per la musica rappresentato nella Villa di Pratolino. Firenze, Vincenzo Vangelisti, 1686.
B Bc; **I** Fc, Fm, Fn, MOe, PAc, Rca, Rn; **US** Wc.

Text: Gio. Cosimo Villifranchi, who is not mentioned. Authorship stated by the *Vita* prefacing the *Raccolta di Opuscoli* and confirmed by Fagiuoli, cited below.

Music (lost): Composer unknown.

Cast: Supplied by manuscript additions to the copy in **I** MOe. Graticcio - Ippolito Fusai; Corinda - Domenico Graziani; Lisetta - Giulio Cavaletti; Delia - Francesco de Castris; Florante - Carl'Antonio Zanardi; Vaiano - Giuseppe Canavesi.

Comment: Diario del Ser.mo Principe Cardinale Francesco Maria records the first date. Fagiuoli I, f. 72r: "A di 17 7mbre [1686]: Andai alla commedia a Pratolino intit[olat]a *Il finto chimico* del Dr. Villifranchi, drama p[er] musica." An entry in Weaver, "Opera," p. 69, no. 12, cites a libretto of this opera dated 1680, an error originating in a cataloguer's error at **I** Fn.

1686[5] 7 vii
S. Maria N.

LE PROVE DELLA SAPIENZA, E DEL VALORE. Festa a cavallo sotto la condotta del Serenissimo Principe di Toscana. Firenze, s.t., 1686.
I Bu, Fn(2), MOe, Rn, Vgc.

Text: Alessandro Segni wrote both the libretto and the description published with it, according to Quadrio III.IV.V, p. 502, substantiated by Fagiuoli: "A dì 7 luglio 1686. Si fece il carosello sù la Piazza di S. M[aria] a Novella la pr.ma volta e fù una festa ricchissima al mag[gio]r segno. Il Teatro non poteva esser più bello, e vago, come gl'abiti, si di chi operava, come anco delle Comparse. Non stò a descriv[er]e la festa

puntualm[en]te essendo q[ues]to stato già fatto del S.r Aless[and]ro
Segni molto meglio di quel che l'avrei fatt'io, come del suo libretto
stampato, che si dispensò avanti cominciasse la festa pred[ett]a della
quale io op[er]ai essendo sul carro tra i musici con l'abito p[er] tale
effetto, e q[ues]to fù un mio sbillo per veder la festa, e così buscar un
p[ai]o di scarpe un p[ai]o calzette di seta, un pezzuola da collo di trina
di Vals.a di 322 e le maniche alla persiana pure con alte funi e nastri,
Q[ues]ta Invenzione il S.r Segni la fece trovar anco ad un suo Nip[o]te
che assieme con me per musici taciti facevamo bellissima armonia."

Music (lost): Composer unknown.

1686[6]

LA TESSALONICA. Dramma per musica del Sig. Niccolo Minato. Firenze,
Pietro Matini, 1686.
I Bc, Fn (lost).

Text: Minato.

Music: Probably Bernardo Pasquini. Sesini assigns the music to Antonio
Draghi who first set the libretto for a performance in Vienna in 1673.
It seems on the surface to be much more likely that the music used here
would have been Pasquini's setting for Rome, 1683. See Crain, pp. 162ff.
He is unaware of this Florentine libretto. The Pasquini score: A Wgm.

1686[7]
Rinvigoriti

Prologo in musica per *La dama spirito folletto.*

Text: Gio: Battista Fagiuoli, published in his *Rime piacevoli* V, p. 278.
The principal drama was probably *La dama folletto ovvero le larve amorose,
commedia nuova di Arcangelo Spagna*, Bologna, Longhi, 1684 (I MOe).

Music (lost): Composer unknown.

1686[8]

LA VERA DAMA ovvero L' INNOCENZA TRIONFANTE. Commedia [in prosa]
di Cosimo Galterotto Bardi. Firenze, Vincenzio Vangelisti, 1686.
I MOe.
No prologue, intermezzi, finale or indications of incidental music.
Dedication makes it plain that the purpose of the publication is to correct
errors in an earlier performance about which no other information is given.

1686[9] 10 xii

Bonazzini I, p. 414 records the death of Antonio Rivani: ". . . doppo aver
guardato il letto oppresso da grave malattia Antonio Rivani detto il
Ciecolino lasso di vivere, et il di lui cadavere fù sepolto nella Chiesa di Santo
Stefano. Questo in vita fù uno de' più singolari musici, che possi mai essere
stato udito nel mondo."

1687[1] 8, 26 i
Cocomero

Lisimaco. Commedia in musica.
Two references exist to performances in this carnival. They probably refer
to the same opera. Luca Degli Albizzi wrote to Card. Francesco de'Medici
(I Fas 5819, no. 1) ". . . domani primiggia le commedia [*sic*] in via del
Cocomero e l'altro colle cose nuove." *L'altro* possibly refers to the other
theater (Tintori?). Unfortunately he does not name the opera. By the end
of the month Francesco has returned to Florence and his Diary records:
"Questa sera andò S.A.R. in Carroza di S.S. Pr.pi di Toscana al *Lisimaco*
commedia in musica."

It is not possible to determine whether this *Lisimaco* is by C. Ivanovich and Gio. Maria Pagliardi, first performed in Venice, 1673 (scores: I MOe, Vnm), or by Giacomo Sinibaldo and Bernardo Pasquini, first performed in Rome in 1681. See 1690[2].

1687[2] 18 ii

Burattini in casa Palmieri.
Mentioned by Luca degli Albizzi (letter no. 3).

1687[3] 26 viii-
16 ix
Pratolino

IL PAZZO PER FORZA. Drama musicale rappresentato nella Villa di Pratolino. Firenze, Vincenzio Vangelisti, 1687.
B Bc; I Bc, Bu, Fc, Fm, Fn.

Text: G.A. Moniglia. The preface to the reprint in the *Poesie dramatiche, parte terza*, p. 99 comments: ". . . dopo 29. anni il Sereniss. Principe di Toscana . . . [si compiacque] esporlo . . . nella Villeggiatura di Pratolino; e perche il Drama era troppo . . . prolisso in quella stagione calda, . . . volle . . . farlo scortare, e ridurre insieme alla foggia moderna." [After listing the omitted characters by reference to the 1658 libretto, it continues:] "Fecelo l'A.S.S. porre in Musica dal Sig. Gio: Maria Pagliardi e l'accompagno con vaghezza, e ricchezza d'abiti, e di Scene, e di Balli . . . "

Music (lost): Pagliardi as stated.

Cast: Ferdinando's correspondence shows that among the *musici ordinari*, Giuseppe Canavese, Francesco de Castris, and Carlo Antonio Zanardi were in Florence and doubtless sang. Degli Albizzi, see below, speaks of an imported singer from "the circle of Card. [Niccola] Acciajuoli,"

Comment: During the summer of 1687, Card. Francesco was again in Rome and the letters of Luca degli Albizzi resume with gossip of the court. July 17, 1687 (I Fas [Arch. Med. 5819, no. 5]): "Circa a Pratolino si pensa p[er] quello crede a poco, benche credo che la commedia si abbia da fare, ma ora se avissi giudicare la villegiatura ha da essere quest'anno corta, la causa poi la sapra più V.A. che io, e il musico di Bologna [Antonio Rinaldi] quello sento ancora non ha ordine di venire ed ora credo che Checchino [Francesco de Castris] pria più di quello." July 24, 1687 (no. 6): ". . . Circa la commedia per quest'ordinario me disdico perche adesso diro che si fa assolutamente, ma a Pratolino al solito, e di più de'musici ordinari ci è uno che fara il ridicolo Romano che opero nel girello del Sig.r Card. Acciajoli, non credo gia abbia da essere con gran lusso, mentre non si fanno alcuni abiti nuovi, ma serviranno in tutto i vecchi." Capponi, p. 244, gives the date of the first performance and adds that on the 30th the Grand Duchess, the Princess, and Prince Gian Gastone, and the Cardinal all went to the performance (recorded in Francesco's diary, f. 96v).

1687[4] 26 xi

Death notice in Fagiuoli, p. 79, for Gio. Michele de Bar "Alias d.º il Basso de Peponi."

1688[1] 11 ii
Sorgenti

Lo sposalizio tra sepolcri. Opera tragicomica (in prose) di G.B. Ricciardi. Francesco de'Medici's Diary, p. 105: ". . . la sera (S.A.R.) andò al Teatro alla commedia in prosa del Dr. Ricciardi stando nel Palchetto colla S.ra Principessa e col S.r Pr.cpe Gio. Gastone." This is amplified by Fagiuoli, I, f. 79v: "A dì [blank but following 29 January] si fece la com[medi]a

a' Sorg[en] ti d[ett] a *le Nozze fra sepolcri*, ov'io recitai." The title is
easily recognizable as a version of the title given. The only publication
of the comedy that has been found is: LO SPOSALIZIO TRA SEPOLCRI,
Opera tragicomica di Giambatista Ricciardi, Fiorentino rappresentata
nel Teatro de' Signori Accademici Sorgenti in Firenze. Bologna, Longhi,
1695 in I Mb and Rn. It is possible that the title actually refers to this
performance rather than one contemporaneous with the publication
since it is quite unusual for a libretto attending a performance to be
printed elsewhere, for obvious practical reasons of transportation. For
a similar instance see 1679[3] and 1694[2].

1688[2] 17 ii
Cocomero

Luca degli Albizzi (no. 4) to Francesco de' Medici: "Jeri si fece la
commedia in via del Cocomero, e quivi si vede il concorso maggiore, e
di molti maggiaticci [*sic*]. La Frumicona vi faceva bene la sua figura."
La Frumicona remains unidentified. He had referred to her earlier in
a letter (no. 8) of October 7, 1687, "Qui si vive al solito ed io ho avuto
di gran trambusti per la Frumicona, e forse ancora non sono finitosi."
No libretto or prose comedy known for this carnival. But a female
performer surely indicates a *dramma per musica*.

1688 11 vii

Ferdinando de' Medici becomes the protector of the Accademia degli
Immobili in what was actually only a legal move necessary in order to
make the Pergola theater available for the wedding celebrations
connected with his marriage to Violante Beatrice di Baviera (see below).
The move did not result in a resuscitation of the academy beyond that
event. Fabbri, *A. Scarlatti*, publishes a facsimile of a *Ricordo* by
Francesco Redi, 1688, of his part in the negotiations between Cosimo
and Ferdinando as the latter's representative in the effort to reopen the
Pergola. The *Ricordo* is inserted in Redi's *Memorie* in I Fm.

1688[3] 25 iv
Centauro

IL FIGLIO DELLE SELVE. Drama musicale di Carlo Sigismondo Capece,
che si rappresenta dalla Conversazione al Canto de' Carnesecchi dal
Centauro. Dedicato al Serenissimo Principe di Toscana. Firenze,
MDCLXXXVIII, Piero Matini, all'Ins. del Lion d'Oro.
I Fn.

Text: Capece. This libretto, listed by Allacci, col. 345 (with an error in
the title) is evidently unknown to Fabbri, *A. Scarlatti*, pp. 33-38, who
cites Allacci and then erroneously "corrects" Allacci's date as being
ab inc. The dedication is signed by Gli Accademici al canto de' Carnesecchi
dal Centauro as shown, which, since it follows the New Year's Day, March
25, *ab inc.*, must be 1688, not 1689.

Music: Cosimo Bani (as the name appears on the score) or Boni (as it is
spelled in a number of sources). First performed in Capece's house in
Rome in 1687 (dedication dated January 18). Score: I MOe. Fabbri
argues against Dent's ascription of the music for the Florentine performance
to Scarlatti. Zanetti registers only Scarlatti's setting in 1708 for Rome
(p. 72).

Comment: The dedication of the Florentine libretto to Ferdinando says:
"La Generosa Benignità, con la quale V.A.S. s'e degnata farci dono del

presente Dramma, porge ora a Noi questo non meno giusto, che riverente ardimento d'esporlo di nuovo al pubblico sotto i felicissimi Auspicj della medesima A.V." Since Francesco de' Medici was in Rome by the end of February, he may very well have seen the performance and sent the score to Ferdinando in Florence.

The insertion of "al Canto de' Carnesecchi" into the name of the Academy would seem to be a location. The via de' Carnesecchi lies outside the city on the way towards Fiesole.

1688[4] 10 v
Tintori

Commedia in musica del Buchino.
Diary of Francesco Maria de' Medici, p. 110: "Lun x (May, 1688). In ferraiolo e zimarra ando S.A.R.mo col S. Principe Gio. Gastone alla commedia in musica del Buchino nel Corso de'Tintori."

1688[5] 2 viii
Pratolino

IL TIRANNO DI COLCO. Drama musicale rappresentato nella Villa di Pratolino. Firenze, Vincenzio Vangelisti, 1688.
A Wn; I Bc, Bu, Fc, Fn, Mb, MOe, PAc; S Uu.

Text: G.A. Moniglia, not mentioned, but reprinted in the *Poesie dramatiche, parte seconda,* pp. 1-68, to which is attached a *Lettera apologetica dell'autore* on pp. 69-78, signed September 15, 1688. The preface, pp. 3-6, describes the prologue (not printed) and its marvelous machine, states that the opera was performed eight times, that it was performed at Pratolino, and mentions the composer.

Music (lost): Gio. Maria Pagliardi, as stated.

Cast: Francesco Grossi and Marc'Antonio Origoni were engaged. De Castris was singing in Venice. Origoni returned to Modena October 10.

Comment: The diary of Francesco de' Medici, p. 116, announces the departure for Pratolino of the usual family: Vittoria, Francesco, Anna Ludovica, and Gio. Gastone on the first of September. Then on the following day: "Dopo le 20 s'ascoltò la Commedia in musica detta *il monarca di Colci.*"

1689 carn

The celebration of carnival season of 1689, probably by Ferdinando's design, coincided with the arrival on January 9 of his bride, Princess Violante Beatrice di Baviera. All of the academies vied with each other in presenting theatrical entertainments. The diarists in turn give their accounts, among which the most important are Settimani (reprinted by Fabbri, *A. Scarlatti* p. 38), Pastoso, Susier, and Bonazzini. In addition, Alessandro Segni wrote the *Memorie de' viaggi e feste per le reale nozze de' Ser. sposi Violante Beatrice di Baviera e Ferdinando principe di Toscana.* Firenze, Ippolito della Nave, 1688 (I Rn).

1689[1] carn
Cocomero

ADELAIDE. Comedia [in prose] rappresentata dagli Accademici Infuocati alla Ser. Violante Beatrice di Baviera, Principessa di Toscana. Firenze, Vincenzio Vangelisti, 1689.
I Fn.
The only known comedy in prose written by G.A. Moniglia. The authorship is established by Martini's repertory. The same subject was converted into an opera by Antonio Salvi (see 1725[7]).

1689² carn
Sorgenti

L'Amicizia tra le sventure (in prose) di Francesco Maria Pazzaglia. Cited by Pastoso and Settimanni. No publication found. I Fas (Med 5876, c. 42): Pazzaglia, Aiutante di Camera to the Duke of Mantua, came to Florence "per assistere ad una virtuosa sua Fatica, che deve rappresentarsi in una di coteste Accademie nella congiuntura di cotesti Festeggiam[en] ti."

1689³ carn
Casine nuove

Bertolina Regina d'Arcadia. Burletta in musica del Sig.r Girolamo Guicciardini. Pastoso, p. 416, no. 1288: "E la conversazione delle Casine nuove fecero recitarsi in musica una delle solite Burlette del Sig.r Girolamo Guicciardini intitolata *Bertolina Regina d'Arcadia* p[er] chi haveva voglia di ridere." Settimanni designates the work an "operetta buffa." Neither libretto nor score known.

1689⁴ 29 i
Tintori

LE FORTUNATE SVENTURE. Commedia [in prose] da recitarsi dai Sig. Accademici Cadenti nel Corso di Tintori l'anno 1689. All'Illustrissimo Sig. Marchese Cosimo da Castiglion. Firenze, Vincenzio Vangelisti, 1689. I Mb, MOe, Rn.

Text: Giuseppe Fivizani, according to Martini's repertory. "Fivizanni" is cited by Allacci in col. 922 as the author of *Roma nascente* (Bologna, s.d.). There is a previous publication of *Le gloriose disaventure* (Lucca, 1685) with the same title in I Rn. Dedication signed 29 genn. 1688 [*ab inc.*] by the Accademici Cadenti. Title page is shown *overleaf.*

Music (lost): Composer unknown. *Prologo* and *Finale* for music, interlocutori: Apollo and Flora.

Comment: Pastoso says: "I Cadenti [recita] un altra commedia composta e recitata in Lucca, intitolata *Le gloriose disaventure di Odoardo figlio del re di Sicilia.*" Weaver, "Opera," p.70, no. 21, erroneously classifies this prose comedy as a comic opera.

1689⁵ 29 i
Pergola

IL GRECO IN TROIA. Festa teatrale rappresentata in Firenze per le nozze de' Serenissimi sposi Ferdinando Terzo, Principe di Toscana, e Violante Beatrice, Principessa di Baviera. Firenze, Stamperia di S.A.S., 1688. I Bc, Fn(3), Mb, MOe, Rca(2), Rn(2 plus a Ms copy); US Wc.

Text: Matteo Noris who signs the dedication December, 1688. Pastoso, p. 407, no. 1263, gives date of first performance and mentions nine more performances until February 21.

Music (lost): Gio. Maria Pagliardi. Pandolfini's *Notizie* identify Noris as the poet and Gio. Maria Pagliardi as the composer.

Cast: Pandolfini lists the cast without roles: Domenico Ballerini, Paolo Rivani, Il Canavese, La Brogina, La Collarettina, Vincenzio Ulivicciani, Siface, Francesco de Castris, Ipolito Fusai, and others. One of the two women is Clara Sassi who was engaged by Ferdinando. Puliti mistakenly identifies Domenico Ballerini as Francesco. Performances ended by February 24 on which date Ferdinando licensed Grossi (I Fas [Med 5876, c.103]).

Comment: The libretto contains seventeen engravings of the scenery by Jacopo Chiavistelli, fourteen reproduced by Molinari, figs. 220-33. Among the various descriptions in the diarists, it is amusing to read

LE

FORTVNATE

SVENTVRE

COMMEDIA

Da recitarsi da i Sig. Accademici Cadenti
nel Corso de' Tintori l'anno 1689.

All'Illustrissimo Sig. Ma ese

COSIMO

DA CASTIGLION

Gentiluomo di Camera di S. A. S.

IN FIRENZE 1689.

Per Vincenzio Vangelisti Stamp. Arciu.
Con licenza de' Supertori.

Bonazzini's cool observation (p. 577): "A dì 29 gen . . . *Il Greco in Troia* composta dal Noris veneziano, con tanta magnificenza, che riuscì cosa di grande stupore, e l'appartenne al S. Principe, ma per il poeta così così."

1689[6] **carn**   Mascherate.
Susier describes briefly the following mascherate:

21 i   "Fù fatto una bellissima Mascherata in un Cocchio tirato da 12 cavalli pieno di Dame, dietro una Carozza a 6 [cavalli] guidata dal Ser.mo Principe Sposo dove vi era la Ser.ma Sposa e Principessa Anna e Principe Gio: Gastone e doppio più Carozze a 6 piene di Dame e Cav.ri con bellissimi habiti e livrai."

10 ii   "Si vede una Mascherata composta di 120 gentiluomini parte in Calessi, e parte a Cavallo, che figuravano gente della Villa venute dalle vicine campagne ad'inchinare la novella Sposa."

22 ii   "Ultimo giorno di Carnevale fù fatto una Mascherata super[bissi]ma che era Ser.mo Prin. Sposo condottiere di Tutti i Potentati dell'Asia et il Ser.mo Gio. Gastone di Tutti i Potentati del'Europa dove si vedero di bellissimi abiti ed la Ser.ma Sposa era vestita da Gran Sultana che aveva in dono il valore di 600 Mila scudi di Gioie. In detto giorno si fece anco una mascherata di zanni con un abbattimento in sulla Piazza di S. Croce." The *zanni* may be a company recommended by Ferdinando to the Elector of Bavaria, **I** Fas (Med 5876, f. 105) 24 ii, 1688 *ab inc.*: "Francesco Contiglio Romano con sua moglie, famiglia, et compagni avendo in questa Città con universale applauso dimostrato la propria agilità, destrezza, et esperienza ne' giuocchi, sopra la corda, salti, et balli . . . "

1689[7] **9 iv**   Rappresentazioni di Fantoccini.
Pal. Pitti   Luca degli Albizzi (Letter to Francesco de'Medici, no. 12): "Nelle due sere passate si è fatta una rappresentazione nelle camere, e vi è stata la Sig.ra Prin[cipes]sa con le dame. Io sono stato uno di quelli che ho maneggiato le figure e mi sono mezzo stropiato per stato chinato." In the next letter of April 12, he again speaks of the *fantoccini* but reassures the Cardinal that he nevertheless will suffer no damage to his veins therefrom.

1689[8] **1 vii**   LA ROSMENE, ovvero L'INFEDELTÀ FEDELE. Melodrama del Signor
Casino   Giuseppe Domenico de Totis. Agl'Illustriss. Sig. della Conversazione del Casino da S. Marco. Firenze, Vincenzio Vangelisti, Stampatore Arcivescovale, 1689.
B Bc; **I** Bc, Bu, Fm, Mb, MOe.

Text: de Totis.

Music: Alessandro Scarlatti. The opera had been performed the preceding year in Naples. Scores: **D** MÜps; **I** Fc; fragments in **I** Nc, Rvat, and **GB** Lbm. (Zanetti, p. 79; Dent, p. 209.)

Comment: Fagiuoli, I, 88v: "A dì p[rim]o Luglio [1689]. Si fece al Casino la *Rosmene* dramma & l'ult[im]a dove recitò Siface." The significance of the last clause is that this was the last performance in

Florence by "Siface" (Francesco Grossi) before his murder in 1697 in which year Fagiuoli records the event on May 30 (Vol. II, f. 21).

1689[9] 22 xi

Festini.

Letter No. 14 of Luca degli Albizzi to Francesco de' Medici is chiefly interesting because of its personal expression and its suggestion that life in a society frantically attempting to be entertained at all times is not always exciting nonetheless. "Ora abbiamo molti festini, ed in specie di ballo dove vengono ogni sera le S.re Prin[cipes]se e S.ri Prin[cipi] per le nozze della Pasquala e Niccolina, per il resto si vivi malinconichissimo; giocando in camera a bambara [gambling game], Checco [Francesco de Castris], che vince tutto, il Prov[editor]e, Ferdinando Ridolfi, Vin[cenz]o Sori, ed io. Che mi anno vinto 200 doppie."

1689[10] aut
Pratolino

LA SERVA FAVORITA. Drama per la musica rappresentato nella Villa di Pratolino. Firenze, Stamperia di S.A.S. alla Condotta, 1689.
B Bc; I Bc, Fc, Fm, Fn, Mb, MOe, PAc, Rca, Rn, Vgc; S Uu; US CA.

Text: Giovanni Cosimo Villifranchi, who is not mentioned. A libretto for a performance in Livorno (Bonfigli, 1692), which is dedicated to Ferdinando and Beatrice, mentions in the letter to the reader the performance at Pratolino, the opera's being a favorite of the prince, and the name of the author, Villifranchi, but not the composer. The *protesta* is reprinted by Robert Freeman, pp. 321-41.

Music (lost): Probably by Alessandro Scarlatti, as may be deduced from the circumstances surrounding the opera. First, it is evident by the number of operas by Scarlatti performed under the patronage of Ferdinando in Siena, Livorno, Pisa, Florence and Pratolino that Scarlatti is by far more favored than any other single composer (Fabbri, *Scarlatti*). Scarlatti is represented by six operas at Pratolino against five of Perti, his closest competitor. But if the field is widened to include the above cities, Alessandro Scarlatti's operas considerably outnumber those of Perti. *La serva favorita* was performed three times under the prince's protection, the third being in 1705 by the Infuocati. No other opera matches the record. Highly circumstantial evidence is to be seen in a link between this repetition in 1705 and a performance in the summer of the same year in Naples of *La serva*; that is, the fact that the leading role, Cleante, is sung by Giuseppe Canavesi in both performances (*La serva favorita* melodrama da rappresentarsi nel Teatro di S. Bartolomeo di Napoli nell'Estate del 1705. Napoli, Mutio, 1705. In I Bu). These circumstances strongly reinforce Fabbri's hypothesis that Scarlatti was the composer based upon three letters in I Fas (Med 5875, cc. 700, 713; F. 5876, c. 20) which concern an unnamed *commedia in musica* which Scarlatti sent to Ferdinando in February, 1689, at the Prince's request. By a process of elimination, Fabbri arrives at the conclusion that *La serva favorita* is the score discussed in the letters (see p. 39).

Cast: None of the singers is identified in Ferdinando's correspondence. However, a lutenist in the service of Ferdinando, Giovanni Gigli, alias il Todeschino, is mentioned. His departure on October 11 for Modena marks the end of the opera at Pratolino.

1690¹ i, ii
Cocomero
Infuocati

LA ROSAURA. Drama per musica rappresentato alla Serenissima Violante Beatrice di Baviera Principessa di Toscana nel Teatro degli Accademici Infuocati. Firenze, Vincenzio Vangelisti, 1690.
I Bc, Bu, Fn, Rn.

Text: Antonio Arcoleo, not mentioned here, but the author signs the Venetian libretto of the previous year. Dedication, signed by the Accademici Infuocati, mentions Massimiliano Emanuele, brother of Violante Beatrice

Music (lost): Probably by G.A. Perti. See Allacci.

Cast: Rosaura - Diana Caterina Luppi; Feraspe - Domenico Sarti; Gelindo - Carlo Antonio Zanatta; Fidauro - Gio. Paolo Tilone; Arsace - Guglielmo Fea; Ersilla - Elena Garofalini; Gilbo - Gio. Batista Tamburini.

Comment: See *Lisimaco* below.

1690² i, ii
Cocomero
Infuocati

IL LISIMACO. Drama per musica rappresentato al Sereniss. Principe Ferdinando di Toscana nel Teatro degli Accademici Infuocati. Firenze, Vincenzio Vangelisti, 1690.
I Bc, Bu, Fn, Mb, Rn.

Text: Giacomo Sinibaldo, not mentioned here, but recognized in the anagram, Comagio Baldosini, in the title of the first Roman publication in 1681.

Music: Bernardo Pasquini, according to Pastoso. See below. Score: D WD. Indexed in Crain, II, pp. 120ff.

Cast: Alessandro - Domenico Sarti; Lisimaco - Carlo Antonio Zanatta; Demetrio - Giovanni Paolo Tiloni; Cleonte - Anton Maria Ristorini; Calistene - Guglielmo Fea; Alcimena - Elena Garofalini; Corebo - Diana Caterina Luppi; [Blank] - Giovanni Batista Tamburini; Anfrisa - Antonio Panichi.

Comment: Both Pastoso and Fagiuoli have entries referring to the performances of this carnival.
    Pastoso, p. 529, no. 1443: "... fatte recitare da Sr. Accademici Infuocati due drami musicale à prezzo che uno s'intitolava [blank] e l'altra il *Lisimaco*, e facevono pagare sul pr[im]o due lire, et un giulio, che non vi fù gran concorso di populo si risolverono poi sbassare il prezzo pensando d'aver far più faccendi facendo pagar lire due per testa, ma si ingannarono [.] Avevano q[ues]ti SS.ri fatto conto d'estinguere una mano di debiti con l'avanzo di dette recite, che detta academia *suncia* [illegible] aveva contrati p[er] i tempi in dietro, ma invece d'avanzare, vi messero su una somma di denari p[er] ciascheduno. E p[er] mettere all'ordine le dette drammi presero a cambio due mila scudi dal P. Prior Cimenes. Successe nel mentre, che recitavano il Drama del *Lisimaco* un fanciulletto, che faceva la comparsa del Leone nel rientrar dentro la scene prese fuoco, essendo ricoperto d'un abito fatto di Lanate assegno, che il povero ragazzo ebbe abruciare

Casa Palmieri

vivo quale fù condotto allo Spedale di Santa Maria Nuova. In Casa del Sig.r Palmieri fù recitata un'operetto del Susini in prosa, e nel Corso

Tintori

de' Tintori gli SS.ri Accademici Cadenti fecero rappresentare un Opera del d[ett]o Susini intitolato *Le False Oppinioni*, quale ebbe grandissimo applauso."

Fagiuoli, I, p. 96. "A dì 30 Gen.o 1689 [*ab inc.*] Fui alla Commedia de' Si.ri Infuocati intitolata Il *Lisimaco* Dramma del'Appolloni, musica del Pasquinj Rom[an]o. Si pagò 32 il bullettino e avanti si era fatto un altro Dramma del Totis, musica dello Scarlatti intitolato la *Rosaura*, e a q[ues]to si pagò 32.13.4. Vi fu sempre poco gente non ost[ant]e lo sbasso [di prezzo]. I, f. 96v. Mart. 7 Feb.o . . . [al calcio] fu il Pr[inci]pe di Neoburgh, che la sera ando alla Commedia agl'Infuocati d[ett]a *La Rosaura*, e poi fu a cena dal S.r Gio: Giorgio Ugolini con Dame, e Cav[alie]ri, e doppo si ballò."

Fagiuoli is wrong in all of his attributions except that of assigning the music of *Lisimaco* to Pasquini. He is confusing *Rosaura* with *Rosaura di Cipro* performed two years later in Florence with Scarlatti's music. But that libretto is by Lucini, not de Totis, whose name suggests further confusion with *La Rosmene* (1689[8]) above. The prices for the tickets are the same in both passages though expressed differently numerically.

1690[3] iii
Volanti

LA MOGLIE DEL FRATELLO. Dramma boschereccio rappresentato in Firenze l'anno 1690. Dedicato al Serenissimo Principe di Toscana. Firenze, Piero Matini, 1690.
I Fn, Mb, Rn.

Text: F. Silvani, according to Fabbri, "Firenze," but who is not mentioned. Season supplied by the *Approvazioni* dated 15 and 19 Marzo 1689 [*ab inc.*]. Dedication signed by Gli Accademici Volanti.

Music (lost): Composer unknown.

Roles: Filli, Tirsi, Rosetta, Berello.

1690[4] 26 iv
Pergola
Nobili

Festa con intermezzi in musica.
Fagiuoli, I, f. 99v: "In via della Pergola il Pr[inci]pe Ferdinando fece una festa consistente d'azioni cavalleresche, come maneggiar la picca, la spada, spiegar l'Insegna, mescolato ciò con Intermezzi in musica da Personnaggi rappre[sen]tanti l'Ozio, la Gloria, la Fama, e l'Honore, e poi termino in festino di ballo, vi furon tutti della Ser.ma Casa, e il S.r Pr.pe di Sassonia ch'era giorni sono ritornato di Roma." Bonazzini, p. 645, has a more lengthy description but on 16 iv Susier announces the arrival of "I primogenito di Duca di Sassonia" on March 4, "e si poso in casa del [Domenico?] Melani in via del Cocomero et ebbe buonissimo Trattamenti dal Sig. Principe Ferdinando e fu fatto de

Cascine

festini e Caccie e Corse di Barberi alle Cascine e Commedie."

1690[5]
Improvisi

L'AMOR VINCE FORTUNA. Drama per musica dedicato alla Altezza Serenissima di Violante Beatrice di Baviera Principessa di Toscana. Composto da Carlo Sigismondo Capece e recitata [*sic*] in Firenze dagli Accademici Improvisi l'anno 1690. Firenze, Vincenzio Vangelisti, 1690.
B Bc; I Bc, Fn, Rn.

Text: Capece, as stated. The dedication, signed by the Accademici Improvisi, recounts, " . . . ci cadde in pensiero d'impiegarci nella presente nuova Stagione in qualche lieto, e giocondo divertimento, e perciò avendo scelto tra molti il Drama intitolato *Amor vince Fortuna*, di Carlo Sigismondo Capece; prendemmo subito ardimento di mandarlo di nuovo alla luce con reverente supplica della sua alta protezione: sperando, che siccome quest'Opera ebbe l'onore di riportare ne'tempi trascorsi sopra altre Scene un'applauso ben singolare sotto i felicissimi auspicj del Sereniss. Elettore Massimiliano Emanuelle Duca dell'una, e l'altra Baviera, glorioso Fratello dell'A.V. . . . ." The reference is to the first performance in Rome in the house of Capece to celebrate the wedding of Maximilian to Maria Antonia Archduchess of Austria. (Libretto in Sonneck, p. 93.)

Music (lost): Composer unknown for either the Roman or the Florentine performance.

(1690⁶ ix)
(Pratolino)

No libretto exists for this year at Pratolino, and probably there was no performance since we did not find in the correspondence of Ferdinando for this year letters dealing with Pratolino.

 Puliti, p. 75, states that Scarlatti composed an opera for Ferdinando and that the Prince engaged several singers in 1690. Ferdinando's letters, however, concern only performances in Livorno in the carnivals of 1690 (Antonio and Ottavia Alamanni, Pietro Paolo Scandalibeni, and three women who could not and did not sing—La Momola, la Lauretta and Angiola Salicola), of 1691 (Scandalibeni and Marc'Antonio Origoni); or else the letters grant permission to the prince's own singers to go elsewhere (Antonio Romolo Ferrini to Venice and Lisi to Genoa). Others listed by Puliti were not located (Gio. Domenico Maggiorini, Domenico Sarti, Elena Garofalini, and Giovanni Battista Tamburini) but in any case these singers, save Maggiorini, performed in 1690².

1690⁷

Il Germanico al Reno. Festa teatrale.
In: G.A. Moniglia, *Poesie dramatiche, parte seconda,* pp. 217-95.
Also in the 1698 edition, *parte seconda,* pp. 225-302. In neither is there any information about any performance. Since Moniglia provides information plentifully for other works, it may be assumed that this libretto was never set to music or performed, at least prior to the first edition of his *Poesie.*

1690⁸
Sorgenti

IL MOCCONE PODESTÀ DEL BAGNO A RIPOLI ovvero DALL'ORDIRE LA FORTUNA. Dramma burlesco da rapp.si in Firenze nel Teatro degli Accademici Sorgenti l'anno 1690. Consacrato all'illustrissimo Sig. Marchese Alessandro Vitelli Gentiluomo della Camera di S.M. Cesarea Governatore dell'Armi di Prato, e Sergente Generale di Battaglia del Serenissimo Granduca di Toscana. Firenze, Cesare, e Francesco Bindi, 1690.
I Bc.

Text: Anonymous. Dedication, signed without date by the Accademici Sorgenti, says it is a "burlesco Drama . . . giudicat[o] degn[o] del Torchio," but it was spared in order to save "il Virtuoso compositor della musica a nuove fatiche di Partitura." One of the reasons for dedicating the opera to Vitelli is to "assicurare questo suo burlesco parto dalla maledicenza degli Aristarchi . . . "

Music (lost): Composer unknown.

Roles: Moccone, Lindora, Serpilla, Clorindo, Paleo, Stradone.

1691^1 9 i
Sorgenti

LA FORZA COMPASSIONEVOLE. Opera scenica da rappresentarsi in Firenze nel Teatro degli Accademici Sorgenti nel corrente anno 1691, dedicata all'illustriss. Sig. Marchese Alessandro Vitelli. Firenze, Vincenzio Vangelisti, 1691.
I Rn.

Text: Bonazzini, p. 684, speaking of a repetition the following year says it was "composta da uno Stanchi Istrione." (See 1692^2). Same subject "reduced" to a music drama by Antonio Salvi (Livorno, Bonfigli, 1694. In I Rn). The text above has no prologue, but in I Fn (Magl. Cl. VII, B 868, f. 646v), there is a prologue for music by Pietro Susini for two *personaggi*: *Innocenza* and *Giustizia*, which mentions the title above. However, the date makes it difficult to accept the attribution of the prologue to Pier Susini.

Music (for the prologue) lost: Composer unknown.

1691^2 1 v

Mascherata che rappresentava Imeneo.
Susier: "Al dì primo di Maggio . . . di più luoghi fece una Mascherata che rappresentava Imeneo con 27 altri fra i Amorini e varie Deità e le tre Grazie con tutti abiti nuovi. Et il Marchese Suigni . . . fece un altra Mascherata di Giunone con 24 altri Deità e tutto a loro spese."

1691^3 9 viii
Oscuri

IL SOSPETTO SENZA FONDAMENTO. Dramma pastorale fatto rappresentare da gli Accademici Oscuri per festivo applauso al giorno natalizio del Sereniss. Principe Ferdinando di Toscana. Firenze, Stamperia di S.A.S. alla Condotta, 1691 ad istanza di Andrea Orlandini.
I Mb, Rn; US Wc.

Text: Francesco Bartolomeo Nencini, according to the score, not Orlandini as Sonneck states (p. 1022).

Music: Alessandro Melani. Score in I Rvat with title *Scherzo musicale*. We are indebted to Lorenzo Bianconi for the identification of what seems to be the first performance of this opera. The libretto, almost identical with the Vatican score, is entitled *Le reciproche gelosie. Operetta in musica fatta recitare e dedicata alle bellissime dame sanese da tre consiglieri nell'occassone* [sic] *del presente carnevale*. In Siena nella Stamparia del Pubblico, 1677 (in I Rvat). The dedication is signed February 27, 1677, by Bonaventura Zondadori, Pandolfo Spannocchi, and Mutio Ugurgieri. See Weaver, "Materiali."

1691^4 aut
Pratolino

IL MARCO AURELIO. Drama per la musica rappresentato nella Villa di Pratolino. Firenze, Stamperia di S.A.S. alla Condotta, 1691.
I Bc, Fc, Fm, Fn, Mb, MOe, PAc, Rn(2); S Uu.

Text: Apostolo Zeno, according to Fabbri, "Firenze," col. 382, on what basis I do not know.

Music (lost): Composer(s) unknown.

Cast: As in 1690, Ferdinando evidently used only his own singers. The sole request for an external performer is for Antonio Rinaldi of Bologna to sing in Livorno in the carnival of 1691. Otherwise the refusal to grant Antonio Ferrini permission to go to Modena until October 12 probably is an indication that his opera was ending at Pratolino about that time.

1691[5]

L'AMAZONE DEL CELIBATO o sia LA VERGINE PARIGINA. Opera sacra [in prosa] di Simone Grassi fiorentino Accademico fra gl'Infecondi di Roma recitata in Firenze l'anno 1691. Dedicata all'illustrissimo Signore Angelo Baldocci gentiluomo di camera del Sereniss. Principe di Toscana. Bologna, Stamperia del Longhi, 1694.
I Bu, Mb.

Text: Simone Grassi, who signs the dedication in Firenze, 8 Gen. 1694. Prologue for music for *Amor divino* and *Amor profano* (no mention of composer).

1691[6]
Sorgenti

LA CORTESIA TRA RIVALI. Opera [in prose] del Sig. Pietro Susini Fiorent. Recitata da' Signori Accademici Sorgenti. Firenze, Vincenzio Vangelisti, 1691.
I Mb, Rn.
Previously performed in 1676[1].

1691[7]
Casino

Il Cid. See 1694[1].

1691[8]
Tintori
Cadenti

LA CADUTA DEL SAVIO INNAMORATA. Opera scenica dell'Signor Mario Calamari, cittad. fiorent., rappresentata dalli Accademici Cadenti l'anno 1691. Firenze, Stamp. di S.A.S. alla Condotta, 1691.
Prose comedy. See 1657[2].

1692[1] 17 v
Cocomero
Innominati

IL RODERICO. Drama per musica fatto rappresentare da' Signori Accademici Innominati nel Teatro di Via del Cocomero al Serenissimo Principe Ferdinando di Toscana. Firenze MDCXCII, Vincenzio Vangelisti, Stamp. Arcivesc.
I Mb.

Text: Gio: Battista Bottalino, not mentioned here, but the author's name appears in the title of the libretto of Milan, 1684 (also in I Mb), which is essentially the same. The dedication, signed May 1692 by Gli Accademici Innominati, speaks of the opera as a "dono della sua mano" and continues somewhat mysteriously, "Supplichiamo pertanto reverentemente l'A.V. . . . voglia riconoscerla coll'alta mercede della sua sublime benignissima Protezione sopra tutti noi, perchè possiamo un giorno meritare, e acquistar quel Nome, che per ancora non abbiamo ardire di prenderci . . ."

Music (lost): Composer unknown.

Comment: *Notizie di Casa Salvini*: "A dì 17 [May, 1692]. Si fece [al Principe di Danemarca] la com[me]dia in Via del Cocomero in musica intitolata il *Rodrigo*, che alcuni cavalieri si preparava per le nozze del Marchese Riccardi."

1692[2] 25 v
Sorgenti

La forza compassionevole. Opera scenica in prosa. Bonazzini, p. 684, records a repetition (see 1691[1]) by the Sorgenti of the prose play of the preceding year, adding that it was composed by a certain Stanchi Istrione. Presumably the prologue in music was also repeated.

1692³ 18, 22 vii
Borgo Ognissanti
Nascenti

LA ROSAURA DI CIPRO ovvero GLI EQUIVOCI IN AMORE. Drama per musica da rappresentarsi dagli Accademici Nascenti. All'Ill.ma Signora Marchese Giulia Spada. Ne' Riccordi [*sic*] Firenze, Vincenzio Vangelisti, 1692.
I Fm.

Text: Giov. Battista Lucini, not mentioned here, but the author is identified in the Roman libretto of 1690, as is the composer, Alessandro Scarlatti. (See Wotquenne, p. 57.) The dedication signed by the Accademici Nascenti on above date.

Music: Scarlatti. Scores: **GB** Lbm(2); fragments I Fc, Nc, Rvat. See Zanetti, p. 71. Excerpts in Eitner, *Publikationen* 14 ii.

Comment: Fabbri, *A. Scarlatti*, p. 41, reports an entry from the *Notizie di Casa Salvini*: "A dì 22 [luglio 1692] una nuova Conversazione di Cavalieri, sotto il nome degli Accademici Nascenti, fecero per la prima volta una loro Commedia in musica in un nuovo e bel Teatro, nel Prato che è avanti al Giardino della Casa del Cavalier Francesco Guglielmo Sangalletti, in Borgo Ognissanti. E i recitanti erano 4 donne e un uomo, e la Commedia [era] intitolata *La Rosaura di Cipro*, ovvero *Gli Equivoci in Amore*, la quale non piacque all'universale."

1692⁴ 12 xi
Borgo Ornissanti?

ALMA FIDA IN AMORE OTTIEN VITTORIA. Dramma pastorale fatto rappresentarsi in Firenze. Dedicato all'illustrissima Signora Marchesa Giulia Spada Riccardi. Firenze, Antonio Navesi ad istanza d'Andrea Orlandini, 1692.
I Bc, Rca, Rn.

Text: Anonymous. Dedication, signed without date by Andrea Orlandini, states: "... ho considerato non poter presentare a V.S. Illustrissima cosa più grata del presente Dramma dolce scherzo d'un Cigno del Tevere, al canto di cui assuefatto il di lei purgatissimo orecchio non gli giungera nuovo sentirlo in riva dell'Arno nel giorno, in cui la Toscana tutta festeggia per la Nascita del Sereniss. Principe Ferdinando suo Signore ..."

Music (lost): Anonymous.

Roles: Eurillo, Clori, Lisa vecchia, Grillo, Rosetta.

Comment: The dedication links this libretto with *La Rosaura* above, which in turn is an opera brought from Rome, just as the dedication says of *Alma fida*. Ademollo, Crain, Kast, etc., do not know of an opera by this title performed in Rome. However, the identification of this opera might be solved by comparison with other pastorale operas performed in Rome at the Palazzo della Cancelleria, the location of the performance of *Rosaura* (*Gli equivoci in amore*) in Rome in 1690.

1692⁵ 7 ix
Pratolino

Trespolo oste.

Text: Giovanni Cosimo Villifranchi. The *Vita* of Villifranchi published as the introduction to the *Raccolta di opuscoli*, p. xxviii, says that Villifranchi reduced Gio: Batista Ricciardi's *La forza del sospetto* to a *commedia in musica* and that it was never published. The *ossia* of Ricciardi's prose play is, in fact, *Il Trespolo oste* (Bologna, Longhi, 1687. Copy in **GB** Lbm). The performance is recorded by the *Notizie di Casa Salvini*: "A dì 7 sett. [1692] si fece per la prima volta lor commedia a Pratolino in musica intitolata *il Trespolo Oste* del Ricciardi messa poi in versi da Giovanni Villifranchi, e non piacque all'universale." No published libretto or manuscript has been found.

Music: No score is known to exist.

Cast: Ferdinando's correspondence does not contain references to this performance, suggesting that only his own singers were used. The performances may have been brief since Antonio Ferrini was given licence to go from Pratolino to Genoa on September 18. Maria Domenica Pini was also engaged to sing in Genoa at the same time.

Comment: Ferdinando wrote to Marchese Decio Fontanelli in Modena, April 22, 1692, his appreciation for the latter's having let him have the original of *Trespolo* and "in addition the libretto of the same drama." However, it is likely that this *Trespolo* is the well-known *Trespolo tutore*, original prose also by Giovanbattista Ricciardi, adapted as a libretto by Villifranchi, set by Stradella, and performed in the Teatro Fontanelli in Modena, 1686 (libretto in I MOe).

**1692⁶
Efimeri**

IL TIRINTO. Drama musicale nuovamente rappresentato de' Signori Accademici Efimeri in Firenze l'anno 1692. Firenze, Vincenzio Vangelisti, 1692.
I Bc, Mb; **US** Wc.

Text: According to Crain, II, 1, by the members of the Accademia degli Sfaccendati, who performed the opera for the first time in Arriccia, 1672, with the title *La sincerità con la sincerità* (copy in **US** Wc and elsewhere). The dedication of the Florentine libretto, signed without date by Domenico Piazzini, declares changes were necessary in order to accommodate the libretto to the "genio del presente secolo" by shortening the verses and adding arias. Crain is of the opinion that the changes are so extensive that the music of Pasquini for the original performance could not have been used.

Music (lost): Composer unknown.

Roles: Filandro, Tirinto, Rosaura, Lisa vecchia, Sireno vecchio, Laurinda, Celindo.

**1693¹ 8 i
Tintori
Cadenti**

Amor nell'odio. Commedia in prosa?
Notizie di Casa Salvini cite the performance in the Teatro dei Cadenti on date shown. No publication known. There is a play of similar title in I MOe: *L'amante per odio*, opera regia di Pompeo Luchese. In Bologna, Longhi, 1679.

**1693² 14 i
Cocomero
Saggiati**

L'INNOCENTE GIUSTIFICATO. Tragicommedia [in prosa] rappresentata dagli Accademici Saggiati nel teatro di via del Cocomero dedicata alla Serenissima Violante Beatrice di Baviera Principessa di Toscana. Firenze, Vincenzio Vangelisti, 1692.
I Rn.

Text: Carlo Calcagnini, according to Allacci, col. 457, who lists earlier editions in Bologna (1650, 1668) and Perugia (1661).

Comment: *Notizie di Casa Salvini*: "Si fece per la prima volta la Commedia in via del Cocomero di una nuova Conversazione messi insieme l'anno passato.

Riuscì l'opera mirabilm[en] te bene e per lor composizione tradotta dallo spagnuolo in francese e da quello in italiano . . . intitolata *l'Innocente giustificato*." The *conversazione* is probably the same which performed *Roderico* at the Cocomero in March, 1692[1], at that time without a name, i.e., *Innominati*. The date of the publication may be a rare instance of the use of the Lady Day calendar for a date of publication. On the other hand, it is not uncommon later to publish the libretto for carnival late in the preceding year.

1693[3] 31 v
Cocomero

Repetition of the above.
Notizie di Casa Salvini: " . . . si rifece al P. Ferdinando la commedia di quest'anno in via del Cocomero."

1693[4] 6 ix
Pratolino

ATTILIO REGOLO. Drama per musica rappresentato nella Villa di Pratolino. Firenze, Stamperia di S.A.S., Gio: Filippo Cecchi, 1693.
B Bc; I Bc, Fc, Fn, Mb, Rca, Rn; S Uu; US Wc.

Text: Matteo Noris, according to Allacci, col. 128, and confirmed by an entry in the *Notizie di Casa Salvini* on above date which also identified Pagliardi as the composer, confirming Puliti, p. 75.

Music (lost): Gio. Maria Pagliardi, as stated.

Cast: Ferdinando's correspondence confirms that Maria Domenico Pini, Antonio Ferrini, Giuseppe Canavesi, and Francesco de Castris were available among his ordinary musicians. In addition, he engaged Maria Maddalena Musi for Pratolino.

1693[5]

IL GIUOCO DELL'ASTROLOGO INDOVINO. Firenze, Vangelisti, 1693.
I Fn.
No further information available.

1694[1] carn
Cocomero

Tintori
Porta Rossa

The *Notizie di Casa Salvini* contain a general survey of the performances for carnival of this year: "Nota come nel[le] Conversazione di quest'anno [1694] fu recitata nell'Accademia degli Infuocati la Com[medi] a intitolata *Il Cid*, fattosi 3 anni sono nel Casino del Cardinale. Ai Cadenti si fece *La pace tra le sventure*. In Porta Rossa *il Trespolo Oste* del Ricciardi. E fecero ancora commedie pubbliche i Frati del Carmine, S.M. Maggiore, Badia, S. Trinita."

1694[2]
Sorgenti

Donna saggia può ciò che vuole. Commedia [in prosa] rappresentata dagli Accademici Sorgenti nel nuovo Teatro. Bologna, Longhi. 1694.

Text: Pietro Susini. No copy of this libretto has been located but it is cited (without author) by Allacci, col. 262, and by Quadrio III, pars II, p. 107. It is probably a reprinting of 1679[3]. For similar republication by Longhi see 1688[1] and 1695[6].

1694 6 iii

Death of Vittoria della Rovere. The theaters remained closed for the rest of the year. However, see following entry.

1694[3] 25 xi
Poggio a Caiano

I tre fratelli rivali per la sorella.

Text: Pietro Susini? Quadrio III, IV. IV, p. 461 attributes *I tre fratelli rivalli* to Susini, the prose text of which was published in Venice, 1683 (I Rn).

Comment: Fagiuoli, on date shown, records, "A dì 25 N[ovem]bre 1694. Essendo in villa a Carmignano dal S.r Pietro Ant[oni]o Susini si fece una commedia del S.r Picio *Scrofe*llo (?) al Poggio a Caiano, dov'era il S.r Pr[inci]pe Ferd[inand]o con la S.ra Pr[inci]pessa [Violante], ed io recitai la parte del ridicolo. La commedia era *i tre fratelli rivali per la sorella* la quale si rifece il dì 28 d[etto] alla pr[esen]za de'med[esimi] pr[inci]pi."

(1695)[1] 2 ii
Corsini

Le stravaganze d'amore, ovv. *Il finto nel vero* (G.A. Lorenzani) melodr. 3a, Firenze, nel Palazzo Corsini, 2 febbraio 1695. Music by Pier Filippo Corsi. Entry under Corsi in Manferrari. No other reference, citation, or publication found. Martini's repertory lists only the prose comedy by Castelletti having the same first title, registered also by Allacci, col. 742, but with no Florentine printing. Lorenzani is, again according to Allacci, col. 237, the author of *Dalle finzioni il vero, oppure la cena e la commedia svanita*. Commedia (in prosa) in Bologna, per gli Eredi di Antonio Pisarri, 1687, which seems related to the *ossia* above.

1695[2] 9 vii
Casino

IL CONTE D'ALTAMURA ovvero IL VECCHIO GELOSO. Drama musicale fatto rappresentare dagli Accademici che s'adunano nel Casino da San Marco, sotto la protezione dell' Serenissimo, e Reverendissimo Signor Princ. Card. de' Medici. Firenze, 1695, ad instanza di Bernardo Rontini Libraio. I Bc, Bu, Fn.

Text: Domenico Tornaquinci, not mentioned, but who is identified in the diary quoted below. The libretto was previously published in Lucca by Ciufetti in 1692 (copy in I MOe), and afterwards in Siena, St. del Publico, 1702 (I Rn); in Rome, s.d. (I Rn), and Modena, by Goliani, 1720 (I Fm), each with alterations.

Music (lost): Composer unknown. But the *Notizie di Casa Salvini* give what may be an important clue: "A dì 9 di Luglio [1695]. Nel Casino del Cardinale se fece per la prima volta la Commedia in musica parole di Domenico Tornaquinci, musica di Roma . . . intitolata *il Conte d'Altamura*, ovvero *Il Vecchio Geloso*."

Roles: Fulderico, Tisbina, Brunello, Leodilla, Iroldo, Ordauro.

1695[3] 9 vii
Pergola
Nobili

L'ACCADEMIA FESTEGGIANTE nel giorno natalizio del Ser.mo Principe Ferdinando di Toscana suo Clemen.mo Protettore. Firenze, 1695, Vincenzio Vangelisti.
I Fn, Mb (title page missing: catalogued under "La Flora"), Rn.

Text: Sig. Avvoc. Francesco Maria Corsignani (p. 7). Dedication signed without date by the Cavalieri dell'Accademia de' Nobili. The names of the participating cavaliers on pp. 3-6.

Music (lost): Martino Bitti, who as stated on pp. 7f composed the "dolce concerto de musicali strumenti." The libretto contains occasional musical items, such as "concerto di trombe e di timpani" on page 15.

1695[4] 26, 29 ix
Pratolino

L'IPOCONDRIACO. Dramma per musica rappresentato nella Villa di Pratolino. Firenze, nella Stamperia di S.A.S., Gio. Filippo Cecchi, 1695.

I Bc, Fc, Fm, Fn, PAc, Rca; **S** Uu; **US** Wc.

Text: Gio. Cosimo Villifranchi, who is not mentioned, on the authority of the *Vita* prefacing Villifranchi's *Raccolta di Opuscoli*.

The *L'Autore a chi legge* is an essay of some interest for its expression of the author's intentions. "Quest'Operetta volevo intitolarla *Heautontimerumenos*, per fare a Terenzio quel ch'egli fece a Menandro, togliendoli il titolo senza toccargli il suggetto, . . . cioè . . . Il tormentatore di se stesso: Ho volsuto non ostante intitolarla *L'Ipocondriaco*, per farmi intender dal Volgo, già che la lingua, e lo stile sono volgari. Non ho lasciato però d'imitare quei due grandi Eroi di Scipione, e Lelio, che ne furono (e non Terenzio come probabilmente si crede) i veri Autori, nel non volere Romanzeggiare Istorie, e chimerizar Romanzi, ma fondar semplicemente il suggetto sopra una passione Umana, . . .

Sarò tacciato, perchè essendomi commesso un Drama giocoso, io l'abbia fondato su l'Ipocondria: . . . Nè mi difende l'averla mescolata con l'Amore, che al parere del Zacuto, è un male della medesima specie: . .

Dubito, che il verso per la sua facilità ti parrà basso, . . . Ma considerando la qualità del Soggetto forse compatirai me, & il Compositore della Musica reflettendo all'industria, che ci vuole per far, ch'il Verso apparisca Prosa, e la Musica un Discorso naturale . . .

Ti supplico in oltre a compatire i più celebri Cantori, se non faranno pompa dell'eccellenza de i loro talenti, non glie n'avendo io data occasione per non guastar l'ordine del Drama, . . . "

Music: Giovanni Battista Benini bolognese, according to a Ms in **I** VO, Ant. Ormanni, "Catalogo di autori volteranni." The Ms catalogue is quoted by Maffei, pp. 21-23. It has been frequently stated that the music was composed by G.M. Buini for the Pratolino performance, which is not a defensible proposition. *L'Ipocondriaco* was performed again in Bologna in 1707 (in **I** Bu. See Ricci, p. 399), but it is not certain that Buini wrote the music until the season of 1717-1718 (Ricci, p. 417).

Roles: Cleone, Limbella, Tarpino, Florinda, Elvira, Cleandro, Gilberto.

Cast: Ferdinando obtained from the Duke of Mantua Gio. Battista Cavani [Puliti, p. 73, spells the name Carani], Maria Maddalena Musi, and from the Duke of Zagarola, Girolamo Bigelli. Among his own singers Carl'Antonio Zanardi, Antonio Ferrini, Francesco de Castris, Giuseppe Canavesi, and a mysterious Carlo Bertini (1694-1695), were available as well as Martino Bitti, composer-violinist, and Giov. Battista Gigli, theorbist.

Comment: Settimani, cited by the Atti dell'Accademia, p.11, records that "riuscirono di grande ammirazione alcuni intermezzi di macchine d'invenzione del cav. Filippo Acciaioli rappresentati insieme coll'opera in musica *L'Ipocondriaco* nell'anno a Pratolino con istraordinario concorso di spettatori." Fagiuoli, I, f. 229, attended September 26 and recorded the final performance on September 29. The first performance would have taken place towards the beginning of the month.

(1695)[5]
(Figline)

GLI EQUIVOCI GELOSI. Drama musicale rappresentato da' Sig. Accademici Illuminati nella Terra di Figline. Dedicato al mento impareggiabile dell' illustriss. Sig. March. Antonio Salviati Cacciator maggiore del Serenissimo

Granduca di Toscana. In Firenze, per Vincenzio Vangelisti, 1695.
I Rn.

Poet and composer unknown. Figline (not Val d'Arno) is north of Prato.
Included here for the benefit of any scholar wishing to do a study of
opera in Figline.

Dedication signed without date by Domenico Piazzini, who also signed
Il Tirinto in 1692[6].

Roles: Olindo, sotto nome d'Idaste; Elisa, sotto nome di Rosalba; Armindo
sotto nome di Eurindo; Clemizia sotto nome di Tempizia; Vafrino, who is
the only one using his own name!

1695[6]
Sorgenti

LO SPOSALIZIO TRA SEPOLCRI. Opera tragicomica [in prosa] di Gianbatista
Ricciardi, Fiorentino, rappresentata nel Teatro de' Signori Accademici
Sorgenti in Firenze. Bologna, Longhi, 1695.
I Mb, Rn.

Text: Ricciardi.

Comment: It cannot be assumed that the date of publication is the date
of the performance by the Sorgenti. See 1688[1]. In 1694 Longhi
published *Donna saggia può ciò che vuole* (according to Allacci, col. 262)
which was likewise a reissue of a comedy performed by the Sorgenti
some years earlier. See 1694[2], 1679[3].

1696[1] 6 ii
Vangelista

LA FORTUNATA DISPERAZIONE DEL PRINCIPE CELIMAURO. Commedia
eroica del D[ott]. A[ntonio]. S[alvi]. [in prose] Rappresentata nel
Teatro della Venerabile Compagnia di S. Giovanni Evangelista di Firenze
l'anno 1695 [*ab inc.*] Firenze, Vincenzio Vangelisti, 1695.
I Rn.

Text: Salvi.

Comment: Fagiuoli, I, f. 234, gives date and cites Salvi as the author.
Fagiuoli played the part of the *servo ridicolo*.

1696[2]
Sorgenti

PIRRO E DEMETRIO. Drama per musica rappresentato in Firenze l'anno
1696 dedicato al Serenissimo Principe Ferdinando di Toscana. Firenze,
il Vangelisti e Matini, 1696.
A Wu; I Bc, Fm.

Text (with alterations): Adriano Morselli who is named in the Venetian
libretto of 1690 (see Sonneck, p. 878). O.T.: *La forza della Fedeltà*.
Dedication mentions theater.

Music: Alessandro Scarlatti, according to Fabbri, *A. Scarlatti*, who equates
this performance to a performance of the preceding year in Siena, which
in turn is the same (with some additions by Domenico Franchini) as the
opera performed in Naples, 1694, and Rome the same year. Scores in B
Br (Fétis) and I Nc; two collections of arias also in I Nc. (Zanetti, p. 78;
Dent, p. 209.)

1696[3]

MUZIO SCEVOLA. Dramma per musica rappresentato in Firenze l'anno
1696. In Firenze, Vincentio Vangelisti, 1696.
I Bc.

Text (with modifications): Niccolo Minato. On the basis of a spot-check, the libretto is identical with the libretto of Rome, 1695 (libretto in **I** Bu, score by Alessandro Stradella in **I** MOe under the title *Oracle sul ponte*) and very close to the Neapolitan libretto of 1698 with music by Alessandro Scarlatti (libretto in **I** Bu, scores according to Zanetti, p. 76, in **I** Bu and Nc). Fabbri, "Firenze," col. 382, ascribes the music to Cavalli, which seems most unlikely. Prudence counsels:

Music (lost): Anonymous.

Roles: Publicola, Tarquinio Superbo, Ismeno, Muzio Scevola, Porsenna, Orazio Cocle, Valeria, Elisa, Vitellia, Lesbina, Milo, Publio.

1696[4]

TEODORA AUGUSTA. Drama per musica da rappresentarsi in Firenze l'anno 1696 dedicato alla Serenissima Violante Beatrice di Baviera Principessa di Toscana. Firenze, il Vangelisti e Matini, 1696.
I Bc, Rn.

Text: Adriano Morselli with additions. Dedication, signed without date by N.N., speaks of a previous performance under the protection of the princess in Livorno, for which performance no libretto has been located. **I** Fn (Landau Finaly 261 [unnumbered manuscript]) contains an anonymous PROLOGO [and QUATRO INTERMEZZI] DELLA TEODORA for music and for three *personaggi*: Clitemnestra, Oreste, e Pilade. But for the title there is no other link with the opera.

Music (lost): Probably by Domenico Gabrielli with additions by Giacomo Antonio Perti. The Florentine libretto is without significant variation from the libretto in **I** Rn of Bologna, 1687 (Recaldini e Giulio Borzaghi). This libretto identifies Morselli and Gabrielli and carefully indicates all additions with quotation marks, for which Perti and Giorgio Maria Rapparini take responsibility by signing the dedication. The Gabrielli score was first performed in Venice in 1686 or somewhat earlier since that libretto already speaks of changes. However, it should not be overlooked that Alessandro Scarlatti set the text for Rome, 1693, of which the score is in **GB** Oc and libretto in **I** Bc (Dent, p. 209). Zanetti, p. 81, lists another score in **I** Fc and various fragments.

1696[5] 20 ix
Pratolino

TITO MANLIO. Drama per musica rappresentato nella Villa di Pratolino. Firenze, Gio. Filippo Cecchi, 1696.
I Bc, Bu, Fc, Fm, Mb, Rn; **S** Uu; **US** Wc.

Text: Matteo Noris, according to Allacci, col. 769.

Music: C. Francesco Pollaroli. The libretto of Venice, 1697 (in **I** Bu) mentions the first performance in Pratolino, a second in Florence "a few months" before the Venetian performance and declares that Pollaroli is the composer. No libretto found for the city of Florence. Date is of Fagiuoli's attendance; first performance would be earlier. Fifty-eight *arie e ariette* in **I** Nc.

Cast: Ferdinando obtained Antonio Rinaldi from Marchese Achille Maria di Grassi (Bologna); Maria Maddalena Musi from the Duke of Mantua. Those of his own singers mentioned in arrangements to sing elsewhere (except during September) are Maria Domenica Pini, Antonio Ferrini, Francesco de Castris, and G.B. Gigli, theorbist.

1697¹ i
Tintori

LA FEDE NE'TRADIMENTI. Drama per musica rappresentato in Firenze l'anno 1696, *ab inc.* Dedicato al Sereniss. Principe Gio. Gastone di Toscana. Firenze, Vincenzio Vangelisti, 1697.
I Bc, Bu, Vgc.

Text: Girolamo Gigli, not mentioned here, but he signs the first libretto of Siena, 1689 (see Sonneck, p. 484). Dedication, signed by the Impresari, Gen. 1696 [*ab inc.*] names the theater but not the academy. The language in fact suggests that the theater is being used by a group especially convening for the production of the opera: "La Conversazione, che si cimenta, in quest'anno, di rappresentare, nel Teatro del Corso de' Tintori, il Drama, sotto il titolo, della FEDE NE' TRADIMENTI . . . ."

Roles: Garzia, Anagilda, Fernando, Elvira, Tisbe, Gillo.

Music: Possibly by Giuseppe Fabbrini, who is named in the Siena libretto. No score known.

1697² carn

IL DOMIZIO. Drama per musica rappresentato in Firenze l'anno 1696 *ab inc.* Firenze, Vincenzio Vangelisti, 1697.
I Bc, Bu, Mb.

Text: Giulio Cesare Corradi, Parmigiano, according to Allacci, there being only one libretto with that title, col. 261. First published in Venice in 1696. No author, composer or theater mentioned.

Music (lost): Possibly by Marc'Antonio Ziani who composed the music for the Venetian performance, according to Allacci, col. 261.

1697³ aut

FLAVIO CUNIBERTO. Drama per musica rappresentato in Firenze nell' autunno del 1697. Firenze, Vincenzio Vangelisti, 1697.
I Bc, Fm.

Text: Matteo Noris, not mentioned here, but he is identified in the title of the Venice, 1682, first publication (see Sonneck, p. 518).

Music: Probably by Alessandro Scarlatti, whose score was used in Rome, 1696, according to Fabbri, *A. Scarlatti*, p. 42. But other settings are possible: G.D. Partenio (Venice, 1682 and 1687), and Domenico Gabrielli, Modena, 1688. The first is the most common attribution for this performance, while the second appears in manuscript in a libretto in I Fm.
Scarlatti's score for 1696 is in B Bc (Dent, p. 208), GB Oc, and fragments in I Nc, Rvat (Zanetti, p. 73). New arias by Scarlatti were substituted in the Pratolino performance in 1702. Scores by Partenio and Gabrielli not known.

1697⁴ 9, 12, 14 ix
Pratolino

Una commedia in musica.
No libretto for this performance has been located. Possibly none was published, as was the case in 1692⁵.

Music (lost): On June 18, 1697, Ferdinando wrote to the Conte di Novellara asking him to concede his *maestro di cappella*, Isidoro Ceruti, "che bramerei tenere appresso di me durante la mia prossima consueta villeggiatura di Pratolino . . ." Ceruti, an old man in failing health, remained in Florence for the rest of his life, dying in late 1698 or early the next year (I Fas [Med 5883, cc. 343, 345, 353, 386, 388]). That Ferdinando called him to

Pratolino suggests that he performed one of Ceruti's operas, and if so, probably not a new one since the procedure of sending the libretto to Ceruti is not recorded in the prince's correspondence. A clue pointing in another direction is found in I Fas (Med 5882, c. 87), which is a letter of recommendation addressed to the Elettrice Palatina in Düsseldorf for Il Virtuoso Boloncini, *professore della musica*. The proximity of the date, October 19, 1697, to the end of the villeggiatura di Pratolino is suggestive.

Cast: Ferdinando engaged Giuseppe Scaccia, virtuoso of the Duke of Parma, to replace Matteo Sassani, who was called to Spain abruptly in July by the King. Scaccia returned to Parma September 28. Among Ferdinando's own singers mentioned in correspondence with various patrons and impresari the following were certainly available: Maria Domenica Pini, Francesco de Castris, Antonio Ferrini, Anna Maria Lisi, and, for the first time after several years of study with Giuseppe Vecchi in Rome, Raffaello or Raffaellino Baldi. Another addition to Ferdinando's singers is Lucrezia Andre detta la Carrò. She was first a singer in the service of the Card. Niccolo Acciajuoli from whom Ferdinando engaged her for Livorno in the carnival of 1697, but by the following year the Duke of Mantua asks Ferdinando's permission to have Carrò sing in his oratorio. Also mentioned is Martino Bitti, violinist and composer.

1697⁵

IL GIRELLO. Drama burlesco per musica rappresentato in Firenze l'anno 1697. Firenze, Vincenzio Vangelisti, 1697.
I Bc.

Text: Filippo Acciajuoli. Protest as usual blames the Signori Musici for the changes in the text.

Music: Probably by Jacopo Melani, with a prologue by Alessandro Stradella (see 1670¹). There was a revival of *Il Girello* in Bologna, 1696 (I Bc) in which the dedication recounts, ". . . Scherzo Dramatico, ingegnosa fatica di Spirito tanto grande, e sublime ben noto a tutto il mondo, e perche questo si trova da tanti anni in qua privo d'un tanto padre, qual'Orfano infelice, dovendo di nuovo comparire su Teatri, e farsi vedere alle Stampe, habbiamo stimato necessario di presentarlo sotto la Tutela di Dame di tanta autorità e prudenza acciò venga assistito, e difeso da qualsivoglia insulto." Since Acciajuoli was still living, the reference to *Il Girello* as an orphan can only be interpreted as a reference to Melani, who died in 1676. See Weaver, "Il Girello."

1697⁶

GL'INGANNI FELICI. Drama per musica da rappresentarsi in Firenze l'anno MDCXCVII. Firenze, Vincenzio Vangelisti, 1697.
I Bn, Bu.

Text: Apostolo Zeno, not mentioned, but reprinted in the *Poesie dramatiche* I, p. 17.

Music: Probably by Carlo Francesco Pollaroli, whose score was used for the Venetian performance of the preceding year (Allacci, col. 451).

1697⁷
Irresoluti

LA SERVA NOBILE. Trattenimento scenico da recitarsi in Firenze nel corrente anno 1697 dagli Accademici Irresoluti. Firenze, Vincenzio Vangelisti, 1697.
I Rn.

Text: A prose reduction of G.A. Moniglia's *commedia in musica.*

1698[1] 26 i
Sorgenti

Fagiuoli II, f. 32r: "Alla commedia in musica recitata nel Teatro
de'Sorgenti nata rissa fra il S.r Cav.r Gio:Batt.a Corboli, e il S.r Gio:Nardi
a conto di far applauso più a una, che a un'altra comica. Il S.r Corboli
diede uno schiaffo al S.r Nardi. Ci furon varij inutili trattati d'aggiustamento;
furon ambedue sequestati, e finalm[en] te essendo il S.r Cav.r Corboli
Gent[iluo] mo di Cam[er] a del S.r Card.le [Francesco de' Medici], q[ues] ti
le prese in petto q[ues] te rifl[ession] i, e finì la festa con pochi sodisfaz[ion] e
del Nardi il dì 26 d[etto] ."

It is not possible to be secure about the opera concerned in these
fisticuffs, but in the absence of indications to the contrary, one of the following,
being the only operas recorded in Florence for this carnival, was possibly
performed at the Teatro de' Sorgenti, not at the Cocomero.

1698[2] carn

BELISARIO IN RAVENNA ovvero I RIVALI GENEROSI. Drama rappresentato
in Firenze nel Carnovale del 1698. Firenze, Vincenzio Vangelisti Stamp.
Arcivesc., MDCXCVIII.
I Bc, Fm, Mb.

Text: Apostolo Zeno with alterations. Reprinted in the author's *Poesie
drammatiche,* vol. V (1744), pp. [267] - 352. On p. 7 of the above libretto,
La stampatore a chi legge says: "È stata necessario mutare alcune arie,
ed aggiungerne altre con pochi versi di recitativo . . . attesoche è convenuto
accomodar la Poesia a Musica già fatta sopra d'altre parole . . . nella stampa
di Venezia . . ." The added words appear at the end of the libretto. The
comments clearly mean that both the words and the music were previously
used in Venice.

Music (lost): Marc'Antonio Ziani by inference based on the above. Venetian
libretto of 1697 listed by Sonneck, p. 942.

1698[3] carn

CAMILLA, REGINA DE' VOLSCI. Drama rappresentato in Firenze nel
Carnovale del 1698. Firenze, Vincenzio Vangelisti, 1698.
I Fn (destroyed), Vgc.

Text: Silvio Stampiglia, not named here, but whose name is in the title of
the libretto of Naples, 1696 (I Bu). *Lo stampatore a chi legge:* "Eccoti
la seconda Opera chi devi ascoltare in questo presente carnovale: anche
in essa è stata necessario mutare alcune cose che non tornavano bene
a' personaggi destinati a rappresentarla. Questa mutazione però non
diversifica punto il Drama dal suo primo essere."

Music: Possibly by Antonio Maria Bononcini, who is not mentioned. A
score in D MÜps is dated Napoli, 1697 (first performance), but ascribed
incorrectly to Giovanni Bononcini. A copy in GB Lbm of the second and
third acts is ascribed to Marc'Antonio. There is also a score by Antonio
Draghi in A Wn for Vienna, 1690, but it is not likely that Draghi's score
was used in Florence. No opportunity has been found for confronting
these scores and librettos.

Cast: Probably includes Cristina Morelli who was given license and a warm
recommendation from Ferdinando on April 3, 1698 (I Fas [Med 5883,
c. 589 bis]). It may be pure coincidence that on March 12, 1698, the Duke

of Mantua requested of Ferdinando the use of Anna Maria Lisi and Lucrezia Andrèe detta la Carrò to sing *Camilla* "già tempo cantato in Napoli," but the fact suggests that the Duke knew that the women were performing or had just performed the opera in Florence (Med 5883, cc. 18, 81).

1698[4] 14 v
Sorgenti

Dov'è uomini è modo, *commedia in musica*.
Fagiuoli II, f. 39: "A dì 14 [May, 1698]. Si fece una commedia in musica ai Sorgenti intitolata *Dov'è uomini è modo*."
 No opera with this or similar, curious title known.

1698[5] 25 ix
Pratolino

ANACREONTE. Drama per musica rappresentato nella Villa di Pratolino. Firenze, Gio. Filippo Cecchi, 1698.
B Bc; I Fm, Fn, Rca, Rn; S Uu.

Text: D. Francesco Bussani with minor alterations by comparison with the edition of Venice, 1678, with the title of *Anacreonte tiranno*.

Music: Francesco de Castris, Martino Bitti, and Alessandro Scarlatti. The composers are identified in seventeenth century manuscript at the end of the Argomento: "I recitativi, e l'Arie contrasegnato con q[ues] to segno # sono tutte poste in musica dal Sig.re Fran[cesc]o de Castris. Il pr[i]mo e 3:o Atto è composizione del Sig.re Martino Bitti, et il 2:o Atto del Sig.re Alessandro Scarlatti, a riserva di q[ues] to che è contrasegnato col segno #."
 No scores by Bitti and de Castris are known. The identity of the score by Scarlatti is confused. In D MÜps there is a full score (all three acts) attributed to Alessandro Scarlatti, but H.C. Wolf, pp. 59-61, asserts that this score is the setting by Antonio Sartorio composed for Venice, 1678. The ascription needs to be re-studied. The D MÜps score probably is not for the performance at Pratolino, though the watermarks (a *giglio* in a double circle) indicate such a provenance. However, the appearance of "Per amor sarò guerriera," Act. II, scene 14, in the 1698 libretto and the score and its absence in the libretto of 1678 casts some doubt upon Wolf's attribution.

Cast: The libretto of I Rn contains the singers in manuscript additions which unfortunately have been cropped. The names can be reconstructed as follows: Anacreonte - S.r [Giuseppe] Canave[si] ; Rosiclea - S.ra Vittoria [Tarquini] Bombac[i] ; Anassarco - S.r Domenico Graz[iani] ; Silena - S.r Raffael[lo] [Baldi] ; Oronte - S.r [Francesco] de C[astris] ; Isifile - Sig.ra [Maria Maddalena Musi detta la] Mign[atta] ; Florimondo - C[arlo] Ant[oni] o Z[anardi] ; Bleno - S.r Gori.

1698[6] aut
(Cocomero)

LAODICEA E BERENICE. Drama per musica rappresentato in Firenze nell'autunno del 1698. Firenze, Vincenzio Vangelisti, 1698.
I Fc, Fm(2), Mb, Rn.

Text: Matteo Noris (Allacci, col. 478).

Music (lost): Possibly by Giacomo Antonio Perti, who composed the music for the first performance in Venice, 1695 (Allacci). However, Bernardo Pasquini was in Florence from September 9, 1698, until March 24, 1699 (I Fas [Med 5883, cc. 339, 379; 5884, cc. 203, 225]). Since he arrived too late to be considered as a possible composer of the Pratolino opera 1697[4], and since he stayed until March, there is a distinct possibility that he furnished a new score for this opera.

Cast: Antioco - Antonio Clara; Laodicea - Lucrezia Andrè detta la Carrò; Berenice - Francesca Vennini; Stesicrate - Filippo Maganini; Origene - Antonio Rinaldi; Gilade - Francesca Borghesi; Delbo - Stefano Coralli.

Comment: Although some of the earlier librettos (beginning notably in 1696) without dedications and signatures of academicians probably belong to the continuing (hereafter) series of operas presented by individual impresarios using a mixture of imported and local singers, the present one is the first to publish the list of singers and therefore make it possible to observe a fairly stable company of singers in Florence. The stability of the company suggests that they have their seat in one theater, which by the following year becomes identified as the Cocomero although the librettos continue not to name the theater. The use of parentheses indicates a libretto that can be identified as being for a performance at the Cocomero by the list of the performers.

(1698)[7]

Apollo geloso.

Text: Pier Jac. Martello; music by G.A. Perti. No libretto found. Cited by Schmidl, "Perti," who errs in saying that it was performed at Pratolino. Probably in error for the performance in Bologna in the same year (see Allacci, col. 97; libretto in **I Rn**). The same statement is repeated in Franz Giegling, col. 1106.

1698[8]
Collegio Tolomei

IL CONCERTO DELLE VIRTÙ SOSTENUTO NELLO SCONCERTO DEGL' ELEMENTI. Accademia di Lettere, e d'Armi tenuti in Firenze da' SS Convittori del Nobil Collegio Tolomei in tributo d'ossequio all beneficenza del Serenissimo Granduca di Toscana Cosimo III. E dedicata al medesimo l'anno M.DC. XCVIII. Firenze, Gio: Filippo Cecchi.
I Fn.
A description containing lists of instrumental performers, dancers, and participants. No composers named.

1698[9]

Filippo Macedone. Dramma per musica.
Text by Gio. Cosimo Villifranchi. The work is listed in the *Vita* prefacing the *Raccolta di opuscoli*, p. xxix, where it is said erroneously that it was recited in the Teatro di via della Pergola. No libretto found. Unknown to bibliographers.

1698[10] 31 xii
(Cocomero)

MASSIMO PUPPIENO. Melodrama rappresentato in Firenze nel Carnovale dell'Anno 1699. Firenze, Vincenzio Vangelisti, 1699.
I Bc, Bu, Fm, Rn.

Text: Aurelio Aureli (not mentioned) by comparison with the Venetian libretto of 1684 (**I Fm**) which is signed by the author. Fagiuoli II, f. 61v: "A dì 31 [Dic. 1698]. Andai all commed.a intitolata [blank] che si fece in musica nel Teatro degli Infuocati." That the entry refers to the above is deduced by comparison with the second opera of the season, *Demofonte.*

Music: Anonymous. The libretto was first set by Carlo Pallavicino for Venice,

1684 (repeated in 1685), librettos in **I** Fm and **US** Wc respectively. The score, according to Loewenberg, is lost. It was set a second time by Alessandro Scarlatti for Naples, 1695 (Dent, p. 208). The latter seems more likely to have been used than the Pallavicino setting. Scarlatti's score in **I** MC; fragments in **I** MOe, Nc, and Vnm (Zanetti, p. 76, who does not list this libretto).

Cast: Massimo Puppieno - Filippo Maganini; Claudia - Giov. Atti Gabrielli; Flavio - Francesca Borghesi; Elio - Antonio Clara; Massimino - Antonio Rinaldi; Decio - Lorenzo Berretta; Sulpizia - Francesca Venini; Gilbo - Stefano Coralli.

1698[11]
Tintori
Cadenti

La Zoraide o pure Amore vince la simplicità, opera scenica [in prosa] recit.a nel Teatro dei S.r Acc. Cadenti 1698.
I Fn (Cl vii, Ms 755). Text probably by Pier Susini, altered by Antonio Fineschi da Radda. See 1700[1].

1699[1] **25 ii**
Cocomero
Infuocati

DEMOFONTE. Drama per musica rappresentato in Firenze nel Carnevale dell'anno 1699. Firenze, Vincenzio Vangelisti, 1699.
I Bc, Bu, Fc, Mb, MOe.

Text: According to the Ms catalogue of **I** MOe, by Francesco Beverini to whom Allacci ascribes a libretto of Rome, 1669, col. 247, copy in **US** Wc. It is, at any rate, totally different from Metastasio's libretto of the same title.

Music (lost): Composer unknown.

Cast: Demofonte - Antonio Clara; Pallante - Antonio Rinaldi; Nerone - Giovanna Atti Gabrielli; Orogia - Maria Caterina Goslerin; Itaura - Maria Domenica Marini; Delmino - Francesca Venini; Eristeo - Filippo Maganini; Golo - Stefano Coralli.

Comment: Fagiuoli II, f. 66v: "Dom. 25 [Feb. 1698/99]. All'accad[emi]a degl'Infuocati l'opera in musica intitolata il *Demofonte* dr." Hence it is the second opera of the season. Putting the two seasons of 1698 and 1699 together, it is apparent that opera is now being presented in Florence on a schedule similar to that of Venice: two operas in the carnival season, one beginning in the week after Christmas, the other in February. Unless Fagiuoli was confused about the theaters (a distinct possibility), the pattern was first set up in the Sorgenti and then in 1699 transferred to the Cocomero. It should also be noted that the Sorgenti retain the rights to a spring season, while the Cocomero resumes with a summer season and a late fall season following the opera at Pratolino. This practical ordering of the operatic seasons to restrain competition among the theaters in Florence will become more clearly documented in the next decades.

1699[2] **12 iii**

Death notice of Giovanni Cosimo Villifranchi in Fagiuoli II, f. 65v.

1699[3] **30 iv-9 v**
Sorgenti

LA VECCHIA SPOSA ovvero L'AMORE MEDESIMO IN TUTTI. Drama rusticale D.P.G.B. rappresentata in Firenze nella Primavera dell'anno 1699. Firenze, Vincenzio Vangelisti, 1699.
I Fn, Rn.

Text: Anonymous. **I** Fn *Notizie storiche di Firenze* (MS Palatino, series Targione, n. 15): "30 April, 1699. Mercoledì si diede principio al Teatro de' Sorgenti all'opera in musica intitolata lo *Sposalizio della vecchia* con il pago una lira per testa avendone fatte sino ad'ora sino in tre, ma si sente grand-applauso." Fagiuoli II, f. 69r: "A dì 9 [Maggio, 1699] . . . La sera a' Sorgenti si recitò un dramma musicale intitolata *Vecchia sposa*."

Music (lost): Composer unknown.

Cast: Mona Mea vecchia - Filippo Rossi; Crezia - Ortenzia Beverini; Gosto - Anton Cammillo Bini; Nanni - Antonio Francesco Gabbrielli; Menca - Angelica Bracci; Maso - (blank).

1699⁴ 5 v   I Fas (Med 5884, cc. 19, 57) is an exchange between Ferdinando and Rinaldo d'Este concerning Giuseppe Londra comico detto Flaminio who arrived in Florence from Modena on date shown. Ferdinando's original request for the service of Londra is in F 5883, c. 115, 19 Aug., 1698, and Rinaldo's reply postponing Londra's departure from Modena is in c. 49. It is not clear whether Londra's function is that of a courier or a performer.

1699⁵ 12 vi   *Chi non sa fingere non sa vivere, ovvero le cautele politiche.* Commedia in prosa.

Text: Giambattista Ricciardi.

Comment: Fagiuoli II, f. 78r. "Merc[oledi] 12 G[iugno, 1699] . . . la sera alla commedia de Paggi in Paggeria, che è del Ricciardi intitolata *le Cautele politiche*." The comedy was published in Bologna by Longhi twice, once without date and once in 1679 (I Rca, but common). G.C. Villifranchi published a *Prologo per musica* for this play in his *Raccolta di Opuscoli*, p. 3. The prologue and play were previously performed in 1672².

1699⁶ 24 iii
(Cocomero)   IL SOSPETTO NON HA FONDAMENTO overo LA COSTANZA NEGLI AMORI. Drama pastorale rappresentato in Firenze nell'estate del 1699. Firenze, Vincenzio Vangelisti, 1699.
I Bc.

Text: Francesco Bartolomeo Nencini with minor changes.

Music: Alessandro Melani. See 1691³ , *Il sospetto senza fondamento*.

Cast: Clori - Maria Domenica Pini; Eurillo - Maria Maddalena Vettori; Lidia - Maria Maddalena Fratini; Rosauro - Raffaello Baldi; Filli - Domenico Fontani.

Comment: Bonazzini II, pp. 324ff., records an altercation between the Proveditore Niccolini and obstreperous auditors of the opera that led to an exchange of blows, thus dating the performance.

1699⁷ 1 x   I Fac: The earliest extant contract for the rental of the Cocomero by the Infuocati. The charter of organization in the same archive bears the same date.

1699⁸ 6, 13 ix
Pratolino   FARAMONDO. Drama per musica rappresentato nella Villa di Pratolino. Firenze, Gio. Filippo Cecchi, 1699.
B Bc; I Bc, Fm, Fn, Rc, Vgc; US CA, Wc.

Text (with alterations): Apostolo Zeno. The Argomento speaks of the changes in what appears to be an understatement. See Sonneck, p. 474.

Music: Anonymous. It is regularly stated by bibliographers that the score is by

Carlo Pollarolo who set the libretto for a performance in Venice in the carnival of 1699. Caution is in order. Pollarolo may have provided a new score, but that score is not the one in **A** Wn which agrees with the Venetian libretto.

Cast: Ferdinando engaged Maria Maddalena Musi from the Duke of Mantua. Mentioned in his correspondence of 1699 among his own musicians are Francesco de Castris, Vittoria Tarquini, Maria Domenica Marini, Lucrezia Andre, Maria Domenica Pini, and Serafina virtuosa (Anna Coltellini).

Comment: Fagiuoli II, f. 82v: "Dom[eni]ca 6 d. [Sett. 1699] Il G. Duca andò a Pratolino alla commedia in musica intitolata *il Faramondo*." Also f. 83v: "Dom[eni]ca 13 7bre [1699]. Con S.r Gio: D[omeni]co Brandi andai a Pratolino all'opera del *Faramondo*, fù ad inchinar il S.r Card.le [Francesco de'Medici].

1699⁹ 25 xi
Cocomero

IL PRIGIONIERO FORTUNATO. Drama per musica rappresentato in Firenze nell'autunno del 1699. Firenze, Vincenzio Vangelisti, 1699.
I Bc, Bu, Mb, MOe.

Text: Francesco Maria Paglia, not mentioned, but identified in the libretto of the first performance in Naples, 1698 (**B** Bc).

Music: Alessandro Scarlatti, according to a diary quoted below. Score and two collections of arias in **I** Nc; score also in **GB** Lbm (Zanetti, p. 79; Dent, p. 209).

Comment: Fabbri, *A. Scarlatti*, p. 42, quotes I Fn Ms II-94, *Diario dal 1600 al 1737*: "Il 'Prigioniero' del sommo Scarlatti ha tenuti tutti prigionieri coloro che erano venuti a goder quest'opera in musica, per la varietà delle vicende, le scene gustose e la musica eccellente . . . Il Serenissimo Principe, che protege quel celebre Professore, fu al solito presente, nel suo palco adorno di fiorami."
    Fagiuoli II, f. 87v: "Fui la sera al Teatro degl'Infuocati all'op[er]a in musica intit[ola]ta il *carcerier fortunato*." Fagiuoli's title is also used in another Ms in **I** Fn by Giulio Santini quoted by Maylender.

1700¹ 21 i
Tintori

Amore vince la semplicità, commedia in prosa, sogg[et]to di Pier Susini vertito da Ant[oni]o Fineschi da Radda.
Fagiuoli II, f. 92v: " . . . agl'Imperfetti, o si chiamivi adesso al [illegible], nel corso de'Tintori," [The new name actually appears to be' written "intromenti."] The above title appears in 1698¹¹ as the *ossia* for *Zoraide*. Neither title known to bibliographers. No publication for this performance found.

1700² 24 i
Cocomero

CARLO RE D'ALEMAGNA. Drama per musica rappresentato in Firenze nel Carnevale dell'anno 1700. Firenze, Vincenzio Vangelisti, s.d.
I Bu, Fc, Mb.

Text: Giacomo Maggi, not mentioned, but this is the same libretto with alterations as that published in Genoa, 1699, which bears the poet's name (**I** Bu). Allacci, col. 167, attributes to Francesco Silvani the Bologna 1713 libretto with music "nuovamente composta" by Giuseppe Maria Orlandini (he does not list an earlier publication). However, this libretto of 1713 which does not mention the poet is in some respects closer to the Genoan than the Florentine libretto is. Hence Allacci is probably in error.

Music (lost): Composer unknown.

Cast: Carlo - Maria Chiara Mozzi; Lotario - Pietro Mozzi; Adalgiso - Antonio Giustacchini; Eduige - Anna Maria Coltellini; Giuditta - Isabella de Angeles; Gildippe - Anna Maria Marchesini; Berardo - Barbera Cristina Morelli; Asprando - Niccolo Giannini; Nerina - Domenico Fontani; Fronzo - Stefano Coralli. (The comic roles differ from Genoa, 1699, where they are Lesba and Edippo.)

Comment: Fagiuoli II, f. 94r, attended with his wife on date shown. Fabbri quotes I Fm Ms. C-27, *Libro di ricordi di Fosco Portinari*, p. 5, 24 i 1700: "Ricordo come in questo passato carnevale s'e recitata nel Teatro di Via del Cocomero la Commedia in Musica intitolata 'Carlo Re d'Alemagna' ove, fra i più celebri musici, hanno recitato la Signora Isabella de Angelis Romana, singolare nell'azione e intelligenza della scena, la Signora Anna Coltellini, detta La Serafina, virtuosa del Serenissimo Principe Ferdinando di Toscana, la più rara e famosa, per la buona e delicata voce, che forse si senta hoggi per i teatri dell'Europa."

**1700³ carn
(Cocomero)**

LA CADUTA DE'DECEMVIRI. Drama per musica rappresentato in Firenze nel Carnevale dell'anno 1700. Firenze, Vincenzio Vangelisti, 1700. I Bc, MOe, Rn.

Text: Silvio Stampiglia, not mentioned here, but identified in the title of Naples, 1697 (**US** Wc). Performed also in Livorno by the Accademici Avvalorati in 1699 (dedicated to Ferdinando de'Medici) (**I** Fm).

Music: Alessandro Scarlatti, not mentioned, composed for Naples, 1697. Scores: **B** Br; **GB** Lbm; **I** Nc (3, plus two collections of arias). See Zanetti, p. 67; Dent, p. 207.

Cast: Appio Claudio - Antonio Giustacchini; Claudia - Anna Marchesini; Valeria - Anna Maria Coltellini; Lucio Verginio - Pietro Mozzi; Virginia - Isabella de Angelis; Icilio - Niccolo Giannini; Servilla - Domenico Fontani; Flacco - Stefano Coralli.

Comment: Fabbri, *A. Scarlatti*, p. 43, claims that the above date should be corrected to read 1701. He is in error. It had not been common for the date on the title page of a publication to be *ab incarnatione* or Lady Day Calendar since the first quarter of the seventeenth century. Dedications are sometimes *ab inc.*, e.g. 1674, *Tacere et amare*, and diaries continue obstinately to maintain the old style into the eighteenth century. Letters, on the other hand, often are signed *ab inc.* but dated at the top of the letter in the Gregorian year. The situation is confusing and we are by no means certain that we have interpreted all dates correctly, but Fabbri's regular translation of dates appearing on the title pages of libretti into following years is simply wrong.

**1700⁴ 17, 19,
23 ii
Tintori**

Amor[e] *e politica.* Commedia in prosa.

Text: Giovanni Cosimo Villifranchi. See 1677.

Music (incidental): Anonymous.

Comment: Fagiuoli II, f. 94v, mentioned this play with incidental music on dates shown. On February 19 he says: "Di nuovo alla com[medi]a d'*Amor, e politica* nel Corso de' Tintori, ne quel Teatro, che allora era degl' Imperfetti, fu recitata la prima volta in vita dell'autore Dr. Villifranchi l'anno 1676. Coll'assist[enz] a d'esso e del S.r Ant[oni] o da Spada [*sic* for Radda?], e fu recitata con altro garbo." Bonazzini II, p. 371, mentions the performances at the Cocomero and Tintori and a fifth at the Casino del Cardinale for this carnival.

Casino

1700[5] sum
Cocomero

Nicomede. Commedia [in prose?].
Maylender V, p. 21, states that such a work was performed by the Infuocati with no further information. Fagiuoli II, f. 102r: "A dì [blank] andai agl' Infuocati alla com[medi] a intitolata il *Nicomede* recitata dai Cav[alie] ri, bella comedia e ben recitata. Ci fu il S.r Card.le de' Medici." No libretto found.

1700[6] 5 ix
Casa Fioravanti

L'amante di se stesso. Commedia [in prose?].
Text by Pier Susini. Fagiuoli II, f. 117v: "Dom.ca 5 [Sett. 1700]. La sera in Casa Fioravanti fu alla com[medi] a intitolata *l'Amante di se stesso* di Pier Susini. Fu recitata altra volta in squola di Ferrara M[aestr?] o di Scherma Fran[ces] co Berti, dove si recitò Stef[an] o suo figlio da Donna assai bene." No publication found.

1700[7] ix
Pratolino

LUCIO VERO. Drama per musica rappresentato nella Villa di Pratolino. Firenze, Stamperia Reale, 1700.
I Bc, Bu, Fc, Fn(2), Mb, Rn; S Sk, Uu.

Text (with alterations): By Apostolo Zeno, reprinted in *Poesie drammatiche* II, p. 59.

Music (lost): Anonymous. According to Puliti by G.A. Perti, which is unlikely. Perti composed the music for Bologna, 1717 (Allacci, col. 491). It is more often attributed to Carlo Francesco Pollaroli who, Allacci says, wrote the music for the first performance in Venice, 1700 (i.e., the carnival preceding the performance at Pratolino). The changes in the text cast some doubt on this standard attribution.

Cast: Ferdinando engaged Maria Maddalena Musi, as usual, and a new singer, Cattarina Azzolini. Available among his own singers were Vittoria Tarquini, Francesco (?) Ballarini, and presumably Francesco de Castris.

Comment: Fagiuoli II, f. 117r: "A dì [?] Fui invitata dal S.r Card.le [Francesco de' Medici] alla Com[medi] a di Pratolino d[ett] a Il *Lucio Vero* Dr. del . . . e in una sua muta mi fece luogo."

1700[8] 12 ix

Fagiuoli II, f. 117v: "Dom[eni] ca 12 [Sett. 1700]. Morì il S.r Aless.ro Acciaioli Tisico d'anni 23 in c[ir] ca, era stato comico buono ed aveva più volte recitato in via del Cocomero nel Teatro degl'Infuocati."

1700[9] 21 ix

Bonazzini, II, p. 483, records the death of G.A. Moniglia.

1701[1] carn
(Cocomero)

ALARICO RE DE' VANDALI. Drama per musica rappresentato in Firenze nel Carnevale del 1701. Firenze, Vincenzio Vangelisti, MDCCI.
F Pn; I Bc, Fc, Rn, Vnm.

Text: Francesco Silvani, not mentioned here, but identified in the title of the Venetian libretto of 1698 (*L'ingratitudine castigata*). The fact that the cast for *Odoardo* is the same as *Alarico* indicates that the operas are the season's offering in the same theater, but lacking any clue as to which is the first, they are listed alphabetically.

Music: Probably a *pasticcio* combining music by Tommaso Albinoni, who set the libretto of Venice, 1698 (Allacci, col. 456) and Francesco Gasparini as well as others. Such a conclusion may be drawn from the apparently close connection between this Florentine performance and another in Palermo, 1705 (I PLcom). We have not seen the Palermo libretto; however, from Sartori's catalogue it may be observed that two actors are the same as those in the Florentine cast: Giuseppe Ferrari who sang Raimondo, and Ortenzia Beverini, who sang Bleno. Also, the *buffa* scenes of the Florentine libretto are contained in the one in Palermo. Beverini had sung the *intermezzi* to *Fede tradita* in 1704[6] in Florence with Filippo Rossi, who sang Bleno at Palermo. A third singer, Gio: Carlo Bernardi, who sang Edeberto in *Fede tradita*, appears also in the Palermo cast. The Palermo libretto says: ". . . abbiamo scelto fra tante altre la musica del celebre signor Maestro Gasparini. . . e per maggiormente arricchirlo abbiamo scelto alcune Arie dell'altre musica del maestro Albinoni, ed altri autori di finissimo gusto. Buona parte dell'arie sono state di nuovo composte di parole e di musica . . . come pure si sono aggiunte tutte le scene buffe del servo con la servetta, poste in musica da vari . . ."

Cast: Alarico - Giovanni Batista Carboni; Raimondo - Giuseppe Ferrari; Enrico - Caterina Azzolini; Ginevra - Maria Domenica Pini; Brunechilde - Regina Pollastri; Astolfo - Girolamo Lorenzo Cerchi; Bleno - Ortenzia Beverini.

1701[2] carn
(Cocomero)

ODOARDO. Drama per musica rappresentato in Firenze nel carnevale del 1701. Firenze, Vincenzio Vangelisti, s.d.
I Mb.

Text: Apostolo Zeno according to Allacci, col. 570, who lists librettos of 1698, Venice, and 1700, Naples (the latter in I Bc, Bu), and Sonneck, p. 814, who reports that Zeno signed the Venetian libretto as author. But, Sonneck further observes, the opera was not ever published in the works of Zeno nor does it appear in Wotquenne's *Verzeichnis* of arias under Zeno. More doubt is cast upon the authenticity of the "signature" by a statement in the *argomento* of *La fortezza al cimento* (1703[1]) which suggests the possibility that it is by Silvani. The *argomento* identifies the source of the plot as Polydore Vergil, *Anglicae historiae*, Book 6.

Music: Alessandro Scarlatti (Naples, 1700) more probably than Marc' Antonio Ziani (Venice, 1698). A collection of forty-four arias by Scarlatti in I Nc (Zanetti, p. 77). Other collections in D Dsl, F Pc (Dent, p. 208).

Cast: Eduino - Girolamo Lorenzo Cerchi; Odoardo - Gio. Batista Carboni; Matilde - Maria Domenica Pini; Gismonda - Regina Pollastri; Riccardo - Caterina Azzolini; Enrico - Giuliano della Scarperia; Lesbina - Ortenzia Beverini; Adolfo - Giuseppe Ferrari.

Comment: Pini wrote to Ferdinando de' Medici who was in Livorno on January 22 that she could not write earlier because she had been rehearsing the second opera, which "ha incontrato assai più che la prima e si va facendo con qualche concorso sin adesso." She unfortunately fails to name either opera.

1701³ carn
Sorgenti
Tintori

Bonazzini II, p. 540, reports that two operas in music were performed at the Cocomero and that prose comedies were done at the Sorgenti and Cadenti theaters, but he names no titles.

1701⁴ spring?
(Cocomero)

ALBA SOGGIOGATA DA' ROMANI. Drama rappresentato in Firenze l'anno 1701. Firenze, Vincenzio Vangelisti, 1701.
I Bc, Rn.

Text: Adriano Morselli, who is identified in the title of the previous publication in Rome, 1694 (*Tullio Ostilio*), with alterations by Silvio Stampiglia (Sonneck, col. 1107).

Music: Probably by Gio. Bononcini, who is named in the Roman libretto. A spot check among the librettos of Rome, 1694 (**I Fn**), Pisa, 1701, and Florence, 1701, reveals no substantial differences. Further, a link is formed among these and Bologna, 1695 (**I MOe**) and Lucca, 1696 (**I Vgc**) by the presence of Pietro Mozzi in the cast in the role of Tullo Ostilio, which suggests that he is both singer and impresario. He sang in the opera as late as 1727 at Macerata (**I MAC**) but in the role of Araspe.

Cast: Personaggi romani: Tullo Ostilio - Pietro Mozzi; Marzia - Vittoria Costa; Valerio - Giuliano Albertini; Irene - Francesco Passerini. Personaggi albani: Sabina - Lodovica Petri; Silvio - Gio. Batista Tamburini; Ascanio - Clara Sassi; Millo - Stefano Coralli.

Six of these performers appear in the libretto of Pisa, 1701, dedicated to Card. Francesco de' Medici. The dedication indicates that the performance took place during the annual visit to Pisa by the Tuscan court in February. Thus the Florentine performance could not have taken place in the carnival, not likely in any case in view of the two known operas of the carnival; therefore, the spring season appears to be the most logical time for a performance of the opera. That the theater is the Cocomero is shown by the fact that six of the singers performed there at other times.

1701⁵ 11, 14
29 ix
Pratolino

ASTIANATTE. Dramma per musica rappresentato nella Villa di Pratolino. Firenze, Stamperia di S.A.R., appresso P. Ant. Brigonci, 1701.
I Bc, Bu, Fm, Fn, Mb, MOe, Rn(2), Rsc(2); S Uu.

Text: Antonio Salvi (Allacci, col. 124) with arias by Pietro Antonio Bernardoni who recalled in a letter of June 13, 1705, to Ferdinando (**I Fas** [Med 5903, c. 152]) that "Sig.r Francesco de Castris mi presentò quattro anni sono di ubbidirla nel cambiare molte Arie dell'*Astianatte*, drama destinato dall'A.V. per il suo divertimento di Pratolino . . ." See 1703³, *Al lettore*. Based upon Racine's *Andromaque*.

Music (lost): Giovanni A. Perti, according to a letter from F.A. Pistocchi to Perti dated August 12, 1702, quoted by Busi, p. 76, which is reproduced because of its implications concerning Ferdinando's patronage. "Ha piaciuto molto . . . al ser.mo Gran Principe la finezza della vostra modestia nel haver negato l'*Astianato* senza la permissione di S.A.S.; e perciò vi dà ampla autorità di darlo, e servirvene in che maniera volete. È certo che se haveste operato diversamente, l'havrebbe havuto a sdegno . . ."

Because of a misreading of Allacci, col. 124, it will be read in
dictionaries that the music for the performance of Salvi's libretto at
Pratolino was composed by Antonio Maria Bononcini.

Cast: Ferdinando engaged Maria Maddalena Musi, Gio. Antonio Archi,
and possibly Maria Maddalena Steffanini (sent by the Duke of Mantua
in May and in June Ferdinando expressed his approval of her [I Fas (Med
5886, cc. 20, 21)]). Among his own singers, Maria Domenica Marini,
Maria Domenica Pini, and Cattarina Galarati (or Galaratia) are mentioned
in correspondence. Galarati, a singer from Venice who entered into
Ferdinando's service in this year, left Florence for Rome on October 8,
1701 (I Fas [Med 5886, c. 187]).

Bibiena was called to Pratolino to design the staging (I Fas [Med 5885,
cc. 27, 48, 51, 57]).

Comment: Fagiuoli II, f. 147r: "Mart. 11 7.bre [1701]. Andai a
Pratolino alla Commedia intitolata *L'Astianatte*. Merc. 14d.o Il Ser.mo
G[ran] D[uca] in un calesso coperto a bilancino andò alla Commedia
a Pratolino." f. 148r. "Lun[edi] 29. [Sett., 1701]. Il S.r Card.e
Panciatichi andò alla Comm[edi] a a Pratolino invitato dal S.r G[ran]
Pr[inci] pe."

1701[6] 18 ix
Fiesole
(Palmieri)

Il Piaccianteo. Commedia [in prose].
Fagiuoli II, f. 147v: "Dom[eni]ca 18 [Sett. 1701] in Fiesole. Si fece la
commedia intitolata *il Piaccianteo*, di Pier Susini, nella stanza delle
commedie da varij villeggianti alla quale io recitai, e gli altri comici furono:
Dom[eni]co Allegri, Cosimo Allegri, Ant[oni]o Lor[enz]o Allegri, Gio:
Ant[oni]o Mattei, Ant[oni]o F[rances]co Piombi, Giuseppe F[rances]co
Rossi, Fran[ces]co Palagi." No publication found. Martini lists it among
his manuscripts.

1701[7] xi
(Cocomero)

LA PARTENOPE. Drama per musica rappresentato in Firenze nell'autunno
1701. Firenze, Vincenzio Vangelisti, 1701.
I Bc, Fc.

Text: Silvio Stampiglia, not mentioned here, but who is identified in the
libretto of Naples, 1699, the earliest publication of this libretto.

Music (lost): Composer unknown. Attributions of the music for this
performance and others in Naples, 1699, and Rovigo, 1699, to Antonio
Caldara are based upon a misreading of Allacci, who does not cite Caldara
except in the performance in Venice, 1707.

Cast: Partenope - Anna Maria Torri Cecchi; Rosmira - Alessandra Scaccia;
Arsace - Gio. Antonio Archi; Armindo - Barbera Cristina Morelli; Emilio -
Giuseppe Scaccia; Ormonte - Giuliano Albertini; Beltramme - Giovanni
Melchior Rapaccioli.

Comment: The Duke of Mantua (I Fas [Med 5886, cc. 28, 58]) sent
Alessandra Scaccia to Ferdinando because of her ability. Ferdinando
responded that he would receive her with partiality on October 25, 1701,
thus effectively establishing the month the opera was done.

1702[1] carn
Cocomero

L'ANALINDA ovvero LE NOZZE COL NEMICO. Drama per musica da
rappresentarsi in Firenze nel Teatro di via del Cocomero nel Carnevale

dell'anno 1702. Firenze, Vincenzio Vangelisti, 1702.
I Bc, Mb, Rn.

Text: Anonymous, first published in Naples, 1695, with the title, *Le Nozze con l'Inimico ovvero l'Analinda* (I Bc).

Music: Probably by Alessandro Scarlatti, composer of the score for Naples. Score in F Pn; fragments in I Nc. (Zanetti, p. 66; Dent, p. 208).

Cast: Analinda - Anna Maria Cecchi; Adraspe - Alessandra Scaccia; Anagilda - Agata Vignali; Oronta - Maria Domenica Marini; Idreno - Giuseppe Scaccia; Osmondo - Giuliano Albertini; Nisco - Giovanni Battista Calvi; Elena - Giovacchini Poggiali.

1702² carn
(Cocomero)

LA FORZA DELLA VIRTÙ. Dramma per musica rappresentato in Firenze nel carnevale dell'anno 1702. Firenze, Vincenzio Vangelisti, 1702.
I Bc, Mb.

Text: Domenico David with many variations (Allacci, col. 375) who is identified in the libretto of Bologna, 1694 (Sonneck, p. 526).

Music: Possibly by Giacomo A. Perti who, according to Allacci, col. 375, almost entirely re-fashioned the music which C.F. Pollaroli had written for the original performance in Venice in 1693 for a second performance in Bologna, 1694. However, Allacci lists the Florentine libretto without comment about who the composer might have been. Fabbri, "Nuova luce," does not consider the possibility that Perti may have written this score.

1702³ vii
Casa Palmieri

Commedia [in prose] in villa del S.r Palmiero Palmieri giù fuori di Porta a S. Gallo.
Fagiuoli II, f. 162r, refers several times to an unnamed comedy attended by the Medici princes.

1702⁴ 6 ix
Pratolino

FLAVIO CUNIBERTO. Drama per musica rappresentato nella Villa di Pratolino. Firenze, Pietro Antonio Brigonci, 1702.
I Bc, Fn, Mb, MOe, Vgc; S Uu; US CA, Wc.

Text: Matteo Noris with many changes, as is stated in the *argomento* (Sonneck, p. 518).

Music: Alessandro Scarlatti. Fabbri, *A. Scarlatti*, pp. 46f., quotes a document in I Fas (Congregazioni religiose soppresse: no. 119:SS Annunziata, Vol. 56, c. 305), that makes it quite certain that Scarlatti composed the score for this opera despite various attributions based on Allacci. Neither Zanetti nor Fabbri seems to have examined the collection of arias in D MÜps, cited by Dent, p. 208, the title of which reads: *Scelta d'arie dell'Opera Intitolata il Flavio Cuniberto - novamente composta in Musica dal Sig. Alessandro Scarlatti e rappresentata in Pratolino per ordine dell'Altezza Serenis.ma di Ferdinando de' Medici, Gran Principe di Toscana in quest'anno 1702.* Watermarks, as well as the title, show that the origins of the manuscript are Florentine and contemporary with the performance. By our count, there are fifteen arias (Dent says sixteen). All except no. 7, *Serbami tu la fe* are found in the libretto of 1702 and not in that of 1697³. Further correspondence between Ferdinando and Scarlatti: I Fas (Med 5887, cc. 783 [Fabbri says 793], 786, 797, 838 [Fabbri, 849]).

Cast: The singers for each aria are identified in **D MÜps** and the resulting
cast is: Sig.ra [Maria Domenica Pini] Tilla, Sig.ra [Maria Maddalena]
Musi, Sig.r [Francesco A.] Pistocchi, Sig.r Francesco de Castris, and Sig.ra
[Vittoria Tarquini] Bombace.

Comment: Fagiuoli II, f. 167r: "Merc[oledi] 6 [Sett.1702]. Il Gran Duca
andò alla com[medi]a a Pratolino, intitolata *Flavio Cuniberto*."

1702⁵ 15 x
Fiesole
(Palmieri)

L'Amazone del celibato. Opera sacra [in prose].
Fagiuoli II, f. 169r: "Dom[eni]ca. 15 d. [Oct. 1702]. Alla commedia a
Fiesole intitolata *l'Amazone del Celibato* del P. [Simon] Grassi
Carmelit[an]o." See 1691⁵.

1702⁶ aut
(Cocomero)

ARIOVISTO. Drama per musica rappresentato in Firenze nell'autunno del
1702. Firenze, Vincenzio Vangelisti, 1702.
I Bc, Fn, Rn.

Text: Pietro d'Averara according to Sesini, p. 399. First published in
Milan, 1699 (Allacci, col. 109).

Music: Anonymous. The music for the Milan performance, Allacci says,
was composed by [Giacomo] Antonio Perti (Act I), Paolo Magni (Act II
and part of Act III) and Francesco Ballarotti (the remainder). It should
be noted, however, that Dent, p. 207, lists a collection of arias by
Alessandro Scarlatti in **D MÜps** for a performance in 1700? A libretto in
I Bu corresponds in time: *Ariovisto . . . nel Teatro di S. Bartolomeo nel
presente anno 1702*, but we have not had the opportunity to make
comparisons.

Cast: Ariovisto - Anton Maria Ristorini; Elinene - Anna Maria Cecchi;
Valerio Procello - Giuseppe Percatio; Olrico - Caterina Gallerati; Labieno -
Giuliano Albertini; Ermosilda - Lucrezio Storni; Giunia - Vittoria Costa;
Golo - Stefano Coralli.

1702⁷
Pergola
Nobili

L'ACCADEMIA FESTEGGIANTE dedicata al Ser.mo Principe Ferdinando di
Toscana suo Clem.mo Protettore. Firenze, Vincenzio Vangelisti, 1720.
I Fc, Fn.
"Esercizi cavallereschi col ballo, e salto a Cavallo" performed by the
Accademia de' Nobili, who are listed. There were three ballets interspersed
with orations, the subjects of which are also given in the libretto. For each
ballet two men are listed as having composed the ballet, but we think that
"composizione" probably refers to the invention and choreography rather
than the music.

First Ballo (unnamed): Stefano Bagni and Adriano Wntrkut [*sic* several
times for Wintergut]; 2nd Ballo all'Italiana: Giov. Battista Fanghi and
Adriano Wntrekut; 3rd Ballo alla Franzese: Wntrkut and Fanghi.

1703¹ carn
(Cocomero)

LA FORTEZZA AL CIMENTO. Drama per musica rappresentato in Firenze
nel carnevale del 1703. Firenze, Vincenzio Vangelisti, MDCCII.
I Bc.

Text: Francesco Silvani. The argomento comments: "L'Autore del Drama
il Sig.r Ab. Francesco Silvani che già due volte cotanto ha dato nel genio
di questa città quella gran forza di Scena, che nel'orrore diletta . . . "

One of the two is *Alarico* (1701[1]), but the second cannot be identified. Naturally a suspicious eye should be cast on the attribution to Zeno of *Odoardo* (1701[2]), the companion piece to *Alarico* in that carnival.

Music (lost): Possibly by Giuseppe Aldrovandini who wrote the music for the first performance of the libretto in Venice, 1699, as stated in the *argomento* of the Venetian libretto (Sonneck, p. 523). The Florentine libretto adds the two comic roles of Alcea and Rullo.

Cast: Nerone - Anton Maria Ristorini; Statilia - Vittoria Costa; Cilone - Giuseppe Percatio; Mitridate - Giuliano Albertini; Oronta - Anna Maria Cecchi; Berenice - Lucrezia Storni; Alcea - Andrea Franci; Rullo - Stefano Coralli.

1703[2] carn
(Cocomero)

GRISELDA. Dramma per musica rappresentato in Firenze nel carnevale del 1703. Firenze, Vincenzio Vangelisti, 1703.
I Bc, Fm, Fn (destroyed), Vgc.

Text: Apostolo Zeno with contrascenes by Girolamo Gigli, as is stated in a note in manuscript preceding the *argomento*: "Questa è opera del Sig.r Apostolo Zeno di Venezia fatta l'anno 1702 nel teatro di S. Casciano di d[ett]a città. Non v'essendo le parti del ridicolo furono dagl'Impresari di Firenze fatti fare le Contrascene dal Sig.r Girol[am]o Gigli Sanese. La musica fu fatta dal Sig.r . . . Albinoni di Venezia, che in d[ett]a [*sic*] Drama suonava il violino." The *argomento* confirms the authors and warns the reader of "qualche piccola novità." (I Fn.)

The contrascenes of Gigli were published with alterations as *La vecchia innamorata, farza sesta*, p. 112 in *Componimenti teatrale del Signor Girolamo Gigli publicati da Vincenzo Pazzini Carli*. Siena, Francesco Rossi, MDCCLIX (I Fn).

Music (lost): Albinoni. Eitner lists three ariette in I Mc.

Cast: Gualtiero - Giuliano Albertini; Griselda - Anna Maria Cecchi; Costanza - Lucrezia Storni; Corrado - Giuseppe Percatio; Roberto - Vittoria Costa; Otone - Anton Maria Ristorini; Elpino - Stefano Coralli; Pernella - Andrea Franci. Note that the cast, save one, is the same as the fall opera preceding (1702[6]).

Comment: The performance was such a success that the libretto of Naples, 1706 (I Bu), recalled it: "Questo Dramatico Componimento parto di quell'ingegno grande del Sig. Apostolo Zeno Veneziano, fu colla musica del Sig. Tomasso Albinoni, ottimo non solo suonatore di Violino, che contrapuntista nell'anno 1703, nel famosissimo Teatro di Firenze da' Virtuosi Cantori di qual Tempo, con tutto applauso possibile rappresentato . . . "

1703[3] 27 ix
Pratolino

ARMINIO. Drama per musica rappresentato nella Villa di Pratolino. Firenze, Stamperia di S.A.S. appresso P.A. Brigonci, 1703.
I Bu, Fm, Fn, Mb, MOe, PAc, Vnm; S Uu; US CA.

Text: Antonio Salvi (Allacci, col. 114, and Quadrio III.IV.IV. p. 487, and Fagiuoli below), who is not mentioned here nor does he sign the *Al Lettore* which does, however, say that the plot was suggested by Capistron and continues: "Non lo dispero dalla tua generosità Lettor Gentile, mentre se avesti la bontà di compatir *l'Astianatte*, a comporre il quale concorse

Serenissima mia Altezza Reale

709.

Somma beneficenza di V. A. Reale, che si è degnata di
mettermi à parte de' suoi benignissimi riflessi ———
honorandomi colla lettera de' 12 med.° de' suoi precetti
Carassei in risconso d'haver graditi i portamenti.
Della Cantatrice maria Anna, si Come promuove
le mie Humiliazioni al più ossequioso rendimento di
grazie, cosi conferma in me quel debito, che ———
contrassi da che hebbi la sorte di nascere nel numero
de suoi sudditi, di sacrificare tutta la mia vita nel
Real servizio di V. A. Reale, alla quale mi sforzerò in
ogni tempo coll'opere far più tosto vedere, che
credere questa verità per meritarmi sempre più
il pregio del suo potentissimo Patrocinio di cui
riverentemente suplicandola mi Humilio a V. A. Reale con
profondissimo Inchino. Roma 20 Maggio 1703

Di V. A. Reale

Umilissimo Dev.mo obbl.mo fed.mo Servo
Alessandro Melani

I Fas, Arch. Med.,
Carteggio del
Principe Ferdinando,
Filza 5888/709.
Letter from
Alessandro Melani,
Roma, 20 v 1703,
expressing thanks
for a necklace
given by
Ferdinando to
Melani for having
obtained a singer,
Maria Anna
(Garberini Benti?)
detta la Romanina,
to perform in
Livorno,
carnival of 1703.

l'ajuto di Rassine gran Tragico della Francia, con tanto più di ratione devi farlo coll' ARMINIO, nella quale sono stato solo." Strom, p. 161, Salvi's statement notwithstanding, says it is based upon *Arminius* by Jean Gualbert de Campistron.

Music: Alessandro Scarlatti. Fabbri, *A. Scarlatti*, p. 51f. publishes two letters from Scarlatti to Prince Ferdinando specifically mentioning the opera by title. The composer urges the Prince to require "la solita puntualità de' Virtuosi, che devono agire in quest'Opera secondo gl' accidenti da me notati, ne' luoghi opportuni, per il portamento dell'Arie secondo l'Idea con cui l'ho partorite; mentre dalla puntuale osservanza del tempo e degl'accidenti segnati dipende principalmente la perfetta dimostrazione de le medesime." I Fas (Med 5888, c. 741). Other letters in same filza: 725, 786 (not in Fabbri), 808, 821.

Cast: Ferdinando's correspondence gives little information this year. Maria Maddalena Musi married degli Antonij, a Bolognese nobleman, and disappears from the cast. Otherwise it probably was the same as in 1702.

Comment: Fagiuoli II, f. 27: "A dì 27 [Sett. 1703] . . . a Pratolino alla commedia dell'*Arminio* del Salvi." The opera would have begun in early September. Antonio Canali di Venezia requested and received an "Esemplare del Drama [*Arminio*]." I Fas (Med 5888, cc. 750, 761, 766, 829, 832). Busi, p. 164, cites letters from Francesco Pistocchi to G.A. Perti, which indicate that Pistocchi was in Pratolino, presumably to sing in *Astianatte*.

1703[4] 15 x
(Cocomero)

AMINTA. Drama regio-pastorale per musica da rappresentarsi in Firenze nell'autunno del 1703 dedicato all'Altezza Sereniss. di Violante Beatrice di Baviera Gran Principessa di Toscana. Firenze, Vincenzio Vangelisti, 1703. I Bc, Fn (destroyed), Mb, MOe; S Uu.

Text: Apostolo Zeno, who signs the dedication "in Venezia li 15 ottobre 1703." It appears in Zeno's *Poesie drammatiche* II, p. 305, with the comment that it was first published in Firenze, 1703.

Contrascene by Gio. Battista Fagiuoli (who is curiously silent about the performance in his diary). Reprinted separately in his *Commedie*, Vol. 7, p. 278, with the note: "Dall'Impresario del Dramma Regio Pastorale, intitolata l'AMINTA, del Famoso Apostolo Zeno, furon richieste all'autore, l'apresso Controscene piacevoli . . ." He records having asked for and received permission from Zeno to write them.

Music (lost): Tommaso Albinoni who is mentioned on p. 9 of the libretto.

Cast: Aminta - Giuliano Albertini; Euridice - Anna Maria Torri Cecchi; Adrasto - Gio. Batista Franceschini; Elisa - Margherita Mencarelli; Silvio - Filippo Balatri; Dionisio - Caterina Azzolini; Elpino - Gio. Batista Simi; Araspe - Andrea Franci.

1703[5] 27? xii
Cocomero

VINCESLAO. Dramma per musica rappresentato in Firenze nel Carnevale del 1704. Firenze, Vincenzio Vangelisti, 1704. I Bc, Mb.

Text: Apostolo Zeno, who is mentioned as author. Reprinted in Zeno's *Poesie drammatiche* II, p. 217. Sources of the plot: Pietro Cornelio and Rotron. Changes with regard to the "stampa di Venezia."

Music (lost): Presumably by Carlo Pollaroli who wrote the music for the first performance in Venice 1703 (or 1702 in a private house).

Cast: Vinceslao - Giovanni Batista Franceschini; Casimiro - Caterina Azzolini; Alessandro - Giulio Falconi; Lucinda - Anna Maria Torri Cecchi; Ernando - Fabbrizio Bertoldi; Erenia - Vittoria Rizzi; Gismondo - Gio. Batista Simi.

Comment: The date is deduced from the postion of *Mitridate* following as the second opera of the season.

1704[1] carn
Cocomero

MITRIDATE IN SEBASTIA. Dramma per musica da rappresentarsi in Firenze nel carnevale del 1704. Firenze, Vincenzio Vangelisti, s.d.
I Bc, Fn, Rn; **US** Wc.

Text: Giacomo Maggi according to Sonneck, p. 766.

Music: Presumably by Giuseppe Aldrovandini who provided the music for the first performance in Genoa, 1701. **I** Bu possesses the libretto of Naples, 1706, in which a note to the reader mentions the Genoese performance and that the music was by G. Aldrovandini. Collection of arias in **I** Nc.

Cast: Mitridate - Fabbrizio Bertoldi; Ericlea - Anna Maria Torre Cecchi; Laodicea - Caterina Azzolini; Alessandro - Giulio Falconi; Nicomede - Clara Sassi; Tigrane - Gio. Batista Franceschini; Filomene - Domenico Francesconi; Eurillo - Giuseppe Maria Vigano; Nesso - Gio. Batista Simi.

Comment: Fagiuoli II, f. 204v: "16 Mercoledi [Feb. 1703/4] Andai alla comedia in musica d[ett]a *Il Mitridate* nel Teatro degli Infuocati in Via del Cocomero." The date indicates that *Mitridate* was the second opera. Therefore, *Vinceslao* was the first.

1704[2] ix
Pratolino

TURNO ARICINO. Dramma per musica rappresentato nella Villa di Pratolino. Firenze, Stamperia di S.A.R., 1704.
I Bc, Fc, Fm, MOe, Rc, Rn, Vgc, Vnm; **US** Wc.

Text: Silvio Stampiglia with variations by comparison with the first publication in Genoa, 1702.

Music: Alessandro Scarlatti, as is proven by letters from Alessandro to Prince Ferdinando de' Medici published by Fabbri, *A. Scarlatti*, pp. 54ff. Scarlatti's letter of August 9, 1704 (**I** Fas Med 5890, c. 473), mentions Stampiglia but not the title of the opera. He attempted to write in "uno stile piutosto ameno ed arioso, che studiato." He continues: "L'andamento dell'arie, oltre d'haverlo segnato a' suoi luoghi proprij, l'ho stesso in minuta al Sig. Matteuccio [Matteo Sassani] come Professore prattico del mio stile, a cui ho pregato di comunicarlo a' Signori Virtuosi attori." Ferdinando's acknowledgement of receipt of the Ms on August 12 in c. 549. Other letters: F. 5889, cc. 459, 526, 587, 602. Dent, p. 209, lists fragments in **D** Bds, MÜps, and **F** Pc.

Cast: Ferdinando engaged Domenico Cecchi il Cortoncino [*sic*]. Since Grimani wrote to Ferdinando to ask for Matteo Sassani, that singer had joined the Prince's musicians; however, since he was too sick for Ferdinando to grant Grimani's request to have him in Venice for the carnival of 1705, he may not have sung at Pratolino. Raffaello Baldi and Maria Domenica Pini were sent to Francesco Thron in Venice for the autumn season following Pratolino's opera.

I Fas, Arch. Med., Carteggio del Principe Ferdinando, Filza 5889/200. Letter from Apostolo [sic] Zeno, Venezia, 12 i 1704, accompanying a presentation to Ferdinando of Zeno's latest drama.

Ser:ma Altezza

Dalla benignità con la q.le si è degnata l'Al.a altre
volte di gradire qualche mia debolezza, come
dal comune compatim.to che incontra il presente mio
Dramma in Musica, prendo l'animo d'inviarlo
all'A.V.S., sperando, che incontrerà la sua maggi[or]
fortuna, e godrà l'onore d'esser ammesso sot[to]
l'occhio benignissimo di l'A.V.S. La supplico dunque ricever questa mia debole fatica in picci[olo]
attestato del mio Umiliss.° Ossequio, come
à compatirmi di tanto ardire, che mi fa go[-]
dere la fortunata occasione d'inchinarmi
con umiliss.a Riverenza. Ven.a 9° Feb.° 1704.

Di V.A.S.

Umiliss.° Dev.° et Ossequiosiss.° S[ervo]
Fran.co Gasparini

I Fas, Arch. Med., Carteggio del Principe Ferdinando, Filza 5889/513. Letter from Francesco Gasparini, Venezia, 1 ii 1704, accompanying a gift of the score, perhaps of *Il più fedele fra i vassali*, performed at the Cocomero in 1704[5], or *La fede tradite e vendicata* in 1704[6].

1704³ 23 x
Villa Imperiale

Fagiuoli III, f. 7v: "A dì 23 Giov. [Ott. 1704]. La Ser.ma G[ran] Pr[incipess]a m'invitò ad una sera commedia recitata da' Paggi alla Villa dell'Imperiale, e mandò a quest'effetto una muta, nella quale mi portai a sentir d[ett]a commedia insieme io: SS.ri P[ie]r Fran[ces]co Baldovini, Ab[at]e Ant[oni]o M[ari]a Salvini, Dr. Antonio Salvi, Dr. Bacci, Massimil[ian]o Poldar.

1704⁴ 26 x
Palmieri Fiesole

Lo speziale in villa. Comedia in prosa.
Fagiuoli III, ff. 7v, 8r: "26 Dom[eni]ca [Ott., 1704]. Fui ad desinare dal S.r Dr. Gio: B.a Giannetti all' sua villa di S. Marco Vecchio, dopo alla Comedia in Fiesole, che si recitò per la 2.a volta in villa di S.r Palmiero Palm[ier]i e fu quella intitolata *lo speziale in villa* portata in prosa dal Dr. [blank] speziale di S. Miniato, da quella in drama di Dr. Gio: Cos[im]o Villifranchi, ch'ei compose per Pratolino." See 1683³.

1704⁵ 28 x
Cocomero

IL PIÙ FEDELE FRA I VASSALI. Drama per musica da rappresentarsi in Firenze nel presente autunno dell'anno 1704 sotto la protezione del Ser.mo Gran Principe di Toscana. Firenze, Vincenzio Vangelisti, 1704. I Bc, Mb, Rn.

Text: Abate Francesco Silvani, who is mentioned on p. iij; variations by comparison with first publication in Venice, 1703 (US Wc).

Music (lost): Francesco Gasparini, also mentioned. Music also first performed in Venice, 1703. I Fas (Med 5889, c. 513, 582), contains an exchange of letters between Gasparini and Ferdinando in which the former sent a *dramma in musica* on February 1, 1704, probably *Il più fedele.*

Cast: See 1704⁶.

Comment: Fagiuoli III, f. 8r: "A dì 28 [Ott. 1704] Mart[edi]. S. Simone. Andai alla Commedia di certi Istrioni miserabili, che recitai in un casotto in Piazza del Gran Duca, si paga, 6.8. In Via del Cocom[er]o si fece l'op[er]a in musica intitolata *Il più fedele tra Vassalli.*"

1704⁶ 27 xii?
(Cocomero)

LA FEDE TRADITA E VENDICATA. Drama per musica da rappresentarsi in Firenze nel presente carnevale dell'anno 1705. Firenze, Vincenzio Vangelisti, MDCCIV.
I Bc, Rsc.

Text: Francesco Silvani, not mentioned here, but who signs the dedication of Venice, 1704. Other titles: *Ernelinda, Ricimero.*

Music: Francesco Gasparini "salvo la mutanza di qualche Aria per compiacimento de' Rappresentanti." Score: I Nc.

Cast: Ricimiero - Gio. Batista Tamburini; Rodoaldo - Niccola Remolini; Ernelinda - Maria Maddalena Buonavia; Edvige - Antonia Toselli; Vitige - Giovanna Albertini; Edelberto - Giovanni Bernardi; Milo - Filippo Rossi; Lesbina - Ortenzia Beverini.

Comment: The choice of this opera as the first of the carnival season (therefore beginning in the last week in December) is somewhat arbitrary. It rests upon the fact that the list of performers is headed: "ATTORI che hanno operato nell'Autunno passato, e che operano nel presente Carnevale."

The actors are then omitted in *Agarista* following, a circumstance that would seem to be sensible were *La fede* the first opera.

There is no indication of the presence of intermezzi in the text of the libretto nor any statement that intermezzi were performed. However, two characters, Milo servo di Corte (sung by Abate Filippo Rossi) and Lesbina Damigella di Eduige (sung by Ortenzia Beverini) are the characters of an intermezzo listed by Mamczarz, p. 431, by an unknown poet and composer, first performed in Naples, 1702 (I Bc). Both singers are recorded as the performers in intermezzi in other years (see catalogue of performers).

1705[1] carn (Cocomero)	AGARISTA ovvero GL'INGANNI FELICI. Drama per musica da rappresentarsi in Firenze nel carnevale dell'anno 1705. Sotto la protezione del Ser. Gran Principe di Toscano. Firenze, Vincenzio Vangelisti, MDCCIV. I Bc, Mb. **Text:** Apostolo Zeno. See 1697[6]. **Music:** Alessandro Scarlatti, "salvo la mutanza di qualche Aria per compiacimento de' Rappresentanti." (P.3). Arias (34) in I Nc (Zanetti, p. 64). First performance in Naples, 1699.
1705[2] 5 ii Tintori	*L'Eraclio.* Commedia [in prose?]. Fagiuoli III, f. 14r: "5 Giov. [Febb. 1704/5]. Io fui da Salvini alla Commedia nel Teatro de' Cadenti alla commedia intitolata *l'Eraclio*. Vi andarono mia mog[li]a, suocera e S.ra Ghiora." Probably a prose translation of Corneille's play.
1705[3] 22 ii Casa Ulivieri Fiesole	*D. Gastone.* Commedia [in prose?]. Fagiuoli III, f. 15v: "A dì 22 [Febb. 1704/5]. Dopo desin[ar]e andai a Fiesole col S.r Giuliano Ulivieri in villa sua, e fummo a veder la commedia del *D. Gastone*." Probably *Don Gastone di Moncada* by G.A. Cicognini published in Rome in 1675 by Lupardi.
1705[4] ix Pratolino	LUCIO MANLIO L'IMPERIOSO. Drama per musica rappresentato nella Villa di Pratolino. Firenze, Stamperia di S.A.R., 1705. I Bc, Fc, Fm(2), Fn, Mb, MOe, Rn(2), Rsc, Vnm. **Text:** Silvio Stampiglia, not named here, but identified in a letter from Ferdinando de' Medici to Scarlatti commissioning him to compose the score (published by Fabbri, *A. Scarlatti*, p. 61). **Music (lost):** Alessandro Scarlatti. **Cast:** Giovanna Albertini (see 1706[4], also I Fas [Med 5903, c. 183]) and Luigi Albarelli, who returned to Modena September 28 well-praised for his singing at Pratolino, can be positively assigned to this cast. Domenico Cecchi returned from Florence to Casale on or before October 29, so he probably sang. The movements of the following *musici ordinari* make their performance likely: Maria Domenica Pini, Raffaello Baldi and Matteo Sassani. **Comment:** Fabbri, *A. Scarlatti*, p. 63-65, publishes a very important letter from Scarlatti to Ferdinando de' Medici concerning *Lucio Manlio*. The following are excerpts: ". . . l'ho veduto posto in luce con velocità e senza opposizione della fantasia, avvezza in me ad accusarne l'idee. L'ho nondimeno posto in giudicio, disappassionatamente, avanti me stesso, e,

recercatolo con diligente esame sullo stile che ha desiderato l'Autor delle parole . . . parmi, se non in tutta l'opera, almeno in tutto quest-atto havervi trovato l'adempimento dell'adorata legge impostami . . . .

. . . dove e segnato grave, non intendo malenconico; dove andante, non presto ma arioso; dove allegro, non precipitoso; dove allegrissimo, tale che non affanni il Cantante ne affoghi le parole; dove andante-lento, in forma che escluda il patetico, ma sia un amoroso vago che non perda l'arioso. E in tutte l'arie, nessuna malenconica . . . . Così nel *Lucio Manlio*, Opera che mi compisce il numero d'Ottant'otto Opere sceniche composte in meno di vintitre Anni . . . " I Fas (Med 5903, c. 165). Other correspondence in same filza: cc. 150, 155, 165, 174, 432, 443, 456. Dent translates some of these letters and comments on their significance, pp. 102ff. See also Morey, p. 58.

1705[5] aut
(Cocomero)

LA SERVA FAVORITA. Melodramma rappresentato in Firenze nell'autunno dell'anno 1705. Firenze, Vincenzio Vangelisti, s.d.
I Bc, Bu, Vgc.

Text: Gio. Cosimo Villifranchi, who is not mentioned, but the libretto is the same as 1689[10] with some variation.

Music: Probably by Alessandro Scarlatti. The link with the Naples performance of the preceding carnival is established by the fact that Giuseppe Canavesi sings Cleante in both performances and by the great consistency between the two librettos.

Cast: Cleante - Giuseppe Canavesi; Dorisbe - Anna Benedetti; Fileno - Gio. Batista Roberti; Cetinda - Anna Maria Sarti; Lidio - Anton Maria Ristorini; Quartille - Giulio Cavaletti; Cordone - Giuseppe Cavana.

1705[6] 22 xi
Casa Corsini

La Penelope. Commedia in musica. (See 27 xii below)
Fagiuoli III, f. 24: "A dì 22 Dom[eni]ca 9bre [1705]. La sera ci fù la comm[edi]a in musica intitolata *Penelope* dove recità la Marg[eri]ta Saligola [Salicola] e festino a casa Corsini."

1705[7]

I DUE BARI. Commedia [in prose]. Firenze, Michele Nestenus, 1705.
I Mbn.
Text by Annibale de Filippi. Not listed by Allacci. No information concerning performance.

1705[8] 27 xii
Cocomero

PENELOPE. Drama per musica rappresentato in Firenze nel carnevale dell' anno 1706. Firenze, Vincenzio Vangelisti, s.d.
I Bc, Fm, Fn, Mb, Rn.

Text: Matteo Noris, not mentioned here, but named in the Roman libretto of 1696 (B Bc).

Music: Possibly by Alessandro Scarlatti. Two settings were produced in 1696: one was by G.A. Perti for Rome, 1696; however, this libretto is too altered for Perti's music to have been used without considerable alteration. The second score was written by A. Scarlatti for Naples. This last libretto is most similar to the Florence one. Eleven arias by Scarlatti in I Nc (Zanetti, p. 77).

Cast: Penelope - Margherita Salicola Suini; Ulisse - Anton Maria Ristorini; Elvida - Anna Maria Sarti; Ariene - Anna Benedetti; Lutezio - Giovanni

Batista Roberti; Gismondo - Giovanni Batista Pieretti; Ambasciatore - Michele Perini, and Gildo - Giuseppe Cavana.

Comment: Fagiuoli III mentions performances on 27, 28 xii, 1705, and 6, 8, 10, 13, and 15 i, 1706.

1706[1] 25 i
Tintori

L'Ermengarda.
Fagiuoli III, f. 67. "25 Martedi [Gen. 1706/7]. *L'Ermengarda* a i [illegible: possibly Cadenti] la p[rim]a volta . . . 29 Ven[erdi] *l'Ermengarda* per la 3a volta."

1706[2] carn
(Cocomero)

LA CLOTILDE D'ARAGONA. Dramma per musica rappresentato in Firenze nel carnevale dell'anno 1706. Firenze, Vincenzio Vangelisti, s.d.
I Bc, Mb.

Text: Giovanni Battista Neri, not mentioned here, but who signs the dedication of the Venice, 1696, libretto. US Wc has this Venetian libretto as well as another entitled *Amar per vendetta*, Venice, 1702 (Sonneck, p. 299).

Music: Anonymous. For the first performance in Venice the music was composed by Giovanni Maria Ruggeri, who is mentioned in the notice to the reader of that libretto. Possibly Ruggeri's music was used in Florence as well.

Cast: Clotilde - Margherita Salicola Suini; Sancio - Anton Maria Ristorini; Garzia - Giovanni Batista Pieretti; Ferdinando - Anna Maria Teresa Benedetti; Anagilda - Anna Maria Sarti; Ramiro - Giovanni Batista Roberti; Consalvo - Giuseppe Cavana.

1706[3] 30 v
Casa Giannetti

Armanda. Commedia [in prose?].
Fagiuoli III, f. 40v: "A dì 30 Dom[eni]ca [Maggio, 1706]. A Sesto dal S.r Piero Giannetti per veder la Commedia dell'*Armanda*."
    This is probably: L'ARMANDA, o vero LE STRAVAGANZE DEL CASO. Opera scenica dell'eccellentiss. Sig. Gio: Cosimo Villifranchi. In Bologna, per Gioseffo Longhi, s.d. The prologue is for music. Personaggi: Heraclito, Democrito, e Commedia.

1706[4] ix
Pratolino

IL GRAN TAMERLANO. Drama per musica rappresentato nella Villa di Pratolino. Firenze, Stamperia di S.A.R. Antonio Maria Albizzini, 1706.
I Bc, Bu, Fc, Fm, Fn, Mb, MOe, Rsc, Rn; US CA.

Text: Antonio Salvi, according to a letter from Scarlatti to Ferdinando (Fabbri, *A. Scarlatti*, p. 82). The *argomento* reveals that the plot was taken from Pradon *francese*, that is, from Pradon's *Tamerlan ou la mort de Bajazet*.

Music (lost): Alessandro Scarlatti. This is the last opera commissioned by Ferdinando from Scarlatti. Remaining correspondence published by Fabbri, *A. Scarlatti*, pp. 85f. and 94ff. in I Fas (Med 5903, cc. 287, 577 and f. 5904, cc. 37, 40, 332, 354) consists of entreaties by Scarlatti answered by the Prince with decorum and disinterest.

Cast: The performers, as usual in these librettos for Pratolino, are not listed, but another letter from Scarlatti, (Fabbri, p. 71) gives the performers of two roles: Vittoria Tarquini sang Asteria and Giuseppe Canavese sang Baiazet.

Altezza Reale

Vostra Altezza Reale, che onora al più alto Segno La m[usica]
e i Professori di questa; anzi che è quel Sole, che la cr[ea]
e nudrisce; Si degna di rimirarne con benigno compatim[ento]
le varie Idee, e diversità di Composizioni, particolarm[ente] in
sto nel Soggiorno di Pratolino, che per la di Lei Real pr[esenza]
za, viene ad essere altamente illustrato; dando il Campo a
comparsa de Madrigali a Tavolino (compiacimento di pur
imo conoscimento dell'Arte Speculativa del Comporre, che da
cipe di Venosa in quà, La fù Regina di Suetia, che fù

I Fas, Arch. Med.,
Carteggio del
Principe Ferdinando,
Filza 5900/224.
Three-page letter from
Alessandro Scarlatti,
Roma, 28 viii 1706,
accompanying a gift
of unidentified
madrigali a tavolino
(table madrigals).

mia Padrona, se ne compiaceu più d'ogn'altra composizione, e Vo

st'Altezza Reale l'hanno sostenuta / ere mi dà l'ardire di pre

sentargliene uno a piedi reali, e qui accluso, sì per continuar

l'esercizio della mia douutale eumilissima seruitù, come perche

eabbia la fortuna d'essere benignamente compatito, ed emenda

de suoi errori, dal profondo intendimento d Cost'Altezza Reale

per cui non tralascierò giamai d scieegliere quei pochi fiori inca

ti della mia debolissima, e conta abilità nel porre in musica,

per tributo della diuuzione del mio Cune, e delle mie ineugli

cabili, infinite obligazioni, che mi rendono schiavo degl' a-
cenni di Vostra Altezza Reale; per la di cui conservazione,
licità prego il Signore Iddio, come sono principalmente te-
e con sommessa obedienza, e profondo rispetto, m'inchino Eum-
te, come sempre

Di Vostra Altezza Reale   Roma 28 Agosto 1706

Eumilissimo, devotissimo, ed obligatissimo Servitore
Alessandro Scarlatti

Scarlatti assumed that Rossane would be sung by La Reggiana [Giovanna Albertini] , who, he says, sang in *Lucio Manlio* in the preceding year. Later he had to rewrite the first act and part of the second because the Prince wished La Tilla [Maria Domenica Pini] , a soprano, to sing the role (pp. 73ff.).

Comment: The correspondence between Scarlatti and Ferdinando de' Medici concerning *Tamerlano* is unusually lengthy and informative. It is published by Fabbri, pp. 69-82. Dent's survey of the contents, pp. 106., is brief, touching upon only the most important bits of information. Correspondence between Ferdinando and Scarlatti in I Fas (Med 5903, cc. 196, 200, 201, 204-6, 208, 213, 217, 219, 224, 497, 499, 503, 507, 509, 511, 516, 520).

1706[5] 27 xii
Tintori

Medico volante. Commedia degli Istrioni.
Fagiuoli III, f. 61. "A dì 27 lun. [Dic. 1706] . Le donne per la p[rim] a volta andarona alla com[edi] a degl'Istrioni del *Medico volante.*" III, f. 64. "Gl'istrioni volevan di nuovo nel Teatro de' Cadenti ricominciar le lor commedie ma per impertinenza usate lor fu proibito fino a nuovi ord[inanz] a dal S.r Ab[at] e Bardi . . . " The last recorded performance by Istrioni in Florence is 1704[5]. The hiatus is perhaps explained by the exchange of letters between the Duke of Mantua and Ferdinando in I Fas (Med 5893, c. 15; 5894, c. 8). The duke, in a letter of June 6, 1706, having requested the prince's protection for Aurelia [Marcello] and her company when they arrived in Livorno, the prince replied on July 6, "Avendo sospeso il Ser.mo Gran Duca e Padre de qualche tempo per diversi motivi le Recite Istrioniche, non vedo di aver luogo di poter giovare all'Aurelia comica di V.A. . . . " Apparently soon afterward the Gran Duca relented, to his sorrow in view of the impertinence of the Istrioni del Medico Volante.

(1706[6])

(*Il trionfo della libertà.*)
Text by Gir. Frigimelica Roberti, music by Scarlatti. Cited by Schmidl only, who says, obviously in error, that it was performed at Pratolino.

1706[7] 29 xii
Cocomero

AMBLETO. Drama per musica rappresentato in Firenze nel carnevale dell' anno 1707 sotto la protezione del Sereniss. Principe di Toscana. Firenze, Vincenzio Vangelisti, 1707.
I Bc, Fc, Fn.

Text: Apostolo Zeno and Pietro Pariati, who are not mentioned, but the text is reprinted in the *Poesie drammatiche* IX, p. 100.

Music (lost): Probably by Francesco Gasparini who set the libretto to music for Venice, 1705 (Allacci).

Cast: Ambleto - Giulio Cavaletti; Tengono - Giuliano Albertini; Gerilda - Maria Anna Garberini Benti; Veremonda - Agata Ginasi; Valdenoro - Antonio Pasi; Sifrido - Angelico Resi; Tisbe - Antonio Pedreri [*sic*] di Bologna; Gilbo - Pietro Paolo Pezzoni.

Comment: Fagiuoli III, f. 64. "A dì 29 Mart[edi] Xbre [1706] . In via del Cocomero per la p[rim] a com[medi] a in musica d[ett] a l'*Ambleto.*"

1707[1] ii ?
Cocomero

ARTASERSE. Drama per musica rappresentato in Firenze nel carnevale dell'anno 1707. Sotto la protezione del Serenissimo Principe di Toscana.

Firenze, Vincenzio Vangelisti, 1707.

I Fc, Fn (destroyed).

Text: Apostolo Zeno and Pietro Pariati, with changes, by comparison with the *Poesie drammatiche* of Zeno, Vol. IX, p. 94. The *A chi legge* of the first publication in Venice, 1705 (I Vnm) says that the libretto is a faithful reduction of a drama previously published in Modena in 1700 by Giulio Agosti Reggiano.

Music (lost): Probably by Giuseppe Maria Orlandini. The first setting in Venice, 1705, was composed by Antonio Zanettini (or Giannettini) according to Allacci, col. 119. This Venetian libretto, however, does not identify the composer (I Vnm). On the other hand, a libretto of 1708 for S. Bartolomeo in Naples in US Wc (Sonneck, p. 166) says that the music was composed by Giuseppe Orlandini with buffa scenes and certain other arias and "accommodations" by Francesco Mancini and further additions to the libretto by Andrea del Po. The notice to the reader observes that the opera had been performed in many cities in Italy before it was adapted for Naples. Hence sometime prior to 1708, the opera was set by Orlandini. The Florentine libretto is most similar to an earlier one published in Livorno in 1706 (I Fm) and dedicated to Ferdinando de' Medici. In I Fas (Med 5909, cc. 139, 140, 142, and 143, are letters to and from Ferdinando's majordomo, Gerini, arranging lodgings for *Musico Orlandini* during the carnival of 1706 in Livorno. If the attribution is correct, *Artaserse* is the earliest known opera written by Orlandini for the Medici.

Cast: Artaserse - Giuliano Albertini; Agamira - Caterina Azzolini; Spiridate - Giulio Cavaletti; Idaspe - Antonio Pasi; Aspasia - Maria Anna Garberini Benti; Berenice - Agata Ginasi; Dario - Cristina Morelli; Semidea - Antonio Pedreri; Lido - Pietro Paolo Pezzoni.

1707² sum
Cocomero

IL MAURIZIO. Drama per musica da rappresentarsi in Firenze nell'estate dell'anno 1707 sotto la protezione del Serenissimo Principe di Toscana. Firenze, Vincenzio Vangelisti, 1707.

I Bc, Fm, Mb, Rn.

Text: Adriano Morselli according to Allacci, which attribution is standard. However, neither the first publication of Venice, 1687, nor the second (also of Venice but 1689-Sonneck, p. 744) nor that of Lucca, s.d., actually states the name of the poet, while the libretto of Rome, 1692, has Niccolò Minati in the title (I Rn).

Music: Possibly by Domenico Gabrielli who composed the music for the opera in Venice, 1687 (Allacci). Score: I MOe.

Cast: Maurizio - Giovanni Antonio Archi; Tibero - Francesco Guicciardi; Cosdroe - Giuliano Albertini; Ergilda - Maddalena Bonavia; Cirene - Maria Anna Garberini Benti; Placilla - Vittoria Costa; Ircano - Domenico Fontani.

Comment: The *Al lettore*: "Il cortese aggradimento che nell'autunno e carnevale dell'anno 1704 dimostrati con l'assidua tua assistenza alle tre Opere in Musica, che sotto la benigna Protezione del Serenissimo Gran Principe feci rappresentare nel Teatro di via del Cocomero mi rende sicuro, che benignamente ancora assisterai con la tua presenza al presente Drama veramente degno della sua aspettazione, tanto più lo spero quanto ti è noto le fatiche, disastri, e spese sofferte per far rappresentare quest'Opera, e superar l'invidio altrui, che ha procurato tutti i modi possibili per impedir questo si nobil divertimento . . ." Signed without date by Michele Giusti, who is the impresario. The operas to which he refers are *Vinceslao*, *Mitridate in Sebastia*, and *Il più fedele fra i vassali*, 1704 above.

1707³ ix
Pratolino

DIONISIO RE DI PORTOGALLO. Drama per musica rappresentato nella Villa di Pratolino. Firenze, Anton Maria Albizzini, 1707.
F Pn; I Bu, Fc, Fm, Fn, Mb, MOe, Rn(2), Vnm; US Wc.

Text: Antonio Salvi (Allacci, col. 255). *Cortese lettore*: "Tutto questo è verità, cavata dall'istoria Portoghese scritta in lingua Franzese da Mons. Lequieu dela Neufuilla . . ."

Music (lost): Giacomo A. Perti. Busi, p. 76, cites a letter in I Bc (Scanz. K, n. 44, Vol. I, p. 21) from Ferdinando to Perti dated June 18, 1707, requesting Perti to send the parts of the *opera comica* for Pratolino as soon as possible so that the singers could memorize them. In I Fas pertinent letters are (Med 5903, cc. 263, 275, 292, 297, 301, 305, and 307) [12 July Perti sends 3rd act].

Cast: In 1709 Ferdinando desired to perform *Dionisio* in Livorno and in a letter to Perti of August 17, 1709, as quoted by Busi, p. 78, he revealed two of the performers. "Pensando di far di nuovo recitare sul Teatro di Livorno il *Dionisio* da Lei già posto in musica, per il mio di Pratolino, le trasmetto col procaccia, che parte domattina, l'originale; acciòcche ella si contenti di apostare la parte d'Isabella, che faceva la Vittoria Tarquini, per la Vienna Mellini, e quella d'Elvide che faceva la Reggiana [Giovanna Albertini] per l'Angiolina della Comare." The scribe's copy is I Fas (Med 5904, c. 551).

Dionisio was beset by grave problems. August 13, 1707, Ferdinando wrote to Modena that Giuseppe Canavesi was in such a state that he could not sing and that he needed Antonio Borosini to replace him [I Fas (Med 5896, cc. 10, 3)]. He had already engaged Luigi Albarelli to sing at Pratolino, but on September 6 Albarelli died (I Fas [Med 5896, cc. 4, 11, 12]). It is not known by whom he was replaced, but a recommendation for Filippo Rossi who left for Naples October 29 may be a clue (I Fas [Med 5896, c. 104]).

1707⁴ 28 x -
27 xi
Cocomero

STRATONICA. Dramma per musica rappresentato in Firenze l'autunno del 1707. Sotto la protezione del Gran Principe di Toscana. Firenze, Vincenzio Vangelisti, 1707.
I Bc, Fm, Mb, MOe.

Text: Antonio Salvi (Allacci, col. 741). A notice to the reader observes: "L'Opera nel suo Idioma Francese ha già ricevuta i suoi Applausi. Nella traduzione non sò, se averà questa fortuna, tant'ò più, che dovendo servire alla Musica, ed alla brevità, è convenuto ristringere, e lasciare molti di quei bellissimi sentimenti de' quali l' ha vestita l'Autore. Qualche Personnaggio, e qualche Scena vi troverai differente dall'Originale, e ciò per meglio accomodarsi al costume Italiano, ed a gli Attori . . ." (without signature). It is clear from the wording that the opera is being given its first performance.

Music (lost): Composer unknown.

Cast: Seleuco - Giuliano Albertini; Antioco - Giulio Cavaletti; Stratonica - Maria Anna Benti; Arsinoe - Giovanna Albertini; Tigrane - Antonio Pasi; Cleone - Alessandro del Ricco; Dorisbe - Antonio Pedreri; Lesbo - Pietro Paolo Pezzoni.

Comment: Fagiuoli III, f. 60. First mention of *Stratonica* on above date (Giovedì): 31 (Domenica) [October,] 2a volta. On f. 62v, "27 Sabato 9bre [1706]. La sera l'ultima com[edi]a della *Stratonica* in via del Cocomero."

1707⁵ xi-xii
Cocomero

VINCER SE' STESSO È LA MAGGIOR VITTORIA. Drama per musica rappresentato in Firenze nell'autunno dell'anno 1707 sotto la protezione del Serenissimo Principe di Toscana. Firenze, Vincenzio Vangelisti, 1707. I Bc, Bu.

Text: Anonymous revision of Francesco Silvani's *Il duello d'amore, e di vendetta*, according to Strom, "Händel," p. 159, who estimates that about three-quarters of Silvani's arias have been retained. He further speculates that the revisions are the work of Antonio Salvi. Silvani's libretto was first performed in Venice, 1700 (see Allacci, col. 272).

Music: Probably by G.F. Handel. Strom, p. 157, identifies this opera as Handel's *Rodrigo*, and therefore the mysterious Handelian opera for Prince Ferdinando, by retracing Handel's movements in Italy (see Kirkendale and Fabbri, (*A. Scarlatti*) and by comparing the Florentine libretto with the text of Chrysander's edition of *Rodrigo* (vol. 56) in the complete works.

Cast: Rodrigo - Stefano Frilli; Esilena - Anna Maria Cecchi; Florinda - Aurelia Marcello; Giuliano - Francesco Guicciardi; Evanco - Caterina Azzolini; Fernando - Giuseppe Perini.

Comment: That this is the second opera of the autumn season is suggested by the known date of the preceding opera and the fact that the cast is identical (save one role) with the following opera while having no performers in common with the first opera of the season above. Strom's speculation that the opera might have been performed at the Pitti Palace must fall since his argument rested upon the supposed uniqueness of the cast. He was unaware of 1707⁶ below.

1707⁶ 27? xii
Cocomero

I PRODIGI DELL'INNOCENZA. Drama per musica rappresentato in Firenze nel carnevale dell'anno 1708 sotto la protezione del Serenissimo Principe di Toscana. Firenze, Vincenzio Vangelisti, 1707. I Bc; US Wc.

Text: An anonymous re-writing of *Ottone* by Girolamo Frigimelica Roberti (Venice, 1694 - US Wc): "A un puntino l' ho sequitata fino a valermi de suoi pensieri (del Conte Roberto Frigimelica [sic]), e in molti luoghi delle sue parole medesime ..."

Music (lost): Composer unknown. The tone of the note to the reader indicates that this is a new work and a first performance.

Cast: Ottone - Stefano Frilli; Eleonora - Aurelia Marcello; Fausto - Caterina Azzolini; Matilde - Anna Maria Cecchi; Ugone - Giuseppe Barelli; Enrico - Giuseppe Perini.

1.ma A 1

Altezza Reale

Doppo infinito contrasto resta in fine terminato l'affare di mio fratello
colli Creditori, mediante lo sborso di buona somma di contante, e con ciò
sostenuta la riputazione del med.mo mio fratello, e della nostra casa.
L'altro prossimo passato si fece la transazione in casa del sig.r Conte
Baldassare Castelli, come destinato dalla somma Clemenza di V.A.R.
per dirrigermi in tanto bisogno, ed infatti questo Cavag.re con immensa pa-
tienza destrità e prudenza, hà condotto à fine un sì imbrogliato negotio,
non s'havendo perdonatone meno ad incommodarsi d'andar sino à trovare
qualche creditore à casa propria per ottenere il suo intento. Insomma
la premura d'ubbidire à riveriti Comandamenti di V.A.R. l'hà reso
tutto foco per favorirmi. Non devo trascurare con V.A.R. questo gius-
tiss.mo passo, perche maggiormente conosca il merito grande del medesim.o
Cavagliere. A tante ed infinite obligazioni, che devo à V.A.R.le
anche per questo Capo, lascio alla mano suprema e Divina la cura
di rimunerare V.A.V.R. per tante grazie, e benefizio ed io haurò quella
di non cessare de mili ardentiss.mi voti perche S.D.M. esaudisca il mio vivo
desiderio, e con profond.mo rispetto humiliandomi à V.A.R. mi protesto
sino all'ultimo respiro
Bologna li 23
V.A.R.
Nouemb.e 1708

Vmiliss.mo Diuot.º Obblig.mo e Oss.mo Ser.re
Antonio Predieri

l Fas, Arch. Med.,
Carteggio del
Principe Ferdinando
Filza 5904/159.
Letter from
Antonio Predieri,
Bologna, 23 xi 1708
thanking the prince
for helping
Predieri's brother
settle a debt.

I Fas, Arch. Med., Carteggio del Principe Ferdinando, Filza 5904/31. Letter from G. A. Perti, Bologna, 17 iii 1708, acknowledging the receipt of the first act of an opera (*Ginevra Principessa di Scozia*, performed at Pratolino, autumn of 1708[2]) and accompanying a gift of two motets.

Comment: The position of the first opera of the season is assigned to
I prodigi because its cast is identical save one role to that of *Vincer se
stesso* (1707[5]) but by comparison with *Statira* (1708[1]), three of the
six performers are changed.

1708[1] ii?
Cocomero

STATIRA. Drama per musica rappresentato in Firenze nel carnevale dell'
anno 1708 sotto la protezione del Serenissimo Principe di Toscana.
Firenze, Vincenzio Vangelisti, 1708.
I Bc.

Text: Apostolo Zeno and Pietro Pariati, not mentioned here, but the text
appears in the *Poesie drammatiche* IX, p. 279.

Music (lost): Composer unknown. However, Allacci, col. 738, ascribes the
music for the libretto of Venice, 1695 (in **US** Wc) to Francesco Gasparini.

Cast: Statira - Anna Maria Torri Cecchi; Barsina - Aurelia Marcello; Dario -
Michele Perini; Arsace - Stefano Frilli; Oribasio - Caterina Azzolini; Oronte -
Domenico Tempesti; Idreno - Angelico Resi.

1708[2] ix
Pratolino

GINEVRA PRINCIPESSA DI SCOZIA. Dramma per musica rappresentato
nella Villa di Pratolino. Firenze, Stamperia di S.A.R. per Anton Maria
Albizzini, M.DCC.VIII.
F Pn; I Bu, Fc, Fm, Fn, MOe, Rn (2), Vnm.

Text: Antonio Salvi, who is mentioned in Perti's correspondence with
Ferdinando (see below). Allacci, col. 403, erroneously lists the date as
1709. See (1709)[4]. A much-altered libretto of Venice, 1716 (in **US** Wc)
also identifies Salvi as the author.

The note to the reader: "Il quinto Canto del nostro Omero Toscano,
[o.t. *Orlando furioso*], l'ingegnosissimo Ariosto m' ha somministrato per
lo presente Drama il Soggetto, il Luogo, l'Azione, i Principali Attori, e i
loro Caratteri ancora; Ho giudicato pertanto superfluo il distenderne
l'Argomento, potendo tu con più diletto leggerlo in quel maraviglioso
Poema. Io mi son preso licenzo di purgare il costume di Dalinda, per
farla un Personaggio più riguardevole, e perche nel nostro secolo non
sarebbe comparso in Scena senza biasimo. Ho caricato alquanto il
Carattere scellerato di Polinesso Duca d'Albania, facendolo operare per
interesse, e per ambizione, non già per amore, perchè nella di lui morte
senta meno di orrore l'Audienza, e perchè maggiormente spicchi la
Virtù degli altri Personaggi. Ho finto Ginevra Figlia unica del Re di
Scozia, benche l'Ariosto la faccia Sorella di Zerbino, perche tutte le
passioni abbiano più forza negli Attori, come la tenerezza del Padre,
l'ambizione in Polinesso, l'amore in Ariodante. Nè ho voluto servirmi
per lo scioglimento del Drama del Personaggio di Rinaldo, perchè nel
rimanente dell'azione non v'avea luogo."

Music (lost): Giacomo A. Perti, whose correspondence with Ferdinando
concerning *Ginevra* and various motets is in I Fas (Med 5904, cc. 31,
which is shown on the *left*, 35, 52, 76, 97, 99, 101, 104, 115, 121, 246,
324, 344, 350, 358, 389, 420, 426, 428, 433, 436, 439, 446). In cc. 350
and 439, Ferdinando says he will use Maria Domenica Pini in the soprano
role of Adalinda, and that he is dissatisfied with three arias which he is
returning to Perti with the instructions: "mi compiacerà col rifare le tre

Arie qui alligate, per contentare chi deve cantarle. Che però io la prego a rifare quella di Adalinda più staccata, acciòche la Tilla [M.A. Pini] abbia più tempo di ripigliar fiato; e l'altre due, che sono d'Ariodante, quella che dice 'Tu preparati a morire' pare che riesca un poco troppo strepitosa perloche si desiderebbe rifatta un poco più moderata." This request is dated August 25; Perti's reply August 28 (c. 121); and the prince's expression of satisfaction, September 1. Busi, p. 77, cites a letter dated April 28, 1708 from Ferdinando to Perti in I Bc (Scanz. K, pp. 94f.) concerning *Ginevra*, and a letter of congratulations from D. Antonio Sgarzi from Rome, October 13, 1708, to Perti: " . . . Godo poi sia ritornato con tutta salute da Pratolino, e mi rallegro che l'opera sia riuscita di gusto alli sigg. sereniss. et a tutti, come pure del regalo havuto della belliss. quantiera d'argento con scudi 300, come m'e stato scritto, regalo meritamente dovuto alla Sua fatica; oltre gl' honori et applausi infiniti . . . "

Cast: Ferdinando's correspondence identifies three singers: Maria Domenica Pini, Francesco Guicciardi, and Antonio Carli. No others of the *musici ordinari* are mentioned.

1708[3] 30 ix
Cocomero

IL NERONE FATTO CESARE. Drama per musica da rappresentarsi in Firenze nell'autunno del 1708 e nel carnevale del 1709 sotto la protezione del Serenissimo Principe di Toscana. Firenze, Vincenzio Vangelisti, MDCCVIII. I Bc, Fn.

Text: Matteo Noris whose name appears in the libretto of Venice, 1693 (in US Wc).

Music: Probably by G.A. Perti, who is mentioned as the composer of the opera in the Venetian libretto. Also, Perti is named in a libretto (I Bu) of Livorno, 1702, which is dedicated to Ferdinando de' Medici, and which, therefore, is circumstantial evidence supporting Perti as the composer. Eitner cites a score in D SW.

Cast: Agrippina - Angiola Augusti; Nerone - Giovanni Maria Morosi; Tigrane - Giovanni Batista Muzzi; Gusmano - Anna Maria Fabbri; Ate - Diana Lucinda Grifoni; Pallante - Giuseppe Berti; Seneca - Michele Salvatici; Zelto - Alessandro del Ricco.

Comment: Fagiuoli IV, f. 53v: "A dì 30 [Sett. 1708]. La nuova commedia in musica il *Nerone* de Noris la p[rim]a volta a gl'Infuocati."

1708[4] x
Cocomero

L'AMOR GENEROSO. Drama per musica da rappresentarsi in Firenze nell' autunno dell'anno 1708 sotto la protezione del Serenissimo Principe di Toscana. Firenze, Vincenzio Vangelisti, 1708. I Bc, Fc.

Text: Apostolo Zeno, not mentioned here, but the libretto is reprinted in the *Poesie drammatiche* III, p. 277.

Music (lost): Giuseppe Orlandini and Rocco Ceruti, as stated on page eight of the libretto: "Il primo atto è musica del Sig. Giuseppe Orlandini. Il secondo atto è musica del Sig. Rocco Ceruti. Il terzo atto, dalla prima scena a tutta la quinta, è musica di detto Sig. Orlandini, ed il restante fino alla fine è musica di detto Sig. Ceruti."

That this is the first performance of Orlandini's and Cerruti's setting is

confirmed by the note to the reader: "Questo Drama fu rappresentato
l'anno passato in Venezia, ora comparisce di nuovo su questo Teatro, di
musica differente."

Cast: Frilevo - Giuseppe Berti; Aldano - Giovanni Batista Muzzi; Cirita -
Angela Augusti; Alvinda - Diana Lucinda Grifoni; Sivardo - Anna Maria
Fabbri; Asmondo - Michele Salvatici.

1709 carn No operas are recorded for this season or for the spring; nor is any reason
known for there having been no performances. Ferdinando's correspondence
contains requests for singers in Livorno only.

1709[1] ix BERENICE REGINA DI EGITTO. Drama per musica rappresentato nella Villa
Pratolino di Pratolino. Firenze, Albizzini, 1709.
GB Lbm; **I** Bu, Fc, Fn, Mb, MOe, Rc, Rn(2), Vnm; **S** Uu.

Text: Antonio Salvi, not mentioned, according to Quadrio III.IV.IV, p. 487
and to Allacci, col. 143. Reprinted in Venice, 1711, with the title, *Le gare
di politica e d'amore*, still anonymous, but identified by Allacci, col. 386,
as also by Salvi. This Venetian libretto refers to the Pratolino performance
without identifying either composer or the poet. See Sonneck, p. 543.
Source (p. 3) of the plot identified as Appian, *Div. Bel. lib I da M. Vailliant*.

Music (lost): Giacomo A. Perti. Busi, p. 77, cites letters of Prince Ferdinando
to Perti concerning *Berenice* (in **I** Bc [Scanz. K, n. 44, Vol. 1, pp. 54ff.]).
Correspondence in **I** Fas (Med 5904, cc. 234, 240, 244, 246, 250, 261, 516,
526, 535, 539, 546, 548, 549, 551, and 556) concerns not only *Berenice*
but also the opera at Livorno in the next carnival and various motets. See
1707[3] for excerpts of letters.

Cast: Ferdinando engaged Francesco Guicciardi and Vienna Mellini from
Rinaldo d'Este. The movements of Vittoria Tarquini, Domenico Tempesti,
Giuseppe Ferrari, and Maria Domenica Pini suggest that they also sang at
Pratolino. Ferrari in librettos of 1701 and 1705 bears the title of *virtuoso
del S. di Mantova*, but in a letter of December 13, 1709, to the March. Neri
Guadagno in Venice (F. 5900, cc. 302, 416) it is Ferdinando who gives
him license to go to Vienna.

1709[2] 4 xi IL RADAMISTO. Drama per musica da rappresentarsi in Firenze nell'
Cocomero autunno dell'anno MDCCIX sotto la protezione del' Serenissimo Principe
di Toscana. Firenze, Vincenzio Vangelisti, 1709.
I Bc, Lg, PS, Rn.

Text: Nicolo Giuvo, who is not mentioned, by comparison with the
publication of the libretto for Venice, 1707, in **US** Wc (Sonneck, p. 913).
Sesini errs in ascribing the Florentine libretto to Antonio Marchi, the author
named on the title page of the Venetian libretto of 1698 (music by Tommaso
Albinoni). The two librettos have only the argomento and three of five or
six characters in common.

Music: Nicola Fago detto il Tarantino, as stated on p. 5. The music is
presumably lost. However, the late ascription of a score in **I** Nc to Albinoni
should not be too readily accepted. See 1728[2]. Fago composed the music
for Venice, 1707, cited above.

Cast: Radamisto - Andrea Pacini; Zenobia - Anna Marchesini; Tiridate - Anton Ristorini; Rosmira - Rosa Ungarelli; Medullina - Ortenzia Beverini; Carasso - Michele Salvatici.

1709³ 27 xii
Cocomero

IL TRIONFO DELLA COSTANZA. Drama per musica da rappresentarsi in Firenze nel carnevale dell'anno 1709 sotto la protezione del Serenissimo Principe di Toscana. Firenze, Vincenzio Vangelisti, 1709.
GB Lbm; I Bc, Mb, Rc.

Text: Apostolo Zeno, not mentioned. O.t. *Lucio Vero*, 1700⁷.

Music (lost): Composer unknown. The text was set first by C.F. Pollaroli for Venice, 1700.

Cast: Berenice - Anna Marchesini; Vologeso - Andrea Pacini; Lucio Vero - Antonio Ristorini; Lucilla - Rosa Ungarelli; Anicelo - Giovanni Maria Morosi; Claudio - Francesco Maria Venturini; Florina - Rosalba Giardi; Giroldo - Michele Salvatici.

Comment: The date in the title is probably merely an error occasioned by the early publication of the libretto in December, 1709, and not an atavistic use of the Lady Day calendar. Fagiuoli V, f. 4 records the first performance on the above date. The second is dated 29 xii and others on 12 i 1709/10, and 26, i, all using the title *Lucio Vero*.

(1709)⁴

Ginevra principessa di Scozia. Text by Salvi, music by C.F. Pollaroli. Performed at Pratolino.
Cited by Manferrari III, p. 101. The entry is erroneous. It is perhaps a misprint for 1708² or a duplication of Allacci's error. See Fabbri, "Nuova luce," p. 157.

1710¹ 3 ii
Acerbi

Gl'inganni lodevoli. Commedia in prosa.
Fagiuoli V, f. 7r: "3. Lun[edi] [Febbraio, 1709/10] da Scalandroni. Si fece la mia commedia intitolata *gl'Inganni Lodevoli* p[er] la p[rim]a volta dagl'Acerbi." No publication of this date known. Reprinted in *Commedie* (1753) V, p. 129.

1710² 5 ii
Cocomero

CAMILLA REGINA DE' VOLSCI. Drama per musica da rappresentarsi in Firenze nel carnevale dell'anno 1710. Firenze, Vincenzio Vangelisti, 1709.
I Mb, Rn.

Text: Silvio Stampiglia, who is not mentioned. See 1698³.

Music: Possibly by Antonio Maria Bononcini.

Cast: Camilla - Anna Marchesini; Latino - Antonio Ristorini; Lavinia - Rosa Ungarelli; Prenesto - Maria Morosi; Turno - Andrea Pacini; Mezio - Francesco Maria Venturini; Attilia - Rosalba Giardi; Memmio - Michele Salvatici.

1710³ 3 iii

Il Baldovino. Commedia [in prose].
Fagiuoli V, f. 9r: "3 Lun[edi] [Feb. 1709]. Alla Commedia ai Frati della Nonz[ia]ta Il *Baldovino*." Martini's repertory includes a prose comedy by "P. Cornelius" by this title.

Per adempire a i pretiosissimi comandamenti
dell'Alt:ª V.Reale accomoderò le due parti delle
Opere di Livorno, al comodo, è bisogno del giovin
Guerri, ed a tempo debito le trasmetterò, acciò
che possano essere le cose mutate, inserite
negl'originali. In quest'opera, che
sino ad ora fà pochissime faccende, y impegno
di Cavalieri, Andreino per verità si porta
bene, tutto che habbi una particella povera
d'intreccio, ed arie, nulla di meno vien da tutti
compatito, ed io ne son contento. Nella secon
da che si comincia a provare, la di lui parte è
di maggior importanza, ma scorciata assieme
con tutte le altre, resterà pure non molta

Above and overleaf: I Fas, Arch. Med., Carteggio del Principe Ferdinando, Filza 5905/111. Two-page
letter from Francesco Antonio Pistocchi, Bologna, 6 vi 1710, concerning performances by Andrea
Guerri of Pisa who was studying with Pistocchi at Ferdinando's command. Pistocchi had been
requested by Ferdinando (Filza 5905/362, letter from Ferdinando, 3 vi 1710) to rewrite two arias,
one for the part of Fedele, for an opera to be performed in Livorno for carnival, 1711, in order to
adjust them for Guerri's voice. The two performances for Bologna are *Il più fedele fra i vassali,* text by
Francesco Silvani and with music by various composers, and *Il Faramondo* by Zeno and various
composers (see Ricci, pp. 404f.). The Bolognese operas are the subject of informative letters from
Fra Pamolo Spada to Ferdinando (Filza 5905/112, 3 vi 1710, and 5905/132, 15 iv 1710).

perche veramente vedono che in questi
giorni il divertimento della seta, non do-
urebbe passare, poco di più delle due ore, e mezza,
E qui umilmente con tutto il rispetto mi riprotesto
Di V. Alt: Reale.

Bologna li 6 Giugno 1710

Vmil: Deu: Obl
Franc.o Antonio Pistocchi

1710⁴ 1 vi
Palmieri

Amor vince la semplicità. Commedia [in prose].
Fagiuoli V, 18v: "1 Dom[eni]ca Giugno [1710]. Andai alla commedia
al Palmieri intitolata *Amor vince la semplicità* commedia d'Ant[oni]o
Fineschi da Radda recitata da Cav[alie]ri." Prince Francesco was in
attendance.

1710⁵ 7- 23 ix
Pratolino

RODELINDA REGINA DE' LONGOBARDI. Dramma per musica rappresentato
nella Villa di Pratolino. Firenze, Stamperia di Anton Maria Albizzini, 1710.
A Wn; I Bc, Bu, Fc(2), Mb, MOe, Rn(3); S Uu; US Wc (not in Sonneck).

Text: Antonio Salvi, according to Fagiuoli (see below) and Quadrio III.
IV.IV. p. 487. Author not named in the libretto. The *argomento* announces
the author's indebtedness to [Pierre] Corneille but that he had dispensed
with "l'ordine, l'episodio, e lo sceneggiamente, . . . ancorche mi sia servito
degli stessi personaggi, e dati loro gl'istessi caratteri [ma con] un'esito più
fortunato . . ." Other title: *Amor costante* (see 1725⁸). Corneille's play
is *Pertharite, Roi des Lombards*.

Music (lost): Giacomo A. Perti. See Busi, p. 78 (Letters in I Bc [Scanz. R,
n. 44, Vol. 1]). Correspondence in I Fas (Med 5905, cc. 63, 66, 124, 190,
329, 334, 363, 366 and 428—a request for an aria with oboe because
Ferdinando has an excellent oboist). Busi reports also that Perti went to
Pratolino to direct the opera.

Roles: Rodelinda, Bertorido, Grimoaldo, Edvige, Garibaldo, Unuflo,
Unoldo, Cuniberto.

Cast: Ferdinando again called Francesco Guicciardi and Vienna Mellini to
Pratolino. Of the regular singers Maria Domenica Pini probably sang.
Three new singers appear among those who must have Ferdinando's
approval for engagements, namely, Maria Maddalena Buonavia, Antonio
Predieri, and Andreino Guerri. Guerri had been studying with F. Pistocchi
in Bologna prior to 1710. The other two singers were familiar to Florentine
audiences because of their performances at the Cocomero.

Comment: Fagiuoli is unusually detailed about the number of performances
thus giving a schedule that probably may be applied to other performances
at Pratolino. V, f. 27r: "7 d[ett]a [Sett., 1710]: A Pratolino alla
Rodelinda Op[er]a del Salvi; entrò alle 22. 9 Mart[edi]: 2a com[edi]a
a Pratolino. 11 Giov.: la 3a com[edi]a a Pratolino. 14 Dom[enic]a:
la 4 com[edi]a a Pratolino. 16 Mart[edi]: 5 comm[edi]a a Pratolino.
18 Giov.: 6 comm[edi]a a Pratolino. 21 Dom[eni]ca: comm[edi]a a
Pratolino 7. 23 Mart[edi]: Comm[edia] a Pratolino 8. Torna il G.P. di
Pratolino a di 24 [Sett.].

1710⁶ 25 x
(Cocomero)

LA FORZA DELL'INNOCENZA. Drama per musica da rappresentarsi in
Firenze nel presente autunno dell'anno 1710 sotto la protezione del
Serenissimo Principe di Toscana e consacrato al medesimo. Firenze,
Vincenzio Vangelisti, 1710.
GB Lbm; I Bc, Mb.

Text: Apostolo Zeno and Pietro Pariati (Allacci, col. 290, with title of
Engelberta; also Quadrio III.IV.IV. p. 483). The libretto above says on
page 5: "[E della] penna del Sig. Francesco [*sic*] Pariati, e le scene
giocose inserite alla mede[si]ma sono di quella non meno celebre del

Sig. Gio: Domenico Pioli ambo poeti di gran credito ne nostri tempi."
The comic characters are Auretta and Gildo. However, no intermezzo
with those characters is listed by Mamczarz and no other libretto known.
Dedication signed by Antonio Guerretti on date shown.

Music (lost): Ascribed by Manferrari II, p. 277, and Fabbri, "Nuova luce,"
p. 155, to Francesco Maria Mannucci. However, two settings would be
equally available: Gasparini's setting for Venice, 1708, and Orefici's and
Mancini's for Naples, 1709. Scores for both of the settings in A Wn.

Cast: Lodovico - Gio. Batista Tamburini; Engelberta - Maria Anna Benti;
Matilde - Lucia Bovarini; Bonoso - Lucinda Diana Grifoni; Arrigo -
Ortenzia Beverini; Ernesto - Chiara Stella Cenachi; Ottone - Lorenzo
Bagnoli; Avretta - Anna Maria Bianchi; Gilda - Ipolito Cigna.

1711¹ 4 - 28 i
Cocomero

La forza dell'innocenza.
Fagiuoli V, ff. 37vff. lists performance of *Engelberta* at the Cocomero as
follows: "4 [Gennaio, 1710/11): Dom[eni]ca la p[rim]a Comm[edi]a
in via del Cocomero; 6 Martedi epifania 2a comm.a della Engelberta; 7.
Merc[oledi] 3. comm.a; 9 Venerdi alla com.a dell'Engelberta la 4.a;
11 Dom[enic]a la comm.a in musica ci fa 5.ta . . . ; 12. Lun[edi] la 6.
com. in musica; 14. la 7a comm.a; 18. Dom[enic]a 8 op[er]a; 25.
l'op[er]a per la xi volta; 28. l'op[era] in musica la xii." No new
publication has been found for this continuation of the fall opera as the
first of the carnival following. Probably the same printing was used again.

1711² 3 ii
Cocomero

LA FORZA DELLA FEDELTÀ. Drama per musica rappresentato in Firenze
nel carnevale del 1711 sotto la protezione del Serenissimo Principe
Ferdinando di Toscana. Firenze, Stamperia di S.A.R. per Jacopo Guiducci,
e Santi Franchi, s.d.
l Bc, Rn.

Text: Adriano Morselli, a repetition of *Pirro e Demetrio* previously
performed in Florence in 1696². Seven of eight singers are the same as
La Forza del'innocenza.

Music: Probably also by Alessandro Scarlatti, as is assumed by Fabbri,
A. Scarlatti, p. 97, where the date is erroneously stated as 1712.

Cast: Pirro - Giovanni Batista Tamburini; Demetrio - Chiara Stella Cenachi;
Deidamia - Lucinda Diana Grifoni; Climene - Anna Maria Benti; Clearte -
Lucia Bovarini; Arbante - Anton Francesco Gabbrielli; Mario - Ortenzia
Beverini; Breno - Ipolito Cigna; Drusilla - Anna Maria Bianchi.

Comment: Fagiuoli V, f. 41r: "3. [Feb., 1710/11] Mart[edi]. Il *Pirro e
Demetrio* in via del Cocomero p[er] la p[rim]a volta."

1711³ carn
Cocomero

BARILOTTO E SLAPINA. Intermezzi per musica.
l Fm (bound in *Lucio Papirio* [Roma, Bernabò, 1714]).

Text: Antonio Salvi, not mentioned here, but who is named in the title
of the libretto of Venice, 1712, as is the composer.

Music (lost): Probably Domenico Sarro, not mentioned here (see Sonneck,
p. 200).

Alterza Reale

254   525

L'innata Clemenza della R. A. V. che si è degnata sempre di benignissimamente compatire la debolezza de' miei componimenti, mi anima a farle comparire avanti in atto di profondissimo rispetto Caio Gracco, Opera da me composta per divertimento di S. M. C.ª nel presente Carnevale: Supplico S. A. V. R. a volersi compiacere di non prendere a sdegno questo umilissimo tributo della mia ossequiosissima servitù, ed a concedermi la gloria che riverentissimamente mi sottoscrivo

Vienna 15 Feb.º 1710

Della R. A. V.

Umil.mo Divot.mo Ossequ.mo Servo
Silvio Stampiglia

I Fas, Arch Med., Carteggio del Principe Ferdinando, Filza 5905/254. Letter from Silvio Stampiglia, Vienna, 15 ii 1710, accompanying a copy of *Caio Gracco* performed in the carnival of that year in Vienna at the Imperial Theater with music by M. A. Bononcini (see Anton Bauer, *Opern und Operetten in Wien*, p. 15. Graz: Böhlaus, 1955.).

Comment: That the intermezzi had to be performed with one or the other operas of the carnival of 1711 is obviously the conclusion drawn from the following entry.

1711 3 ii

Death of Francesco Maria de' Medici. His death must have cut short the performances of the second opera of the season and occasioned the closure of the theaters for the remainder of the year.

1712^1 3 - 17 i
Cocomero

LA COSTANZA FRA GL'INGANNI. Drama per musica da rappresentarsi in Firenze nel presente carnovale dell'anno 1711. Sotto la protezione del Serenissimo Principe di Toscana. Firenze, Stamperia di Caesare Bindi, MDCCXI.
I Bc, Mb, MOe.

Text: Apostolo Zeno, referred to here indirectly as "uno de' più culti professori della comica poesia"; reprinted in the *Poesie* III, pp. 89ff., with title of *Il Teuzzone*.

Music (lost): Possibly by Giuseppe Maria Orlandini who is named by Tagliavini, "Orlandini," as the composer of *Teuzzone* in Ferrara in the spring of the same year. It was set also by Antonio Lotti, who is named in the libretto of Venice, 1707, and whose score was used in Bologna, 1711, according to Allacci, col. 763.

Cast: Teuzzone - Gaetano Bernstatt; Zidiana - Francesca Borghesi; Zelinda - Rosaura Mazzanti; Gino - Chiara Stella Cenachi; Silvenio - Francesco Bernasconi; Argonte - Rosalba Giardi; Egaro - Luca Mengoni.

Comment: The date on the title page is shown to be erroneous by Fagiuoli VI, ff. 3rff., where the dates given are 3 Jan, 1711/12, "la prima il *Teuzzone*," 4, 8, 9, 17, January. Further confirmation is the fact that five of the seven performers are the same in the following opera.

1712^2 24 i
Cocomero

L'AMOR TIRANNICO. Drama per musica da rappresentarsi in Firenze nel presente Carnovale dell'anno 1712 sotto la protezione del Serenissimo Principe di Toscana. Firenze, Michele Nestenus, e Ant. Maria Gorghigiani ad Istanza di Domenico Ambrogio Verdi, MDCXII.
B Bc; I Fn, MOe, Rn.

Text: Domenico Lalli, not mentioned here, but identified in the title of the first publication in Venice, 1710 (Sonneck, p. 92).

Music (lost): Composer unknown. Quadrio III.IV.IV. p. 519, lists Lalli's libretto among the works of Carlo Francesco Gasparini (whose setting is lost) without identifying the location and date of the performance. (Allacci, col. 66, does not mention the composer.) However, the Venetian performance would be the logical choice, and the attribution is generally accepted. Since the Florentine is the second known libretto, it is likely that Gasparini's music was used. Francesco Feo is cited as the composer of the Neapolitan libretto of 1713 which is, however, much shortened and altered by comparison with the Florentine libretto, and, therefore, his setting cannot be considered. Giuseppe Maria Orlandini should not be discarded quickly on the other hand. Pavan, who supplies the information for Schatz (cf. Schatz Material in US Wc), states that Orlandini composed the music (lost) for Rome, 1712, at the Capranica theater, an attribution

either unknown or rejected by Tagliavini, "Orlandini." The libretto of
Pesaro, 1722, in **I** Bc, says: "musica di Giuseppe Maria Orlandini con
aggiunta di molte arie et altro di Agostino Tinazzoli, maestro di cappella
in detta cittã e direttore dell'opera." That is, Orlandini's setting precedes
the Pesaro performance. Since Orlandini was known in Florence as early
as 1708[4] above and by 1713 had been appointed as maestro di cappella
to Gian Gastone di Toscana (he is given the title in the libretto of *Carlo
Re d'Alemagna*, nuovamente composta for Bologna, 1713 [libretto in
I Bc]), he becomes a likely composer for Florence, 1712.

Cast: Tiridate - Giovanni Batista Franceschini; Polissena - Maria Caterina
Ghossler; Farasmane - Francesco Bernasconi; Radamisto - Gaetano
Berenstatt; Zenobia - Francesca Borghesi; Tigrane - Chiara Stella Cenachi;
Fraarte - Rosalba Giardi.

1712 20 vii

First meeting of the Immobili for the purpose of reestablishing the academy.

**1712 ix
Pratolino**

No performance took place at Pratolino owing to the prince's illness.

1712[3]

Il parassito. Intermezzo.

Text: Antonio Salvi. Cited by Mamczarz, p. 449, who locates a copy of
the libretto in **F** Pn, the existence of which has been denied by that library.
It is, however, listed by Allacci, col. 598, "in Firenze senza Stampatore."

Music (lost): Composer unknown. Mamczarz attributes the music to
"Lucignano." This is perhaps a misreading of Allacci who says "di Antonio
Salvi, di Lucignano."

**1712[4] 26 xii
Cocomero**

IL TIRANNO EROE. Drama per musica rappresentato in Firenze nel
carnevale del 1713. Sotto la protezione [*sic*] del Serenissimo Ferdinando
Principe di Toscana. Firenze, Stamperia di S.A.R. per Jacopo Guiducci, e
Santi Franchi, MDCCXIII.
I Mb, Rn.

Text: Vincenzo Cassani, not mentioned here, but who signs the dedication
of the Venetian libretto of 1710 (see Sonneck, p. 1076) and who is
identified in the libretto of 1715, Milano (**I** Bu). *Argomento* states the
source to be Appian and Plutarch.

Music: Possibly by Tommaso Albinoni who is mentioned as the composer
in the Venetian libretto of 1710. No score known.

Cast: Silla - Carlo Antonio Mazza; Emilia - Anna Marchesini; Bocco -
Lorenzo Porciatti; Pompeo - Antonio Bernacchi; Domizio - Alessandro
del Ricco; Valeria - Maria Caterina Goslerin; Albino - Pietro Sbaragli.
Per gl'Intermedii: Vespetta - Anna Maria Bianchi; Pimpinone - Filippo
Rossi. Bernacchi sang the same role in Venice, in 1710.

Comment: From the list of *personaggi*, it is to be observed that the
intermezzo *Vespetta e Pimpinone*, attributed by Mamczarz to Pietro
Pariati with music by Albinoni, was performed. However, the text is not
printed with the opera. Intermezzo first performed in Venice in 1708.

1713¹ 31 i
Casino

Tito e Berenice.
Fagiuoli VI, f. 49v: "31 Mart[edi] [Genn. 1712/13] . . . al Casino *Tito e Berenice.*" Identification is obviously not possible with the title alone. It may be a repetition of *Berenice* (1709¹), or an earlier performance of *Tito, e Berenice* by Capece and Caldara (Allacci, col. 769), performed in Rome the following carnival, or it may be a prose translation of Corneille's play. That it was a revival of opera at the Casino is indicated by Fagiuoli's reference to the Casino in 1713⁴.

1713² 13 ii
Pergola
Nobili

IL VERO ONORE. Festa teatrale fatta dall'Accademia de' Nobili di Firenze per la venuta dell'Altezza Reale del Serenissimo Principe Elettorale di Sassonia, descritta da Gio. Batista Casotti, reggente e lettore della stessa Accademici. Firenze, Michele Nestenus e Anton Maria Borghigiani, 1713. I Bc, Fn, MOe, Vgc.

Text: Francesco Maria Corsignani, mentioned on p. 55 of the libretto.

Music (lost): Francesco Maria Mannucci, *maestro di cappella dell' Altezza Reale.*

Cast: Mercurio - Carlo Antonio Mazza; Giunone - Lisabetta Brandi; Venere - Anna Marchesini; Fama - Antonio Bernacchi; Flora - Maria Caterina Goslerin; Arno - Anton Francesco Gabbrielli; Vizio - Pietro Sbaragli.

Comment: The date is supplied by a report in the Portinari Diary in I Fm (Ms c-27), p. 77, where it is observed, "Gl'esercizi in vero sono riusciti benissimo in tutte le loro parti, ed applauditi al sommo grado siccome gl'intermezzi della squisita musica ed orchestra; . . . " Susier notes the occasion briefly.

1713³ 25 ii
Cocomero

MEROPE. Drama per musica rappresentata in Firenze nel carnevale del 1713 sotto la protezione [*sic*] del Serenissimo Ferdinando Principe di Toscana. Firenze, Stamperia di S.A.R. per J. Guiducci e L. Franchi, 1713. I Fm, Mb, Vgc; S Uu.

Text: Apostolo Zeno, not mentioned here, but the libretto is published in the *Poesie drammatiche* IV, p. 95.

Music (lost): Possibly by Carlo Francesco Gasparini who is mentioned as the composer of the music for Venice, 1711 (Sonneck, p. 756). G.A. Orlandini at some time wrote at least settings of the arias. These were substituted for portions of Gasparini's music in Bologna, 1717 (See Ricci, "I teatri di Bologna," p. 417).

Cast: Polifonte - Lorenzio Porciatti; Merope - Anna Marchesini; Epitipe - Antonio Bernacchi; Argia - Maria Caterina Goslerin; Lirico - Pietro Sbaragli; Trasimede - Carlo Antonio Mazza; Anastandro - Alessandro del Ricco. Intermezzi: Parpagnacco - Filippo Rossi; Pollastrella - Anna Maria Bianchi.

PARPAGNACCO E POLLASTRELLA. Intermezzi.
Bound in the copy of I Fm. Mamczarz, p. 449, reports other copies in I Bc, Rc, and Vgc.

Text: Pietro Pariati, music possibly by Gasparini, both attributions appearing in Sonneck, p. 850 (Allacci, col. 600: *d'incerto autore*).

Comment: Fagiuoli VII, 1v, reports: "Sab[ato] 25. [Feb., 1712/13]

Al Casino p[er] veder la nuova burletta di Co: Pecori dopo il com[medi]a che fu l'ultima, alla *Merope* in via del Cocom[er]o." The reference is the basis for the following entry:

1713⁴ 25 ii
Casino

Burletta [in musica?].
See Fagiuoli entry immediately above. The facts that the term *burletta* is consistently used to mean comic opera and that the Conte Pecori appears in 1718⁴ and 1719¹ as the impresario of operas at the Pergola strongly suggest that this is an unknown comic opera.

1713⁵ aut
Cocomero

LA SILVIA. Drama pastorale per musica da rappresentarsi in Firenze nell' autunno dell'anno 1713 nel teatro di via del Cocomero sotto la protezione del Serenissimo Ferdinando . . . Firenze, Stamperia di S.A.R. per Jacopo Guiducci e Santi Franchi, 1713.
l Bc, Fm.

Text: Conte Enrico Bissaro, Vicentino, not mentioned here but identified by comparison with the libretto of Venice, 1711 (I Fm). Also Allacci, col. 721.

Music: Possibly D. Bartolommeo Cordans, Veneziano, who wrote the music for the Venetian performance of 1711 (Allacci, col. 721).

Cast: Silvia - Lucinda Diana Grifoni; Nerina - Maria Rosny; Egisto - Rosaura Mazzanti; Elpina - Ortensia Beverini; Marte - Lorenzo Porciatti; Faustolo - Florido Matteucci.

1713 30 x

Death of Ferdinando di Toscana. Since the autumn season normally began in late September or early October, the performance of *Silvia* above was probably cut short. Evidently no performance at Pratolino took place after September of 1710 because of the prince's illness. State mourning continued for one year, as was the convention.

1714 29 xi

Giovanni Gastone de' Medici becomes the protector of the Immobili, preparing the way for the re-opening of the theater.

1714¹ 25, 30 xi
Cocomero

SESOSTRI RE D'EGITTO. Drama per musica da rappresentarsi in Firenze nell'autunno dell'anno 1714 sotto la protezione dell'Altezza Reale del Serenissimo Gio: Gastone Gran Principe di Toscana. Firenze, Anton Maria Albizzini ad istanza di Domenico Ambrogio Verdi, MDCCXIV.
I Rn(2).

Text: Apostolo Zeno and Pietro Pariati, not mentioned here, but the libretto is reprinted in the *Poesie drammatiche* X, p. 199. The *argomento* announces that the plot was taken from "Amasi Re di Egitto del Sig. de la Grange, un moderno Tragico francese."

Music: Francesco Gasparrini [*sic*], as stated beneath the *Attori*. No score known. First performed in Venice, 1709 (libretto in I Bu; US Wc).

Cast: Sesostri - Gio: Maria Morosi, Amasi - Domenico Tempesti; Artenice - Francesca Miniati; Nitocri - Rosaura Mazzanti; Fanete - Gaetano Mossi; Organte - Gaspero Geri; Canopo - Filippo Rossi.

Comment: Fagiuoli VII, f. 84r: "30 Ven[erdi] [Nov., 1714]. La sera tornai col Co. Pecori e andai alla Com[medi]a in musica in via del Cocom[er]o d[ett]a Sesestri [*sic*]." Gian Gastone de' Medici attended 25 xi. See p. 42.

(1714)²

(*Lucio Papirio*)
(Text by Antonio Salvi; music by Antonio Predieri.) Allacci, col. 490, Schmidl and Sonneck, p. 704, state that the opera was performed in 1714 at Pratolino, which is clearly incorrect, no more operas being performed there after Ferdinando's death. It is most likely a misreading of the libretto of Rome, 1714, a copy of which is in **US** Wc and listed on p. 703 by Sonneck himself.

1714³ 27 xii
Cocomero

I VERI AMICI. Dramma per musica da rappresentarsi in Firenze nel teatro di via del Cocomero nel carnevale dell'anno 1715. Firenze, Anton Maria Albizzini, 1715.
I Bc, Mb, Rn.

Text: Francesco Silvani and Domenico Lalli, not mentioned but according to Allacci, col. 811 (but see also Sonneck, p. 1128). *Argomento* credits P. Corneille's *Heraclius* as the source.

Music (lost): Again the most likely composer is G.A. Orlandini who, according to Tagliavini, "Orlandini," provided a setting for Naples, 1715. But, of course, Andrea Paulati's score, used, according to Allacci, in Venice, 1713, is a possibility.

Cast: Amasi - Giovanni Batista Franceschini; Lagide - Gimignano Ramondini; Candace - Aurelia Marcello; Evergete - Antonio Bernacchi; Niceta - Margherita Caterina Zani; Tilame - Antonia Margherita Merighi.

1715¹ 11 ii
Cocomero

AMOR VINCE L'ODIO, overo TIMOCRATE. Drama per musica da rappresentarsi nel teatro di via del Cocomero l'anno 1715 sotto la protezione dell'Altezza Reale del Serenissimo Gio: Gastone Gran Principe di Toscana. Firenze, Anton Maria Albizzini, 1715.
I Bc, Fc, Mb, Rn(2), Vgc.

Text: Antonio Salvi, not mentioned, but see Fagiuoli below and Allacci, col. 67. *Cortese lettore* identifies the source of the plot as Thomas Corneille's *Timocrate*.

Music (lost): The composer, Francesco Gasparini, identified on page 5. This may be the first performance. The opera is listed without date at the end of a list of Gasparini's operas in Martin Ruhmke's article in MGG. Allacci's reference is to a libretto of Rome, 1715, which has not been located and for which he cites no composer.

Cast: Anfia - Aurelia Marcello; Erifile - Margherita Caterina Zani; Timocrate - Antonio Bernacchi; Nicandro - Gimignano Ramondini; Trasillo - Antonia Margherita Merighi; Arcade - Giovanni Batista Franceschini. Balli di Monsieur Antonio Saron.

Comment: Fagiuoli VIII, f. 6r: "Lun[edi] 11 Feb., 1714/15]. In via del Cocom[er]o l'op[er]a in musica *Il Timocrate* del Dr. Salvi la p[rim]a."

1715² 30 vi -
12 vii
Cocomero

AMORE, E MAESTÀ. Tragedia per musica da rappresentarsi in Firenze nel teatro di via del Cocomero nell'estate dell'anno MDCCXV sotto la protezione dell'Altezza Reale del Serenissimo Gio: Gastone Gran Principe di Toscana. Firenze, Anton Maria Albizzini, MDCCXV, Ad istanza di Domenico Ambrogio Verdi.
l Bc, Bu, Fn, Mc, Mb, Rn; US BL.

Text: Antonio Salvi, not mentioned, but cited by Fagiuoli (see below), and the author is named in later libretti, notably for Naples, 1718 (see Sonneck, p. 158, under the alternate title *Arsace*).

Music: Giuseppe Orlandini, "Maestro di Cappella dell'A.R. del Sereniss. Gio: Gastone," etc., as is stated on page 5 of the libretto. Score in A Wn (*Arsace*).

Cast: Statira - Margherita Durastanti; Arsace - Francesco Bernardi detto il Senesino; Rosmiri - Lucinda Diana Grifoni; Mitrane - Gio: Carlo Bernardi; Magabise - Matteo Berscelli; Artabano - Gaetano Mossi.

Comment: Fagiuoli VIII, f. 24r: "30 dom[enic]a [June, 1715]. P[rim]a recita del Dr[ama] *Amor'e Maestà* del Salvi in via del Cocom[er]o." Other performances recorded on July 3, 5, 7, 10, and 12.

In the *Cortese Spettatore* the author comments: "Eccoti una Tragedia in Musica, col fine veramente Tragico, Novità, per quanto è a mia notizia, non più veduta, almeno sulle Scene d'Italia. Se incontrerà, come spero, il tuo gentil compatimento, mi pregierò io d'essere il primo a farti sortir dal Teatro con le lagrime, fra le dolci armonie della Musica.

Il Soggetto è l'istesso, che già espose sulle Scene di Francia il famoso Tommaso Cornelio, sotto il nome del Conte d'Essex; ma dovendo questa servire alla Musica, alla Compagnia, ed al Teatro Italiano, m'è convenuto fingere la Scena in Persia, scemare il numero degli Attori, variar lo Scenario, far comparire varie azioni, ed alterarla molto dal Suo Originale. Ho pero conservato i caratteri de' principali Personaggi, e resa la catastrofe più spessi gli incidenti, conforme puoi riscontrar dalla lettura dell'uno, e dell' altro Dramma." The libretto seems to have been popular, but the Neapolitan libretto of 1718 already discards the tragedy and speaks of added comic scenes and a happy ending.

1715³ 6 xi
Cocomero

IL COMANDO NON INTESO ED UBBIDITO. Drama per musica da rappresentarsi in Firenze nel teatro di via del Cocomero nel autunno dell' anno 1715 sotto la protezione dell'Altezza Reale del Serenissimo Gran Principe di Toscana. Firenze, da Antonmaria Albizzini, 1715. Ad istanza di Domenico Ambrogio Verdi.
l Bc, Fn, MOe.

Text: Francesco Silvani, not mentioned, but whose name appears in the title of the first publication for Venice, 1709 (I Mb and US Wc. See Sonneck, p. 303).

Music (lost): Francesco Gasparrini [sic] as is stated on p. 5. The first Venetian performance of this opera was performed with the music of Antonio Lotti. There followed performances in Naples, 1713, and Genoa in the same year (librettos in l Bu), but without identification of the composer. This may be then the first performance of Gasparini's setting.

Cast: Zoe - Aurelia Marcello; Isacio - Antonia Margherita Merighi; Teodora -

Anna Vincenzia Dotti; Argiro - Gio: Battista Minelli; Constantino - Matteo Berscelli; Maniace - Domenico Tempesti; Leone - Lorenzo Porciatti.

1715[4]
Cocomero

INTERMEZZI COMICI MUSICALI da rappresentarsi nel teatro di via del Cocomero l'anno 1715. Sotto la protezione del Serenissimo Gio: Gastone Gran Principe di Toscana. Firenze, Antonio Maria Albizzini, 1715.
I Bc, Fn.

Text: Anonymous. These intermezzi are probably the same as those listed under *Lisetta, e Delfo* by an unknown author in Allacci, col. 487, and by Mamczarz, p. 433, for Rome, 1713 (libretti in I Rsc and Vnm).

Music (lost): Composer unknown.

Cast: Lisetta - Ortenzia Beverini detta la Lucertolina; Delfo - Lucrezia Borsari.

Comment: These intermezzi could have been performed with any of the operas for this year.

1715[5] 26 xii
Cocomero

LUCIO PAPIRIO. Drama per musica da rappresentarsi in Firenze nel teatro di via del Cocomero nel carnovale dell'anno 1716. Sotto la protezione dell'Altezza Reale del Serenissimo Gran Principe di Toscana. Firenze, Anton Maria Albizzini, 1716.
I Bc, Mb, Rn.

Text: Antonio Salvi, according to Allacci, col. 490, and confirmed by Fagiuoli (see below); also Salvi's name appears in the libretto of Venice for the same carnival but with a score by L.A. Predieri (Sonneck, p. 704). Plot derived from Livy, according to the *Argomento*.

Music (lost): Francesco Gasparini, as stated. This score had been performed in Rome the preceding year (Sonneck, p. 703).

Cast: Lucio Papirio - Domenico Tempesti; Marco Fabio - Pietro Paolo Laurenti; Quinto Fabrio - Battista Minelli; Emilia - Aurelia Marcello; Claudio Papirio - Antonia Margherita Merighi; Sabina - Anna Dotti; Appio - Lorenzo Porciatti.

Comment: Fagiuoli VIII, f. 53r: "26 Dic. [1715]. La Commedia in Musica *il Papirio* del Salvi con gran concorso, essendo pieno affatti il Teatro." Cited also on f. 53v for December 27.

1715[6]

Amazzoni vinte da Ercole. Dramma per Musica. In Firenze, 1715.

Text: Antonio Salvi. The entry is found only in Allacci, col. 45.

Music (lost): Probably by Giuseppe Maria Orlandini. The only surviving libretto of this opera is published in Reggio by Vedrotti in 1718, wherein the music is declared to be by Orlandini, mastro di capella [*sic*] del gran prenc. di Toscana. Since the libretto speaks of the usual accommodations, particularly in the arias, giving in justification the distance of the author and the brevity of time available, the opera must have been performed previous to the performance in Reggio. This would seem to be the first performance. However, without a full title it is not possible to be sure whether the performance took place in Florence or Livorno since the librettos of Livorno are commonly published in Florence.

1716¹ carn
Cocomero

ARMINIO. Drama per musica per rappresentarsi in Firenze nel teatro in via del Cocomero nel carnovale dell'anno 1716. sotto la protezione dell' Altezza Reale del Serenissimo Gran Principe di Toscana. Firenze, Anton Maria Albizzini, ad istanza di Domenico Ambrogio Verdi, 1716.
I Bc, Fn, Mb, Rn.

Text: Antonio Salvi, not mentioned, but a repetition of the 1703³ libretto with the same *Cortese lettore* and a few substitute arias performed at Pratolino with the music of Scarlatti.

Music: Composer unknown. Despite Morey's statement on p. 98 that the Florentine libretto is altogether different by comparison with either the 1703³ or the Naples, 1714, librettos, there is great similarity between the two Florentine librettos, and the music of Scarlatti could very well have been used. As for Fabbri's statement in "Firenze" that this is the first performance of Carlo Francesco Pollaroli's setting (otherwise composed for Venice, 1722 [Allacci, col. 114]), we know of no evidence to support it.

Cast: Arminio - Domenico Tempesti; Tusnelda - Aurelia Marcello; Segeste - Pietro Paolo Laurenti; Varo - Gio: Battista Minelli; Sigismondo - Antonia Margherita Merighi; Ramise - Anna Dotti; Tullio - Lorenzo Porciatti.

1716² 8 ii
Casino

Il Mitridate. Commedia in musica?
Fagiuoli IX, f. 8r: "8 [Feb., 1715/16] . . . alla com[medi]a al Casino *Il Mitridate.*" Probably a repetition of *Mitridate in Sebastia* (1704¹).

1716³ 17 vi
Cocomero

ASTIANATTE. Dramma per musica da rappresentarsi in Firenze nel teatro in via del Cocomero nell'estate dell'anno MDCCXVI. sotto la protezione dell'Altezza Reale del Serenissimo Gio: Gastone Gran Principe di Toscana. Firenze, Anton Maria Albizzini, 1716.
I Bc.

Text: Antonio Salvi. See 1701⁵.

Music: Possibly by G.A. Perti if it is indeed a repetition. The comment for the first performance concerning the attribution of the music to Antonio Maria Bononcini for 1701⁵ applies equally to this performance.

Cast: Pirro - Gaetano Borghi; Oreste - Pietro Casati; Ermione - Santa Cavalli; Creonte - Alessandro del Ricco; Pilade - Rosalba Giardi; Andromaca - Aurelia Marcello.

Comment: Fagiuoli IX, f. 27r, provides the date.

1716⁴
Cocomero

INTERMEZZI COMICI MUSICALI da rappresentarsi in Firenze nel teatro di via del Cocomero nell'estate dell'anno MDCCXVI. sotto la protezione dell'Altezza Reale del Serenissimo Gran Principe di Toscana. Firenze, Anton Maria Albizzini, 1716.
I Bc.
Poet and composer unknown. No intermezzo listed by Mamczarz with the two *personaggi* below.

Cast: Nerina - Santa Marchesini; Ginone - Filippo Rossi.

Comment: There being no other opera known for this summer season, the intermezzi must have been performed with *Astianatte* above.

1716⁵ 26? xii
Cocomero

IL TAMERLANO. Drama per musica da rappresentarsi in Firenze nel teatro di via del Cocomero nel carnevale dell'anno 1717. sotto la protezione dell' Altezza Reale del Gran Principe di Toscana. Firenze, Michele Nestenus, 1716. I Bc, Fc, Fn, Mb.

Text: Agostino Piovene, who is not mentioned, but who is so credited by Allacci, col. 749, and Quadrio III.IV.IV, p. 488. *Al lettore*: "Eccoti il *Tamerlano* poco tempo fa comparso nelle Scene della bellissima Capitale della Liguria . . . " The reference is to the first performance in Venice, 1710 (Sonneck, p. 1049).

The separation between Piovene's text and Salvi's (see 1706⁴) is not always clearly maintained in references. Indeed, it is to be suspected that a pasticcio may have been made of the two operas, pratcularly in the case of the Roman libretto of 1717 entitled *Il Trace in Catena* (**GB** Lbm), an alteration of Salvi's libretto set, according to the libretto itself, by Gasparini and two of his students. Thus, it appears that Gasparini, having set both texts, might have borrowed from them both. The same may be true of the Reggio, 1719, *Bajazet* (**US** Wc). Only a line-by-line comparison is likely to clarify the matter. Generally, the distinction may be made by the presence of the characters Leone, Rossane, and Tamur in Salvi's text and Irene and Idaspe or Morteno in Piovene's.

Music: Probably by Carlo Francesco Gasparini. A score in **A** Wn is dated Reggio 1719.

Cast: Tamerlano - Giuliano Albertini; Bajazete - Matteo Luchini; Asteria - Anna Marchesini; Irene - Caterina Borghi; Andronico - Antonia Maria Laurenti; Idaspe - Raffaello Signorini.

Comment: Fagiuoli IX, f. 49r, attended January 11, 1716/17. The date of the publication reinforces the presumption that this is the first opera of the carnival, hence the date given.

1717¹ carn
Cocomero

IL PRINCIPE CORSARO. Drama per musica da rappresentarsi in Firenze nel teatro di via del Cocomero nel carnovale dell'anno 1717. sotto la protezione dell'Altezza Reale del Serenissimo Gran Principe di Toscana. Firenze, Michele Nestenus, 1717.
I Bc, Fn, MOe, Rn.

Text: Anonymous. Manferrari ascribes this libretto to G.B. Giardini on the basis of a libretto of the same title listed by Allacci, col. 645, for Modena, 1674, which may, in turn, be a poetic reduction of the translation of a *tragedia di M. Quinault tradotta* (*in prosa*), in Bologna, per il Longhi, 1662, listed in col. 918. However, Quadrio III.II.III, p. 360, cites a *tragicommedia del Quinault trasporta in Italiano da L.P.*, Bologna, Longhi, 1716 (**I** MOe), and this one seems more likely.

Music (lost): G.C.M. Clari, according to Sesini, Manferrari, and Fabbri, "Firenze," on what grounds we do not know.

Cast: Nicandro - Matteo Luchini; Aminta - Antonia Maria Laurenti; Elisa - Anna Marchesini; Irene - Caterina Borghi; Alcandro - Giuliano Albertini; Sebaste - Raffaello Signorini.

Comment: Unfortunately Fagiuoli did not record this performance. It has been placed in second position because the dates of the preceding opera are

known and because the cast was exactly the same as *Tamerlano* (1716[5])
while varying by two singers from *Il potestà* (1717[3]).

1717[2] 27 i
Cascine

Attilio Regolo. Commedia.
Fagiuoli IX, f. 51r: "27 Merc[oledi], [Genn. 1716/17]. Al Cascine
com[medi] a l'*Attilio Regolo*." Possibly a repetition of the opera of 1693[4].

1717[3] 8 ii
Cocomero

IL POTESTÀ DI COLOGNOLE. Dramma per musica da rappresentarsi in
Firenze nel teatro di via del Cocomero nel carnovale dell'anno 1717. sotto
la protezione dell'Altezza Reale del Seren. Gran Principe di Toscana.
Firenze, Anton Maria Albizzini, s.d.
I Bc, Fn.

Text: A reduction of G.A. Moniglia's libretto of 1657[1]. The recitatives are
preserved, but all of the arias are substitutes.

Music (lost): Composer unknown. It is doubtful that any of the recitatives
of the original score of Jacopo Melani survived.

Cast: Leandro - Giuliano Albertini; Anselmo - Matteo Luchini; Isabella -
Antonia Maria Laurenti; Flavio - Raffaello Signorini; Vespino - Celestino
Ligi; Leonora - Anna Maria Mangani.

Comment: Fagiuoli IX, f. 52r, attended on the above date. Apparently
this was the third opera of this season, an exceptional event.

1717[4] 21 vi
Cocomero

TACERE ET AMARE. Drama per musica da rappresentarsi in Firenze nel
teatro di via del Cocomero l'estate dell'anno 1717. sotto la protezione
dell'Altezza Reale del Serenissimo Gran Principe di Toscana. In Firenze,
da Anton Maria Albizzini, 1717.
I Bc, Mb.

Text: G.A. Moniglia, not mentioned, with many changes. The same libretto
was published in Siena in the same summer (I Bc).

Music: Composer unknown, the changes being too significant to presume a
repetition of Jacopo Melani's music (see 1674).

Cast: Leonora - Francesca Cuzzoni; Bruscolo - Cosimo Ermini; Anselma -
Andrea Franci; Vespino - Celestino Ligi; Pancrazio - Matteo Luchini; Drusilla -
Maria Giustina Turcotti; Leandro - Giuliano Albertini. This is the same cast
as that appearing in the Siena libretto of the same summer.

Comment: Fagiuoli X, f. 7v: "21 Lun[edi], [Giugno, 1717]. P[rim]a
Commedia agl'Infuocati *Amar e Tacere* [sic] del D[ottore] Moniglia."
Cited again on July 27.

1717[5] 28 x
Fiesole
Villa di Gorini

La nobil contadina. Commedia [in prosa?].
Fagiuoli X, f. 21r: "28 Giov[ed]i SS. Simone [Oct. 1717]. da Fiesole alla
Villa di Gorini alla Comm[edi] a intito[lat] a *la Nobil Contadina* alle
20 . . ."

1717[6] 7 xi
Settignano

La finta serva. Commedia in prosa.

Text: Pier Francesco Minacci. Previously published by Longhi in Bologna,
1683. Martini's repertory confirms the entry in all particulars.

Comment: Fagiuoli X, f. 23r: "7 Dom[enica] [9bre, 1717] Comm[edi]a a Settignano intitolata *la Finta Serva* commedia di Pier Francesco Minacci." It is possible that the entries for 1717[5] and 1717[6] are the same prose comedy but moved from one private theater to another.

1718[1] 12 i
Cocomero

ALESSANDRO SEVERO. Dramma per musica da rappresentarsi in Firenze nel teatro di via del Cocomero nel carnevale dell'anno 1718. sotto la protezione dell'Altezza Reale del Serenissimo Gran Principe di Toscana. Firenze, Anton Maria Albizzini, 1718.
I Bc, Fm, Fn, Mb.

Text: Apostolo Zeno, not mentioned here, but the libretto is published in the *Poesie drammatiche* IV, p. 353.

Music (lost): Probably by various composers. For unknown reasons, Manferrari ascribes the music to Fortunato Chelleri, who is mentioned as the composer in the libretto of Brescia, 1719, in **I** Vcg. Antonio Lotti is named as the composer by the libretto of the first performance of the text in Venice, 1717 (**I** Bc). Allacci, col. 29, says that the Bolognese performance of 1718 was by diverse composers, which is probably the case for Florence in view of the fact that three of the singers listed below (Laurenti, Guglielmini and Amaini) sang the same roles in Florence and Bologna (autumn). It should be noted also that G.A. Orlandini set this text for Milan, 1723, according to Tagliavini, "Orlandini."

Cast: Giulia - Agata Landi; Alessandro - Gio: Antonio Archi; Sallustia - Antonia Maria Laurenti; Albinia - Anna Guglielmini; Claudio - Giuseppe Cassani; Marziano - Carlo Amaini.

Comment: Fagiuoli X, f. 32r, attended on January 12 and 30. Since this is the first opera of the season, the performances probably began on December 26 or 27, 1717.

1718[2] 6 ii
Cocomero

IL CIRO. Drama per musica da rappresentarsi in Firenze nel teatro di via del Cocomero nel carnevale dell'anno 1718. sotto la protezione dell'Altezza Reale del Serenissimo Gran Principe di Toscana. Firenze, Anton Maria Albizzini, ad istanza di Domenico Ambrogio Verdi, 1718.
I Bc, Fn, Mb, Rn, Vnm.

Text: Anonymous. The characters and text differ entirely from the Venetian libretto of 1709 (**I** Rn, **US** Wlc: Sonneck, p. 287) which is signed by P[ietro] P[ariati]. Allacci, col. 194, lists the Florentine libretto as being by an unknown author.

Music (lost): Composer unknown. Fabbri, "Firenze," col. 383, states that Tommaso Albinoni composed the music for Florence, presumably because he set Pariati's text for Venice, 1709. But since the above is not Pariati's text, the attribution is erroneous. Allacci, col. 194, cites a libretto of Naples, 1712 (**I** Bc, Rn) by an unknown author with music by Alessandro Scarlatti. But again the Florentine libretto is not the same.

Cast: Tomiri - Agata Landi; Telesia - Anna Guglielmini; Ciro - Gio: Antonio Archi; Arbace - Antonia Maria Laurenti; Silace - Giuseppe Cassani; Miceno - Carlo Amaini; Gildo - Giuseppe Galletti.

Comment: Fagiuoli X, f. 32v, attended the first performance on date stated.

SCANDERBEG

DRAMA PER MUSICA

DA RAPPRESENTARSI IN FIRENZE

Nel Teatro degl'Illuſtriſſ. SS. Accademici Immobili
poſto in Via della Pergola.

Nell'Eſtate dell'Anno M.DCC.XVIII

5

SOTTO LA PROTEZIONE

DELL' ALTEZZA REALE

DEL SERENISSIMO

GRAN PRINCIPE

DI TOSCANA.

70
E
11

IN FIRENZE,

Da Anton-Maria Albizzini: da S. Maria in Campo.
Con Licenza de' Superiori.

1718³ 22 vi -
15 viii
Pergola

SCANDERBEGH. Drama per musica da rappresentarsi in Firenze nel teatro degli Ill.me SS. Accad. Immobili posto in via della Pergola nell'estate dell' anno 1718 sotto la protezione del Gran Principe di Toscana. Firenze, Anton Maria Albizzini, s.d.
I Bc, Bu, Fn, MOe, Rn.

Text: Antonio Salvi, not mentioned, but identified by Pandolfini, f. 1r, and Allacci, col. 697. Title page shown on *page 233*.

Music (lost): Antonio Vivaldi, as stated in the libretto below the *Attori*. First performance of both music and text.

Cast: Scanderbegh - Gio. Battista Carboni; Doneca - Francesca Cuzzoni; Aroniz - Antonio Ristorini; Ormondo - Gio. Pietro Sbaraglia; Climene - Anna Guglielmini; Amurat II - Gaetano Mossi; Asteria - Agata Landi; Acomat - Rosa Venturini. Impresario - Cav. Antonio Ridolfi.

Comment: Fagiuoli records 22 vi as the "prima." I Fas (Med. Misc. d'Acquista 308): 18 performances from 25 vi to 15 viii.

1718⁴ 11 ix
Pergola

LA FEDE NE' TRADIMENTI. Drama per musica da rappresentarsi in Firenze nel teatro degl'illustriss. SS. Accademici Immobili posto in via della Pergola sotto la protezione dell'Altezza Reale del Serenissimo Gio: Gastone Gran Principe di Toscana. Firenze, Anton Maria Albizzini, 1718.
I Fn, Lg, Mb.

Text: Girolamo Gigli, not mentioned, but the libretto is the same as that of Siena, 1689 (I Fn) with minor changes. *Argomento* identifies the source of the plot as "Padre Rogatis nelle sue Storie della Spagna."

Music (lost): Luc'Antonio Predieri (p. 5). First performance of the music.

Cast: Garzia - Gio. Battista Pinacci; Anagilda - Agata Morelli; Fernando - Giovanni Battista Rapaccioli; Elvira - Anna Maria Bombasari. *Per gl'intermezzi. I quali per convenienti motivi non si stampano* - Rosa Ungherelli, Antonio Ristorini. Pandolfini names Francesco Pecori as the impresario.

Comment: Fagiuoli X, f. 58v: "Il Dom[eni]ca [Sett. 1718]. In via della Pergola la comedia del Co: Franc[esc]o. *La Fede ne' Tradim[en]ti* con Intermedij . . . 5 Merc. [Ottobre] Andai alla Comedia del Co. Pecori 2a la *Fede nei tradimenti* con Intermezzi del *Medico guarisci*."

1718⁵
Pergola

INTERMEZZO DI ERIGHETA, E D. CHILONE per il drama, che si rappresenta in Firenze nel teatro degl'illustriss. SS. Accademici Immobili posto in via della Pergola sotto la protezione dell'Altezza Reale del Serenissimo Gio: Gastone Gran Principe di Toscana. Firenze, Anton Maria Albizzini, 1718.
I Rn.

Text: Anonymous, but attributed to N. De Castelli by Mamczarz, p. 365 (first performed in Venice, 1713, music by Conti with the title, *L'Ammalato imaginario*).

Music: Attributed as above to Francesco B. Conti.

Cast: No performers are listed, but since Ristorini and Ungherelli were singing the intermezzi at the Pergola in this year, doubtless they sang these roles as well.

Comment: On the reverse side of the title page the sub-title is "Il carnovale di Venezia," which is cited by Mamczarz on pages 381 and 512, without recognizing it as another title for *Erighetta, e D. Chilone* or *Ammalato imaginario*. It is, of course, possible that Fagiuoli's *Medico guarisci* is still another title for this libretto, though the statement in the libretto of *La fede ne' tradimenti* that the intermezzi were not published makes it unlikely.

1718[6]
Pergola

INTERMEZZI DI VESPETTA, E PIMPINONE. Per il drama che si rappresenta in Firenze nel teatro degl'illustriss. SS. Accademici Immobili posto in via della Pergola sotto la protezione dell'Altezza Reale del Serenissimo Gio: Gastone Gran Principe di Toscana. Firenze, Anton Maria Albizzini, 1718. I Rn.

Text: Pietro Pariati, not mentioned, but cited by Allacci, col. 629, as the author of the Venetian libretto of 1708 (**US** Wc).

Music (lost): Possibly by Tommaso Albinoni, composer of the music for Venice, 1708. See Sonneck, p. 875.

Cast: Performers are not listed but from evidence of other librettos Rosa Ungherelli and Antonio Ristorini undoubtedly were the performers.

Comment: It is not possible to be certain with which opera these intermezzi were performed. The simplest arrangement would be to link the above with *Scanderbegh*. But the absence of any reference to them or to the actors in the libretto or in Pandolfini makes the link weak. It is possible that the intermezzi were changed in the course of the performances of *La fede ne' tradimenti* so that both of the 1718 intermezzi were performed with that opera. Or the date on the libretto of these intermezzi could be interpreted to coincide with autumn (November-December) and carnival of 1719 thereby linking the intermezzi with the performance of *La finta pazzia di Diana* (1719[1]).

1718[7] 26? xii
Cocomero

PARTENOPE. Dramma per musica da rappresentarsi in Firenze nel teatro di via del Cocomero nel carnevale dell'anno 1719. sotto la protezione dell' Altezza Reale del Serenissimo Gran Principe di Toscana. Firenze, Dom. Ambrogio Verdi, s.d.
I Fc.

Text: Silvio Stampiglia with changes and reduction. See 1701[7].

Music (lost): Luca Antonio Predieri as stated at the end of the libretto. According to Allacci, col. 601, Predieri composed the music first in 1710 for Bologna. The opera, presumably with the same music, was currently being performed again in Bologna in 1719 (I Bc libretto).

Cast: Partenope - Cecilia Belisani; Rosmira - Antonia Pellizzari; Arsace - Paolo Mariani; Armindo - Giuseppe Bigonzi; Emilio - Marco Antonio Berti; Ormonte - Giovanna Fontani.

Comment: The position of first opera (therefore beginning in December, 1718) has been assigned because of the established dates of *Griselda*, 20 i 1719[2], and *Lo speziale di villa*, 13 ii 1719[4]. The cast, as is usual in a single season, is the same in *Partenope* and *Griselda*.

1719[1] carn
Pergola

LA FINTA PAZZIA DI DIANA. Drama per musica da rappresentarsi in Firenze

nel teatro degl'illustriss. SS. Accademici Immobili posto in via della Pergola. Firenze, Anton Maria Albizzini, 1719.
I Bc, Rn.

Text: Anonymous. Revived, still anonymous, for Venice, 1748 (**US** Wc: Sonneck, p. 541).

Music: Luc'Antonio Pedrieri [*sic*, for Predieri] as stated on p. 5 of the libretto. First performance of both libretto and music.

Cast: Marchione - Anton Francesco Carli; Fileno - Gaetano Borghi; Eurilla - Anna Bombasari; ——— - Diana Vico. Performers for the intermezzi: Rosa Ungherelli, e Antonio Ristorini. Pandolfini identifies Francesco Pecori as the impresario.

Comment: Pandolfini assigns this opera to the autumn of 1718 although the libretto is dated as shown. He lists one set of performers for both operas, *La fede ne' tradimenti* (summer) and *La finta pazzia* (autumn) which is normal for the procedures of the theater in later seasons. However, the libretto for *La finta pazzia* lists performers completely different from those for *La fede* while, on the other hand, having four singers in common with the casts for summer and autumn of 1719. Therefore, it seems probable that Pandolfini is in error and the date of the libretto is correct.

Allacci, col. 391, lists an intermezzo, *Il Geloso*, Firenze, 1719, by Antonio Salvi (composer unknown), which is unknown to bibliographers.

1719² 20 i
Cocomero

GRISELDA. Dramma per musica da rappresentarsi in Firenze nel teatro di via del Cocomero nel carnevale dell'anno 1719, sotto la protezione dell' Altezza Reale del Serenissimo Gran Principe di Toscana. Firenze, Dom. Ambrogio Verdi, s.d.
I Fn.

Text: Apostolo Zeno. See 1703² above.

Music: Possibly by Giuseppe Maria Orlandini whose setting was composed for Brescia in 1716 (Tagliavini, "Orlandini," col. 398) and performed in Mantova, 1717, with the title *La virtù nel cimento* (**US** Wc: Sonneck, p. 577). Six arias from Orlandini's setting in **A** Wn. However, it should be noted the *contrascenes* of Gigli are contained also in this libretto, suggesting a repetition of Albinoni's score of 1703² which was revived as late as 1728 in Venice (**US** Wc).

Cast: Gualtiero - Giuseppe Bigonzi; Griselda - Antonia Pellizari; Costanza - Cecilia Belisani; Corrado - Marco Antonio Berti; Roberto - Giovanna Fontani; Otone - Paolo Mariani; Elpino - Francesco Belisani; Pernella - Lucia Bonetti.

Comment: Fagiuoli XI, f. 2v, attended on date shown. Performances probably began at the end of December for this opera.

1719³ 23 i
Casa Mattei

Amor vince fortuna.
Fagiuoli XI, f. 3v: "[23 Gen., 1718/19] Alla commedia in casa Marian Mattei *Amor vince fortuna*." A revival of Capece's melodrama (see 1690⁵), probably without music.

1719⁴ 13, 16 ii
Cocomero

LO SPEZIALE DI VILLA. Drama per musica da rappresentarsi nel teatro di via del Cocomero nel carnevale dell'anno 1719. sotto la protezione dell'Altezza

Reale del Serenissimo Gran Principe di Toscana. Firenze, Dom. Ambrogio Verdi, s.d.
I Fc, Fm, Fn.

Text: Gio. Cosimo Villifranchi; see 1683[3] above.

Music (lost): Anonymous.

Roles: Cartoccio, Rosaura, Filarco, Delmira sotto nome di Lisardo, Damone, Tranella.

Comment: Fagiuoli XI, f. 6r: "13 Lun[edi] [Feb., 1718/19]. In via del Cocom[er] o la com[edi] a di *Cartoccio Sp[ezia]le*. ... 16 Giov. [Feb.] In via del Cocom[er] o *Il Cartoccio Speziale di Villa* del Villifr[anchi]."

**1719[5] carn
Cocomero**

INTERMEZZI COMICI MUSICALI da rappresentarsi nel teatro di via del Cocomero nel carnevale dell'anno 1719. sotto la protezione dell'Altezza Reale dell' Serenissimo Gran Principe di Toscana. Firenze, Dom. Ambrogio Verdi, 1719.
I Bc.

Text: Anonymous. Identified by its characters, Zamberlucco and Palandrana, as the intermezzo set by Francesco Gasparini for Venice in 1709 and by A. Scarlatti for Naples, 1716 (see Mamczarz, pp. 491f.).

Music: Possibly by either of the above.

Cast: Zamberlucco - Giovanni Menzini; Palandrana - Lucia Bonetti.

Comment: This intermezzo and the one following cannot be assigned specifically to one or the other of the two operas for the carnival of 1719 at the Cocomero.

**1719[6] carn?
Cocomero?**

INTERMEZZI COMICI MUSICALI. Firenze, Dom. Ambrogio Verdi, 1719.
I Rn.

Text: Anonymous. By its characters, Cola and Aurilla, it can be equated with an intermezzo for Venice, 1720 (I Vnm) with the same characters listed by Mamczarz on p. 386, also anonymous.

Music (lost): Composer unknown.

Cast: Aurilla - Anna Maria Faini; Cola - Francesco Belisani.

**1719[7] 14 vii -
6 viii
Pergola**

IL TRIONFO DI SOLIMANO, ovvero IL TRIONFO MAGGIORE E VINCERE SE STESSO. Drama per musica da rappresentarsi in Firenze nel teatro degli Accademici Immobili posto in via della Pergola sotto la protezione dell' Altezza Reale del Serenissimo Gio: Gastone Gran Principe di Toscana. Firenze, Anton Maria Albizzini, 1719.
GB Lbm; I Mb, Rn.

Text: Anonymous.

Music (lost): Luc'Antonio Predieri, not mentioned in the libretto but according to Pandolfini. First performance of libretto and music.

Cast: Solimano - Gaetano Borghi; Asteria - Anna Bombasari; Giuba - Anton Francesco Carli; Isabella - Francesca Cuzzoni; Giustiniano - Diana Vico. Pandolfini adds the name of the impresario, Francesco Pecori. (The *ballerini*, Rochefort e Aquilanti, which Pandolfini lists, performed in 1719[8] and not in this opera.) Pandolfini also reverses the order between 1719[7] and 1719[8] as is proven by Fagiuoli's entries. Finally, he adds the names of Antonio Ristorini and Rosa Ungherelli as actors in the intermezzi. In neither libretto, 1719[7] or 1719[8], is there any indication that intermezzi were performed.

Comment: Fagiuoli XI, f. 23v: "14 Ven. [Luglio 1719] Il S.r Pr[inci]pe andò alla Commedia del Conte Pecori: *Il Trionfo di S.* [sic!] *Solim*[an]*o* . . . f. 28r: 6 Dom[eni]ca Agosto. Fui con Peppino alla Com[edi]a in via della Pergola al *Trionfo di Solimano*."

1719[8] 11 viii
Pergola

IL TRIONFO DELLA VIRTÙ. Festa teatrale dedicata all'Altezza Elettorale la Serenissima Anna Maria Luisa elettrice Palatina del Reno, da rappresentarsi in Firenze nel giorno del glorioso suo nome nel teatro degl' illustriss. SS. Accademici Immobili in via della Pergola. Firenze, Anton Maria Albizzini, 1719.
I Bc, Rn; US A.

Text: Apparently by Francesco Pecori, who signs the dedication without date.

Music (lost): Luca Antonio Pedrieri [*sic*] as stated on page 8 of the libretto. First performance of music and text.

Cast: La Virtù morale - Francesca Cuzzoni; Pallade - Diana Vico; Marte - Gaetano Borghi; Vulcano - Antonio Carli; Venere - Anna Bombasari. Pandolfini adds Ungherelli and Ristorini "per gl'intermezzi" (without distinction between this opera and *Il trionfo di Solimano*), Rochefort, and Aquilanti as ballerini and Girolamo Tacciato as the "Inventore della Grotta, e Macchine." Francesco Pecori continues as impresario.

Comment: The date shown is Anna Maria's birthday.

1719[9] 10 ix
Pergola

Il trionfo di pazzia.
Fagiuoli XI, f. 33v: "Dom[enico] [Sett. 1719]. La comedia in via della Pergola del Co. Francesco Pecori la p[rim]a *Il Trionfo di Pazzia*."

Comment: A curious entry. Pandolfini provides no information about such an opera at the Pergola and the title used by Fagiuoli is on the surface inappropriate to the *Trionfo della virtù* above unless it is to be interpreted as irony. But Morini, p. 40, refers to the *Trionfo della virtù* as a *farsa in musica*, which it certainly is not. Is he erroneously connecting other references to the above (which may be, from the title, a farce) with the libretto for the *Trionfo della Virtù*? As for Pandolfini's silence, regular variations in spelling indicate that his primary source is the collection of libretti that must have existed (and may still) in the Immobili archives, and if the libretto of the *Pazzia* was not published, his lack of information would be explained.

1719[10] xi?

Scherzo scenico fatto ad istanza della M.R. Madre D. Angelo M. Ridolfi monaca in S. Donato in Polverosa mia Nipote. Recitata pel carnevalino innanzi l'avvento da D. Angelica M. Ridolfi e da D. Maria Lucrezia Vignali l'anno 1719.

Text: G.B. Fagiuoli. Ms Cod. Ricc. 3279 in I Fr. See Baccini, *G.B. Fagiuoli*, p. 165.

1720[1] carn
Pergola

EUMENE. Drama per musica da rappresentarsi nel teatro degl'Illustrissimi
SS. Accademici Immobili in via della Pergola nel carnevale dell'anno 1720.
Firenze, Anton Maria Albizzini, 1720.
I Bc, Fc, Mb.

Text: Apostolo Zeno, not mentioned here, but the text is published in the
Poesie drammatiche I, pp. 235-318.

Music (lost): By various composers, according to Pavan. Pandolfini and the
libretto do not identify the composer or composers. It should be noted,
however, that Francesco Gasparini set this libretto for Reggio, 1714
(I Bu), a libretto unknown to Ruhmke.

Cast: Eumene - Silvia Lodi; Laodicea - Maria Anna Laurenzani; Artemisia -
Girolama Moreni; Aminta - Raffaele Canini; Antigene - Gio: Batista Roberti;
Leonato - Paola Besonzi; Penceste - Antonio Carli; Nesso - Antonio Lottini.

Comment: Performances presumably began in December since this is the
first opera.

1720[2] 11 ii
Pergola

ASTARTO. Drama per musica da rappresentarsi in Firenze nel teatro degli
Illustrissimi SS. Accademici Immobili in via della Pergola nel carnevale
dall'anno 1720.
I Bc, Fm.

Text: Apostolo Zeno and Pietro Pariati, not mentioned, but the text is
published in the *Poesie drammatiche* X, pp. 97-198. First performed in
Venice, 1708, with the music of Tommaso Albinoni (Allacci, col. 123).
Argomento states source as "Libro Decimo di Gioseffo contra Appione,
ed all'Idea favolosa ha dato qualche motivo il Tragico Francese Quinault,
nelle sue Tragedie intitolate *l'Astarto*, e *l'Amalasunta*."

Music (lost): Luc'Antonio Pedriere [*sic*], as stated on page 5. First
performance.

Cast: Elisa - Marianna Laurenzani; Astarto - Giovan Battista Roberti;
Sidonia - Giustina Turcotti; Fenicio - Anton Francesco Carli; Nino -
Silvia Lodi; Agenore - Girolama Moreni; Geronzio - Paola Besonzi.

Comment: Fagiuoli XI, f. 55v, records performance on above date.

1720[3] 12 ii
Cocomero

LA SERVA NOBILE. Drama per musica da rappresentarsi in Firenze nel
teatro di via del Cocomero nel carnevale dell'anno 1720. sotto la
protezione dell'Altezza Reale del Serenissimo Gran Principe di Toscana.
Firenze, Anton Maria Albizzini, 1720.
I Bc, Fc.

Text: Based upon Giovanni Andrea Moniglia's comic opera of 1660.

Music (lost): Composer unknown. Certainly this is not a repetition of
Anglesi's score as Sesini assumes in the catalogue of I Bc.

Cast: Desso - Giovanni Baldini; Fernando - Anton Francesco Carli;
Isabella - Anna Cosimi; Anselmo - Alessandro del Ricco; Bruscolo -
Antonio Lottini; Leandro - Giustina Turcotti; Leonora - Anna
Maria Bianchi.

Comment: Fagiuoli XI, f. 55v, provides the date shown.

1720⁴ 8, 16 v
Cocomero

IL FINTO CHIMICO. Drama per musica da rappresentarsi in Firenze nel teatro di via del Cocomero primavera nell'anno 1720. sotto la protezione dell'Altezza Reale del Serenissimo Gio: Gastone Gran Principe di Toscana. Firenze, Anton Maria Albizzini, 1720.
GB Lbm; I Bc.

Text: Giovanni Cosimo Villifranchi. See 1686⁴.

Music (lost): Composer unknown.

Cast: Delia - Anna Guglielmini; Graticcio - Alessandro del Ricco; Florante - Gaetano Borghi; Vaiano - Anton Francesco Carli; Lisetta - Anna Cosimi; Corinda - Maria Teresa Cotti.

Comment: Fagiuoli XI, f. 67v, supplies the dates as shown.
 The revival of this libretto seems to have been popular, the following having been found: Modena, 1723, "diverso dall'Originale stampato in qualche piccole parte ultimamente in Firenze . . ." (I MOe), Livorno, 1723 (I Bam, Fn, Mb), Bologna, 1729 (I Bc, Rn).

1720⁵ 31 vii
Pergola

LUCIO VERO. Dramma per musica da rappresentarsi in Firenze nell'estate dell'anno 1720. nel teatro degl'Illustrissimi SS. Accademici Immobili in via della Pergola sotto la protezione dell'Altezza Reale il Serenissimo Gio: Gastone Gran Principe di Toscana. Firenze, Gaetano Tartini, e Santi Franchi, 1720.
I Bc, Fc.

Text (with extensive changes): Apostolo Zeno, not mentioned here. See 1700⁷ and 1709³ (*Il Trionfo della Costanza*).

Music: By various composers, according to Pavan. However, it should be noted that G.A. Perti had written a setting in 1717 for Bologna.

Cast: Lucio Vero - Gaetano Borghi; Lucilla - Teresa Cotti detta la Francese; Vologeso - Gaetano Berenstadt; Flavio - Anton Francesco Carli; Aniceto - Alessandro del Ricco. Pandolfini adds Co. Francesco Pecori as the impresario.

Comment: Fagiuoli XI, f. 75v, attended on date shown.

1720⁶ 11 ix
Cocomero

TEMISTOCLE. Azione scenica musicale da rappresentarsi in Firenze nel teatro di via del Cocomero nell'autunno dell'anno 1720. sotto la protezione dell'Altezza Reale il Serenissimo Gio: Gastone Gran Principe di Toscana. Firenze, Anton Maria Albizzini, 1720.
I Fc, Mb.

Text: Apostolo Zeno, not mentioned here, but the text is reprinted in the *Poesie drammatiche* II, pp. 5-58. The *Argomento* states the source to be Thucydides.

Music (lost): Composer unknown. It is unlikely that Marc'Antonio Ziani's music for the original performance in Venice, 1700, was revived. However, the possibility exists that this is the first performance of the music of G.M. Orlandini. See 1737².

Cast: Artaserse - Gio: Batista Pinacci; Temistocle - Andrea Pacini; Palmide - Francesca Cuzzoni; Eraclea - Maria Giustina Turcotti; Cambise - Gio: Pietro Sbaraglia; Clearco - Maria Maddalena Pieri. For the intermezzi (not published with the libretto): Rosa Ungherelli and Antonio Ristorini.

Comment: Fagiuoli XII, f. 3v, provides the date shown.

1720[7] 11 ix? *Il marito giocatore e la moglie bacchettona*. Intermezzi per musica.

Text: Antonio Salvi. Allacci lists this libretto three times under different titles: col. 133, *Bacchetona*; col. 417, *il Giuocatore*, both dated 1720 in Florence; and col. 507, *il Marito*, etc., as above, dated 1729, Venice, this time without author. Loewenberg, p. 70, and Mamczarz, p. 437, assure us these are the same intermezzi and that another title is *Serpilla e Bacocco* (or *Barotto*).

Music: Giuseppe Maria Orlandini (Loewenberg, p. 70). Scores: **A** Wn, **B** Bc, **D** MÜps (with final duet by J.A. Hasse), **D** ROu (arrangement by Leonardo Vinci), and **I** Fc. See Sonneck, pp. 730ff., and Lazarevich.

Comment: Loewenberg and Allacci give 1720 as the year. Tagliavini says 1721. Mamczarz does not locate libretto, but she must have seen one since on p. 653 (but erroneously dated 1729) and on p. 636, she identifies Ristorini and Ungherelli as the performers, thus forming a link with *Temistocle* above.

1720[8] *L'Avaro*. Intermezzi rappresentati l'anno 1720 nella città di Firenze. Firenze, 1720.

Text: Antonio Salvi, according to Allacci, col. 129. Listed by Mamczarz, p. 372, without the location of a libretto.

Music (lost): Francesco Gasparini, according to Mamczarz. Unknown to Ruhmke.

1721[1] carn
Pergola

L'INNOCENZA DIFESA. Dramma per musica da rappresentarsi in Firenze il carnevale dell'anno 1721. nel teatro di via della Pergola sotto la protezione dell'Altezza Reale del Serenissimo Gran Principe di Toscana e dedicato all'Eccellenza Illustrissima del Signor Duca Francesco Bonelli Baron Romano Duca di Montenara, ecc. Firenze, Dom. Ambrogio Verdi, 1720.
I Bc, MOe.

Text: Francesco Silvani (with numerous changes), not mentioned, but his name is in the title of the original libretto of Venice, 1699 (Sonneck, p. 632). Allacci, col. 460, lists the latter and, among others, a libretto of Verona, 1714, with the title of *L'innocenza difesa* (with changes), music by Giuseppe Orlandini, and finally a repetition of the same libretto in Rome, 1720, a copy of which is in **US** Wc (Sonneck, as above). Sonneck incorrectly interprets Allacci to mean that Orlandini's music was used in Rome. The Florentine libretto above remarks in the dedication signed by Michele Giusti (impresario): "Il presente Dramma, il quale avendo fatta di se vaga mostra sulle Latine Scene, la farà più bella sulle nostre Toscane," a statement that can be taken with certainty to apply only to the libretto.

Music: Anonymous. The above comment forms a tenuous link with the music of Orlandini. However, Sesini catalogues the libretto under Fortunato Chelleri, presumably as an arbitrary choice of Chelleri's setting, which Sonneck says was first performed in Milan, 1714, and which Allacci cites as the setting for Venice, 1722. There is an anonymous score in **I** MOe.

Cast: Giuditta - Margherita Albinoni; Gildippe - Maria Anna Laurenzani; Lotario - Vittoria Tesi; Adalgiso - Gio: Antonio Archi; Berardo - Andrea Guerri; Asprando - Lorenzo Berretti. Pandolfini identifies the impresario as Michele Giusti.

Comment: The two operas for this season are listed alphabetically and in Pandolfini's order, there being no clue as to the chronological order. Both librettos bear the publisher's date of 1720, which is unusual.

1721² carn
Pergola

TITO MANLIO. Dramma per musica da rappresentarsi in Firenze il carnevale dell'anno 1721. nel teatro di via della Pergola sotto la protezione dell' Altezza Reale del Serenissimo Gran Principe di Toscana. Firenze, Dom. Ambrogio Verdi, 1720.
I Bc, Fn, Rn; **US** Wc.

Text: Matteo Noris (see 1696⁵) with changes "onde si rende assai diverso da quel che lo compose l'autore," as is stated in the notice addressed to the Altezza Reale and signed by Michele Giusti (impresario).

Music: Anonymous. Luca Antonio Predieri, according to Pavan. Tagliavini, "Predieri," lists the above performance and the same opera for Bologna both, however, in 1721. Ricci, *I teatri di Bologna*, p. 422, does not cite a performance of this opera in 1721 but rather *Astarte* by Predieri. Sesini, on the other hand, catalogues this libretto under Pollaroli, i.e., a revival of both text and music of the 1696⁵ performance. Pandolfini does not identify the composer, nor does the libretto itself. The archives of the Pergola may be Pavan's resource, but in other cases Pavan can be shown not to be entirely reliable.

Cast: *Romani*: Ramerin - Vittoria Tesi; Vitellia - Maria Anna Laurenzani; Tito Manlio - Gio. Antonio Archi; Decio - Lorenzo Berretta; *Latini*: Servilia - Margherita Albinoni; Lucio - Andrea Guerri; Geminio - Lorenzo Berretta. Pandolfini adds the name of the impresario, Michele Giusti.

1721³ 21 i
Cocomero

IL CONTE DI CUTRO. Drama per musica da rappresentarsi nel presente carnevale in Firenze nel teatro di via del Cocomero sotto la protezione dell' A.R. il Sereniss. Gio: Gastone Gran Principe di Toscana. Firenze, 1721, s.t., Ad istanza di Giuseppe Magnolfi e Vettorio Borghesi.
I Bc, Fc, Fn.

Text: Giovanni Andrea Moniglia, not mentioned here.

Music: Anonymous. Declared to be by Lorenzo Cattani (see 1682¹) by Sesini and by the catalogue of **I** Fc, although the libretto does not identify either the poet or the composer. Despite the faithfulness of the libretto above to the original, there being only a few omissions of arias, to assume the revival of Cattani's music is unwarranted.

Cast: Ottavio - Sig. [Anna Maria] Mangani; Leandro - Maria Caterina Negri; Isabella - M. Maddalena Visconti; Laura - M. Giustina Turcotti; Davo - Giovanni Baldini; Bruscolo - Alessandro del Ricco; Fiammetta - Anna M. Faini. Il Direttore de' Balli: Francesco Miriggioli.

Comment: Fagiuoli XII, f. 19v. 21 Genn. 1720/21: "al *Conte di Cutro* con Zeppo."

1721⁴ 10 ii   *Attilio Regolo.*
Fagiuoli XII, f. 21v, on 10 ii: "Alla com[edi]a a S.M.N.a [Santa Maria Novella?] *Attilio Regolo.*" Possibly the same text by Matteo Noris as in 1693⁴. Possibly without music. See also 1717².

1721⁵ carn   *Il bottegaro gentiluomo* ovvero *Larinda e Vanesio.*

Text: Antonio Salvi.

Music: Giuseppe Maria Orlandini.

Comment: The notice of this performance is to be found in Tagliavini, "Orlandini" and in Mamczarz, p. 378 (without location of libretto). The former specifies that it was performed in the Pergola. The absence of any indication in the librettos and lists of actors in Pandolfini is not reassuring. For what it is worth, Anna Maria Faini, who sings in London in 1737 in the above intermezzo (see Sonneck, p. 230), is in the cast of *Il conte di Cutro* at the Cocomero, 1721³. See 1722.

1721⁶   DEMODICE. Tragedia [in versi sciolti] del Sig. G[iambatista] R[ecanati]. Firenze, Giuseppe Manni, 1721.
I Mb.

Comment: Allacci, col. 247. Poetic tragedy without music. The text contains no duets, arias, etc. No indications of the performance.

1721-22
Pergola   Morini states: "Della stagione di Carnevale 1721-22, di cui ebbero l'impresa diversi interessati e della stagione di Estate dell'anno 1722, nella quale il teatro fu affidato all'impresa dei Sigg. Buonazzoli e Orlandini, mancano in Archivio (degl'Immobili) le notizie delle opere che si rappresentarono alla Pergola ..." Pandolfini asserts that the theater was closed because of the death on September 19, 1721, of the Granduchessa Aloisia d'Orléans," i.e., Marguerite Louise d'Orléans, the estranged wife of Cosimo III.

1722   *Artigiano gentiluomo.* Intermezzi per musica. Firenze, 1722.

Text: Antonio Salvi. Cited by Allacci, col. 121. No copy found. It is plainly another title for *Il bottegaro gentiluomo.*

Music (lost): Giuseppe Maria Orlandini.

Comment: To accommodate the year with Pandolfini's statement quoted above concerning the closure of the Pergola because of offical mourning, it must be presumed that the intermezzi were performed in the fall of 1722, after the anniversary of the death of Marguerite d'Orléans on September 19, 1721. The libretto may on the other hand be connected somehow with 1721⁵.

1723¹ carn
Cocomero   L'ANDRONICO. Drama per musica da rappresentarsi in Firenze nel teatro di via del Cocomero nel carnovale dell'anno 1723. Sotto la protezione dell'Altezza Reale del Serenissimo Gran Principe di Toscana. Firenze, Stamperia di Sua Altezza Reale, 1723.
I Bc, Fn, Rc.

Text (with variations): By Apostolo Zeno and Pietro Pariati with the title of *Antioco*. The notice to the reader explains: *"L'Antioco*, Poesie Drammatica d'una rinominata penna dell'Adria è questo, che ti si rappresenta sotto il nome d'*Andronico* . . . [per] che il medesimo Autore ne a preso il soggetto dalla Tragedia di Monsù Capistron, intitolata *l'Andronico*, a cui per dare un fine lieto, e terminar colle nozze, ha stimato meglio appogiarla [sic] all'Istoria d'*Antioco*." The variations, by comparison with Zeno's *Poesie drammatiche* IX, pp. 95-184, are very slight.

Music: Anonymous. Possibly by Francesco Gasparini who composed the music for the first performance in Venice, 1705, according to Allacci, col. 95. Allacci lists no other composer before 1723.

Cast: Gian Paleologo - Angiol Maria Zannoni; Andronico - Giovanni Rapaccioli; Irene - Margherita Caterina Zani; Palmira - Diacinta Spinola; Marziano - Pietro Baratti; Leonzio - Rosa Mignatti.

Comment: The choice for the first opera of this season is arbitrary, there being no clues.

1723² carn
Cocomero

GINEVRA, PRINCIPESSA DI SCOZIA. Dramma per musica da rappresentarsi in Firenze nel teatro di via del Cocomero nel carnevale dell'anno 1723. sotto la protezione dell'Altezza Reale del Serenissimo Gran Principe di Toscana. Firenze, Stamperia di Sua Altezza Reale, 1723.
I Bc.

Text: Antonio Salvi with considerable alteration. The notice to the reader states: "Ciascuna volta, che si è ristampato il presente Drama, in occasione di rappresentarsi in diversi Teatri è stato molto alterato dal suo primo Originale, come è convenuto fare questa volta ancora per accomodarsi alla Compagnia."

Music: Anonymous. Sesini catalogues the libretto under Carlo F. Pollarollo. In view of the extensive changes the attribution is doubtful. A more likely candidate is a score used in Livorno, 1722, the libretto of which says that the music is by Sarto [sic] di Napoli. A score dated 1720 attributed to Domenico Sarri exists in I Nc. Perti composed the music for 1708².

1723³ 9 vii
Pergola

FLAVIO ANICIO OLIBRIO. Dramma per musica da rappresentarsi nel teatro di via della Pergola nella presente estate dell'anno 1723. sotto la protezione dell'Altezza Reale il Serenissimo Gran Principe di Toscana all'Altezza Reale della Serenissima Violante Beatrice Gran Principessa di Toscana. Firenze, Dom. Ambrogio Verdi, ad istanza di Gio: Angiolo Targioni, s.d.
GB Lbm; I Bc, Fc(2), Fn, Mnb, Rn; US Wc(2).

Text: By Apostolo Zeno, not mentioned here, but the text appears in the *Poesie drammatiche* X, p. 96. The *Argomento* identifies the source: "Vedi Evagno I. 2 cap. 7. Procop. lib I. Hist. Vand. Paol. Diac. lib. 6. ed altri." The dedication, signed by Michele Giusti, the impresario, speaks of the "benigno aggradimento, che V.A.R. si compiacque avere delle due Opere, che nel Carnevale dell'Anno 1720. feci rappresentare nel Teatro di Via della Pergola." Other evidence attests to the interest and participation of Violante Beatrice in the operatic performances of Florence.

Music: Possibly by Francesco Gasparini who wrote the setting for the first performance in Venice in 1707. Pavan suggests Nicola Antonio Porpora.

Cast: Flavio Anicio Olibrio - Carlo Scalzi; Placidia - Faustina Bordoni; Ricimero - Gio: Batista Pinacci; Teodelinda - Vittoria Tesi; Olderico - Rosalia Bombasari; Fausto - Giuliano Albertini; Massimo - Anton Domenico Biscardi.

Comment: Fagiuoli XIV, f. 15v, supplies the date as shown.

1723[4] sum
Rimoti

IL GIOCATORE. Intermezzi per musica da rappresentarsi in Firenze nel teatro della Ill.ma Accademia de' Rimoti l'estate dell'anno 1723. Firenze, Giseffantonio Archi, 1723.
I Rn.

Text: Antonio Salvi (see 1720)[7].

Music: Possibly by Giuseppe Maria Orlandini. See Sonneck, pp. 730f.

1723 31 xi

Death of Cosimo III. Theaters are closed until the carnival of 1725.

1725[1] 17 i
Pergola

DIDONE ABBANDONATA. Drama per musica da rappresentarsi in Firenze nel teatro in via della Pergola nel carnevale dell'anno 1725. sotto la protezione dell'Altezza Reale il Serenissimo Gio: Gastone I. Gran Duca di Toscana. Firenze, Dom. Ambrogio Verdi, s.d.
I Bc, Fc(2).

Text: Metastasio, not mentioned here. Text published again in his *Opere* II, pp. 47-82. Dedication signed without date by the Cavalieri Interessati nell' Opera.

Music: Anonymous. The *Opere* state that the first performance took place in Naples, 1724, with the music of Domenico Sarri, a copy of whose score is in I Nc. In the same carnival of 1725 the opera was performed in Venice with the music of Tommaso Albinoni (Sonneck, p. 381). And in the following year it was performed in Rome with the music of Leonardo Vinci (scores in A Wn and D MÜps).

Cast: Didone - Margherita Guallandi; Enea - Gio: Battista Minelli; Jarba - Gio: Battista Pinacci; Selene - Antonina Tozzi; Osmida - Giovanni Drejer; Araspe - Rosa Croci. Negli Intermedii (not published with the libretto) - Rosa Ungherelli and Antonio Ristorini. Architetto, e Pittore delle scene nuove - Giacomo Monari.

Comment: Fagiuoli XI, f. 34v, provides the date as shown adding that this was "l'ultima opera della pr[im]a recita." The position of first opera (with December opening) is confirmed by the dedication of the next entry.

1725[2] 23 i
Pergola

LUCIO PAPIRIO. Drama musicale da rappresentarsi in Firenze nel teatro di via della Pergola nel carnovale dell'anno 1725. Sotto la protezzione dell' Altezza Reale il Serenissimo Gio: Gastone I. Gran Duca di Toscana. Dedicato all'Altezza Reale la Serenissima Violante Beatrice di Baviera, ecc. In Firenze, Dom. Ambrogio Verdi, s.d.
I Bc, Fc(2), Vnm.

Text: Apostolo Zeno, not mentioned. Text reprinted in the *Poesie drammatiche* V, p. 86. This libretto conforms to initial and final scenes of Piovene's "mutilation" for Venice, 1721 (Sonneck, p. 705). Confused in sources with Salvi's libretto of the same name (see 1715[5]). The dedication, signed by the *Cavalieri della Conversazione* without date, comments: "La generosa Clemenza, con cui si è degnata V.A.R. di onorare più volte le Recite della prima Opera, che si è fatta in Teatro di via della Pergola, ha dato agli ossequiosi animi nostri un forte impulso . . ." Hence, this is the second opera of the season.

Music: Possibly by Antonio Pollaroli who composed the music for the Venetian performance.

Cast: Lucio Papirio - Gio: Bat.a Pinacci; Papiria - Margherita Guallandi; Marco Fabio - Pietro Pertici; Rutilio - Antonina Tozzi; Quinto Fabio - Gio: Battista Minelli; Cominio - Rosa Croci; Servilio - Giov. Drejer.

Comment: Morini, p. 41: "L'Opera 'Lucio Papirio' fu anche decorata di un superbissimo carro trionfale, di bellissimi trofei, e tirato da quattro cavalli leardi e seguito da sedici comparse a cavallo." The comment appears to be taken from Pandolfini (see *Farnace* 1725[12]) but associated with the wrong opera.
Fagiuoli XI, f. 36v, records the opera "per la prima volta."

1725[3] carn
Pergola

L'ammalato immaginario. Intermezzi in musica.

Text: N. de Castelli, according to Mamczarz, p. 514, and Tagliavini, "Orlandini," col. 399. Libretto unknown to Sartori.

Music: Giuseppe Orlandini, according to Morini, p. 41.

1725[4] carn
Pergola

Le bourgeois gentil-homme. Intermezzi in musica.

Text: Antonio Salvi (see 1721[5]), according to Mamczarz and Tagliavini.

Music: Giuseppe Orlandini, according to Mamczarz and Tagliavini.

1725[5] carn
Pergola

Un vecchio innamorato. Intermezzi in musica.

Text: Anonymous.

Music: Giuseppe Orlandini, according to Morini, p. 41, and Mamczarz, p. 484.

NOTE The source for both Mamczarz and Tagliavini is probably Morini, whose habit of listing all works performed in the carnival season as a double-year misled Mamczarz into listing the first and third under two separate years, i.e., under 1724 and 1725. (She omits the second intermezzo for unknown reasons.) No librettos have been uncovered for these three. They may not indeed have been published. Only one of the librettos of the two operas at the Pergola in the carnival of 1725 states that intermezzi were performed: *Didone abbandonato*, which adds Ungherelli and Ristorini to the performers of the opera. One intermezzo (1725[6]) has been located, not mentioned by Morini but known to Mamczarz, p. 474, bringing the total of the intermezzi proposed for the Pergola in this season to four, something of a record surely. Presumably Ungherelli and Ristorini would have performed them all.

1725[6] carn
Pergola

INTERMEZZI MUSICALI da rappresentarsi in Firenze nel teatro di via della Pergola nel carnevale dell'anno 1725. Firenze, Dom. Ambrogio Verdi, 1724. I Fc, Rn.

Text: Anonymous.

Music: Anonymous.

Cast: Tarpina - Rosa Ungherelli; Zelone - Antonio Ristorini.

1725[7] carn
Cocomero

ADELAIDE. Dramma musicale da rappresentarsi in Firenze nel teatro di via del Cocomero l'anno 1725. sotto la protezione dell'A.R. del Serenissimo Gio. Gastone I. Gran Duca di Toscana. Dedicato alla medesima Altezza Reale. Firenze, Stamperia di S.A.R., le Tartini e Franchi, 1725.
I Bc, Fc, Vnm.

Text: Antonio Salvi, according to Allacci, col. 8. The *Al lettore* speaks of other publications and performances *su' Forastieri Teatri* by comparison with which the Florentine libretto has a few changes. However, we have not seen an earlier libretto than the Florentine. Dedication signed without date by the *Interessati dell'Opera*.

Music: Anonymous. The music has been attributed by Sesini and others to G.M. Buini, who composed the music for a performance in the same year in Bologna (libretto in I Bc, Bu) according to Allacci, col. 8. But Allacci's attribution for the Bologna performance may not be presumed to apply to the Florentine, as has almost universally been done. A more tenable proposition is that Giuseppe Orlandini composed the music. The opera was performed again in Livorno in the carnival of 1726, and the libretto there (I Fn) is dedicated to Gian Gastone as well. It was performed again in Venice, 1729, when the libretto identifies Orlandini as composer. A comparison among Bologna, 1725 (Buini's setting), Florence, 1725, and Venice, 1729, shows a significantly closer relationship between the latter than between these and the Bologna libretto. Since Orlandini was the maestro di cappella to Gian Gastone it is reasonable to suppose that his music was performed in Florence before being performed elsewhere.

Cast: Adelaide - Margherita Zani; Ottone - Innocenzio Baldini; Berengario - Giuliano Albertini; Matilde - Margherita Stagi; Idelberta - Antonio Pasi; Everardo - Giuseppe Ristorini; Clodomiro - Giuseppe Casorri. Abiti di Antonio Torricelli. Since this cast is identical with *L'Amor costante* below, it is clear that the opera is a carnival opera despite the title.

1725[8] carn
Cocomero

L'AMOR COSTANTE. Dramma per musica da rappresentarsi in Firenze nel teatro di via del Cocomero nel carnevale dell'anno 1725 sotto la protezione dell'Altezza Reale di Gio: Gastone I. Granduca di Toscana. Firenze 1725, Stamperia di S.A.R. ad istanza di Vettorio Borghesi, e Melchiorre Alberighi.
GB Lbm; I Fn, Mb.

Text: Antonio Salvi, a repetition with a few changes of *Rodelinda Regina dei Longobardi* (1710)[5].

Music: Anonymous. No score known. However, the libretto in I Mb attributes the music in Ms to Passoti.

Cast: Rodelinda - Margherita Zani; Bertarido - Antonio Pasi; Grimoaldo - Innocenzo Baldini; Eduige - Margherita Stagi; Garibaldi - Giuliano Albertini; Unulfo - Giuseppe Ristorini; Unoldo - Giuseppe Casorri. Abiti di Antonio Torricelli.

1725[9] sum
Pergola

ARMINIO. Drama per musica da rappresentarsi in Firenze nel teatro di via della Pergola nel estate dell'anno MDCCXXV. Sotto la protezione dell'Altezza Reale di Gio. Gastone I. Gran Duca di Toscana. Firenze, Fabio Benedetto Maria Verdi, Stampatore dell'Academia. Ad istanza di Cosimo Pieri. 1725.
I Bc, Fc, Fn, Mb; US CA, Wc(2).

Text (with a few changes and substitute arias): Antonio Salvi.

Music: Anonymous. Morini ascribes the music to Carlo Francesco Pollaroli. Pavan indicates *Diversi Autori*. Pandolfini does not identify the composer.

Cast: Arminio - Niccola Grimaldi; Tusnelda - Antonia Margherita Merighi; Segeste - Antonio Barbieri; Varo - Luca Mengoni; Sigismondo - Domenico Gizzi; Ramise - Maria Teresa Cotti; Tullio - Giuseppe Casorri. Pandolfini lists the *Sarto*, Antonio Torricelli, and the impresari: "diverse accademici . . ."

(1725)[10]

(*Astianatte*)
Manferrari III, p. 382, is in error in citing a performance at Pratolino of this opera by Antonio Salvi and Leonardo Vinci in 1725.

1725[11] 26 xii
Cocomero

LA MARIANE. Drama per musica da rappresentarsi in Firenze nel teatro di via del Cocomero nel carnevale dell'anno MDCCXXVI sotto la protezione dell'Altezza Reale del Serenissimo Gio. Gastone I. Gran Duca di Toscana. Firenze, Dom. Ambrogio Verdi, s.d.
I Bc, Fc, Mb, Rn; US Wc.

Text: Domenico Lalli (Sonneck, pp. 420f.), by comparison with *Gl'eccessi della Gelosia* (Venice, 1722), but with mostly new arias.

Music: Anonymous. Generally ascribed to Albinoni and Giovanni Porta who wrote the music for 1722 (Albinoni) and 1724 (additions of Porta) in Venice. But, according to Sonneck, not much of the music of either could have been preserved in this edition. Manferrari ascribes the Florentine music to Antonio Cortona for unknown reasons.

Cast: Agrippa - Anibal Pio Fabbri; Mariane - Rosaura Mazzante; Arminda - Anna Guglielmi; Ottavio - Castoro Anton Castori; Tolomeo - Anna Maria Antonia Bagnolesi; Decio - Stefano Posi [Pasi]. Mazzante sang the same role in Venice, 1722, and 1724.

Comment: Fagiuoli XVI, f. 28r, supplies the date.

1725[12] 26 xii
Pergola

FARNACE. Drama per musica da rappresentarsi in Firenze nel teatro di via della Pergola nel carnovale dell'anno MDCCXXVI sotto la protezione dell'A.R. di Gio: Gastone I. Gran Duca di Toscana. Firenze, Fabio Benedetto Mario Verde, s.d.
I Bc, Fc(3), Fn, Rn(2).

Text: Antonio Maria Lucchini, according to Allacci, col. 327, (not to be confused with Domenico Lalli's libretto of Venice, 1718, with the same title). The text is substantially the same as that of 1733 below. *Farnace* was performed a third time in Florence in 1749, the libretto of which retains the plot and characters but changes the text almost completely.

Sonneck, p. 477, lists only this last and still identifies it by comparison
with a libretto of Venice, 1739, as Lucchini's which makes the whole
series of attributions shaky. Sesini equates Florence, 1726, with Rome,
1724, attributing both to Lucchini. The question is to be solved only by
detailed study of all librettos beginning with Lalli's for Venice, 1718, for
Lalli signs the dedication of the 1739 Venice libretto!

Music: Anonymous. Sesini and Morini say Leonardo Vinci (who composed
the music for Rome, 1724, scores: **D MÜps**; **F Pc**); Pavan says Nicola
Antonio Porpora. Nor is there any reason to overlook the fact that Vivaldi
composed the score for the concurrent performance in Venice, or that
A Wn possesses a score by Leonardo Leo.

Cast: Farnace - Andrea Pacini; Tameri - Margherita Guallandi; Berenice -
Maddalena Pieri; Selinda - Anna Faini; Gilade - Antonio Pellizzari; Pompeo -
Gio: Batista Pinacci; Aquilio - Lorenzo Berretta.
Pandolfini adds: "Pittore delle quattro mutazioni di Scene nuove - Giacomo
Monari. Direttore per l'Abbattimento Bartolomeo Pagnini. Sarto -
Antonio Torricelli. Impresarj - Diversi Accademici. La prima volta, che
si vedde in scena il carro tirato dai cavalli di fronte, e accompagnato da altri
16. cavalli a sella."

Comment: Fagiuoli XVI, f. 28r, supplied the date.

1726 31 i
Coletti

Earliest known record of the Teatro del Sig.ʳ Coletti in via del Giardino
(**I Fr**, Fagiuoli Carteggio 3011): a request for admission addressed to
Fagiuoli by Francesco Bencino, a merchant of Florence.

1726¹ 25 ii
Pergola

LA FORZA DEL SANGUE. Dramma per musica da rappresentarsi in Firenze
nel teatro di via della Pergola nel carnevale dell'anno MDCXXVI. Sotto
la protezione dell'A.R. di Gio: Gastone I. Gran Duca di Toscana. Firenze,
Dom. Ambrogio Verdi, s.d.
I Bc, Mc.

Text: Francesco Silvani, not mentioned, but he signs the author's
dedication of the first edition of Venice, 1711 (Sonneck, p. 525). Variant
arias are listed at the end of the libretto. The argument warns: ". . .
si avvisa il Lettore non esser questa la medesima Zoe, la di cui Istoria diede
l'Argomento al Dramma intitolato, *Il Comando non inteso, ed ubbidito*,
che fù rappresentato nell'Autunno dell'Anno 1715 nel Teatro di Via del
Cocomero. Questa regno l'anno 912, e fù moglie come s'è detto dell'Imp.
Leone; e quella resse l'Imperio d'Oriente l'anno 1018 e fu moglie di
Romano Imperadore . . ."

Music: Anonymous. Antonio Lotti composed the music for the performance
of 1711 in Venice, according to Allacci, col. 374. Several sources from
Pavan to Fabbri, "Firenze," col. 385, ascribe the music to G.M. Buini who,
Allacci says, composed the music for a repetition of Silvani's libretto in
Bologna, 1728. The attribution to Buini of the Florentine opera must be
questioned on the basis of Sesini's observation on p. 73 (catalogued under
Antonio Lotti) that the libretto of Bologna 1728 is "affatto diverso da
quello di Francesco Silvani, musicato da Ant. Lotti."

Cast: Zoe - Margherita Guallandi; Foce - Gio: Batista Pinacci; Elena - Maria
Maddalena Pieri; Alessandro - Anna Faini; Eraclio - Andrea Pacini; Basilio -

Lorenzo Berretta; Argiro - Antonia Pellizzari. Pandolfini adds the same information for *La forza del Sangue* as for *Farnace* (above), since regularly he does not distinguish between first and second operas of one season.

Comment: Fagiuoli XVI, f. 35r, provides the date.

1726² ii
Cocomero

L'INGRATITUDINE GASTIGATA. Drama per musica da rappresentarsi in Firenze nel teatro di via del Cocomero nel carnevale dell'anno MDCCXXVI. sotto la protezione dell'Altezza Reale di Gio: Gastone I. Gran Duca di Toscana. Firenze, Domenico Ambrogio Verdi, s.d.
I Bc, Fm, Fn, Mb, Rn(2).

Text (with many changes): Francesco Silvani, who is not mentioned, but who is named in the title of the original publication in Venice, 1698 (Sonneck, p. 630). The *Protestà* says, "Nel presente Drama, che dopo di essere tante, e tante volte Stampato in diversi luoghi d'Italia, comparisce adesso di nuovo alla Stampa assai gastigato, e diverso da quel ch'egli era . . ."

Music: Anonymous. Fabbri, "Firenze," ascribes the music to Albinoni, who composed the music for the original performance in Venice, 1698, and probably for the Florentine performance 1701[1], but the present libretto is so transformed that the same music could not have been used again.

Cast: Alarico - Castoro Antonio Castori; Raimondo - Anibal Pio Fabbri; Enrico - Anna Bagnolesi; Ginevra - Rosaura Mazzanti; Brunechilde - Anna Guglielmini; Astolfo - Stefano Pasi.

1726³ 3 vii
Cocomero

SIROE RE DI PERSIA. Drama per musica da rappresentarsi nel teatro di via del Cocomero nella estate dell'anno MDCCXXVI. Sotto la protezione dell'A.R. di Gio: Gastone I. Granduca di Toscana. Firenze, Bernardo Paperini, ad istanza di Vettorio Borghesi e Melchiore Alberighi, 1726.
I Fn, Mb, Vgc.

Text: Pietro Metastasio, not mentioned here, but the libretto is reprinted in his *Opere* II, p. 119. The *Protestà*: "Il presente componimento fù recitato la prima volta in Venezia, nel passato Carnevale, dove incontro un applauso universale; E se adesso comparisce in qualche parte diverso . . ." etc.

Music: Giovanni Porta, as stated on page 7. The original music for Venice was composed by Leonardo Vinci (score in D MÜps, GB Cfm). No score by Porta known.

Cast: Cosroe - Gio. Batista Minelli; Siroe - Giovanni Carestini; Medarse - Elisabetta Uttini; Emira - Anna Bagnolesi; Laodice - Anna Cosimi; Arasse-Giuseppe Casorri. Carestini sang Medarse in the Venetian performance and Minelli sang Siroe in Rome, 1727 (both in I Fm).

Comment: Fagiuoli XVI, f. 58r, gives date as *la prima*.

1726⁴ 27 ix
Coletti

Comedia de Vaganti.
Fagiuoli XVII, f. 12v: "27 Ven[erdi] Sett. [1726]. 3ª Comedia de Vaganti nel Teatro Coletti. Vi fu M.ʳ Gualtieri."

1726⁵ 27 ? xii

IL NERONE. Drama per musica da rappresentarsi in Firenze nel teatro di

Pergola

via della Pergola nel carnovale dell'anno MDCCXXVII. sotto la protezione dell'Altezza Reale il Serenissimo Gio: Gastone I. Gran Duca di Toscana. Firenze, Domenico Ambrogio Verdi, s.d.
I Bc.

Text: Anonymous. This is not the same as Noris' *Nerone fatto Cesare* of 1708[3].

Music (lost): Giuseppe Bencini, Virtuoso di Camera di S.A.R. il Serenissimo Gran Duca di Toscana, as stated on page 5.

Cast: Nerone - Anibal Pio Fabbri; Oronta - Rosaura Mazzanti; Berenice - Barbera Stabili; Rutilio - Raffaello Signorini; Mitridate - Lucia Lanzetti; Stalia - Giustina Eberhard. Pandolfini adds: "Per gl'Intermezzi, Rosa Ungherelli, e Antonio Ristorini; Impresarj, Diversi Accademici." The librettos of this opera and of *Ipermestra* do not mention the two singers or contain the texts for the intermezzi. Moreover, Pandolfini as usual does not distinguish between the two operas of this season; hence, it cannot be determined which opera was accompanied by intermezzi.

Comment: This opera is chosen as the first at the Pergola for the 1727 season because Fagiuoli dates the other opera, *Ipermestra*, 26 January.

1726[6] 27 xii
Cocomero

LA SERVA FAVORITA. Dramma per musica da rappresentarsi in Firenze nel teatro di via del Cocomero il carnevale dell'anno MDCCXXVII. sotto la protezione dell'Altezza Reale del Sereniss. Gio: Gastone I. Gran Duca di Toscana. Firenze, Stamperia di Bernardo Paperini, ad istanza di Melchiore Alberighi, Librajo di Orsan Michele, 1727.
I Bc, Fn, PSc.

Text: Gio. Cosimo Villifranchi with extensive changes by comparison with the last performance in 1705[5].

Music (lost): Giovanni Chinzer, as stated on page 6. No previous performance of Chinzer's music known.

Cast: Cleante - Giuseppe Toselli; Fileno - Mariano Lena; Celinda - Anna Maria Mangani; Lidio - Maria Margherita Costa; Dorisbe - Paola Corvi; Quartilla - Maria Penni; Gardone - Carlo Amaini. Inventor de' Balli: Gio. Domenico del Fede.

Comment: Fagiuoli XVII, f. 19r: "27 Ven[erdi], 1726. P[rim]a com[edia] agl'Infuocati *Serva Fav[orit]a*." He also attended Sunday, 29 December.

1727[1] 26 i
Pergola

IPERMESTRA. Drama per musica da rappresentarsi in Firenze nel teatro di via della Pergola nel carnevale dell'anno 1727. sotto la protezione de Gio: Gastone I. Gran Duca di Toscana. Firenze, Domenico Ambrogio Verdi, s.d.
I Bc, Fc(3).

Text: Antonio Salvi, who is not mentioned, on the authority of Quadrio III.IV.IV, p. 487, and Allacci, col. 467, both of whom attribute the Venetian libretto of 1724 to Salvi. Allacci comments: "Sentitosi prima altrove." Sonneck, p. 638, states that Salvi's name appears neither in the

Venetian libretto nor any other libretto he lists.

Music (lost): Antonio Vivaldi, as stated on page 4 of the libretto.

Cast: Danao - Anibal Pio Fabbri; Ipermestra - Rosaura Mazzanti; Delmira - Barbera Stabili; Nicandro - Raffaello Signorini; Linceo - Lucia Lanzetti; Argia - Giustina Eberard. Pandolfini adds: "Per gl'intermezzi; Rosa Ungherelli, Antonio Ristorini; Impresarj, Diversi Accademici." (No intermezzi appear in the libretto and the performers are not mentioned.)

Comment: Fagiuoli XVII, f. 22r, supplies the date shown.

1727² 26? i
Cocomero

IL POTESTÀ DI COLOGNOLE. Dramma per musica da rappresentarsi in Firenze nel carnevale dell'anno MDCCXXVII. sotto la protezione dell' Altezza Reale del Sereniss. Gio: Gastone I. Gran Duca di Toscana. Firenze, Bernardo Paperini, ad istanza di Melchiorre Alberighi, 1727. I Bc, Fn, PSc.

Text: Giovanni Andrea Moniglia, but with new arias. The *Cortese Lettore* comments: "Nella reduzione del medesimo, ci siamo regolati quasi omninamente con quella, che nell'Anno 1717. sopra questo istesso Teatro, ricevè un sommo applauso, e che fu fatta da una dottissima Penna, alla quale pure si professa ogni stima: Facendoti ancora noto, che si sarebbero lasciate stare tutte l'Arie, che allora furono cantate, se quelle, per essere state in quel tempo tanto applaudite, non fossero presentemente per la bocca d'ognuno. Quindi è, che per apportarti qualche novità, si è stimato necessario il mutarle . . ." See 1717³. The roles are the same.

Music (lost): Composer unknown. The music has been attributed to Giuseppe Maria Buini on the basis of Allacci's attribution of the Bolognese performance of 1730 to Buini (col. 634).

Comment: The date is chosen by reason of the dates of the first opera of the season, *La serva favorita*, and the date for the second opera at the Pergola, it being usual for all of the theaters to change on the same day.

1727³ 22, 25 vi,
2 vii
Cocomero

LA CACCIA IN ETOLIA. Dramma per musica da rappresentarsi in Firenze nel teatro di via del Cocomero in questa estate dell'anno 1727. sotto la protezione dell'Altezza Reale del Sereniss. Gio: Gastone I. Gran Duca di Toscana. Firenze, Bernardo Paperini, 1727. I Bc, Fn, Rn.

Text: Belisario Valeriani, according to Allacci with reference to the libretto of Ferrara, 1715. Valeriani signs the dedication of the Ferrara libretto (Sonneck, p. 259). The narrative text of the Florentine edition is virtually the same as that of Ferrara. The arias, however, are almost entirely different. On page 45 are printed the intermezzi, *Monsieur di Porsugnacco* (next entry).

Music: Various "professori," as stated on page 5.

Cast: Atalanta - Cecilia Buini; Irene - Giovanna Gasparini; Melagro - Antonio Pasi; Aminta - Anibal Pio Fabbri.

————

MONSIEUR DI PORSUGNACCO. Intermezzi per musica. [Page 45 of the libretto above.]

Text: Anonymous. Cited by Allacci, col. 639, who does not know the poet or composer.

Music: Possibly Giuseppe Maria Orlandini who composed the music for the performance in Venice in the autumn of the same year, according to Sonneck, p. 773. In the absence of an earlier libretto, the performance in Florence may be considered to be the first performance. Score: D Bds.

Cast: Grilletta - Rosa Ungherelli; Porsugnacco - Antonio Ristorini. The actors' names are found below rather than adjacent to the roles.

Comment: Fagiuoli XVII, f. 47r: "22 Dom[enica] [Giugno, 1727]: La prima com[edi]a d[ett]a *la Caccia in Etolia* in via del Cocom[er]o. 25 Giugno: Nuova che il Cav.e Piero Ughi abbia bastonato il Paperini stampatore a causa che nella com[edi]a che ora si recita in via del Cocom[er]o intitolata *La Caccia in Etolia* non ha detto nel Teatro Ughi ma ha detto nel Teatro di Via del Cocom[er]o. 2 luglio: Fui alla Commedia in via del Cocomero, Impresario il Guerretti: *La Caccia in Etolia.*" Ughi was the actual owner of the theater which was leased to the academy. The archives of the Infuocati are filled with litigation between the academy and the proprietors.

1727[4] 26, 31 xii
Pergola

L'ERNELINDA. Drama per musica da rappresentarsi in Firenze nel teatro di via della Pergola nel prossimo carnevale dell'anno 1728. sotto la protezione di Gio: Gastone I. Gran Duca di Toscana. Firenze, Domenico Ambrogio Verdi, s.d.
I Bc, Fm, Fn, Rn.

Text (revised): Francesco Silvani's *La fede tradita e vendicata*, 1704[6].

Music: Leonardo Vinci, as stated on page 7. A score by Vinci dated November 1726 in I Nc.

Cast: Ricimero - Gaetano Berenstadt; Vitige - Castoro Anton Castori; Rodoaldo - Pietro Baratta; Ernelinda - Maria Maddalena Salvai; Eduiga - Teresa Pieri; Edelberto - Diamante Gualandi. Inventore de' Balli - Antonio Dannacci. Pandolfini adds the name of the impresario, Antonio Torricelli (who signs the dedication).

Comment: Fagiuoli XVIII, f. 10v, 11v, provides the dates shown.

1728[1] 10 ii
Pergola

L'ANDROMACA. Drama per musica da rappresentarsi in Firenze nel teatro di via della Pergola nel prossimo carnevale dell'anno 1728. sotto la protezione dell'Altezza Reale del Serenissimo Gio: Gastone I. Gran Duca di Toscana. Firenze, Domenico Ambrogio Verdi, s.d.
I Bc, Fc(2); US CA, Wc.

Text: Antonio Salvi, with much alteration. Last performed in Florence in 1716[3] with the title *Astianatte*.

Music (lost): Composer unknown. Morini and Manferrari erroneously ascribe the music to Antonio Caldara. Caldara set the libretto of the same name by Zeno (Sonneck, p. 113). Previous settings: Ferrara, 1723, by Gius. Maria Orlandini and Modena, 1726, by Pietro Vincenzo Chiocchetti.

Cast: Andromaca - Maddalena Salvai; Ermione - Teresa Pieri; Pirro - Gaetano Berenstadt; Oreste - Castoro [Anton] Castori; Pilade - Pietro Baratta; Clearte - Diamante Guallandi. Pandolfini adds the "Maestro de Balli in due persone, Antonio Dannacci. Sarto e Impresario, Antonio Torricelli." The significance of the "in due persone" is unclear. No other dancers are listed.

Comment: Fagiuoli XVIII, f. 16v: "10 Feb [1727/28] L'op[er]a dell' *Andromaca* in via della Pergola la mattina, e termino alle 20."

1728² 18 vi
Cocomero

IL RADAMISTO. Drama per musica da rappresentarsi in Firenze nel teatro di via del Cocomero l'estate dell'anno MDCCXXVIII. sotto la protezione dell'Altezza Reale del Serenissimo Gio: Gastone I. Gran Duca di Toscana. Dedicato all'Altezza Reale della Serenissima Violante Beatrice di Baviera Gran Principessa di Toscana, e Governatrice della Città e Stato di Siena. Firenze, ad istanza di Melchiorre Alberighi, e Giuseppe Pagani, 1728.
I Bc, Fn; US Wc.

Text: Nicolo Giuvo, who is not mentioned. The libretto is the same as 1709² with a few changes. Also published in Bologna, 1715 (in I Bc), with the intermezzi, *La preziosa ridicola*, beginning on page 71, as is the case with the libretto above. Dedication signed on date shown by Antonio Guerretti, Impresario.

Music (lost): Composer unknown. Previous settings (excluding the intermezzi) include Tommaso Albinoni, Venice, 1698 and Niccola Fago, Florence, 1709².

Cast: Radamisto - Elisabetta Uttini; Zenobia - Maria Giustina Turcotti; Tiridate - Filippo Giorgi; Rosmira - Elena Riva; Floro Pastore - Grisogono Marchi. Per gl'intermezzi: Santa Marchesini, Antonio Lottini.

————

LA PREZIOSA RIDICOLA. Intermezzi per musica. [Pages 71-88 of the above libretto.]

Text: Marchese Trotti, according to Sesini, under "Orlandini." The authorship is unknown to Ricci, p. 419, and Allacci, col. 642.

Music: Probably by Giuseppe Orlandini. His setting (lost) was first performed, according to Tagliavini, "Orlandini," col. 398, in Reggio Emilia in 1715.

Comment: The roles are not identified but obviously Madama Dulcinea was sung by Marchesini and Il Cuoco del Marchese del Bosco by Lottini.

1728³ 9 viii - 22 ix
Pergola

ARIANNA E TESEO. Drama per musica da rappresentarsi in Firenze nel teatro di via della Pergola nell'estate dell'anno 1728. sotto la protezione dell'A.R. del Serenissimo Gio: Gastone I. Gran Duca di Toscana. Firenze, Stamperia di Dom. Ambrogio Verdi, s.d.
I Fc, Fm, Fn (destroyed), Mb.

Text: Pietro Pariati, according to Allacci, col. 107.

Music: Niccola Porpora, as stated on page 4 of the libretto. First performed in Vienna, 1714 (Sonneck, p. 142). Score in A Wn, 18 arias and score "in Londra, 1734," in GB Lk.

Cast: Arianna - Maria Maddalena Pieri; Teseo - Niccola Grimaldi; Minosse - Felice Novello; Carilda - Benedetta Soresina; Alceste - Carlo Broschi; Tauride - Anna Maria Faini. Inventore de' Balli: Francesco Aquilanti. Pandolfini adds: "La compagnia intera de Balli in otto per la prima volta in Firenze sotto la direzzione di Francesco Aquilante di Firenze. Impresarj: Diverse Accademici."

Comment: Fagiuoli XVIII, f. 49v, on 20 August. Closing date of September 22 stated by Morini, p. 47.

1728⁴ 30 xii
Cocomero

Commedia de' nuovi Istrioni.
Fagiuoli XVIII, f. 63v: "La p[rim]a com[edi]a de' nuovi Istrioni in Via del Cocomero è male." Also 31 December.

1728⁵

L'impresario delle canarie. Intermezzi. In Firenze, 1728.
I Fn (destroyed).

Text: Pietro Metastasio, according to the card catalogue. Allacci, col. 442, lists a libretto of Venice, 1705, without the name of the composer.

Music (lost): Composer unknown. Mamczarz lists settings by D. Sarro (Naples, 1724) and Tommaso Albinoni? (Venice, 1725). Paumgartner, cc. 297f., does not cite a setting by Albinoni of this text.

1728⁶ 29 xii
Pergola

L'ATENAIDE. Drama per musica da rappresentarsi in Firenze nel teatro di via della Pergola nel carnovale dell'anno 1729. sotto la protezione dell' Altezza Reale del Serenissimo Gio: Gastone I. Gran Duca di Toscana. Firenze, Domenico Ambrogio Verdi, s.d.
I Bc, Fc, Fn, Mb.

Text: Apostolo Zeno, not mentioned, but text is printed in the *Poesie drammatiche* IV, pp. 267-352. First performance in Venice, 1714, music by M.A. Ziani, Antonio Negri and Antonio Caldara (I Nc).

Music (lost): Antonio Vivaldi, as stated on page 5. First performance of Vivaldi's setting.

Cast: Teodosio - Gaetano Valletta; Atenaide - Giustina Turcotti; Pulcheria - Anna Girò; Varani - Lisabetta Moro; Leontino - Anibal Pio Fabbri; Marziano - Anna Maria Faini; Probo - Gaetano Baroni. Pandolfini adds: "Impresarj, Diversi Accademici."

Comment: Fagiuoli XVIII, f. 63v: "29 Dic. [1728] In via della Pergola, la p[rim]a opera *l'Atenaide*." Also 31 December.

1729¹ 7 ii-1 iii
Pergola

CATONE IN UTICA. Drama per rappresentarsi in Firenze nel teatro in via della Pergola nel carnovale dell'anno 1729. sotto la protezione dell'Altezza Reale del Serenissimo Gio: Gastone I. Gran Duca di Toscana. Firenze, Domenico Ambrogio Verdi, 1729.
I Bc, Fc, Mb, Rn.

Text: Pietro Metastasio, not mentioned, but the text is published in his *Opere* II, pp. 157-204, which locates the first performance in Rome, 1727, music by Leonardo Vinci. Page 4: "L'Arie che sono notate con questo segno* non sono dell'Autore dell'Opera."

Music: Leonardo Vinci as stated on page 5. Scores in I MAC and D MÜps (dated Rome, 1728). Some of the music in the latter score is, however, attributed to Feo. There is also an anonymous score in I MOe, but we have not been able to make comparisons.

Cast: Catone - Anibal Pio Fabbri; Cesare - Gaetano Valletta; Marzia - Giustina Turcotti; Arbace - Lisabetta Moro; Emilia - Anna Girò; Fulvio - Anna Maria Faini. Pandolfini adds: "Impresarj, Diversi Accademici."

Comment: Pandolfini appends the following note. "In questo anno fu concesso nell'ultimo del carnevale per la prima volta l'ingresso alle maschere nel Teatro le sere dell'opera." Morini, p. 47, cites performances on February 17, 22, and 28, and March 1. He states also that for the first time performances took place during daytime. However, Fagiuoli recorded a previous daytime performance in 1728[1].

1729[2] sum
Cocomero

VIRIATE. Drama per musica da rappresentarsi in Firenze nel teatro di via del Cocomero nell'estate dell'anno MDCCXXIX. sotto la protezione dell' Altezza Reale del Serenissimo Gio: Gastone I. Gran Duca di Toscana. Firenze, Domenico Ambrogio Verdi, s.d.
I Bc, Fc (see comment to *La finta Tedesca* below), Rn.

Text: Pietro Metastasio, who is not mentioned. The text is not reprinted in any of his works. See Sonneck, p. 1005, under the other title, *Siface*, for history of this attribution.

Music (lost): Don Gio. Nicola Ranieri Redi, whose dedication to the Grand Duke declares that the composer, until this work, had composed only sacred music and undertook this task only at the urging of the Grand Duke.

Cast: Viriate - Vittoria Tesi; Siface - Carlo Scalzi; Ismene - Anna Peruzzi; Erminio - Gaetano Majorano; Oronte - Giuliano Albertini; Libanio - Caterina Visconti. Intermezzi: Anna Marchesini, Antonio Lottini.

————

LA FINTA TEDESCA. Intermezzi per musica.
I Fc (bound with *Il Viriate*).

Text: Anonymous.

Music (lost): Possibly Johann Adolph Hasse, who set the text for the first performance in Naples, 1728, according to Sonneck, p. 513, among others. Other title: *Pantaleone e Carlotta*.

Cast: Given only in the libretto for *Viriate* where the roles are not designated. It may be presumed, however, that Marchesini sang Carlotta and Lottini, Pantaleone.

Comment: We are again prevented from checking the accuracy of an entry because of a protracted closing of a library, this time the Cherubini Conservatory in Florence which, up to the present, is undergoing restoration and renovation necessitated by the disastrous flood of 1966. Our original notation was based upon the card catalogue only and not the libretto itself. The catalogue carries the date of 1725, which would seem to be an error since it precedes by three years the generally accepted first performance of the intermezzi. Until the libretto can again be examined, this entry must remain in doubt.

1729[3] 26? xii
Pergola

MEROPE. Drama per musica da rappresentarsi in Firenze nel teatro di via

della Pergola nel carnovale dell'anno 1730. sotto la protezione dell'Altezza Reale del Serenissimo Gio: Gastone I. Gran Duca di Toscana. Firenze, Domenico Ambrogio Verdi, s.d.
I Fc, Fm, Fn, Vgc; US CA.

Text: Apostolo Zeno, not mentioned. Text reprinted in the *Poesie drammatiche* IV, pp. 95-184, first performed in Venice, 1711 (US Wc), with music by Carlo Francesco Gasparini.

Music (lost): Possibly Luca Antonio Predieri, according to Clement and Morini. Predieri composed the music for a performance in Livorno in 1718, for which the libretto published in Florence is in I Fn. G.M. Orlandini set the libretto for Bologna, 1717. See 1713[3].

Cast: Polifonte - Gaetano Berenstadt; Merope - Giustina Turcotti; Epitide - Gaetano Valletta; Argia - Antonia Maria Laurenti; Lisico - Pellegrino Tomii; Trasimede - Francesca Barlocci; Anassandro - Maddalena Barlocci. Inventore de' Balli: Francesco Pagnini. Pandolfini adds: "Compagnia de Balli, Maestro da med.a Francesco Pagnini; Impresarj, diversi accademici."

Comment: Position as the season's first opera determined by Fagiuoli's entry for *Il Gran Tamerlano*.

1730[1] 25 i
Pergola

IL GRAN TAMERLANO. Dramma per musica da rappresentarsi in Firenze nel teatro di via della Pergola nel carnevale dell'anno 1730. sotto la protezione dell'A.R. del Serenissimo Gio: Gastone I. Gran Duca di Toscana. Firenze, Domenico Ambrogio Verdi, s.d.
I Fc, Vgc.

Text (altered): Antonio Salvi. See 1706[4].

Music (lost): Giovanni Porta, as stated on page 5. This is the first performance known.

Cast: Tamerlano - Gaetano Berenstadt; Bajazet - Pellegrino Tomii; Asteria - Giustina Turcotti; Andronico - Gaetano Valletta; Rossane - Antonia Maria Laurenti Novelli; Leone - Francesca Barlocci. Additons by Pandolfini as above for 1729[3].

Comment: Fagiuoli XVIIII, f. 51r: "25 [Gen. 1729/30]. In via della Pergola il *Tamerlano* dopo la *Merope*."

1730[2] 19 x
Cocomero

L'Artaserse.

Text: Pietro Metastasio, judging by the number of singers required as registered in the Archives of the Infuocati, Busta 44. Published in the *Opere* I, pp. 1-41.

Music: Possibly by J.A. Hasse, who composed the score for Metastasio's text for Venice, carnival of 1730 (Sonneck, p. 165), or by Leonardo Vinci, who set the same libretto for Rome, carnival, 1730. On the other hand, a cryptic reference to a payment to Gaetano Bracci "per *l'Artaserse*" in the archives may refer to a payment for the composition of the score since Bracci also composed two acts of *Amor vince l'odio* for the carnival of 1731 (see 1731[3]).

Cast: The cast is probably contained in Item #1, Busta 44, of the Infuocati Archives (I Fac). Since the libretto of Metastasio's *Artaserse* requires six singers, those most probably singing in this performance from the list, which includes both the opera and the burletta below, are: [Gregorio] Babbi, [Anna] Landuzzi, [Antonio] Baldi, [Antonia] Cerminati, [Maria Marta] Monticelli, and [Maria Maddalena] Salvai. The cast, except for the additional seventh singer necessary for the carnival opera, is the same as that for *Il Fratricido innocente* below. The fact accords with a practice previously recorded whereby the cast for the autumn opera is retained for the carnival opera. [Gaetano Maiorana detto] Caffariello [*sic*] heads the list. However, he probably would not have sung in the *burletto* and there is no role for him in *Artaserse* unless the libretto was enlarged by an additional role. Antonio Guerretti was impresario in autumn and the next carnival.

Comment: Item 7 in the same Busta is a list of performances which shows the schedule of the season with the irregular alternation between the opera and the burletta (*Lo speziale*), the opera beginning on 19 October and having fifteen performances by the 19th of November. The burletta began November 13 and was performed seven times until November 28. Fagiuoli XX, f. 13v, places the *prima* of *Artaserse* on October 18. The discrepancy is unexplained except by the possibility that Fagiuoli attended the dress rehearsal or a private performance for the academicians, the 19th being the first performance with a paying public.

1730[3] 13 xi
Cocomero

LO SPEZIALE DI VILLA. Drama per musica da rappresentarsi in Firenze nel teatro di via del Cocomero l'autunno dell'anno 1730, e carnevale 1731. sotto la protezione dell'Altezza Reale del Serenissimo Gio: Gastone I. Gran Duca di Toscana. Firenze, Domenico Ambrogio Verdi, s.d.
I Bc, PSc, Rn.

Text: Giovanni Cosimo Villifranchi with new arias. See 1719[4] and 1683[3].

Music (lost): Composer unknown; however, a possibility would be Giuseppe Maria Orlandini, who, since he signed the contracts in the Infuocati Archives for the engagement of Maria Maddalena Salvai and her husband, which is shown on the *right*, was the musical director, and the possibility that he wrote scores for this opera and *Il fratricidio innocente* cannot be discounted.

Cast: By a study of the fees, the number of singers needed, and a process of elimination, the cast for *Lo speziale* can be adduced as follows, using the order of the list cited above: [Felice] Fontini, [Santi] Barbieri, [Pietro] Pertici, [Maria] Penna, [Antonio] Lottini and [Anna] Faini. Roles: Cartoccio, Rosaura, Filarco, Delmira, Damone, and Nice.

(1730)[4]

Berenice regina d'Egitto.

Text: Antonio Salvi. See 1709[1]. Music by Araya, according to Schmidl, who says it was performed in "un Castello del Granduca," which Manferrari converts into "Pratolino."

(1730)[5]

La Forza dell'Amicizia in Oreste e Pilade, dr. 3a.
Text anonymous. Music by Caldara for a performance in the Pergola theater. Information extracted from Manferrari. The entry is highly suspect since no authority on the Pergola includes it.

Di 20 Maggio 1730.

Io sottoscritto m'obligo con il Sig.r Antonio Guerretti Fiorentino, e suoi
Sig.ri Compagni conduttori delle opere, che si faranno in Firenze nel
Teatro di via del Cocomero nel prossimo venturo autunno e carnevale
le stanche la scrittura fatta con Madama Maddalena moglie di
Monsieur Salvai di cento cinquanta Doppie di spagna, non le forse
fatta la reduzione nel tempo del pagamento del suo onorario in Me cento
cinquanta Doppie d'Italia e di paoli trenta l'una ed il quartiere
li sia tenuto a sborsar il rimanente, che ci corre tra i Luigi, o delle
Doppie di spagna, e le Doppie d'Italia da trenta paoli, in ogni luogo
subito senza eccezione alcuna in fede di che di propria mano affermo
e mi sottoscrivo Giuseppe M.a Orlandini

I Fac, Accademia degl'Infuocati, Busta I, Foglio 28.
Contract signed 20 v 1730, by Giuseppe Maria Orlandini with
Maddalena Salvai for performances at the Cocomero
during the autumn and carnival seasons in 1730-31. See 1730[3].

1730⁶ 26 xii
Cocomero

IL FRATRICIDO INNOCENTE. Drama per musica da rappresentarsi in
Firenze nel teatro di via del Cocomero nel carnovale dell'anno 1731.
sotto la protezione dell'Altezza Reale del Serenissimo Gio: Gastone I.
Gran Duca di Toscana. Firenze, Domenico Ambrogio Verdi ad istanza
di Melchiorre Alberighi e Giuseppe Pagani, s.d.
I Bc.

Text: Apostolo Zeno, not mentioned. O.t. *Vinceslao.* See 1703⁵.

Music (lost): Composer unknown. The libretto was first set in 1703 by
Carlo Francesco Pollaroli for Venice, then by Giacomo Antonio Perti in
1708 for Bologna and thereafter, a number of pasticci are listed by
Allacci, col. 804. Since Giuseppe Orlandini signed the contracts in the
archives of the Infuocati for Maria Maddalena Salvai, the possibility that
he composed a score for this or for any of the four operas at the Cocomero
in this season cannot be discounted.

Cast: Vinceslao - Antonio Baldi; Casimiro - Gregorio Babbi; Alessandro -
Anna Landuzzi; Lucinda - Maria Maddalena Salvai; Erenice - Antonia
Cermenati; Ernando - Maria Marta Monticelli; Gismondo - Francesco
Biancalana. Biancalana does not appear in any of the payment records of
the Infuocati for this season, and it is to be supposed that after the printing
of the libretto something prevented his singing. Maria Penni does appear in
the payments, on the other hand, and probably was his substitute (Busta 44,
Item #6). Payments on the fifth of January to Antonio Lottini and on
January 10 to Anna Faini "per le scarpe e calze per gli intermezzi" indicate
that intermezzi were performed with *Il fratricido innocente.*

Comment: Fagiuoli XX, f. 23v, supplies the date shown.

1730⁷

CANTATA fatta stampare e mettere in musica di Signori Antonio Paoli e
Vicenzio Coletti . . . Firenze, Michele Nestenus e Francesco Moŭcke, 1730.
I PEc.
No further information. Libretto not seen.

1731¹ 13? i

LO SPEZIALE DI VILLA.
See 1730³ above. Only one printing of the libretto sufficed for both
performances. It cannot definitely be demonstrated by reference to the
payments record that the order in the carnival was, in fact, as here stated.
The first two operas might have been performed in alternation as in the fall
or *Lo speziale* might have been added at the end of the season. The choice
is made solely upon practicality: it would be easier to perform the above
before introducing new burlettas rather than afterwards. The date is
suggested by the first payment in 1731 for Pietro Pertici, who at the
Cocomero was always involved in the performance of burlettas. A payment
on January 13 to Francesco Tagliasacchi *impresario di Pistoia* may identify
the impresario of this performance. Finally, an expense registered on
January 20 "a spese di calze per gl'attori della *nova* Burletta," that is, on
the day before Fagiuoli announces the *prima* of *Serva nobile* (see below),
implies a burletta preceding it and hints that it was not new. Since all of
the actors listed for the first performance were still being paid during the
carnival, presumably the cast would be the same.

1731² 21 i
Cocomero

LA SERVA NOBILE. Drama per musica da rappresentarsi in Firenze il carnevale dell'anno 1731. nel teatro di via del Cocomero sotto la protezione dell'Altezza Reale del Serenissimo Gio. Gastone I. Gran Duca di Toscana. Firenze, Stamp. allato alla Chiesa di Sant'Appollinare, per Giuseppe Pagani e Melchiorre Alberighi, 1731.
I Bc, PSc.

Text: Giovanni Andrea Moniglia, not mentioned, but the libretto is very similar to that of 1720³ with a few substitute arias.

Music (lost): Composer unknown. The Infuocati *Uscite* cited above contain two references concerning this burletta: "A dì 15 d.o [Dic., 1730] A Natale Gonnelli sc. 2.4 tanti sono per suo onorario dell'essere andato a Livorno per lo spartito della *Serva Nobile* e ritornato a Firenze." Thereafter follows: "A dì d[ett]o [15 Dic., 1730] Al S.r Gregorio Barsotti sc. 7 per lo spartito della *Serva Nobile*, come per mand[at]o." It should not be thought that Barsotti composed the score. He appears elsewhere in the Archives as having rented the theater, i.e., as an impresario. Moreover, sc. 7 is not sufficent for the composition of a full opera, as is shown by the amounts paid for the composition of *Amor vince l'odio*, below.

Cast: The cast is probably contained in item #3, Busta 44: [Felice] Fontana, [Santi] Barbieri, [Gregorio] Babbi, [Pietro] Pertici, [Maria Marta] Monticelli, [Anna] Faini. Antonio Lottini is listed but without a payment, perhaps an oversight by the person recording the payments.

Roles: Anselmo, Leonora, Isabella, Leandro, Bruscolo, Desso, Fernando.

Comment: Fagiuoli XX, f. 28f, supplies the above date (a Sunday).

1731³ 2? ii
Cocomero

AMOR VINCE L'ODIO, overo TIMOCRATE. Drama per musica da rappresentarsi nel teatro di via del Cocomero nel carnevale dell'anno 1731. sotto la protezione dell'Altezza Reale del Serenissimo Gio. Gastone I. Gran Duca di Toscana. Firenze, Dom. Ambrogio Verdi, s.d.
I Bc, Fc.

Text: Antonio Salvi, being the same with some additions as the libretto of 1715¹ above. Even the *Cortese Lettore* is the same.

Music (lost): Giovanni Chinzer (first act) and Gaetano Bracci (second and third acts), as stated on page 5. Busta 44, *Uscite*, registers the payments to the composers: "A dì 26 d. [dic., 1730] A S.r Gio. Chinzer S[cudi] 8.4 porto di contj per suo mercede della composiz[ion]e del Pr[im]o Atto del *Timocrate*." "A S.r Gaet[an]o Bracci 17.1 per suo onorario della composizione fatta alli due atti del Dramma intitolata *Timocrate*."

Cast: Anfia - Maria Maddalena Salvai; Erifile - Antonia Cermenati; Timocrate - Gregorio Babbi; Nicandro - Antonio Baldi; Transillo - Maria Marta Monticelli; Arcade - Anna Landuzzi. Vestiario - Ermanno Compstoff.

Comment: There is not an equal number of cast lists in Busta 44 to the number of operas performed. The missing opera is probably the present one, in spite of discrepancies. Between February 2 and 11 a series of payments occurs in the *Uscite* in the same Busta to Landuzzi, Baldi, Cermenati, and Salvai. These are singers who sing the *opere serie* only. The other two, Babbi and Monticelli, sing both operas and burlettas. Their payments, perhaps significantly, follow on February 18 at a time conjectured as coinciding with the performance of the burletta, *La maschera* (see below). Unexplained payments go on February 4 to Domenico Palafuti and on February 11 to Maria Penna, neither of whom appears in the lists of singers published in the librettos. Payments on February 2 and 3 to Antonio Lottini and Anna Faini indicate that, as usual, the *opera seria* was accompanied by intermezzi.

1731⁴ 18? ii   *La maschera levata al vizio*. Burletta in musica.

Text: Francesco Silvani? Giuseppe Maria Buini? Allacci, cc. 513f., cites a libretto by Silvani written for Venice, 1704, with music by Francesco Gasparini, and repeated in Bologna, 1730, with music by Buini, the latter obviously being a better candidate than the former for the Florentine performance. On the other hand, Quadrio III.IV.IV, p. 490, attributes the text to Buini, who on other occasions supplied his own libretto.

Music (lost): Possibly by G.M. Buini.

Cast: In the *Uscite* of Busta 44, between February 18 and 23 occurs a series of payments, this time to the actors (or some of them at least) who are associated with Pertici and therefore with the burlettas. These are Pietro Pertici, Felice Fontana, Gregorio Babbi, Marta Monticelli, Santi Barbieri. Busta 44, Item #2, is a list of payments to actors and may pertain to this burletta since it includes all of the above plus Antonio Lottini and Anna Faini.

Comment: The date is, again, a hypothetical interpretation of the *Uscite*. The reference to the above occurs in the *Entrata e uscite* on December 20; a payment to D. Gio. B.a Tappi for the "spartito della Burletta intitolata *La Maschera Levata al Vizio*." The performance possibly coincided with the series of payments between February 18 and 23 as stated above. Mardi Gras in 1731 fell on February 23, and the performances would have ceased on that date. Significantly, it is Pertici who receives the final payment on that date.

1731⁵ carn   Feste di ballo con maschere.
Pergola   Pandolfini, f. 8, states: "In quest'anno non vi furono opere, e nell'ultimo del carnevale si fecero no. 6. Feste di Ballo con maschere." Morini, p. 43, adds that the theater was undergoing restoration.

Fagiuoli records these *festini* in XX, ff. 29r-31r. The first one, without exact date, but February 18, 1731, probably, reads: "Alla commedia de Portughesi. Festino in via della Pergola alle Maschere con pagare 32. a testa." The commedia should not be presumed to have taken place at the Pergola. The last is dated February 23, and the price has been raised to 37.

1731⁶ 30 v   Death of Violante Beatrice di Baviera.

1731⁷ 2 xi   LA VANITÀ DELUSA. Dramma per musica da rappresentarsi in Firenze
Cocomero   nell'autunno dell'anno 1731. nel teatro di via del Cocomero sotto la protezione dell'A.R. del Serenissimo Gio: Gastone I. Gran Duca di Toscana. Firenze, Giuseppe Pagani e Melchiorre Alberighi, 1731. I Bc, PSc, Rn; US Wc.

Text: Anonymous. Page 4 in the *argomento*: "La discretezza del benigno

Lettore me fa sperare qualche compatimento per questo mio difettosissimo aborto, pregandolo a considerare l'angustia del Tempo, in cui me è convenuto comporto . . . nulladimeno per purgarmi della taccia di avere io fatta una Satira diretta contro la Nobilità . . ." etc. Characteristics suggest Francesco Vanneschi is the author.

Music (lost): Giovanni Chinzer, as stated on page 6. Repeated in Arezzo, 1737 (**I** Vgc).

Cast: Panicone - Pietro Pertici; Lisaura - Agata Giannelli; Bellalba - Elisabetta Duparc; Don Sancio - Carlo Signoretti; Leandro - (Blank); Orazio - Maddalena Frizzi; Lisetta - Alessandra Stabili; Ficca - Giovanni Manzuoli.

Comment: Fagiuoli XX, f. 61v, supplies the date as shown.

1731[8] aut
Cocomero

LA COMMEDIA IN COMMEDIA. Drama per musica da rappresentarsi in Firenze nell'autunno dell'anno 1731. nel teatro di via del Cocomero sotto la protezione dell'A.R. del Serenissimo Gio: Gastone I. Gran Duca di Toscana. Firenze, Stamperia allato alla Chiesa di Sant'Apollinare, 1731. I Bc, PSc, Vgc.

Text: Abate Francesco Vanneschi. The original form of the comedy is, on the authority of Allacci, col. 860, a prose comedy by Cosimo Antonio Pelli. In col. 206 he cites two publications in Lucca, 1731 and 1734. Erroneously Groppo, *aggiunta*, p. 30, attributes the libretto of Venice, 1744, entitled *L'ambizione delusa* to Giovanni Gualberto Barlocci, Romano. Allacci, who normally depended upon Groppo, drops the attribution when listing the same libretto in col. 841 as anonymous. Others to present-day bibliographers have reinstated Groppo's attribution.

The Venetian libretto of 1744 does not identify the author (Sonneck, p. 305). In no libretto that we have seen is the name of Barlocci attached, including the libretto of Rome, 1738. The dedication of a libretto of Ferrara, 1747 (**US** Wc) is signed by Eustacchio Bambini who calls it his second musical drama, but he is surely speaking as an impresario. He apparently performed some such function for Pietro Pertici's company, for he signed the dedication of *Madama Ciana*, Milan, 1745 (**I** Ma) which was also in the company's repertory (but he never appeared in the list of singers).

The libretto of London, 1748 (**I** Rn), uses the name of Francesco Vanneschi in the title. The choice of Vanneschi as the. true author rests on several circumstances. He wrote four librettos for Florence in a few years about the same time: *Enrico* (1731[10]), *Serva padrona* (1732[9]), *La moglie accorta* (1735[5]), and *Pimpinone* (1735[6]). *La serva padrona* was written for Pertici's company as was *Commedia in commedia*, whoever wrote it. The latter then continued to be performed by Pertici's company beginning with Florence, 1741[8], and continuing with Venice, 1744 and 1745, where the title was changed to *L'ambizione delusa*; Milan, 1745 and 1746; Torino, 1747, where the title changed again to *Il vecchio amante*; Brescia, 1747; Mantua, 1747; and finally London, 1748. (Later performances were not performed by Pertici's company.) Pertici's long association with the comedy makes the use of Vanneschi's name in London quite convincing.

Groppo's error is understandable. He also attributes another comedy, *Madama Ciana*, to Barlocci, and Melzi concurs that Barlocci wrote an *opera scenica* by that title published in Bologna, 1733, and Milan, 1737. (Allacci says it is anonymous!) In the autumn of 1744 it was transformed into an opera with music by Latilla and performed in S. Cassano. In the preceding carnival *L'ambizione delusa*, i.e., *Commedia in commedia*, had been performed in the same theater. But in Torino, 1747, *Madama Ciana* was published with the title of *L'ambizione delusa* while *Commedia in commedia* assumed the title of *Il vecchio amante*! The curiosity is that Pertici's company is responsible for the exchanges of titles since it performs both operas as part of its repertory.

Music: Giovanni Chinzer as stated on page 3. Beginning possibly in 1741[8] or definitely by Venice, 1744, the music of Rinaldo di Capua replaces Chinzer's.

Cast: Pandolfo - Pietro Pertici; Nobilia - Agata Giannelli; Lucinda - Elisabetta Duparc; Celindo - Carlo Signoretti; Fiorlindo - (Blank); Marchionne - Bartolomeo Papi; Dorina - Alessandra Stabili; Vespino - Giovanni Manzuoli.

Comment: Fagiuoli does not record this performance but see 1732[3].

1731[9] 26? xii
Pergola

ARSACE. Drama per musica da rappresentarsi in Firenze nel teatro di via della Pergola nel carnevale dell'anno 1732. sotto la protezione dell'Altezza Reale del Serenissimo Gio: Gastone I. Gran Duca di Toscana. Dedicato alla medesima Altezza Reale. Firenze, Domenico Ambrogio Verdi, s.d. I Bc, Fc; **US** Wc(2).

Text: Antonio Salvi, not mentioned, by comparison with *Amore e Maestà* (1715[2]), with the usual alterations and substitute arias. Dedication signed without date by the *impresari*.

Music (lost): Giuseppe [Maria] Orlandini, as stated on page 7, who, since he was the *maestro di cappella* (Pandolfini), probably supplied new music for the alterations in the text himself. See 1715[2].

Cast: Arsace - Andrea Pacini; Rosmiri - Francesca Cuzzoni; Statira - Antonia Margherita Merighi; Mitrane - Dorotea Lolli; Megabise - Maria Caterina Aureli; Artabano - Giuseppe Ristorini. Pandolfini adds: "Per gl'Intermezzi, Rosa Ungherelli di Bologna, Antonio Ristorini di Bologna. Maestro di Cappella, Giuseppe Orlandini . . . Impresarj. diversi Accademici."

Comment: The choice of *Arsace* as the first of the season is made by reason of Fagiuoli's date for *Ifigenia in Aulide* below. The two librettos for operas at the Pergola for this carnival do not mention intermezzi (only Pandolfini adds them to his list). However, one libretto and one reference identify the intermezzi performed at the Pergola. They follow at the end of carnival for the lack of any clue concerning their actual order or the operas with which they were performed. See 1732[6], 1732[7].

1731[10] 26 xii
Cocomero

L'ENRICO. Dramma per musica da rappresentarsi in Firenze nel teatro di via del Cocomero nel carnevale dell'anno 1732. sotto la protezione dell' A.R. del Serenissimo Gio: Gaston I. Gran Duca di Toscana. Dedicata alla medesima Altezza Reale. Firenze, Giuseppe Pagani, e Melchiorre Alberighi, 1732.

I Bc, Rn, Vgc; **US** Wc.

Text: Abate Francesco Vanneschi, as stated on page 7.

Music (lost): Composer unknown. Caselli for unknown reasons attributes the music to B. Galuppi.

Cast: Enrico - Innocenzio Baldini; Elvida - Costanza Posterli; Siffredi - Pietro Baratti; Costanza - Maddalena Molarini; Don Ferdinando - Gaspero Geri; Roberto - Giuliano Albertini.

Comment: Fagiuoli XX, f. 66v, supplies date shown.

1732[1] 29 i, 25 ii
Cocomero

ALESSANDRO NELL'INDIE. Drama per musica di Pietro Metastasio fra gli Arcadi Artino Corasio da rappresentarsi in Firenze nel teatro di via del Cocomero nel carnevale dell'anno 1732. sotto la protezione dell'Altezza Reale del Serenissimo Gio: Gastone I. Gran Duca di Toscana. Dedicato alla medesima Altezza Reale. Firenze, si vendono da Giuseppe Pagani, 1732.
I Nn.

Text: Pietro Metastasio. The libretto was first published in Rome, 1729, and set to music by Leonardo Vinci (Sonneck, p. 58). Reprinted with variants in his *Poesie* II, p. 243.

Music: Possibly Leonardo Vinci (score in **B** Bc; **GB** Lbm; **I** Nc), but also Luca Antonio Predieri, who is mentioned as the composer in a libretto for Milan, 1731 (**I** Bc), and whose music is lost.

Cast: Alessandro - Giuliano Albertini; Poro - Innocenzo Baldini; Cleofile - Costanza Posterli; Erissena - Maria Maddalena Molarini; Gandarti - Pietro Baratti; Timagene - Agata Giannelli.

Comment: Fagiuoli XX, f. 76r, provides the dates shown.

1732[2] 18 ii
Tintori

La moglie in calzoni. Commedia in prosa.
Text undoubtedly by Jacopo Angelo Nelli. Allacci registers in col. 535 a publication in Lucca, 1731.

Comment: Fagiuoli XX, f. 75v: "18 [Febb. 1731/32] in corso de' Tintori, *La moglie in calzoni*, commedia.

1732[3] 21 ii

La commedia in commedia.
Fagiuoli XX, f. 76r: "21 Febb. [1731/32]. Alla com.a ai frati alla Nunz[iata]. *La Commedia in Commedia.*" The entry is problematic. If the *frati* indulged in theatricals (not at all unusual), the work performed would probably be the prose comedy by Pelli (see 1731[8]). On the other hand, he may have attended an unnamed comedy performed by the frati, and simply noted the opera, a repetition in the carnival of the autumn opera without further detail. The practice of such a repetition is commonly found in the schedule of the Cocomero.

1732[4] carn
Cocomero

IL VINCITOR CORALBO. Drama per musica da rappresentarsi nel teatro in via del Cocomero dalla compagnia de' comici di S.A.R. dedicata da Anton Bartolomeo Panacci unito a' Comici alla medema A.R. Firenze, Piero Matini Stamp. Arciv. 1732.

I Rc, Rn.

Text: Anton Bartolomeo Panacci after Salvador Rosa (see below), which is curious since no work by Rosa is known that would be identifiable as the antecedent of this burlesque.

Music (lost): Panacci.

Comment: This brief (16 pages) libretto is a lampoon of not great subtlety. The dedication in an era of fulsome dedications is so fulsome that only satire could have been intended: "Quella inparaggiabile intelligenza, che tra le altre infinitissime doti, che adornano l'A.V.R. tiene il principal posto; Anima non solo i suoi fortunatissimi Sudditi, ma ancora le più remote Nazioni a tributare avanti al suo Real Trono, in atto d'adorazione il Vassallaggio dei proprj cuori per ottenere il sublime merito d'incontrare in qualche forma il suo Reale compatimento. Quindi è, che io pure mosso da un così glorioso motivo, mi fo lecito assieme con i Comici miei compagni di presentare all'A.V.R. questa Operetta di poche righe, e note di Musica intitolata IL VINCITORE CORALBO, per recitarsi dai miei Compagni, e da me nel Teatro di Via del Cocomero dove già al presente godiamo la bella sorte, mercè le grazie di V.A.R. di fatigare, con le nostre comiche operazioni . . ." Signed without date by Panacci.

The Attori are quoted entirely for the sake of the burlesque of the usual list of *personaggi* of a melodrama.

CORALBO Re di Menfi. Il Sig. Antonio Feramonti Pantalone Virtuoso di Camera di S.M. la Regina del Giappone negli spazj immaginarj.

STELLA Regina. La Sig. Pierina Veronesi Musica senza saperlo al servizio del gran Mogor [*sic*].

COLOMBINA Cameriera. La Sig. Domenica Panacci Servetta Virtuosa per accidente al servizio di chi per anco non ha ritrovato per Padrone.

ASTOLFO Buffone di Corte. Il Sig. Antonio Costantini Gradellino Musico Majorchino al servizio dell'Isole Canarie nelle Catatube del Nilo.

La Poesia e del Sig. moderno Imitatore dell'ultimo gusto, cioè più sul copiare, che sul comporre, per maggiormente avvalorare il detto di Salvator Rosa, cioè raro è quel Libro, che non sij un centone di cose a questo, e a quello tolte, e rapite sotto il pretesto dell'imitazione.

La Musica di Anton Bartolommeo Panacci Brighella dilettante per non aver Rendita da Professore, e questi è incognito per non dare spesa a' Comici, essendo anch'esso interessato per i medesimi.

Li Balli sono d'invenzione alla Chinese, poiche chi fa peggio, fa meglio.

La Scena si finge in Regia di Menfi, e sara delle medeme Scene, che ora si ritrovan fatte nel Teatro in Via del Cocomero.

The last remark is the clue that suggests the date chosen. The scene is the location of *Alessandro nell'Indie* and not *Enrico* which takes place in Sicily. The company may have been performing in some schedule of alternations with the opera during the latter part of the season.

1732⁵ 4 ii
Pergola

IFIGENIA IN AULIDE. Drama per musica da rappresentarsi in Firenze nel teatro di via della Pergola nel carnovale dell'anno 1732. sotto la protezione di Gio: Gastone I. Gran Duca di Toscana. Firenze, Domenico Ambrogio Verdi, s.d.
I Bc, Vgc; US BE.

Text: Apostolo Zeno, not mentioned, but the text is published in the *Poesie drammatiche* IV, pp. 185-266.

Music (lost): Giuseppe Orlandini, as stated on page 7.

Cast: Ifigenia - Francesca Cuzzoni; Clitemnestra - Antonia Margherita Merighi; Agamennone - Andrea Pacini; Achile - Antonio Pasi; Elisena - Teresa Pieri; Ulisse - Giuseppe Ristorini; Teucro - Maria Caterina Aureli; Arcade - Dorotea Lolli; Calcante - Giuseppe Casorri. Pandolfini adds the same information for this opera as for *Arsace* above.

Comment: Fagiuoli XX, f. 73v, provides the date shown. In addition, the dedication identifies the opera as the second of the season at the Pergola.

1732⁶ carn
Pergola

L'AMMALATO IMMAGINARIO. Intermezzi da rappresentarsi dalla Signora Rosa Ungarella e Sig. Antonio Ristorini nel teatro di via della Pergola nel carnevale dell'anno 1732. In Firenze, Domenico Ambrogio Verdi, s.d. I Rn.

Text: N. Castelli (?), a repetition of the performance of 1725³.

Music (lost): Giuseppe Maria Orlandini.

Cast: As above.

1732⁷ carn
Pergola

Baronessa d'Arbella. Intermezzo per musica.
Cited by Morini (using the above title).

Text: Antonio Salvi.

Music (lost): Giuseppe Orlandini.

1732⁸ 6 iv

Susier records the appointment of Giuseppe Maria Orlandini as *maestro di cappella* in place of Mannucci.

1732⁹ 22 vi
Cocomero

LA SERVA PADRONA. Drama per musica da rappresentarsi in Firenze nel teatro di via del Cocomero nell'estate dell'anno 1732. sotto la protezione dell'A.R. del Serenissimo Gio: Gastone I. Gran Duca di Toscana. Firenze, Giuseppe Pagani, 1732.
I PSc, Rn.

Text: Abate Francesco Vanneschi. A poetic version of a prose comedy by Jacopo Angiolo Nelli of the same title (Allacci, col. 715) written by Vanneschi as stated in the *Al lettore*. The author speaks of his changes from the original: "L'Aver dovuto l'Autore della presente Traduzione addattarsi al gusto delle Burlette per Musica, l' ha obbligato a diminuirla di Personaggi, siccome a variarla in qualche parte . . . "

Music (lost): Luca Antonio Predieri, as stated.

Cast: Pasquina - Anna Faini; Arnolfo - Pietro Pertici; Giacinta - Caterina Castelli; Flaminio - (Blank); Berenice - Margherita Bonistalli; Cleante - Sebastiano Barzi; Brunetto - Giovanni Manzuoli; Dragoncello - Lorenzo Saletti.

Comment: Faguoli XXI, f. 16r: "22 Dom. [Giugno, 1732] . . . la sera in via del Coco[mer]o la com[edi]a in musica messa in versi del Vanneschi, che e la *Serva P[a]drona* del Nelli."

1732[10] sum
Pergola

LA FEDE NE' TRADIMENTI. Drama per musica da rappresentarsi in Firenze nel teatro di via della Pergola nell'estate dell'anno 1732. sotto la protezione dell'A.R. del Serenissimo Gio: Gastone I. Gran Duca di Toscana. Firenze, Domenico Ambrogio Verdi, s.d.
I Bc, Fc(2).

Text: Girolamo Gigli. It is the same as the libretto of 1697[1] but without the two comic roles and considerably shortened.

Music (lost): Anonymous. Pavan and Sesini ascribe the music to Gaetano Maria Schiassi, on the basis, one supposes, of the fact that his score was performed in the same year in Bologna.

Cast: Anagilda - Anna Peruzzi; Garzia - Anibal Pio Fabbri; Ferdinando - Francesco Bilancioni; Elvira - Barbera Stabili. Pandolfini adds: "Maestro de Balli, Francesco Aquilanti; Impresarj, Mhse [Marchese?] Bernardino Riccardi, e Prior Vincenzio Antinori."

1732[11] 31 viii
Cocomero

LA FINTA PAZZA. Dramma per musica da rappresentarsi in Firenze nel teatro di via del Cocomero nell'autunno dell'anno 1732. sotto la protezione dell'A.R. del Serenissimo Gian Gastone I. Gran Duca di Toscana. In Firenze, Giuseppe Pagani. 1732.
I Bc, Fn, Rn.

Text: Alteration of G.C. Villifranchi's *Finto Chimico* (1686[4]), written by Damiano Marchi, on the authority of Fagiuoli.

Music (lost): Composer unknown.

Roles: Pandolfo, Corinda, Lindora, Delfa, Florante, and Dorino. The choice of the role of Pandolfo to replace the original Graticcio suggests that Pertici's company performed.

Comment: Fagiuoli XXI, "31 Dom[eni]ca Agosto [1732]. La *finta pazza* tratto dal *Finto Chimico* del Villifranchi guastata dal Dr. Damiano Marchi."

1732[12] aut
Coletti

LA POTENZA DEL VINO, E LA DEBOLEZZA DELLA VECCHIAIA. Intermezzi da recitarsi da Domenico Guagni, autore di detti, e da Gaetano Ciarli nel teatro Coletti nel presente autunno, dedicato al merito impareggiabile del medesimo Signor Benedetto Coletti ad istanza del Sig. Giuseppe Wiseman. Firenze, da A.M. Albizzini, 1732.
I Rn.

Text and music (lost): Domenico Guagni.

Dedication: "Mio Sig. e Padron Colendiss. Suole accadere spesso che taluno trovandosi ad una lautissima Mensa, dopo guasto molte preziose vivande, da ultimo vada trastullandosi (avendo di già la pancia piena) con una crochetta di Finocchio. Il simile accaderà adesso a V.S. che avendo il gusto ripieno da tante bellissime Commedie non solo ne' primi Teatri di Firenze recitate, ma nel Suo proprio, che non è inferiore agli altri, ed essendo già fazio, pigliata questa lappola di Finocchio della nostra Burletta, con questi miei Intermezzi a mal tempo anderà trastullandosi qualche sera nel presente Autunno. Se riusciranno di Suo gusto non lo sò, e non lo credo; io di già glie ve dò per Finocchio, ch'è l'ultima vivando; che volendogli mettere per Piatto di mezzo, guasterebbero la Tavola. Mi son'eletto la Parte di Cotto, perchè spesso soglio rappresentarla al naturale. La Musica credo che sappia già, che l'Autore si è regolata secondo la Poesia, ed il genio di Musici salvatici, come noi due, che tanto aviam cognizione delle note, quanto i ciechi de i colori. La prego dunque che con la Sua solita benignità, voglia non solo gradire questa mia bagatella, che io umilmente Li dedico, ma compatire ancora (e non solo Lei, ma tutti gli Ascoltanti) tutti gli errori, che nel cantare potessin succedere, ricordandogli, che i Rappresentanti, uno è Linajolo, e l'altro Legniajolo, che vuol dire faticanti, ma gente però di bel tempo; e con ogni maggior ossequio La reverisco." Signed by Domenico Guagni without date. Three intermezzi *a due* follow.

1732[13] 26? xii
Pergola

IL DEMETRIO. Drama per musica da rappresentarsi in Firenze nel teatro di via della Pergola nel carnevale dell'anno 1733. sotto la protezione dell' Altezza Reale del Serenissimo Gio: Gastone I. Gran Duca di Toscana. Firenze, Domenico Ambrogio Verdi, s.d.
I Bc, Fc.

Text: Pietro Metastasio, not mentioned, but the text is published in his *Opere* I, p. 79.

Music: According to Morini and Loewenberg, by Giovanni Battista Pescetti, who composed the music for a performance in 1737 in London (Sonneck, p. 358). Walsh, London, 1737, published *Favourite Songs* (**GB** Lbm).

Cast: Cleonice - Maria Maddalena Pieri; Alceste - Giovanni Carestini; Barsene - Rosa Mancini; Fenico - Giovanni Batista Pinacci; Olinto - Anna Bagnolesi; Mitrane - Cristofano Roperini. Maestro di Balli - Francesco Masimiliano Pagnini.

Comment: The position of first opera of the season is based solely upon Pandolfini's order, which is not a very dependable criterion.

1733[1] carn
Pergola

FARNACE. Drama per musica da rappresentarsi in Firenze nel teatro di via della Pergola nel carnovale dell'anno 1735. sotto la protezione dell'A.R. del Serenissimo Gio: Gastone I. Gran Duca di Toscana. Firenze, Domenico Ambrogio Verdi, s.d.
I Fc.

Text: Antonio Maria Lucchini (?), not mentioned, but the libretto is quite similar to the libretto of 1725[12]. Some of the substitute arias in 1725 are retained in 1733, which is otherwise somewhat shortened.

Music (lost): Composer unknown.

Cast: Farnace - Giovanni Carestini; Tamiri - Maria Maddalena Pieri; Berenice - Anna Bagnolesi; Selina - Rosa Mancini; Pompeo - Giovanni Battista Pinacci; Gilade - Cristofano Roperini; Aquilio - Giuliano Albertini. Maestro dei balli - Francesco Mass.o Pagnini. Le scene nuove sono d'invenzione del Sig. Pietro Righini Parmigiano. Pandolfini adds that the *Impresarj* were *Diversi Accademici*.

Comment: Susier. "A dì 6 Feb. [1732/33] ... licenza di maschere la notte solamente per l'opera in via della Pergola si come per i due festini ... "

1733[2] 5 v-18 vi
Casa del
Sig. Gio. Fortini

UN VERO AMORE NON CURA INTERESSE. Dramma rusticale del Signore Gio: Batista Fagiuoli. Da rappresentarsi in Piccolo Teatrino di Fantoccini, per semplice divertimento de' Giovani del Fortini scultore, e architetto

di S.A.R. In questa Primavera dell'Anno 1733. Firenze, stamperia di
Bernardo Paperini, 1733.
I Fn.

_____

*Prologo fatto pel Sig. Giovacchino Fortini, per una burletta dell'Autore
che fe recitare co'i fantocini.* In *Rime piacevoli* V, pp. 246-52.

Text of both prologue and opera: G.B. Fagiuoli. The libretto without the
prologue was reprinted in vol. VII, p. 5 of his *Commedie* (1736) and again,
p. 147, in the edition of 1753. Prologue in *Commedie*, vol. VII, p. 271.
Fabbri, "Firenze," dates the first performance 1725.

Music (lost): Composer unknown for both.

Roles: Anselmo Taccagni, Ciapo, Lena, Orazio, Nanni.

Comment: Fagiuoli XXI, f. 54v, [5 Maggio, 1733] " . . . Dal Fortini la mia
com[edia] in musica. 6 Merc[oledi]. La mia com[edia] al Fortini la 2a
volta a dame e a cav[alie]ri." References continue until June 18.

1733³ 5 v
Cocomero?

La pazzia d'Orlando. Melodrama?

Text: Prospero Bonarelli? See 1682².

Comment: Fagiuoli XXI, f. 54v: "5 [Maggio, 1733]. Agl'Istrioni *la
Pazzia d'Orlando* ..."" Without further information it is obviously not
possible to be certain of the identity. However, the concession of the
Cocomero to Antonio Ricci Strione on pp. 53-56 of the I Fac (Infuocati)
index coincides with this period.

1733⁴ 13 ix
Pergola

L'ARDELINDA. Drama per musica da rappresentarsi in Firenze nel teatro
di via della Pergola nell'autunno dell'anno 1733. sotto la protezione dell'
Altezza Reale del Serenissimo Gio: Gastone I. Gran Duca di Toscana.
Dedicato alla medesima Altezza Reale. Firenze, Domenico Ambrogio
Verdi, 1733.
I Bc, Fn, Rn.

Text: Bortolamio Vitturi, not mentioned, but his name, spelled as shown,
appears in the Venetian libretto of 1732 (Sonneck, p. 136; also Sesini, p. 5).

Music (lost): Possibly Tommaso Albinoni, the composer of the score for
the performance in Venice above. The dedication is signed September 12,
1733, by Antonio Foster, Impresario, who speaks of having been invited
to Florence from Venice specifically to direct this opera, thus giving
weight to the supposition that he used the Venetian score as well.

Cast: Eumene - Andrea Costa; Ardelinda - Barbera Stabili; Ateste - Pietro
Murigi; Aspazia - Giovanna Guaetta; Fernando - Teresa Zanardi. Inventore
de' Balli - Michele Saroni. (A ballet corps of four men and four women
are also named.)

Comment: Fagiuoli XXI, f. 70v, gives date as shown for the first performance,
recording also performances on September 14 and October 9.

1733⁵ 26 xii?
Pergola

ADRIANO IN SIRIA. Dramma per musica da rappresentarsi in Firenze nel
teatro di via della Pergola nel carnevale dell'anno 1734. sotto la protezione
dell'Altezza Reale del Serenissimo Gio: Gastone I. Gran Duca di Toscana.

Firenze, Domenico Ambrogio Verdi, ad istanza di Bernardo Bellandi, s.d.
I Fc.

Text: Pietro Metastasio, not mentioned here, but text is published in the
Opere I, pp. 42-78, where the first performance is stated to be in Vienna,
1731, with the music of Caldara.

Music (lost): Composer unknown. Pavan declares it to be the work of various
composers. Morini ascribes the music to Gio. Battista Pergolesi (score in
I MC). Nor should it be ignored that it was being performed in Venice at
the same time with music (lost) by Giminiano Giacomelli (Allacci, col. 11).

Cast: Adriano - Luigi Antinori; Osroa - Gaetano Berenstadt; Sabina -
Rosaura Mazzanti; Emirena - Maria Maddalena Monarini [sic]; Farnaspe -
Giovanna Guaetta; Aquilio - Giovanni Mancini. "I balli sono d'invenzione
del Sig. Francesco Sabbioni di Venezia. Inventore degl'Abiti. Il Sig. Ermano
Compstoff." Pandolfini correctly spells the name of Molarini and adds that
the Impresarj were "Diversi Accademici."

1734[1] carn
Pergola

SEMIRAMIDE. Dramma per musica da rappresentarsi in Firenze nel teatro
di via della Pergola nel carnevale dell'anno 1734. sotto la protezione dell'
Altezza Reale del Serenissimo Gio: Gastone I. Gran Duca di Toscana. In
Firenze, Domenico Ambrogio Verdi, s.d.
I Bc, Fc, Mb.

Text: Francesco Silvani, not mentioned, but Allacci, col. 709, ascribes
the Venetian libretto of 1714, of which the above is a version, to Silvani.
This is the same libretto used in Livorno in 1728 (in I Mb). No relation to
either Zeno's or Metastasio's librettos of the same title.

Music (lost): Composer unknown.

Cast: Semiramide - Rosaura Mazzanti; Atalo - Maria Maddalena Molarini;
Nino - Giovanna Guaetta; Zomira - Luigi Antinori; Arbace - Gaetano
Berenstadt; Idaspe - Giovanni Battista Mancini. Pandolfini gives the same
ballet master, costumer and impresari as above for Adriano.

1734[2] 4 ix
Pergola

L'INNOCENZA GIUSTIFICATA. Dramma per musica da rappresentarsi in
Firenze nel teatro degl'Illustrissimi Signori Accademici Immobili di via
della Pergola nell'estate dell'anno MDCCXXXIV. sotto la protezione dell'
A.R. del Serenissimo Gio: Gastone I. Gran Duca di Toscana. Dedicato alla
medesimo Altezza Reale. Firenze, Anton Maria Albizzini, s.d.
I Bc, Fc, Rn; US CA.

Text: Anonymous. Sesini, p. 347, ascribes this libretto to Francesco
Silvani as another title for Innocenza difesa (see 1721[1]). However, the
characters are totally different and a cursory comparison fails to reveal
any similarity.

Music (lost): Composer unknown. Morini, p. 44, as well as Sesini, attributes
the music to Giuseppe Maria Orlandini, but their basis apparently was the
supposition that the libretto was Silvani's. That not being the case, the
attribution fails.

Cast: Feraspe - Angiolo Amorevoli; Statira - Vittoria Tesi Tramontini;
Astiage - Carlo Broschi; Rosane - Caterina Fumagalli; Arbace - Giovanna
Guaetta; Artabano - Lorenzo Saletti. Pandolfini adds that "si veddero in

quest'opera due cammelli. Sarto, Ermanno Compostoff; Impresario, Conte Filippo Canale." Canale signed the dedication without date.

Comment: Fagiuoli XXII, f. 28r, attended on date shown.

1734³ 2 x
Cocomero

L'UMILTÀ ESALTATA. Dramma per musica da rappresentarsi in Firenze nel teatro di via del Cocomero nell'autunno dell'anno 1734. sotto la protezione dell'Altezza Reale del Serenissimo Gio: Gastone I. Gran Duca di Toscana. Firenze, Anton Maria Albizzini, 1734.
I Bc, Fn.

Text: Apostolo Zeno. An abridged version of *La Griselda*, previously performed with the music of Albinoni in 1703².

Music: Antonio Vivaldi, according to Fabbri, "Firenze," of whose score this is the first performance. His source is not revealed and unknown to Rudolf Eller, cols. 1857-58.

Cast: Gualtieri - Luc'Antonio Mengoni; Griselda - Rosaura Mazzanti; Costanza - Lucia Panichi; Roberto - Filippo Finazzi; Otone - Gregorio Babbi; Corrado - Santi Barbieri.

Comment: Fagiuoli XXII, f. 39r, October 2, 1734: "In via del Cocom[er]o la *Griselda*, sotto nome dell'*Umiltà esaltata* recitata la p[rim]a volta."

1734⁴ 26 xii
Tintori

L'aver cura di donna è pazzia. Commedia [in prosa].
Fagiuoli XXII, f. 44r, December 26, 1734: "La mia commedia a' Cadenti la prima intitolata *L'aver cura di donna è pazzia*. La p[rim]a dr[ama] in via della Pergola." (Without name of opera!) Baccini, *G.B. Fagiuoli*, p. 122, cites a publication in Milan, 1738, with above title and an *ossia*, *il cavaliere Parigino*. Published also in his *Commedie*, Moücke, 1724, and again, vol. III, p. 3 (1753).

1734⁵ 26 xii
Pergola

DIDONE ABBANDONATA. Dramma per musica da rappresentarsi in Firenze nel teatro della via della Pergola nel carnevale dell'anno 1735. sotto la protezione dell'Altezza Reale del Serenissimo Gio: Gastone I. Gran Duca di Toscana. Firenze, Antonio Maria Albizzini, s.d.
I Fc(2), Rn.

Text: Pietro Metastasio, not mentioned, but the libretto is virtually identical, including arias, to the libretto of 1725¹.

Music: Composer unknown. Morini, p. 44, ascribes the music to Domenico Sarro without revealing his grounds for doing so. Sarro composed the music for the first performance of the libretto in Naples, 1724 (Sonneck, p. 383; score in I Nc). However, without a detailed comparison of librettos and scores, Albinoni's setting for Venice, 1725, and Leonardo Vinci's for Rome, 1726 (score of Acts I and II in A Wn), may not be discounted.

Cast: Didone - Caterina Visconti; Selene - Lucia Bassi Barbieri; Enea - Agostino Fontana; Jorba - Antonio Barbieri; Araspe - Lisabetta Uttini; Osmida - Agata Elmi. I Balli sono d'Invenzione del Sig. Francesco Aquilanti. Pandolfini adds the customary *sarto*, Ermanno Compostoff, and the *impresarj, diversi accademici*.

Comment: Morini classifies *Didone* as the second opera. Pavan and Pandolfini list it as the first. Having no other clues, the latter are accepted here.

1734[6] 26 xii
Cocomero

ALESSANDRO SEVERO. Dramma per musica da rappresentarsi in Firenze nel teatro di via del Cocomero il carnevale dell'anno 1735. sotto la protezione dell'A.R. dell Serenissimo Gio: Gastone I. Gran Duca di Toscana. Firenze, Giuseppe Pagani, 1735.
I Vgc.

Text: Apostolo Zeno (see 1718[1] above). Dedication to Marchese Vincenzo Maria Ticcardi signed by Antonio Guerretti as Impresario.

Music: Gaetano Maria Schiassi, as stated.

Cast: Alessandro Severo - Lorenzo Saletti; Giulia Mammea - Anna Marini; Sallustia - Elisabetta Duparch; Albina - Prudenza Sani; Claudio - Sebastiano Naldi; Marziano - Domenico Bonifaci. For the intermezzi: Rosa Ruvinetti and Domenico Cricchi. Costumer - Ermanno Compostoff.

Comment: The position of the first opera is deduced from the known date of the second opera, *Adelaide*, below.

1735[1] 2,17 ii
Cocomero

ADELAIDE. Dramma per musica da rappresentarsi in Firenze nel teatro di via del Cocomero il carnevale dell'anno MDCCXXXV. sotto la protezione dell'A.R. del Serenissimo Gio: Gastone I. Gran Duca di Toscana. Firenze, Stamperia allato alla Chiesa di Sant'Apollinare ad istanza di Giuseppe Pagani, 1735.
I Fn, Rn.

Text: Antonio Salvi. A somewhat abbreviated version with frequent substitute arias of 1725[7]. The dedication to MY LORD CONTE DI EUSTON (whose name does not, as is customary, appear on the title page) is signed by Antonio Guerretti, Impresario, without date.

Music: Composer unknown. A simultaneous performance in Bologna used the music of Antonio Vivaldi, according to the libretto in I Mb.

Cast: Attone - Lorenzo Saletti; Adelaide - Marianna Marini; Berengario - Giuliano Albertini; Matilde - Lisabetta Duparch; Idelberto - Prudenza Sani; Everardo - Domenico Bonifaci; Clodimiro - Sebastiano Naldi. For the intermezzi: Rosa Ruvinetti, Domenico Cricchi. Inventore degli Abiti il Sig. Ermanno Compstoff. The intermezzi are not printed with the libretto. Note that Albertini sang the same role in 1725.

Comment: Fagiuoli XXII, f. 50r, February 6, 1734/35. "L'*Adelaide* in via del Cocom[er]o la p[rim]a volta." He attended also on February 17.

1735[2] 2 ii
Cocomero

LA CONTADINA. Intermezzi in musica per rappresentarsi in Firenze nel teatro di via del Cocomero il carnevale dell'anno 1735. Firenze, ad istanza di Giuseppe Pagani, 1735.
I Mb.

Text: Bernardo Saddumene, at least in part. See Frank Walker, pp. 310ff., for a discussion of the attributions of this text.

Music: Probably G.A. Hasse by reference to the same source. Scores in B Br (Fétis) and D SW. Published in *opera omnia* of Pergolesi in error.

Cast: Scintilla - Rosa Ruvinetti; D. Tabarano - Domenico Cricchi. The date is chosen by reference to *Adelaide* where these performers will be found for the intermezzi. Moreover, *Adelaide* is the only recorded opera at the Cocomero for this carnival.

1735³ carn
Pergola

EZIO. Drama per musica da rappresentarsi in Firenze nel teatro degli Ill.mi Sig. Accademici Immobili in via della Pergola nel carnevale dell'anno 1735. sotto la protezione dell'Altezza Reale del Serenissimo Gio: Gastone I. Gran Duca di Toscana. Firenze, Anton Maria Albizzini, s.d.
I Bc, Fc.

Text: Pietro Metastasio, not mentioned here, but the text is published in his *Opere* II, p. 3.

Music: Composer unknown. In the *Opere*, the first performance is stated to have been in Rome, 1728, with the music of Pietro Auletta. However, Sonneck, p. 466, lists a previous libretto of Venice dated November 20, 1728, which identifies Niccolo Porpora (score in B Bc) as the composer, and Morini, p. 44, believes that to be the score for Florence, 1735 and 1744[14]. But a setting by Riccardo Broschi for Torino, 1731/32 (Sonneck, p. 464) should not be overlooked.

Cast: Fulvia - Caterina Visconti; Onoria - Lucia Bassi Barbieri; Ezio - Agostino Fontana; Massimo - Lisabetta Uttini [Pandolfini spells the name Ottini] ; Varo - Agata Elmi; Valentiniano - Antonio Barbieri. Pandolfini adds: "Inventore de' Balli, Francesco Aquilanti; Sarto, Ermanno Compostof; Impresarj, Diversi Accademici."

1735⁴ 22 vi
Cocomero

LI VERI AMICI. Dramma per musica da rappresentarsi in Firenze nel teatro di via del Cocomero nell'estate dell'anno MDCCXXXV. sotto la protezione dell'Altezza Reale del Serenissimo Gio: Gastone I. Gran Duca di Toscana. Firenze, allato a Sant'Apollinare, da Paperini, e Barchesi, 1735.
I Fc, Fn. Mb.

Text: Francesco Silvani and Domenico Lalli, not mentioned here but according to Allacci's attribution of the Venetian libretto of 1713 (col. 811). *Al Lettore*: "L'Idea del presente Drama è presa dalla famosa Tragedia di Mons. Pietro Cornelio, intitolata l'*Eraclio*." This statement also appears in the Venetian libretto (Sonneck, p. 1128).

Music (lost): Possibly by G.A. Orlandini in a repetition of 1714³. In addition to Andrea Paulati's setting for Venice, 1713 and 1723, Tommasso Albinoni provided a score for Munich, 1722 (Sonneck, p. 1128), but both seem unlikely for Florence, 1735.

Cast: Amasi - Angelo Amorevoli; Candace - Barbera Stabili; Lagide - Paola Corvi; Evergete - Gaetano Valletta; Niceta - Margherita Giacomazzi; Tilame - Lucia Panichi. Inventore degli Abiti il Sig. Ermanno Compstoff.

Comment: Fagiuoli XXII, f. 70v, June 22: "In via del Cocomero la p[rim]a op[er]a *I veri amici*." The position of the concession to Luigi Pitti "per l'opera" in I Fac (Infuocati) makes the association with this opera reasonable.

1735⁵
Abbozzati

LA MOGLIE ACCORTA. Scherzo drammatico da rappresentarsi nel teatrino delle figurine degli Accademia Abbozzati in questo presente anno 1735. Firenze, Pietro Gaetano Viviani, 1735.
I Bc, Rn (without title page: #35.7.B.6,5).

Text: Original author unknown. Abate Francesco Vanneschi is credited on page 3 with the *reduzione delle parole*.

Music (lost): Various composers, as stated on page 3. "Alla fine d'ogni Parte

vi sono alcuni Intermezzi in Prosa [lacking in the libretto] , con suo
Balletto diverso."

Cast: Cialdone - Francesco Biancalana; Sorbina - Gio. Battista del Bianco;
Ciarlino - Giovanni Mulinari.

1735[6]
Abbozzati

PIMPINONE. Scherzo drammatico da rappresentarsi nel teatro delle
figurine dagli Accademici Abbozzati in questo presente anno 1735. Firenze,
Stamperia di Pietro Gaetano Viviani, 1735.
I Rn.

Text: "Reduzione delle parole del Sig. Abate Francesco Vanneschi."
Apparently a greatly altered version of Pietro Pariati's *Vespetta e Pimpinone.*

Music (lost): Sig. Giovanni Chinzer, as stated.

Cast: Pimpinone - Francesco Biancalana; Vespetta - Giovanni Mulinari;
Lesbino - Giovanni Rutini.

1735[7] 26? xii
Pergola

CESARE IN EGITTO. Dramma per musica da rappresentarsi in Firenze nel
teatro in via della Pergola nel carnevale dell'anno 1736. sotto la protezione
dell'Altezza Reale del Serenissimo Gio: Gastone I. Gran Duca di Toscana.
Lucca, s.t., 1735.
I Bc, Fc(2).

Text: Giacomo Francesco Bussani, not mentioned, but on the authority
of Allacci, col. 181, who also names the composer for the first performance
in Venice, 1735, as Giminiano Giacomelli. However, in **I** Rc there is an
earlier libretto of Rome, 1728.

Music: Possibly by Giminiano Giacomelli. The score was performed also
in Milan, 1735, the libretto of which (**I** Bc, **US** Wc: Sonneck, p. 274)
mentions the composer. Score in **B** Bc.

Cast: Giulio Cesare - Francesco Grisi; Tolomeo - Pietro Baratta; Cornelia -
Anna Girò; Cleopatra - Teresa Baratta; Lentulo - Natalizia Bisagi; Achilla -
Maria Maddalena Frizzi. Inventore de' Balli - Alessandro Mion Francese;
Inventore degli abiti - Ermano Compstoff. Pandolfini adds: "Impresarj,
Diversi Accademici."

Comment: Position as the first opera at the Pergola chosen solely on the
basis of Pandolfini's order.

1736[1] carn
Pergola

GINEVRA PRINCIPESSA DI SCOZIA. Dramma per musica da rappresentarsi
in Firenze nel teatro di via della Pergola nel carnevale dell'anno 1736.
sotto la protezione dell'A.R. del Serenissimo Gio: Gastone I. Gran Duca
di Toscana. Lucca, s.t., 1735.
I Fc.

Text: Antonio Salvi. Previously performed in 1708[2] and 1723[2].

Music (lost): Antonio Vivaldi, as stated. First performance of this score.

Cast: Re di Scozia - Pietro Baratta; Ginevra - Anna Girò; Ariodante -
Francesco Grisi; Lurcanio - Natalizia Bisagi; Dalinda - Teresa Baratta;
Polinesso - Settimio Canini; Odoardo - Maria Maddalena Frizzi. Inventore,
e compositore de' Balli - Francesco Alessandro Neron, Maestro dell'
Accademia Reale di Musica di Parigi. Pandolfini gives the name of the

inventor of the ballets as Alessandro Mion Francese. He adds: "Sarto, Ermanno Compostof; Impresarj, Diversi Accademici." He does not list Vivaldi as the composer.

Comment: The position of second opera is based entirely upon Pandolfini's order.

1736² carn
Prato

ALESSANDRO NELL'INDIE. Dramma per musica da rappresentarsi nel teatro Pubblico della città di Prato nel carnevale dell'anno 1736. Firenze, Bernardo Paperini, 1736.
I Fm.

Text: Pietro Metastasio, not mentioned, but the text is printed in the *Opere* II, p. 243. See 1732¹.

Music (lost): Composer unknown.

1736³ 17 ii

L'aver cura di donna è pazzia. Commedia in prosa.

Text: G.B. Fagiuoli. Performance cited in his diary XXII, f. 60r. See 1734⁴.

1736⁴ carn
Prato

Arsace, ovvero *Amore e maestà.* A. Salvi, libr. riformato da G. Boldini, dr. 3a. Prato di Toscana. Tr. Pubblico., carnevale 1736. Music by Geminano Giacomelli. Cited by Manferrari, II, p. 53, and Allacci, col. 116.

1736⁵ 15 iv
Cocomero

LA CLEMENZA DI TITO. Dramma per musica da rappresentarsi in Firenze nel teatro di via del Cocomero nella primavera dell'anno 1736. sotto la protezione dell'A.R. del Serenissimo Gio: Gastone I. Gran Duca di Toscana. Firenze, Anton Maria Albizzini, 1736.
I Rn.

Text: Pietro Metastasio. A shortened version of the libretto published in his *Opere* II, p. 83, where the first performance is designated that of Vienna, 1734, with music by Antonio Caldara.

Music: Possibly Leonardo Leo, who composed the music for Venice, 1735 (Sonneck, p. 295). A contemporaneous setting by Pietro Vincenzo Chiocchetti was performed in Genoa, 1736 (*ibid*.).

Cast: Tito Vespasiano - Stella Cantelli; Vitellia - Maria Maddalena Gerardini; Servilia - Francesca Poli; Sesto - Lorenzo Saletti; Annio - Angeliza Cantelli; Publio - Francesco Biancalana.

Comment: Fagiuoli XXII, f. 26r. April 15: ". . . la *Clemenza di Tito* la 3a volta." I Fac (Infuocati) indexes on p. 62 the concession of the theater to Mazzini e Secchioni, probably the impresari.

(1736)⁶

Siroe, Rè di Persia.
Cited only by Loewenberg who states that this was a performance of Metastasio's and Hasse's opera. See 1726³.

1736⁷ 26? vii
Pergola

IL CID. Dramma per musica da rappresentarsi in Firenze nel teatro di via della Pergola il carnevale dell'anno 1737. sotto la protezione dell'Altezza Reale del Serenissimo Gio: Gastone I. Gran Duca di Toscana. Firenze, Anton Maria Albizzini per Cosimo Maria Pieri, s.d.

I Fc, Fn, Mb.

Text: Gio. Giacomo Alborghetti, "benchè in gran parte variata," according to Allacci, col. 188. The libretto had been performed in 1715 in Livorno (**I Fn**) and again in 1717 (**I Rn**), both without indication of the composer. Allacci lists another edition of Massa, 1715, with music by Giambatista Stuk.

Music (lost): Composer unknown. Morini, p. 46, states that in this carnival "furano poste in scene le opere Il *Cid* e il *Temistocle* del Maestro Caldara." Since the libretto of the latter names Orlandini as the composer, the attribution of the former to Caldara is called into question.

Cast: Ferdinando I - Diacinta Forcellini; Rodrigo - Filippo Finazzi; Cimene - Marianna Marini; Leonora - Caterina Bassi; Diego - Settimio Canini; Duarte - Prudenza Sani. Inventore de' Balli - il Sig. Gio. Batista Nesti, detto Scaramuccia. Inventore degli Abiti, il Sig. Ermano Comstoff. Date based upon Fagiuoli's date for *Temistocle.* Pandolfini adds that the *Impresarj* were *Diversi Accademici.*

1736[8] sum
Cocomero?

Commedie.
I Fac (Infuocati) index contains on p. 60 a reference to Giuseppe Imer. Goldoni's *Memoirs,* p. 179, state that Imer passed the summer in Florence.

1737[1] 3 ii
Pergola

TEMISTOCLE. Drama per musica da rappresentarsi in Firenze nel teatro di via della Pergola il carnevale dell'anno 1737. sotto la protezione dell' Altezza Reale del Serenissimo Gio: Gastone I. Gran Duca di Toscana. Firenze, Anton Maria Albizzini, s.d.
I Fc.

Text: Pietro Metastasio, not mentioned, but the text is published in his *Opere* III, p. 79, where the first performance is stated to have been in Vienna, 1736, with the music of Caldara.

Music: Giuseppe Orlandini, as stated. See 1720[6].

Cast: Serse - Settimo Canini; Temistocle - Filippo Finazzi; Aspasia - Marianno Marini; Neocle - Diacinta Forcellini; Rossana - Caterina Bassi; Lisimaco - Prudenza Sani; Sebaste - Santi Barbieri. Pandolfini adds the same information as above for the first opera (1736[7]).

Comment: Fagiuoli XXIII, f. 58v, cites February 3 as the first performance of *Temistocle* at the Pergola.

(1737)[2] carn?

La pupilla. Intermezzi a 3.

Text: Carlo Goldoni.

Music (lost): Giacomo Maccari.

Comment: Cited by Mamczarz, p. 457. The edition is said to be Venetian. Other discrepancies make the entry suspect. If genuine, the carnival is the only possible season in 1737. Not listed in Sartori's catalogue.

1737[3] carn?

IL MARITO SAVIO FATTO VIZIOSO PER GASTIGO DELLA MOGLIE VANA. Intermezzi per musica. Firenze, Francesco Moücke, 1737.
I Fc, Mb, Rn.

Text and music: Anonymous.

Roles: Erminia and Tiburzio.

Comment: No indications of season or theater. Some clue about the identity of the intermezzi is provided by the fact that the roles were sung in Venice (S. Samuele) in the same year by Agnese Muratte and Giuseppe Imer respectively (see 1736[8]).

1737[4] carn
Cocomero

IL MATRIMONIO PER FORZA. Intermezzi da recitarsi nel teatro di via del Cocomero di Firenze il carnevale dell'anno MDCCXXXVII. Firenze, allato alla Chiesa di Sant'Appollinare, 1737.
I Mb.

Text: Anonymous. First published in Venice, 1729 (Allacci, cols. 516f).

Music: Anonymous. Mamczarz, p. 440, tentatively attributes the music to Giuseppe Maria Buini. The Venetian score was probably used in Florence also since Bertelli sang the same role in Venice and Florence.

Cast: Rosmene - Antonia Bertelli; Gerondo - Giuseppe Lironi.

Comment: The intermezzi probably were performed with a spoken drama at the Cocomero. At least, no operatic performance has been recorded for this year at the theater.

1737[5] 20 ii

Susier. Death notice of Padre Paulucci, who sang bass each evening in Ferdinando de' Medici's academy. Age 75.

1737[6] 2 vi
Pergola

L'Olimpiade.
See 1738[4].

Cast: (All information supplied by Pandolfini): Anibal Pio Fabbri, Francesca Cuzzoni, Lucia Panichi, Angelo Maria Monticelli, Natalizia Bisagi, Pietro Baratta, and Rosa Costa. Sarto - Ermanno Compostof. Impresario - Cav. Luigi Pitti. [Added in Pandolfini's hand:] "Stante la morte seguita del Ser.mo G.D. Gio: Gastone di questa Opera ne furono fatte tre sole Recite."

Comment: Fagiuoli: "23 Dom[eni]co [Giugno, 1737] Opera in via della Pergola L'Olimpiade."

1737 9 vii

Death of Gio: Gastone Gran Duca di Toscana.

1737[7] 29 xii
Cocomero

CHI NON SA FINGERE NON SA GODERE. Drama per musica da recitarsi in Firenze nel teatro di via del Cocomero nel carnevale dell'anno 1738. Dedicato a sua eccellenza La Signora Principessa di Craon. Firenze, Bernardo Paperini, 1738.
I Bc, Rn.

Text: Anonymous. Dedication signed without date by the Impresarij.

Music: Giovanni Chinzer, "maestro di cappella fiorentina, Professore di tromba, privilegiato da Sua Maestà Cesarea e da tutto il Sacro Romano Impero," as stated on page 5.

Cast: Falcone - (Blank); Lindora - Anna Mecheri; Uberto - Anna Maria Mangani; Ortenzia - Domenica Taus; Annuccia - Caterina Dons; Dorina - Caterina Brogi; Pepino - Gaetano Nesi; Balocco - Giuseppe Ferrini.

Comment: I Fac (Infuocati) records that the theater was conceded to Benedetto Nanni for the *opera in musica* in the carnival of 1738.

Fagiuoli XXIV, f. ultima, 29 [Dic., 1737] "Dom[eni]ca. Alla 3.a comm[edia] in musica intitolata *Chi non sa fingere non sa godere* in via del Cocomero agl'Infuocati." The performances would then have begun the 26th or 27th. It is interesting to note the brevity of the official mourning for the last of the Medici by the new dynasty.

1738[1] 5,13 i
Pergola

ORMISDA. Drama per musica da rappresentarsi in Firenze nel teatro di via della Pergola nel carnevale dell'anno 1738. Firenze, Anton Maria Albizzini, s.d.
I Bc, Fc.

Text: Apostolo Zeno, not mentioned here, but the text is published in his *Poesie* V, p. 167, where the first performance is stated to be Vienna, 1721, with music by Antonio Caldara (Sonneck, p. 834).

Music: Composer unknown. Morini, p. 46, says that Caldara's setting was used in Florence (score in A Wn). But other possibilities are Giuseppe Maria Orlandini, who composed the music for Bologna, 1722 (Allacci, col. 583) and Bartolommeo Cordans, who set the second Venetian libretto of 1728 (Sonneck, p. 834).

Cast: Ormisda - Pellegrino Tomii; Cosroe - Francesco Bernardi; Artemice - Francesca Cuzzoni; Palmira - Caterina Negri; Arsace - Francesca Fantoni; Mitrane - Santi Barbieri; Erismeno - Giovanni Redi. Pandolfini adds: "Sarto, Ermanno Compostof; Impresarj, Diversi Accademici."

Comment: Fagiuoli XXIV, f. 30. Dates of performances as above. Susier: "13 i 1738 . . . in via della Pergola si recitava la Cuzzoni et il Senesino [Bernardi] che valse suoi ruspi [zecchini]. Ma vi andava poca gente."

1738[2] 29 i
Tintori

L'Amante esperimentato ovvero *Anche le donne sanno far da uomo*. Commedia [in prosa].

Text: G.B. Fagiuoli. Printed in vol. VI, p. 3, of his *Commedie* (1753). Performance cited in his diary XXIV, f. 32v, *dai Cadenti*.

1738[3] 2 ii

L'Astuto balordo. Commedia [in prosa].
Text by G.B. Fagiuoli. Printed in vol. I, p. 147 of his *Commedie* (1753). Performance cited in his diary, XXIV, f. 33r.

1738[4] 2 ii
Pergola

L'OLIMPIADE. Drama per musica da rappresentarsi in Firenze nel teatro di via della Pergola nel carnevale dell'anno 1738. Firenze, Anton Maria Albizzini per Cosimo Maria Pieri, s.d.
A Wu; US Wc.

Text: Pietro Metastasio, not mentioned, but the text is printed in his *Poesie* I, p. 123, where it is stated that the first performance took place in Vienna in 1733 with the music of Antonio Caldara.

Music: Anonymous. Manferrari, Pavan and Schmidl say G.M. Orlandini composed the score. Tagliavini, "Orlandini," does not recognize this opera. Morini ascribes the score to Leonardo Leo (scores in D Bds; F Pn; GB Lbm; I Mc, Nc, and Vnm). Previous settings, apart from the original: Antonio Vivaldi, Venice, 1734; Giovanni Battista Pergolesi, Rome, 1735; and Giuseppe Ferdinando Brivio, Torino, 1737; all three librettos are listed in Sonneck, pp. 816ff.

Cast: Clistene - Pellegrino Tomii; Aristea - Francesca Cuzzoni; Argene - Francesco Bernardi; Licida - Caterina Negri; Megache - Santi Barbieri; Aminta - Francesca Fantoni; Alcandro - Giovanni Redi. Pandolfini adds: "Sarto, Ermanno Compostof; Impresarj, Diversi Accademici."

Comment: Date supplied by Fagiuoli XXIV, f. 33.

1738[5] 2 ii?
Cocomero

LA GIARDINIERA FINTA CONTESSA. Drama per musica da recitarsi in Firenze nel teatro Cocomero nel Carnovale dell'anno MDCCXXXVIII. Dedicato all'Eccellenza di Mylord Raymond Pari d'Inghilterra. Firenze, Giuseppe Pagani, 1738.
I Bc, Mb.

Text: Anonymous. Loewenberg states that a performance of Giovanni Barlocci's *La finta cameriera* took place in Rome and Florence in 1738. This citation of a Florentine performance, for which no libretto or reference has been found, is probably an error. Since he says also that *La finta cameriera* was performed in Hamburg, 1741, with the title of *La Giardiniera contessa*, it may be assumed that he is confusing the Florentine libretto above with Barlocci's comedy because of the similarity of the titles of Florence and Hamburg. Actually the Roman and Florentine librettos have nothing in common.

Music (lost): Composer unknown.

Cast: Delmira - Domenica Taus; Lauretta - Caterina Brogi; Celindo - Anna Maria Mangani; Filauro - Giuseppe Ferrini; Serpilla - Gaetano Nesi; Corina - Caterina Dons.

Comment: The date is assumed from the dating of the first opera at the Cocomero, *Chi non sa*, above and from the frequently observed habit of changing plays and operas at about the same time in the theaters.

1738[6] 9 iv
Pergola

LE NOZZE DI PERSEO E DI ANDROMEDA. Azione drammatica da cantarsi nel teatro di via della Pergola in dimostrazione d'umilissimo ossequio e di gratitudine all'Altezza Reale di Francesco III Duca di Lorena e di Bar, Granduca di Toscana, etc. Firenze, Anton Maria Albizzini, 1738.
I Fm(2), Vgc.

Text: Damiano Marchi, as stated.

Music: Giuseppe Maria Orlandini, as stated. Score: A Wn.

Cast (provided by Pandolfini): Francesca Cuzzoni, Francesco Bernardi, Prudenza Sani, Settimo Canini, Giuliano Albertini. Pandolfini adds: "Le parole furono del Dottore Damiano Marchi. La musica fu di Giuseppe Orlandini ad istanza di quale fu fatta la spesa con grand'apparato, e vi sonarono n.ro 80 strumenti. [In Pandolfini's hand:] suonatori."

Comment: The *Gran Cantata*, as Pandolfini calls it, celebrated the patronage of Francesco di Lorena as the new protector of the academy.

Susier: "A dì 9 Aprile Mercoledi. In ringraziamente d'essere stato graziato da S.A.R. tutti i suonatori che erano stipendiati dalla reale casa di

Toscana, il Sig. Orlandini, maestro di cappella, volse mostrare atto di
gradimento con farne una dimostrazione pubblica come fece nel Teatro
di via della Pergola una superbissima cantata in lode del Ser. Gran Duca
intitolata *Le Nozze di Perseo et Andromeda* composta dal Sig. Marchi,
musica del Orlandini. I Cantori furono il Senesino, la Cuzzoni, la Sani,
il Canini, e Giuliano Albertini. Fu cosa assai magnifica e maestosa, che
la teneva . . . in una grande scalinata tutta piena di cantori che passavano
Cento cinquanta sicome sonatori di diversi strumenti. Era tutta arrichiata
di Lumi sicome il Gran Teatro circondato tutto di lumiere di Cristallo,
che pareva un Paradiso. Fu mandato a Vienna a S.A.R. la detta
composizione e musica." [The omitted words are difficult to decipher.
They are perhaps *un retta*, i.e., the singers and performers were arranged
in straight lines on risers.]

1738[7] spring
Cocomero

Compagnia di Strioni Carlo Veronese.
I Fas (Reggenza 631, c. 1) records the request and permission granted to
the company to perform. Also indexed in I Fac (Infuocati).

1738[8] aut
Cortona

LA BARONESSA. Intermezzo in musica da rappresentarsi nel teatro de'
Sigg. Accademici di Cortona l'autunno dell'anno 1738. Firenze, Viviani, s.d.
I Rn, Vgc.
Text and music anonymous. Obviously not performed in Florence.

1738[9] aut
Cocomero

Compagnia di Strioni di S[ua] Ecc[ellenz]a [Michele] Grimani.
I Fas (Reggenza 631, c. 4) contains the request and permission granted to
the Grimani company to perform at the end of June. But apparently their
arrival was postponed. I Fac (Infuocati) entry on p. 80 carries the date of
aut., 1738. References on pp. 91 and 94 to Vitalba who was at about this
time a member of the Grimani company. See Goldoni, p. 171.

1738[10] 22 xii

Susier: Death notice of Giovanni Lavinio Barsotti, "uomo assai virtuoso in
musica perche era un bravo suonatore di cembalo e compositione d'anni 72."

1738[11] 28 xii
Cocomero

SIRBACE. Dramma per musica da rappresentarsi in Firenze nel teatro di
via del Cocomero nel carnevale dell'anno 1739. Dedicato all'A.R. del
Serenissima Maria Teresa, Arciduchessa d'Austria, etc. Firenze, appresso
Bernardo Paperini, 1739.
I Bc, Rn.

Text: Claudio Nicola Stampa, according to Sonneck, p. 953, who is quoting
material collected by Schatz, who says that the original title was *Eurene*
without locating the libretto. Two previous librettos are known: Arezzo,
1736, autunno, with music by Geminiano Giacomelli (in I Rn, published
with the title of *Rosbale* by Viviani in Firenze), and Venice, autumn of
1737, in which Nicola Porpora is mentioned as the composer (US Wc).
The libretto of Arezzo is still not the earliest performance since the libretto
declares it to be "nuovamente in Iscena."

Music (lost): Carlo Arrigoni, as stated.

Cast: Sirbace - Giuseppe Galletti; Rosbale - Giuseppe Ciacchi; Eurene -
Maddalena Gerardini; Nirena - Prudenza Sani; Astarbo - Francesca Barlocci;

Lesbano - Francesca Fantoni.

Comment: Date given by Fagiuoli XXV, f. 1v.

1738[12] 29 xii

Susier: Death notice of il [Gasparo] Geri musico.

1739[1] 14, 21 i
Pergola

ARIANNA E TESEO. Drama per musica da rappresentarsi in Firenze nel teatro di via della Pergola nel carnevale dell'anno 1739. Firenze, Anton Maria Albizzini ad istanza di Cosimo Maria Pieri, s.d.
I Bc, Fc, Rn.

Text: Pietro Pariati. See 1728[3]. The present libretto varies only in minor degree.

Music (lost): Composer unknown. Pavan and Tagliavini propose Giovanni Maria Orlandini; Morini, Niccolo Porpora.

Cast: Teseo - Francesco Bernardi; Arianna - Lucia Facchinelli; Carilda - Caterina Aschieri; Alceste - Antonia Costa; Tauride - Caterina Brigonzi; Minosse - Antonio Raaff. Pandolfini adds in his own hand: "Il Ser. G. Duca colla Ser. Granduchessa, e Principe Carlo furono p[er] la pr[i] ma volta all'Opera a *21*. Gennaio.

Comment: Fagiuoli XXV, f. 4v, registers his attendance on date shown.

1739[2] ii ?
Cocomero

SCIPIONE NELLE SPAGNE. Dramma per musica da rappresentarsi in Firenze nel teatro di via del Cocomero nel carnevale dell'anno 1739. Dedicato all' Altezza Reale della Serenissima Maria Teresa Archiduchessa d'Austria, Duchessa di Lorena, E di Bar, e Gran Duchessa di Toscana. Firenze, Stamperia di Piero Matini, 1739.
I Bc.

Text: Apostolo Zeno, who is mentioned in the *Argomento* in the usual apology for changes. Published in the *Poesie* IV, p. 94, where the first publication is identified as Barcelona, 1710 (with music by Antonio Caldara, according to Sonneck, p. 977).

Music (lost): Carlo Arrigoni, compositore di camera di S.A.R. il Serenissimo Gran Duca di Toscana, as stated on page 7;

Cast: Scipione - Giuseppe Galletti; Sofonisba - Maddalene Gerardini; Elvira - Prudenza Sani; Lucejo - Francesca Barlocci; Marzio - Giuseppe Ciacchi; Cardenio - Francesca Fantoni; per gli Intermezzi - Anna Faini, Giuseppe Ristorini. The intermezzi are not identified or printed.

Comment: The month is adduced from the fact that it is the second opera of the season at the Cocomero.

1739[3] 10 ii
Pergola

ARSACE. Drama per musica da rappresentarsi in Firenze nel teatro di via della Pergola nel carnevale dell'anno 1739. sotto la protezione dell'Altezza Reale del Serenissimo Francesco III., [etc.] , Gran Duca di Toscana. Firenze, Anton Maria Albizzini, s.d.
I Bc, Fc.

Text: Antonio Salvi. About half of the arias are changed by comparison with 1731[9], *Amore e maestà* (o.t.).

Music: Anonymous. Pavan believes this to be a repetition of Giuseppe

Maria Orlandini's music used in 1731[9], and corroboration is found in a
manuscript notation on the title page of the I Fc copy: *La Musica e del
Sig.r Giuseppe Orlandini*. The ascription appears to be possibly
eighteenth century and the use of the polite form of address would seem
to rule out an addition by a later librarian. However, Morini assigns the
music (lost) to Geminiano Giacomelli who, according to Allacci, col. 116,
composed the music for a performance in the Teatro Pubblico di Prato
in 1736.

Cast: Arsace - Francesco Bernardi; Statira - Lucia Facchinelli; Rosmiri -
Caterina Aschieri; Megabise - Antonia Costa; Mitrane - Caterina Brigonzi;
Artabano - Antonio Raaf. Inventore degli Abiti - Sig. Ermanno Compstoff.

Comment: Fagiuoli XXV, f. 10v. 10 February 1738/39: "In via della
Pergola l'opera dell'Arsace la mattina all'ore 16."

1739[4] 30 iii-11 v
Pergola

TEMISTOCLE. Dramma per musica da rappresentarsi in Firenze nel teatro
di via della Pergola nella primavera dell'anno 1739. sotto la protezione dell'
Altezza Reale del Serenissimo Francesco III., [etc.]. Firenze, Cosimo
Maria Pieri, s.d.
I Bc, Fc.

Text: Pietro Metastasio, not mentioned. See 1737[1].

Music: Anonymous. Pavan assumes this to be a repetition of the music of
Giuseppe Maria Orlandini. Morini attributes the music, however, to
Antonio Caldara who wrote the music for the first performance in Vienna
in 1736.

Cast: Serse - Giovanni Batista Pinacci; Aspasia - Anna Bagnolesi; Lisimaco -
Natalizia Bisagi; Neocle - Giovanni Tedeschi; Temistocle - Francesco
Bernardi; Rossane - Caterina Aschieri; Sebaste - Caterina Brigonzi. Sarto -
Ermanno Compostoff. Impresarj - Diversi accademici. Pandolfini:
"Opera di primavera a richiesta del Ser.mo Gran Duca."

Comment: Fagiuoli XXV, f. 16v. 30 March, 1739. "Il *Temistocle* di
Metastasio in via della Pergola la p[rim]a volta." Susier attended the
same date.

1739[5] 30 iii-11 v
Pergola

*Tre balli: Il trionfo chinese, La favola di Promoteo quando da l'anima
alla statua prendendo il fuoco dal sole per animarla*, and *Un divertimento
campestre.*
Ballets by Francesco Aquilanti. Cited by Morini, p. 47, and in I Fas (Med.
Acquista misc., 308, p. 8), where the third is entitled *La campagna*. No
librettos or scenarios known.

Music (lost): Composer(s) unknown.

Ballerine: Barbera Campanini, Domitilla Campanini, Zannetta Cortini,
Angela Lugani. Ballerini: Giuseppe Brunoro, Giuseppe Valenti, Gio:
Battista Nesti, Domenico Lensi. Inventor de' Balli: Francesco Aquilanti.

The dancers are listed by Pandolfini under *Temistocle* without the
titles of the ballets themselves. Probably the ballets were intermezzi for
the opera.

1739[6] spring
Cocomero

Truppa dei commedianti Michel Grimani.

I Fas (Reggenza 631, c. 5). The Grimani Company was granted permission to perform after Easter until September and to go to other cities in Tuscany when for S. Giovanni (June 24 and the season thereof) there might be *opere in musica*. Indexed in I Fac (Infuocati, F. I).

1739[7] 5 vii

Death notice in Susier: "Morosini detto Scerna, Poeta Ridicolo del Ser. Princ. Ferdinando . . . e recitava la parte di Brighetta. Farsai bene nelle commedie a l'improviso e aveva anni 84."

1739[8] 26 xii
Pergola

CATONE IN UTICA. Drama per musica da rappresentarsi in Firenze nel teatro di via della Pergola nel carnovale dell'anno 1740. Sotto la protezione di Francesco III, Duca di Lorena, [etc.]. Firenze, Anton Maria Albizzini, s.d. I Bc, Fn (destroyed).

Text: Pietro Metastasio. See 1729[1] which is basically the same libretto. The above is expanded somewhat by comparison.

Music: Anonymous. Pavan and Morini agree upon Egidio Romualdo Duni, whose score is in E Mn but this is dated 1746, San Carlo, Naples. On the other hand, Frank Walker, p. 308, reports the curious information that the poet Thomas Gray acquired in Florence in 1740 a copy of "Confusa, smarrita," an aria from this libretto, which is attributed to G.B. Pergolesi (published in vol. XV of *The Golden Treasury of Music* [New York, 1910] by H.E. Krehbiel and Max Spicker). The coincidence suggests that at least some of the music may have been Pergolesi's.

Cast: Catone - Cesare Grandi; Marzia - Giustina Turcotti; Cesare - Dionisio Bonfigli; Emilia - Antonia Cermenati; Arbace - Margherita Alessandri; Fulvio - Elisabetta Guerrini. Sarto - Ermanno Compstof. Impresarij - Diversi accademici. Pandolfini adds: "Scena nuova per le Feste da Ballo fu dipinta da Giuseppe Zocchi di Firenze."

Comment: Fagiuoli XXV, f. 46v, provides the date shown.

1739[9] 28 xii
Cocomero

ARTASERSE. Drama per musica da rappresentarsi in Firenze nel teatro di via del Cocomero nel carnevale dell'anno 1740. sotto la protezione dell' Altezza Reale del Serenissimo Francesco III Duca di Lorena, [etc.]. Firenze, s.t., s.d. I Fm.

Text: Pietro Metastasio, not mentioned, but the text is printed in his *Opere* I, p. 1, where the first performance is stated to be in Rome, 1730, with music by Leonardo Vinci. The *Argomento* observes: "[Il drama] è in qualche parte diverso dal suo primo originale, a riserva di qualche Aria, è però totalmente nella forma medesima, che fu ridotto in Bologna, in occasione di esservi stato recitato con applauso nel Teatro Malvezzi l'anno 1730."

Music: Leonardo Vinci, as stated on page 7. Scores: A Wgm, Wn; B Bc; I Nc; others listed by Eitner.

Cast: Artaserse - Gio. Domenico Ciardini; Mandane - Maria Natalizia Bisagi; Artabano - Filippo Laschi; Arbace - Prudenza Sani; Semira - Maria Giuditta Fabiani; Megabise - Maria Fabiani. Inventore degl'abiti il Sig. Ermano Compstoff.

Comment: Fagiuoli XXV, f. 46v, attended on date shown. Susier reports that on January 16 (probably still during the performances of *Artaserse*): "Mentre che si recitava l'opera in Via della Pergola, casco un uomo Legniaiolo che tirava la scene [*sic*] e dette sopra il palco che si roppe una Gamba in maniera tale che conviene andare [al] la Misericorda . . ." Index in I Fac (Infuocati) records concession to Luigi Pitti twice (pp. 94, 95) *per l'opera*, corresponding to the two carnival operas in this season.

1740[1] ii?
Pergola

ALESSANDRO NELLE INDIE. Dramma per musica da rappresentarsi in Firenze nel teatro di via della Pergola nel carnevale dell'anno 1740. sotto la protezione dell'Altezza Reale del Serenissimo Francesco III, Duca di Lorena, [etc.]. Firenze, Anton Maria Albizzini per Cosimo Maria Pieri, s.d.
I Fc.

Text: Pietro Metastasio, not mentioned, but text printed in his *Opere* II, p. 243. See 1736[2].

Music: Anonymous. Pavan chooses Baldassare Galuppi, who wrote a setting for Venice, 1755 (!), while Morini prefers Gaetano Maria Schiassi, who, according to Allacci, col. 28, wrote the music for Bologna, 1734. More likely is the lost setting by J.A. Hasse for Venice, 1734 and 1743. See Sonneck, p. 60.

Cast: Alessandro - Dionisio Bonfigli; Poro - Cesare Grandi; Cleofide - Giustina Turcotti; Erissena - Antonia Cermenati; Gaudarte - Margherita Alessandri; Timagene - Elisabetta Guerrini. Inventore degli Abiti - Ermanno Compstoff. Pandolfini adds: "Maestro dell'Abbattimento per l'*Alessandro nell'Indie*, Domenico dell'Agata; Impresarij, Diversi accademici."

Comment: The position as second opera deduced from known date of *Catone in Utica*, 1739[8].

1740[2] ii?
Cocomero

SEMIRAMIDE RICONOSCIUTA. Drama per musica da rappresentarsi in Firenze nel teatro di via del Cocomero nel carnevale dell'anno 1740. sotto la protezione dell'Altezza Reale del Serenissimo Francesco III Duca di Lorena, [etc.]. Firenze, Pietro Matini, 1740.
I Bc.

Text: Pietro Metastasio, not mentioned, but the text is printed in his *Opere* III, p. 213.

Music: Anonymous. Leonardo Vinci composed the music for Rome, 1729, and Nicola Antonio Porpora for Venice in the same year. (Both listed in Sonneck, p. 990.) Tagliavini, "Orlandini," attributes a setting for Turin, 1722, to G.A. Orlandini.

Cast: Semiramide - Maria Natalizia Bisagi; Sibari - Maria Fabiani; Tamiri - Maria Giuditta Fabiani; Scitalce - Prudenza Sani; Ircano - Filippo Laschi; Mirteo - Giovanni Domenico Ciardini.

Comment: I Fac (Infuocati), p. 95, concedes the theater to Luigi Pitti as the impresario.

1740[3] 1 iii

Don Pilogio.
Susier states that at this time there were comedies being performed at the

Tintori
Pergola
Cocomero
Coletti

Pergola, the Cocomero, and "in via del Giardino e Corso dei Tintori, ove fecero il *D. Pilogio* del Gigli di Siena." Probably another title for *Don Pilone ovvero il Bacchettone falso. Commedia tratta nuovamente dal Francese* [Molière's *Tartuffe*] *da Girolamo Gigli.* In Lucca, Marescandoli, 1715. (I MOe) The play in prose is accompanied by *intermezzi per musica.* The play with its intermezzi were first performed in Siena, 1701, according to a statement in the 1715 publication.

1740[4] spring
and summer
Cocomero

Compagnia di commedianti Filippo Coluccj.
I Fas (Reggenza 631, c. 8). Coluccj was granted permission to perform in the spring and summer of 1740, and to continue in other Tuscan cities. A subsequent request specifically names April 26.
    Between 1740[4] and 1740[5], I Fac (Infuocati) indexes a concession of a company of *Saltatori Inglesi.*

1740[5] 1 x
Cocomero

ORAZIO. Commedia per musica da rappresentarsi in Firenze nel teatro di via del Cocomero nell'autunno dell'anno 1740. Firenze, Stamperia di Pietro Matini, 1740.
I Fc, Fm, Vgc.

Text: By common consent of bibliographers, by Antonio Palomba, who is not mentioned. But we have not traced the attribution to its source. Some portion of it, however, is by Luigi Maria Stampiglia (see comment below).

Music: Anonymous, but probably Gaetano Latilla and Giovanni Battista Pergolesi, named in the libretto of Venice, 1743 (Sonneck, p. 826). However, for a detailed analysis of a score in I Fc, see Frank Walker, p. 307.

Roles: Lamberto, Giacomina che poi si scopre Ginevra, Leandro che poi si scopre Elisa, Lauretta, Bettina, Mariuccio, Colagianni.

Comment: Susier on date shown: "[Nella via del Cocomero] *Orazio* recitata in musica. E ridicola, parole del figlio di Stampiglia." I Fas (Reggenza 631, c. 10) contains the request and permission to Luigi Maria Stampiglia to recite an opera in September following the end of the recitation of the comedians (1740[4]).

1740[6] 1 x
Tintori

La sposa alla moda. Commedia in prosa.
Susier, in the continuation of the entry immediately above, says: "La seconda [commedia] nel teatro di via de' Tintori int[itolata] *La Sposa alla moda* Commedia ridicola Composizione di Roma e vi era gl'Intermedi in Musica." The intermezzi were published and are recorded below. The comedy is most probably *La moglie alla moda* by Girolamo Gigli, who, while Sienese in fact, was so frequently in Rome that he might have been thought of as being Roman. *La moglie* was published in his *Componimenti teatrale*, p. 127, his seventh farce.

1740[7] 1 x
Tintori

LE STRAVAGANZE DELL'UBBRIACHEZZA. Intermezzi rusticali da recitarsi nel teatro del corso de' Tintori nell'autunno dell'anno 1740. sotto la protezione di S.A. Reale il Ser.o Francesco III, ecc. Firenze, Chiesa di Sant'Apollinare, 1740.
I Rn.

Text: Domenico Guagni. The same with changes as 1732[12].

Music (lost): Guagni.

Cast: Silvio - Domenico Guagni; Lisa - Gaetano Ciarli.

1740[8]
Cocomero

Didone.
I Fas (Reggenza 631, c. 11): Request and permission granted to Giuseppe
Fantini di Arezzo "che e stato Impresario, che si è recitata nella passata
Estate a Pistoia, e a Lucca fa istanza di venir con la med[esim]a
compagnia di musici p[er] far recitar la *Didone* nel Teatro di via di
Cocomero nel prossimo novembre."
Text and music unidentified. No libretto found.

1741 carn

Pandolfini records that the Pergola was closed during this carnival because
of the official mourning for Emperor Charles VI of Austria who died
October 20, 1740. His death would also account for the absence of operas
in November of the preceding year. Susier, however, reports that some
public entertainment was allowed towards the end of the carnival (see below).

1741[1] 9 ii
Porta a S. Niccolò

La forza della magia. Commedia in prosa.

Text: Giovanni del Cataldi.

Comment: Susier, on date shown, remarks: " . . . stante la morte dell'
Imperatore non fu visto maschere ne si fece opere ne festini; in questi
ultimi giorni fu permesso di recitare alcune comedie in prosa, cioè nel

Tintori

Teatro dei Cadenti. E dalla Porta a S. Niccolò fu da Giovanni del Cataldi
recitato una comedia in prosa intitolata: *La Forza della magia*, e da

Mercato nuovo

Mercato Nuovo fu recitata una comedia di Burattini in musica, e si pagava
un paolo per entravi." First references to theaters at S. Niccolò and
Mercato nuovo.

1741[2] 9 vi-2 vii
Cocomero

DEMOFONTE. Dramma per musica da rappresentarsi in via del Cocomero,
1741. Firenze, Albizzini, s.d.
I Fn (destroyed).

Text: Probably Pietro Metastasio. See 1746[8].

Music: Composer unknown.

Comment: I Fas (Reggenza 631, cc. 13-23) concerns the tangled commitments
of the Cocomero during the summer and fall seasons. Emmanuel de
Richecourt, who, with the Principe di Craon, was one of the officials of the
Regency, complains that the academy committed the theater without his
permission thus creating confusion. A concession by Richecourt dated
April 2, 1741, establishes the following schedule: In June and until July 2,
the theater is conceded to Francesco Pepi for an *opera in musica*; July 2
until September 1 to Giuseppe Giannetti *cittadino fiorentino* for a *burletta*
or a *drama in musica*; from September 1 onward to [Antonio] Berti [the
I Fac index adds *strumentaio* to his name] who is acting in the name of the
academician Cav. Luigi Pitti, who, according to the index, performed an
opera in musica.
   Giannetti apparently was unable to perform during his time, for on
June 14 the Regency conceded the theater to Giovanni Vitalba e compagni

"di rappresentare le loro commedie" for the next two months of July and August. It is probably significant that Giannetti does not appear in the I Fac (Infuocati) index.

Demofonte is assigned to Pepi's period by elimination. Fagiuoli XXVI, f. 34v, mentions a performance of a *commedia in via del Cocomero* on 9 ii but fails to give the title. Susier likewise mentions a commedia on the same day with no more information.

1741³ 24 vi
Pergola

ARMINIO IN GERMANIA. Dramma per musica da rappresentarsi in Firenze nel teatro di via della Pergola nell'estate dell'anno 1741. sotto la protezione dell'Altezza Reale del Serenissimo Francesco III. Duca di Lorena, e Bar, Granduca di Toscana, ecc., dedicato alla Maestà della Regina d'Ungheria, e di Boemia, Arciduchessa d'Austria, Duchessa di Lorena, e Bar, Granduchessa di Toscana, ec., ec., ec. Firenze, Anton Maria Albizzini, per Cosimo Maria Pieri, 1741.
I Bc, Rc, Rn.

Text: Anonymous. The credit for the composer indicates that the libretto had been previously performed with other music, but no such libretto is known.

Music (lost): Giuseppe Scarlatti, *tutta nuova*, as stated on page 7 and confirmed by Pandolfini and Susier.

Cast: Arminio - Felice Salimbeni; Rosmonda - Giustina Turcotti; Segeste - Angiolo Amorevoli; Germanico - Agata Elmi; Ersinda - Margherita Chimenti; Valerio - Maria Maddalena Parigi. Ballerini: Pietro Gugliantini, Francesco Piccioli, Giuseppe Cavicchi, Tommaso Ricciolini. Ballerine: Anna Bresciana, Angela Lugana, Felice Banti, Gaspera Becheroni. Inventore de' Balli- Maestro Pietro Gugliantini. Inventore degli Abiti - Ermanno Compostoff. Impresario - Antonio Gaspero Guerretti (but see Susier below).

Comment: Fagiuoli XXVI, f. 36r, gives date shown. Susier on the same date speaks of "*Arminio in Germania* alla Pergola, composizione di un Scarlatti e vi cantava La Turcotti, Amorevoli, Salimbeni, una Romana [Chimenti] ed altri. Impresario Cataldi." Given the usual plurality of impresari as a common Florentine practice, Cataldi, who has been recorded as active at a theater at the Porta S. Niccolò (1741¹), may have been collaborating with Guerretti.

(1741)⁴ carn
(Pergola)

Issipile, text by P. Metastasio, music by D.M.B. Terradeglias, Pergola theater. Listed by Manferrari under the composer's name. Since no other authority on the Pergola recognizes such a performance, it is unlikely to have occurred. *Issipile* was performed in 1744³ at the Cocomero.

1741⁵ 2 vii-30 viii
Cocomero

Commedie.
I Fas (Reggenza 631, c. 23) records the concession of the theater to the company of Giovanni Vitalba. The index in I Fac (Infuocati) calls Vitalba a *strione* and does not crosslist his entry under either *opera in musica* or *burletta*. Consequently the comedies were *all'improvviso*. See 1741².

1741⁶ 12 viii

Susier: Death notice of Dr. Isidoro Maria Salvetti, cellist in the Cappella Reale.

1741[7] 3 ix
Cocomero

L'IMPRESARIO. Commedia per musica da rappresentarsi in Firenze nel teatro di via del Cocomero nell'autunno dell'anno 1741. sotto la protezione dell'Altezza Reale del Serenissimo Francesco III, Duca di Lorena, etc. Firenze, Anton Maria Albizzini, s.d.
I Bc.

Text: Anonymous. No relation to *L'impresario alla moda* (Firenze, 1752: I Bc) or Metastasio's intermezzi, *L'impresario* or *L'impresario delle Canarie*, etc. (I Bc; Sonneck, p. 615).

Music (lost): Anonymous.

Roles: Scartaffia, Leonora, Don Ciccio, Elisa, Nuccetta, Simone, Giberto, and Volpino.

Comment: Fagiuoli XXVI, f. 45r. *La prima* on date shown. I Fas (Reggenza 631, cc. 13-19) concedes the theater to [Antonio] Berti who is acting in the name of Cav. Luigi Pitti. The index in I Fac (Infuocati) identifies Berti as a *strumentaio*.

1741[8] 26 ix
Cocomero

LA COMMEDIA IN COMMEDIA. Dramma per musica da rappresentarsi in Firenze nel teatro di via del Cocomero nell'autunno del 1741. sotto la protezione dell'Altezza Reale il Sereniss. Francesco III, Duca di Lorena, etc. Firenze, Anton M. Albizzini, s.d.
I Bc, Fc.

Text: Francesco Vanneschi. The libretto is the same as 1731[8].

Music: Anonymous but probably by Rinaldo di Capua. Rinaldo is mentioned in the librettos of Rome, 1738; Milan, 1745; Venice, 1745; Milan, 1746; Venice, 1746; and London, 1745. Mantua, 1747, mentions Gaetano Latilla, whose setting is hardly to be considered for Florence. Walsh published in London (s.d.) favourite songs (GB Lbm).

Roles: Pandolfo, Lucinda, Nobilia, Celindo, Fiorlindo, Marchionne, Dorinda, Vespino.

Comment: Susier, on date above, "Si fece un opera in musica nel Teatro di via del Cocomero e dopo un altra intitolata *La Serva Favorita* per durare tutto Novembre." Since there is no additional concession of the theater in I Fas or I Fac between that to Berti and Pitti for September 1 and the next concession to Carlo Veronese in the carnival of 1742, both 1741[8] and 1741[9] are probably the product of their labors. The company performing, one suspects, is Pietro Pertici's but no trace has been found of him in connection with this performance.

1741[9] 29 ix
Cocomero

LA SERVA FAVORITA. Dramma per musica da rappresentarsi in Firenze nel teatro di via del Cocomero nell'autunno 1741. Firenze, Albizzini, s.d.
GB Lbm(2); I Bc, Fm(2), Rn, Vnm; US Wc.

Text: Giovanni Cosimo Villifranchi. See 1726[6].

Music (lost): Giovanni Chinzer, who signs the dedication as the impresario as well.

Comment: Fagiuoli XXVI, f. 51r, 29 October [1741]. "All'opera in via del Cocom[er]o *la Serva favorita* per la pr[i]ma volta - male." Susier quoted above. This and the preceding opera were performed in alternation.

1741¹⁰ x
Tintori

Commedie di burattini.

Susier (continuation of 26 x, 1741, above): "In detto tempo fu nel Teatro del Cadenti recitare commedie di burattini i quale erano maneggiate da una Compagnia di Forestieri come Strioni. Se facevano cose maravigliose in balli e trasformazioni e Giuochi di Picca e di Bandiera, e Cacci e di tutte sorte d'Animati chi parevano vivi. Dimenavono gli occhi e la bocca. Si vedeva de Burattini suonare il violino, chi la Chitara, chi il Flauto, e Tamburo, et ogni sera mutavano Commedia. Uno scenario bellissimo di Prospettiva; e si pagava quattro Crozie per entravi."

1741¹¹ 27 xii
Cocomero

Didone abbandonata.

Both Fagiuoli XXVI, f. 56v, and Susier register on 27 xii this performance for which no libretto has been found. It is probably a repetition of Metastasio's opera performed in 1734⁵.

The lack of a libretto possibly indicates that the performance is by the company of Carlo Veronese, "di sua Ecc. Grimani" (see 1738⁹), to whom the Cocomero was conceded on December 4, 1741, for the next carnival for his comedies. The plural might allow the same company for 1742¹ and the presence of the Imer sisters tends to confirm the possibility. However, it should be noted that I Fac (Reggenza 631) lacks a page indexed in I Fas (Infuocati) that is a concession to Giuseppe Rosselli for an *opera in musica* which by its page number ought to be during this time.

1741¹² 27 xii
Pergola

VENCESLAO. Dramma per musica da rappresentarsi in Firenze nel teatro di via della Pergola nel carnovale dell'anno 1742. sotto la protezione dell' Altezza Reale del Sereniss. Francesco III, Duca di Lorena, [etc.]. Firenze, Cosimo Maria Pieri, s.d.
I Bc.

Text: Apostolo Zeno, substantially rewritten by comparison with 1703⁵.

Music: Anonymous. However, Pandolfini lists Giuseppe Orlandini as Maestro di Cappella, which may be taken as an attribution of the music. Schmidl, Pavan, and Fabbri, "Firenze," col. 385, assign the music to him. Morini unaccountably attributes the music to Giuseppe Boniventi who composed the music for Torino, 1721 (Sonneck, p. 1121).

Cast: Venceslao - Domenico Bonifaci; Casimiro - Antonio Bernachi; Alessandro - Caterina Brigonzi; Lucinda - Anna Bagnolesi Pinacci; Ernando - Giovanni Tedeschi; Gismondo - Maria Maddalena Parigi; Berenice - Francesca Fabiani. Pandolfini adds: "Maestro di Cappella, Giuseppe Orlandini; Sarto, Ermanno Compostof; Impresario, Sig. M[arc]h[e]se Giuseppe Ridolfi.

Comment: Fagiuoli XXVI, f. 56v, attended on 29 xii. Susier on 27 December writes: ". . . si aprirono tutte i Teatri. In via della Pergola si recità il *Vinceslao* in musica con gran comparse di Cavalli e vi recitava Bernacca [sic]. In via del Cocomero fece *Didone abbandonata* in musica.

Coletti
Tintori
Orsanmichele

Nel Teatro Coletti si fece la *Squola delle Fanciulle* del Gigli in prosa [a translation of Molière's *École des femmes*?]. Nel Teatro del Corso dei Tintori vi era una compagnia di Strioni (et nel teatro di Orsanmichele una compagnia di burattini,) et ogni sera mutavano e in tutte si pagava." [Parentheses indicate reconstructed passage.]

1742¹ 22 i
Cocomero

TITO MANLIO. Dramma per musica da rappresentarsi in Firenze nel teatro
di via del Cocomero nel carnevale dell'anno 1742. sotto la protezione dell'
Altezza Reale del Sereniss. Francesco III. Duca di Lorena, [etc.]. Firenze,
Piero Matini, s.d.
I Mb.

Text: Matteo Noris, a shortened version of 1721².

Music (lost): Michele Fini Napolitano, as stated on page 5.

Cast: Tito - Giuseppe Ciacchi; Manlio - Girolama Tearelli; Vitellia - Teresa
Imer; Decio - Maria Angiola Paganini; Servilia - Mariana Imer; Geminio -
Maria Angiola Paganini; Lucio - Nunziata Scardabelli. Inventore degli
Abiti - Ermano Compstoff.

Comment: Susier sets the date of the changing of the operas at both the
Pergola and Cocomero without giving the titles. He then identifies *La
costante Rosalba* as the prose play at the Teatro del Giardino (Coletti)
and a company of *Strioni nel Corso de' Tintori*.

Coletti
Tintori

1742² 26 i
Pergola

VOLOGESO RE DE' PARTI. Dramma per musica da rappresentarsi in Firenze
nel teatro di via della Pergola nel carnevale dell'anno 1742. sotto la
protezione dell'Altezza Reale del Sereniss. Francesco III. Duca di Lorena,
[etc.]. Firenze, Anton Maria Albizzini per Cosimo Maria Pieri, s.d.
I Bc, Fc, Fm, Fn.

Text: Apostolo Zeno with alterations. Performed with other titles in
1709³ (*Il trionfo della costanza*) and 1700⁷ (*Lucio Vero*).

Music: Anonymous. Pavan and Tagliavini, col. 399, nominate Giuseppe
Maria Orlandini, while Morini chooses Leonardo Leo, who composed the
music for Torino, 1744, in the carnival season (Sonneck, p. 1147).
Schmidl lists this Florentine performance under Pollaroli! Still another
possibility is Rinaldo di Capua, who is mentioned in a libretto in **GB** Cfm
for Rome, 1739.

Cast: Vologeso - Antonio Bernacchi; Berenice - Anna Bagnolesi Pinacci;
Lucio Vero - Giovanni Tedeschi, detto Amadori; Lucilla - Francesca
Fabiani; Aniceto - Domenico Bonifaci; Flavio - Maria Maddalena Parigi.
Inventore degli Abiti - Ermanno Compstoff. Pandolfini identifies
Giuseppe Orlandini as maestro di cappella (making him the probable
composer) and Giuseppe Ridolfi as impresario.

Comment: Fagiuoli XXVI, f. 59v, provides the date shown.

1742³ 1 iii
Coletti

LA FINTA CAMERIERA. Divertimento giocosò per musica da rappresentarsi
in Firenze nel teatro Coletti nella primavera del corrente anno 1742.
Dedicato a sua eccellenza il Signor Marco di Beauvau Principe di Craon,
Grande di Spagna di Prima Classe, Cavaliere del Toson d'Oro, Presidente
di Reggenza di S.A.R., ec., ec., ec. Firenze, Anton Maria Albizzini, s.d.
I Bc, Fn (destroyed), Mb.

Text: Giovanni Barlocci, who is not mentioned. The attribution is found
in Allacci, col. 880, with references to the librettos of Venice, 1743, 1744,
and 1747. The first Venetian libretto (and another of Vicenza, 1743) is,
except for considerable omissions, virtually identical with the Florentine
libretto above. The earliest performance of the libretto was in Rome, 1738,

first in the carnival and then with the substitution of three arias in the spring (**I** Rn; also Schatz Materials *Rome*, in **US** Wc), but we have not seen either Roman libretto. Other titles: *Don Calascione* (London, 1749) and *Giardiniera contessa* (Hamburg, 1744), but see 1738[5]. Title page is shown on the *right*.

Music: Gaetano Latilla, as stated on page four of the libretto. The first performance of the music and libretto took place in Rome, 1738, according to Loewenberg. Score (Venice, 1743) in modern copy in **B** Bc; twelve arias in **DK** Kk.

Roles: Pancrazio, Erosmina, Giocondo, Betta, Don Calascione, Filindo, Moschino, Dorina. Inventore degli Abiti - Ermanno Compstoff.

Tintori

Comment: Fagiuoli XXVI, f. 65v, "Istrioni nel corso de' Tintori. Com[medi]a in musica in via del Giardino *la Finta cameriera*." Assuming Fagiuoli's date to be correct, it presents a remarkable departure from the usual proscription of comedies in Lenten and pre-Easter seasons. Easter fell on March 25 in this year.

1742[4] 1, 4, 8 iv
Cocomero

DALISA. Dramma per musica da rappresentarsi in Firenze nel teatro di via del Cocomero nella primavera dell'anno 1742. sotto la protezione dell'Altezza Reale del Sereniss. Francesco III. Duca di Lorena, [etc.]. Firenze, Piero Matini, s.d.
I Bc.

Text: Niccolo Minato with alterations by Domenico Lalli. Lalli's version was first performed in Venice, 1730, with the music of J.A. Hasse (Sonneck, p. 346).

Music (lost): Possibly by J.A. Hasse since the libretto is very close to the Venetian libretto of 1730 which identifies Hasse as the composer. It varies only by the addition of another scene at the beginning, a few substitute arias and a new final chorus.

Cast: Ottone - Margherita Alessandri; Dalisa - Caterina Baratti; Edita - Clorinda Landi; Enrico - Maria Maddalena Parigi.

Comment: Fagiuoli XXVI, f. 65v, records performances on April 1 and 8. Susier attended April 4. **I** Fas (Reggenza 631, c. 26) contains permission to use the theater granted to Guido da Bagnano "di far recitare un opera in musica dalla Domenica in Albis [April 1] prossima avvenire alla metà di maggio."

1742[5] 3 iv
Coletti

DIVERTIMENTO GIOCOSO PER MUSICA da rappresentarsi in Firenze nel teatro Coletti nella primavera del corrente anno 1742. dedicato a sua eccellenza il Signor Marco di Beauvau Principe di Craon, [etc.]. Firenze, Anton Maria Albizzini, s.d.
I Bc, Mb.

Text (which is better known by the title of *Madama Ciana*)**:** Giovanni Barlocci, not mentioned, but according to Groppo, *Aggiunta*, p. 30, and Sonneck, p. 710, *et al.* However, no libretto bears his name, and Allacci lists both the prose (presumably original) comedy, col. 493 (Bologna, Longhi, 1733) and the libretto of Venice, 1744, with music by Gaetano Latilla, as anonymous, col. 896. The only circumstantial evidence

LA FINTA CAMERIERA

Divertimento Giocoso per Musica

Da rappresentarsi in Firenze nel
Teatro COLETTI, nella Primavera
del corrente Anno 1742.

DEDICATO

A SUA ECCELLENZA IL SIGNOR

MARCO DI BEAUVAU

PRINCIPE DI CRAON

Grande di Spagna di Prima Classe, Cavaliere del Toson d'Oro, Presidente
di Reggenza di S.A.R. ec. ec. ec.

IN FIRENZE,

Nella Stamperia d'Anton Maria Albizzini.
Con Licenza de' Super.

Si vende allato alle Scalere di Badia.

I Mb, Racc. Dramm. 268. *La finta cameriera*, 1742[3]. First in series of comic operas at Coletti Theater.

supporting the attribution is a manuscript addition to a copy of the earliest known publication of the prose comedy, that is, in Rome by Giovanni Zempel, 1731 (**I** Vgc, another copy in **F** Pc), which says, "p. Giovanni Barbon (*sic*) prete romano." Assuming that the prose comedy is by Barlocci, the author of the libretto is still unknown. Further research is needed.

Music (lost): Gaetano Latilla, as stated in the libretto. Other librettos which name Latilla are: Venice, 1744 (**I** Bc), Milan, 1745 (**I** Ma), Livorno, 1748 (**I** Fm), and Torino, 1747 (**US** Wc - entitled *Ambizione delusa*), and Bologna, 1749 (**I** Bc). Thus, the Florentine is the first performance known.

Cast: With *Commedia in commedia*, this is in the repertory of the company of Pietro Pertici.

Comment: Susier provides the date, calling the drama by the title of *Madama Ciana*. He also speaks of the continuation of *strioni* at the Tintori.

Tintori

1742⁶ 7 iv

Death notice in Susier of Antonio Salvi: "È morto di febbre acuto il Salvi, dottore di medicina [damaged page] . . . detta famiglia. Questo era figlio del Dott. Salvi, similmente in Medicina, e bravo compositore di drammi che si ne scriva per il Ser.mo G[ran] P[rincipe Ferd[inando] per comporre l'opere che si recitava nella villa di Pratolino."

1742⁷ 24 iv-25 vi; SIROE RE DI PERSIA. Drama per musica da rappresentarsi in Firenze nel
18-24 viii teatro in via della Pergola. Firenze, Albizzini, 1742.
Pergola I Fn (destroyed).

Text: Pietro Metastasio. Printed in his *Opere* II, p. 119. No other copy known to Sartori.

Music: Giuseppe Scarlatti, according to Pandolfini and Susier.

Cast (all information supplied by Pandolfini): Ottavio Albuzzi, Gioacchino Conti detto Gizziello; Agata Elmi, Prudenza Sani, Maria Maddalena Caselli, Gio: Domenico Ciardini. Musica di Giuseppe Scarlatti, di Napoli. Maestro di Cappella - Giuseppe Orlandini, di Firenze. Sarto - Ermanno Compostof. Pittore p[er] alcune scene - Giuseppe Chamant Pittore del Ser.mo Gran Duca. Impresario - Sig.r Cav.r Luigi Pitti.

Comment: Susier on date shown mentions the opera, *Siroe*, *Musica del nuovo Scarlatti*, at the Pergola and then continues, "Vi cantava Tiezzello [*sic* for Gizziello] soprano di Grido e La Sana Fiorentina protetta da Principe Ottaviano de Medici, chi spende lire [?] in mantenerla del tutto e la ritiene a canto al suo Palazzo in via del Cocomero che a correlazione con la casa del detta Sana e si vede che spende ancora in fare detta Opera." On 25 vi 1742 Susier records the suspension of the opera because of the illness of Tiezzello. Performances resume 18 viii and continue until 24 viii.

1742⁸ sum LE VICENDE D'AMORE, E DI FORTUNA. Dramma per musica da
Cocomero rappresentarsi in Firenze nel teatro di via del Cocomero nell'Estate dell' anno 1742. sotto la protezione dell'Altezza Reale del Sereniss. Francesco III. Duca di Lorena, [etc.]. Firenze, Piero Matini, s.d.
I Rn.

Text: Anonymous. Allacci, col. 814, and Sonneck, p. 1134, list a libretto of this title published in Venice in 1709 (or 10) which is a version of *Tiberio imperadore d'Oriente* published in Venice in 1702 (Sonneck, p. 1072) by Giovanni Domenico Pallavicino. But a check of first and final scenes and of characters reveals no connection between these Venetian librettos and the Florentine.

Music: Anonymous.

Cast: Fidaspe - Caterina Baratti; Delia - Maria Maddalena Parigi; Elinda - Clorinda Landi; Seleno - Gio. Batista Bianchi; Adrasto - Giuseppe Ciatti. Inventore de' Balli - Gio. Batista Nesti. The ballerini (four women and four men) are listed; however, they were omitted in our original notation and at the moment the materials of I Rn are not available.

Comment: The opera is not mentioned by either Susier or Fagiuoli. But the opera season seems normally to have begun at about the same time in all theaters. Therefore, performances probably began on June 24, the date on which *Siroe* opened at the Pergola.

1742⁹ 18 viii
Cocomero

LA LIBERTÀ NOCIVA. Dramma giocoso per musica da rappresentarsi nel teatro di via del Cocomero nell'autunno dell'anno 1742. sotto la protezione dell'Altezza Reale del Serenissimo Francesco III. Duca di Lorena, [etc.]. Firenze, s.t., 1742.
I Bc, Rn.

Text: Anonymous, attributed to Giovanni Barlocci by Sonneck, p. 682, with a first performance in Rome, 1740, a libretto which we have not seen, nor is it registered in Sartori's catalogue.

Music (lost): Rinaldo di Capua, as stated under the list of actors. Rinaldo's score was also used in Rome, 1740, and again Venice, 1744, in autumn (Sonneck, p. 682).

Cast: Giorgiano - Pietro Pertici; Flaminia - Caterina Castelli; Baron Zuffre Tedesco - Filippo Laschi; Dorimene - Elisabetta Vestri; Flavio - Gaetana Nesi; Ormindo-Caterina Chiaveri; Dirindina - Caterina Brogi; Piaccola - Gaspera Becheroni.

Cocomero

Comment: Susier on date shown records the performance at the Cocomero of *Don Pilogio* (*sic* for *Don Pilone*) "... Ma gli fu proibito dal Archiv[esco]. Ne fanno un altra che è intitolata *La Libertà nociva*, burletta, tradotta da una Commedia in prosa fatta in Roma." This comment refers to *La libertà nociva. Opera ischenica rappresentata nel teatro della Pallacorda di Firenze nel Carnevale dell'anno 1718. Dedicato all Em.mo e Rev.mo Principe il Sig. Cardinale Pietro Ottoboni ...* Roma e Bologna, Longhi, 1718 (I Rn). The Florentine libretto is a very faithful translation into poetry of the original prose play. At times even the words are the same. Unfortunately, the prose version is also anonymous.

The theater is conceded to Francesco Pepi for a burletta during the months of August and September.

1742¹⁰ 6 ix
Coletti

IL MARCHESE SGRANA. Divertimento giocoso per musica da rappresentarsi in Firenze nel teatro Coletti nell'autunno del corrente anno 1742. Dedicato a sua eccellenze il Signor Marco di Beauvau Principe di Craon, Grande di Spagna di Prima Classe [etc.]. Firenze, Pietro Matini, 1742.

I Bc.

Text: Antonio Palomba, not mentioned, but whose name is in the title of the libretto published in Naples, 1738 (Sonneck, p. 721).

Music: Anonymous, but probably by Pietro Auletta who is named in the Neapolitan libretto cited above.

Cast: Checchina - Maria Angiosa Paganini; Cammillo - Anna Rigacci; Flaminio - Gaetano Lanetti; Rosalba - Lucrezia Longini; Celia - Maria Longini; Giampersio - Antonio Lottini.

Comment: Susier supplies the date shown for the "opera in musica nel via del Giardino intitolata *Marchese Sgrana*." Other performances listed: *La caduta d'amore* at the Sorgenti and the usual *strioni* by the Cadenti. We have no information concerning *La caduta*.

Sorgenti
Tintori

1742[11] fall
Coletti

AMORE VUOL SOFFERANZA. Divertimento giocoso per musica da rappresentarsi in Firenze nel teatro Coletti all'autunno del corrente anno 1742. Dedicato a sua eccellenze il Signor Marco di Beauvau Principe di Craon, [etc.]. Firenze, Piero Matini, 1742.
I Bc, Rn.

Text: Gennaro Antonio Federico, not mentioned, whose name appears in the first publication of the libretto in Naples, 1739 (**F** Pn).

Music: Leonardo Leo, as stated on page 6. Scores: **A** Wn; **F** Pc; **GB** Lk; **I** Nc.

Cast: Fazio Lucchese - Filippo Laschi; Alessandro - Gaetano Lanetti; Vastarella Ortolana - Angiola Paganini; Eugenia - Lucrezia Longini; Cammilla - Maria Longini; Mosca Procaccia - Antonio Lottini; Ridolfo Genovese - Anna Rigacci. Abiti di Ermanno Compstoff.

Comment: The position as the second opera of the season at the Coletti is determined by a comment in the dedication indicating that it was the second dedicated to Beauvau.

1742[12] fall
Cocomero

ORAZIO. Commedia per musica da rappresentarsi in Firenze nel teatro di via del Cocomero l'autunno dell'anno 1742. sotto la protezione dell'Altezza Reale del Sereniss. Francesco III. Duca di Lorena, [etc.]. Dedicato all' Illustrissimo Sig. Barone Giuseppe Leopoldo Giovanni Libera Barone di Petrasch, Signore di Zemech. Firenze, Pietro Gaetano Viviani, 1742.
I Bc.

Text: Antonio Palomba, not mentioned. See 1740[5]. Dedication signed by Viviani as publisher.

Music: Probably a pasticcio but primarily by Gaetano Latilla. See 1740[5].

Cast: Bettina - Gaspera Becheroni; Lauretta - Caterina Brogi Pertici; Giacomina - Caterina Castelli; Leandro - Niccola Gori; Mariuccio - Caterina Chiaveri; Elisa - Elisabetta Vestri; Colagianni - Filippo Laschi; Lamberto - Pietro Pertici.

Comment: The index of the Infuocati (**I** Fac) lists a rental to Niccola Pezzana (or Piazzani), but the record is missing in **I** Fas (Reggenza 631).

1742[13] fall

LA SERVA PADRONA. Intermezzo per musica da rappresentare in Firenze

Cocomero

nel teatro di via del Cocomero nell'autunno dell'anno 1742. Firenze, s.t., 1742.
I Rn; US CA.

Text: Gennaro Antonio Federico, not mentioned, but his name is published in the libretto of Naples, 1733.

Music: Anonymous. Giovanni Battista Pergolesi, as is known from many sources. Scores: A Wn; B Bc, Br; I Nc, etc.

Cast: Serpina - Caterina Brogi; Uberto - Pietro Pertici.

Comment: Since the singers are the Pertici, it is unlikely that these intermezzi were performed with *Orazio* (1742[12]) because the Pertici had important roles in the opera also. While not inconceivable, it would be most unusual at this time for the singers of the intermezzi to be also in the opera. Another possibility is suggested by applications for permission (I Fas [Reggenza 631, c. 34]) by Andre Cambi with Domenico Guagni and Filippo Medici to perform *commedie in prosa* in the fall of 1742, which then might have been accompanied by these intermezzi.

1742[14] 26 xii
Pergola

ANDROMACA. Dramma per musica da rappresentarsi in Firenze nel teatro della Pergola nel carnevale dell'anno 1743. sotto la protezione dell'Altezza Reale del Serenis. Francesco III. Duca di Lorena, [etc.]. Firenze, Cosimo Maria Pieri, s.d.
I Fn, Mb.

Text (altered): Antonio Salvi, not mentioned. See 1728[1], 1716[3], and 1701[5], the last two with the title of *Astianatte*.

Music: Anonymous. Pavan does not suggest any composer; Morini, p. 48, ascribes the music to Francesco Feo, who is named as the composer of the Roman performance, 1730. More likely is Leonardo Leo who composed the music for a performance in Naples, November, 1742 (both in US Wc: Sonneck, p. 113). Leo's score is in I Nc.

Cast: Andromaca - Anna Bagnolesi Pinacci; Pirro - Gio. Batista Andreoni; Ermione - Maria Anna Venturini; Oreste - Rosa Mancini; Pilade - Carlo Carlani; Clearte - Caterina Brigonzi; Vestiario e d'Invenzione - Ermanno Compstoff. Pandolfini adds "Impresario - Sig. M.se Giuseppe Ridolfo." He leaves the space under Maestro di Cappella blank.

Comment: Susier: "A dì 26 Dic. [1742] fu aperto tutti i teatri conforme al solito, nel Teatro di via della Pergola rappresentava la *Andromaca* in

Tintori
Cocomero

musica; nel Corso dei Tintori la *Pimpa Locandiera*, Burletta del Capece in prosa; in via del Cocomero fecero *l'Ifigenia* trasportata dal Francese in prosa e tutte a pago. Fu visto in diversi Teatri altre Burlette con Pastorale e per tutto si pagare. In detto anno [during carnival] non ci fu altro che un teatro in musica, che fu ordinato dalla regenzia."

Aside from *Andromaca*, it is not possible to identify the works mentioned. No work by Capece with that title is known; however, the same title appears in 1744[6] and 1750[18], and a variant in 1748[3]. *Andromaca* evidently had little success (see next entry).

1743[1] 18 i
Cocomero

Susier: "A dì 18 Gennaio [1742/43]. Tutti questi Teatri anno mutato l'opera, cioè in via del Cocomero si fà il *Filosofo maritato*, nei Cadenti

Tintori
Pergola

la *Schiava per amore* tutte in prosa. In via della Pergola è piaciuta poco, e ne vanno mettendo su un altra intitolata: *La Merope* con musica nuova."

We interpret this to mean that *Andromaca* was not very pleasing but *Merope* was in preparation and not opened until February 2, below. Concerning the two prose plays, we have nothing to report. Acton, p. 309, mentions Filippo Medici as the impresario at the Cocomero.

1743² 2 ii

Death notice of Martino Bitti in Susier: "È morto similmente Martino Bitti Genovese virtuoso di violino e compositore singolare e provisionato nella Reale Cappella, il detto Martino serviva il Ser[enissim]o Gran Principe Ferdinando di Gloriosa Memoria, et ogni sera interveniva nelle belle accademie che si faceva nella sua Reale camera et aveva anni 87."

1743³ 11 ii
Pergola

MEROPE. Dramma per musica da rappresentarsi in Firenze nel teatro di via della Pergola nel carnevale dell'anno 1743. sotto la protezione dell' Altezza Reale del Serenis. Francesco III. Duca di Lorena, [etc.]. Firenze, Cosimo Maria Pieri, s.d.
I Fc, Fn (destroyed).

Text: Apostolo Zeno, not mentioned. See 1713³.

Music: Anonymous. Pavan and Morini attribute the music to Domingo Miguel Barnabas Terradellas, who is named as the composer in the libretto of Rome, 1743, during the same carnival (copy in I Bc). The score exists in GB Cfm, marked "alle Dame, 1743." Susier's comment quoted in 1743¹ that the music was new does not exclude Terradellas since the performances in Florence and Rome were simultaneous.

Cast: Polifonte - Carlo Carlani; Merope - Anna Bagnolesi Pinacci; Trasimene - Rosa Mancini; Anassandro - Caterina Zipoli; Epitide - Gio. Batista Andreoni; Argia - Maria Anna Venturini; Lisico - Caterina Brigonzi. Pandolfini adds, "Sarto, Ermanno Compostoff; Impresario, Sig.r M[arche]se Giuseppe Ridolfi."

Cocomero
Tintori

Comment: Susier: A dì 11 Febbraio [1742/43]. Tutti questi Teatri anno mutate l'opere. In via della Pergola fanno la *Merope*, opera buona e musica cattiva. In via del Cocomero fanno l'*Astarto* tradotto dal Francese e con il prologo tradotto dall'Inglese. Nel Corso de' Tintori fanno *l'invecchia e l'impazza* [sic] del Fagiuoli." The last named was published together with another play in prose, *Gli sponsali in maschere*, in Firenze, 1752, by G.B. Stecchi. See Baccini, *G.B. Fagiuoli*, p. 80. The title reads *S'invecchia e s'impazza.*

1743 18 ii

Death of Anna Maria Luisa de' Medici, wife of the Elector of the Palatine, and the last child of Cosimo III. Acton, p. 309, quotes Horace Mann's wry commentary on the interruption of the carnival season.

1743⁴ 15 iv
Cocomero

Commedie.
I Fas (Reggenza 631, c. 35). Request and permission for "Antonio Marchesini, Capo di una comp[agni]a di commedianti" to perform during the first week following Easter (April 14).

1743⁵ 5 v

Un pazzo guarisce l'altro. Opera serioridicola in prosa.

Tintori

Text: Girolamo Gigli. Published in Venice, per lo Rossetti, 1704, according to Quadrio I.I.VIII, p. 343.

Comment: Susier records the performance as *la prima* at the Tintori and that the Avocato Piero Cini was the *Capo degl'Interessati.*

1743⁶ 25 v
Coletti

IPOCONDRIACO. Commedia per musica da rappresentarsi in Firenze nel teatro Coletti nella primavera del corrente anno 1743. Dedicato a sua eccellenza il Sig. Marco di Beauvau Principe di Craon [etc.]. Firenze, Cosimo Maria Pieri, s.d.
I Bc.

Text: Anonymous. There is no similarity between this libretto and Villifranchi's homonymous libretto.

Music: Giuseppe Lirone di Firenze, as stated on page 7, "a riserva di tutte le arie di Flavia, di una di Cleante, che dice *non hai Cleante niente giudizio,* ec., e dell'Aria di Gilberto dell'atto terzo."

Cast: Cleante - Pellegrino Gaggiotti; Flavia - Anna Maria Querzoli; Elisa - Agata Sani; Leandro - Filippo Laschi; Gilberto - Pietro Venturini; Dorilla - Giovanna Poli; Vespino - Antonia Alberti.

Comment: Date supplied by Susier.

1743⁷ 25 v
Tintori

Il podestà di Malmantile. Commedia in prosa.

Text: Cosimo Antonio Pelli, under pseudonym Simone Falconio Pratoli, according to Allacci, col. 917, from a publication of Florence, 1749, by Paperini.

Comment: Susier, on date shown, registers the change of comedies at the Tintori, performed, as he remarks, by Strioni. He cites the title only.

1743⁸ 7 vii
Cocomero

CHI NON FA NON FALLA. Commedia per musica da recitarsi in Firenze nel teatro di via del Cocomero l'estate dell'anno 1743. Firenze, Pietro Gaetano Viviani, 1743.
I Rn.

Text: Giuseppe Maria Buini, not mentioned, by comparison with the first edition of Bologna, 1729 (I Bc) and a second edition of Venice, 1732 (Sonneck, p. 278).

Music: Anonymous. Giuseppe Maria Buini possibly, simply for the lack of a record of any other setting; however, the changes are extensive, only four out of eight characters of the original 1729 are retained in Florence, 1743.

Cast: Diacinta - Anna Querzoli; Lispina - Agata Sani; Tintiminia - Giovanna Poli; Monser' Voragine - [blank] ; Saltobello Impresario - Filippo Laschi; Alippio Musico - Pietro Venturini; Mammolo - Antonia Alberti.

Comment: Susier is very nearly illegible but he mentions *Chi non fa non falla* on the date shown. The concession is missing in I Fas (Reggenza 631); however, the index in I Fac lists Innocenzio Vanni "per le burlette" in an entry between Marchesini (1743⁴) and Pertici (1743⁹). The plural gives some support to the interpretation of Susier's statement, at least to the supposition that two *burlette* were performed in this season.

1743⁹ 25 viii
Cocomero

GIRAMONDO. Commedia per musica da rappresentarsi in Firenze nel teatro di via del Cocomero nell'autunno dell'anno 1743. sotto la protezione dell'Altezza Reale del Sereniss. Francesco III. Duca di Lorena, [etc.]. Firenze, Anton Maria Albizzini, 1743.
I Bc.

Text: Anonymous. Caselli, no. 4446, attributes the text to A. Palomba. This is not, however, a dependable source.

Music: Anonymous. Sesini names Leonardo Leo, to whom the music for intermezzi by the same title in Venice, 1749, is also attributed.

Cast: Pancrazio - Pietro Pertici; Emilia - Anna Querzoli; Giulia - Caterina Brogi [Pertici]; Giramondo - Filippo Laschi; Clarice - Ottavia Nunziata Barberini; Odoardo - Niccola Gori; Don Giov. Andrea - Pellegrini Gaggiotto.

Comment: The concession of the theater is to *Il musico* Pertici for *una burletta in musica* from August 20 and for the remainder of the autumn. This is the first occasion on which the company has been engaged under the name of Pertici.

Susier supplies the date of the first performance. He mentions in the same passage *Strioni* at the Cadenti.

Tintori

1743¹⁰ 8 ix - 29 x
Pergola

BAJAZET. Dramma per musica da rappresentarsi in Firenze nel teatro di via della Pergola l'autunno dell'anno 1743. sotto la protezione dell'Altezza Reale del Ser. Francesco III. Duca di Lorena, [etc.]. Firenze, Cosimo Maria Pieri, s.d.
I Fc, Vgc.

Text: Agostino Piovene, not mentioned by comparison with 1716⁵.

Music: Anonymous. Pavan says E.R. Duni, while Morini says Leonardo Leo, both without visible reasons. No score by either composer known.

Cast: Bajazet - Gio. Batista Pinacci; Tamerlano - Francesca Barlocci; Asteria - Vittoria Tesi Tramontini; Irene - Maria Maddalena Parigi; Andronico - Santi Barbieri; Clearco - Margherita Alessandri; Morteno - Giuseppe Caterini. Ballerini: Francesco Sauter di Francia; Gaspero Cacioni di Firenze; Giuseppe Fabiani di Firenze; Giuseppe Turchi. Ballerine: Anna Pagnini; Placida Cacioni; Margherita Falchini; Caterina Anichini. Inventore de Balli: - Francesco Sauter; Sarto - Ermanno Compostof. Impresario - Gio: Batista Pinacci.

Comment: Susier supplies the date. He mentions it again on 29 October "con grandi applausi." In this same entry he continues, "nel corso de' Tintori una Compagnia di Ballerine Romane e Veneziane e ballarano sopra la Corda tirata, et in ultimo recitarano una Burletta Ridicola. In detto tempo, [quattro teatri si aprono, e nel teatro di vai del] Giardino, *Ciapo* commedia ridicola del Capece di Roma." No play by Capece with that title is known. Susier may be mistaken. Giovanni Battista Fagiuoli wrote a prose play entitled *Ciapo tutore*, published in volume four of his comedies by Moücke, Firenze, 1738 (Allacci, col. 186) and again, vol. IV, p. 3 (1753). (See 1747¹.)

Tintori

Coletti

1743¹¹ 29 ix
Cocomero

LA FIAMMETTA. Commedia per musica da rappresentarsi in Firenze nel teatro di via del Cocomero, nell'autunno del corrente anno 1743.

sotto la protezione dell'Altezza Reale del Sereniss. Francesco III. Duca
di Lorena, [etc.] . Firenze, Anton Maria Albizzini, 1743.
I Mb, Rn.

Text: Anonymous. The same libretto was published anonymously the
preceding carnival in Venice (Sonneck, p. 502) and again in Venice in 1744
(copy in I Mb).

Music: Anonymous, and also anonymous in the first Venetian libretto above,
while Allacci assigns the second to *diversi autori*.

Cast: Fiammetta - Caterina Brogi [Pertici] ; Rosalba - Anna Querzoli;
Flaminio - Niccola Gori; Geronio - Pietro Pertici; Ernesto - Pietro Venturini;
Filaura - Ottavia Nunziata Barberini; Monsu' Bigio Sarto Francese - Filippo
Laschi; S. Imbroglio - Pellegrin Gaggiotti. Inventore degli Abiti -
Ermanno Compstoff.

Comment: Date supplied by Susier, who calls it *Fiammetta buffa in musica
ridicola*. Querzoli and Laschi sang the same roles in Venice, 1743/44,
while Gaggiotti sang Geronio. A memorandum from Scipione Capponi to
the Reggenza (I Fas 631, c. 40) probably applies to this or to a missing
burletta. On November 2, 1743, Capponi reports that he had permitted
the impresario, [Filippo] Medici, to perform on Sunday because the latter
had said he had the permission to do so from the Reggenza. The original
concession of the theater for November is missing in Reggenza 631, but it
is indexed in I Fac (Infuocati).

1743^{12} xi?
Cocomero
Tintori

Susier, on an undecipherable date in November, lists a prose comedy at
the Cocomero entitled *La fedeltà nei disprezzi* (not identified) and at the
Tintori a continuation of the "Strioni e donne Ballerine di Corda."

1743^{13} 1 xii
Cocomero

Il marito alla moda. Comedia in prosa.

Text: Giov. Battista Fagiuoli. Published in vol. V of his comedies by
Moücke in Firenze, 1738 (Allacci, col. 506).

Tintori

Comment: Susier supplies the date, theater, and author, and remarks a
third time upon the "strioni e ballerine di corda" at the Tintori.

1743^{14} 26 xii
Pergola

ALESSANDRO NELLE INDIE. Dramma per musica da rappresentarsi in
Firenze nel teatro di via della Pergola nel carnevale dell'anno 1744. sotto
la protezione dell'Altezza Reale del Sereniss. Francesco III. Duca di Lorena,
[etc.] . Firenze, Cosimo Maria Pieri, s.d.
I Fc, Fn (destroyed).

Text: Pietro Metastasio, not mentioned. See 1740^{1}, from which it differs
only in two substitute arias listed at the end.

Music: Anonymous. Two of the singers, Pinacci and Tramontini, sang the
same roles in Venice, 1743 (Sonneck, p. 60) the libretto of which states
that the music (lost) is by Gio. Adolfo Hasse; thus there is a small basis
for ascribing some of the music to Hasse in this case. Susier is otherwise
doubtless correct in ascribing the music to *diversi* (see below).

Cast: Alessandro - Gio. Battista Pinacci; Poro - Giuseppe Santerelli;
Cleofide - Vittoria Tesi Tramontini; Erissena - Margherita Chimenti;
Gandarte - Girclama Tearelli; Timagene - Giuseppe Caterini. Inventore

de' Balli - Monsieur Sauter; Inventore dell'Abbattimento - Domenico Dell'Agata; Il Vestiaro è d'Invenzione del Sig. Ermanno Compstoff. Pandolfini lists the ballerini: "Francesco Sauter Francese, Pietro Gugliantini, Giuseppe Fabiani, Francesco Turchi. Ballerine: Anna Pagnini, Maria Maddalena Cacioni, Margherita Falchini, and Maria Maddalena Magherini. Impresario Gio: Battista Pinacci, che non ha nell'Impresa altro che il nome, e la direzione, essendo l'Interesse di alcuni de SS. Accademici, e di altri Cavalieri."

Comment: Susier provides the date adding "parole di Metastasio, musica di diversi."

1743[15] **26 xii**
Cocomero

LE FURBERIE DI SPILLETO. Commedia per musica da rappresentarsi in Firenze vel [*sic*] teatro di via del Cocomero nel carnevale dell'anno MDCCXLIV. sotto la protezione dell'Altezza Reale del Serenissimo Francesco III. Duca di Lorena, [etc.]. Firenze, Gio: Paolo Giovannelli, s.d. I Bc, Rn.

Text: Anonymous. Unknown to bibliographers.

Music: Girolamo Abos, Maestro di Cappella Napoletano, as stated on page 4. No earlier performance known. Sartori's catalogue does not contain a prior libretto.

Cast: Cipriano Taccagni - Pietro Costantino Compassi; Cammilla - Caterina Chiaveri; Alessandro - Gaetano Nesi; Elisa - Anna Gaschi; Lelio - Anna Maria Vittori; Spilleto and Armellina - Giovanna Falconetti Poli; Bozza - Pietro Venturini.

Comment: Susier provides the date, designates the opera a *burletta in musica*. In the same list he mentions also a "buona compagnia d'Istrioni" at the

Tintori
Orsanmichele

Tintori, "[e] nel Teatrino di Orsanmichele si rappresentava una pastorale con figurine e per tutto si pagava." I Fas (Reggenza 631, c. 39) contains a request dated October 27, 1743, made by Filippo Medici, impresario, to perform two *burlette in musica* during the next carnival. The second opera, *Issipile*, turned out not to be a *burletta*. However, the fact that Medici's company was the performers is shown by the several singers common to both casts.

Additional entertainment was permitted by the Reggenza (c. 41-43): fireworks on January 3 and masques on January 7. During the second opera, a *festa in ballo* took place on Saturday, February 8.

(1743)[16] **carn**

Artemisia. Text: Anonymous. Music: Dom. Terradeglias. Cited by Schmidl in error. Perhaps a confusion with *Merope*, 1743[3] which Pavan attributed to Terradeglias.

(1743)[17]

Demofonte. Text: Metastasio. Music: Gluck. Cited by Loewenberg. But no evidence found to support such a performance.

(1743)[18]

La scuffiara. Text: Anonymous. Music: Fr. Maria Paci romano. This and other operas performed at the Roman theater *detto Pallacorda di Firenze* have been located in Florence because of the name of the theater and because towards the end of the eighteenth century, a theater with a similar title was in operation in Florence. The error has been made notably by Manferrari who is the source of the present entry (III, p. 8) and Mamczarz. According to Fabbri, "Firenze," col. 388, the Florentine theater was founded in 1778 by the Accademia degli Intrepidi. In both Mamczarz and Manferrari earlier performances in Florence at Pallacorda should be assumed to have taken place in Rome.

1744[1] 12 i
Coletti

Don Pilogio con il coro delle Zovolette. Commedia in prosa del Gigli. Susier on date shown. *Don Pilogio* is probably *Don Pilone*, the former title having been used also in 1740[3]. *La zoccoletta* is the seventh *farza* published in Gigli's *Componimenti teatrale*, p. 152.

1744[2] 23 i
Pergola

ARTASERSE. Dramma per musica da rappresentarsi in Firenze nel teatro di via della Pergola nel carnovale dell'anno 1744. sotto la protezione dell' Altezza Reale del Serenissimo Francesco III. Duca di Lorena, [etc.]. Firenze, Cosimo Maria Pieri, s.d.
I Vgc.

Text: Pietro Metastasio, not mentioned, but by comparison with 1739[9].

Music: Anonymous. Pavan and Morini both agree on E.R. Duni. Pandolfini is silent. An anonymous score in I MOe. Whether it is a setting for Florence is unknown.

Cast: The singers are not named in the libretto but it may be assumed that they are the same as 1743[14].

Comment: Date supplied as shown by Susier.

1744[3] 23 i
Cocomero

ISSIPILE. Dramma per musica da rappresentarsi in Firenze nel teatro di via del Cocomero nel carnevale dell'anno 1744. sotto la protezione dell' Altezza Reale del Sereniss. Francesco III. Duca di Lorena, [etc.]. Firenze, nuova Stamperia di Gio. Paolo Giovanelli, 1744.
I Bc.

Text: Pietro Metastasio, not mentioned. Text published in his *Opere* I. First performed in Vienna, 1732.

Music: Anonymous. Previous settings are abundant. The first, 1732, in Vienna, was by Francesco Conti, according to the *Opere*. Allacci, col. 476, cites Giovanni Porta as the composer for Venice, 1732. Sonneck lists Baldassare Galuppi for Torino, 1738, as well as Porta, Venice, 1732, and Manferrari lists a setting by Dom. Miguel Terradeglias performed in the Pergola, 1741[4], which is certainly an error in location at least.

Cast: Giasone - Caterina Chiaveri; Toante - Pietro Costantino Compassi; Rodope - Anna Gaschi; Eurinome - Gaetano Nesi; Learco - Pietro Venturini; Issipile - Anna Maria Vittori.

Comment: Date supplied by Susier.

1744[4] carn
Cocomero

LA PREZIOSA RIDICOLA. Intermezzo per musica da rappresentarsi in Firenze nel teatro di via del Cocomero nell'carnevale dell'anno 1744. Firenze, Gio: Paolo Giovannelli.
I Rn.

Text: Marchese Trotti, not mentioned. See 1728[2].

Music: Anonymous, but doubtless by Giuseppe Maria Orlandini. Tagliavini, "Orlandini," does not include this performance.

Cast: Madama - Anna Faini; Cuoco - Costantino Compassi.

Comment: These intermezzi probably accompanied *Issipile*, an *opera seria*, rather than the first opera at the Cocomero, *Le Furberie di Spilleto*, a burletto.

1744[5] 4 iv Cocomero	Commedie di commedianti Istrionj. I Fas (Reggenza 631, c. 45): Request by Paolo Arrighi for permission of the Reggenza to perform during the octave of Easter (April 5).

1744[6] 6 vii Coletti	"*La Pimpa locandiera* del Capece di Roma accomodata al uso di Firenze. I comici fiorentini erano [Domenico] Guagni, [Gaetano] Ciarli, Civili, Dori, il Giamberini." - Susier. See comment, 1742[14], and 1750[18]; also p. 115.

1744[7] 9 viii Cocomero	LA SERVA PER AMORE. Commedia per musica da rappresentarsi in Firenze nel teatro di via del Cocomero nell'estate dell'anno 1744. sotto la protezione dell'Altezza Reale del Senerissimo [*sic*] Francesco III. Duca di Lorena, [etc.]. Firenze, Stamperia dirimpetto a S. Apollinare, s.d. I Bc, Mb, Rn.

Text: Anonymous. No other performance has been identified.

Music (lost): Anonymous.

Cast: Pandolfo - Pietro Pertici; Leonora - Elisabetta Ronchetti; Isabella - Caterina Brogi [Pertici], Rosalba - Lucrezia Minardi; Silvio - Luigi Ristorini; Davo Gobbo Tartaglia - Giuseppe Ristorini; Orlando - Bartolommeo Cherubini; Moschetto - Margherita Cavalli.

Comment: Susier gives date, denominates the work "commedia ridicola in musica, la prima" [of the season at the Cocomero]. The permit is not found in I Fas, but the I Fac index includes a reference to Pertici at the right time, i.e., a permit on the page following Paolo Arrighi.

1744[8] viii	Death notice in Susier of "Carlo Arrighani [*sic*] fiorentino d'anni 55. Compositore di camera e suonatore di leuto del G. Duca." See 1738[11], and 1739[2].

1744[9] 28 viii	Death notice in Susier of Stefano Frilli "d'anni 80 . . . detto Frilli è stato bravo soprano e servi per molto tempo l'Elettore di Baviera. Lascia molti danari."

1744[10] 14 ix Cocomero	LO SCIALAQUATORE. Commedia per musica da rappresentarsi in Firenze nel teatro di via del Cocomero nel'autunno dell'anno 1744. sotto la protezione dell'Altezza Reale del Serenissimo Francesco III. Duca di Lorena, [etc.]. Firenze, Stamperia dirimpetto a S. Apollinare, s.d. I Bc, Mb, Rn.

Text: Anonymous, attributed by Sesini, Manferrari, and Tagliavini (all under G.M. Orlandini) to Ambrogio Borghesi.

Music: Anonymous, but probably by Giuseppe Maria Orlandini who is named in the libretto of Venice, 1745, as the principal (among several) composer of the score (Sonneck, p. 976).

Cast: Pancrazio - Pietro Pertici; Don Pasquale - Giuseppe Ristorini; Rosaura - Elisabetta Ronchetti; Delfina - Anna Faini; Lindora - Lucrezia Minardi; Flavio - Luigi Ristorini; Pierotto - Bartolommeo Cherubini; Mommolo - Margherita Cavalli. Vestiario - Ermanno Compstoff.

Comment: The date is set by Susier.

1744[11] fall
Cocomero

LA FEDE NE' TRADIMENTI. Drama per musica da rappresentarsi in Firenze nel teatro di via del Cocomero nel'autunno dell'anno 1744. sotto la protezione dell'Altezza Reale del Serenissimo Francesco III. Duca di Lorena, [etc.] . Firenze, Giuseppe Pagani, s.d.
I Bc, Vgc.

Text: Girolamo Gigli, not mentioned, but see 1697[1].

Music: Anonymous. See 1732[10].

Roles: Artabano, Anagilda, Sebaste, Aspasia. Negl'intermezzi: Moschetta, Grullo. (See below.)

Comment: Susier mentions the opera but imprecisely: 14 ix, 1744: "In detto tempo d'autunno nel teatro di via del Cocomero si recitava un opera intitolata *La Fede ne' Tradimenti* del Gigli e vi cantava Il [Gregorio] Babbi tenore che ebbe gran applauso." Since 1744[10] opened the season, this opera probably began towards the end of November.

————
Cocomero

MOSCHETTO E GRULLO. Intermezzi per musica.

Text: Anonymous, published at the end of the above libretto without any further information.

Music: Anonymous. Mamczarz, p. 423, attributes the music for Venice, 1732, to Giuseppe Maria Orlandini, as does indeed Sonneck, p. 581, Tagliavini, "Orlandini," and many others, chiefly upon the strength of the London libretto of 1737 which names Orlandini as the composer. But that libretto is altered greatly, according to Sonneck, which raises some doubt that the London attribution can be accepted as valid for Venice, 1732, and Florence, 1744.

S. Fridiano

Comment: Susier, 14 ix, 1744, continues: "Fuori la porta a S. Fridiano a Navicella in un nuovo teatro si recitava *Gli Sponsali tra nemici* del [Simone] Grassi [Fiorentino] , e per tutto si pagava." Grassi's prose play was published by Longhi in Bologna, 1688, according to Allacci, col. 931.

1744[12] 27 xii
Cocomero

CATONE IN UTICA. Drama per musica da rappresentarsi in Firenze nel teatro di via del Cocomero nel carnevale dell'anno 1745. sotto la protezione dell' Altezza Reale del Sereniss. Francesco III. Duca di Lorena, [etc.] . Firenze, Gio. Battista Stecchi, 1745.
I Bc.

Text: Pietro Metastasio, not mentioned. See 1739[8].

Music: Anonymous.

Cast: Catone - Giuseppe Ciacchi; Cesare - Chiara Minucciani; Emilia - Maria Maddalena Parigi; Marzia - Elizabetta Ronchetti; Arbace - Agata Sani;

Fulvio - Pietro Venturini. Per gli'Intermezzi; Caterina Brogi Pertici, Pietro
Costantino Compassi, "sotto la protezione di S. Eccellenza il Sig. Generale
Barone di Braittevitz." Inventori degli abiti, Ermanno Compostoff.

Comment: Susier lists the theaters and the works which opened on date
shown: "Pergola, *Ezio* (1744[14]) di Metastasio; Cocomero, *Catone in Utica*
(1744[12]); Giardino [Coletti], *Il furto onorato* di Pad[re] Pelli in prosa;
Corso de' Tintori, Istrioni; Orsanmichele, *Pastorale di Burattini*; diversi
commedie in case particulare." Nothing is known about *Il furto onorato*.

Coletti
Tintori
Orsanmichele

I Fas (Reggenza 631, c. 49) contains the request of Filippo Medici for
permission to perform an *opera in musica* during the carnival of 1745.

1744[13] 27 xii
Cocomero

AMOR FA L'UOMO CIECO. Intermezzi in musica da rappresentarsi in
Firenze nel teatro di via del Cocomero nel carnevale del corrente anno
1745. Firenze, Giov. Battista Stecchi, 1745.
I Fc, Rn.

Text: Carlo Goldoni, not mentioned, but the text is published in his *Opere
teatrali* XXXV, p. 141.

Music: Anonymous. Manferrari III, p. 55, attributes the music to Davide
Perez for this Florentine performance. Mamczarz, p. 356, recognizes a
setting only by Pietro Chiarini. Both of these are, however, unreliable
sources. Frank Walker, p. 299, observes this to be a *rifacimento* by
Goldoni of *La contadina astuta* with some music by Pergolesi and some
by Gaetano Latilla, specifically "La carrozza ci sarà," a Ms in B Bc dated
Rome, Teatro Valle, May, 1738.

Roles: Livietta, Mengono, Cardone.

Comment: The date is determined by the fact that only one opera, *Catone
in Utica* above, was performed at the Cocomero in this carnival owing to
the closure of the theater in official mourning by January 10 (see below).

1744[14] 27 xii
Pergola

EZIO. Drama per musica da rappresentarsi in Firenze nel teatro di via della
Pergola nel carnevale dell'anno 1745. sotto la protezione dell'Altezza Reale
del Sereniss. Francesco III. Duca di Lorena, [etc.]. Firenze, Cosimo Maria
Pieri, s.d.
I Bc.

Text: Pietro Metastasio, not mentioned. See 1735[3].

Music: Anonymous. The libretto is quite the same as 1735[3].

Cast: Fulvia - Giustina Turcotti; Valentiniano III - Francesca Barlocci;
Onoria - Clorinda Landi; Varo - Rosalba Buini; Ezio - Ventura Rochetti;
Massimo - Anibal Pio Fabbri. Pandolfini lists the ballerini: Frediano
Salvetti Maestro, Luigi Biscioni, Melchior Monti, Filippo Vicedomini, and
ballerine: Giovanna Passini, [Anna or Maria Maddalena] Biscioni; ———
Messeri, Caterina Anichini, Maria Maddalena Magherini. Sarto - Ermanno
Compostof. Impresario - Luigi Stampiglia Ministro per diversi Signori
Accademici, ed altri Cavalieri. "Nota, che dopo la prima recita fù levata la
prima Coppia de Ballerini per non aver incontrato, e preso per Maestro
Pietro Gugliantini, e ridotti i Ballerini a no. 8. Di quest'opera non se ne
fecero più che quattro Recite per essere stato proibito il Carnevale per il
Lutto per la Madre del Ser. Gran Duca morta il dj [blank, but 10] Gennaio."

1744[15] **9 xii**
Pergola

Festa di ballo con maschere.
Pandolfini in the Ms at I Fn inserts the following notice: "Il dì 9 Dicembre:
di poi per Festeggiare La Nascità del Principe Carlo Giuseppe fu concesso
una Festa di Ballo con Maschere gratis, ed altre tre a pagamento negl'ultimi
giorni del Carnevale."

1744[16]

CANTATA in applauso de' felicissimi sponsali di sua eccellenza my lord
Giovanni Carteret con sua eccellenza my lady Sofia Farmor. Composta in
musica dal Sig. Giuseppe Orlandini, maestro di cappella di sua altezza
reale il Granduca di Toscana. Firenze, s.t., 1744.
GB Lbm; I Rn.

1744[17]
Pergola?

IL NARCISO. Favola pastorale per introduttione de balletti.
I Fas (Med., F. 6424).

Text: Anonymous.

Music (lost): Composer unknown.

Cast: Narciso - Sig.r Con[te] Moricke; Filli - La Sig.ra Con[tes] s[a]
Sincendorff; Clori - La Sig.ra Cons. Konige; Echo - La Sig.ra Cons. Ferrari;
Daliso - Sig.r Mutio; Aminta - Sigr. Francesco Sauter.

Comment: The general date is estimated on the basis of the presence in the
cast of Francesco Sauter who danced in various operas at the Pergola
between 1743 and 1747. Since Pandolfini records *feste di ballo* in 1744[15],
1745[3], and 1745[5], the above date seems reasonable.

1745[1] **26 iv**
Cocomero

Commedie.
I Fas (Reggenza 631, c. 51) contains the request for and concession of the
theater to Antonio Marchesini for after the octave of Easter. No libretto
or further record. C. 52 is a request and permission for Marchesini to
continue to perform comedies until the middle of August. Two pages
indexed in I Fac (Infuocati) of missing materials that should concern the
remainder of 1745 or early 1746 indicate Marchesini continued his
performances at the Cocomero.

1745[2] **22 viii**
Cocomero

I VECCHI AMANTI. Commedia per musica da rappresentarsi in Firenze nel
teatro di via del Cocomero nell'estate dell'anno 1745. sotto la protezione
dell'Altezza Reale del Seren.mo Francesco III. Duca di Lorena, [etc.].
Firenze, Giuseppe Pagani, 1745.
I Rn.

Text: Anonymous. No other publication or performance known. No
other libretto known to Sartori.

Music: Anonymous.

Cast: Elisa - Caterina Bassi; Filauro - Regina Gonzales; Asdrubale - Pietro
Costantino Compassi; Pandolfo - Pietro Pertici; Flavia - Angiola Tani;
Nobilio - Matteo Bevilacqua; Dorina - Caterina Brogi Pertici; Cacocco -
Dionisia Lepri.

Comment: Date supplied by Susier. I Fas (Reggenza 631, c. 52) contains
the request and permission granted to Pertici to perform a *burletta in musica*
from the middle of August for the remainder of the autumn.

1745³ 26, 27 ix
Pergola

Gran feste di ballo con maschere.

Pandolfini in the I Fn copy inserts: "A dì 26, e 27 Settembre 1745. Furono in Teatro due Gran' Feste di Ballo, con Maschere fatte in ossequio del nostro Imperiale Sovrano, stato in quest'anno apunto al Trono Imperiale. Vi fù grande Illuminazione, tanto dentro in Teatro, quanto fuori in strada, e furono dati generosi rinfreschi tutto a Spese de' Sig.re Accademici."

I Fas (Reggenza 631, c. 53) contains a permission granted to Gaetano Antinori on behalf of the *Nazione Ebrea* to perform a Te Deum in the Duomo and to give public balls (one of the two at the Cocomero). The second *gran festa* was requested by Pier Francesco de Ricci on behalf of Gio. Batt.a Vanetti di Pistoia.

1745⁴ 28 ix
Cocomero

LA VEDOVA ACCORTA. Commedia per musica da rappresentarsi in Firenze nel teatro di via del Cocomero nell'autunno dell'anno 1745. sotto la protezione di sua Eccellenza il Signor Principe di Craon, etc. Firenze, Giuseppe Pagani, 1745.
I Bc, Fc, Fm, Mb, Rn.

Text: Ambrosio Borghesi, not mentioned, according to Sonneck, p. 1119, and the catalogues of most of the indicated libraries. Manferrari I, p. 116, attributes the libretto to C. Goldoni. The Venetian libretto of 1745, carnival, does not mention the author.

Music: Anonymous, portions possibly by Ferdinando Bertoni who is mentioned in the Venetian libretto of the preceding carnival as the composer of the recitatives and nine arias. The remainder of the score is anonymous.

Cast: Rosaura - Caterina Bassi; Isabella - Angiola Tani; Filberto - Matteo Bevilacqua; Lisetta - Caterina Brogi Pertici; Ernesto - Regina Gonzales; Monsu della moda - Pietro Costantino Compassi; Giorgione - Pietro Pertici; Pasquino - Dionisia Lepri.

Comment: Date supplied by Susier.

1745⁵ 3 x
Pergola

Gran festa di ballo con maschere.

Pandolfini, immediately following 1745³, inserts: "A dì 4 Ottobre 1745. Fu prestato [*sic*] il Teatro a Sig.ri Ufiziali Militari quali ve fecero altra con simile Festa a tutte Loro Spese."

1745⁶ 3 xi - 18 xii
Cocomero

Orazio. Burletta.

Susier, on date shown, records, "Nel teatro di Via del Cocomero mutavano la Burletta e fecero l'*Orazio*." This is doubtless the comic opera performed in 1740⁵ and 1742¹². This corresponds to the request and permission granted by the Reggenza (I Fas [Reggenza, c. 50]) to Gaetano di [del] Ricco to perform an *opera in musica* from October 9 until December 18. Susier's notice suggests that another opera preceded *Orazio*.

Coletti

On the same date shown above, Susier continues, "Nel teatro di via del Giardino [T. Coletti] vi fu un teatro d'apparenze mattematiche che mostravano diverse figure le quale tutte si muovano, e in ultimo una marina con vascelli e tempesta di mare con tuoni baleni, e grandine che disperse tutti i vascelli marinari che erano sopra."

1745[7] 26 xii
Pergola

ADRIANO IN SIRIA. Dramma per musica da rappresentarsi in Firenze nel teatro di via della Pergola nel carnevale dell'anno 1746. sotto la protezione della Sac. Ces. Real Maestà di Francesco I. Imperadore de' Romani, [etc.]. Firenze, Cosimo Maria Pieri, s.d.
I Fc (3).

Text: Pietro Metastasio, not mentioned, but the libretto is very close to 1733[5]. Dedication to Marco di Beauvau unsigned.

Music: Anonymous. Pavan attributes the music to Girolamo Abos; Morini, to G.B. Pergolesi. There are a number of other possibilities.

Cast: Adriano - Gio. Triulzi; Osroa - Gaetano Pompeo Basteris; Emirena - Isabella Gandini; Sabina - Artemisia Landi; Farnaspe - Giacomo Catilini; Aquilio - Nonziata Garrani. I Balli sono d'invenzione del Sig. Gio. Batista Nesti di Firenze detto Scaramuccia. Inventore degli Abiti - Il Sig. Giuseppe Compstoff. Pandolfini's list of dancers: Gio: Batta. Nesti, Maestro. Paolo Borromeo, Luigi Biscioni, Vincenzio Nesti, Niccolo Cambi, Tommaso Ricciolini, Placida Cacioni, Caterina Anichini, Margherita Falchini, Anna Ermini, Anna Pacini, Anna Biscioni. Impresario - Innocenzio Vanni.

Comment: Date supplied by Susier and Morini.

1745[8] 26 xii
Cocomero

ROSMIRA. Drama per musica da rappresentarsi in Firenze nel teatro di via del Cocomero nel carnevale dell'anno 1746. sotto la protezione della Sac. Ces. Real Maestà di Francesco I. [etc.]. Firenze, Gio. Batista Stecchi, 1746.
I Bc, Rn; **US** Wc.

Text: Silvio Stampiglia, not mentioned. Sesini observes that it is the same as Stampiglia's *Rosmira fedele*, first performed in Venice, 1725. Sonneck, p. 959, adds, however, that some of the arias and much of the dialogue of the Florentine libretto are from Stampiglia's libretto, but that most of the arias are substitutes, some of which can be traced to Metastasio.

Music: Anonymous. Sesini and Schatz attribute the music to Giuseppe Antonio Paganelli [di Padova?] who may or may not be the Paganelli singing the role of Armindo below since the singer is from Forlì. (See Sonneck cited above).

Cast: Rosmira - Barbera Stabili; Arsace - Giovanni Angeli; Partenope - Caterina Bassi; Armindo - Giuseppe Paganelli; Emilio - Domenico Negri; Ormonte - Anna Galeotti. Attori degl'Intermezzi (not published in the libretto) - Caterina Brogi Pertici and Pietro Pertici.

Comment: Date supplied by Susier. The permission granted to Pertici's company is missing in I Fas (Reggenza 631); however, it is indexed in I Fac (Infuocati) and confirmed by the fact that the Pertici are singing in the intermezzi. See 1745[9].

1745[9] 26 xii
Cocomero

LA CONTADINA. Intermezzi comici musicali da rappresentarsi in Firenze nel teatro di via del Cocomero nel carnevale 1746. Firenze, Gio. Batista Stecchi, 1746.
I Bc, Rn.

Text: Anonymous. This has no similarity with Saddumene's *La Contadina*, 1735[2]. The characters and initial texts do not coincide with those of *La contadina astuta* (Livietta e Tracollo: see Sonneck, p. 690, and Frank Walker,

p. 310), performed with the music of Pergolesi in Naples, 1734. Finally, Mamczarz lists no intermezzo with the characters below.

Music (lost): Anonymous.

Cast: Pancrazio vecchio - Pietro Pertici; Crezia - Caterina [Brogi] Pertici; Ciapo Contadino servo di Pancrazio che non parla.

Comment: The position following the first opera of the season at the Cocomero is arbitrarily chosen: it may well have been performed with *Siface*, the second opera.

1745[10] **26 xii**
Tintori

Coletti
Borgo de' Greci

Susier, after listing *Adriano in Siria* (1745[7]) and *Rosmira* (1745[8]) above, adds the following: At the Teatro de' Cadenti, "*Il Superbo* tradotta da francese che lo mutarono e fecero *La Moglie giudice e parte* in prosa di Roma. In via del Giardino, *Non sempre le donne s'attengono al peggio* [in prose]. Nel Teatrino nuovo di Borgho de' Greci, *Non a cuore che non senta pietà* del Fiuizzani di Lucca."

    La moglie giudice was published anonymously in Bologna, 1748 (I Fn). Allacci, col. 562, lists *Non ha cuore* in a Bolognese publication by Longhi without date, but he attributes it to Ferrante Scarnelli. In Martini's repertory it is attributed to Fiuizani. We have no information regarding the other plays.

1746[1] **2 i**
Pergola

SEMIRAMIDE RICONOSCIUTA. Dramma per musica da rappresentarsi in Firenze nel teatro di via della Pergola nel carnevale dell'anno 1746. sotto la protezione della Sac. Ces. Real Maestà di Francesco I. [etc.]. Firenze, Cosimo Maria Pieri, s.d.
I Bc.

Text: Pietro Metastasio, not mentioned. See 1740[2].

Music: Domenico Terradellas, maestro di Cappella Napolitano, as stated on page 9.

Cast: Semiramide - Isabella Gandini; Tamiri - Artemisia Landi; Sibari - Nonziata Gar[r]ani; Scitalce - Giovanni Triulzi; Ircano - Gaetano Pompeo Basteris; Mirteo - Giacomo Catilini. Pandolfini adds the same dancers as appear in *Adriano*, 1745[7], as well as costumer, and impresario. But: "Maestro di Scherma p[er] l'abbattimento nella seconda Opera - Giovanni Cini."

Comment: Susier provides the date.

1746[2] **2 ii**
Cocomero

SIFACE. Dramma per musica da rappresentarsi in Firenze nel teatro di via del Cocomero nel carnevale dell'anno 1746. sotto la protezione della Sac. Ces. Real Maestà di Francesco I Imperadore de' Romani, [etc.]. Firenze, Gio. Battista Stecchi, 1746.
I Bc.

Text: Pietro Metastasio, not mentioned, but see Sonneck, p. 1005, where a letter written by Metastasio establishes the authorship. Largely, however, a pasticcio.

Music: Anonymous. Sonneck states that Schatz's notes refer to a performance in Naples, 1723, with the music of Francesco Feo. The performance which Metastasio declares to be the first is Niccola Porpora's setting for Venice, 1726. Allacci, col. 720, adds a Bolognese performance in 1737, music of Leonardo Leo and Sonneck cites a performance in Venice in 1744 set by Francesco Maggiore!

Cast: Siface - Giovanni Angeli; Ismene - Caterina Bassi; Libanio - Maria Anna Galeotti; Orcano - Domenico Negri; Erminio - Giuseppe Paganelli; Viriate - Barbara Stabili. Per gli Intermezzi: Caterina Brogi Pertici and Pietro Pertici. (Intermezzi not published with the libretto.)

Comment: Date set by Susier. The second opera performed by Pertici's company. See 1745[8].

1746[3] 2 ii
Tintori
Coletti

Borgo de' Greci

Susier continues after the above two operas to list the changes at the theaters. At the "teatro in Corso de' Tintori, *Avere cura di donne è pazzia* del Fagioli (see 1734[4]), in via del Giardino, *La Dame ideale*, che non incontra e faranno *I Guardiani de' Pazzi* del Bartorelli. In Borgo de' Greci *L'Armanda* del Villifranchi, tutte in prosa (see 1706[3])."

1746[4] 8 ii
Tintori

Coletti

Susier's next list: "in via del Cocomero, *Siface* e festa di ballo; In via della Pergola, *Semiramide riconosciuta*, l'impresario, il Gobbo Vanni. Nel Teatro de' Cadenti, *Marito alla moda* del Fagiuoli [in *Commedie* (1753), vol. V, p. 227]. In via del Giardino, *Lo spedale de' Pazzi* del Bartorelli." [With this title, *Lo spedale* di Bonarelli is curiously echoed. See Allacci, col. 733.]

1746[5] 23 vi - 3 vii
Coletti

LE GARE FRA GLI DEI. Dramma pastorale per musica da rappresentarsi nel teatro Coletti in via del Giardino l'estate dell'anno 1746. Dedicato al merito sempre grande dell'Illustriss. Giorgio Rice. Firenze, Gio. Paolo Giovanelli, 1746.
I Bc.

Text: Pietro Metastasio (*L'Endimione ovvero Il trionfo d'amore*, first performed in Naples, 1720, according to the edition of his *Opere* X, p. 111 [Paris, 1782]) but considerably altered by Ferdinando Caldari, according to Susier.

Music: Anonymous. The alterations make the use of any previous setting of Metastasio's *serenata* unlikely.

Cast: Amore - Anna Sani; Nice - Dionisia Lepri; Diana - Rosa Scarlatti.

Comment: Susier sets the first performance on date shown; on 3 vii he identifies the poet as Metastasio and says that it was "ridotto dal Sig. Ferdinando Caldari. Cattivo."

1746[6] iv - 3 vii
Cocomero

Tintori

Commedie.
I Fas (Reggenza, c. 58) records the request of and permission to the Compagnia di S. Luca di Venezia protetta dal Sig.r Vendramini for the spring of 1746 (following Easter, April 10). The final date of their performance is given by Susier on July 3. The same day there was in Corso de' Tintori "una compagnia di ballerine e ballerini" who performed various farces.

1746[7] 6 viii

SERENATA a due voci fatta la sera del VI. di Agosto MDCCXLVI. In Firenze, s.t., s.d.
I Rn.

Text anonymous. A brief seven pages. Begins "Al dolce sonno in sen / Riposo il caro ben."

Music: Anonymous.

Roles: Clori, e Aminta.

1746⁸ 3 ix
Pergola

DEMOFOONTE. Dramma per musica da rappresentarsi in Firenze nel teatro della via della Pergola nell'autunno dell'anno 1746. sotto la protezione della Sac. Ces. Real Maestà di Francesco I. [etc.] . Firenze, Cosimo Maria Pieri, s.d.
I Bc, Fc.

Text: Pietro Metastasio, not mentioned, but published in his *Opere* II, p. 205, where the first performance is stated to be Vienna, 1733, with the music of Caldara. Dedication to Giulia Strozzi signed by Gio. Gaetano del Ricco Impresario.

Music: Anonymous. Pavan does not know the composer; Morini assigns it to Antonio Caldara which, in view of the known policy of the Imperial court to prohibit performances elsewhere of their operas, is unlikely.

Cast: Demofoonte - Gregorio Babbi; Dircea - Giovanna Babbi; Timante - Filippo Elisi; Creusa - Margherita Parisini; Cherinto - Agata Elmi; Matusio - Giovanni Redi; Adrasto - Pietro Venturini. Pandolfini lists dancers (for this opera and *Ciro riconosciuto* below): Inventore de Balli - Pietro Gugliantini. Ballerini: Monsiur [Jean] Denis, Luigi Biscioni, Gio: Battista Galantini, Gaetano Andreozzi, Margherita Falchini, Maddalena Biscioni, Maddalena Formigli, Lucrezia Berardi. Sarto - Giuseppe Compostof. Impresario - Giuseppe [*sic*, for Giovanni] Gaetano del Ricco.

Comment: Susier on date shown remarks that Orlandini was *il direttore*.

1746⁹ 4 x
Pergola

CIRO RICONOSCIUTO. Drama per musica da rappresentarsi in Firenze nel teatro di via della Pergola nel Autunno dell'anno 1746. sotto la protezione della Sac. Ces. Real Maestà di Francesco I. [etc.] . Firenze, Cosimo Maria Pieri, s.d.
I Bc; S Uu.

Text: Pietro Metastasio, not mentioned, but published in his *Opere* III, p. 37, where the first performance is stated to be Vienna, 1736, with the music of Caldara. Dedication to Marchesa Teresa Capponi signed by Gio. Gaetano del Ricco Impresario.

Music: Anonymous. Pavan follows Allacci who attributes the music of Venice, 1737, to *diversi autori*; Schatz (Sonneck, p. 289), however, attributes the Venetian score to Baldassare Galuppi, whose music would then be a possibility for Florence (score in **B** Bc). Morini prefers Leonardo Leo (score in **I** Mc, Nc, and **D** Tmi, the last dated Milan, 1737). Sonneck lists other settings; Bologna, 1744, Niccolo Jommelli; and Roma, 1737, Rinaldo di Capua.

Cast: Mandane - Giovanna Guaetta Babbi; Arpalice - Margherita Parisini; Arpago - Agata Elmi; Ciro - Filippo Elisi; Cambise - Gregorio Babbi; Astiage - Giovanni Redi; Mitridate - Pietro Venturini. Inventore de' Balli, Ballerini, etc., as above for *Demofoonte*, 1746⁸.

Comment: Susier supplies the date and mentions Metastasio as the poet.

Del Ricco's dedication contains interesting glimpses of the functions of the impresario:

"Nulla altro avendo in mira nell'intrapreso mio impegno, che di accostarmi quel più che fosse possibile al punto difficilissimo d'incontrare il genio, e compatimento del Pubblico, non ho remorso finora d'avere omessa veruna di quelle diligenze, che io mi sia persuaso potermi al bramato fine condurre. Quindi doppo pensato alla scelta di eccellenti Cantori, e a ravvivare la rappresentanza delle Opere coll'ornamento de' Balli, scopertone il desiderio di molti, senza che il maggior dispendio ne ritenesse, condescesi ben volentieri a trasferire dal Teatro di Via del Cocomero, nel quale erano destinate le Recite, all'altro più magnifico di Via della Pergola, ed alle persuasioni parimente di altri fu mio pensiero il megliorare la Compagnia destinata a' Balli, con procurare di aggiugnervi [*sic*] il celebre Ballerino Monsieur Denis, conformemi potè riuscire. Era pel secondo de' Drammi da rappresentarsi stato determinato, e promesso l'*Arminio*, ma presentito, che di maggior sodisfazione sarebbe riuscita la rappresentanza del *Ciro Riconosciuto*, non mai per anche in Musica sentitasi in Firenze, anche a questo, partendomi dalla prima risoluzione, mi son tosto adattato . . . ."

Del Ricco's request (and permission) to use the Cocomero is found in I Fas (Reggenza 631, c. 61) dated 9 iii 1745 *ab inc.* Two years later he made the same transfer from the Cocomero to the Pergola, but not so gladly. His difficulties in 1748 occasioned the theatrical regulations of that year. See page 109.

1746[10] 15 x

Susier's death notice for Maria Domenica Pini, detta la Tilla "fiorentina d'anni 75. Questa Tilla è stata una brava cantatrice allieva del Sig. Martini [Bitti] e recitava a Pratolino al tempo del Ser.mo Principe Ferdinando, si come a Livorno et andava per tutti i Teatri d'Italia."

1746[11] 15 x,
16 x, 11 xii
Cocomero

La vita di Cartoccio, ladro famoso di Parigi.
Susier on dates shown refers to the Istrioni at the Cocomero which he calls a *brava compagnia*. The title used appears only on the last date. I Fas (Reggenza 631, c. 59) is probably the request and permission (18 iii, 1746) for this commedia. Though the season is not designated the position in the carteggio is appropriate. The permission is issued to "comico Giuseppe Campioni con la sua compagnia."

1746[12] 26 xii
Pergola

IL DEMETRIO. Dramma per musica da rappresentarsi in Firenze nel teatro di via della Pergola nel carnevale dell'anno 1747. sotto la protezione della Sac. Ces. Real Maestà di Francesco I. [etc.]. Firenze, Cosimo Maria Pieri, s.d.
I Bc, Fc.

Text: Pietro Metastasio, not mentioned, but see 1732[13].

Music: Anonymous, but Pavan says Georg Christoph Wagenseil (scores in A Wn and I Nc). Morini says E.R. Duni.

Cast: Mitrane - Angela Tani; Cleonice - Caterina Fumagalli; Alceste - Lorenzo Gherardi; Olinto - Livia Segantini; Barsene - Orsola Strambi;

Fenicio - Carlo Carlani; Pandolfini adds: "Inventore de' Balli, Monsiur Sauter. Ballerini: Monsieur Sauter, Giacomo Brighenti, Francesco Fabri detto Puttanina. Ballerine: Anna Beccari detta Spaccatavole, Caterina Anichini, Giovanna Moglie di Francesco Fabri, Maria Maddalena Biscioni, Margherita Falchini. Sarto, Giuseppe Compostof; Primo violino - Pianta Nida; Impressarj; Diversi Cavalieri Accademici, ed altri Cavalieri."

Comment: Susier records the opera on date shown and that the orchestral director was Giuseppe Orlandini. On January 10, that is, before the change of operas, he recounts the following scandalous behavior:

"Essendo nel teatro di via della Pergola Balli assai belli di Ballerini e Ballerine, e fu essi il più bravo che si chiamava Beni [M. Sauter] - il quale ballava assieme soli con una Ballerina [Anna Bechani or Beccari, who is the only dancer listed by Pandolfini without an Italian city attached] tutti e due francesi, e nel accostarsi assieme Mons. Beni baciò la Ballerina. Vedendo questo l'Auditor Fiscale la mattina mandò per il Bargiello; egli diede ordine da sua parte, che per quella sera lo perdonare, e guardasse bene quello, che faceva per l'avvenire, che l'averebbe fatto baciare pubblicamente dal Boia."

1746[13] 26 xii
Cocomero

LA SEMPLICE SPIRITOSE. Commedia per musica da rappresentarsi in Firenze nel teatro di via del Cocomero nel carnevale dell'anno 1747. sotto la protezione della Sac. Ces. Real Maestà di Francesco I. [etc.]. Firenze, Gio. Paolo Giovanelli, s.d.
I Bc, Fc, Rn.

Text: Anonymous. Neither Allacci, col. 926 ("d'incerto Autore - musica di diversi") nor Sonneck, p. 991, knows the author of the Venetian libretto of the following year.

Music: Anonymous.

Cast: Rosmira - Maria Masi; Ergasto - Francesco Paolo Guerrieri; Doralba - Maria Barchetti; Orazio - Bartolomeo Cherubini; Agnesa - Ginevra Magagnoli; Arnolfo - Francesco Carattoli; Menichina - Anna Sani; Belfiore - Petronio Manella; Inventor de' Balli - Monsieur Jan Denis di Parigi.

Comment: Susier provides the date shown and the fact that il Gobbo Vanni [Innocenzio] was the Impresario. In I Fas (Reggenza 631, c. 77) permission is granted to Alessandro Caldari, e compagnj to perform "alcune Burlette in musica, con decorazionj, e Balli" during the carnival of 1747.

1746[14] 26 xii
Tintori

Susier, after recording the preceding two operas, continues: "Al teatro de' Cadenti *La Mariene* ornata da contrascene in musica con abbattimento e balli." [Besides the *opera tragica* of Cicognini performed in 1683[1], another possibility is presented by Allacci: *Marianne*. Tragedia di tristo fine (in prosa). Bologna, della Volpe, 1728, d'Incerto Autore.]

Coletti
"*Farnace*, opera in prosa decorata con contrascene e ballo."

Borgo de' Greci
"Burattini a l'improviso."

Orsanmichele
"*Gli scambi lodevoli* che termina in una Pastorale."

1747[1] 9 i
Tintori

Susier's first list for 1747 on this date is as follows: "Commedia [in prosa] *I vizj correnti a l'ultima moda* del Gigli Sanese . . ." [Allacci, col. 944, cites the title with the designation of *commedia tratta dal Francese di M. Palaprat*.

Firenze, 1745. Copy in **I** Sc.]

Orsanmichele   "Sua prima commedia *La costante Rosalba*." [Previously performed
in 1742[1].]

Vangielisto   "*Bajazet* opera" [in musica?] .

Borgo S.   "*Ciapo Tutore* del Fagiuoli." [Published as *Il Ciapo Tutore o sia il Potesta*

Appostolo [*sic*]   *di Capraja*. Commedia (in prosa)." Firenze, Moücke, 1738; in Fagiuoli's
Commedie, vol. IV (1738), and again (1753), vol. IV, p. 129.

1747[2] 10 i   *La rota della fortuna*. Commedia in prosa.

Coletti

Text: Giambattista Ricciardi. Published in Bologna, 1686, by Longhi
(**GB** Lbm), entitled *La ruota*, etc.

Susier announces the change to the second performance of the season on
date shown. Fabbri, "Firenze," col. 388, says that in 1747-1748, the
Coletti was operated by the Accademia dei Risoluti.

1747[3] 24 i   IL TRIONFO DELLA GLORIA. Drama per musica da rappresentarsi in Firenze

Pergola   nel teatro di via della Pergola, il carnevale di 1747. sotto la protezione della
Sac. Ces. Real Maestà di Francesco I. [etc.] . Firenze, Cosimo Maria Pieri, s.d.
I Bc.

Text: Pietro Metastasio, not mentioned, but text published in his *Opere* III,
p. 1. Substitutions indicated by an asterisk. Original title: *Achille in Sciro*.

Music: Anonymous. Pavan does not know the composer; Morini proposes
Schauensee. More reasonable would be Pietro Chiarini (Venice, 1739) or
Gio. Batt. Runcher (Venice, 1747), both librettos in Sonneck, pp. 26f.

Cast: Achille - Vittoria Tesi Tramontini; Ulisse - Lorenzo Gherardi; Teagene -
Livia Segantini; Deidamia - Caterina Fumagalli; Licomede - Carlo Carlani;
Nearco - Orsola Strambi; Arcade - Angela Tani. Inventore de Balli -
Monsiur [Francesco] Sauter. Pandolfini adds: "Ballerini: Monsieur Sauter,
Giacomo Brighenti, Franco Fabri detto Puttanina, Luigi Biscioni, Gio:
Battista Galantini, Anna Beccari detta la Spaccatavole, Caterina Anichini,
Giovanna Moglie di Franco Fabri, Maria Mad. Biscioni, Margherita Falchini.
Sarto, Giuseppe Compostof. Primo violino, Pianta Nida. Impresari,
Diversi Cavalieri Accademici, ed altri Cavalieri."

Comment: On date shown Susier notes, "Adorna con macchine et Balli
superbi e vi recitò la Tesi."

1747[4] 24 i   IL GIUOCATORE. Commedia per musica da rappresentarsi in Firenze nel

Cocomero   teatro di via del Cocomero il carnevale dell'anno 1747. Firenze, Giovanni
Paolo Giovanelli, s.d.
I Bc, Fc, Rn.

Text: Anonymous.

Music: Giuseppe Scarlatti, as stated on page 5. Score in **D** Bds.

Cast: Isabella - Maria Masi; Dorante - Francesco Paolo Guerrieri; Petronilla -
Maria Barchetti; Mascarillo - Bartolommeo Cherubini; Nerina - Ginevra
Magagnoli; Rinaldo - Francesco Carattoli; Gelinda - Anna Sani; Barone
Buongusto - Petronio Manella.

Comment: On date shown Susier comments, " . . . et adorna di Balli superbi, e per tutto sempre v'era gran concorso di popolo e maschere." This is the second of the two burlette performed by Alessandro Caldari (see 1746¹³).

1747⁵ 24 i   Omitting the references to the preceding on this date, Susier's list of other performances includes:

Coletti   "*Gli inganni lodevole* del Fagiuoli." [Allacci, col. 452, cites a publication by Moücke in 1738 of this *commedia in prosa*. Published again in vol. V, p. 129 (1753) of his *Commedie*.]

Tintori   "*L'Adulatore* e doppo *l'Avaro* tradotte dal francese, e in ultimo *l'invecchia* [*sic*] *e s'impazza* del Fagiuoli." [The first is possibly the prose comedy cited by Allacci, col. 12, published in Venice, 1740. It is too early to be the commedia of Goldoni by the same title which, according to MGG, was first performed in Venice in 1750. The second, which like the first, is a translation, was most likely Moliere's comedy. For the last, see Comment, 1743³.]

via S. Zanobi   "Nella nuova conversazione di Via S. Zanobi *Pulchinella* [*sic*] *in giostra del Capeci di Roma*."

Borgo S. Apostolo   "*Il fanciullo eroe*, Pioli." [Allacci, col. 325: *Il Fanciullo eroe ovvero, Artemio all'Imperio*. Opera Tragicomica (in prosa) Bologna, Longhi, 1716. -di Gio. Domenico Pioli.]

1747⁶ 11 ii   Susier records that on "Mercoledi, e primo giorno di quaresima, fu preso e messo in prigione il Gobbo Vanni impresario dalle Commedie dal [*sic*] Teatro di Via del Cocomero."

1747⁷ 26 ii   *Baiazette* [?].

Vangielista   Susier records that "Con tutto che sia di Quaresima il Sig. Principe di Craun [*sic*] fece fare la Commedia al Vangielista intitolata *Baiazette* e vi intervenne tutte Dame e Cavalieri . . ." Possibly Racine's tragedy.

1747⁸ 9 iv   SESOSTRI. Dramma per musica da rappresentarsi in Firenze nel teatro di
to middle of vi   via del Cocomero nella primavera dell'anno 1747. Firenze, Giovanni
Cocomero   Paolo Giovanneli, s.d.
I Bc, Fc, Fm; S Uu.

Text: Apostolo Zeno and Pietro Pariati, not mentioned, but the text is published in their *Poesie* X, p. 199. This is a somewhat abbreviated version of *Sesostri Re d'Egitto* (1714¹).

Music: Anonymous.

Cast: Amansi - Domenica Pansacchi; Nitocri - Livia Segantini; Sesostri - Giovanni Tedeschi; Fanete - Agata Elmi; Artenice - Caterina Fumigalli; Orgonte - Violante Masi.

Comment: Susier supplies the date and adds, ". . . con balli. Continua anche nel Maggio e per la nascita di Pietro Leopoldo vi furono ammesse anco le maschere." I Fas (Reggenza 631, c. 70) contains the request and permission granted to Antonio Berti to perform an *opera in musica* beginning with the octave of Easter (April 2) and continuing to the middle of June.

1747⁹ 24 vi   Commedie.

- mid ix
Cocomero

I Fas (Reggenza 631, cc. 80, 68) contain the request and permission granted to a Compagnia di commediante della Casa [Michele] Grimanj ... "per esser queste una delle miglior compagnie," to perform from the middle of June until the middle of September. C. 68 is a request for passports issued in the name of Tommaso Simonetti, an actor in the company. I Fac (Infuocati) does not register Michele Grimanj but does list Giuseppe Imer Strione on p. 154 between Aless. Caldari (1747[4]) and Medebac. Imer was the head of the Grimanj company. He was previously in Florence in 1736[8].

Antonio Marchesini, head of a Florentine company, is also indexed on p. 150, but there seems to be no vacant space on the schedule of the theater.

1747[10] 30 viii
Pergola

L'ANTIGONO. Dramma per musica da rappresentarsi in Firenze nel teatro di via della Pergola nell'estate del 1747. sotto la protezione della Sac. Ces. Real Maestà di Francesco I. [etc.]. Firenze, Cosimo Maria Pieri, s.d.
I Fc (2).

Text: Pietro Metastasio, not mentioned, but text published in his *Opere* III, p. 79, where the first performance is stated to be Dresden, 1744, music by J.A. Hasse.

Music: Anonymous, a pasticcio, according to Susier. Pavan does not know the composer; Morini cites Antonio Bernasconi who composed the music for Rome, 1745, according to Allacci, col. 94.

Cast: Antigono - Ottavio Albuzzi; Berenice - Caterina Visconti; Demetrio - Gaetano Majorana Caffarelli; Ismene - Domenica Taus; Alessandro - Caterina Zipoli; Clearco - Maria Anna Galeotti. Inventore de' Balli - Monsieur Jean Denis. Pandolfini adds the following giving the dancers in pairs. "Ballerini: Giovanni Denis, Giovanna Cortini detta La Pantalonesina; Lodovico Romi, Anna Romi; Giovanni Gallini, Anna Becheroni; Giacomo Brighenti, Caterina Anichini; Giuseppe Cinti, Caterina Martini; Francesco Benucci, Anna Cortini. Primo Violino, il Sabatini. Sarto, Giuseppe Compostof. Impresario, Gaetano Del Ricco." Another impresario named below.

Comment: On date shown Susier states: "... musica di diversi e vi recitava Caffariello soprano et altri virtuosi ... gran concorso."

Impresario Raimondo Niccolai requested permission to perform on the evening of September 23 (Sunday) in I Fas (Reggenza 631, c. 78).

1747[11] 29 ix
Pergola

CAIO MARIO. Dramma per musica da rappresentarsi in Firenze nel teatro di via della Pergola nel'autunno dell'anno 1747. sotto la protezione della Sac. Ces. Real Maestà di Francesco I. [etc.]. Firenze, Cosimo Maria Pieri, 1747.
I Bc, Fc, Rn.

Text: Gaetano Roccaforte, not mentioned, but who is named in the libretto of Rome, 1746 (I Fm).

Music: Anonymous. Niccolo Jommelli (score in D MÜps dated Rome, 1746) is named as the composer in the libretto of Rome cited above. Morini says Caldara, probably a confusion with *Caio Marzio Coriolano* (Vienna, 1717).

Cast: Cajo Mario - Ottavio Albuzzi; Marzia Calpurnia - Caterina Visconti; Annio - Gaetano Majorana Caffarelli; Rodope - Domenica Taus, detta la

Fanesina; Lucio - Caterina Zipoli; Aquilio - Maria Anna Galeotti. Inventore de' Balli - Monsieur [Jean] Denis. Pandolfini adds, "Ballerini: Lodovico Romi, Anna Romi, Giovanni Gallini, Anna Becheroni, Giacomo Brighenti, Caterina Anichini, Giuseppe Cinti, Caterina Martini, Francesco Benucci, Anna Cortini, Francesco Sautter, Anna Beccari detta Spaccatavole. Primo Violino, il Sabatini. Sarto, Giuseppe Compostof. Impresario, Gaetano Del Ricco."

Comment: Susier, on date shown, adds weight to the attribution of the libretto to Roccaforte by adding: ". . . Composizione d'un Romano."

The Reggenza permitted masques from October 4th until the 20th, but it also attempted to regulate an interesting custom. During periods when masques were permitted, customarily the academicians were permitted to go up on the stage the better to see the dancers. The Reggenza wished to curb the practice, but Del Ricco vigorously protested that to do so would cause him to lose patrons. I Fas (Reggenza 631, cc. 81, 83).

1747[12] 29 ix
Coletti

Almansor, re della China.
Susier says of this *opera in prosa* in via del Giardino: "I personaggi erano tutto gobbi si come tutti quelli che operavano, che rendeva ridicolo agli auditori che sempre era pieno il Teatro per la novità de' suggetti."
Fabbri, "Firenze," col. 388, cites an unidentified chronicle that gives the date of September 18, 1747, and a title of *Almansor, re della Clinca* (which may be a typographical error).

1747[13] 31 ix - xii
Cocomero

Commedie.
I Fas (Reggenza 631, cc. 72-76) records the request and permission granted to Girolamo Medebach Romano and his *Istrioni* to perform from the middle of September until Advent. In c. 73, the company requested permission to continue until *Novena* in order to recover the time lost while opera was being performed during its allotted time. Susier noted the performances of the *istrioni* at the Cocomero until October 11.

1747[14] 26 xii
Cocomero

Susier's list for the new carnival is as follows:
"*Didone abbandonata* di Metastasio." No libretto has been found. Last performed in 1734[5] but see 1741[11]. Several settings are possible, including Johann Adolph Hasse's for Dresden, 1742 (Sonneck, p. 382). The request and permission granted to Antonio Berti to perform *opere in musica* is contained in I Fas (Reggenza 631, c. 70). See second opera, 1748[5].

Tintori   "*Le Donne virtuose* et *il Francese in Londra*, in prosa tradotte dal francese."
Coletti   "*La Costanza ne' tradimenti* in prosa."
Borgo de' Greci   "*Le nozze per amore e per forza* in prosa."
Orsanmichele   "*Pastorale.*"

1747[15] 26 xii
Pergola

L'OLIMPIADE. Dramma per musica da rappresentarsi in Firenze nel teatro di via della Pergola nel carnevale dell'anno 1748. Firenze, Cosimo Maria Pie [*sic*], s.d.
I Bc, Fc.

Text: Pietro Metastasio, not mentioned. See 1738[4]. Somewhat abbreviated.

Music (lost): Gio. Batista Lampugnani as stated in libretto, "musica è tutta nuova." Morini unaccountably ascribes the music to G.B. Pergolesi.

Cast: Clistene - Gaetano Pompeo Basteris [Pandolfini says Gio. Domenico] ; Aristea - Caterina Visconti; Argene - Maria Maddalena Parigi; Licida - Caterina Zipoli; Megaole - Domenico Buccella (Pandolfini records that Buccella "si amassò dopo la p[ri]ma op[er]a e in suo luogo canto Gio. Batta Andreoni soprano di Lucca."); Aminta - Domenica Taus. Maestro di Cappella - Gio. Battista Lampugnani. Inventore de' Balli - Giuseppe Valenti. Pandolfini adds, "Ballerini: Giuseppe Valenti, Vincenzio Nesti, Albuzio Albuzi, Antonio Niccoli, Niccolo Cambi, Vincenzio Gallini, Anna Nardi, Lucrezia Berardi, Maddalena Tedesca, Nunziata Martini, Regale Becheroni, Rosa Stagi. Primo Violino, Sabatini. Sarto, Giuseppe Compostof. Impresario, Gaetano Del Ricco." [Also a painter is mentioned.]

Comment: The date is Susier's.

1747[16]
Coletti

IL TUTORE. Intermezzi in musica per rappresentarsi in Firenze nel teatro di via del Giardino l'anno 1747. Firenze, Stamperia Imperiale, 1747. I Rn.

Text: Anonymous.

Music: Possibly by Johann Adolphus Hasse whose music was performed in the first setting in Naples, 1730, and continued to be performed until 1739 (Venice) and 1747 (Vienna), with the titles respectively *Pandolfo* and *Il tutore e la pupilla*.

Cast: Lucilla - Maria Maddalena Parini; Pandolfo - Filippo Marioni.

1748[1] 8 i
Borgo de' Greci

Susier lists the following changes:
"*Gli amanti senza vidersi* [*sic*], commedia del Fagioli [in prosa]."
Published in vol. II (1734) of his *Commedie* and again vol. VI, p. 257 (1753).

1748[2] 14 i
Tintori
Coletti

"*La pittura e la poesia in gara per amore*, del Fagiuoli." Apparently not published in the various editions of his comedies.
"*Il Don Gastone di Moncardo* [*sic*], del Cicognini." [See 1705[3]].

1748[3] 17 i
Tintori

"*La locanda di Pimpa e di Baggio* del Capece." [See comments for 1742[14], 1744[6]].

1748[4] 21 i
Orsanmichele

"*L'Innocenza trionfante*, commedia." [Of the two works with this title listed by Allacci, col. 462, this is probably the *scenico trattenimento* (in prosa, Roma, Mascardi, 1676. -di Prospero Mandosio).]

1748[5] 28 i
Cocomero

"*Alessandro nelle Indie* di Metastasio." See 1743[14].
This is the second opera of the season at the Cocomero for which no libretto has been located.
    The theater is conceded to Antonio Berti according to the page (162) in the I Fac (Infuocati) index. That, as before, he is acting for Cav. Luigi Pitti is shown by the index on pp. 176,7 where Luigi Pitti is given permission to perform *feste di ballo*. The permit in I Fas (Reggenza 631, c. 102) probably refers to this opera and another impresario, Giuseppe Beltrami.

1748[6] 4, 18 ii

IL GRAN TAMERLANO. Dramma per musica da rappresentarsi in Firenze

Pergola

nel teatro di via della Pergola nel carnevale dell'anno 1748. sotto la protezione della Sac. Ces. Real Maestà di Francesco I. [etc.]. Firenze, Cosimo Maria Pieri, s.d.
I Bc, Fc.

Text: Agostino Piovene, not mentioned, but the libretto is the same as 1716[5].

Music: Gio. Batista Lampugnani as stated on page 4.

Cast: Tamerlano - Giovanni Battista Andreoni; Bajazet - Gio: Domenico Basteris; Asteria - Caterina Visconti; Irene - Maria Maddalena Parigi; Clearco - Maria Eleonora Castelli; Andronico - Caterina Zipoli; Idaspe - Domenica Taus. Inventore de' Balli - Giuseppe Valenti. Pandolfini adds, "Ballerini: Giuseppe Valenti, Vincenzio Nesti, Albuzio Albuzi, Antonio Niccoli, Niccolo Cambi, Vincenzio Gallini; Ballerine: Anna Nardi, Lucrezia Berardi, Maddalena Tedesca, Nunziata Martini, Regale Becheroni, Rosa Stagi. Primo Violino, Sabatini. Sarto, Giuseppe Compostof. Impresario, Gaetano Del Ricco. La prima scena nuova e d'invenzione e Pittura del Sig. Pietro Anderlini di Firenze." He calls Lampugnani *maestro di cappella*.

Comment: Susier provides the dates shown. On the first occasion he adds: ". . . decorata con carri e si vedeva venire no. 24 cavalli. In via del Giardino,

Coletti

Don Ciccio Cucco, commedia [in prosa]."

1748[7] 18 ii
Tintori
Borgo de' Greci
Orsanmichele

Changes listed by Susier:
"*S'invecchia e s'impazza* del Fagioli [See 1743[3] and 1747[5]]."
"*L'Ospedale de' pazzi*."
"*Amore nella statua*."

1748[8] 21 iv
Tintori

Orsanmichele

Cocomero

Susier:
"Compagnia di Burattini detti la *Marittanetta*; e presen il Teatro de Cadenti et in detta sera fu la prima recita."
"*Giochi di magia bianca*." Although Susier does not mention performances, I Fac (Infuocati) lists on p. 179 Niccolini and company at the Cocomero.

1748[9] 12 v
Cocomero

LA FACCENDIERA. Drama per musica da rappresentarsi in Firenze nel teatro Cocomero nella primavera, 1748. sotto la protezione del Sac. Ces. Real Maestà di Francesco I. [etc.]. Firenze, Giovanni Battista Stecchi, 1748.
I Bc, Fc.

Text: Anonymous. Allacci lists a Venetian libretto of 1746 *d'incerto autore*, *musica di diversi* for a performance at Teatro di S. Moise (col. 321). Another libretto for a performance in Padua, Fiera, 1746, published in Venice (I Mb), also says the music was by *diversi Maestri*.

Music: Anonymous, doubtless the same *diversi Maestri* of Padua.

Cast: Checchina, Faccendiera - Mariangiola Paganini; Elisa - Margherita Landi; Filauro - Gaetano Lanetti; Flavia - Anna Barchetti; Baldone - Carlo Paganini; Lelio - Giuseppe Ducci; Don Scialappa - Antonio Valletti, detto Brigido; Bacocco, muta - Giuseppe Compstoff (who doubtless was also in charge of costumes).

Comment: The dates are Susier's. He adds, "Messe in iscene dal Orlandini.

Burlette in musica." The plural of *burletta* probably is meant to include
La Vedova spiritosa below.

I Fas (Reggenza 631, c. 104) registers the request and permission granted
to Carlo Paganini to perform *burlette in musica* (I Fac [Infuocati] indexed
on pp. 182, 3). His being the head of the company reinforces the hypothesis
that the Padua score was repeated in Florence.

1748[10] **13 vi -** **11 vii** **Cocomero**	LA VEDOVA SPIRITOSA. Dramma giocoso per musica da rappresentarsi in Firenze nel teatro di via del Cocomero nella primavera dell'anno 1748. sotto la protezione di . . . Francesco III. Firenze, Giovanni Battista Stecchi, 1748. I Fm, Rn.

Text: Ambrosio Borghese, not mentioned, but this is the same libretto
with modifications as *La vedova accorta*, 1745[4].

Music: Anonymous, probably a pasticcio. See previous entry.

Cast: Lisetta - Mariangiola Paganini; Rosauro - Margherita Landi; Ernesto -
Gaetano Lanetti; Isabella - Anna Barchetti; Giorgione - Carlo Paganini;
Filiberto - Giuseppe Ducci; Monsu' La Mod. - Antonio Valletti; Pasquino -
Maria Maddalena Parrini. Inventori de' Balli - Giovanni Scali.

Comment: Susier provides the dates. 11 vii: "Terminavano le Burlette, e
fecero delle composizione drammatiche come oratori del Metastasio, et
intermedi e balli." Orlandini probably was the director of music and Carlo
Paganini was the head of the troupe, again as in the case of *La facciendiera*
preceding.

1748[11] **11 vii** **Cocomero**	COMPONIMENTO DRAMMATICO che introduce ad una festa teatrale da rappresentarsi in Firenze nel teatro di via del Cocomero nell'estate dell'anno 1748. sotto la protezione di . . . Francesco III. [etc.]. Firenze, Giovanni Battista Stecchi, 1748. I Bc.

Text: Anonymous. The intermezzi, also anonymous, are printed beginning
on page 16 with the title LA VIRTUOSA MODERNA. According to Mamczarz,
the intermezzi were published previously in Pisa, for the carnival of 1747
(I Vgc).

Music: Anonymous.

Cast: Attori nella Cantata: Lisinga - Mariangola Paganini; Sivene -
Margherita Landi; Tangia - Niccola Berardi. Nell'Intermezzo: Elisa -
Mariangola Paganini, Scartaffia Impresario - Carlo Paganini.

Comment: See Susier's entry quoted immediately above. Neither Pandolfini
nor modern scholars mention this *Componimento*. The term *festa teatrale*
may have been used here merely to indicate a grand ball in the theater
rather than the festival opera in the meaning of the term in the seventeenth
century.

1748[12] **1 ix** **Pergola**	SIROE. Dramma per musica da rappresentarsi in Firenze nel teatro di via della Pergola nell'autunno dell'anno 1749. sotto la protezione della Sac. Ces. Real Maestà di Francesco I. [etc.]. Firenze, Cosimo Maria Pieri, s.d. I Bc, Fc.

Text: Pietro Metastasio, not mentioned, but same as 1726[3].

Music: Anonymous. Pavan says "diversi autori"; Morini, Leonardo Vinci, whose music was used in the first performance in Venice, 1726!

Cast: Siroe - Gaetano Maiorana; Cosroe - Giovanni Battista Pinacci; Medarse - Pietro Venturini; Emira - Girolama Tearelli; Laodice - Anna Medici; Arasse - Caterina Luzzi. Pandolfini adds, "Attori ne' Balli: Gaetano Andreozzi, Giovanni Battista Galantini, Filippo Vicedomini, Andrea Marchi, Giuseppe Paoli, Teresa Colonna, Maddalena Formigli detta la Mora (ballò sola), Felice Banti, Teresa Romolini, Giuditta Falchini, Stella Bicocchi."

Comment: Susier records on date shown: "L'impresario fu il Cav.e Grifoni con altri Cavalieri e vi cantava Caffariello, et altri virtuosi. Il detto Cav.e Grifoni seguiterà anco questo Carnevale et il Direttore della musica fù l'Orlandini Maestro di Cappella."

1748[13] 29 ix
Pergola

L'ARTASERSE. Dramma per musica da rappresentarsi in Firenze nel teatro di via della Pergola nell'autunno dell'anno 1748. sotto la protezione della Sac. Ces. Real Maestà di Francesco I. Imperadore de' Romani [etc.]. Firenze, Cosimo Maria Pieri, 1748.
S Uu.

Text: Pietro Metastasio, not mentioned, but same as 1739[9] and 1744[2].

Music: Anonymous. Pavan says Davide Perez; Morini, Leonardo Vinci. Scores by both composers in I Nc and Vnm.

Cast: Artaserse - Pietro Venturini; Arbace - Gaetano Majorana Caffarelli; Mandane - Girolama Tearelli; Semira - Anna Medici; Artabano - Gio: Batista Pinacci; Megabise - Caterina Luzzi. Ballets are listed. Pandolfini adds, "Attori ne' Balli: Gaetano Andreozzi, Gio. Battista Galantini, Filippo Vicedomini, Andrea Marchi, Giuseppe Paoli, Teresa Colonna, Maddalena Formigli detta la Mora (ballò sola), Felice Banti, Teresa Romolini, Giuditta Falchini, Stella Bicocchi."

Comment: Susier records the performance on date shown.

1748[14] 15 x
Cocomero

Susier: Compagnia d'Istrioni venuti per stare tutto il carnevale." I Fas (Reggenza 631, c. 103) records the permission granted to Antonio Marchesini for performances during autumn and the following carnival (in I Fac [Infuocati], p. 197). In c. 105 permission is granted to perform after the octave of Easter (14 iv).

1748[15] 6 xi

Death notice in Susier for "Pellegrino Sabatini che sonava la viola e aveva l'incumbranza d'invitare a tutte le musiche di Palazzo."

1748[16] 26 xii
Pergola

ARMINIO. Dramma per musica da rappresentarsi in Firenze nel teatro di via della Pergola nel Carnovale dell'anno 1749. Firenze, Cosimo Maria Pieri, s.d.
I Fc, Rn.

Text: Anonymous rewriting of Salvi's *Arminio* of 1703[3]. Characters and plot are the same but the text is new.

Music: Anonymous, but by Gio. Battista Pescetti, whose music is lost. Morini assigns the music to Galuppi who composed the music for Venice, 1747 (Sonneck, p. 154). Pavan does not hazard a guess. Pandolfini, see below, says that Pescetti was the maestro di cappella and Susier positively asserts that he was the composer. He also wrote the music for the second opera of the season, *Farnace*.

Roles: Arminio, Segeste, Tusnelda, Ramise, Sigismondo, Varo.

Cast: Clorinda Landi, Anna Medici, Caterina Luzzi, Girolama Tearelli, Giovanni Battista Pinacci, Pietro Venturini. Maestro di Cappella: Giovanni Battista Pescetti di Venezia. Attori ne' Balli: Giuseppe Bedotti, Gaetano Andreozzi, Giovanni Battista Galantini, Filippo Vicedomini, Giovanni Andrea Galloni, Angelo Alberti, Teresa Colonna, Maddalena Formigli detta la Mora, Placida Cacioni, Ancilla Cardiori, Teresa Romolini, Anna Franceschi. Inventore de' Balli: Pietro Gugliantini; Sarto - Giuseppe Compostof. Impresario: Sig. Cav.re Ugolino Grifoni. (All information supplied by Pandolfini.)

Comment: Susier on date shown: "[In via della Pergola] *Arminio* drama per musica et il compositore della musica fu il Pescietti fatto venire di Venezia dal Cav. Grifoni impresario." See p. 54 for the contract with Landi.

1748[17] 26 xii
Tintori

Susier lists the following addition to *Arminio*:
"Nel Corso de' Tintori *La Zaira* tradotta dal Francese e *L'oracolo* con applauso." [Allacci, col. 945: *La Zaira*. Tragedia di M. Voltaire tradotta (in prosa). -in Firenze, nella St. Imperiale. 1748. -di Giuseppe Finoti.]

Coletti

"Nel teatro in via del Giardino *Sesostri* in prosa." [This is perhaps the *opera in prosa* listed by Allacci, cols. 927f., published in Venice, by Rossetti in 1716, written by Pietro Pariati.]

Borgo de' Greci

"*Le gelose cautele* del [Mattias Maria] Bartolommei tutte in prosa, e non vi fu altro opere in musica che in via della Pergola che così ordinò la Reggenza." [Allacci, col. 388, cites publications in Bologna, Manolessi, 1669, and Longhi, s.a., di M.M.B.]

Orsanmichele

"Nel teatrino da Orsanmichele cominciarno con *Pastorale*. Et in molte case particolare recitavano pastorali, et per tutto si pagava."

Cocomero

"Nel teatro di via del Cocomero vi fu una compagnia d'Istrioni." The company is Antonio Marchesini's. See 1748[14].

1749[1] 6 i
Tintori

AVARIZIA PIÙ ONORATA NELLA SERVA CHE NELLA PADRONE ovvero LA SORELLINA DI DON PILONE. Commedia [in prosa] recitata in Siena dagli Accademici Rozzi l'anno 1712 e di nuovo nel carnevale dell'anno 1749. Firenze, Paperini, 1749.
I Fn.

Text: Girolamo Gigli. See 1740[3].

Comment: Susier records date and further, "Nel teatro de' Cadenti *Il Don Pilone* del Gigli commedia non più sentita per essere stata proibita per costume cattivo." Concerning the Coletti he continues, "Mutarono anche e fecero *Il Coriolano* opera." [Possibly the *tragedia* recorded by Allacci, col. 219, published in Bologna, Lelio della Volpe, 1734, composed in *versi sciolti* by Giovanni Pietro Cavazzoni.]

Coletti

1749² 7 i
Cocomero

Il principe Eugenio in Belgrado.
Susier: "Nel teatro di via del Cocomero gli Istrioni fecero un opera intitolata il *Principe Eugenio in Belgrado* con molti abbattimenti, che molto piacque e la fecero tre volte con gran concorso di popolo, che non è così del Teatro di Via della Pergola, che fanno pochi Bullettini." [This unsuccessful opera would have been *Arminio*, 1748¹⁶, continuing in January.] The concession of the theater to Giuseppe Maleci is on p. 207 in I Fac (Infuocati) which is cross-indexed among *opere in musica*.

1749³ 10 i
Borgo de' Greci

Susier records the following changes:
"Mutarono commedia e fecero una commedia intitolata *Ciò che pare non è* del Fagioli." [Allacci, col. 192, adds the ossia, il *Cicisbeo sconsolato*. Commedia (in prosa) -in Firenze, per il Moücke, 1732, vol. VI, p. 139.]

Orsanmichele

"Fecero *la Fortunata disperazione del Principe Celimauro* del Dott. Salvi." [See 1696¹.]

Tintori

"*Il Bugiardo* tradotto dal francese." [Allacci, col. 853, cites this *commedia di Pietro Cornelio tradotta* (in prosa) -in Firenze, per il Viviani, 1749 -d'Incerto.]

1749⁴ 10 i
Pergola

FARNACE. Dramma per musica da rappresentarsi in Firenze nel teatro di via della Pergola nel carnevale dell'anno 1749. sotto la protezione del Francesco I. [etc.]. Firenze, Cosimo Maria Pieri, s.d.
I Bc, Fc(2); US Wc.

Text: Antonio Maria Lucchini, not mentioned, but identified by comparison with the Venetian libretto of 1739, with which it shares at least some of the text and roles (Sonneck, p. 477).

Music (lost): Gio. Batista Pescetti di Venezia as stated on page 5.

Cast: Farnace - Girolama Tearelli; Tamiri - Clorinda Landi; Selinda - Anna Medici; Aquilio - Giovanni Battista Pinacci; Pompeo - Pietro Venturini; Gilade - Caterina Luzzi. Maestro di Cappella: Gio. Battista Pescetti di Venezia. Pandolfini adds, "Attori ne' Balli: Giuseppe Bedotti [etc. as for *Arminio*, 1748¹⁶. Also same inventori, sarto, and impresario.]"

Comment: The date is Susier's. He erroneously attributes the libretto to Metastasio.

1749⁵ 24 i
Tintori

Susier comments that all the theaters continue their performances and that *Zaira* is the most successful (1748¹⁷, Tintori). This may be a new translation, however, by Padre Ambrogi Gesuita (Allacci, cols. 945f).

1749⁶ 26 i
Coletti

Susier's list of new plays:
"*Lo Stilicone*." [Allacci, col. 932, lists a translation of this tragedy by Thomas Corneille in Bologna, Longhi, s.d. Crescimbeni, pp. 106-108, identifies Padre Don Felippo Merelli as the translator for a performance in Rome. It is probably the same as that used in Florence. See Freeman, p. 325.]

Borgo de' Greci

"[*Un vero*] *Amor non cura interesse* del Fagioli." See 1733².

Tintori

"*L'Inquieto* [sic] e *i Letigante* tradotti dal francese." [The second is possibly *I Litiganti overo il Giudice impazzito* opera satiri comica in prosa di Girolamo Gigli published in his *Opere Nuove* (1704), copy in I MOe.]

Orsanmichele	"*L'Amico nemico*, burletta."

1749[7] 3 ii
Cocomero

Coletti
Tintori

Susier: "Nel teatro di via del Cocomero ove recitano gli Istrioni, facevano la loro commedia e nel isteso tempo nel salone dove giocano vi era festa da Ballo ove concorreva molte maschere ... Nel teatro di via del Giardino mutarno opera e fecero *il Cidd'* con nuovi balli. Nel teatro de' Cadenti poco piacquerò le opere del *Inquieto* e *Letiganti* tradotte dal Francese e rimesserò su la *Zaira* con gran concorso."

1749[8] 5 ii
Tintori

Susier: "Nel detto teatro de' Cadenti mutarono commedia e fecero *Il Giocatore* tradotto dal francese."

1749[9] 19 ii
Tintori

Susier: "Nel teatro del Corso de' Tintori detto i Cadenti tutte le Domeniche di Quaresima vi fu accademia di canto e suono, fatte fare da varii Cavalieri."

1749[10] 13 iv
Cocomero

CATONE IN UTICA. Dramma per musica da rappresentarsi in Firenze nel teatro di via del Cocomero nella Primavera dell'anno 1749. Firenze, Giovanni Battista Stecchi, 1749.
I Fc.

Text: Pietro Metastasio, not mentioned, see 1729[1]. Dedication to Cassandra Cerretani calls it "primo della corrente Primavera." Page 4, "... il presente dramma in qualche parte alterato ..."

Music: Anonymous, but probably G.M. Orlandini who composed the music for the second opera of the season below.

Cast: Catone - Giuseppe Meisner; Cesare - Giuseppe Porna; Marzia - Angiola Paganini; Emilia - Rosa Tagliarini; Arbace - Caterina Bartolini; Fulvio - Eleonora Castelli.

Comment: On date shown, Susier: "... la prima *Catone in Utica* di Metastasio. Direttore fu Orlandini." Also mentions *La costanta Rosalba* at Orsanmichele, probably the same work performed at the Coletti in 1742[1] (see comment).

Orsanmichele

1749[11] 1 v
Albergo del
Vecchio

Il pazzo furbo, burletta.
Susier provides the above information. Burletta is normally used to indicate a comic opera, but none by that title is known.

1749[12] 21 v
Cocomero

ARSACE. Dramma per musica da rappresentarsi in Firenze nel teatro di via del Cocomero nella Primavera del corrente anno 1749. sotto la protezione di Francesco I. [etc.]. Firenze, Giovanni Battista Stecchi, 1749.
I Fm.

Text: Antonio Salvi. It is his *Amore e maestà* (1715[2]) with changes.

Music: Giuseppe Maria Orlandini, as stated on page 7.

Cast: Arsace - Giuseppe Porna; Mitrane - Caterina Bartolini; Megabise - Maria Eleonora Castelli; Artabano - Giuseppe Meisner; Statire - Maria Angiosa Paganini; Rosmiri - Rosa Tagliarini.

Comment: The date is Susier's. He also records the performance of *Zaira*, opera regia at Orsanmichele, which presumably is a testimony to the play's great success since it was performed in the preceding carnival.

Orsanmichele

1749[13] **14 vii**
Cocomero
Tintori

Susier records a company of *Istrioni* at the Cocomero following *Catone* above and at the Tintori, a company of *figurine*.

1749[14] **28 vii**
Orsanmichele

Susier notes the change at Orsanmichele to *l'Oracolo*, continuing its repetition of the successful plays performed at the Tintori in the preceding carnival.

1749[15] **20 viii**
Pergola

IPERMESTRA. Dramma per musica da rappresentarsi in Firenze nel teatro di via della Pergola nel'autunno dell'anno 1749. sotto la protezione di Francesco I. [etc.]. Firenze, Cosimo Maria Pieri, s.d.
I Fc; S Uu.

Text: Pietro Metastasio, not mentioned, but the text is published in his *Opere* III, p. 149, where the first performance is stated to be Vienna, 1744, with the music of J.A. Hasse.

Music: Anonymous, but possibly Gio. Battista Pescetti who is named as the director of the music by Susier. Pavan does not know the composer; Morini proposes Giuseppe Bertoni, who composed the music for Venice, 1748 (Sonneck, p. 637).

Cast: Danao - Giuseppe Baratti; Ipermestra - Maria Maddalena Parigi; Linceo - Filippo Elisi; Elpinice - Caterina Pilai; Plistene - Angiola Tani; Adrasto - Casimiro Venturini. Inventore de' Balli: Sig. Pietro Gugliantini.
Pandolfini adds: "Ballerini: Francesco Turchi, Gaspero Pieri, Andrea Marchi detto Morino, Giovanni Michele Costa, Niccolo Nastri; Ballerine: Barbera Cambi, Adriana Sacco, Maddalena Formigli, Anna Pacini, Maria Burgioni, Libera Sacco, Giuditta Falchini.

Comment: Susier on above date records *Impermestra* [*sic*] at the Pergola, "Ugolino Grifoni fu Impresario, e direttore della musica il Pescietti veneziano, fatto venire di detta città a posto."

1749[16] **24 ix**
Pergola

LA CLEMENZA DI TITO. Dramma per musica da rappresentarsi in Firenze nel teatro di via della Pergola nell'autunno dell'anno 1749. sotto la protezione (di) Francesco I. [etc.]. Firenze, Cosimo Maria Pieri, s.d.
I Bc, Fc.

Text: Pietro Metastasio, not mentioned, but same as 1736[5].

Music: Anonymous. Unknown to Pavan; Morini supposes Antonio Gaetano Pampani who composed the music for Venice, 1748 (Sonneck, p. 296). Since the cast, the ballet master, and the dancers are the same for the summer opera, *Ipermestra* above, it is likely that Grifoni served again as impresario in the fall and that Pescetti was again asked to compose the music.

Cast: Tito Vespasiano - Giuseppe Baratti; Vitellia - Maria Maddalena Parigi; Servilla - Caterina Pilai; Sesto - Filippo Elisi; Aumio - Angiola Tani; Publio - Casimiro Venturini; Balli di Direzione del Sig. Pietro Gugliantini.
Ballerini: [same as *Ipermestra*, 1749[15]].

Comment: The date is Susier's.

1749[17] **26 xii**

MEROPE. Drama per musica da rappresentarsi in Firenze nel teatro di via

Pergola

della Pergola nel Carnevale dell'anno 1750. sotto la protezione della Sac. Ces. Real Maestà di Francesco I. [etc.]. Firenze, Cosimo Maria Pieri, s.d. I Bc, Fc, Rsc.

Text: Apostolo Zeno, as stated. It has been greatly altered by comparison with 1743[3].

Music: Anonymous. Pavan's and Morini's assumption of a repetition of D.M.B. Terradeglias's music, probably used in 1743[3], is unwarranted because of the extensive changes in the text. The first scene is the same and the scene-structure is also the same thereafter, but the text is different. Possibly a continuation of Pescetti's cooperation with Grifoni.

Cast: Merope - Maddalena Parigi; Epitide - Filippo Elisi; Polifonte - Giuseppe Baratti; Argio - Caterina Pilai; Trasimede - Angiola Tani; Licisio - Casimiro Venturini; Amassandro - Lorenzo Giorgetti. Inventore de' Balli: Pietro Gugliantini; Sarto, Giuseppe Compostof; Impresario, Sig. Cav.e Ugolino Grifoni. Same dancers as *Ipermestra*, 1749[15].

Comment: Susier on date shown: "A dì 26 Dicembre. In detta sera s'aprirono i teatri ordinati della reggenza, p[er] tante che il Cav.e Ugolino Grifoni Impresario del Teatro di Via della Pergola si trovava molto al disotto, et indebitato, ne fare ricorso in Reggenza et ottenere, molti Teatri non facessero Comedie con speranza d'avessi a ricattare che si crede che non vogli riuscire. Fu ordinato che il teatro di Via del Cocomero facessi quando non fa via della Pergola, et il Teatro de' Cadenti solamente le feste, et tutti gli altri Teatri stiano serrati, si come molti pastorali che si facevano in diverse case e teatri a pagho sono tutte levate, eccettate alcune, che non si paga." His list, condensed, is *La Merope* at the Pergola, *La Z[a]ira* in

Cocomero
Tintori
Borgo de' Greci

prose at the Cocomero, *Ines tragedia* and *Il Fiorentino* [?] "in prosa tradotte dal Francese" at the Cadenti, and *Bass'in fuga* at the Borgo de' Greci, "pero senza pago." See Allacci, col. 138, for last.

1750[1] 1 i
Cocomero

La squola delle madri e Le grazie [in prosa] tradotte dal francese. Susier on date shown. The first is doubtless Molière. See Comment, 1741[12]. For explanation of the silence in 1750 of all theaters except the Pergola and Cocomero see pp. 113 to 116.

1750[2] 4 i
Cocomero

L'avaro, tradotto dal francese. Susier. See 1747[5].

1750[3] 16 i
Cocomero

Irrisoluti, tradotta dal francese. Susier. Probably the same as the play cited by Allacci, col. 893, *L'Irresoluto*. Commedia di M. Destouches tradotta (in prosa) -in Milano, per gli Eredi dell'Agnelli, 1754. Nel Tomo I del Teatro Comico dell'autore.-da Madama Serbelloni.

1750[4] 20 i
Pergola

ARIANNA E TESEO. Dramma per musica da rappresentarsi in Firenze nel teatro di via della Pergola nel carnevale dell'anno 1750. sotto la protezione della Sac. Ces. Real Maestà di Francesco I. [etc.]. Firenze, Cosimo Maria Pieri, s.d. I Fc, Rn.

Text: Pietro Pariati, not mentioned, but the text is the same as 1728[3] with many variations.

Music: Gio. Batista Pescetti, as stated on page 4.

Cast: Arianna - Maddalena Parigi; Teseo - Filippo Elisi; Minosse - Giuseppe Baratti; Laodice - Caterina Pilai; Alceste - Angiola Tani; Tancrede - Casimiro Venturini. [Rest as in *Ipermestra*, 1749[15]].

Comment: Susier records the change of the opera at the Pergola.

1750[5] 25 i
Cocomero

Il superbo, tradotta dal francese.
Susier. The seventh in the marathon of French plays in translation at the Cocomero! See 1745[10].

1750[6] 23 iii

Susier: "Lunedi Santo. Fù l'ultimo giorno del Carnevale degli Ebrei e fecero in Ghetto una commedia in prosa del Fagioli e vi era maschere, cosa insolita ne' mai costumata nei tempi passati."

1750[7] 5 iv; 21 vi
Cocomero

La maestra. Burletta in musica.

Text: Probably this is the libretto by Antonio Palomba (with or without alterations by Carlo Goldoni [Venice, 1748, entitled *La scuola moderna*]). Palomba's libretto was first performed in Bologna, 1747, with the music of Gioacchino Cocchi, according to Ricci, p. 462 and Sonneck, p. 712. Other titles are: *La maestra di scuola*, and *La maestra di buon gusto.*

Music: Doubtless a pasticcio, perhaps retaining some of Cocchi's music, but the presence of the composer, Alessandro Felici, as the director of the opera, would make it highly likely that he supplied some of the music also.

Comment: Susier is the only source for this performance. He identifies the impresario as *il Pertici* [Pietro] and the *direttore* as *il Felici* [Alessandro]. This is designated *P[rima] burletta*. On June 21, *La Maestra* again returns, replacing *La commedia in commedia* (1750[11]).

Pertici was in Florence by the invitation of Count Richecourt who was planning to establish at the Cocomero a permanent national Tuscan theater. His project was accomplished in 1751 and Pertici became the permanent director of the Cocomero. See p. 113 for a *Memorial* in I Fas concerning this Tuscan theater.

1750[8] 3 v
Cocomero

I CICISBEI DELUSI. Drama giocoso per musica da rappresentarsi in Firenze nel teatro di via del Cocomero nella primavera dell'anno 1750. Firenze, Giovanni Battista Stecchi, 1750.
I Bc, Mb.

Text: Carlo Antonio Vasini Bolognese, not mentioned, but the libretto is the same as *Li tre cicisbei ridicoli* published in Bologna, 1748, by Sassi (unknown to Ricci), in which the author is named.

Music: Anonymous. The composer for the Bolognese libretto was Natale Resta, Maestro di Cappella Milanese.

Roles: Giscone, Bice, Modulina, Lidia, Lindoro, Ottavio, Cuccamondo, Corina.

Comment: Susier on date shown announces the "2a burletta." On 13 v he reports: "Nascita dell'Imperator. In detta sera nel Teatro di via del Cocomero vi fu la solita Burletta in musica, et il Sig. Conte di Richecourt fece trattenimento di gioco."

1750⁹ 18 v
Cocomero

Il Tamburo notturno tradotto dal francese.
This translation was published, according to Allacci, col. 933, whose notice reads: "*il Tamburro*. Commedia (in versi). — in Firenze, per il Bonducci, 1750 in 8 — del Senatore Giulio Ruccellai, Fiorentino, Cavaliere di S. Stefano. — Questa Commedia fu trasportata in prosa Francese dall'Originale Inglese per M. Destouches, e dal Francese mirabilmente tradotta, e parafrasata dal Cavaliere suddetto." Being in verse, it is possible that it contained at least incidental music. But we have not seen a copy.
Susier gives no further information than the above.

1750¹⁰ 29 v
Cocomero

Ines tragedia tradotta dal fran[ces]e.
Susier is the only source. Allacci records an earlier translation: "Ines de Castro. Tragedia (in prosa, in cinque atti) tradotta dal Francese di M. Houdard de la Motte, e recitata da' Signori Cavalieri del Collegio Clementino (di Roma) nelle vacanze del Carnevale dell'anno 1728 - in Roma, nella Stamperia del Chracas. 1728 -d'Incerto." See 1749¹⁷.

1750¹¹ 2 vi
Cocomero

La commedia in commedia. Burletta in musica.
Text: Francesco Vanneschi (see 1731⁸).
Music: Probably by this time thoroughly a pasticcio but based upon Rinaldo di Capua's score (see 1741⁸).
Comment: Susier again is the only source. That this is the much-performed opera by Vanneschi and di Capua is indicated by the presence of Pietro Pertici at the Cocomero in April and May (see 1750⁷ and 1750⁸).

1750¹² 5 vi

Death notice in Susier for Giovanni Battista Pinacci: "Nella Chiesa S. Maria in Campo fu esposto G. Batt.a Pinacci di anni 55, morto d'un accidente in poche ore senza poter parlare. Il detto Pinacci era fiorentino, e musico, e comico bravo. Cantava di tenore, aveva preso per moglie la Bagniolesi [*sic*] Musica, e ne ebbe figli che son vivi; andava assieme con la sua moglie a recitare per i primi Teatri de gl'Italia, et a lasciato della roba."

1750¹³ 9 viii
Cocomero

ATTILIO REGOLO. Dramma per musica, ultimo drama del Sig. Abate Pietro Metastasio da recitarsi nel teatro in via del Cocomero l'estate dell' anno 1750. Nuovamente stampato e ricorretto e dedicato al merito ragguardevole della Illustrissima Signora Contessa Claudia Feroni ne' Guicciardini. Firenze, Stamperia Imperiale, 1750.
I Bc, Fn, Vgc.

Text: As stated. Published in his *Opere* III, p. 29, where the first performance is stated to be Dresden, carnival of 1750, with music by J.A. Hasse. Dedication signed by Domenico Umiliano Guagni, Impresario.
Music: According to Susier, it was recited without music, probably because of the regulations imposed by the Reggenza. For a full discussion, see p. 111.

Roles: Regolo, Manlio, Attilia, Publio, Barce, Licinio, and Amilcare.

Comment: On date shown, Susier records: "Nel teatro di via del Cocomero preso dal Guagni fu fatta la p[rim]a commedia intitolata *Attilio Regolo* del Abate Metastasio in versi ma recitata come in prosa con balli e decorazioni."

1750[14] 6 ix
Cocomero

Don Pilogio [equals *Don Pilone* di Girolamo Gigli] e doppo *Lo Sciocco* e *L'Oracolo*.
Susier provides the dates. For *Don Pilogio* see 1740[3]. Allacci, col. 702, lists two possibilities for the second comedy: *Lo Sciocco*, commedia, Venice, Collesini, 1604 (and later editions) by Cesare Caporali, and *Lo Sciocco deluso*, commedia in prosa, Vienna, Heyninger, 1729, by an unknown author. *L'Oracolo* was performed previously 1748[17] and 1749[14].

1750[15] 20 ix
Cocomero

La pupilla and *l'Inquieto*, tradotte dal francese.
Cited by Susier. The title of the first suggests Goldoni's intermezzi (see 1737[2]), but the stated character of a translation makes it unlikely. The second was performed in 1749[6] and 1749[7].

1750[16] 4 x

Susier: "E venuto ordine della Reggenza che possi andare le Maschere la sera al Teatro di via del Cocomero per durare tutto il dì 20 detto mese." There is no mention of the work being performed. However, Chatfield-Taylor, p. 605, cites a performance in September, 1750, of Carlo Goldoni's *Il Padre di Famiglia* at the Cocomero.

1750[17] 15 x
Cocomero

"*Quanto più si vanta, peggio si fa*, commedia" [in prosa?].
Susier's report.

1750[18] 4 xi
Cocomero

"*La Pimpa Locandiera* del Capeci di Roma in prosa, è stata fatta cinque anni fa ne' Cadenti" [see 1742[14] and 1744[6]].

1750[19] 29 xi
Cocomero

"*Arlecchino Medico per forza*," [in prosa?].
Susier's report.

1750[20] 1 xii
Cocomero

Jefte, opera sacra.
Susier: "Nel Teatro di via del Cocomero benche fusse entrato l'avvento recitorno un opera sacra intitolata *Jefte*."

1750[21] 26 xii
Pergola

MITRIDATE. Dramma per musica da rappresentarsi nel teatro di via della Pergola nel carnevale dell'anno 1751. sotto la protezione della Sac. Ces. Real Maestà di Francesco I. Firenze, Cosimo Maria Pieri, 1751.
I Fm.

Text: Apostolo Zeno, not mentioned, but the text was published in vol. VII, p. 153 of his *Poesie* where the first date of publication is stated to be Vienna, 1728. The music was by Caldara.

Music: Anonymous. This libretto was performed in Venice, 1730, with the music of Giovanni Antonio Giai, and Rome, 1730, with the music of Nicolà Porpora. However, Giuseppe Orlandini again is the most likely composer since he is also the impresario for this performance. No score known by any of the three composers.

Cast: Mitridate - Giuseppe Ciacchi; Farnace - Maria Maddalena Parigi; Ladige - Rosa Scarlatti; Aristia - Isabella Gandini; Euridea - Rosa Tagliavini; Gordio - Luigi Ristorini; Dorilao - Anna Barchetti. Pandolfini adds: "Non ci furon Balli, ma bensì gl'Intermezzi Buffi, e recitarono Agata Paganini, Carlo Paganini, Niccola Petri, Anton Valletti. Sarto, Giuseppe Compostof. Impresario, Giuseppe Orlandini e altri." The libretto omits the intermezzi and any mention of the actors, etc.

Cocomero

Comment: Susier records on date shown. "Si aprirano i Teatri. E la Reggenza ordinò che non vi fusse altro che, due Teatri a pago, cioè quello di Via della Pergola che fa l'Orlandini, e quello di via Cocomero che fa il Guagni in Prosa. Nel teatro di via della Pergola rappresentano *Mitridate*, dramma per musica. Nel Teatro di via del Cocomero *La Vedova scaltra* in prosa che ebbe applauso grande." Pandolfini appends a note: "In quest'anno stante il Bruno p[er] la morte della madre del'Imperatrice non furon p[er] messe le Maschere, e così il Teatro ebbe poco concorso." *La vedova scaltra*, probably by Carlo Goldoni, had been performed for the first time in Modena the previous summer. See Chatfield-Taylor, p. 605.

FOR THE PURPOSES OF PRESENTING THE ENTIRE CONTENTS OF PANDOLOFINI'S CHRONOLOGY OF THE PERGOLA, THE REMAINING THREE YEARS ARE PRINTED BELOW ALTHOUGH THEY EXTEND BEYOND THE LIMITS OF OUR CHRONOLOGY.

1751

Opere del Carnevale

Mitridate
(See 1750[21])

Massimiano
(Information duplicates that found under *Mitridate*, 1750[21])

1752   *Antigona*   *Semiramide* (I Bc 7122)

Musici

Natalizia Bisagi Fini di Firenze
Agata Colizi Romana
Anna Galosti
Teresa Migliorini Romana
Orazio Mannotti Senese
Antonio Donnini di Sinigaglia

Inventore de' Balli - Pietro Gugliantini

Ballerini

Vincenzio Nesti di Firenze
Baldassare Albrizi
Giulio Salamon
Gio: Franchi di Bologna
Niccolo Nastri di Firenze
Maria Franchi di Bologna
Teresa Bavanzini
Maria Udini
Vittoria Udini
Eufemia Moretti

Sarto - Gius.e Compostof

Pittore Pietro Anderlini, che rifiori di nuovo la scena di Bosco.

Impresario

Michele Fini Maestro di Musica, quale ammalatosi dopo l'ultima recita del'*Antigona*, ed aggravatosi il male nel di 24. Genn.o ando all'altro mondo nella sera del di 25. giusto nel tempo, che s'era messa in Palco l'opera nuova della *Semiramide*, della quale si proseguiron le Recita per tutto Carnevale, non ostante che la prima Donna fosse moglie di detto Fini.

1753   Opere del Carnevale

Didone abbandonata   e   Cesare in Egitto
    (I Bc 6210)

Musici

Margherita Giacomazzi
Maria Maddalena Parigi
Monaca Bonanni
Chiara Minucciani
Teresa Migliorini
Andrea Masoro

Inventore de' Balli

Brunoro

Giuseppe Brunoro
Niccolo Cambi
Gaetano Montelatici
Filippo Beccari
Maria Burgioni
Caterina Bartolini
Colomba Beccari
Caterina Stachini

Maestro di cappella

Giuseppe Orlandini

Sarto

Giuseppe Compostof

Impresari tutti gli accademici in corpo, e per loro furono eletti Deputati
il Sig. Marche.e Pier Anton Guadagni Principe, Sig. March.e Francesco
de' Frescobaldi Guardaroba maggiore, Sig. March.e Mattias Bartolommei
Provveditore.

ENTRIES WITHOUT DATES

Most of the dateless entries are prologues, intermezzi, and finales. If these have usable titles they are catalogued alphabetically under these titles in capital letters. If there is no convenient title and the work with which they were associated is known, they are catalogued under the title of the associated principal work, the title of which will be in italics.

L'Amor fra i nemici. Prologo per la commedia intitolata . . . . Text probably by Giovanni Cosimo Villifranchi. Ms in I Fn (Magl. VII, B 868, f. 672). Although the prologue is anonymous, it is preceded and followed by prologues by Villifranchi.

The principal comedy is probably that cited by Allacci, col. 842, with the title *Amor tra' nemici* by G.A. Cicognini published in Venice in 1662.

The prologue is preceded by a brief description of the scene. Interlocutori: Natura, Fato, and il Genio.

Amore difende l'innocenza. Prologo [e finale] rappresentato in musica dagli Accademici Imperfetti alla commedia intitolata . . . . In: *Raccolta di opuscoli del Dr. G[iovanni] C[osimo] V[illifranchi]*, pp. 109-124. On page xvi, the author of the comedy is identified as Antonio Fineschi da Radda. A manuscript copy in I Fn (Magl. VII, B 868). Roles: Verità and Interesse. The Imperfetti are active in 1669, 1672 and 1676-1678.

Amore non vuol vendetta. Prologo rappresentato in musica dagli Accademici Imperfetti alla Commedia intitolata . . . . In: *Raccolta di opuscoli del Dr. G[iovanni] C[osimo] V[illifranchi]*, (1737), p. 95.

The author of the principal comedy is identified on page xvi as Antonio Fineschi da Radda. The comedy was published in Bologna, 1691 by Longhi (I MOe, Rca). See preceding.

Astrea. See *Innocenza e giustizia.*

La civil villanella. Prologo per la commedia intitolata . . . . In: *Raccolta di opuscoli del Dr. G[iovanni] C[osimo] V[illifranchi]*, (1737), p. 55.

CONTRASTO DI APOLLO E AMORE. Intermedio.
I Fn (Magl. VII, 356). The Ms is catalogued under [Antonio] Malatesti in a volume of various poetry actually containing works by other poets. Dated 1650 as the date of the Ms itself. The *Contrasto* is obviously intended for music, but no composer is mentioned.

La dama spirito folletto. Prologo rappresentato in musica per la commedia intitolata . . . . In: *Raccolta di opuscoli del Dr. G[iovanni] C[osimo]*

V[*illifranchi*], (1737), p. 125. On page xvi, the author of the principal comedy is identified as Giov. Battista Ricciardi.

DIALOGO DI POESIA GIOCOSA E POESIA GRAVE. Prologo [per musica]. Text possibly by Pietro Susini. Ms in I Fas (Med. F. 6424/7), is apparently a collection of prologues, etc., some of which were performed on the birthdays of Vittoria della Rovere, wife of Ferdinando II. The dialogue is anonymous but it appears among other works by Susini. References to *La bella Partenope.*

DIALOGO PER MUSICA.
Text: Francesco Panciatichi. Ms in I Fn (Magl. VII, 363, p. 245); anon. copy in I Fas (Med. 6424, no. 2), *Pastorale.* Roles: Lidia, Rosalba, and Fileno.

IL DON GILE. Opera del Sig.r Radda Fiorentino [Antonio Fineschi da Radda]. Prose comedy without prologue or intermedii. Ms in I Fn (Magl. VII, B 868).

Il giocatore innamorati. Prologo e finale per .... In: *Rime piacevoli di Gio. Batista Fagiuoli*, parte quinta (1733), p. 268.

IL LADRO BURLATO. Farsa. In: *Rime piacevoli di Gio. Batista Fagiuoli*, parte quinta (1733), p. 349. Roles: Marchionne vecchio, Meo suo servitore.

LE MINIERE DELL'ORO. Prologo rappresentato in musica dagli Accademici del Casino alla commedia intitolata *Il trionfo del savio in corte.* In: *Raccolta di opuscoli del Dr. G*[*iovanni*] *C*[*osimo*] *V*[*illifranchi*] (1737), p. 19. On page xvi the author of the principal comedy is identified as Marchese Mattias Maria Bartolommei. The Accademici del Casino flourished from 1678-1686.

IL MUGNAJO DI SEZZATE, E IL PAGGIO DEL SIG. BENEDETTO FEDINI. Prologo fatto nella villa di esso nel sud[ett]o luogo.
Text: Anonymous. Ms in I Fn (Magl. VII, B 868, f. 639).

LA PIETÀ DI SABINA. Drama musicale. In: *Poesie dramatiche di Giovanni Andrea Moniglia*, parte terza (1698), pp. 157-224. From the argument: "Questo drama fu composto per servire alla Serenissima Granduchessa Vittoria di Toscana, e messo in musica dal Padre Lorenzo Cattani Maestro di Cappella dell'Illustrissima, e Sacra Religione de' Signori Cavalieri di S. Stefano in Pisa, ma per ancora non è comparito su le scene, nè alle Stampe."

Polifemo geloso. Dramma musicale rappresentato alle Altezze di Toscana sotto nome di Vegghia. Genova, Pavoni, 1622. Text by Gabriello Chiabrera published by Pavoni with other works (see 1608[1]) by Chiabrera. See Allacci, col. 636, but when it was performed is unknown.

Prologo per una commedia in villa. In: *Rime piacevoli di Gio. Batista Fagiuoli*, parte quinta (1733), p. 277.

SERVA SCALTRITA SA FARSI PADRONA. Intermezzi. In: *Rime piacevoli di Gio. Batista Fagiuoli*, parte quinta (1733), p. 317. Roles: Dorina Serva, Vanesio Padrone.

Il trionfo del Savio. See *Le miniere dell'oro.*

Il veglino. Finale alla P.a commedia del Casino Intitolato . . . .

Text: Cosimo Villifranchi. Ms in I Fn (Landau Finaly 261, pp. 5-55), and a second Ms of which we have recorded only the title but which gives the authorship shown. Roles: Primo Gentilhuomo (or Cavaliere), Secondo Gentilhuomo (or Cavaliere), and Dottore. See above *Le Miniere dell'oro.*

NOTICES OF COMPOSERS AND SINGERS
EXTRACTED FROM
THE DIARY OF NICOLO SUSIER AFTER 1750

1752 24 i   Morto Michele Fini Napoletano e Compositore di Musica e direttore dell'
opere in musica che si fanno presentemente in Via della Pergola. E morto
di Colica in tre giorni. Aveva moglie che presentemente recitava da prima
donna in d[ett]o t[eatr]o.

1753 2 i   Morta Maddalena Pieri detta la Polpetta. Musica . . . di anni 70 . . . era di
bassa nascità che per vivere raccoglieva per le strade lo sterco di cavallo e
per ciò gli rimase il nome detto Le Polpette con la Teresa sua sorella, che
si è maritata al Branchi speziale, che era ajutante di camera del Gran Duca
Gio: Gastone, et in oggi tiene Bottegha in Mercato Nuovo.
   La detta Polpetta era protetta dal Marchese Casimiro del [sic] Albizzi
(La sorella [i.e. Teresa] dal Marchese Vincenzio) e Torrigiani, i quali vi
spesero di gran danari e elle messero insieme molte migliaia di scudi.

1753 14 iv   Morta Vittoria Tesi. [Susier describes the public sale of her property,
then continues:] La detta Tesi detta la Moretta per sopranome stante che
suo Padre era Lacche detto il Moretto e serviva Checco de Castris Musico
e Favorito del Serenissimo Principe Ferd[inando] figlio di Cos[imo]
Terzo, et avendo questa sua unica figlia la messe a fare la Ballerina e dopo
la Musica et era brava Comica.
   Seguì l'accidente che Checco suo Padrone perse la grazia del Principe
gli convenne andarsene a stare a Roma e poco doppo seguì la Morte di
detto Principe Ferdinando.
   Il povero Moretto rimase senza Provisione, Miserabile e se ne andò
con detta sua Figlia ad abitare a Bologna e di li se ne andò in Pollonia,
ove il ne s'innamoro di Lei e fece gran ricchezze, e per vari accidenti
seguiti gli convenne ritornare a Bologna, ove s'innamoro d'un bel giovine
del Casato de Tramontini che esercitava il mestiere del Barbiere.
   Doppo poco tempo venne ad abitare a Firenze e si trattava come
una Principessa.
   Presentemente si trova a Vienna e con tutto ciò che sia in stà assai
avanzata vi a fatta gran Fortuna e richezza per essere Favorita da un
ricco Principe d'Ungheria.

1756 3 vi   Morto Il Marchese Giuseppe Ridolfi, protettore di Musiche e fra esse vi
era la Bagniolessi Pinacci che era sua favorita.

1756 3 viii   Morto il Rapacioli musico morto d'Idropisia d'anni 67. Era fiorentino e
musico soprano, et era stato molto tempo fuori in particolare in Ispagna
al servizio di Filippo V.

1759 27 i   È venuto nuove di Siena che sia morto Antonio Bernardi detto il Senesino
musico soprano famosissimo ove fece gran richezza in Inghilterra et in altro
parti d'Italia.

1760 25 v   È venuto di Bologna che sia morto in detta Città Carestino Musico Soprano.

INDEX
BY
CATEGORY

LIBRETTISTS

If the author is known with some degree of probability, then the title and date are given.
If the author is mentioned as one of a number of possible librettists, or if he is mentioned
for some other reason, only the date is given.

Acciajuoli, Filippo (N.N.). *Girello*, 1670[1], 1697[5]; 1695[4]; pp. 16, 28, 29, 41, 74.

Adimari, Alessandro. *Caramogi*, 1629[2]; *Giudizio di Paride: Astrea*, intermezzo, 1608[3];
Mascherata cappriciosa di Calai e Zeti, 1628[5]; *Mascherata di donzelle di Ghinea*, 1625[4];
Mascherata fatta in Arno, 1628[6]; Unnamed ballet, 1613[2].

Adimari, Lodovico. *Amante di sua figlia*, 1683[4]; *Carceriere di se medesimo*, 1681[1]; *Gare
dell'amore e dell'amicizia*, 1679[4]; p. 37.

Alborghetti, Giovanni Giacomo. *Cid*, 1736[7].

D'Ambra, Francesco. *Cofanaria*, 1613[4].

Ambrogi, Padre Gesuita. 1749[5].

Apolloni, Giovanni Apollonio. *Dori*, 1661[5], 1670[2]; 1690[2]; p. 28.

Apolloni, Giovanni Filippo. *Con la forza d'amore si vince amor*, 1679[2]; *Dori*, 1661[5], 1670[2];
pp. 28, 70.

Aquilante, Francesco. *Divertimento campestre*, 1739[5]; *Favola di Promoteo*, 1739[5]; *Trionfo
chinese*, 1739[5].

Arcoleo, Antonio. *Rosaura*, 1690[1].

Aureli, Aurelio. *Erismena*, 1661[3]; *Fortune di Rodope e Danira*, 1662[2]; *Massimo Puppieno*, 1698[10].

D'Averara, Pietro. *Ariovisto*, 1702[6].

Azzi, Bernardino. *Sforza del cortigiano*, 1620[5].

Bardi, Cosimo Galterotto. *Vera dama*, 1686[8].

Barlocci, Giovanni. *Finta cameriera*, 1742[3]; *Giardiniera finta contessa*, 1738[5]; 1731[8]; 1742[5]; 1742[9].

Baroncini, Andrea. *Griselsa*, 1638[1].

Bartolommei, Mattias Maria. *Amore opera a caso*, 1668[2]; *Gelose cautele*, 1748[17]; *Inganno vince l'inganno*, 1684[2]; *Sofferanza vince la fortuna*, 1669[3]; *Trionfo del savio*, p. 337; 1672[1], 1673[1]; pp. 28, 32, 74.

Bartolommei, Girolamo, già Smeducci. *Fedeltà d'Alceste*, 1661[7].

Bartorelli, ———. *Guardiani de' pazzi*, 1746[3]; *Spedale de' pazzi*, 1746[4].

Benedetti, Giovanni Battista. *Senarbia*, 1638[2].

Berardi, Cristofan. *Con la moglie e con l'amico ci vuol flemma*, 1680[1]; *Innocenza trionfo degl'inganni*, 1660[2].

Bernardoni, Pietro Antonio. *Astianatte*, 1701[5].

Beverini, Francesco. *Demofonte*, 1699[1].

Biancardi, Bastiano. *See* Lalli, Domenico, pseudonym.

Bisaccioni, Majolino (Conte). *Veremonda, l'Amazzone d'Aragona*, (1652)[3].

Bissaro, Vicentino, Conte Enrico. *Silvia*, 1713[5].

Boldini, Giovanni. *Arsace*, 1736[4].

Bonarelli, Pietro (Conte). *Valore*, 1634[2].

Bonarelli, Prospero. *Pazzia d'Orlando*, 1682[2], 1733[3].

Bonini, Don Severo. *Canzone*, 1608[6].

Borghesi, Ambrogio. *Vedova accorta*, 1745[4]; *Vedova spiritosa*, 1748[10]; 1744[10].

Bottalino, Giovanni Battista. *Roderico*, 1692[1].

Bracciolini, Francesco. *Festa di S. Maria Maddalena*, 1629[1].

Buchino, ———. 1688[4].

Buini, Giuseppe Maria. *See* index of COMPOSERS.

Buonarroti, Michelagnolo. *Balletto della cortesia*, 1614[6]; *Descrizione*, 1600[4]; *Fiera*, 1619[1]; *Giudizio di Paride*: *La nave di Amerigo Vespucci* and *Tempio della pace*, intermezzi, 1608[3]; *Natal d'Ercole*, 1605; *Siringa*, 1634[1]; *Tancia*, 1611[3].

Bussani, D. Giacomo Francesco. *Anacreonte*, 1698[5]; *Cesare in Egitto*, 1735[7]; p. 70.

Calamari, Mario. *Caduta del savio innamorato*, 1657[2], 1691[8]; Commedia senza titolo, 1662[1]; *Forza d'amore e di fortuna*, 1659[2]; 1680[1]; pp. 32, 74.

Calcagni, Carlo. *Innocenza giustificato*, 1693[2].

Caldari, Ferdinando. *Gare fra gli dei*, 1746[5].

Capece, Carlo Sigismondo. *Amor vince fortuna*, 1690[5], 1719[3]; *Ciapo*, 1743[10]; *Figlio delle selve*, 1688[3]; *Locanda di Pimpa e Biaggio*, 1748[3]; *Pimpa locandiera*, 1742[14], 1744[6], 1750[18]; *Pulchinella in giostra*, 1747[5]; 1713[1].

Caporali, Cesare. *Sciocco*, 1750[14].

Cassani, Vincenzo. *Tiranno Eroe*, 1712[4].

Castelletti, Cristoforo. 1695[1].

De Castelli, N. *Ammalato immaginario*, 1725[3], 1732[6]; *Erighetta, e D. Chilone*, 1718[5].

Cavazzoni, Giovanni Pietro. *Coriolano*, 1749[1].

Cecchi, Giammaria. *Ammalata*, 1630; *Serpe*, 1620[2].

Gelli, Giovanni Battista. *Errore*, 1603.

Giacomini, Giuseppe. *Corindo*, 1680[2]; *Rosalba*, 1681[2]; *Sidonio*, 1680[3]; pp. 69, 70.

Giardini, Giambatista. 1717[1].

Gigli, Girolamo. *Avarizia più onorata nella serva che nella padrone*, 1749[1]; *Don Pilogio*, 1740[3], 1744[1], 1750[14]; *Don Pilone*, 1740[3], 1749[1]; *Fede ne' tradimenti*, 1697[1], 1718[4], 1732[10], 1744[11]; *Geneviefa*, 1685[5]; *Griselda*, 1703[2]; *Un Pazzo guarisce l'altro*, 1743[5]; *Squola delle fanciulle*, 1741[12]; *Sposa alla moda*, 1740[6]; *Vizi correnti a l'ultima moda*, 1747[1]; 1749[6].

Ginori, Alessandro. *Ballo di donne turche*, 1615[3].

Ginori, Giovambattista. *Scherzi e balli di giovanette montanine*, 1614[2].

Giuvo, Nicolo. *Radamisto*, 1709[2], 1728[2].

Goldoni, Carlo. *Amor fa l'uomo cieco*, 1744[13]; *Padre di famiglia*, 1750[16]; *Pupilla*, (1737)[2]; *La scuola Moderna*, 1750[7]; *Vedova scaltra*, 1750[21]; 1745[4], 1747[5], 1750[15].

Grassi, P. Simone. *Amazone del celibato*, 1691[5], 1702[5]; *Sponsali fra nemici*, 1744[11].

Guagni, Domenico. *Potenza del vino*, 1732[12]; *Stravaganze dell'ubbriachezza*, 1740[7] (o.t. of preceding); p. 48.

Guarini, Battista. *Dialogo cantato nel Convito Reale da Giunone e Minerva*, 1600[4]; 1595.

Guicciardini, Girolamo. *Bertolina regina d'Arcadia*, 1689[3].

Guidiccioni, Laura. *Disperazione di Fileno*, 1590[2]; *Giuoco della cieca*, 1595; *Satiro*, 1590[1].

Herrico, Scipione. *Deidamia*, 1650[1].

Ivanovich, Cristoforo. 1687[1].

Lacchi, Jacopo. *Ninfe d'Ardenna*, (1616)[6].

Lalli, Domenico (pseudonym of Biancardi, Bastiano). *Amor tirannico*, 1712[2]; *Dalisa*, 1742[4]; *Mariane*, 1725[11]; *Veri amici*, 1714[3], 1735[4]; 1725[12].

Lenzini, Camillo. *Clori*, 1626[4].

Lorenzani, Gianandrea. 1695[1].

Lucchini, Antonio Maria. *Farnace*, 1725[12], 1733[1], 1749[4].

Luchesi, Pompeo. *Amante per odio*, (1693)[1].

Lucini, Giovanni Battista. *Rosaura di Cipro*, 1692[3]; 1690[2].

Maggi, Giacomo. *Carlo re d'Alemagna*, 1700[2]; *Mitridate in Sebastia*, 1704[1], 1716[2]; p. 64.

Malatesti, Antonio. *Alidoro il costante*, 1650[3]; *Contrasto di Apollo e Amore*, prologo, p. 335; *Mascherata di Galeone*, 1657[7]; *Prologo*, 1649.

Mandosio, Prospero. *Innocenza trionfante*, 1748[4].

Manni, Pietro. *Regina floridea*, 1678[2].

Marchi, Antonio. 1709[2]; 1728[2].

Marchi, Damiano (Dottore). *Finta pazza*, 1732[11]; *Nozze di Perseo e d'Andromeda*, 1738[6].

Martello, Pier Jacopo. *Apollo geloso*, 1698[7].

Melosio, Francesco. 1680[3].

Merelli, Don Felippo. *Stilicone*, 1749[6].

Metastasio, Pietro. *Adriano in Siria*, 1733[5], 1745[7]; *Alessandro nelle Indie*, 1732[1], 1736[2], 1740[1], 1743[14], 1748[5]; *Antigono*, 1747[10]; *Artaserse*, 1730[2], 1739[9], 1744[2], 1748[13]; *Attilio Regolo*, 1750[13]; *Catone in Utica*, 1729[1], 1739[8], 1744[12], 1749[10]; *Ciro riconosciuto*, 1746[9]; *Clemenza di Tito*, 1736[5], 1749[16]; *Demetrio*, 1732[13], 1746[12]; *Demofonte*, 1741[2], (1743)[17]; *Demofoonte*, 1746[8]; *Didone abbandonata*, 1725[1], 1734[5], 1741[11], 1747[14], 1753; *Ezio*, 1735[3], 1744[14]; *Gare fra gli dei* (o.t. of *Endimione*), 1746[5]; *Impresario delle canarie*, intermezzi, 1728[5]; *Ipermestra*, 1749[15]; *Issipile*, (1741)[4], 1744[3];

Puccetti, Carlo. 1654[2].

Racine, Jean. 1701[5], 1703[3], 1747[7].
Radda, Antonio Fineschi da. *Amore difende l'innocenza*, p. 335; *Amore non vuol vendetta*, p. 335; *Amore vince la semplicità*, 1698[11], 1700[1], 1710[4]; *Don Gile*, p. 336.
Recanati, Giovambattista. *Demodice*, 1721[6].
Riccardi, Riccardo. *Rime cantate nel giardino*, 1600[6].
Ricci, Agnolo. *Alta Maria*, 1614[5]; *Ballo delle grazie*, 1615[1]; *Ballo delle zingare*, 1615[2]; *Imperiale*, 1614[3]; *Mascherata di ninfe di Senna*, 1613[3]; *Mascherata di villanelle di castello*, 1613[1]; *Nozze degli dei*, 1637[1]; 1611[2]; 1614[4]; 1614[6]; 1616[1]; 1616[5]; 1620[3]; 1637[2]; 1639[1].
Ricciardi, Dott. Giambatista. *Chi non sa fingere non sa vivere*, 1672[2], 1699[5]; *Dama spirito folletto*, p. 335; *Ruota della fortuna*, 1747[2]; *Sposalizio tra sepolcri*, 1695[6]; *Trespolo oste*, 1694[1]; 1688[1]; 1692[5]; p. 23.
Rigogli, Benedetto. *Combattimento e balletto a cavallo*, 1652[2].
Rinuccini, Ottavio. *Dafne*, 1598, 1599, 1600[1], 1600[2], 1600[3], 1604, 1611[1]; *Descrizione*, 1608[3], 1608[5]; *Descrizione della barriera*, 1613[2]; *Euridice*, 1600[5], 1600[8], 1602[3]; *Mascherata di ninfe*, 1611[2]; *Mascherata di ninfe di Senna*, 1613[3]; *Mascherata di selvaggi*, 1614[1]; pp. 74, 75.
Roberti, Girolamo Frigimelica. *Trionfo della libertà*, 1706[6]; 1707[6].
Roccaforte, Gaetano. *Caio Mario*, 1747[11].
Rondinelli, Simone Carlo. *Fonti d'Ardenna*, 1623[1].
Rosa, Salvador. 1732[4]; p. 23.
Rospigliosi, Giulio. 1658[3]; p. 74.
Ruccellai, Giulio (Senatore). *Tamburo notturno*, 1750[9].

Saddumene, Bernardo. *Contadina*, 1735[2]; 1745[9].
Salvadori, Andrea. *Battaglia tra tessitori e tintori*, 1619[2]; *Canzone delle lodi d'Austria*, 1624[2]; *Canzonette in lode della Befana*, 1620[1]; *Caramogi*, 1629[2]; *Descrizione della barriera*, 1613[2]; *Disfida d'Ismeno*, 1628[4]; *Flora*, 1628[3]; *Fonti d'Ardenna*, 1623[1]; *Giuditta*, 1626[3]; *Guerra d'amore*, 1616[1]; *Guerra di bellezza*, 1616[5]; *Intermedi*, 1626[1]; *Liberazione di Tirreno e d'Arnea*, 1617; *Medoro*, 1619[4]; *Olimpia abbandonata da Bireno*, 1622[2]; *Precedenza delle dame*, 1625[3]; *Regina Sant'Orsola*, 1620[4], 1623[4], 1624[3], 1625[1]; *Seraglio degl'Amori*, 1628[1]; *Sposalizio di Medoro ed Angelica*, 1619[4]; p. 74.
Salvi, Antonio. *Adelaide*, 1725[7], 1735[1]; *Amazzoni vinte da Ercole*, 1715[6]; *Amor costante*, 1725[8]; *Amor vince l'odio*, 1715[1], 1731[3]; *Amore e maestà*, 1715[2]; *Andromaca* (o.t. of *Astianatte*), 1728[1], 1742[14]; *Arminio*, 1703[3], 1716[1], 1725[9], 1748[16]; *Arsace* (o.t. of *Amore e maestà*), 1731[9], 1736[4], 1739[3], 1749[12]; *Astianatte*, 1701[5], 1716[3], (1725)[9]; *Avaro*, (1720)[8]; *Barilotto e Slapina*, intermezzi, 1711[3]; *Baronessa d'Arbella*, 1732[7]; *Berenice regina di Egitto*, 1709[1], (1730)[4]; *Bottegaro gentiluomo, Bourgeois gentilhomme*, 1721[5], 1722, 1725[4]; *Dionisio re di Portogallo*, 1707[3]; *Fortunata disperazione del Principe Celimauro*, 1696[1], 1749[3]; *Geloso*, intermezzo, 1719[1]; *Ginevra, Principessa di Scozia*, 1708[2], (1709)[4], 1723[2], 1736[1]; *Giocatore*, 1723[4]; *Gran Tamerlano*, 1706[4], 1730[1]; *Ipermestra*, 1727[1]; *Lucio Papirio*, 1714[2], 1715[5]; *Marito giocatore e la moglie bacchettona*, 1720[7]; *Parassito*, 1712[3]; *Rodelinda regina dei Longobardi*, 1710[5]; *Scanderbegh*, 1718[3]; *Stratonica*, 1707[4], 1689[1]; 1691[1]; 1701[4]; 1707[5]; 1716[5]; 1742[6]; pp. 17, 41, 42, 43, 69, 70, 74, 75.
Sanseverino, A. R. *Ballo e giostra de' venti*, 1608[4].
Saracinelli, Ferdinando. *Armida e l'Amor pudico*, 1637[2]; *Balletto fatto nel battesimo del terzogenito delle Serenissime Altezze di Toscana*, 1614[4]; *Balletto rusticale di contado fiorentini*, 1616[2]; *Ballo delle zingare*, 1615[2]; *Descrizione dell'arrivo d'Amore in Toscana*,

COMPOSERS

If the composer is known with some degree of probability, the title and date are given. If the composer is mentioned as one of a number of possible composers, or if he is mentioned for some other reason, only the date is given.

Abos, Girolamo. *Furberie di Spilletto*, 1743[15]; 1745[7].

Agostino, Pier Simeone. *Adalinda*, 1679[1]; 1678[2].

Albinoni, Tommaso. *Alarico re de' Vandali*, 1701[1]; *Aminta*, 1703[4]; *Ardelinda*, 1733[4]; *Griselda*, 1703[2]; *Tiranno eroe*, 1712[4]; *Vespetta e Pimpinone*, 1712[4], 1718[6]; 1709[2]; 1718[2]; 1719[2], 1720[2]; 1725[1]; 1725[11]; 1726[2]; 1728[2]; 1728[5]; 1734[3]; 1734[5]; 1735[4]; pp. 42, 75.

Aldrovandini, Giuseppe. *Fortezza al cimento*, 1703[1]; *Mitridate in Sebastia*, 1704[1]; p. 68.

Allegri, Lorenzo (Lorenzo del Liuto). *Alta Maria*, 1614[5]; *Balletto* "Elysian Fields," 1614[4]; *Balletto rusticale di contado fiorentini*, 1616[2]; *Ballo delle grazie*, 1615[1]; *Descrizione della barriera*, 1613[2]; *Imperiale*, 1614[3]; *Mascherata di ninfe*, 1611[2]; *Mascherata di ninfe di Senna*, 1613[3]; *Mascherata di villanelle di castello*, 1613[1]; *Notte d'amore*, 1608[2], 1609[1].

Anglesi, Domenico. *Alidoro il costante*, 1650[3]; *Mondo festeggiante*, 1661[2]; *Serva nobile*, 1660[1]; 1720[3].

Araya, Antonio. *Berenice regina d'Egitto*, (1730)[4].

Archilei, Vittoria. *Mascherata di ninfe*, 1611[2]; *Mascherata di ninfe di Senna*, 1613[3]; 1590[1]; 1600[5].

Arrigoni, Carlo. *Scipione nelle Spagne*, 1739[2]; *Sirbace*, 1738[11]; 1744[8]; p. 75.

Auletta, Pietro. *Marchese sgrana*, 1742[10]; 1735[3].

Baglioni, Baccio. *Celio*, 1646[1].

Ballarotti, Francesco. 1702[6].

Bani, Cosimo. *Figlio delle selve*, 1688[3].

Bati, Luca. *Rapimento di Cefalo*, 1600[7].

Belli, Domenico. *Andromeda*, 1618[3]; *Orfeo dolente*, 1616[3].

Bencini, Giuseppe. *Nerone*, 1726[5]; p. 47.

Benini, Giovanni Battista. *Ipocondriaco*, 1695[4]; p. 70.

Bernasconi, Antonio. 1747[10].

Bertoni, Ferdinando. 1745[4].

Bertoni, Giuseppe. 1749[15].

Bitti, Martino. *Accademia festeggiante*, 1695[3]; *Anacreonte*, 1698[5]; 1695[4]; 1697[4]; 1743[2]; 1746[10]; pp. 41, 69, 70, 74.

Boni, Cosimo. *See* Bani, Cosimo.

Boniventi, Giuseppe. 1741[12].

Bononcini, Antonio Maria. *Camilla, regina de' Volsci*, 1698[3], 1710[2]; 1701[5]; 1716[3]; p. 17.

Bononcini, Giovanni. *Alba soggiogata da' Romani*, 1701[4]; 1698[3].

Botti, A. Pietro. *S. Giorgio liberatore di Silena*, 1621[2].

Lotti, Antonio. 1712[1]; 1715[3]; 1718[1]; 1726[1].

Maccari, Giacomo. *Pupilla*, 1737[2].

Maggiore, Francesco. 1746[2].

Magni, Paolo. 1702[6].

Mancini, Francesco. 1707[1]; 1710[6]; p. 73.

Mannucci, Francesco Maria. *Vero onore*, 1713[2]; 1710[6]; 1732[8]; p. 75.

Mariani, Giovanni Battista. *Amor vuol gioventù*, 1662[3], 1664.

Melani, Alessandro. *Carceriere di se medesimo*, 1681[1]; *Sospetto non ha fondamento*, 1699[6]; *Sospetto senza fondamento*, 1691[3]; p. 16.

Melani, Jacopo. *Amor vuol inganno*, 1663; *Una Commedia all'improvviso*, 1657[3]; *Donna più costante*, 1655[3]; *Ercole in Tebe*, 1661[1]; *Forza del destino*, 1658[5]; *Girello*, 1670[1], 1697[5]; *Pazzo per forza*, 1658[1]; *Potestà di Colognole*, 1657[1], 1661[6]; *Scipione in Cartagine*, 1657[5]; *Tacere et amare*, 1674; *Vecchio balordo*, 1659[1]; *Vedova*, ovvero *Amor vuol inganno*, 1680[4]; 1654[1]; 1717[3]; 1717[4]; pp. 16, 24, 26, 32, 61, 69, 74.

Negri, Antonio. 1728[6].

Orefici, Antonio. 1710[6], 1711[1]

Orlandini, Giuseppe Maria. Impresario and Maestro di Cappella. *Amazzoni vinte da Ercole*, 1715[6]; *Ammalato immaginario*, 1725[3], 1732[6]; *Amor generoso*, 1708[4]; *Amore, e maestà*, 1715[2]; *Arsace*, 1731[9], 1739[3], 1749[12]; *Artaserse*, 1707[1]; *Artigiano gentiluomo*, 1722; *Baronessa d'Arbella*, 1732[7]; *Bottegaro gentiluomo*, 1721[5]; *Bourgeois gentilhomme*, 1725[4]; *Cantata*, 1744[16]; *Catone in Utica*, 1749[10]; *Ifigenia in Aulide*, 1732[5]; *Marito giocatore*, 1720[7]; *Monsieur di Porsugnacco*, 1727[3]; *Nozze di Perseo e di Andromaca*, 1738[6]; *Preziosa Ridicola*, 1728[2], 1744[4]; *Scialacquatore*, 1744[10]; *Speziale di villa*, 1730[3]; *Temistocle*, 1737[1]; *Un Vecchio innamorato*, 1725[5]; *Vinceslao*, 1741[12]; 1700[2]; 1712[1]; 1712[2]; 1713[3]; 1714[3]; 1718[1]; 1719[2]; 1720[6]; 1721[1]; 1721-22; 1723[4]; 1725[7]; 1728[1]; 1729[3]; 1730[6]; 1732[8]; 1734[2]; 1735[4]; 1736[7]; 1737[6]; 1738[1]; 1738[4]; 1739[1]; 1739[4]; 1740[2]; 1742[2]; 1742[7]; 1744[11]; 1746[8]; 1746[12]; 1748[9]; 1748[10]; 1748[12]; 1750[21]; 1753 - p. 333; pp. 42, 44, 49, 75, 76.

Paci, Francesco Maria, romano. *Scuffiara*, (1743)[18].

Paganelli, Giuseppe Antonio. 1745[8].

Pagliardi, Giovanni Maria. *Attilio Regolo*, 1693[4]; *Caligula delirante*, 1685[4]; *Greco in Troia*, 1689[5]; *Pazzo per forza*, 1687[3]; *Tiranno di Colco*, 1688[5]; 1658[1]; 1687[1]; pp. 41, 69, 70, 74.

Pallavicino, Carlo. 1698[10].

Pampani, Antonio Gaetano. 1749[16].

Panacci, Anton Bartolomeo. *Vincitor Coralbo*, 1732[4].

Paoli, Antonio. *Cantata*, 1730[7].

Partenio, Giovanni Domenico. 1697[3].

Pasquini, Bernardo. *Donna ancora è fedele*, 1684[1]; *Idalma* overo *chi la dura la vince*, 1685[1]; *Lisimaco*, 1690[2]; *Tessalonica*, 1686[6]; 1687[1]; 1692[6]; 1698[6]; p. 74.

Passoti, ———. 1725[8].

Paulati, Andrea. 1714[3]; 1735[4].

Perez, Davide. 1744[13]; 1748[13].

Pergolesi, Giovanni Battista. *Serva padrona*, 1742[13]; 1733[5]; 1735[2]; 1737[6]; 1738[4]; 1739[8]; 1740[5]; 1744[13]; 1747[7]; 1747[15].

Peri, Jacopo. *Balletto della cortesia*, 1614[6]; *Balletto fatto nel Battesimo*, 1614[4]; *Balletto rusticale di contado fiorentini*, 1616[2]; *Canzone delle lodi d'Austria*, 1624[2]; *Dafne*, 1598,

Schauensee, Francesco Giuseppe. 1747[3].
Schiassi, Gaetano Maria. *Alessandro Severo*, 1734[6]; 1732[10]; 1740[1]; p. 73.
Signorini, G.B. *Guerra d'amore*, 1616[1].
Stradella, Alessandro. *Girello* (prologue), 1670[1], 1697[5]; 1692[5]; 1696[3].
Strozzi, Pietro. *Rapimento di Cefalo*, 1600[7].
Stuk, Giambatista. 1736[7].

Terradeglias (Terradellas), Domenico M.B. *Artemisia*, (1743)[16]; *Issipile*, (1741)[4]; *Merope*,
1743[3]; *Semiramide riconosciuta*, 1746[1]; 1744[3]; 1749[17].
Tinazzoli, Agostino. 1712[2].

Venturi del Nibbio, Stefano. *Rapimento di Cefalo*, 1600[7].
Vinci, Leonardo. *Artaserse*, 1730[2], 1739[9], 1748[13]; *Astianatte*, (1725)[10]; *Catone in Utica*,
1729[1]; *Ernelinda*, 1727[4]; 1720[7]; 1725[1]; 1725[12]; 1726[3]; 1732[1]; 1734[5]; 1740[2]; 1748[12];
1748[13]; p. 73.
Vitali, Filippo. *Cocchiata delli Accademici Rugginosi*, 1628[2]; *Intermedii*, 1623[3], 1626[2]; p. 23.
Vivaldi, Antonio. *Atenaide*, 1728[6]; *Ginevra Principessa di Scozia*, 1736[1]; *Ipermestra*,
1727[1]; *Scanderbegh*, 1718[3]; *Umiltà esaltata*, 1734[3]; 1725[12]; 1735[1]; 1737[6]; 1738[4];
pp. 47, 74, 75.

Wagenseil, Johann Christoph. 1746[12].

Zanettini, Antonio. *See* Giannettini.
Ziani, Marc'Antonio. *Belisario in Ravenna*, 1698[2]; *Domizio*, 1697[2]; 1701[2]; 1720[6]; 1728[6].
Ziani, Pietro Andrea. *Fortune di Rodope e Damira*, 1662[2]; 1701[2].

SINGERS AND ACTORS

Singers without surnames are listed at the end of this index. Women performing under both maiden and married names are listed under the former with the married name in parentheses.

Acciaioli, Alessandro, Tisico. 1700[8].

Acciari, Jacopo. 1661[1].

Alamanni, Ottavia. 1690[6].

Albarelli, Luigi, detto il Luigino. Contralto. Virt. del Ser. di Modena. 1705[4], 1707[3].

Alberti, Antonia. 1743[6], 1743[8].

Albertini, Giovanna, detta la Reggiana. Virt. del Ser. di Mantova. 1704[6], 1705[4], 1706[4], 1707[3], 1707[4].

Albertini, Giuliano, di Firenze. Contralto. Virt. della Gran Principessa di Toscana in 1725. Singer primarily at the Cocomero. 1701[4], 1701[7], 1702[1], 1702[6], 1703[1], 1703[2], 1703[4], 1706[7], 1707[1], 1707[2], 1707[4], 1716[5], 1717[1], 1717[3], 1717[4], 1723[3], 1725[7], 1725[8], 1729[2], 1731[10], 1732[1], 1733[1], 1735[1], 1738[6], p. 68.

Albinoni, Margherita. Soprano. 1721[1], 1721[2].

Albuzzi, Ottavio, di Milano. Tenor. 1742[7], 1747[10], 1747[11].

Alessandri, Margherita, di Bologna. 1739[8], 1740[1], 1742[4], 1743[10].

Allegri, Antonio Lorenzo. Comico. 1701[6].

Allegri, Cosimo. Comico. 1701[6].

Allegri, Domenico. Comico. 1701[6].

Amadori, detto. *See* Giovanni Tedeschi.

Amaini, Carlo, di Bologna. 1718[1], 1718[2], 1726[6].

Amerighi, Antonia. *See* Merighi, Antonia.

Amorevoli, Angelo (or Angiolo), di Venezia. Tenor. 1734[2], 1735[4], 1741[3], p. 73.

Andrè, Lucrezia, detta La Carrò. Virt. del Prin. di Tocana. 1697[4], 1698[3], 1698[6], 1699[8], p. 68.

Andreoni, Giovanni Batista, di Lucca. Soprano. 1742[14], 1743[3], 1747[15], 1748[6].

Angeli, Giovanni, di Siena. 1745[8], 1746[2].

Angelis, Isabella de. 1700[2], 1700[3], p. 36.

Antinori, Luigi, di Bologna. Tenor. 1735[5], 1734[1], p. 73.

Archi, Giovanni Antonio, detto il Cortoncino, di Faenza. Al servizio del Marchese Strozzi di Mantova. 1701[5], 1701[7], 1707[2], 1718[1], 1718[2], 1721[1], 1721[2], p. 67.

Archilei, Vittoria. *See* index of **COMPOSERS**.

Argenti, Gioseppe. P. 67.

Aschieri, Caterina, di Roma. Soprano. Virt. del Duca di Modena. 1739[1], 1739[3], 1739[4].

Augusti, Angiola, di Venezia. 1708[3], 1708[4].

Aureli, Maria Caterina, di Bologna. 1731[9], 1732[5].

Azzolini, Caterina, di Ferrara. Al servizio del Duca di Mantova. 1700[7], 1701[1], 1701[2], 1703[4], 1703[5], 1704[1], 1707[1], 1707[5], 1707[6], 1708[1], p. 41.

Azzurrini, Verginia. 1660[1].

Babbi, Giovanna Guaetta. *See* Guaetta.

Babbi, Gregorio, di Cesena. Tenor. Virt. di Camera di S.A.R. (Gian Gastone). 1730[2], 1730[6], 1731[2], 1731[3], 1731[4], 1734[3], 1744[11], 1746[8], 1746[9], pp. 44, 45.

Bagnolesi, Anna Maria Antonia (Pinacci), di Firenze. Contralto. Virt. della Gran Principessa Violante Beatrice di Toscana. 1725[11], 1726[2], 1726[3], 1732[13], 1733[1], 1739[4], 1741[12], 1742[2], 1742[14], 1743[3], 1750[12], 1756 - p. 339.

Bagnoli, Lorenzo, di Firenze. 1710[6].

Balatri, Filippo, di Firenze. 1703[4], p. 41.

Baldi, Antonio. 1730[2], 1730[6], 1731[3], pp. 44, 45.

Baldi, Raffaello (Raffaellino). Virt. di S.A.R. di Toscana (Cosimo III). 1697[4], 1698[5], 1699[6], 1704[2], 1705[4], pp. 64, 67, 68.

Baldini, Giovanni, di Firenze. 1720[3], 1721[3].

Baldini, Innocenz(i)o, di Firenze. 1725[7], 1725[8], 1731[10], 1732[1].

Balino, detto il. See Fabbri, Anibal Pio.

Ballarini, Francesco, detto Il Ballarino. Al servizio del Duca di Mantova. 1700[7], p. 66.

Ballerini, Domenico. 1689[5], p. 66.

Ballerini, Leonora Falbetti. 1654[3], 1657[1], 1658[1], 1660[1], 1661[1], 1663.

Bambagia, detta la. See Tarquini, Vittoria.

Bar, Giovanni Michele de, detto il Basso di Peponi. 1658[1], 1660[1], 1661[1], 1661[4], 1662[2], 1662[5]-63, 1663, 1687[4].

Baratta(i), Pietro, di Massa. Virt. del Principe di Modena. 1723[1], 1727[4], 1728[1], 1731[10], 1732[1], 1735[7], 1736[1], 1737[6].

Baratta, Teresa. Soprano. Possibly Teresa Pieri. 1735[7], 1736[1].

Baratti, Caterina. 1742[4], 1742[8].

Baratti, Giuseppe, di Bologna. 1749[15], 1749[16], 1749[17], 1750[4].

Barberini, Ottavia Nunziata. 1743[9], 1743[11].

Barbieri, Antonio. Tenor. Virt. del S.o Prin. Darmstat. 1725[9], 1734[5], 1735[3].

Barbieri, Lucia Bassi. 1734[5], 1735[3].

Barbieri, Santi, di Firenze. Contralto. 1730[3], 1731[2], 1731[4], 1734[3], 1737[1], 1738[1], 1738[4], 1743[10], pp. 44, 45.

Barchetti, Anna or Maria. 1746[13], 1747[4], 1748[9], 1748[10], 1750[21].

Barelli, Giuseppe. 1707[6].

Barlocci, Francesca, di Roma. Virt. della S. Duchessa Vedova di Guastalla. 1729[3], 1730[1], 1738[11], 1739[2], 1743[10], 1744[14].

Barlocci, Maddalena, di Roma. Virt. della S. Duchessa Vedova di Guastalla. 1729[3].

Baroni, Gaetano, di Firenze. 1728[6].

Bartolini, Caterina, di Roma. 1749[10], 1749[12].

Barzi, Sebastiano, Pesciatino. 1732[9].

Bassi, Caterina, di Modena. Virt. di S.A.S. di Modana. 1736[7], 1737[1], 1745[2], 1745[4], 1745[8], 1746[2].

Bassi, Lucia. See Barbieri, Lucia Bassi.

Basso di Peponi, il. See De Bar, Giovanni Michele.

Basteris, Gaetano Pompeo, detto Perini, di Bologna. Tenor. Virt. del Re di Sardegna. 1745[7], 1746[1], 1747[15], 1748[6].

Batistoni, ———. 1657[1].

Beccaretta, detta la. See Fachinelli, Lucia.

Beccarina, detta la. See Cecchi, Anna Maria Torri.

Becheroni, Gaspera. 1742[9], 1742[12].

Belisani, Cecilia (Buini), di Bologna. Serva del Principe del Darmstat. 1718[7], 1719[2], 1727[3].

Belisani, Francesco, di Ferrara. 1719[2], 1719[6].

Bellieri, S. 1679[2].

Bellucci, Domenico. 1657[1], 1658[1], 1661[1], 1663.

Benedetti, Anna Maria Teresa, di Bologna. Virt. del S. di Mantova. 1705[5], 1705[8], 1706[2].

Bonfigli, Dionisio, di Siena. 1739[8], 1740[1].

Bonifaci, Domenico. Tenor. 1734[6], 1735[1], 1741[12], 1742[2].

Bonistalli, Margherita. 1732[9].

Bordoni Hasse, Faustina, di Venezia. Soprano. Virt. di Camera dell'Elettor Palatino, e poi del Re di Polonia. 1723[3].

Borghesi, Francesca. 1698[6], 1698[10], 1712[1], 1712[2].

Borghi, Caterina. 1716[5], 1717[1].

Borghi, Gaetano. Tenor. 1716[3], 1719[1], 1719[7], 1719[8], 1720[4], 1720[5].

Borgonzoni, Lucretia. P. 67.

Borosini, Antonio. Virt. del Duca di Modena. 1707[3].

Borsari, Lucrezia. Virt. dell'Archiducale Cappella di Mantova, 1715[4].

Boschi, Giuseppe Maria. P. 67.

Bovarini, Lucia, detta la Mantovanina. 1710[6], 1711[2].

Bracci, Angelica. Entitled Naples, 1705, virt. dell'Eminentissimo de' Medici. 1699[3], p. 67.

Brandi, Antonio. 1600[5], 1611[2].

Brandi, Lisabetta, di Firenze. 1713[2].

Brigido, detto. *See* Valetti, Antonio.

Brigonzi, Caterina, di Venezia. Contralto. 1739[1], 1739[3], 1739[4], 1741[12], 1742[14], 1743[3], p. 58. Quadro III.IV.VI.II, p. 539, says soprano.

Brogi, Caterina (Pertici, 1742). 1737[7], 1738[5], 1742[9], 1742[12], 1742[13], 1743[9], 1743[11], 1744[7], 1744[12], 1745[2], 1745[4], 1745[8], 1745[9], 1746[2], pp. 58, 71.

Brogina, detta la. 1689[5].

Broschi, Carlo, detto Farinello, di Napoli. Soprano. Virt. di Camera di Filippo V. Re delle Spagne. 1728[3], 1734[2].

Buccella, Domenico. 1747[15].

Buini. *See* Belisani, Cecilia.

Buini, Rosalba. 1744[14].

Buonavia, Maria Maddalena. *See* Bonavia, Maria Maddalena.

Buzzoleni, Giovanni, P. 66.

Caccini, Francesca. *See* index of COMPOSERS.

Caccini, Giulio. *See* index of COMPOSERS.

Caccini, Paola. 1620[1], 1637[1].

Caccini, Settimia. *See* index of COMPOSERS.

Caffarello, detto. *See* Maiorana, Gaetano.

Calvi, Giovanni Battista. 1702[1].

Campagniolo, Francesco. 1624[2].

Campaspe, detta la. *See* Sardelli, Anna Maria.

Campioli, detta la. *See* Guallandi, Margherita.

Canavese, Giuseppe, di Genova. Tenor. 1684[3], 1686[4], 1687[3], 1689[5], 1689[10], 1693[4], 1695[4], 1698[5], 1705[5], 1706[4], 1707[3], p. 68.

Canini, Raffaello, di Firenze. 1720[1].

Canini, Settim(i)o Canizoni, di Firenze. Tenor. 1736[1], 1736[7], 1737[1], 1738[6].

Cantelli, Angelic(z)a. 1736[5].

Cantelli, Stella Fortunata, di Bologna. 1736[5].

Carattoli, Francesco. 1746[13], 1747[4].

Carboni, Giovanni Batista. Virt. del S. di Mantova. 1701[1], 1701[2], 1718[3].

Carestini, Giovanni, detto il Cusanino. Contralto. Virt. del Duca di Parma. 1726[3], 1732[13], 1733[1], 1760 - p. 339, p. 73. Quadro III.IV.VI.II, p. 532, says he was a soprano.

Carlani, Carlo, di Bologna. Tenor. 1742[14], 1743[3], 1746[12], 1747[3].

Clementi, Antonio. 1661[1].

Clerici, Carl'Andrea. P. 67.

Colizi, Agata, di Roma. 1752 - p. 332.

Collarettina, detta la. 1689[5].

Coltellini, Anna Maria, detta la Serafina. Virt. del Ser. Prin. Ferdinando di Toscana. 1699[8], 1700[2], 1700[3], p. 68.

Compassi, Pietro Costantino, di Pisa. 1743[15], 1744[3], 1744[4], 1744[12], 1745[2], 1745[4].

Conti, Gioacchino, detto Gizziello, di Napoli. Soprano. 1742[7].

Coralli, detta la. *See* Laurenti, Antonia Maria.

Coralli, Stefano, di Bologna. Virt. del Ser. di Mantova (1701). 1698[6], 1698[10], 1699[1], 1700[2], 1700[3], 1701[4], 1702[6], 1703[1], 1703[2].

Coresi, Niccola. 1658[1], p. 32.

Cortona, detto il. *See* Cecchi, Domenico.

Cortoncino, detto il. *See* Archi, Giovanni Antonio.

Corvi, Paola, detta Morotti Piacentina. Virt. del Ser. Prin. Antonio di Parma. 1726[6], 1735[4].

Cosimi, Anna, di Roma. Virt. del Prin. ereditario di Modena. 1720[3], 1720[4], 1726[3].

Costa, Andrea, di Venezia. Virt. della ducal capp. della Repubblica di Venezia. 1733[4].

Costa, Anna Francesca. Protected by Leopoldo de' Medici. 1654[1], p. 27.

Costa, Antonia, di Milano. 1739[1], 1739[3].

Costa, Maria Margherita, di Bologna. 1726[6].

Costa, Rosa. 1737[6].

Costa, Vittoria, di Bologna. 1701[4], 1702[6], 1703[1], 1703[2], 1707[2].

Costantini, Antonio, comico. 1732[4].

Cotti, Maria Teresa, detta la Francese, di Modana. Contralto. Virt. di Camera del Duca di Modena. 1720[4], 1720[5], 1725[9].

Cricchi, Domenico, di Bologna. Bass. Virt. di S.A.S. Il Sig. Principe d' Hasse-Darmstat. 1734[6], 1735[1], 1735[2].

Croci, Rosa, di Bologna. Contralto. Virt. del Princ. Darmstat. 1725[1], 1725[2].

Curzio, biccheria, la figluola del Sigr. 1620[2].

Cusanino, detto il. *See* Carestini, Giovanni.

Cuzzoni, Francesca, detta la Parmigiana. Soprano. Virt. di Camera della Gran Principessa di Toscana Violante Beatrice. 1717[4], 1718[3], 1719[7], 1719[8], 1720[6], 1731[9], 1732[5], 1737[6], 1738[1], 1738[4], 1738[6], pp. 51, 68, 74.

Del Bianco, Giovanni Battista. 1735[5].

Del Borgo, Jacopo. 1679[4].

Del Maures, Mauro. P. 67.

Del Ricco, Alessandro, di Firenze. 1707[4], 1708[3], 1712[4], 1713[3], 1716[3], 1720[3], 1720[4], 1720[5], 1721[3], p. 69.

Della Comare, Angiolina. 1707[3], p. 68.

Della Donna, Sergio. P. 67.

Della Scarperia, Giuliano. Virt. dell'Ill. Sig. Generale, Marchese del Borro. 1701[2].

Donnini, Antonio, di Sinigaglia. 1752 - p. 332.

Dons, Caterina. 1737[7], 1738[5].

Dori, ———. 1744[6], pp. 58, 59.

Dotti, Anna Vincenzia, di Bologna. 1715[3], 1715[5], 1716[1].

Dreino, detto il. *See* Guerri, Andrea.

Drejer, Giovanni, detto il Tedeschino, di Firenze. 1725[1], 1725[2].

Droghierina, detta la. *See* Chimenti, Margherita.

Francese, detta la. *See* Cotti, Maria Teresa.

Franci, Andrea, di Firenze. Virt. del Ser. di Modena. 1703[1], 1703[2], 1703[4], 1717[4].

Franci, Ippolito. P. 66.

Fratini, Maria Maddalena. Virt. del Card. de' Medici. 1699[6], pp. 67, 68.

Frilli, Stefano. 1707[5], 1707[6], 1708[1], 1744[9], p. 58.

Frizzi, Maria Maddalena, di Firenze. Contralto. 1731[7], 1735[7], 1736[1].

Frumicona, la. 1688[2].

Fuma(i)galli, Caterina, detta la Romanina. Virt. del Duca di Guastalla. 1734[2], 1746[12], 1747[3], 1747[8].

Fusai, Ippolito. Basso. 1661[1], 1661[3], 1679[2], 1686[4], 1689[5], pp. 36, 66, 68, 71.

Gabbrielli, Antonio Francesco. 1699[3], 1711[2], 1713[2].

Gabrielli, Giovanni Atti. 1698[10], 1699[1].

Gaggiotti, Pellegrino. 1743[6], 1743[9], 1743[11].

Galarati(a). *See* Gallerati.

Galeotti, Maria Anna. 1745[8], 1746[2], 1747[10], 1747[11].

Gallerati, Caterina, di Venezia. Virt. del Princ. di Toscana (1705). 1701[5], 1702[6], pp. 67, 68.

Galletti, Domenico Giuseppe, di Cortona. Contralto. 1718[2], 1738[11], 1739[2].

Galletti, ———. 1661[1], 1661[3].

Galli, Pietro. 1661[1].

Galosti, Anna. 1752 - p. 332.

Gandini, Isabella, di Venezia. Soprano. 1745[7], 1746[1], 1750[21].

Garberini, Maria Anna (Benti), detta la Romanina. Virt. della Princ. di Modana. 1706[7], 1707[1], 1707[2], 1707[4], 1710[6], 1711[2].

Garofalini, Elena, di Bologna. Virt. del S. di Mantova. 1690[1], 1690[2], 1690[6], pp. 35, 67.

Garrani, Nonziata, di Bologna. Soprano. 1745[7], 1746[1].

Gaschi, Anna. 1743[15], 1744[3].

Gasparini, Giovanna, di Bologna. Soprano. 1727[3].

Genari, Andrea. P. 66.

Gerardini, Maria Maddalena, detta la Sellarina. 1736[5], 1738[11], 1739[2].

Geri, Gaspa(e)ro. 1714[1], 1731[10], 1738[12].

Gherardi, Lorenzo, detto Puttello. Virt di Camera di S.A. Elettorale di Baviera. 1746[12], 1747[3].

Ghossler, Maria Caterina. *See* Goslerin.

Giacomazzi, Margherita, di Venezia. 1735[4], 1753 - p. 333, p. 73.

Giamberini, ———. Comico. 1744[6], p. 58.

Giannelli (Giamelli), Agata, di Firenze. 1731[7], 1731[8], 1732[1].

Giannetti, Marco. 1661[1].

Giannini, Niccolo. 1700[2], 1700[3].

Giardi, Rosalba, di Firenze. 1709[3], 1710[2], 1712[1], 1712[2], 1716[3].

Ginasi, Agata. 1706[7], 1707[1].

Giorgetti, Lorenzo. 1749[17].

Giorgi, Filippo, di Napoli. 1728[2].

Girò, Anna, di Venezia. Contralto. 1728[6], 1729[1], 1735[7], 1736[1].

Giustacchini, Antonio. Virt. del Ser. di Mantova. 1700[2], 1700[3].

Giusti, Jacopo. 1600[5].

Gizzi, Domenico, di Napoli. Soprano. 1725[9].

Gizziello, detto. *See* Conti, Gioacchino.

Gonzales, Regina. 1745[2], 1745[4].

Gori, (Signor). 1698[5].

Laschi, Anna Querzoli. *See* Querzoli, Anna.

Laschi, Filippo, di Firenze. Virt. di Camera del Princ. Carlo Duca di Lorena e di Bar. 1739[9], 1740[2], 1742[9], 1742[11], 1742[12], 1743[6], 1743[8], 1743[9], 1743[11].

Laurenti, Antonia Maria (Novelli), detta la Coralli, di Bologna. Virt. di Camera della Maestà del Re Augusto di Pollonia. 1716[5], 1717[1], 1717[3], 1718[1], 1718[2], 1729[3], 1730[1].

Laurenti, Pietro Paolo. Virt. del Ser. Princ. Antonio di Parma. 1715[5], 1716[1].

Laurenzani, Maria Anna Romana. *See* Lorenzani.

Lauretta, la. 1690[6].

Lena, Mariano, di Lucca. 1726[6].

Lepri, Dionisia. 1745[2], 1745[4], 1746[5].

Ligi, Celestino. 1717[3], 1717[4].

Lionardi, Francesco. 1658[1].

Lironi, Giuseppe, di Firenze. 1737[4].

Lisi, Anna Maria. Virt. della Gran Princ. di Toscana. 1690[6], 1697[4], 1698[3], p. 68.

Lodi, Silvia, detta la Spagnoletta, di Bologna. 1720[1], 1720[2].

Lolli, Dorotea, di Bologna. 1731[9], 1732[5].

Longini, Lucrezia. 1742[10], 1742[11].

Longini, Maria. 1742[10], 1742[11].

Lorenzani, Maria Anna. Soprano. Virt. del Princ. d' Harmstadt. 1720[1], 1720[2], 1721[1], 1721[2].

Lottini, Antonio, di Pistoia. 1720[1], 1720[3], 1728[2], 1729[2], 1730[3], 1730[6], 1731[2], 1731[3], 1731[4], 1742[10], 1742[11], pp. 44, 45, 71.

Lucchese, detta la. *See* Pontissi, Lucrezia.

Lucchesina (La), di Casale di Bonferrata. *See* Minucciani.

Lucchesino, detto. *See* Pacini, Andrea.

Lucertolina, detta la. *See* Beverini, Ortenzia.

Luchini, Matteo. Virt. della Corte di Polonia. 1716[5], 1717[1], 1717[3], 1717[4].

Luigino, detto il. *See* Albarelli, Luigi.

Luppi, Diana Caterina, di Ferrara. Virt. del Sig. Conte Ercole Estense Mosti. 1690[1], 1690[2].

Luzzi, Caterina. 1748[12], 1748[13], 1748[16], 1749[4].

Maestina, detta la. *See* Negri, Maria Caterina.

Magagnoli, Ginevra. 1746[13], 1747[4].

Maganini, Filippo. 1698[6], 1698[10], 1699[1].

Maggiorini, Giovanni Domenico. Tenor of Santa Maria Maggiore in Rome. 1690[6].

Magliani, Angiola. P. 67.

Maichigiano, detto. *See* Murigi, Pietro.

Maiorana, Gaetano, detto Caffarello, di Napoli. Soprano. Virt. della Real Cappella del Re delle due Sicilie. 1729[2], 1730[2], 1747[10], 1747[11], 1748[12], 1748[13], p. 44.

Mancini, Giovanni Batista, di Ascoli. 1733[5], 1734[1].

Mancini, Rosa, di Firenze. Soprano. 1732[13], 1733[1], 1742[14], 1743[3].

Manella, Petronio. 1746[13], 1747[4].

Mangani, Anna Maria, di Firenze. Virt. dell'Altezza Reale la S. Gran Principessa Violante di Toscana. 1717[3], 1721[3], 1726[6], 1737[7], 1738[5].

Mannini, Livia. P. 67.

Manotti, Orazio, di Siena. 1752 - p. 332.

Mantovanina, detta la. *See* Bovarini, Lucia.

Manzuoli, Giovanni. 1731[7], 1731[8], 1732[9].

Marbizzi, ———. P. 58.

Marcello, Aurelia, di Venezia. Soprano. Al serv. del Duca di Mantova (1707); virt. di Camera della Princ. Violante di Baviera, governatrice di Siena (1720). 1706[5], 1707[5], 1707[6], 1708[1], 1714[3], 1715[1], 1715[3], 1715[5], 1716[1], 1716[3], p. 67.

Pignattino, detto il. *See* Romani, Stefano.

Pilai, Caterina, di Roma. 1749[15], 1749[16], 1749[17], 1750[4].

Pinacci, Anna Bagnolesi, *See* Bagnolesi,

Pinacci, Giovanni Battista, di Firenze. Tenor. Virt. del Principe d' Harmstadt. 1718[4], 1720[6], 1723[3], 1725[1], 1725[2], 1725[12], 1726[1], 1732[13], 1733[1], 1739[4], 1743[10], 1743[14], 1744[2], 1748[12], 1748[13], 1748[16], 1749[4] 1750[12], p. 71.

Pini, Maria Domenica, detta la Tilla. Virt. del Gran Principe di Toscana. Quadrio, III.IV.VI.II, p. 535, misspells Pini as Tini and erroneously entitles her virtuosa del Gran Duca di Toscana. 1692[5], 1693[4], 1696[5], 1697[4], 1699[6], 1699[8], 1701[1], 1701[2], 1701[5], 1702[4], 1704[2], 1705[4], 1706[4], 1708[2], 1709[1], 1710[5], 1746[10], pp. 67, 68.

Piombi, Antonio Francesco. Comico. 1701[6].

Pistocchi, Francesco A. Musico di S.A.S. Rannuccio II Duca di Parma. 1701[5], 1702[4], 1703[3], pp. 34, 68.

Poggi, Domenico. 1611[2].

Poggiali, Giovacchini. 1702[1].

Poli, Francesca. 1736[5], p. 73.

Poli, Giovanna Falconetti. 1743[6], 1743[8], 1743[15].

Pollarolina, la. 1663.

Pollastri, Regina. 1701[1], 1702[2], p. 41.

Pontissi, Lucrezia. P. 66.

Porciatti, Lorenzo. Virt. della Ser. Violante Gran Principessa di Toscana. 1712[4], 1713[3], 1713[5], 1715[3], 1715[5], 1716[1], p. 68.

Porna, Giuseppe. 1749[10], 1749[12].

Posterli, Costanza. Virt. del Principe d'Armstat. 1731[10], 1732[1], p. 73.

Predieri, Antonio, di Bologna. Virt. de' Ser. di Mantova, e di Parma, e poi anche del Gran Prin. di Toscana. 1706[7], 1707[1], 1707[4], 1710[5], pp. 66, 67.

Puccini, Sig.[ra] P. 58.

Puttello, detto. *See* Gherardi, Lorenzo.

Querzoli, Anna (Laschi). 1743[6], 1743[8], 1743[9], 1743[11].

Raaff, Antonio, di Colonia. Tenor. 1739[1], 1739[3].

Raffaellino, detto il. *See* Baldi, Raffaello.

Ramondini, Gimignano. Virt. del Ser. di Modena. 1714[3], 1715[1].

Rapaccioli, Giovanni Battista, di Firenze. Soprano. 1701[7], 1718[4], 1723[1], 1756 - p. 339, p. 69.

Rasi, Francesco. 1600[5], 1600[7].

Redi, Giovanni, di Firenze. Tenor. 1738[1], 1738[4], 1746[8], 1746[9].

Reggiana, detta la. *See* Albertini, Giovana; Besonzi, Paola.

Remolini, Niccola. Virt. della Maestà del Re de' Romani, e del S. Elettore di Brounsuith Hannover. 1704[6].

Resi, Angelico. 1706[7], 1708[1].

Riccardini, Giacomo. P. 66.

Riccioni, Barbara. P. 66.

Ridolfi, Donna Angelica M. 1719[10].

Rigacci, Anna. 1742[10], 1742[11].

Righensi, Carlo. 1657[1], 1658[1], 1660[1], 1661[1], 1661[3], 1663.

Rinaldi, Antonio, di Bologna. Contralto. Cantante del Marchese Grassi. 1687[3], 1691[4], 1696[5], 1698[6], 1698[10], 1699[1].

Ristorini, Antonio (Maria), di Firenze. Tenor. Virt. del Princ. d' Harmstadt. 1690[2], 1702[6],

Scaccia, Alessandra, di Mantova. Al servizio del Duca di Mantova. 1701[7], 1702[1].

Scaccia, Giuseppe, di Mantova. Al servizio del Duca di Mantova. 1697[4], 1701[7], 1702[1], pp. 66, 67.

Scalzi, Carlo, di Voghera. Soprano. 1723[3], 1729[2].

Scandalibeni, Pietro Paulo. Al serv. del Duca di Mantova. 1690[6].

Scardabelli, Nunziata. 1742[1].

Scarlatti, Rosa. 1746[5], 1750[21].

Segantini, Livia, di Roma. 1746[12], 1747[3], 1747[8].

Sellarina, detta la. See Gerardini, Maria Maddalena.

Senesino, detto il. See Bernardi, Francesco.

Serafina, detta la. See Coltellini, Anna Maria.

Siface. See Grossi, Giovanni Francesco.

Signoretti, Carlo. 1731[7], 1731[8].

Signorini, Raffaello, di Firenze. Soprano. Virt. della repubblica di Venezia. 1716[5], 1717[1], 1717[3], 1726[5], 1727[1].

Simi, Giovanni Batista, di Lucca. 1703[4], 1703[5], 1704[1].

Simonetti, Tommaso. 1747[9].

Sincendorff, Contessa. 1744[17].

Sirt, Antonio. 1657[1].

Sorbi, ———. P. 58.

Sorentino, ———. 1661[1].

Soresina, Benedetta, di Venezia. Soprano. 1728[3].

Spagnoletta, detta la. See Lodi, Silvia.

Speroni, detta la. See Muzzi, Giovanni Batista.

Spinola, Diacinta, di Firenze. Sotto la protezione di S.A.S. il Princ. Antonio di Parma. 1723[1].

Stabili, Alessandra. 1731[7], 1731[8].

Stabili, Barbera, di Firenze. Contralto. 1726[5], 1727[1], 1732[10], 1733[4], 1735[4], 1745[8], 1746[2], p. 73.

Stagi, Margherita, detta la Romanina, di Roma. 1725[7], 1725[8].

Steffanini, Maria Maddalena. Al serv. del Duca di Mantova. 1701[5].

Stella, Santa. P. 67.

Storni, Lucrezia, di Venezia. 1702[6], 1703[1], 1703[2].

Strambi, Orsola, di Lucca. 1746[12], 1747[3].

Suini, Margherita Salicola. Virt. del Duca di Modena. 1705[6], 1705[8], 1706[2].

Tagliar(v)ini, Rosa, di Bologna. 1749[10], 1749[12], 1750[21].

Tamburini, Giovanni Batista, di Siena. Virt. del Cardinale de' Medici. 1690[1], 1690[2], 1690[6], 1701[4], 1704[6], 1710[6], 1711[2], 1712[2], p. 68.

Tani, Angiola (Angela), di Firenze. 1745[2], 1745[4], 1746[12], 1747[3], 1749[15], 1749[16], 1749[17], 1750[4].

Tarquini, Vittoria, detta la Bombace o Bambagia. Virt. del Princ. di Toscana. 1698[5], 1699[8], 1700[7], 1702[4], 1706[4], 1707[3], 1709[1], p. 68.

Taus, Domenica, detta la Fanesina. 1737[7], 1738[5], 1747[10], 1747[11], 1747[15], 1748[6].

Tearelli, Girolama. 1742[1], 1743[14], 1744[2], 1748[12], 1748[13], 1748[16], 1749[4].

Tedeschi, Giovanni, detto Amadori. Soprano. 1739[4], 1741[12], 1742[2], 1747[8].

Tedeschino, detto il. See Drejer, Giovanni.

Tempesti, Domenico, di Firenze. Contralto. 1708[1], 1709[1], 1714[1], 1715[3], 1715[5], 1716[1], p. 69.

Tesi, Vittoria (Tramontini), detta la Moretta, di Firenze. Virt. del S. Prin. Antonio Farnese di Parma. 1721[1], 1721[2], 1723[3], 1729[2], 1734[2], 1743[10], 1743[14], 1744[2], 1747[3], 1753 - p. 339, pp. 63, 69, 71, 73.

Tilla, detta la. *See* Pini, Maria Domenica.

Tiloni, Giovanni Paolo, di Ferrara. Musico del Sig. Conte Pinamonte Buonacosa. 1690[1], 1690[2].

Toci, Giuseppe. 1660[1].

Tollini, Domenico. P. 67.

Tolve, ———. P. 73.

Tomii, Pellegrino, di Vicenza. Tenor. 1729[3], 1730[1], 1738[1], 1738[4]. Quadrio, III.IV.VI.II, p. 533, says Viniziano.

Tommaso, D. 1661[4].

Torri, Anna Maria. *See* Cecchi, Anna Maria Torri.

Toselli, Antonia, di Venezia. 1704[6].

Toselli, Giuseppe. Virt. del S. Princ. Antonio di Parma. 1726[6].

Tosi, ———. P. 58.

Totti, ———. P. 58.

Tozzi, Maria Antonia, di Firenze. Contralto. Virt. del Princ. Antonio di Parma. 1725[1], 1725[2].

Tramontini, Vittoria Tesi. *See* Tesi, Vittoria (Tramontini).

Triulzi, Giovanni, di Milano. Tenor. 1745[7], 1746[1].

Turcotti, Maria Giustina, di Firenze. Soprano. 1717[4], 1720[2], 1720[3], 1720[6], 1721[3], 1728[2], 1728[6], 1729[1], 1729[3], 1730[1], 1739[8], 1740[1], 1741[3], 1744[14], p. 73.

Ulivicciano, Vincenzio. Member of the Grandducal *musici ordinarii*. 1689[5], pp. 68, 71.

Ungherelli (or Ungarelli), Rosa. Soprano. Virt. del Principe d' Harmstadt. 1709[2], 1709[3], 1710[2], 1718[4], 1718[5], 1718[6], 1719[1], 1719[7], 1719[8], 1720[6], 1720[7], 1725[1], 1725[5], 1725[6], 1726[5], 1727[1], 1727[3], 1731[9], Note - p. 246, pp. 44, 71, 74.

Uttini, Elisabetta, di Bologna. Contralto. 1726[3], 1728[2], 1734[5], 1735[3], p. 73.

Valle(n)ti, Antonio, detto Brigido. 1748[9], 1748[10], 1750[21].

Valletta, Gaetano, di Milano. Soprano. Virt. di Camera di S.A.R. il S. Gio: Gastone Primo Gran Duca di Toscana. 1728[6], 1729[1], 1729[3], 1730[1], 1735[4].

Vecchi, Giuseppe. P. 68.

Vennini (or Vanini or Venini), Francesca (Boschi?). Al serv. del Duca di Mantova. 1698[6], 1698[10], 1699[1], p. 67.

Venturi, Anna Caterina. 1666.

Venturini, Casimiro, di Firenze. 1749[15], 1749[16], 1749[17], 1750[4].

Venturini, Francesco Maria, di Firenze. Baritone. Virt. di S.A. Elettorale di Baviera. 1709[3], 1710[2]. Quadrio, III.IV.VI.II, p. 532, says Viniziano.

Venturini, Maria Anna, di Venezia. 1742[14], 1743[3].

Venturini, Pietro, di Arezzo. 1743[6], 1743[8], 1743[11], 1743[15], 1744[3], 1744[12], 1746[8], 1746[9], 1748[12], 1748[13], 1748[16], 1749[4].

Venturini, Rosa, di Parma. Virt. di Camera di S.A.S. di Parma. 1718[3].

Veronesi, Pierina. Comica. 1732[4].

Vestri, Elisabetta. 1742[9], 1742[12].

Vettori, Maria Maddalena, detta la Marsuppina. Virt. del Gran Prin. di Toscana (1701). 1699[6], p. 68.

Vico, Diana, di Venezia. Contralto. Virt. di S.A. Elettoral di Baviera. 1719[1], 1719[7], 1719[8].

Vienna, detta la. *See* Mellini, Vienna.

Vigano, Giuseppe Maria, di Milano. 1704[1].

Vignali, Agata, di Bologna. 1702[1].

Vignali, Donna Maria Lucrezia. 1719[10].

Vincentino, ————. 1686[3].

Visconti, Caterina, di Milano. Soprano. 1729[2], 1734[5], 1735[3], 1747[10], 1747[11], 1747[15], 1748[6].

Visconti, M. Maddalena, di Milano. 1721[3].

Vittori, Anna Maria. 1743[15], 1744[3].

Zanardi, Carl'Antonio, di Bologna. Soprano. Virt. del Gran Princ. di Toscana (1686). 1684[3], 1686[4], 1687[3], 1695[4], 1698[5], pp. 66, 67, 68.

Zanardi, Teresa. 1733[4].

Zanatta(i), Carlo Antonio, di Bologna. 1690[1], 1690[2]. Possible misspelling of Zanardi above.

Zani, Margherita Caterina, di Bologna. 1714[3], 1715[1], 1723[1], 1725[7], 1725[8], p. 71.

Zannoni, Angiol Maria, di Venezia. Virt. di Camera del Princ. d' Harmstadt. 1723[1].

Zipoli, Caterina. 1743[3], 1747[10], 1747[11], 1747[15], 1748[6].

SINGERS WITHOUT SURNAMES

Anna. 1661[3].

Bastianino, del Fusai. 1685[3].

Gabbriela, di Lucca. 1662[5]-63.

Girolamo. 1662[2], 1662[5]-63.

Giulia. 1661[4].

Orazio. P. 67.

Signor, del Sig. Niccolini. 1661[3].

Vettoria. 1661[3], 1661[4].

DANCERS (*EXCLUDING NOBILITY*),
IMPRESARIOS, INSTRUMENTALISTS, COSTUMERS, PAINTERS, ETC.

Brunoro, Giuseppe. Inventor de' Balli and Ballerino. 1739[5], 1753 - p. 333.

Buonazzoli. Impresario. 1721-22.

Burgioni, Maria. Ballerina. 1749[15], 1749[16], 1753 - p. 333.

Cacioni, Gaspero, di Firenze. Ballerino. 1743[10].

Cacioni, Maria Maddalena. Ballerina. 1743[14], 1744[2].

Cacioni, Placida, di Firenze. Ballerina. 1743[10], 1745[7], 1746[1], 1748[16], 1749[4].

Caldari, Alessandro. 1746[13], 1747[4], 1747[9].

Cambi, Andre. Impresario. 1742[13].

Cambi, Barbera. Ballerina. 1749[15], 1749[16].

Cambi, Niccolo, Fiorentino. Ballerino. 1745[7], 1746[1], 1747[15], 1748[6], 1753 - p. 333.

Campanini, Barbera, di Parma. Ballerina. 1739[5].

Campanini, Domitilla, di Parma. Ballerina. 1739[5].

Campioni, Giuseppe. Impresario. 1746[11].

Canale, Conte Filippo. Impresario. 1734[2].

Cantagallina, Remigio. Engraver. 1608[3], 1608[5].

Capponi, Scipione. 1743[11], pp. 14, 31, 49, 52, 56.

Cardiori, Ancilla. Ballerina. 1748[16], 1749[4].

Cataldi, Giovanni del. Impresario. 1741[3].

Cavicchi, Giuseppe, di Firenze. Ballerino. 1741[3].

Chamant, Giuseppe. Pittore del Ser. Gran Duca. 1742[7].

Chiavistelli, Jacopo. Pittore. 1689[5].

Cini, Giovanni. Maestro di Scherma p[er] l'abbattimento. 1746[1].

Cini, Piero (Avocato). Capo degl'Interessati. 1743[5].

Cinti, Giuseppe. Ballerino. 1747[10], 1747[11].

Colonna, Teresa. Ballerina. 1748[12], 1748[13], 1748[16], 1749[4].

Comesari, Santino. Maestro di ballo. 1614[2], 1615[3].

Compostof, Ermanno. Inventor degli'Abiti. 1731[3], 1733[5], 1734[1], 1734[2], 1734[5], 1734[6], 1735[1], 1735[3], 1735[4], 1735[7], 1736[1], 1736[7], 1737[1], 1737[6], 1738[1], 1738[4], 1739[3], 1739[4], 1739[8], 1739[9], 1740[1], 1741[3], 1741[12], 1742[1], 1742[2], 1742[3], 1742[7], 1742[11], 1742[14], 1743[3], 1743[10], 1743[11], 1743[14], 1744[10], 1744[12], 1744[14].

Compostof, Giuseppe. Inventor degli'Abiti. 1745[7], 1746[1], 1746[8], 1746[9], 1746[12], 1747[3], 1747[10], 1747[11], 1747[15], 1748[6], 1748[9], 1748[16], 1749[4], 1749[17], 1750[4], 1750[21], 1752 - p. 332, 1753 - p. 333.

Contiglio, Francesco, di Roma. Impresario. 1689[6].

Cortini, Anna. 1747[10], 1747[11].

Cortini, Zanetta (or Giovanna), di Venezia, detta la Pantalonesina. Ballerina. 1739[5], 1747[10].

Costa, Giovanni Michele, di Torino. Ballerino. 1749[15], 1749[16].

Dannacci, Antonio. Maestro de' Balli. 1727[4], 1728[1].

Dei, Sig.[ra]. P. 58.

Del Fede, Giovanni Domenico. Inventor de' Balli. 1726[6].

Del Ricco, Giovanni Gaetano. Impresario. 1745[6], 1746[8], 1746[9], 1747[10], 1747[11], 1747[15], 1748[6], p. 51.

Del Zanca, Michele. Pp. 58, 59.

Dell'Agata, Domenico. Maestro dell'Abbattimento. 1740[1], 1743[14].

Dell'Armajolo, Casimiro. Maestro di Scherma. 1611[2].

Della Bella, Stefano. Engraver. 1637[1].

Denis, Jean (Jan or Giovanni), di Parigi. Ballerino, inventore de' Balli. 1746[8], 1746[9], 1746[13], 1747[10], 1747[11]. *See* Sauter, Francesco.

Stachini, Caterina. Ballerina. 1753 - p. 333.
Stagi, Rosa. Ballerina. 1747[15], 1748[6].
Stampiglia, Luigi. Impresario. *See* index of **LIBRETTISTS.**
Susier, Nicolò. Theorbist. Pp. 14, 35, 43, 49, 50.

Tacca, Ferdinando. Architect. 1661[1], pp. 25, 32.
Tacciato, Girolamo. Inventore. 1719[8].
Tagliasacchi, Francesco. Impresario. 1731[1].
Tappi, Giovanni Battista. Copyist. 1731[4].
Tedesca, Maddalena. Ballerina. 1747[15], 1748[6].
Todeschino (or Tedeschino). *See* Gigli, Giovanni Battista.
Torricelli, Antonio. Costumer. 1725[7], 1725[8], 1725[9], 1725[12], 1726[1], 1727[4], 1728[1]
   (also Impresario).
Turchi, Francesco, di Firenze. Ballerino. 1743[14], 1744[2], 1749[15], 1749[16].
Turchi, Giuseppe, di Firenze. Ballerino. 1743[10].

Udini, Maria. Ballerina. 1752 - p. 332.
Udini, Vittoria. Ballerina. 1752 - p. 332.

Valenti, Giuseppe. Inventore de' Balli and Ballerino. 1739[5], 1747[15], 1748[6].
Vanetti, Giovanni Battista. Impresario. 1745[3].
Vanni, Innocenzio (Gobbo). Impresario. 1743[8], 1745[7], 1746[1], 1746[4], 1746[13], 1747[6].
Vannini, Luigi. Impresario. P. 56.
Veronese, Carlo. *See* index of **THEATERS, ACADEMIES, COMPANIES, AND** *CONVERSAZIONI.*
Vicedomini, Filippo. Ballerino. 1744[14], 1748[12], 1748[13], 1748[16], 1749[4].
Vitalba, Giovanni. Impresario. *See* index of **THEATERS, ACADEMIES, COMPANIES, AND**
   CONVERSAZIONI.
Vitelli, Camillo. Impresario. P. 31.

Wintergut, Adriano. 1702[7].

Zocchi, Giuseppe. Pittore. 1739[8].

THEATERS,
ACADEMIES, COMPANIES,
AND *CONVERSAZIONI*

Ricomposti, Accad. (Terra d'Anghiari). P. 34.
Rifritti, Accad. 1682[2], p. 37.
Rimoti, Accad. 1723[4], p. 48.
Rinaldi, Palazzo. 1618[3], p. 22.
Rinascenti, Accad. (Poppi). P. 34.
Rinvigoriti, Accad. 1672[1], 1673[2], 1686[7], pp. 32, 37.
Risoluti, Accad. 1747[2].
Riuniti, Accad. (Ravenna). 1686[2].
Rozzi, Accad. (Siena). 1749[1].
Rugginosi, Accad. 1623[1], 1627[2], 1628[2], p. 23.

S. Bartolomeo, teatro (Naples). 1689[10], p. 67.
S. Cassiano, teatro (Venice). 1646[2], 1650[2], p. 67.
S. Fridiano a Navicella. 1744[11], p. 50.
S. Giorgio, compagnia di. 1622[1], 1622[3], p. 22.
S. Giovanni Evangelista. *See* Vangelista.
S. Luca di Venezia, compagnia di. 1746[6].
S. Maria Maggiore, Frati del. 1694[1].
S. Remigio, teatro. 1679[3], p. 32.
S. Trinita, Frati del. 1694[1]
S. Zanobi, via. (*Nuova conversazione*). 1747[5], p. 50.
SS. Apostoli, Borgo, teatro. 1747[1], 1747[5].
Saggiati, Accad. 1693[2], p. 37.
Saltatori Inglesi, compagnia di. 1740[4], p. 50.
Santo Egidio, teatro. P. 56.
Settignano. 1717[6].
Sfaccendati, Accad. (Rome). 1692[6].
Sorgenti, Accad. 1652, 1654[2], 1655[1], 1655[2], 1655[3]-56, 1655[4]-56, 1657[2], 1657[3], 1657[5]
    1658[5], 1659[2], 1660[2], 1661[3], 1661[4], 1661[5], 1662[1], 1662[2], 1662[5]-63, 1665[2], 1679[3],
    1684[2], 1684[5], 1686[1], 1688[1], 1689[2], 1690[8], 1691[1], 1691[6], 1692[2], 1694[2], 1695[6],
    1696[2], 1698[1], 1698[4], 1699[3], 1701[3], 1742[10], pp. 25, 27-32, 37, 38, 47, 48, 50.
Sorpresi, Accad. 1654[2].
Spensierati, Accad. (Venice). P. 91.
Stanzone de Fiorenza Franco. 1645[1].
Storditi, Accad. 1618[3].
Strioni, compagnie di. 1738[7], 1738[9], 1741[5], 1741[10], 1741[12], 1742[1], 1742[3], 1742[5],
    1742[10], 1743[7], 1743[9], 1743[12], 1743[13], 1743[15], 1744[5], 1744[12], 1747[13], 1748[14],
    1748[17], 1749[7], 1749[13], pp. 51, 52, 58. *See also Comici* and *Zan(n)i.*
Strozzi, Palazzo. 1614[1], p. 22.

Teatro Mediceo. *See* Uffizi, Palazzo degli.
Tegolaia, Borgo, Teatro. 1669[4], 1673[2], 1679[4], pp. 32, 37, 47.
Tintori, teatro nel Corso dei. (The theater, erected about 1676, was used by the Imperfetti,
    then by the Cadenti from 1689[4]. The following entries refer to the theater by the name
    of the Corso or by the academy *and* the Corso.) 1676[1], 1677, 1678[1], 1688[4], 1689[4],
    1690[2], 1691[8], 1693[1], 1694[1], 1697[1], 1698[11], 1700[1], 1700[4], 1732[2], 1738[2], pp. 32, 37,
    47, 50, 56, 58. From 1740 through 1749 performances occur in every year.

Uffizi, Palazzo degli. 1600[5], 1600[7], 1608[3], 1613[2], 1617, 1619[1], 1624[3], 1625[1], 1626[1],
    1628[3], pp. 21, 22.

TITLES

L'Accademia festeggiante. 1695[3], 1702[7].
Achille in Sciro (Bentivoglio, Bologna). Pp. 66, 68.
Achille in Sciro (Metastasio). 1747[3].
Achille placato (Venice). P. 67.
Adalinda. 1679[1].
Adelaide. 1689[1], 1725[7], 1735[1], p. 37.
Adriano in Siria. 1733[5], 1745[7].
L'Adulatore. 1747[5].
Agarista. 1705[1].
Aiace (Milan). P. 66.
Alarico Re de' Vandali, 1701[1].
Alba soggiogata da' Romani. 1701[4]; (Reggio), p. 66; (Bologna), p. 67.
Alcibiade (Aureli, Modena). P. 66.
Alessandro nell'Indie. 1732[1], 1736[2], 1740[1], 1743[14], 1748[5], p. 73.
Alessandro Severo. 1718[1], 1734[6].
Alessandro vincitor di se stesso. 1654[1], p. 27.
Alidoro il costante. 1650[3].
Alma fida in amore ottien vittoria. 1692[4].
Almansor re della China. 1747[12], p. 52.
Alta [Altera?] Maria, balletto. 1614[5].
L'Amante di se stesso. 1700[6].
L'Amante di sua figlia. 1683[4].
L'Amante esperimentato. 1738[2].
L'Amante per odio. 1693[1].
Gl'Amanti generosi (Naples). P. 67.
Gli Amanti disperati. 1619[3].
Gli Amanti ladri notturni cocchiata. 1667[2].
Gli Amanti senza vidersi. 1748[1].
Amar per vendetta. 1706[2].
L'Amazone del celibato, with prologue. 1691[5], 1702[5].
Amazzoni vinte da Ercole. 1715[6].
L'Ambizione delusa. 1731[8], 1742[5].
Ambleto. 1706[7].
L'Amicizia costante. 1600[9], 1601.
L'Amicizia tra le sventure. 1689[2].
L'Amico nemico. 1749[6].
Aminta. 1703[4].
L'Ammalata. 1630.
L'Ammalato immaginario. 1718[5], 1725[3], 1732[6].
L'Amor costante. 1710[5], 1725[8].
Amor'e Signoria non voglion comparsa. 1686[1].
Amor fa l'uomo cieco. 1744[13].
L'Amor fra i nemici, prologo. Undated, p. 335.
L'Amor generoso. 1708[4], p. 75.
Amor nell'odio. 1693[1].
L'Amor tirannico. 1712[2].
Amor vince fortuna. 1690[5], 1719[3].
Amor vince l'odio. 1715[1], 1731[3].

Amor vince la semplicità. 1710[4].

Amor vuol gioventù. 1662[3], 1664.

Amor vuol inganno. 1663, 1680[4].

Amore difende l'innocenza, prologo. Undated, p. 335.

Amore e maestà. 1715[2], 1731[9], 1736[4], 1739[3], 1749[12].

Amore e politica. 1677, 1700[4].

L'Amore medesimo in tutti. 1699[3].

Amore nella statua. 1748[7].

Amore non vuol vendetta, prologo. Undated, p. 335.

Amore opera a caso. 1668[2].

Amore sbandito. 1608[1].

Amore vince la semplicità. 1698[11], 1700[1].

Amore vuol sofferanza. 1742[11].

Gli Amorosi affanni. 1601, p. 23.

Anacreonte. 1698[5], p. 70.

L'Analinda. 1702[1].

Anche le donne sanno far da uomo. 1738[2].

L'Andromaca. 1728[1], 1742[14].

L'Andromeda. 1618[3].

L'Andronico. 1723[1].

Antigona. 1752.

L'Antigono. 1747[10].

L'Antioco. 1669[2], 1723[1], p. 28.

Apollo, l'inganno, e' l giovane, prologo. 1684[2].

Apollo geloso. (1698)[7].

L'Arcangelo Raffaello. 1624[1].

L'Ardelinda. 1733[4].

L'Argonautica. 1608[5].

Arianna e Teseo. 1728[3], 1739[1], 1750[4], p. 49.

Ariovisto. 1702[6].

Arlecchino medico per forza. 1750[19].

Armanda, with prologue. 1669[4], 1706[3], 1746[3].

L'Armi d'Achille dell'isola degl'eroi, intermedio. 1626[1].

Armida e l'Amor pudico. 1637[2].

Arminio. 1703[3], 1716[1], 1725[9], 1748[16], pp. 41, 43, 70.

Arminio in Germania. 1741[3].

Arrivo d'Amore in Toscana, descrizione. 1615[4].

Arsace. 1715[2], 1731[9], 1736[4], 1739[3], 1749[12], p. 47.

L'Artaserse (Metastasio). 1730[2], 1739[9], 1744[2], 1748[13], p. 46.

Artaserse (Zeno). 1707[1].

Artemio all'Imperio. 1747[5].

Artemisia. 1666, (1743)[16], p. 28.

Artigiano gentiluomo, intermezzi. 1722.

Astarto. 1720[2].

Astarto, tradotto dal francese. 1743[3].

Astianatte. 1701[5], 1716[3], (1725)[10], 1728[1], pp. 41, 70.

Astrea (Adimari). 1608[3].

Astuto balordo. 1738[3].

Atenaide. 1728[6].

Atlante, intermedio. 1626[1].

Canzonette in lode della Befana. 1620[1].

I Caramogi. 1629[2].

Il Carcerier fortunato. 1699[9].

Il Carceriere di se medesimo. 1681[1].

Carlo re d'Alemagna. 1700[2], p. 64; (Bologna), p. 75.

Il Carnovale di Venezia. 1718[5].

Il Cartoccio speziale di villa. 1719[4].

Catone in Utica. 1729[1], 1739[8], 1744[12], 1749[10].

Le Cautele politiche, with prologue. 1672[2], 1699[5].

Il Cavaliere Parigino. 1734[4].

La Celeste guida, o vero l'Archangelo Raffaello. 1624[1].

Celio. 1646[1].

Cesare in Egitto. 1735[7], 1753.

Chi la dura la vince. 1685[1].

Chi non fa non falla. 1743[8].

Chi non sa fingere non sa godere. 1737[7].

Chi non sa fingere non sa vivere, with prologue. 1672[2], 1699[5].

Ciapo. 1743[10].

Ciapo tutore. 1747[1].

I Cicisbei delusi. 1750[8].

Il Cicisbeo sconsolato. 1749[3].

Il Cid(d). 1691[7], 1694[1], 1736[7], 1749[7], p. 33.

Ciò che pare non è. 1749[3].

Il Ciro. 1718[2].

Ciro riconosciuto. 1746[9].

La Civil villanella, prologo. Undated, p. 335.

La Clemenza di Tito. 1736[5], 1749[16].

Clori, 1626[4].

La Clotilde d'Aragona. 1706[2].

Cocchiata delli Accademici Rugginosi. 1628[2].

Cocchiata e musica. 1625[4].

La Cofanaria. 1613[4].

Cola e Aurilla, intermezzi. 1719[6].

Il Comando non inteso ed ubbidito. 1715[3], 1726[1].

Combattimento e balletto a cavallo. 1652[2].

Comedia de Vaganti. 1726[4].

Commedia all'improvviso, una. 1657[3].

Commedia de' nuovi Istrioni. 1728[4].

La Commedia in commedia. 1731[8], 1732[3], 1741[8], 1750[7], 1750[11], pp. 46, 56.

Commedia in musica, una. 1697[4].

Commedia in musica del Buchino. 1688[4].

Commedia in villa del S.r. Palmiero Palmieri. 1702[3].

Commedia rapp.ta dalli Accad. Rinvigoriti. 1673[2].

Commedia recitata da' paggi. 1704[3].

Commedia senza titolo. 1662[1].

Commedie. 1736[8], 1741[5], 1743[4], 1744[5], 1745[1], 1746[6], 1747[9], 1747[13].

Commedie all'improvviso, due. 1655[1].

Commedie di burattini. 1741[10].

Commedie in musica. 1671.

Componimento drammatico. 1748[11].

La Donna ancora è fedele. 1684[1].
La Donna più costante. 1655[3]-56.
Donna saggia può ciò che vuole. 1679[3], 1694[2], 1695[6], p. 32.
Le Donne virtuose. 1747[14].
La Dori. 1661[5], 1670[2], pp. 28, 33.
Dov'è uomini è modo. 1698[4].
I Due bari. 1705[7].
Il Duello d'amore, e di vendetta. 1707[5].

Gl'Eccessi della gelosia. 1725[11].
Egisto. 1646[2], 1667[1], p. 28.
L'Endimione. 1746[5].
Engelberta. 1710[6], 1711[1].
L'Enrico. 1731[10].
Gli Equivoci gelosi. (1695)[5].
Gli Equivoci in amore. 1692[3].
L'Eraclio. 1705[2].
Ercole in Tebe. 1661[1], pp. 26, 68.
Erighetta e Don Chilone, intermezzo. 1718[5].
Erismena. 1661[3], 1662[5]-63, p. 25.
Ermengarda. 1706[1].
L'Ernelinda. 1704[6], 1727[4].
Lo Errore. 1603.
Eumene. 1720[1].
Eurene. 1738[11].
L'Euridice. 1600[5], 1600[8], 1602[3].
Ezio. 1735[3], 1744[14].

La Facciendiera. 1748[9].
Le False oppinioni. 1690[2].
Il Fanciullo eroe. 1747[5].
Fantoccini. 1689[7].
Faramondo. 1699[8], p. 70.
Farnace. 1725[12], 1733[1], 1749[4].
Farnace, opera in prosa. 1746[14].
La Favola di Prometeo. 1739[5].
La Fede ne' tradimenti. 1697[1], 1718[4], 1732[10], 1744[11].
La Fede tradita e vendicata. 1704[6], 1727[4].
La Fedeltà d'Alceste. 1661[7].
La Fedeltà nei disprezzi. 1743[12].
Festa con intermezzi in musica. 1690[4].
Festa di ballo. 1744[15], 1745[3], 1745[5], 1746[4].
Festa di S. Maria Maddalena. 1629[1].
Festa in musica. 1645[2].
Festa rappresentata da gl'Accademici Sorgenti. 1654[2].
Feste di ballo con maschere. 1731[5].
Festini. 1689[9].
La Fiammetta. 1743[11].
La Fiera. 1619[1].
Il Figlio delle selve. 1688[3].

Ginevra, principessa di Scozia. 1708², (1709)⁴, 1723², 1736¹, pp. 42, 70.
La Giocasta, regina d'Armenia (with prologue). 1676².
Il Giocatore, intermezzi. 1720⁷, 1723⁴.
Il Giocatore, tradotto dal francese. 1749⁸.
Il Giocatore innamorati, prologo e finale. Undated, p. 336.
Giochi di magia bianca. 1748⁸.
Giostra rappresentata in Firenze. 1652¹.
Giramondo. 1743⁹.
Il Girello, with prologue. 1670¹, 1697⁵, pp. 28, 38, 41, 42.
Il Giudice impazzito. 1749⁶.
La Giuditta. 1626³.
Il Giudizio di Paride. 1608³.
Il Giugurta. 1680⁶.
Il Giuocatore. 1747⁷.
Il Giuocatore, intermezzi. *See* Il Giocatore, intermezzi.
Il Giuoco dell'astrologo indovino. 1693⁵.
Il Giuoco della cieca. 1595.
Le Gloriose disaventure di Odoardo. 1689⁴.
Gneo Marzio Coriolano. 1686³.
Gran festa di ballo. 1745³, 1745⁷.
Il Gran natale di Christo Salvator nostro. 1622⁴.
Il Gran Tamerlano. 1706⁴, 1730¹, 1748⁶, p. 70.
Le Grazie. 1750¹.
La Greca schiava. 1618¹.
Il Greco in Troia. 1689⁵, pp. 37, 68.
Griselda. 1703², 1719², 1734³.
La Griselsa. 1638¹.
I Guardiani de' Pazzi. 1746³.
Guerra d'amore. 1616¹.
Guerra di bellezza. 1616⁵.

L' Hipermestra. 1658³, p. 26.

L'Idalma. 1685¹
Ifianassa e Melampo. 1685³, p. 70.
Ifigenia (in prosa). 1742¹⁴.
Ifigenia in Aulide. 1732⁵, p. 47.
L'Imperiale. 1614³.
L'Imperio di casa d'Austria, intermedio. 1626¹.
L'Impresario. 1741⁷.
L'Impresario alla moda. 1741⁷.
L'Impresario della Canarie, intermezzi. 1728⁵.
L'Incostanza del Fato. 1672¹, pp. 28, 32.
Ines, tragedia tradotta dal francese. 1749¹⁷, 1750¹⁰.
L'Infedeltà fedele. 1689⁸.
Gl'Inganni felice. 1697⁶, 1705¹.
Gl'Inganni lodevole. 1710¹, 1747⁵.
L'Inganno vince l'inganno (with prologue). 1684².
L'Ingratitudine c(g)astigata. 1701¹, 1726².
L'Innocente giustificato. 1693².

Il Martirio di S. Agata. 1622^1, 1622^3.
Il Martirio di S. Caterina. 1627^1.
La Maschera levato al vizio. 1731^4, p. 46.
Mascherata. 1620^3.
Mascherata cappricciosa di Calai e Zeti. 1628^5.
Mascherata che rappresentava Imeneo. 1691^2.
Mascherata di covielli. 1618^2.
Mascherata di donzelle di Ghinea. 1625^4.
Mascherata di Galeone. 1657^7.
Mascherata di ninfe. 1611^2.
Mascherata di ninfe di Senna. 1613^3.
Mascherata di selvaggi. 1614^1.
Mascherata di vecchi inamorati. 1627^2.
Mascherata di villanelle di castello. 1613^1.
Mascherata fatta in Arno. 1628^6.
Mascherate. 1689^6.
Massimiano. 1751.
Massimo Puppieno. 1698^{10}.
Il Matrimonio per forza. 1737^4.
Il Maurizio. 1707^2.
Medico guarisci. 1718^4, 1718^5.
Medico volante. 1706^5.
Il Medoro. 1619^4.
Merope. 1713^3, 1729^3, 1743^3, 1749^{17}.
Le Miniere dell'oro, prologo. Undated, p. 336.
Il Mitridate. 1716^2.
Mitridate (Zeno). 1750^{21}.
Mitridate in Sebastia. 1704^1, 1716^2.
Il Moccone podestà del Bagno a Ripoli. 1690^8.
La Moglie accorta. 1735^5.
La Moglie alla moda. 1740^6.
La Moglie del fratello. 1690^3.
La Moglie in calzone. 1732^2.
La Moglie giudice e parte. 1745^{10}.
Il Monarca di Colci. 1688^5.
Il Mondo festeggiante. 1661^2.
Monsieur di Porsugnacco. 1727^3.
I Morti e i vivi. 1602^2, p. 22.
Moschetto e Grullo, intermezzi. 1744^{11}.
Il Mugnajo di Sezzate, prologo. Undated, p. 336.
Muzio Scevola. 1696^3, p. 38.

Il Narciso. 1744^{17}.
Il Natal d'Ercole. 1605.
Il Natal de' Fiori. 1628^3.
La Nave di Amerigo Vespucci. 1608^3.
Nerina e Ginone, intermezzi. 1716^4.
Il Nerone. 1726^5.
Il Nerone fatto Cesare. 1708^3.
Nicomede. (1670)^3, 1700^5.

La Pimpa locandiera. 1742^{14}, 1744^6, 1750^{18}.

Pimpinone. 1735^6.

Pirro e Demetrio. 1696^2, 1711^2.

La Pittura e la poesia in gara per amore. 1748^2.

Il Più fedele fra i vassalli. 1704^5, p. 38.

Il Podestà di Malmantile. 1743^7.

Polifemo geloso. Undated, p. 336.

Pompeo (Livorno, 1688). P. 34.

La Potenza del vino, e la debolezza della vecchiaia. 1732^{12}, 1740^7, p. 48.

Il Potestà di Capraja. 1747^1.

Il Potestà di Colognole. 1657^1, 1661^6, 1717^3, 1727^2, pp. 26, 28.

La Precedenza delle dame. 1625^3.

La Preziosa ridicola. 1728^2, 1744^4.

Il Prigioniero fortunato. 1699^9.

Il Principe Corsaro. 1717^1.

Il Principe Eugenio in Belgrado. 1749^2.

I Prodigi dell'innocenza. 1707^6.

Prologo fatto pel Sig. Giovacchino Fortini. 1733^2.

Prologo per musica. 1649.

Prologo per una commedia in villa. Undated, p. 336.

Le Prove della sapienza, e del valore. 1686^5.

Pudicizia schernita. 1655^4-56.

Pulchinella [sic] in giostra. 1747^5.

La Pupilla. $(1737)^2$, 1750^{15}.

Quanto più si vanta, peggio si fa. 1750^{17}.

La Querele amorose, dialogo. 1651^2.

Quinto Lucrezio proscritto. 1681^3.

Il Radamisto. 1709^2, 1728^2.

Il Rapimento di Cefalo. 1600^7.

Rappresentazione del Agniolo Raffaello et Tobia. 1624^1.

Il Raro esempio di costanza e fede. 1680^3.

Le Reciproche gelosie. 1691^3.

La Regina floridea. 1678^2, pp. 31, 33.

La Regina Sant'Orsola. 1620^4, 1623^4, 1624^3, 1625^1.

Ricimero. 1704^6.

Rime cantate nel giardino del Signor Riccardo Riccardi. 1600^6.

Rime della barriera fra i Traci, e l'Amazone. 1609^2.

I Rivali generosi. 1698^2.

La Rivalità favorevole. 1668^1, pp. 28, 30.

Rodelinda regina de' Longobardi. 1710^5, 1725^8.

Il Roderico. 1692^1.

Rodrigo. 1707^5.

Rosalba. 1681^2, p. 70.

La Rosaura. 1690^1.

La Rosaura di Cipro. 1692^3.

Rosbale. 1738^{11}.

La Rosmene. 1689^8.

Rosmira. 1745^8.

La Sofferenza vince la fortuna. 1669[3].
La Sorellina di Don Pilone. 1749[1].
Il Sospetto non ha fondamento. 1699[6], pp. 38, 42.
Il Sospetto senza fondamento. 1691[3].
Gli Spazj immaginarj. 1669[4].
Lo Spedale. 1673[1].
Lo Spedale de' Pazzi. 1746[4].
La Speranza guidata da Mercurio. 1615[1].
Lo Speziale di villa. 1683[3], 1684[3], 1704[4], 1719[4], 1730[3], 1731[1], p. 70.
Gli Sponsali in maschere. 1743[3].
Gli Sponsali tra nemici. 1744[11].
La Sposa alla moda. 1740[6].
Lo Sposalizio della vecchia. 1699[3].
Lo Sposalizio di Medoro ed Angelica. 1619[4].
Lo Sposalizio tra sepolcri. 1688[1], 1695[6].
Squola delle fanciulle. 1741[12].
La Squola delle madri. 1750[1].
Statira. 1708[1].
Lo Stilicone. 1749[6].
Stratonica. 1707[4].
Le Stravaganze d'Amore. 1695[1].
Le Stravaganze del caso. 1669[4], 1706[3].
Le Stravaganze dell'ubbriachezza. 1740[6].
Il Superbo, tradotta dal francese. 1745[10], 1750[5].

Tacere et amare. 1674, 1717[4], pp. 28, 74.
Il Tamburo notturno. 1750[9].
Il Tamerlano. 1716[5].
La Tancia. 1611[3].
Tarpina e Zelone, intermezzi. 1725[6].
Temistocle. 1720[6], 1737[1], 1739[4], p. 47.
Il Tempio della pace. 1608[3].
Teodora Augusta, with prologue and four intermezzi. 1696[4].
La Tessalonica. 1686[6].
Il Teuzzone. 1712[1].
Tiberio imperadore d'Oriente. 1742[8].
Timocrate. 1715[1], 1731[3], p. 46.
Il Tiranno di Colco. 1688[5], p. 70.
Il Tiranno eroe. 1712[4].
Il Tirinto. 1692[6].
Tito, e Berenice. 1713[1].
Tito Manlio. 1696[5], 1721[2], 1742[1], p. 70.
Li Tre cicisbei ridicoli. 1750[8].
I Tre fratelli rivali per la sorella. 1694[3].
Trespolo oste. 1692[5], 1694[1], p. 70.
Trespolo tutore. 1692[5].
Il Trace in Catena. 1716[5].
Il Trionfo chinese. 1739[5].
Il Trionfo d'Amore. 1746[5].
Il Trionfo de' brutti. 1683[2].

Viriate. 1729[2], p. 47.
La Virtù nel cimento. 1719[2].
La Virtuosa moderna, intermezzi. 1748[11].
La Vita di Cartoccio, ladro famoso di Parigi. 1746[11].
La Vita è un sogno, with prologue. 1684[5].
I Vizj correnti a l'ultima moda. 1747[1].
La Vlasta. 1673[1].
Vologeso re de' Parti. 1742[2].
Il Voto d'Jefette. 1623[2].
Il Voto d'Oronte. 1623[2].
Vulcano. 1608[3].

Xerse. 1647.

La Zaira. 1748[17], 1749[5], 1749[7], 1749[12], 1749[17].
Zamberlucco e Palandrana, intermezzi. 1719[5].
La Zoccoletta. 1744[1].
La Zoraide. 1698[11].

BIBLIOGRAPHY

BOOKS AND ARTICLES

Acton, Harold. *The Last Medici.* Revised edition. London: Methuen, 1958.

Ademollo, Alessandro. *I primi fasti del teatro di via della Pergola (1657-1661).* Milano: Ricordi, 1885.

———. *I primi fasti della musica italiana a Parigi.* Milano: Ricordi, 1884.

Allacci, Lione. *Drammaturgia di L.A.* (Facsimile of Venice: Pasquali, 1755). Torino: Bottega d'Erasmo, 1966.

d'Amico, Silvio. "Buonarroti, M.A.," *Enciclopedia dello spettacolo* II, cc. 1331-1333.

Baccini, Giuseppe. *Giovanni Batista Fagiuoli, poeta faceto fiorentino.* Firenze: Soliani, 1886.

———. *Notizie di alcune commedie sacre in Firenze nel secolo XVII.* Firenze: Libreria Dante, 1889.

Baldinucci, Filippo. *Notizie de' professori del disegno.* Firenze: 1748.

Baur-Heinhold, Margarete. *Theater des Barock.* Munich: Callwey, 1966.

Beccherini, B. "Andrea Salvadori," *Enciclopedia dello spettacolo* VIII, c. 1438.

Bianconi, Lorenzo. "Caletti-Bruni, Francesco," *Dizionario Biografico degli Italiani.* Istituto della Enciclopedia Italiana. Roma, 1973.

Bianconi, Lorenzo, and Thomas Walker. "Dalla 'Finta pazza' alla 'Veremonda': storie di Febiarmonici," *Rivista italiana di musicologia* X (1975), pp. 379-454.

Bonaventura, Arnaldo. *Saggio storico sul teatro musicale italiano.* Livorno: Raffaello Giusti, 1913.

Brunelli, Bruno. "Giacinto Andrea Cicognini," *Enciclopedia dello spettacolo* III, cc. 742-744.

Busi, Leonida. *Il padre G.B. Martini musicista-letterato del secolo XVIII. Notizie raccolta da Leonida Busi.* Bologna: Ditta Nicola Zanichelli, 1891.

Carini, Isadore. *L'Arcadia dal 1680 al 1890: Memorie storiche.* Vol. I. Roma: Cuggiani, 1891.

Caselli, Aldo. *Catalogo delle opere liriche pubblicate in Italia.* Firenze: Olschki, 1969.

Castello, Giulio Cesare. "Pagliardi," *Enciclopedia dello spettacolo* VII (1960), cc. 1484f.

Chatfield-Taylor, Hobart C. *Goldoni: a Biography.* New York: Duffield & Co., 1913.

Cochrane, Eric. *Florence in the Forgotten Centuries 1527-1800.* Chicago and London: The University of Chicago Press, 1973.

Crain, Gordon F. *The Operas of Bernardo Pasquini.* Unpublished dissertation. New Haven: Yale University, 1965. University Microfilms, Inc. #65-15,026.

Crescimbeni, Giovanni Mario. *Istoria della volgar poesia.* 6 vols. Roma: de' Rossi, 1702-1711.

De la Fage, A. *Essais di diphtherographie musicale.* Vol. II. Paris: Legouix, 1864.

Della Corte, Andrea and Guido Pannain. *Storia della musica.* 2nd ed. 3 vols. Torino: Unione Tipografico-Editrice Torinese, 1944.

Dent, Edward J. *Alessandro Scarlatti: his life and works.* New edition with preface and additional notes by Frank Walker. London: Edward Arnold, 1960.

"Diario istorico fiorentino di autore anonimo dal 1600 al 1640," *Notizie istoriche italiane,* ed. M. Rastrelli, Vol. III. Firenze: Benucci, 1781.

Dizionario letterario Bompiani I. Firenze: 1956.

Eitner, Robert. *Biographische-Bibliographische Quellen-Lexikon.* 10 vols. Leipzig: Breitkopf und Härtel, 1900-1904.

——. *Publikationen aelterer praktischer und theoretischer Musikwerke.* 33 vols. Leipzig: Breitkopf und Härtel, 1873-1905.

Eller, Rudolf. "Vivaldi," *Die Musik in Geschichte und Gegenwart* XIII, cc. 1857-1858.

Enciclopedia dello spettacolo. Ed. by Silvio and Sandro d'Amico. 10 vols. and supps. Firenze-Roma: Le Maschere-Sansoni, 1954-1968. (Individual articles listed by author.)

Fabbri, Mario. *Alessandro Scarlatti e il Principe Ferdinando de' Medici.* Firenze: Olschki, 1961.

——. "Firenze," *Enciclopedia dello spettacolo* V, cc. 379-395.

——. "Nuova luce sull'attività fiorentina di Giacomo Antonio Perti, Bartolomeo Cristofori e Giorgio F. Haendel," *Chigiana rassegna annuale di studi musicologici* XXI. Firenze: Olschki, 1964.

Freeman, Robert. "Apostolo Zeno's Reform of the Libretto," *Journal of the American Musicological Society* XXI (1968), pp. 321-341.

Galeazzo, Gualdo. *Relazione della città di Firenze, e del Gran Ducato di Toscana sotto il Gran Duca Ferdinando II.* Colonio: Pietro de la Place, 1668.

Galluzzi, Riguccio. *Istoria del Granducato di Toscana sotto il governo della casa Medici.* Firenze: G. Cambiagi, 1781.

Garboli, Cesare. "Chiabrera," *Enciclopedia dello spettacolo* III, c. 625.

Ghisi, Federico. *Alle fonti della monodia.* Milan: F. Bacci, 1940.

——. "An Early Seventeenth Century Manuscript," *Acta Musicologica* XX (1949), pp. 51ff.

——. "Ballet Entertainments in the Pitti Palace," *Musical Quarterly* XXXV (1949), pp. 429ff.

——. "Contributo bibliografico alla musica italiana antica," *Rassegna dorica,* Anno VII (1936), no. 4, p. 64.

——. *Studi e testi di musica italiana dall'Ars Nova a Carissimi.* Bologna: A.M.I.S., 1971.

Contains reprints of "Ballet entertainments," and "An early seventeenth century."

Giegling, Franz. "G.A. Perti," *Musik in Geschichte und Gegenwart* X, c. 1106.

Goldoni, Carlo. *Memoirs Written by Himself.* Trans. by John Black. New York: Knopf, 1926.

Goldschmidt, Hugo. *Studien zur Geschichte der italienischen Oper im 17 J.* Leipzig: Breitkopf und Härtel, 1901.

Groppo, Antonio. *Catalogo di tutti i drammi per musica recitati ne' teatri di Venezia dall' anno 1637 . . . sin all'anno presente 1745.* Venezia: Antonio Groppo, 1745.

Haas, Robert. *Die Musik des Barocks. Handbuch der Musikwissenschaft*, ed. by Ernst Bücken, Vol. III. New York: Musurgia Publishers, 1928.

Hill, John Walker. "Le relazione di Antonio Cesti con la corte e i teatri di Firenze," *Rivista italiana di musicologia* XI (1976/1), pp. 27-47.

Kirkendale, Ursula. "The Ruspoli Documents on Handel," *Journal of the American Musicological Society* XX (1967), pp. 222-273.

Lazarevich, Gordana. "Eighteenth-Century Pasticcio: The historian's Gordian Knot." In *Analecta Musicologica* XVII.

Litta, Pompeo. *Famiglie celebri italiane.* Milano: presso l'autore, 1833.

Livingston, A. *La vita veneziana nelle opere di Gian Francesco Busenello.* Venezia: 1913.

Loewenberg, Alfred. *Annals of Opera*, 1597-1940. 2nd. ed., revised and corrected. 2 vols. Genève: Societas Bibliographica, 1955.

Il luogo teatrale a Firenze. Vol. I of *Spettacolo e musica nella Firenze Medicea: Documenti e restituzioni.* Catalogo a cura di Mario Fabbri, Elvira Garbero Zorzi, and Anna Maria Petrioli Tofani. Firenze: Electa Editrice, 1975.

Lustig, Renzo. "Per la cronistoria dell'antico teatro musicale. Il teatro della Villa Medicea di Pratolino," *Rivista musicale italiana* XXVI (1929), pp. 2ff.

Maffei, Raffaello. *Tre volterrani: Enrico Ormanni, G.C. Villifranchi, Mario Guarnacci.* Pisa: Nistri, 1881.

Mamczarz, Irene. *Les intermèdes comiques italiens au XVIIIe siècle en France et en Italie.* Paris: Editions du Centre National de la Recherche Scientifique, 1972.

Manferrari, Umberto. *Dizionario universale delle opere melodrammatiche.* 3 vols. Firenze: Sansoni Antiquariato, 1955.

Maylender, Michele. *Storia delle accademie d'Italia.* 5 vols. Bologna: L. Cappelli, 1926-1930.

Mazzuchelli, Giammaria. *Gli scrittori d'Italia cioè notizie storiche e critiche intorno alle vite.* Brescia: Presso Ag. Bosen, 1743-1763.

Mazzuoli, Enrico. "Le donne, i cavalier, l'arte, i tenori," *Teatro della Pergola.* Firenze: Ente teatrale italiano, 1967.

Melzi, Gaetano. *Dizionario di opere anonime e pseudonime di scrittori italiane, o come che sia aventi relazione all'Italia.* 3 vols. Milano: Torchi di Luigi di Giacomo Pirola, 1848.

Molinari, Cesare. *Le Nozze degli Dei: un saggio sul grande spettacolo italiano del seicento.* Roma: Mario Bulzoni, 1968.

Morey, Carl. *The late Operas of Alessandro Scarlatti.* Unpublished dissertation. Bloomington: University of Indiana, 1965. University Microfilms, Inc. #65-10870.

Morini, Ugo. *La Reale Accademia degli Immobili e il suo teatro La Pergola.* Pisa: Simoncini, 1926.

Die Musik in Geschichte und Gegenwart. Friedrich Blume, ed. 14 vols. Kassel u. Basel: Bärenreiter-Verlag, 1949-1968. (Individual articles listed by author.)

Nagler, Alois Maria. *Theatre Festivals of the Medici 1539-1637.* New Haven and London: Yale University Press, 1964.
Notizie istoriche italiane. Vol. II. Firenze: Benucci, 1781.

Osthoft, W. "Antonio Cesti's 'Alessandro vincitor di se stesso,' " *Studien zur Musikwissenschaft* XXI (1960), pp. 13-43.

Panum, Hortense. (Two arias from *Dafne*), *Musikalisches Wochenblatt* XIX, (1888), pp. 346f.
Panum, Hortense and W. Behrend. (Two arias from *Dafne*), *Illustreret Musikhistorie,* (1905), pp. 218f.
Paumgartner, Bernhard. "Albinoni," *Musik in Geschichte und Gegenwart* I, cc. 297-299.
Pavan, Giuseppe. *Saggio di cronistoria teatrale fiorentina: serie cronologica delle opere rappresentate al teatro degli Immobili in via della Pergola, nel secolo XVII e XVIII.* Milano: G. Ricordi, 1901.
Piccini, G. (Pseud. Jarro). *Storia aneddotica dei teatri fiorentini: I. Il teatro della Pergola.* Firenze: Bemporad, 1912.
Pirotta, Nino. "Apolloni," *Enciclopedia dello spettacolo* I, cc. 736f.
———. "Tre capitoli su Cesti," *La scuola romana. Accademia musicale chigiana* X. Siena: Ticci, 1953.
Porter, William. "Peri and Corsi's *'Dafne,'* " *Journal of the American Musicological Society* XVIII (1965), pp. 170-196.
Puliti, Leto. *Cenni storici della vita del Serenissimo Ferdinando de' Medici Granprincipe di Toscana e della origine del pianoforte.* Estratto degli Atti dell'Accademia del R. Istituto Musicale di Firenze, 1874.

Quadrio, Francesco Saverio. *Della storia e della ragione d'ogni poesia.* 7 vols. Venezia, Bologna: P. Pisarri; Milano: Agnelli, 1739-1752.

Ricci, Corrado. "Un melodramma ignoto," *Rivista musicale italiana* XXXII (1926), pp. 51-79.
———. *I teatri di Bologna nei secoli XVII-XVIII.* Bologna: Succesori Monti, 1888.
Riemann, Hugo. *Handbuch der Musikgeschichte.* 2nd. ed. 2 vols. Leipzig: Breitkopf und Härtel, 1921-1922.
Rolandi, Ulderico. *Il libretto per musica attraverso i tempi.* Roma: Ateneo, 1951.
Ruhmke, Martin. "Gasparini," *Musik in Geschichte und Gegenwart* IV, c. 1414-1418.

Salvioli, Giovanni and Carlo. *Bibliografia universale del teatro drammatico italiano.* Vol. I, A-C (only volume published). Venezia: C. Ferrari, 1903.
Sartori, Claudio. *Primo tentativo di catalogo unico dei libretti italiani a stampa fino all'anno 1800.* Milano: Bibl. Nazionale Braidense, s.d. (Typsecript available on Xerox or microfilm from Dr. Sartori at via Clerici 5, 20121 Milano.)
Schlitzer, Franco. "Fortuna dell' Orontea', " *La scuola romana. Accademia musicale chigiana* X. Siena: Ticci, 1953.
———. "Intorno alla 'Dori' di Antonio Cesti," *Biblioteca degli eruditi e dei bibliofili* XXVII. Firenze: Sansoni, 1957.
———. "A letter from Cesti to Salvator Rosa," *Monthly Musical Record* LXXXIV (1954). Translated by Frank Walker from the next entry.
———. "Una lettera inedita di A. Cesti e un frammento di lettera inedita di Salvator Rosa," *La scuola romana. Accademia musicale chigiana* X. Siena: Ticci, 1953.
———. "L'Orontea di Antonio Cesti," *Biblioteca degli eruditi e dei bibliofili* XLII. Firenze: Sansoni, 1960.

Schmidl, Carlo. *Dizionario universale dei musicisti.* 2 vols. Milano: Sonzongo, 1929.

Schmidt, Carl B. "Antonio Cesti's 'La Dori': a study of sources, performance traditions and musical style," *Rivista italiana di musicologia* X (1975), pp. 455-498.

―――. *The Operas of Antonio Cesti.* Unpublished dissertation. Cambridge: Harvard University, 1973.

Schneider, M. *Die Anfänge des Basso Continuo und seiner Bezifferung.* Leipzig: Breitkopf und Härtel, 1918.

Sesini, Ugo. *Catalogo della Biblioteca del Liceo Musicale di Bologna. Vol V. Libretti d'opera.* Tomo 1º. Bologna: Libreria Romagnoli dall'Acqua, 1943.

Solerti, Angelo. *Gli albori del melodramma.* Milano: R. Sandron, 1905.

―――. "Emilio de' Cavalieri e Laura Guidiccioni Lucchesini," *Rivista musicale italiana* IX (1902), p. 797.

―――. *Musica, ballo e drammatica alla Corte Medicea dal 1600 al 1637: Notizie tratte da un diario con appendice di testi inediti e rari.* Firenze: Bemporad, 1905.

―――. *Le origini del melodramma.* Torino: Fratelli Bocca, 1903.

Sonneck, Oscar G.T. *Catalogue of opera librettos printed before 1800 in the Library of Congress.* 2 vols. Washington: Government Printing Office, 1914.

―――. " 'Dafne,' the first opera," *Sammelbände der internationalen Musikgesellschaft* XV (1913-1914), p. 105.

"Storia d'Etichetta ovvero Diario di Corte," *Miscellanea fiorentina di erudizione e storia diretta da Jodoco del Badia.* Vols. I, II. Firenze: Salvadore Landi, 1902.

Strom, Reinhard. "Händel in Italia: nuovi contributi," *Rivista italiana di musicologia* IX (1974), pp. 152-174.

Strunk, Oliver, ed. *Source Readings in Music History.* New York: W.W. Norton, 1950.

Tagliavini, Luigi Ferdinando. "Orlandini," *Musik in Geschichte und Gegenwart* X, c. 398-400.

―――. "Predieri," *Musik in Geschichte und Gegenwart* X, c. 1604-1607.

Vogel, Emil. *Bibliothek der gedruckten weltlichen Vocalmusik italiens.* 2 vols. Hildesheim: Olms, 1962.

Walker, Frank. "Two centuries of Pergolesi forgeries and misattributions," *Music and Letters* XXX (1949), pp. 297-320.

Walker, Thomas. "Gli errori di 'Minerva al tavolino': osservazioni sulla cronologia delle prime opere veneziane," Atti della tavola rotonda "Venezia e il melodramma nel Seicento," ed. by M.T. Muraro. Firenze: 1976, pp. 7-16.

Weaver, Robert L. *Florentine Comic Operas of the Seventeenth Century.* Unpublished dissertation. Chapel Hill: University of North Carolina, 1958. University Microfilms, Inc. #58-5975.

―――. "*Il Girello,* a seventeeth century burlesque opera," *Memorie e Contributi alla musica dal medioevo all'età moderna. Offerti a F. Ghisi nel settantesimo compleano (1901-1971).* Bologna: A.M.I.S., 1971.

―――. "Materiali per le biografie dei Fratelli Melani," *Rivista italiana di musicologia* XII (1977/2).

―――. "Opera in Florence: 1646-1731," *Studies in Musicology in memory of Glen Haydon.* Chapel Hill: University of North Carolina Press, 1969.

Wolf, H.C. *Die venezianische Oper in der zweiten Haelfte des 17. Jahrhunderts. Theater und Drama,* H Knudsen, ed., Bd. 7. Berlin: O. Elsner, 1937.

Wotquenne, A. *Catalogue de la bibliothèque du Conservatoire Royal di Musique. Annexe I. Libretti d'operas et d'oratorios italiens du XVIIe siècle.* Bruxelles: O. Schepens, 1901.

Young, G.F. *The Medici.* New York: Modern Library, 1930.

Zanetti, E. e C. Sartori. "Contributo a un catalogo delle opere teatrali di A.S. esistenti nelle biblioteche italiani," *Gli Scarlatti*, numero unico dell'Accademia Musicale Chigiana per la [II] settimana celebrativa dell'Accademia Musicale Chigiana, Siena, 1940.

MANUSCRIPTS
(*EXCLUDING MANUSCRIPTS OF SINGLE LETTERS, DESCRIZIONI, AND LIBRETTOS*)

Accademia degli Infuocati. Archivio. *Buste* 1-40. I Fac.
Adimari, Alessandro. *Poesie varie.* I Fn: Magl. II.I.92.

Bonazzini, Francesco. *Bisdosso* o vero *diario di F.B.* I Fn: Magl. XXV, no. 42. 2 vols.

Capponi. *Diario di cose domestiche (sino al 1690).* I Fn: Serie Capponi 273.
Cappuzi. *Diario inedito della Collezione Cappuzi 1600-1620.* I Fas: Arch. Med. Misc. di
Acquista 308/8.

Fagiuoli, Giov. Battista. *Memorie e ricordi di quello accederà alla giornata di Ma. Gio: Batta.
Fagiuoli, 1692.* Vols. I-XXVI (1742). Firenze, I Fr.

Marmi, A.F. *Notizie* [*della vita del Principe Ferdinando de'Medici*]. Miscellany catalogued
under Pietro Susini. I Fn: Magl. VIII, 74.
Martini, Gaetano. *Indice generale di commedie, in prosa stampate, manoscritte, in musica,
e verso lirico o sia sdrucciolo le quali commedie sono ad uso di Gae. M., sacerdote e
cittadino fiorentino, sec. XVII.* I Fn: Raccolta Tordi 186.
Medici, Francesco Maria de'. *Diario del Ser.mo Prin. Card.* (*1686-1691*). I Rvat, lat. 10437.
———. Letters to Francesco de Castris, 1704-1706. I Fas: Arch. Med. 5869.

Notizie di Casa Salvini. I Fm: Ms A139.
Notizie storiche di Firenze. I Fn: Palatino, Serie Targione, no. 15.

Pandolfini, Palmieri. *Notizie dell'origine dell'Accademia degli'Immobili, e dell'erezione, e
progressi della fabbrica del loro teatro posto in via della Pergola. Parte prima. Raccolte
l'anno 1753 dal loro segretario Palmieri Pandolfini a di i 23 Agosto 1753.* I Fn: Mss di
ordinare vol. 59.
———. *Notizie di tutte le opere, che si sono recitate in Firenze nel teatro di via della
Pergola dall'anno 1718 in poi.*[*] Mss in US Wc.
Pastoso. *Diario del, da 10 dicembre 1640 al 5 giugno 1690.* I Fr: Cod. Moreniano 167.
Second copy in I Fn: Serie Capponi, Cod. 55.
Pavan, Giuseppe. *Schatz Material* Mss ii. Correspondence of Pavan to Schatz on the subject
of Schatz's libretto collection. US Wc.
Poesie varie. I Fas: Arch. Med. 6424. Collection of prologues, pastorales, oratorios, etc.,
many of which are associated with Vittoria della Rovere, wife of Ferdinando II.
I Fn: Magl. VII, nos. 252, 356, 359, 364, 757, 868, 934. Landau-Finally 261, 277.
Portinari. *Diario.* I Fm: Ms C-27.

---

[*] The second is chronologically the first, in which a professional scribe continues until 1748 with a
few additions in a hand that is to be identified as Pandolfini's. This latter hand continues the chronology
from 1749 until the carnival of 1753 where the list ends, which date agrees with the date in the title of
the first Ms in I Fn. The I Fn Ms contains more material, specifically information prior to 1718. From
1718 onwards I Fn is a copy of US Wc whose precedence is established by an error in the former, which
skips a page by proceeding from the title of Atenaide (1728-1729) to the actors of *La Merope* and
Tamerlano (1729-1730) omitting these last two titles altogether.

Repertorio granducale. I Fn: Magl. VIII, 40. Inventory of all plays and librettos of the Medici library.

Settimanni. *Diario fiorentino*. I Fas: Arch. Med. 1532-1737.

Susier, Niccolo. *Diario di tutto quello che e seguito nella città di Firenze*. 32 vols. Vol. 1-6 are copies of other diaries including Bonazzini and Capponi and are of little interest. Vol. 7, 1688 through 1728, is a copy of a diary "scritto dal Martini fiorentino." Vols. 8-17 are Susier's own record to 1750. We have culled the later volumes for death notices of singers active during the period of our chronology.

Teatri: Regolamento sopra i medesimi dal 1737 al 1766. I Fas: Reggenza, F. 629-632.

Il teatro della Pergola. I Fas: Arch. Med. Miscellanea di Acquista 308. Anon. nineteenth century Ms based on the Archives of the Immobili; includes material (financial) unknown to Morini. Contains little about operas performed.

Villifranchi, Gio. Cosimo. *Prologhi*, etc. I Fn: Magl. VII, 187. Contains one prologue by Cosimo Villifranchi.

COLLECTIONS OF
LIBRETTOS AND MUSIC

Allegri, Lorenzo (Lorenzo del Liuto). *Primo libro delle musiche.* Venezia: Gardano, 1618.

Bartolomeo, Girolamo già Smeducci. *Drammi musicali morali, parte prima; Drammi musicali sacri, parte seconda.* Firenze: G.A. Bonardi, 1656. (There is no information concerning performances or composers; therefore, the dramas indicated do not appear in the chronology.)
Bonarelli della Rovere, Pietro. *Poesie dramatiche.* Ancona: Ottavio Beltramo, 1651.

Caccini, Giulio. *Le nuove musiche* (1601).
Chiabrera, Gabriello. *Opere.* Naples: Giordani, 1831.

Fagiuoli, Gio. Batista. *Rime piacevole.* 7 vols. [Vol. 5: *Prologhi e finali*]. Firenze: Moücke, 1729-1736.
———. *Commedie.* 7 vols. [Vol. 7: *Drammi per musica*]. Firenze: Moücke, 1734-1738.
———. *Commedie.* 7 vols. [republication of the Florentine edition]. Venezia: Geremia, 1753.

Gagliano, Marco da. *Musiche a una, due e tre voci.* Venetia: Amadino, MDCXV.
———. *Sesto libro de' madrigali a cinque voci.* Venezia: Gardano, 1617.
Gigli, Girolamo. *Opere nuove.* Venezia: Rossetti, 1704.
———. *Componimenti teatrali.* Siena: Rossi, 1759.

Metastasio, Pietro. *Opere del Signor Abate P.M. Poeta Cesareo Giusta le ultime correzioni ed aggiunte dell'Autore.* 7 vols. Venezia: Zatta, 1783.
Moniglia, Giovanni Andrea. *Poesie dramatiche.* 3 vols. Firenze: Vangelisti, 1689 (*Parte prima*); Bindi, 1690 (*P. seconda*); Stamperia della S.A.S., 1689 (*P. terza*). Reprint of all three volumes, Firenze: Vangelisti, 1698.

Salvadori, Andrea. *Le poesie del Sig. Andrea Salvadori.* Rome: Ercole, 1668.

Villifranchi, Giovanni Cosimo. *Raccolta di opuscoli del Dr. G.C.V.* Firenze, 1737.

Zeno, Apostolo (and Pietro Pariati). *Poesie drammatiche.* Orleans: Couret de Villeneuve, 1785-1786.

DESCRIZIONI

Descrizioni are to be found for the following performances: 1600^4, 1608^2, 1611^2, 1613^2, 1618^5, 1637^1, 1658^3, 1661^1, 1686^5, 1689 carn.

GENERAL INDEX

In order to preserve the variety of seventeenth-century nomenclature and to avoid requiring the reader to search for a reference in the index to a term that has been subsumed under a different wording, the original Italian terminology is indexed with only the most obvious adjustments, e.g., drama *or* dramma per *or* in musica *will be found indistinguishably indexed under* dramma per musica. *The reader is warned, therefore, that he must use ingenuity to discover all of the terminological variants used to denote a single type of work, for example:* commedia pastorale, favola pastorale, favola boschereccia, *etc.*

Kings, Queens, Emperors, and the Medici and their wives are indexed according to their given or Christian names, e.g., Anne, Queen of France; Ferdinando II de' Medici, etc.

Italian ducal families, Habsburgs not Emperors, and commoners are indexed under their family names, e.g., Farnese, Odoardo, Duca di Parma. Whenever the original reference, such as a dedication, gives only the title but the man is known who possesses the title, we index the item under the man's name. In a few instances the occupant is unknown and only the title is therefore indexed.

Italian spelling of names and titles is used since names and titles will appear in the chronology only in Italian.